Praise for
Hitler's American Gamble

"This is history at its scintillating best. The fate of the world tilted on the decisions made in those few days—hours even—in December 1941, and Simms and Laderman brilliantly strip away the many myths surrounding them in this hard-hitting, revelatory, and superbly researched work."

—ANDREW ROBERTS, author of *Churchill: Walking with Destiny*

"Brendan Simms and Charlie Laderman show how Hitler's mad decision to declare war on the United States on December 11, 1941, proved suicidal for the Axis, ensured a global catastrophe, and would radically redefine how World War II would end. And yet was Hitler really as unhinged and reckless as it has seemed? Warring with America was predictably consistent with the Nazi's Final Solution ideology. It was consistent with Germany's allegiance with Japan and the idea of Americans and British suddenly bogged down in a new two-front war—and at the time seen as far more strategically advantageous than allowing a neutral America to continue to supply Germany's enemies, the British Empire and Soviet Union. *Hitler's American Gamble* is revisionist, but in the best sense of sound research, rare originality, singular analysis, and riveting prose."

—VICTOR DAVIS HANSON, the Hoover Institution,
Stanford University, author of *The Second World Wars*

"All too often, historians narrate the past as if the end were preordained at the beginning. But history is not a novel or a play; it is more like a big game, in which the difference between victory and defeat depends on split-second decisions and hair's breadths. In *Hitler's American Gamble*, Brendan Simms and Charlie Laderman grippingly retell the story of five days that not only shook but also shaped the world—the days between the Japanese attack on Pearl Harbor (December 7, 1941) and

Hitler's declaration of war on the United States (December 11). All students of both World War II and the Holocaust will learn, as I did, from their careful use of neglected documents and their attention to 'counterfactuals' that, for contemporaries, were at least as likely as what actually happened."

—NIALL FERGUSON, Milbank Family Senior Fellow, the Hoover Institution, and author of *The War of the World*

"The greatest grand strategic blunder of all time may well have been Nazi Germany's declarations of war, within six months in 1941, on *both* the Soviet Union and the United States. 'Don't try this at home,' I've always told my students, but I've never been able to explain to them why Hitler chose to. Brendan Simms and Charlie Laderman have now come to the rescue with a rare achievement: a microhistory that's global in scope. Filled with fresh insights, excitingly written, and meticulously documented, *Hitler's American Gamble* is sure to become an instant classic."

—JOHN LEWIS GADDIS, Yale University

"*Hitler's American Gamble* is a thrilling and authoritative study of five crucial days in the Second World War: December 7–11, 1941. Using a wide array of hitherto-neglected sources and their own deep understanding of the period, Laderman and Simms provide an altogether outstanding account of what transpired between the Pearl Harbor attack and Hitler's declaration of war against the United States. A gripping tale, expertly told."

—FREDRIK LOGEVALL, author of *Embers of War*

"This outstanding book by two of the best historians around revolutionized what I thought I knew about strategy by the Axis powers and how it shaped post-war order. Written like a thriller, it pulls you along breathlessly as Hitler makes his fateful decision."

—DR. KORI SCHAKE, senior fellow and director of foreign and defense policy studies, American Enterprise Institute

HITLER'S AMERICAN GAMBLE

**PEARL HARBOR AND
GERMANY'S MARCH TO
GLOBAL WAR**

Brendan Simms and
Charlie Laderman

BASIC BOOKS
NEW YORK

Basic Books
Hachette Book Group
1290 Avenue of the Americas, New York, NY 10104
www.basicbooks.com

Printed in the United States of America
First Edition: November 2021

Published by Basic Books, an imprint of Perseus Books, LLC, a subsidiary
of Hachette Book Group, Inc. The Basic Books name and logo is a trademark
of the Hachette Book Group.

The Hachette Speakers Bureau provides a wide range of authors for speaking
events. To find out more, go to www.hachettespeakersbureau.com or call
(866) 376-6591.

The publisher is not responsible for websites (or their content) that are not
owned by the publisher.

Print book interior design by Linda Mark.

Library of Congress Cataloging-in-Publication Data
Names: Simms, Brendan, author. | Laderman, Charlie, author.
Title: Hitler's American gamble : Pearl Harbor and Germany's march to global
   war / Brendan Simms, and Charlie Laderman.
Other titles: Pearl Harbor and Germany's march to global war
Description: First edition. | New York : Basic Books, 2021. | Includes
   bibliographical references and index.
Identifiers: LCCN 2021016054 | ISBN 9781541619098 (hardcover) |
   ISBN 9781541619081 (ebook)
Subjects: LCSH: World War, 1939–1945—Causes. | World War, 1939–1945—
   Germany. | Strategy. | United States—Strategic aspects. | World War,
   1939–1945—United States.
Classification: LCC D742.G4 S56 2021 | DDC 940.53/43—dc23
LC record available at https://lccn.loc.gov/2021016054

ISBNs: 9781541619098 (hardcover), 9781541619081 (ebook)

LSC-C

Printing 1, 2021

CONTENTS

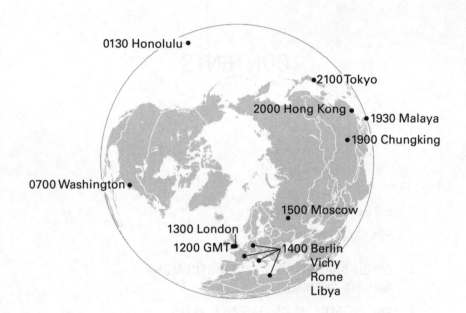

0130 Honolulu •

•2100 Tokyo

2000 Hong Kong •

•1930 Malaya

•1900 Chungking

0700 Washington •

1500 Moscow
•

1300 London

1200 GMT•

1400 Berlin
Vichy
Rome
Libya

TIME ZONES

01:30	Honolulu
07:00	Washington
12:00	Greenwich Mean Time (GMT)
13:00	London*
14:00	Berlin, Vichy, Rome, Libya
15:00	Moscow
19:00	Chungking
19:30	Malaya
20:00	Hong Kong
21:00	Tokyo

* During World War II, British Double Summer Time—two hours ahead of GMT—was temporarily introduced for the period when ordinary daylight saving would normally be in effect. During the winter months, clocks continued to be one hour ahead of GMT to enhance productivity. See "Why Do the Clocks Change?," Royal Museums Greenwich, www.rmg .co.uk/stories/topics/british-summer-time-bst-daylight-saving#:~:text=During%20the %20Second%20World%20War,of%20GMT%20to%20increase%20productivity.

PREFACE

T HE FIVE DAYS FROM THE JAPANESE ASSAULT ON PEARL HARBOR to Adolf Hitler's declaration of war on the United States were among the most fraught, but remain some of the least understood, of the twentieth century. The dominant narrative holds that Japan's surprise attack led inexorably to the outbreak of a truly global conflict. In this view, American opposition to involvement in both the Pacific and European wars simply melted away on December 7, 1941. As the stridently anti-interventionist Senator Arthur Vandenberg subsequently claimed in an oft-quoted remark: "That day ended isolationism for any realist."[1] It is assumed that the United States' entry into the war against Germany was inevitable from the moment that Japan struck Pearl Harbor. This perspective has been encouraged by no less a witness than Winston Churchill himself, who later spoke of having "slept the sleep of the saved and thankful" after hearing the news of Japan's attack. In his memoirs, he would declare that "now at this very moment I knew the United States was in the war, up to the neck and in to the death. So we had won after all!"[2]

Yet at the time, Churchill did not regard America's full-scale entry into the war against Germany as a foregone conclusion. Nor was he alone. Across the world, politicians and military leaders tried to fathom what had happened in Hawaii and where it might lead. In fact, it would take almost one hundred hours from Pearl Harbor for the situation to resolve itself—five agonizing days in which the fate of the world hung in the balance. In the end, it was Hitler who declared war on the United States on December 11, rather than the other way around. Among those who do remember this order of events, the declaration is considered an inexplicable strategic blunder by Hitler, sealing the fate of his regime. But in reality, Hitler's declaration of war was a deliberate gamble, driven by his geopolitical calculations, his assessment of the balance of manpower and matériel, and, above all, his obsession with the United States and its global influence.

The world that emerged on December 12, 1941, was not inevitable a week earlier, nor even immediately after the Pearl Harbor attack. Before December 1941, Asia and Europe were the scenes of cataclysmic conflicts, but these struggles raged across the Eurasian landmass and on the surrounding oceans, essentially siloed in their separate theaters. Between the Pearl Harbor attack and Hitler's declaration of war on the United States, five days passed during which the future of those disconnected struggles was decided, and every major power was forced to commit to one of two camps.[3] This interval was the crucible for a new global alignment that would dramatically alter the course of the conflict and reverberate far beyond the war, with implications we still feel today.

Churchill's actions and comments during this pivotal period demonstrate unease and anxiety more than triumphal relief. Immediately upon hearing news of Pearl Harbor, Churchill made urgent plans to travel to Washington. As he informed King George VI, he was desperate to ensure that the influx of aid from the United States, on which Britain's fighting capacity depended, "does not suffer more than is, I fear, inevitable."[4] His fears were exacerbated when, on the night of December 7, the US Army and Navy stopped all defense aid shipments to foreign governments to ensure that sufficient supplies were available for America's own war in the Pacific. From Washington, the British ambassador,

Lord Halifax, warned Churchill that Roosevelt was reluctant to agree to his visit. The American public, Halifax said, was now focused on Japan. Worse, many Americans remained unconvinced that the United States needed to entangle itself in an additional conflict with the German Reich. Indeed, Senator Vandenberg himself wrote in his diary on December 8 that although he and his fellow "non-interventionists" were now ready to "go along" with war against Japan, they remained wedded to "our beliefs."[5] They showed little sign of embracing a wider war.

President Franklin Roosevelt was well aware of the national mood. Roosevelt had spent more than a year carefully educating his fellow countrymen about the threat posed by Hitler's Germany. He had established the United States as the "arsenal of democracy," providing as much aid as was politically feasible to the Allied nations fighting Hitler. While Roosevelt prioritized Europe, he had evinced comparatively less concern about Japanese ambitions in the Pacific. But now, on December 7, 1941, the United States found itself at war not with Nazi Germany, against whom Roosevelt had devoted so many American resources, but with Imperial Japan. An immediate declaration of war on Hitler was a tremendous political risk at a time when the nation's attention and anger were directed against Japan.

Cables from Berlin to Tokyo, intercepted and decoded by US intelligence, suggested that Germany would join any war that Japan fought against the United States, but Hitler's behavior was not so easy to predict. As Roosevelt's speechwriter Robert Sherwood later noted, the Nazis "were in honour bound by their pledges to the Japanese, but they had not previously shown much inclination to let such bourgeois-democratic considerations interfere with their own concepts on self-interest."[6]

Japan's leadership was no more certain that Hitler would keep his word. Emperor Hirohito and other members of the Japanese elite had repeatedly expressed their fear that Hitler, who had previously described the Japanese as a second-class race, would reconcile with the other "white powers"—the "Anglo-Saxon" United States and British Empire—leaving Japan to fight alone.[7] There was indeed considerable ambivalence in Berlin about helping to bring down the so-called white British Empire, even though Hitler had increasingly reshaped himself as the defender of those he termed the global "have-nots" against the Anglo-Saxon "haves" as the war progressed.

Moreover, Hitler was being advised that, as Japan had initiated the conflict with the United States, Germany was under no obligation to support its ally by joining in a declaration of war. German diplomats made their leader aware that Roosevelt was determined to avoid simultaneous hostilities in the Pacific and Atlantic and had no intention of issuing a declaration against Germany. If Germany avoided a formal state of war with the United States, then, with America's attention fixed on Japan, Britain might be deprived of any further meaningful support from Washington and left isolated against the Axis powers in the Atlantic. Keeping the struggles separate might well give Germany the advantage against the British and the Soviets.

In Moscow, Pearl Harbor came at a time when the tide of war with Germany seemed to be turning. Stalin's master spy in Tokyo, Richard Sorge, had previously reported that the Japanese intended to strike against the Anglo-Americans and not the Soviet Union, and the attack vindicated Stalin's decision to move much of the Far Eastern army west to deal with the Germans. Yet Pearl Harbor triggered profound anxiety in the Kremlin. First, because it brought American pressure to declare war on Japan and thus plunge the Soviet Union into a two-front war after all. Second, because the new needs of the US armed forces, and those of the embattled British Empire in Asia, threatened to reduce the flow of vital military aid to the Soviet Union.

The world, then, held its breath. The global sense of confusion and unpredictability after Pearl Harbor was captured by the American diplomat George Kennan, then stationed at the US embassy in Berlin. With all communication lines now cut by the Nazis, Kennan and his colleagues could only speculate whether a US-German war was imminent, debating among themselves whether to burn their diplomatic codes and declassified files lest they fall into enemy hands. As Kennan later recalled, "We lived in excruciating uncertainty."[8]

ON DECEMBER 11, 1941, it was Hitler who let Roosevelt, the American interventionists, and the Allies off the hook. His declaration of war on the United States turned two potentially separate conflicts into a truly world war. For almost every other major world leader, the Pearl Harbor attack initially brought confusion. For Hitler, it was a moment of "murderous clarity."[9] The terrible consequences were felt not only by combatants and the civilian population the world over, but also by European Jews. The Nazi dictator was convinced that the US president, international "plutocratic" capitalism, and "world Jewry" were together bent on his destruction. For Hitler, Jews were not only responsible for the actions of Roosevelt, but potentially a weapon that could be used against him. For three years, Hitler had explicitly held European Jewry hostage to secure the good behavior of the Americans. Inspired by his conspiratorial view of worldwide Jewish influence, Hitler believed that the threat of further violence against European—especially central and western European—Jews would deter their supposed agent, President Roosevelt, from intervening directly in the European war.

Of course, Hitler's genocidal ambitions had already been barbarically and brutally demonstrated well before December 1941. The murders of at least a million mainly Soviet Jews were proof of his long-standing intentions. But as 1941 came to an end, millions of western and central European Jews were still alive, if in great peril. Nazi leaders had discussed their systematic destruction for some time, but the timing and technical details were still not agreed, and, most important, the Führer himself had not yet communicated a final decision to the party leadership. Following his declaration of war on the United States, Hitler would tie the fate of surviving European Jewry inextricably to the collapse of US-German relations. When he declared war on the United States, he also pronounced a sentence of death on the Jews of western and central Europe. In 1939, Hitler had delivered his infamous warning that the consequences of a world at war would be the annihilation of the Jews. In the subsequent two years, he had repeatedly invoked this "prophecy," which was by its very nature, for someone with his radically anti-Semitic worldview, ultimately a self-fulfilling one. But it was only after his declaration of war on the United States on December 11, 1941, that he would move to fully realize this apocalyptic vision.

If for Hitler the die was cast, things were still very much uncertain in Washington and London. At the start of December history seemed open, and this sense of uncertainty persisted in the immediate aftermath of Pearl Harbor as well. Yet over time, the participants would remember their experiences in ways shaped by the outcome. Memories and stories came to reflect the ultimate, decisive defeat of the Axis nations by the combined Allied powers. Looking back, the Axis fate appeared inescapable, and so the uncertain events that led to it seemed inevitable.[10] This tension between determinacy and contingency is what makes these five days in December so dramatic—and why we must unpick the days, hours, and minutes to turn back the clock and get closer to the truth of these moments as they were lived.

Powerful narratives like Churchill's "sleep of the saved" have distorted our memory of this period, but history was being rewritten before 1941 was even over. Days mattered. For example, Roosevelt's trusted pollster Hadley Cantril, on whom the president relied to gauge public opinion before embarking on any major policy decisions, would also contribute to the impression that an American declaration of war against Germany was inevitable as soon as the Pearl Harbor attack occurred. In his survey of American public opinion around World War II, Cantril would reproduce a poll, ostensibly from December 10, 1941, in which an overwhelming 90 percent of respondents were in favor of Roosevelt asking Congress for a declaration of war on Germany as well as Japan.[11] Historians have pointed to this poll as evidence that American public opinion was settled on the question of war with Germany in the immediate aftermath of the Pearl Harbor assault and that a declaration of war by Roosevelt was imminent, irrespective of what Hitler did.[12] Yet Cantril's account of the poll's date was misleading. The poll question was finalized on December 10, but it was not actually put to Americans until two days later. That is, the question was asked on the day after Hitler declared war on the United States. A resounding affirmative response was, therefore, unsurprising. Those Americans polled on this question between December 12 and 17 were, in effect, simply validating what their government had already done in answering Hitler's declaration of war on December 11 with a reciprocal American declaration that same day.[13]

For five momentous days, while clocks ticked in chancelleries and war rooms across the world, the minds of the major leaders inevitably went back to the last great conflict, which many had experienced firsthand, either as soldiers or statesmen. To truly comprehend the mentalité of these men at this time, we must first understand how the global strategic picture had evolved in the almost quarter century since the First World War and the ways in which these powerful individuals experienced, and contributed to, that transition. We begin, therefore, by charting the emergence of an Anglo-American world hegemony, which was furiously resisted by the self-described have-nots of the international system: Imperial Japan, Italy—another Fascist regime in Europe that saw territorial expansion as the route to great-power status—and, above all, the Third Reich.

Our story thereafter is largely metropolitan in focus, concentrating not only on the battlefronts but on how the political intrigue and breaking news was reported and received by the leadership, the press, the military, and the wider public in major capitals around the world. We draw on a broad range of often neglected sources, especially German, British, and American, the three powers at the center of our story. Of particular significance is the correspondence of the German Foreign Office; the records of those responsible for the procurement and distribution of American military aid on both sides of the Atlantic, which, while largely overlooked by other analysts of this critical juncture, reveal the potentially fatal threat posed by the new US-Japanese war to vital defense support to Britain and the USSR; the papers of Roosevelt's domestic political opponents; and the files of leading Americans in Germany and Italy who, more than most, experienced the "excruciating uncertainty" of those momentous days. We also draw on diaries, memoirs, newspaper reports, and other accounts by individuals across all the major combatant nations to show how the events of these five days were perceived and experienced by ordinary people across the globe.

Above all, this book emphasizes and recreates the uncertainty of these five crucial days in global history. It is the first study to investigate this critical period in such extensive detail.[14] Rather than adopting a geographical approach, we provide an hour-by-hour and sometimes minute-by-minute account of these days in a truly global and nonstop narrative. The fate of the world hung on decisions made in multiple countries but, between December 7 and 11, Britain was the only power at war in both the Atlantic and Pacific theaters. Consequently, each day begins at midnight in London, by which time it is already 1 a.m. in Berlin and Rome, 2 a.m. in Moscow, and 8 a.m. in Tokyo, but still 6 p.m. the previous day in Washington. This blow-by-blow account enables us to reconstruct the drama and complexity of the events as they unfolded, sequentially and sometimes simultaneously, across four continents and more than half a dozen time zones. What played out over these five days was as consequential as any crisis in twentieth-century diplomatic history, because it transformed that century's second great conflagration into a war that was even more destructive and world-encompassing than the first. In challenging the prevailing deterministic interpretation of this critical turning point in the Second World War, our book uncovers the rationale behind what proved to be Hitler's greatest strategic error and offers a new perspective on the background to America's rise to world power.

1

ORIGINS

Anglo-American Hegemony and Its Enemies

O N December 11, 1941, Adolf Hitler stood before the German Reichstag. Four days had passed since Japan had launched a devastating assault on Pearl Harbor and unleashed a series of attacks against American and British possessions across Asia. Japan was now at war with the British Empire and United States. For the other Axis powers, Germany and Italy, much remained unresolved. The Asian and European conflicts were not yet fully conjoined. The United States was a belligerent in the former but not formally in the latter. The Tripartite Pact between Germany, Italy, and Japan committed each to go to the others' aid if they were attacked, but as other world powers were aware, the pact required nothing if they were the aggressor. Hours turned to days as the world waited to see how Hitler would respond.

When Hitler began to speak, no one outside of his closest confidants could be certain exactly what he would say or what the consequences would be. After a ramble across the different war fronts, the Führer arrived at America. He began by declaring that there was no reason why Germany and the United States, who were racially akin and who had no clashing national interests, should be at odds. Despite this, he claimed,

Washington had launched an unprovoked attack on the German Reich in 1917 and was now preparing to do the same again. Hitler argued that the US president during that first conflict, Woodrow Wilson, had been driven by "a group of interested financiers" who hoped for "increased business." The misery that the German people had suffered after defeat in the First World War was primarily the responsibility of Wilson and this shadowy clique. Although Hitler did not discuss it on this occasion, that cataclysm had been the decisive turning point in his life, and his first encounter with Americans on the battlefield had indelibly shaped his worldview.[1]

As open hostilities again loomed with the United States, Hitler lamented to the Reichstag: "Why is there now another president of the USA who regards it as his only task to intensify anti-German feeling to the pitch of war?" For Hitler, the answer was simple: it was "a fact that the two conflicts between Germany and the USA were inspired by the same force and caused by two men in the USA—Wilson and Roosevelt."[2] The "force" to which Hitler alluded was Jewish international finance, which he claimed was once more at work, manipulating the incumbent president, Franklin Delano Roosevelt, to follow in Wilson's footsteps. Although the Wilhelmine Reich had awaited the blow passively, Hitler vowed to strike first, announcing the start of open hostilities against the United States. Only now would the war become a world war.

IT HAD BEEN almost twenty-five years since American intervention had turned the tide of a major international conflict. While the Great War engulfed Europe, President Wilson had struggled for almost three years to keep his country out. In 1915, he secured a pledge from the Germans to suspend their aggressive U-boat offensive in the Atlantic. Yet in January 1917—as the Allied blockade threatened to strangle Germany into submission and Allied armies used munitions supplied by American manufacturers against German troops—the military-controlled government in Berlin announced the resumption of unrestricted submarine warfare.

Even then Wilson did not immediately declare war. Noninterventionist sentiment remained strong, particularly in the American Midwest, and Wilson feared leading a divided nation into war. Yet after the interception of the Zimmerman telegram, in which Germany's foreign minister proposed an alliance with Mexico in the event of a US-German war, and the subsequent sinking of American vessels by German U-boats, a reluctant Wilson decided that he had no choice. In April 1917, he brought the United States into the war "to make the world safe for democracy" and, in doing so, revolutionized international politics.[3]

At the beginning of the First World War, the United States was unrivaled as the world's most powerful industrial nation, producing far more coal and oil than any other country, a third of the world's manufactured goods, and a fifth of global economic output. Its navy was the third largest in the world, and although its military remained small, even by the standards of a midsize European nation, its potential was vast. At a time when steel production was regarded as a key indicator of prospective military capacity, American output was almost equal to that of the next four countries combined.[4] As Winston Churchill recalled, his then cabinet colleague, the foreign secretary Sir Edward Grey, compared the prewar US economy to "a gigantic boiler. Once the fire is lighted under it there is no limit to the power it can generate."[5]

Upon America's entrance into the war, industrial and military production surged. Reinforced by the power of their American associate, the Allies finally forced Germany to sue for peace in November 1918. Among the major powers other than Japan, only the United States emerged vastly stronger. The war witnessed the collapse of the German, Russian, Austro-Hungarian, and Ottoman Empires. Even among the victors, Britain and France suffered great losses.[6] The United States now possessed economic power on a scale unprecedented in world history and had intervened militarily to help determine events on the European continent for the first time.[7] The US president seemed poised to shape a new international order, centered on a League of Nations and underpinned by principles of open diplomacy, national self-determination, arms control, freedom of the seas, and a liberal trading order.[8]

The war raised the specter of American power, but political fissures promptly demonstrated its limits. After Wilson was forced to make concessions at the Paris Peace Conference to secure Allied agreement to the Versailles Treaty and the Covenant of the League of Nations, he then proved unable to convince the Republican-controlled Congress to ratify the treaty or join the new international organization. The Republican administrations that presided over American diplomacy for the next dozen years adopted a more restrained international role. While helping to limit naval armaments in East Asia at the 1921–1922 Washington Conference and using American economic power to help create the conditions that underpinned relative stability in Europe during the 1920s, these presidents, backed by the overwhelming majority of Americans, were determined to avoid any international political commitments.[9] They kept the United States aloof from the League, whose dominant powers, Britain and France, were regarded by many American officials as immoral imperialists who put their own narrow national interests above broader international harmony and were committed to upholding an unjust settlement.[10]

As the United States effectively withdrew from a leading role in international politics, the burden of maintaining the fragile international political and economic order largely rested on Britain. But the First World War had exacted a heavy toll. The conflict had destroyed London's dominance of international finance and left Britain deeply indebted to the United States.[11] Nevertheless, although it no longer enjoyed the industrial supremacy of its mid-to-late-nineteenth-century heyday, Britain remained relatively more economically powerful than its European rivals. Its political system had weathered the war better than those on the continent, accommodating the arrival of mass democracy in 1918. It presided over an empire that had reached its territorial zenith—albeit one in which anti-colonial nationalism was on the rise, particularly in India and Egypt, and in which the Dominions (Australia, Canada, the Irish Free State, Newfoundland, New Zealand, and South Africa) could no longer be automatically relied on to stand with the metropole in case of conflict. Even so, in the decade after the First World War, Britain's global influence was unparalleled and, with the United States on the sidelines, it was perceived by its strategic competitors as the central power in almost every major diplomatic issue.[12]

The interwar Anglo-American relationship was ambivalent. Signs of serious naval rivalry were evident in the 1920s, and in retrospect it is clear that the process of "hegemonic transition" from British to US dominance was already underway.[13] But to much of the rest of the world, US-British accord appeared to prevail based on a shared heritage and common strategic, economic, and racial interests.[14] British leaders had hoped to formalize this in an alliance to govern global affairs after World War I but were thwarted by America's rejection of League membership, a decision motivated, at least in part, by popular American perceptions that Britain was simply seeking to exploit US international ideals for its own selfish ends.[15] Nevertheless, many American politicians and businessmen came to believe that US interests were well served by British primacy outside the Western Hemisphere, as long as it enabled American companies equal access to global markets. Few articulated this as clearly as the US governor-general of the Philippines, who spoke in the late 1920s of the need to defend "Anglo-Saxonism . . . in the Western Pacific, in the Far East, [and] in India."[16] As we shall see, this hegemony was resented as keenly by the populations of the formal and informal "Anglo-Saxon" empires as it was by the European and Asian powers pursuing imperial ambitions of their own. Hatred and envy of the Anglo-Saxon world system was something that German racists, Japanese expansionists, Soviet Communists, and anti-colonial activists could all agree on.

MEANWHILE, THE NAZI leader Adolf Hitler spent the 1920s in relative obscurity, imagining a world in which the German Reich would coexist as an equal with the British Empire and the United States. He feared and admired the "Anglo-Saxons," as he also came to call them, who he believed wielded the power of international capitalism, which he otherwise associated with "world Jewry." In his view, Germany had been racially hollowed out by the emigration of its "best" elements to "fertilize" the new world, especially the United States. These same men, Hitler believed, had then come back to scourge the Reich as enemy soldiers during the First World War. He also blamed Germany's defeat on a conspiracy between the British, the Americans, and Jewish plutocracy, which had starved the Reich through the naval blockade, undermined it from within through Communist subversion, and overwhelmed it with men and shells on the battlefield. In his view, the Germans had subsequently been "negrified" by the victors, reduced to the status of "slaves" on a "plantation."

Throughout the decade, Hitler focused intensely on the industrial power, natural resources, territorial extent, and supposed "racial" quality of the United States. "One should take America as a model," he proclaimed while in prison after his failed putsch of 1923. The main focus of his unpublished *Second Book* in 1928 was the overwhelming power of Anglo-America, and especially of the United States. "The American Union," Hitler argued, "has created a power factor of such dimensions that it threatens to overthrow all previous state power rankings" and had the capacity to challenge even the British Empire. This view survived the Wall Street crash of 1929 largely unchanged. Reviewing the list of Germany's rivals, he stated in early February 1931 that the United States had become a "competitor on the world market," especially "since the war," because it was "a giant state with unimaginable productive capacities." Unless Germany could match this power, Hitler feared, it would stay in the state of subjection to which it had been condemned by the outcome of the First World War.[17]

The solution, Hitler argued, lay in the removal of Jewish influence from Germany and in the seizure of new Lebensraum (living space) in the east, into which he would channel future German settlement. When he took power in 1933, Hitler acted on these views without delay. He moved to isolate the Jews, rearm Germany, and, at first unopposed, harvest low-hanging fruit through the reoccupation of the Rhineland, the Anschluss of Austria, and the annexation of the formerly Czech Sudetenland.[18]

On the other side of the world, imperial Japan was on a similar journey. Like the German Reich, Japan had been fast-tracked to great power status, defeating an ailing China in 1895, besting mighty Russia in 1905, and annexing Korea in 1910. Like the Germans, the Japanese had primarily taken this course in order to avoid external domination. But unlike the German Reich, Japan had emerged from the First World War a victor. Nevertheless, Japan also felt increasingly constrained and humiliated by the West, especially the American insistence that China not become a colony of Tokyo, but that the "door" should remain "open" to all trade. Despite the Anglo-Japanese alliance of 1902—which showed that, for the British at least, race was subordinate to strategic considerations—and US president Theodore Roosevelt's acceptance of the Japanese as an "honorary white race" at the time of the Russo-Japanese War, the established powers rebuffed Japanese attempts to have the principle of racial equality between member states incorporated into the League of Nation charter.[19] For Tokyo's part, protecting Japanese emigrants, rather than an abstract commitment to racial equality, had been a prime motivation. American and European fears of unchecked immigration from Japan made this concession impossible in 1919.[20]

This rejection left a deep wound in the Japanese elite, exacerbated by the white racism many experienced firsthand during their travels and in diplomatic encounters. One of these elite was Prince Konoye, who would later become Japanese prime minister at a critical time leading up to Pearl Harbor. "The white people—and the Anglo-Saxon race in particular," he wrote in 1919, "generally abhor coloured people," something that was "blatantly observable in the US treatment of its black people."[21] One Japanese daily paper spoke of "Anglo-Saxon dominance in defiance of racial equality."[22] As the Japanese pushed back against white domination, there were many in Asia and across the world who saw Japan, as the African American campaigner James Weldon Johnson put it, as "perhaps the greatest hope for the coloured race of the world."[23] Defining or overcoming the global color line became an increasingly vital aspect of the looming struggle for the challenger powers.

To the leadership in Tokyo, the Washington Naval Treaty of 1922, which institutionalized Japan's numerical inferiority in warships, epitomized their sense of discrimination. In their minds, imperial Japan was "surrounded" by the Communist Soviet Union and the British Empire, but the "enemy number one" was the United States.[24] This perception was shared by many outside Japan. Weldon Johnson, for example, claimed that the Washington agreement was designed "to isolate Japan and put her more at the mercy of the two great Anglo-Saxon nations," the United States and the British Empire.[25] Japanese humiliation was then completed by the US Immigration Act of 1924, which discriminated against arrivals from Asia and eastern Europe. This was both a psychological and a political blow, because emigration had served a crucial role as a demographic safety valve for overcrowded Japan. Western rejection boosted Japanese pan-Asianism, the idea that the Japanese Empire might lead to the emancipation of the Asian peoples from white tutelage.[26]

But Tokyo was no avatar of global racial equality. What Japan wanted was "civilized" status and not to be colonized, two aims the regime expressed by maintaining colonies of its own. This is why Western objections to Japan's colonization of China grated so much. "Read your history," the Japanese envoy to the League of Nations fulminated in the early 1930s. "Would the American people agree to such control of the Panama Canal Zone? Would the British permit it over Egypt?"[27] The looming conflict between Japan and the Anglo-Saxon powers was thus both a traditional territorial contest and a new racial struggle.[28]

Japan suffered from critical shortages of raw materials to support its industries and armaments programs, however. Like Hitler, the Japanese leaders thought they, too, had learned the lessons of the German experience in World War I. The Japanese sought to address these material deficiencies through autarky and pursuit of their own living space by means of territorial expansion into China, beginning with the occupation of Manchuria in 1931, which was widely seen as an attempt by a subordinate power to escape its inferior status. Imperial Japan was—as Stanley Hornbeck, chief of the State Department's Division of Far Eastern Affairs, put it in 1934—one of the "have-nots" of the world, destined to clash with "haves" such as the United States.[29] This policy culminated in a full-scale assault on China in 1937, and the outbreak of a Sino-Japanese war that pitched Japan against the nationalist leader Chiang Kai-shek and his Anglo-American backers, as well as against the then-obscure Communist movement of Mao Tse-Tung.

For a white supremacist, Hitler's view of Japan was remarkably positive.[30] In his manifesto *Mein Kampf*, penned in the 1920s, he claimed to have sympathized with Tokyo during the Russo-Japanese War. The Führer also expressed admiration for Japanese naval and foreign policy, which he contrasted with the ineffectiveness of the Wilhelmine Reich.[31] He saw the Japanese as fellow victims of Jewish machinations.[32] He admired the way they had acquired "European science and technology with Japanese characteristics."[33] That said, there was also an element of skepticism, evident in his view that Japan's rise to power had been driven by an "Aryan impulse" and in his reluctance until the late 1930s to choose Japan over China, which was still favored by the army and the Foreign Office.[34] For example, Hitler refused, for now, to recognize the Japanese annexation of Manchuria.

Fascist Italy, for its part, was determined not to be left out of any global redistribution of power. The former socialist Benito Mussolini seized power in 1922 with the promise to reclaim the "mutilated victory" Italy had secured as one of the Allies in World War I through a program of domestic transformation and external expansion.[35] He attacked Abyssinia (Ethiopia) in 1935, eventually occupying the whole country. His main focus, though, was the Mediterranean, which he hoped—at least rhetorically—to turn into an "Italian lake." There, Mussolini threw down the gauntlet to France and especially Britain. Building a large fleet of surface warships, Italy set out to become a formidable foe for the overstretched Royal Navy, which had bases in Gibraltar, Malta, and Alexandria. Mussolini claimed to want "neither monopolies nor privileges," but rather asked "those countries who have already arrived [the United States, the British Empire, and France], those who are satisfied and conservative" not to "try to block on every side the spiritual, political and economic expansion of Fascist Italy."[36] This was the same rhetoric of resentment that Hitler and the Japanese were using, and an early portent of the subsequent alliance between the three countries.

The three challenger powers began to collaborate. In October 1936, Germany and Italy moved closer together with a declaration of friendship. Shortly afterward, Mussolini remarked that world politics had begun to revolve around a Berlin-Rome "axis," and the term stuck. In November 1936, a Germany-Japan treaty—the Anti-Comintern Pact—followed. This was initially directed against the Soviet Union, but the pact also increasingly targeted the British Empire and the United States. In due course, it became routine to refer to the Third Reich, Italy, and Japan collectively as the Axis powers. Shortly after the agreement with Japan was signed, the Nazi propaganda minister Joseph Goebbels wrote in his diary that "the Führer thinks the fruits of this agreement will only ripen in five years' time. He really pursues policy in the long term."[37] This turned out to be an uncannily precise prediction.

In the United States, disenchanted policy makers bitterly observed the rise and growing cooperation of these aggressive authoritarian regimes. Just under two decades after their country's crusade "to make the world safe for democracy," Americans had little confidence or interest in their capacity to heal a fallen world. Europe, in particular, was regarded as inherently war-torn, and it was widely believed that the United States should do everything possible to avoid re-entangling itself in the affairs of that benighted continent.[38] This view, of course, was built on deeper American beliefs about Europe as an essentially corrupt and hierarchical continent that so many Americans, or their ancestors, had left behind.[39] In any case, the United States' power and favorable geographical position, separated by vast oceans from the storm centers of Europe and Asia, convinced most Americans that their security would hardly be impaired even if the dictatorships overturned the existing order there. Polls consistently showed that Americans now regarded intervention in the last global war as a mistake. An investigation led by the Republican senator Gerald Nye between 1934 and 1936 blamed America's entrance into that previous conflict on munitions makers and bankers, arguing that their aid to the Allies had precipitated the German submarine campaign. Public outrage energized Congress to pass a raft of legislation that prohibited loans to warring governments, imposed a mandatory arms embargo on all sides, and banned travel on belligerent ships.[40]

For much of the 1930s, it was generally agreed that the overriding goal of US foreign policy was to avoid involvement in a major foreign war. This was an objective to which President Franklin Roosevelt—though privately an advocate of greater international engagement and scornful of the idea that the United States could remain idle as the global environment deteriorated—publicly committed himself. He had served as assistant secretary of the navy under Woodrow Wilson, and the fate of the former president remained at the forefront of Roosevelt's mind during his own time in office. As his speechwriter, Robert Sherwood, observed, whenever Roosevelt worked on a significant address, he "would look up at the portrait of Woodrow Wilson over the mantelpiece" in the White House's Cabinet Room. Sherwood maintained that "the tragedy of Wilson was always somewhere within the rim of his consciousness," and "no motivating force" in shaping Roosevelt's foreign policy was "stronger than the determination to prevent repetition of the same mistakes."[41] Above all, Roosevelt was determined to avoid committing the United States to policies that Americans were ultimately unwilling to fulfill, as Wilson had after the First World War. Acutely conscious that the bulk of the nation was opposed to ever again dispatching forces overseas to a large-scale conflict, Roosevelt declared during his 1936 re-election campaign that Americans were "not isolationists except insofar as we seek to isolate ourselves completely from war."[42]

Four years after being elected to deal with the debilitating economic depression, Roosevelt started his second term in 1937 facing a stalled recovery and steep recession. An acrimonious showdown over the president's attempts to extend his New Deal domestic reforms by enlarging the Supreme Court and reorganizing the federal government further consumed his agenda in the year that followed. While there was widespread popular sympathy for China in its struggle with Japan, most Americans were focused on domestic matters and disinclined to extend meaningful assistance.[43]

Yet Roosevelt seized the opportunity presented by the China-Japan conflict to challenge this sentiment in an October 1937 speech in Chicago, one of the strongest bastions of isolationism. "Let no one imagine that America will escape, that America may expect mercy, that this Western Hemisphere will not be attacked" when Germany, Italy, and Japan have so flagrantly violated "the sanctity of international treaties and the maintenance of international morality," Roosevelt warned his audience. In response to the "disease" represented by the totalitarian aggressors, he wanted the United States to join with the democracies in a "quarantine of the patients."[44] The three transgressor powers were identified as what we might today call an axis of evil.

A domestic backlash forced Roosevelt to clarify that any "quarantine" would not involve joining any collective sanctions.[45] Despite the president's rhetorical denunciation of the dictatorships, the public's continuing opposition to international commitments prevented him from offering guarantees that the United States would do much to deter the Axis powers' aggression. Though Roosevelt regularly condemned Japan's brutal policies in East Asia and its encroachment on America's interests and treaty rights in China, his administration avoided active involvement in any initiative to curtail the conflict. In Europe, the Roosevelt administration initially suggested an openness to aligning the United States with any League of Nations sanctions on exports, most notably oil, to Italy after its Abyssinian invasion. But the League ultimately decided against an oil embargo, in part because its leading members suspected that American neutrality legislation left Roosevelt powerless to place any effective constraints on exports.[46] Although publicly committed to peaceful resolution of disputes and privately inclined toward cooperation with the Western democracies, Roosevelt could provide little tangible aid to stiffen British and French resolve.[47]

Nevertheless, the substantial expansion of the US Navy during the thirties ensured that American power remained on standby. America's military spending still lagged behind that of Germany and Japan in 1937. But with a national income that equaled that of those two powers, the British Empire, Italy, and the Soviet Union combined, the United States' potential productive power was staggering if utilized to anything like its full capacity.[48] The following year, as Japan continued its assault on China and Germany annexed Austria, the US Congress passed legislation, revealingly nicknamed the "Navy Second to None Act," to massively expand the fleet. And as Roosevelt became increasingly convinced that a Berlin-Rome-Tokyo axis threatened to encircle the Western Hemisphere, he began to explore measures to coerce the dictators short of declared war. That is, as the president put it to his cabinet, he hoped to achieve the "same result" as fighting, which the American public would not abide, but without needing "to go to war to get it."[49]

To Britain's prime minister Neville Chamberlain and his chief advisers, Roosevelt looked weak, trapped by isolationist opinion and more concerned with domestic politics than an emerging international crisis. Like many British leaders of the era, Chamberlain was resentful that Britain had committed itself to the League of Nations in 1919 to satisfy the Americans and was then left to pick up the pieces when the US Congress rejected membership.[50] As a result, he dismissed Roosevelt's proposals for an international conference, designed to reduce tensions and sow division among the Axis powers, as just more evidence that it was "always best and safest to count on nothing from the Americans except words."[51]

Instead, Chamberlain's government focused on reaching separate agreements with Britain's potential adversaries. Confronted with three revisionist powers in three separate theaters, Britain faced grave strategic challenges. The maintenance of Britain's imperial possessions, especially in the Far East, was seen as central to the nation's global standing, with implications for its influence in Europe. "It is our imperial position which gives this country its great voice in the world," the first sea lord and chief of the naval staff, Sir Ernie Chatfield, wrote. "Unless we are willing to maintain that imperial position," he continued, "we shall become once more nothing but an insignificant island in the North Sea" carrying "as much weight in the councils of the world as Italy or Spain."[52]

Yet with an empire stretched across the world, Britain's leaders were acutely aware of the limited resources at their disposal to meet all these potential threats at the same time. They resorted to clandestine compromises to appease the aggressors, such as the abortive Hoare-Laval Pact of 1935, which would have granted Italy part of Ethiopia in the hopes of separating Mussolini from Hitler. When this ill-fated attempt was exposed, it was roundly condemned not only by the British public but by Americans as well. Roosevelt regarded British appeasement as evidence of a lack of moral fiber, privately noting that "what the British need today is good stiff grog, including not only the desire to save civilization but the confirmed belief that they can do it," in which case they would "have more support from their American cousins."[53]

After it became clear that the Munich Agreement of September 1938 had done nothing to sate Hitler's appetite and after the anti-Semitic outrages of Kristallnacht in November 1938 had confirmed Nazi barbarism, the attitude of Chamberlain's government hardened.[54] In turn, these events led the majority of Americans to regard Germany with hostility, and Roosevelt requested a substantial rearmament program from Congress—particularly in warplanes, which he intended primarily for purchase by Britain and France in order to deter Hitler.[55] While the defense program sailed through Congress, Roosevelt's attempt to revise the neutrality legislation and repeal the arms embargo was rejected. Roosevelt's increasing willingness to countenance cautious cooperation raised the hopes of Britain's leaders. But they remained uncertain whether they could expect substantive support from the world's most powerful nation and concerned that, if it did come, the price would be steep.[56]

All the while, the Soviet dictator Joseph Stalin watched the rise of Nazi Germany and Imperial Japan with concern. He was particularly keen to avoid being "encircled" by them from west and east, forcing the Red Army to fight on two fronts.[57] In Europe, Stalin tried to block the advance of the Axis through the establishment of "popular fronts"—that is, alliances of Communists and socialists designed to contain the threat of "fascism." In Asia, Stalin sent pilots and advisers not to his fellow Communist Mao Tse-Tung but to the Chinese nationalist leader Chiang Kai-shek and his Kuomintang regime.[58] This was because he saw the latter as the more credible barrier to Japanese expansionism. At the same time, Stalin never lost sight of the fact that his ultimate enemies were the principal powers of the capitalist and imperialist world: the British Empire and the United States. On the lookout for any Western attempts to divert Hitler's attention east, Stalin was determined not to "take their chestnuts out of the fire."

BY THE LATE 1930s, the time of easy Axis victories was over. From the autumn of 1937, it became clear to Hitler that both London and Washington were deeply opposed to his aims. Globally, he reserved particular venom for Roosevelt, furious that his Quarantine Speech had targeted Nazi Germany along with Fascist Italy and Imperial Japan.[59] In 1938, the cautious German ambassador to Washington, Hans-Heinrich Dieckhoff, was recalled in retaliation for Roosevelt's withdrawal of the US ambassador from Berlin after the Kristallnacht pogrom.[60] From the Reich capital, Dieckhoff continued to warn of the dangers of conflict with the United States. His place was taken by the chargé d'affaires, Hans Thomsen, whose reports, along with those of the military attaché Friedrich von Boetticher, Hitler read attentively.[61] In Europe, Hitler identified "England [as] the motor of opposition to us."

With London and Washington firmly identified as hostile, Nazi Germany was now on a collision course with the haves, the established Anglo-American global powers who were denying Berlin, Rome, and Tokyo—the three have-nots—their rightful place at the world table.[62] This reframing had fearsome implications not only for world peace but also for European Jewry. In January 1939, Hitler connected the emerging global coalition against him with the "Jewish question" in a notorious speech to the Reichstag. "The German people," he said, "must know who the men are who are trying to provoke a war at all costs," and for this reason all propaganda should be focused on the "Jewish world enemy." Hitler then issued a coded but clear warning to Roosevelt and "world Jewry." "If Jewish international finance in and outside Europe should succeed in plunging the peoples into another war," Hitler announced, "then the result will not be the Bolshevization of the earth and thus

15

the victory of Jewry, but the destruction of the Jewish race in Europe." Hitler was sending an explicit message, at least as he saw it: European Jews would be held responsible for the behavior of "international finance Jewry" not just in Europe but also in New York and in Roosevelt's America generally.[63] The Jews were in effect to be his hostages.[64]

That same month, Boetticher warned Berlin about the "president and his Jewish friends [and] their boundless armament plans and their attempts to paint a German specter on the wall." Even if the immediate capacity of the United States to wage war was limited, the attaché cautioned, its potential was massive. Hitler told Boetticher that he would destroy Roosevelt by proving to the world that the president was of Jewish descent. He now asked the Washington embassy and other experts to establish the date by which the United States could practically intervene if war broke out in Europe in the course of the next year. It was no longer a question of whether war with America would come, but when.

Hitler's determination to match the United States was even reflected in his architectural visions. In January 1939, he met with Fritz Todt, his armaments minister, and Albert Speer, the general building inspector, in the imperial chancellery to discuss the planned remodeling of Hamburg and the construction of a huge San-Francisco-style bridge over the Elbe. Hitler explained his thinking to the German high command. Such monumental construction projects were part of his plan to show the German people "that it is not second-rate, but the equal of any other people on earth, even America."

Militarily, Hitler reacted by giving the navy priority in arms procurement and resource allocation. In January 1939, he secretly authorized the Z-Plan, a massive program of construction designed to culminate in the mid-1940s, the moment by which Hitler expected the confrontation with the United States to be unavoidable.[65]

Meanwhile, Japan was mired in an interminable conflict against the Chinese nationalist regime of General Chiang Kai-shek.[66] Rather than alleviating Japan's shortage of raw materials, the war proved to be a drain on scarce resources. Worse still, it put Tokyo under scrutiny internationally: Japan's global reputation never recovered from the notorious

Rape of Nanking in December 1937. For London, Japan was a threat to the empire, while for Washington, it was a challenge to the integrity of China and the US domination of the Pacific. This mattered because Japan was painfully dependent on US supplies of oil and scrap iron for its industries and shipyards. That said, the emerging solution to Japan's resource scarcity—namely, southward expansion toward the oil fields of the Dutch East Indies (today's Indonesia)—threatened to provoke open conflict. Tension with the British Empire and the United States rose. Japan invested even more heavily in its navy, and especially in naval aviation.[67] In November 1938, Prince Konoye proclaimed a "new order in East Asia," with Tokyo at its heart. This pan-Asian vision was synonymous with Japanese leadership and, in effect, domination.[68]

Hitler now finally opted for Japan over China.[69] After seven years of stalling, Germany recognized the annexation of Manchuria. In the autumn of 1938, Hitler authorized the construction of a huge new Japanese embassy on Berlin's Tiergarten park, not far from the Italian one. This was slated to be part of the complete remodeling of the entire city as Germania, the capital of the new Reich.[70] Hitler was dissatisfied, though, with the Japanese caution in embracing the Axis wholeheartedly. This reportedly resulted in an outburst in which Hitler traduced Emperor Hirohito as "weak, cowardly, and irresolute" and the Japanese as "at best lacquered half monkeys."[71] There is good reason to doubt that he said these words, but even if he did, he soon relented, because he needed Japanese help. Moreover, though Hitler occasionally toyed with the idea of encouraging Japan to attack the Soviet Union, he saw Tokyo mainly as an ally against London and a deterrent against Washington.

In September 1939, Hitler invaded Poland as a first step toward capturing living space further east in the Soviet Union. Britain and France declared war in response and imposed a blockade. The United States remained neutral, but the vast majority of Americans, including the president, made no secret of their sympathy for the Allied cause. The administration now succeeded in repealing the arms embargo. Roosevelt's cash-and-carry policy, which secured congressional approval in early November, was intended to favor the Allies, because they were able to pay for military supplies, take possession in American ports, and ship them across the Atlantic. Yet in order to prevent "incidents and controversies which tend to draw us into conflict," Roosevelt also maintained the prohibition on US ships entering the combat zones, and loans to the belligerents remained forbidden.[72] While Chamberlain saluted the revocation of the embargo as a "momentous event" that reopened for "the Allies the doors of the greatest storehouse of supplies in the world," the continued American resistance to any risk of war, and Britain's need to husband its limited dollar and gold reserves, initially restricted its practical impact.[73]

Hitler accompanied his military confrontation with the Western powers with an escalation of his anti-Semitic rhetoric, framing the war as a contest between the satiated and the deprived nations. He asserted that the aim of the "Jewish-capitalist world enemy" was to "destroy Germany" and "the German people." This was because the Third Reich represented a youthful, dynamic, and popular challenge to the international ruling elite, which he understood in national and generational rather than in class terms. The Germans, he claimed in late January 1940, were one of the "young peoples" of the world. They were challenging the "so-called propertied classes among the people" who had "robbed" Germany and were sitting on their ill-gotten gains. In this spirit, Hitler professed sympathy with the other wretched of the earth who groaned under the weight of imperialism and capitalism, particularly that of the British Empire. He argued that the blockade of Germany was simply the latest version of Britain's age-old method of waging war against women and children.[74]

In April 1940, Hitler overran Denmark and Norway; a month later he crushed the French Army and the British Expeditionary Force. Northern France, Belgium, and the Netherlands came under more or less direct German military occupation.[75] The southern half of France was run by a collaborationist regime under Marshal Philippe Pétain based at Vichy. A small group of London-based Free French fought on under a little-known colonel and acting brigadier general, Charles de Gaulle, who reminded his listeners that the conflict was a "world war" in which the United States stood behind Britain.[76] On the high seas, German submarines attacked British shipping in the hope of starving out the home islands. The Royal Navy, which had given up key bases in the now-neutral Irish Free State, was under severe pressure. If Italy entered the conflict and, worse still, if Japan did so in the Far East, the navy would be stretched beyond endurance without US aid.

Hitler's domination of Europe and his assault on Britain's control of the Atlantic sea-lanes left Americans fearful for their own country's security. Germany's Blitzkrieg campaign shocked the American public. Even high-ranking military officials, who had previously expected an Allied victory, grew alarmed. Roosevelt had warned since the Munich Agreement of 1938 that Germany might emerge triumphant, and he now moved to step up rearmament.[77] Two leading anti-isolationist Republicans, Henry Stimson and Frank Knox, were brought into the cabinet as secretary of war and the navy, respectively. Roosevelt told Americans that their country risked becoming "a lone island in a world dominated by the philosophy of force." Alongside building up US defenses, therefore, he wanted to "extend to the opponents of force the material resources of this nation."[78]

Military preparedness enjoyed overwhelming support, but provision of aid to the anti-Axis nations was consistently controversial. Polls that summer showed that most Americans were against supplying or selling munitions if it hindered America's own defense mobilization, and the America First Committee was formed to oppose it. Determined to retain supplies for its own build-up, the US military balked at transferring matériel to Britain. As a result, the administration responded slowly and cautiously to desperate requests from the new British prime minister, Winston Churchill, for aircraft and warships as the Battle of Britain raged.[79] After protracted wrangling with the service chiefs, Roosevelt agreed to transfer fifty World War I–era destroyers to Britain in exchange for leases on bases in the Western Hemisphere and a British pledge not to surrender to the Germans and, if necessary, to scuttle the Royal Navy to prevent it from falling into Hitler's hands. This was another psychologically significant departure from neutrality. But the high price exacted for these antiquated vessels and the emphasis on securing America's own continental defense reflected Roosevelt's concern to cover himself against isolationist attacks, particularly with an election for a historic third term looming that November.[80]

The outbreak of war was accompanied by the radicalization of Nazi measures against the Jews. Hitler viewed European Jewry both as a fifth column that had to be eliminated and, as we have seen, as a hostage for the good behavior of the United States. The emigration of German Jews, once encouraged, now slowed. Worst off, at this point, were the Jews of Poland. Though there was no systematic policy of extermination as yet, tens of thousands of Jews were already being shot or dying of disease and starvation in the ghettos.[81]

For now, Japan bided its time. Unlike in Berlin and Rome, there was no one dominant leader in Tokyo, just a congeries of competing personalities and interest groups. Politics divided, broadly speaking, between doves who wished to avoid conflict with the Anglo-Saxons—not least because they were aware of Japan's crushing industrial inferiority—and hawks, who either embraced conflict or saw no other way out of the growing impasse. The war party, though, was itself split between those, mainly in the army, who wanted to attack the Soviet Union, and those, mainly in the navy, who saw the Anglo-Saxons, especially the United States, as the main threat. Advocates of conflict with Russia received a cold shower in 1938, and then again in July 1939, when the Red Army made short work of the Japanese at Lake Khasan and at Nomonhan in Outer Mongolia.[82] These defeats were to resonate in Tokyo over the next two years.

Italy also stayed out of the war between Germany and the Britain-France alliance, at least at first. But when France was about to fall, Italy scrambled to attack in June 1940 to avoid being left out of the distribution of spoils. After that, Rome conducted a parallel war loosely coordinated with Berlin.[83] Its offensive in North Africa soon petered out. Most of the Italian empire in East Africa was rolled up by the British within a year.[84] In October 1940, Mussolini fell upon Greece with disastrous results. His troops were quickly bogged down in the mountains of Epirus and western Macedonia. A month later, the Italian fleet was badly mauled in harbor at Taranto by British torpedo bombers. British troops were deployed to Crete and the Peloponnese, threatening the vital Romanian oil fields from the air. In North Africa, the British Western Desert Force steadily pushed back the Italians. To prevent Churchill from opening up a fresh flank to his south, Hitler deployed a force to Libya in March 1941 under General Erwin Rommel, soon dubbed Afrika Korps. Shortly afterward, Germany occupied Yugoslavia and Greece, including Crete. Hitler now dominated the entire continent between the English Channel and the Soviet border.

The USSR did not openly take sides in the Britain-Germany contest, but the Soviet dictator leaned strongly toward Hitler, at least after Paris and London ignored Moscow's overtures. Stalin effectively partitioned eastern Europe with the Third Reich through the notorious Molotov-Ribbentrop Pact, cashing in his chips in eastern Poland in late September 1939 and then occupying the Baltic states in the summer of 1940.[85] In between, Stalin launched an unprovoked war of aggression against Finland, hacking off a large slice of its territory. Throughout this period, Stalin supplied Hitler with copious amounts of raw materials and foodstuffs vital for the functioning of the Nazi war machine. Nazi and Soviet propaganda went easy on each other; Goebbels gave strict instructions that world Jewry should be attacked in all its guises *except* for the Soviet Union.[86] German minister of foreign affairs Joachim von Ribbentrop notoriously remarked of his trip to Moscow to conclude the pact that he felt as if he were in a "circle of old comrades."[87] The mutual enemy of Hitler and Stalin from late 1939 to the summer of 1940, and perhaps beyond, was referred to by both as "Anglo-Saxon capitalism"— that is, the British Empire and the United States.[88]

Tokyo watched these developments with anxiety. The shock of the Hitler-Stalin pact, which one senior Japanese diplomat described as a "bolt from the blue," brought down the whole government.[89] Japan feared that Hitler had given the Soviet Union the green light to continue the attack in Mongolia; his move left a legacy of suspicion of German motivations that went well beyond the Japanese elite.[90] Nevertheless, the stalemate in China and the empire's critical lack of vital raw materials remained the Japanese leadership's foremost concerns, and the United States stood as the main obstacle on both fronts. In August 1940, Tokyo proclaimed a "Greater East Asia Co-prosperity Sphere"—the phrase was that of the minister of foreign affairs, Yosuke Matsuoka—which would incorporate not only Manchuria, Korea, and China but also much of Southeast Asia as Japan's living space.[91] A month later, with Vichy France's acquiescence, Japan occupied the northern part of the French colony of Indochina (today's Cambodia, Laos, and Vietnam), the first tangible sign of an ambition to seize the oil fields and rubber plantations of the Dutch East Indies.[92]

The American reaction was sharp. The US Pacific Fleet had already been moved from the West Coast to its new base at Pearl Harbor in May to safeguard against Japan exploiting the situation in Europe to expand southward. In July and August, the United States imposed restrictions on the export of aviation fuel, lubricants, and alloys to Japan. A month later, Japan's move into Indochina prompted a ban on the sale of steel and scrap iron as well.[93] The purpose of these moves was to sober up the Japanese because Hitler's successes, as the American ambassador to Tokyo remarked at the time, "had gone to their heads likes strong wine."[94] Roosevelt, of course, had seen Germany and Japan as working in tandem ever since the Quarantine Speech three years earlier. Likewise, he was well aware—as his close adviser Admiral William Leahy would warn him—of "the certain advantage to Germany of getting us involved in the Pacific."[95] As a result, Roosevelt aimed to deter Japan from attacking the British Empire in the Far East and thus undermining the British effort against Nazi Germany. London followed suit in December 1940 by extending a large loan to Chiang Kai-shek and reopening the Burma Road, which the British had briefly closed beforehand in response to Japanese pressure. This enabled supplies that had landed in the Bay of Bengal to reach the Chinese nationalists. Meanwhile, Mao's Communists were becoming an ever-bigger headache for Japan in the northern province of Yenan. Luckily for Tokyo, though, Mao took his cue from Moscow and still saw the capitalist "Anglo-American alliance" as a bigger enemy than Hitler or the Japanese.[96]

Tokyo's growing estrangement from Washington and London was by no means uncontested in the Japanese elite. Many of them were mindful that the British Empire had been Japan's first ally at the start of the century and during the First World War. Many others had studied there and in the United States. Foreign Minister Matsuoka, for example, studied law at the University of Oregon. These men admired and imitated the United States; they were also in awe of its industrial capacity.[97] Nobody was more conscious of this than Admiral Isoroku Yamamoto, commander in chief of the Combined Fleet since August 1939, who had served as naval attaché in Washington.[98] But so long as Anglo-Saxons and "plutocrats" refused to share the resources of the world with the Japanese—that is, recognize their right to enslave and exploit others on equal basis with the established global empires—Japan would someday have to take them on. Besides, the implications for Japan of the German victories in Europe in 1940 were overwhelming: an extraordinary vista opened up for Japanese rule over Southeast Asia.

The emerging Axis's common ideological platform was thus far more anti-Anglo-American and anti-plutocratic than it was anti-Soviet or anti-Bolshevik. The Tripartite Pact between Berlin, Rome, and Tokyo of September 1940 was not directed against Moscow. It specified that the "agreement affects in no way the political status existing at present between each of the three contracting powers and Soviet Russia." Both Hitler and Foreign Minister Matsuoka hoped that Stalin would soon join the pact, but in the end his price (Finland, Bulgaria, and the Turkish straits) was too steep. The three parties agreed to support each other militarily in the event that they were attacked by a "power at present not involved in the European War or in the Japanese-Chinese conflict."[99] This was widely expected to be Roosevelt, whose intervention to prevent the partition of the British Empire seemed to be only a matter of time. The main target of the Tripartite Pact, therefore, was the United States; a subsidiary purpose was to deter the Soviet Union from attacking Japan. For Tokyo, the pact also reflected fears that the Germans would attempt to inherit the Vichy French colonies in Indochina.[100] This anxiety about Hitler's intentions remained with the leadership in Tokyo throughout the prewar period, and indeed beyond.

For Roosevelt's part, the Tripartite Pact confirmed his belief that the conflicts in Asia and Europe were part of a broader global struggle between dictatorship and democracy. In that larger campaign, however, Hitler's Germany was seen as the more serious and imminent threat.[101] This was confirmed by the analysis of Roosevelt's handpicked head of the navy, Admiral Harold Stark, in an influential memorandum that tied American security to a favorable balance of power in Europe, which was now threatened by Britain's collapse and the destruction of its fleet. This overriding strategic priority meant that the US military must plan for "an eventual strong offensive in the Atlantic as an ally of the British, and a defensive in the Pacific." The United States simply did not possess the ships to project power in both oceans and as a result, Stark suggested, must maintain a defensive posture in the Pacific, not provoking Japan if possible.[102] While Roosevelt did not explicitly endorse this plan, clearly recognizing that direct US intervention remained politically unfeasible at this time, it did reflect his focus on Hitler and consequent commitment not to risk unnecessarily antagonizing Japan. The president and his secretary of state, Cordell Hull, were against expanding America's naval presence in the western Pacific or imposing a complete oil embargo, in case this precipitated a Japanese attack on the Dutch East Indies to secure an alternative supply.[103] Meanwhile, in the Atlantic, the president publicly committed that the United States would provide Britain "all aid short of war" to ensure the defeat of Germany.[104]

Hitler knew that pacts and rhetoric, though important, were not enough to knock the British out of the war. Britain would have to be either crushed militarily, starved out through the submarine campaign, or awed into giving way. Britain had previously managed to get most of its expeditionary force out of France during the legendary evacuation from Dunkirk. Then British pilots saw off the Luftwaffe in the skies over southern England. Production leaped and soon outperformed that of Germany in every sphere except rifles, though the quality of British armored vehicles left much to be desired.[105]

While the US economy cranked up in support of Britain's war effort, RAF Bomber Command carried the war to German cities, causing, at this stage of the war, little physical damage and few casualties but widespread anxiety and disruption.[106] Every day, ships arrived from the Dominions, bringing men, equipment, foodstuffs, raw materials, and pilots who had completed the Empire Air Training Scheme. Far from accepting German domination of the continent, Churchill stepped up support for the Free French movement of General de Gaulle in London and in July 1940 vowed "to set Europe ablaze."[107] Clearly, Britain was not going to surrender any time soon.

So, in the autumn of 1940, the Third Reich went into diplomatic overdrive. Foreign Minister Ribbentrop sought to assemble a "continental bloc"—consisting of Japan, the Soviet Union, and the German Reich—that would rally the whole of Eurasia from Yokohama to Brest to partition the British Empire and deter the United States.[108] Ribbentrop and Hitler also tried to corral the Italians, Spaniards, and Vichy French into a coalition in the Mediterranean. Both endeavors failed. There was no shortage of would-be scavengers but there was little appetite for taking on Britain directly. Stalin politely declined the share of the empire offered to him in India, as did, ultimately, Spain's Francisco Franco and Vichy's Philippe Pétain. Perhaps most important, Hitler failed, for now, to persuade the Japanese to move. It was still unclear whether they would attack the British Empire, or the United States, or the Soviet Union, or all three, or none at all.

To make matters worse for the Führer, Roosevelt's hostility to the Third Reich became ever more explicit after his reelection in November 1940. During the campaign, US foreign policy had been hamstrung and the Democrats were forced to combat the Republican charge that Roosevelt was a warmonger by committing that "we will not participate in foreign wars, and we will not send our army, naval or air forces to fight in foreign lands outside of the Americas, except in case of attack." When the Republican challenger Wendell Willkie persisted in charging Roosevelt with planning to send troops to Europe if reelected, the president moved to reassure "you mothers and fathers" that "your boys are not going to be sent into any foreign wars."[109] With victory secured, however, Roosevelt could once more intensify his campaign against Hitler by new measures short of war.

By now, Britain was confronted with a financial and military crisis, encapsulated by the British ambassador Lord Lothian's pithy, although possibly fictitious, declaration to American reporters: "Well boys, Britain's broke: it's your money we want!"[110] During his postelection Caribbean cruise, the president struck on an ingenious plan that enabled the administration to circumvent the web of neutrality legislation by lending Britain supplies while deferring payment. In late December, the president declared that the United States would become the "arsenal of democracy."[111] And in the new year, he introduced legislation to Congress that would grant him authority to transfer war supplies to any country that he deemed "vital" to American security. It was entitled "an Act Further to promote the Defense of the United States."[112] With the overwhelming majority of Americans still opposed to committing troops overseas, the Lend-Lease bill would enable the United States to make a critical contribution to defeating Nazi Germany without direct military intervention.

From Berlin, the prominent American journalist William Shirer reflected at the start of December 1940 on the looming clash between America and Germany. The Third Reich, he wrote, could not "master the world as long as the United States stands unafraid in its path." "The clash," Shirer went on, "is as inevitable as that of two planets hurtling inexorably through the heavens towards each other." Hitler himself spoke of the conflict as one between "two worlds," and only one could triumph. Shirer went on to report a disconcerting conversation with a member of the German high command. "You think," his interlocutor warned, "[that] Roosevelt can pick the moment most advantageous to America and Britain for coming into the war." Then he asked, "Did you ever stop to think that Hitler, a master of timing, may choose the moment for war with America—a moment which he thinks will give him the advantage?"[113]

Seeing the writing on the wall, the German Foreign Office had already drawn up a memorandum to assess how much leeway Roosevelt had in foreign policy. The conclusion was not encouraging. While the president did not have the right to declare war unilaterally, the author warned that "as leader of the executive he had the opportunity to create a situation as a result of which war could not be avoided." Roosevelt could, for example, break off relations with foreign countries and impose a blockade without consulting Congress.[114] Hitler was therefore deeply conscious of the need not to provoke the United States more than absolutely necessary, at least not yet. It was for this reason that the Führer had tried to dissuade Mussolini from launching his invasion of Greece until after the US presidential elections.[115]

Nazi moves to create a continental bloc were accompanied by anti-Anglo-American, anti-capitalist, anti-Semitic, and anti-imperialist rhetoric. Echoing a common theme in contemporary discourse, Hitler described the British Empire and the United States as the haves of the world order, and the German Reich as the leader of the have-nots. "I have been a have-not all my life," Hitler claimed in December 1940. "I consider myself a have-not and have always fought for them." For this reason, Hitler announced, he "acted in the world as a representative of the have-nots."[116] In Hitler's reading, inequality was manifested at both the national and the class levels, and the two were connected. Germany as a whole was subject to an international ruling class, which had divided Germans from each other. This meant that Germany had been left behind in the global distribution of territory, with less space per person than any other major European state. The implication was clear: Germany might own large tracts of Europe, but in global terms it was still poor. It did yet not have enough, and the combination of British resistance and a likely future American intervention blocked Hitler from seizing what Germany required.

In December 1940, Hitler decided to break the deadlock through an attack on Russia. He did so not because he considered Stalin his main enemy—quite the contrary. Hitler still had the Anglo-Saxon and plutocratic powers firmly in his sights.[117] Rather, the elimination of the Soviet

Union would, in his view, kill several birds with one stone. First, it would force the British to give up any hopes of Stalin entering the war on their side, and thus make them amenable to a negotiated peace. Second, it would deter the United States from intervening by creating an over-whelming German preponderance in Europe and denying Roosevelt a potential major ally on the mainland. Third, control of the cornfields of the Ukraine and the minerals of the Donbass and Caucasus would allow the Reich to outlast the British blockade. And fourth, the seizure of living space in the east would put the future of the German people on the sounder footing Hitler had been calling for since the 1920s. The Führer now moved to his new headquarters in East Prussia, the Wolfsschanze (Wolf's Lair) at Rastenburg (today's Ketrzyn, Poland), from which he would direct the campaign, Operation Barbarossa.

Hitler's decision to invade the Soviet Union was accompanied by an escalation of the war on the Jews. In mid-March 1941, Hitler instructed the leader of the SS, Heinrich Himmler, to establish four *Einsatzgruppen* (task forces) of the Sicherheitspolizei and Sicherheitsdienst (SD, the intelligence agency of the SS). These Einsatzgruppen totaled about three thousand men and were created to carry out "special tasks"—in other words, murders—behind the front lines.[118] These planned killings were not the purpose of Operation Barbarossa, but a consequence of it. Soviet Jews were targeted as Communist partisans—that is, as enemy combatants—and Bolshevik ideological adversaries.[119] Hitler did not need to invade the Soviet Union to murder Jews or take them hostage; he already had millions of central and western European Jews under his control.

The campaign against the Soviet Jews was embedded in a broader ideological war against Bolshevism, which was now brought to the fore in Nazi rhetoric. In late March 1941, Hitler pronounced the coming conflict as not merely a war for resources such as land and raw materials, but also a "contest between two worldviews." For this reason, the Führer demanded, German soldiers must abandon the customary rules of war.[120] On May 12, he issued a commissar order, according to which Communist "political leaders" were to be eliminated immediately after capture. Partisans, he decreed the next day, were to be "dispatched without mercy," all other opposition was to be "crushed," and, where German units were attacked behind the lines, "measures of collective violence" were to be undertaken against the local population.[121] Operation Barbarossa was to be a "war of annihilation."

Meanwhile, the American challenge loomed ever larger. In January, President Roosevelt spoke of a "world at war," and by March he was referring to "the second World War" beginning "a year and a half ago."[122] Throughout this period, the president relentlessly widened the scope of American "national security"—a term he used in the four years after the Quarantine Speech more frequently than all previous presidents combined—to preclude the possibility of coexistence with the Third Reich under any circumstances.[123] He continued not only to lambast Hitler and the Third Reich but also to send military assistance to Britain. On March 11, 1941, the Lend-Lease Act finally came into force after a fractious political battle in Congress.[124] This allowed the British to lease tanks, artillery, ships, and aircraft.

Hitler was infuriated by Lend-Lease. Later that month, he told a group of senior military and political leaders that "the Americans have finally let the cat out of the bag." The Führer claimed that while it would be "legitimate to interpret [Lend-Lease] as an act of war," it was still something he wanted to avoid for the moment. "The war with the US," he continued, "was sure to come sooner or later anyway." This was because, in his view, "Roosevelt and the Jewish financiers have no other choice than to strive for this war, since a German victory in Europe would mean enormous financial losses for the American Jews." He also expressed his desire to "teach" American Jewry "a lesson."[125] The connection in Hitler's mind between the Jews, capitalism, and American policy toward Germany was thus clear. As we shall see, Lend-Lease would loom large in Axis calculations over the next nine months.

From the German perspective, signs of a forthcoming direct American intervention were accumulating.[126] In January 1941, Roosevelt sent his confidant Colonel William "Wild Bill" Donovan to the Balkans and the Mediterranean on a two-month mission. His attempts to strengthen opposition to the Third Reich there were closely followed by German intelligence and reported to Hitler.[127] On March 1, 1941, the US Atlantic Fleet's Support Force was instructed to protect convoys to Britain, greatly increasing the chances of clashes with German submarines. Toward the end of the month, British and American military leaders agreed during secret staff talks that in the event of a world war involving Japan they would nonetheless pursue a "Germany first" strategy. If Hitler was unaware of this meeting, he could not mistake the meaning of the seizure of all German and Italian ships in US harbors, ordered by Roosevelt three days later. In April, with Britain suffering heavy shipping losses in the Atlantic, the US president reinforced the Atlantic Fleet and extended the American defense zone as far as Greenland. The United States had absorbed the central North Atlantic into its sphere of influence and ensured a regular naval presence in those waters, which presented the German naval command with a dilemma: limit its operations or risk an incident that might precipitate formal US-German hostilities.[128]

London and Washington were increasingly engaged in what Roosevelt speechwriter Robert Sherwood termed a "common-law alliance."[129] Dozens of officials from both countries were crisscrossing the Atlantic, procuring armaments, swapping intelligence, and determining military strategy for a war that the United States was not officially fighting.[130] In public, too, advocates of US involvement in the war were articulating more and more openly the idea of a joint management of the world, based on Anglo-American kinship and commitment to democratic values. "Tyrannies may require a large amount of living space," Henry Luce, the legendary publisher of *Time* magazine, wrote in a much-discussed February 1941 article, but "Freedom requires and will require far greater living space than Tyranny." He continued, "Peace cannot endure unless it prevails over a very large part of the world."[131] A clash of two ordering concepts—Nazi Lebensraum and Anglo-American liberty, one even more limitless than the other—was inevitable. The message to Hitler from Roosevelt and his supporters in the American public could not have been clearer. There was no room for the Third Reich, and Hitler knew it. If the Americans were securing the Western Hemisphere today, tomorrow it would be the world.[132]

Yet Churchill remained far more anxious in private about American aid than his public statements suggested. The British prime minister greeted the passage of the Lend-Lease bill through the US House of Representatives in February by bullishly declaring in a radio broadcast: "Give us the tools and we will finish the job."[133] By March, however, Churchill was expressing outrage to colleagues about the hidden economic costs that the Americans were attaching to this aid, which included a renunciation of the imperial preference system that had governed tariffs since 1932. As Churchill remarked to the chancellor of the exchequer, Sir Kingsley Wood, "I am sure we will have to come to a showdown. . . . As far as I can make out we are not only to be skinned but flayed to the bone."[134] Churchill's aide Jock Colville noted that the prime minister feared that "the Americans' love of doing good business may lead them to denude us of all our realizable resources before they show any inclination to be the Good Samaritan."[135]

The president's attitude toward Britain was certainly ambivalent, fluctuating between a feeling that the two powers must work together to police the world and a belief that British imperialism was a baleful influence.[136] On the one hand, Roosevelt told confidants that he "favoured concentration of military power in Anglo-American hands" after the war.[137] On the other, he remarked to correspondents that "there never has been, there isn't now, and there never will be any race of people on earth fit to serve as masters of their fellow men," and "we believe that any nationality, no matter how small, has the inherent right to its own nationhood."[138] Whether this was foremost in the president's mind or if he was focused on the high price he might exact from Britain for American supplies, Churchill recognized that, with Britain's dollar reserves exhausted, there was no other way to secure the weapons required to continue fighting effectively. As Churchill told King George VI in March, without Lend-Lease, "we should be unable to carry on and win the war."[139]

Even with this support, however, Churchill was soon telling Roosevelt's special envoy to Europe and Lend-Lease coordinator, W. Averell Harriman, that "there was a limit to the length of time Britain could hold out alone." The prime minister's entire strategy depended on withstanding the German onslaught until the Americans "came into the war."[140] Britain's plight worsened in early 1941, with defeats in mainland Greece, Crete, and North Africa, and, most concerningly, U-boats devastating the merchant fleet on which Britain relied for importing half the nation's food supplies and most of its raw materials. In response, Churchill lamented that "we are being left to our fate."[141] He warned Roosevelt in May that without American belligerence soon, "the vast balances may be tilted heavily to our disadvantage."[142]

Yet American public opinion continued to hamper Roosevelt from acting. A series of Gallup polls throughout the spring consistently suggested that around 80 percent of Americans would vote to stay out of the war.[143] In May, despite Britain's perilous position, a new poll revealed that only 50 percent of Americans were prepared to enter the conflict, even if the president was "certain" that otherwise Britain would be defeated.[144] Other than the United States' growing assertiveness in the Atlantic—which the administration justified on the grounds of hemispheric security rather than the more controversial basis of shared US-British interests—Roosevelt's support for Britain would have to take the form of productive potential and cargo capacity.[145] At Churchill's request, Roosevelt issued a powerful directive to accelerate the production of tanks, which were vital to Britain's North African campaign.[146] That summer, tanks, trucks, and ammunition sailed for the Mediterranean on forty-four US vessels, which went some way to replacing the tonnage that Britain was losing from U-boat attacks.[147]

For the most part, however, American munitions were supplied on a first-aid basis, involving intermittent bulk reinforcements to help Britain overcome particular emergencies.[148] In order to establish a continuous flow of munitions to Britain and for US forces, the Roosevelt administration put Major Albert G. Wedemeyer in charge of a committee entitled the Joint Board Estimates of United States Over-All Production Requirements. A German American who had spent a stint at the *Kriegsakademie* in Berlin, Wedemeyer commenced work in May 1941 on a report that would go down in history as the Victory Program. His projections were based on the United States having to defeat both Germany and Japan, but the main thrust was clearly directed against the Third Reich.[149]

Hitler was under no illusions about the magnitude of the danger he faced. He saw himself in a battle of production not only with the formidable British Empire but also (via Lend-Lease) with the United States.[150] It was a war that he expected to fight at sea and in the air. His main emphasis in early 1941 was thus not on immediate output for the planned attack on Russia, but investment to enable subsequent increases in aerial and naval production to fight Britain and America.[151] Given the immense potential of the United States—and despite its nominal nonbelligerence—Hitler was at pains to stress publicly that "we are in a position today to deploy more than half the European labor force in this struggle."[152] Occupied Europe—which Nazi planners dubbed the *Grossraum*—was indeed to contribute substantially to the German war economy, but bringing the combined resources of Europe to bear against the United States and Britain was far from the panacea the Führer publicly claimed.

At first glance, the area under Hitler's direct or indirect control in 1941 represented a formidable continental bloc. It had a combined population of some 290 million people—which was larger than that of the United States, metropolitan Britain, and the Dominions put together—and its aggregate prewar GDP was greater than that of either the British Empire or the United States.[153] However, the combined economies of the British Empire and United States—now beginning to mobilize against Hitler through Lend-Lease—considerably exceeded that of the German Grossraum. Besides, prewar figures were inflated, because the British blockade had unplugged the continental economies not just from many of their traditional markets but also from their supply of raw materials. Worse still, Hitler's victories in 1940 had brought him no substantial new sources of energy or foodstuffs but millions of new mouths to feed.

Globally, Hitler's strategy now hinged upon Japan. In early March 1941, he issued directive 24. "The aim of the collaboration under the Tripartite Pact," Hitler announced, "must be to persuade Japan to act in the Far East as quickly as possible." "This would tie down substantial British forces," he continued, "and divert the attention of the United States of America to the Pacific." He elaborated that the "common aim of [Axis] strategy" was "to subdue Britain quickly and thereby keep the United States out of the war." Direct attacks on America should be undertaken only if war with that power "cannot be avoided." Hitler made no mention of any Japanese action against the Soviet Union; the alliance with Japan was primarily conceived as an instrument against Britain and a deterrent against the United States.[154]

In late March 1941, the chief Nazi ideologist Alfred Rosenberg spelled out once again the connection the regime had made between the global situation and the fate of the Jews in a major speech on "The Jewish Question as a World Problem." The war of 1914, Rosenberg claimed, had been "a war of encirclement of Jewish-British high finance" to establish a "rule of gold" over the Germans and other resisting peoples. The United States, he continued, had entered the conflict because the interests of its "Jewish and non-Jewish bankers" were identical with those of Britain. The result was a "rule of Anglo-Saxon-Jewish global and money power over the great German nation." History was now repeating itself as Roosevelt and his "Jewish advisers" ganged up with Britain against the Third Reich. For this reason, Rosenberg warned, "for Germany the Jewish question is only then solved when the last Jew has left the Greater German area."[155]

On the far side of the world, Japan was also scrambling to cope with growing American hostility. Embracing Ribbentrop's vision, Japanese foreign minister Matsuoka wanted to extend the Tripartite Pact to include the Soviet Union, creating a "Eurasian continental alliance." This would contain the Anglo-Saxons and enable what he, like Hitler, called the have-nots to hedge against the global haves. Matsuoka was as yet unaware, of course, that Hitler had already decided to seek strategic depth at the expense of Stalin, rather than in continued collaboration with him. Matsuoka's ultimate objective, in any case, was not confrontation with the Western powers but its avoidance. "To shake hands with Germany," he argued, "is a temporary excuse to shake hands with the Soviet Union, but that handshaking with the Soviet Union is also nothing more than an excuse to shake hands with the United States."[156]

In late March 1941, Hitler received Matsuoka.[157] The Führer reassured his interlocutor that the danger of greater US involvement in the war had "already been taken into consideration," but it was not expected to take on "more tangible forms" until 1942. Hitler explained that his aim was to "break" the "British hegemony" in Europe and to exclude any "American interference" there. In this context, the great merit of the Tripartite Pact was that it had deterred the United States from "formally entering into the war." Hitler concluded that while there would always be a "certain risk," now was the best chance Japan would ever have of attacking the British Empire. Matsuoka agreed, in particular with the need to seize Singapore, and said that it was only "a question of time" when Japan would attack. The Japanese foreign minister added that during his meeting with Stalin on the journey through the Soviet Union, he had told the Russian dictator that the Anglo-Saxons—a phrase he used repeatedly—were the common foes of Japan, Germany, and Soviet Russia.[158]

A week later, on April 4, 1941, the two men met again. The Führer repeated his assurance that while a conflict with America was "unwelcome" it had already been "taken into account." For this reason, Hitler promised to intervene immediately in the case of a conflict between Japan and the United States. This was a commitment going well beyond the terms of the Tripartite Pact, which only guaranteed assistance in the event of an American attack on one of the contractants and not—as Hitler now implied—if Japan took the fight to the United States. "Providence," the Führer told Matsuoka, "favors those who do not wait for danger to come to them, but those who courageously confront it."[159] Taking on the Americans was thus always a gamble in Hitler's eyes, but one that was justified, provided it could be undertaken at the right time.

Hitler, as we have seen, did not expect to need Japanese help fighting the Soviet Union, preferring them to remain focused on the United States and Britain. For this reason, Hitler was entirely unperturbed by the Japan-USSR nonaggression pact of April 13, 1941. This was negotiated by Matsuoka on his return to Japan via the Soviet Union. Stalin's hope was explicitly to deflect Japanese aggression away from his eastern border, especially the Japanese fight against what he pejoratively called the "Anglo-Saxons." It is likely that the Soviet dictator agreed with the Japanese foreign minister's contention that Chiang was the "agent of Anglo-Saxon capital."[160]

Matsuoka also saw Mussolini on this trip. The Duce told him that the United States was the main enemy, more dangerous still than the Soviet Union. Not long after this meeting, Mussolini—who like Hitler harbored an intense hatred for the US president—dismissed Roosevelt as "a paralytic who when he wants to go to the toilet or dinner must be assisted by other men." The Duce was already growing uneasy about the extent of German power in Europe, but on the malevolence of Roosevelt he and the Führer were in complete agreement.[161]

OPERATION BARBAROSSA BEGAN on June 22, 1941, as German armies plunged deep into Russia. At first, all seemed to go well.[162] The invaders captured vast swaths of territory and millions of prisoners, many of whom were either shot immediately or starved to death in camps.[163] Flanking the German advance were allied formations of Finns, Romanians, Hungarians, Slovaks, Italians, and, from September 1941, the Spanish Blue Division, named after the blue shirts worn by Franco's Falange party.[164] By the autumn of 1941, the Germans were approaching Leningrad in the north, which was effectively cut off from September 8; they were well past Smolensk in the center; and they were poised to reach the Don river in the south. A descent on the Caucasus before the end of the year seemed likely. Behind the spearheads came the *Einsatzkommandos*, who together with the Wehrmacht murdered about a million Soviet Jews in mass shootings that summer and autumn.[165] In August 1941, Reichsführer-SS Heinrich Himmler and his adjutant Karl Wolff attended mass shootings at Minsk in White Russia (today's Belarus). That month, there was a shift to the systematic killing of Jewish women and children as well, an important milestone in the Holocaust.

Deep inside German-occupied Europe, the apparatus of repression was growing by leaps and bounds. The transit camp at Auschwitz, headed by Rudolf Höss, was greatly expanded, and in the autumn of 1941 construction began on the later notorious site, Birkenau.[166] This was not yet a death camp, but rather a place where Soviet prisoners of war, political prisoners, and Poles were incarcerated. The mass murder of the Soviet Jews was not publicly announced, but it was so frequently reported back home by Wehrmacht soldiers that it must have been widely known in German society.[167]

For Japan, Operation Barbarossa created a new strategic reality. Tokyo made no official response, but as the Germans advanced, there were many voices in the army command and the political leadership (among them Matsuoka) who wanted to take advantage of Stalin's predicament.[168] There was also anxiety that Hitler might take the lot and then come to terms with the Western powers. As the debate raged, the Japanese reinforced their Kwantung Army in Manchuria, which now totaled seven hundred thousand men. Stalin, who was aware of these discussions from his spy Richard Sorge in Tokyo, kept a substantial force in the Far East as a deterrent.

Despite initial appearances, the Red Army was far from defeated. To be sure, it lost millions of men and huge quantities of equipment in the opening months of the campaign. Industrial production was seriously disrupted due to territorial losses and the evacuation of key plants beyond the Urals. But there were always more Soviet troops to call on. Churchill recognized that the greater the Soviet resistance, the less likely an impending German invasion of Britain. Brushing off his long-standing hostility to Communism—telling his private secretary that "if Hitler invaded Hell I would make at least a favourable reference to the Devil in the House of Commons"—he immediately offered assistance.[169] British supplies soon flowed to Russia through the Arctic and later through Iran, which was occupied by Britain and the Soviet Union that August.

Roosevelt, too, pushed his administration to support the Soviets, despite deep-seated American opposition to extending Lend-Lease to Stalin's Communist regime. Secretary of the Treasury Henry Morgenthau reflected Roosevelt's position when he declared: "This was the time to get Hitler," and the Soviets "have just got to get this stuff and get it fast."[170] Roosevelt's principal aide and Lend-Lease administrator, Harry Hopkins, who was in London to facilitate a first wartime meeting between the president and prime minister, embarked on a hazardous journey to Moscow in July to assess the Soviet situation. In doing so, he hoped to "bring Roosevelt and Stalin closer."[171] Charmed by the "dictator of Russia," Hopkins reported back that he was "ever so confident about this front," stressing the "exceptionally good" morale of the people and their "unbounded determination to win."[172] This reinforced Roosevelt's commitment to secure more supplies from his reluctant military establishment, and he told Wayne Coy, the administrator overseeing Soviet aid, to "use a heavy hand—and act as a burr under the saddle and get things moving."[173]

Some British and Americans, mindful of Soviet crimes and duplicity, were deeply skeptical about their new friends. "I avoid the expression 'allies,'" the vice chief of the British imperial general staff, Sir Henry Pownall, stated, "for the Russians are a dirty lot of murdering thieves themselves, and double crossers of the deepest dye." He continued, "It is good to see the biggest cut-throats in Europe, Hitler and Stalin, going for each other."[174] Many American lawmakers agreed with him. It was a pity, they felt, that the Nazis and the Soviets could not both lose.

Hitler's position was increasingly fraught. Behind the German lines, partisan groups, mostly composed of trapped Red Army soldiers, were forming, although these were still largely ineffective.[175] Even staunchly anti-Soviet Ukrainian nationalist groups—such as those loyal to far-right nationalist Stepan Bandera—were both expecting and hoping for an Allied victory. To make matters worse for Hitler, the autumn rains turned the dirt roads in Russia into mud, and the temperature was dropping. Things were not going well against Britain either. After a terrible spring, British fortunes revived throughout the summer and autumn of 1941. In May, the battleship *Bismarck*, pride of the Kriegsmarine, was sunk by the Royal Navy. That same month, a nationalist coup in Iraq was suppressed, dashing German hopes of a lunge at the Persian Gulf, and the movement's leader, Rashid Ali al-Gailani, fled. In July 1941, Bomber Command subjected the historic Westphalian city of Münster to raids that were very mild by later standards but that caused widespread alarm at the time. Across the Atlantic, the U-boat campaign to starve out Britain stalled following a shortage of submarines and the vigor of the countermeasures.[176] In North Africa, the Axis armies were unable to make headway against the greatly reinforced British Western Desert Force.

All the while, Roosevelt steadily increased the pressure on the Third Reich. Maintaining the Soviet fight against the Nazis was becoming the focal point of his global strategy, and the United States was expanding its naval presence in the Atlantic to ensure that the supply line to Hitler's enemies was kept open.[177] There was a clear risk now that the British and Russians would be able to grind down the Reich with American logistical support alone, rather than the United States' active entry into the war. In July 1941, American troops relieved the British garrison in Iceland, effectively taking over securing the area against Germany. In the middle of August, Roosevelt met with Churchill in Placentia Bay off Newfoundland and issued what came to be known as the Atlantic Charter. In it, the British prime minister and the as-yet-nonbelligerent US president explicitly looked forward to the defeat of Nazi Germany. The charter made a deep impression on the Führer.[178] Despite his focus on Russia, Hitler was following events in the United States closely and in late August 1941 he even suggested that Nazi chargé d'affaires Hans Thomsen's reports from Washington, which he rated highly, should be made available to the Japanese.[179]

By September, Roosevelt was publicly referring to the Reich as a "rattlesnake," ready to strike unless it was crushed. This followed a clash in the North Atlantic between a U-boat and the American destroyer *Greer*. Roosevelt accused the Nazi raider of initiating the skirmish "without warning" in an act of "piracy."[180] The submarine had indeed fired first on the *Greer*, but only after a lengthy pursuit by the US vessel, operating alongside a British bomber. Roosevelt was also informed by his naval leaders that there was no indication that the U-boat commander was aware of the ship's nationality.[181] Nevertheless, the president used the incident as the basis for publicizing a new policy, agreed at Placentia Bay with Churchill, that American warships would escort British vessels in the Atlantic. He placed the *Greer* within the broader context of a "Nazi design to abolish the freedom of the seas," already manifest in previous attacks on US and Latin American ships. The president now warned German warships that they entered Atlantic waters "at their own peril" and directed the fleet to "shoot on sight," a policy approved by almost two-thirds of Americans according to a Gallup poll.[182] All the while, US Lend-Lease material flowed to the British, and some of it from them to Stalin, a fact of which the Führer was only too aware.[183] From Hitler's perspective, therefore, it looked like the United States would soon be at war with the Third Reich, and in some ways already was.

As if all this were not bad enough, the Roman Catholic bishop of Münster, Clemens August Graf von Galen, launched an open attack on Nazi "euthanasia" policies in July and August 1941. The contents of his sermons were not only broadcast by the BBC, and listened to by many Germans, but also were dropped as propaganda leaflets by the RAF, especially in Westphalia. The regime monitored the popular response closely, registering mounting alarm as the autumn wore on.[184] Cumulatively, these stresses took their toll on Hitler's health, and he suffered a brief collapse in early August 1941; it took a hefty dose of stimulants from his doctor Theo Morell to revive him.[185] The Führer did not yet know it, but much more stress loomed in the months to come.

MEANWHILE, JAPAN'S POLICY was still completely up in the air. As the Germans became bogged down, appetite for attacking the Soviet Union waned. There were still strong forces in Tokyo inclined toward a compromise with the Western powers. One of these was the former ambassador to London, who had been recalled in June 1941.[186] In mid-July 1941, much to Ribbentrop's distress, the doves forced the resignation of the pro-German foreign minister, Matsuoka.[187] His successor was an Anglophile, Admiral Teijiro Toyoda. The Germans, who were well-informed about the progress of the negotiations between Tokyo and Washington through their surveillance of the Japanese embassy in Berlin, were anxious.[188] If Hitler broadly welcomed the USSR-Japan rapprochement, which left Tokyo free to confront Washington and London, he greatly feared an understanding between Tokyo and the Anglo-Saxon powers. It was for this reason that in mid-August 1941, the Führer once again assured the Japanese that "if a clash occurs by any chance between Japan and the United States, Germany will at once open war against the United States."[189]

In July 1941, Hitler broke off relations with nationalist China and recognized the Nanjing-based, collaborationist "central government" of Wang Jingwei. The Führer had no particular animus against Chiang Kai-shek but wanted to signal solidarity with Japan.[190] The British and the Americans, especially the latter, stepped up their support for Chiang, who was more or less impregnable in Chungking, though his forces and Chinese civilians suffered badly from Japanese air attacks.[191] One way or the other, the war in China dragged on, tying down most of the Japanese Army.

Japan now took a momentous step. In late July 1941, with the permission of Vichy authorities, the Japanese moved into southern Indochina. The coup brought the Japanese air force within striking distance of the British bases in Singapore and Malaya (present-day Malaysia), and a great deal closer to the vital oil fields in Dutch East Indies.

The Anglo-Saxons struck back swiftly, aided by Roosevelt's foreknowledge of the attack. American intelligence officers had broken the Japanese diplomatic code the previous September, and what were subsequently referred to as MAGIC decrypts allowed Roosevelt to learn of the Japanese plans for occupation a fortnight beforehand from Tokyo's cables to the ambassador at Vichy. As a result, the president moved quickly to freeze Japanese assets in the United States, effectively imposing an embargo on the supply of oil and other vital materials. One of the principal reasons for this was to deter Japan from exploiting the German attack on the Soviet Union to launch its own invasion through Siberia.[192] In addition, the Roosevelt administration announced the establishment of a full-scale army in the Philippines. This had been an

American colony since 1898, but little had been done so far to rein-force the archipelago. General Douglas MacArthur was brought out of retirement to lead the new force, and a squadron of heavy bombers was sent to defend the islands.[193] In turn, Britain disavowed its trade treaties with Japan and froze Japanese sterling accounts.[194]

Japan was now increasingly boxed into a corner.[195] Long bogged down in China, Japan felt the clock ticking with regard to the United States. If it did not get the oil and iron embargo lifted soon or secure alternative sources, the country would begin to eat into its reserves, and eventually its industries and armed forces would be immobilized. More generally, Japanese strategists looked to Southeast Asia, just as Hitler had fixed on the Soviet Union, for solutions to their food and raw-material problems.[196] The impending conflict was conceived of by many Japanese as both a racial and a redistributional struggle. In August 1941, the Min-istry of Education in Tokyo brought out a substantial document entitled *The Way of the Subject*, which saw Japan engaged in a life-and-death con-test with the exploitative Anglo-Americans.[197]

Churchill was determined to tie the United States as closely as possi-ble to Britain in the containment of Japan. At Placentia Bay, he pressured Roosevelt to join the British Empire and the Dutch East Indies in issuing parallel warnings to Japan that any further aggression in the southwest Pacific might lead to a war involving all three nations. While Roosevelt eventually agreed to issue a warning in line with Churchill's proposal, the State Department watered the threat down and the president conveyed a far weaker message to the Japanese ambassador, making no mention of the potential for war, in order to pave the way for negotiations.[198] An anxious Churchill feared that Britain, without American aid, would be left vulnerable to a Japanese assault that would demolish its merchant fleet in the region and leave its Dominions isolated: "The blow to the British Government might be almost decisive."[199] He disguised his disappoint-ment with a public declaration that presented the Americans as Japan's primary nemesis and promised that Britain would "of course" stand "un-hesitatingly at the side of the United States."[200] Privately, however, Chur-chill was in despair. He told Roosevelt's principal adviser, Harry Hopkins, that the president's continued assertions that he was no closer to bringing the United States into the war were causing "waves of depression through Cabinet and other informed circles here." He warned Hopkins, "If 1942 opens with Russia knocked out and Britain left again alone all kinds of dangers may arise."[201]

Despite the demands of the war against Hitler, the British prepared to deter a Japanese attack in the Far East if possible, and to resist one if necessary. In October, the garrison in Hong Kong was reinforced with a contingent of Canadian infantry, and its defenses were strengthened.[202] That same month, the government overcame opposition from the Admiralty and ordered the battleship *Prince of Wales* to join the battle cruiser *Repulse* in the Indian Ocean and deploy to Singapore.[203] The purpose of Force Z, as these ships were later christened, was not to grapple with the Japanese fleet in the confined waters of the South China Sea, but, as Churchill told Stalin, to "keep Japan quiet" and out of the Indian Ocean.[204] Proudly informing Roosevelt that the *Prince of Wales*, the vessel that had hosted their meeting in Placentia Bay, could "catch and kill anything," Churchill urged him, "The firmer your attitude and ours, the less chance of their taking the plunge."[205]

At the same time, Anglo-American thinking about the threat in the Far East was bedeviled by a systematic underestimation of Japanese capabilities. In part, this was driven by the fact that Tokyo was struggling so mightily against the comparatively disorganized and divided Chinese. Mainly, though, it reflected underlying racist assumptions. There was a reluctance to believe that the Japanese could build and deploy sophisticated weaponry, and there was widespread skepticism about their fighting qualities. This sentiment was epitomized by the reaction of the commander in chief of British forces in the Far East, Robert Brooke-Popham, to the sight of Japanese troops just across the border from Hong Kong. "I had a good close-up," he reported, "of various sub-human specimens dressed in dirty grey uniform." Brooke-Popham could not "believe that they would form an intelligent fighting force."[206]

On the American side, a similar complacency abounded. In February, the cocksure assistant naval attaché at the US embassy in Tokyo told an audience at the American Club that "we can lick the Japs in twenty-four hours." The following month, a member of the US House of Represen-tatives military affairs committee confided to a reporter, after hearing secret testimony from Secretary of War Henry Stimson and army chief of staff George Marshall, that "our naval people hold the Japanese to be very inferior, and I gather they would like to knock them off any time." Two months later, the same reporter, after learning of an off-the-record briefing from the head of the Atlantic Fleet, Admiral Ernest King, pri-vately noted that naval leaders "feel we should have knocked off the little brown brother years ago."[207]

Contempt for Tokyo's military capacity masked concerns among American and British officials that, in light of the buildup in the Atlan-tic, each currently lacked the regional resources to curb Japan if it did attack. A sense that the Japanese were erratic and irrational only added to the confusion. The uncertainty around Japanese intentions also had profound ramifications for the war in Europe. In particular, it threatened to drive Australia and Britain apart. If it came to war in East Asia, the role of the Australian Imperial Force in Libya would be placed in question. From this point of view, the appointment of the Labor Party leader John Curtin as prime minister of Australia in October was not reassuring. He had refused to serve in the First World War, and it was feared that he would put narrowly Australian concerns over those of the British Empire as a whole.

It was Stalin who first achieved certainty with regard to the Far East. In the late summer, he received word from his spy Sorge in Tokyo that unless Russia collapsed suddenly, Japan did not intend to strike west but south.[208] This ultimately enabled the Soviet dictator to transfer twenty divisions from Siberia to shore up the defense of Moscow and even pre-pare a counterattack. Still, American production was struggling under the strain of supplying the Soviet Union, Britain, and China—which had become a recipient of Lend-Lease in May—not to mention its own forces. As Churchill ruefully remarked, the Soviet Union was a "welcome guest" but at a "hungry table."[209]

With Roosevelt increasingly prioritizing Soviet needs, the British government feared the consequences for its own war effort, particularly the upcoming offensive in Libya. Nor did it help that many leading American military officers were disdainful of the British performance in the desert and resistant to diverting munitions that they wanted for themselves. The Battle of Britain was now a receding memory, and Britain's military prestige in America was low on account of recent fiascos in Greece and North Africa. The Australian ambassador in Washington, Richard Casey, observed that senior US officers "consistently fought the proposal that a large part of current productions should go to the British" and took "the attitude that it is a waste of equipment that is sorely needed in the U.S. to send it to the Middle East," which was regarded as a "hopeless cause." While Casey was grateful that Roosevelt was more supportive and had handled the situation with his "accustomed political skill," it was clear that altering "the attitude of mind adopted by the U.S. Army must be a gradual business; not even the President can knock the Army Chiefs on the head and tell them to reverse their thinking."[210]

In September 1941, Major Wedemeyer completed his monumental report on how the US war economy and armed forces should mobilize to defeat the Axis. This involved intensive planning for a US-British intervention in mainland Europe in 1943.[211] When Roosevelt received the report, however, he expressed disapproval to Secretary of War Stimson at the suggestion that "we must invade and crush Germany."[212] With the latest polls showing that public support for direct intervention in the war still hovered around 20 percent, he clearly regarded this as a political impossibility.[213] Furthermore, Roosevelt's strategic advisers continued to believe that the United States would "be more effective for some time as a neutral, furnishing aid to Britain, rather than as a belligerent," as American combat strength was not yet "sufficiently developed." The deployment of America's own military forces remained very much "weapons of last resort."[214] As a result, the Victory Program, according to the official War Department history, was still "a hypothesis without real influence."[215]

The principal impact of the report was to reveal that, at this rate, American war production would not outstrip that of Britain and Canada until late 1942 and needed to be at least doubled to ensure sufficient supplies for all parties. With his proxy-war strategy in jeopardy, Roosevelt moved to step up industrial mobilization, squeeze US military allocations, and streamline the provision of aid. He created the Office of Lend-Lease Administration, under the former executive of General Motors and US Steel Edward Stettinius, to expedite the shipment of matériel to the armies fighting America's enemies before it was too late. In Lend-Lease headquarters there hung a single poster with the warning: "Time Is Short."[216]

By the autumn of 1941, Europe had been at war for over two years and China for more than four, but the rest of the world was still at peace. The United States was still officially nonbelligerent and enjoying the first fruits of its recovery from the Depression. Pearl Harbor was not yet a word synonymous with "infamy." Japan was embroiled on the Asian mainland, but the Dutch East Indies, Malaya, and the Philippines appeared, for all the background turbulence, oases of peace. The future was still open, or seemed so. The conflict was yet to go global and become, as the Italian dictator Benito Mussolini would put it, a "war between continents."

2

THE WORLDS OF DECEMBER 6, 1941

As winter 1941 approached, Berlin and Tokyo were increasingly seized by the feeling that they were running out of time. The Russian campaign was stagnant, U-boats were struggling in the Atlantic, and the British continued to harry the Nazis on the southern and western fronts. Increasingly certain that open hostilities with the United States loomed, Hitler took two far-reaching steps. First, he launched an offensive on Moscow, Operation Typhoon, in early October 1941, which was designed finally to capture the city in hopes of knocking the Soviet Union out of the war, shocking Britain into suing for peace, and precluding Roosevelt's intervention.[1] Second, Hitler further intensified his war on the Jews and Anglo-American plutocracy. This was intended to punish "the Jews" for their alleged support for the Allied cause, and was meant to send the president one last warning, even if it was only in Hitler's mind.

On the other side of the world, under pressure as the American oil and scrap-metal embargo began to take effect, the Japanese government opted for a twin-track policy at a series of meetings of the Imperial Conference between September 6 and November 5, 1941. The empire would continue negotiations with the Americans to secure Japan's access to raw materials and interests in China, but also prepare for war in case talks broke down. Driving the decision was the belief, as the minutes of one conference put it, that "the policy of the United States toward Japan is based on the idea of preserving the status quo in order to dominate the world and defend democracy." In order to do this, the document continued, "it aims to prevent our Empire from rising and developing in East Asia." A clash was thus "historically inevitable" and would "ultimately lead to war."[2] In that event, the conflict would open with a devastating first strike against the American battle fleet moored at Pearl Harbor in Hawaii. In late September 1941, Commander Mitsuo Fuchida, an experienced naval aviator, was briefed to lead the attack.[3]

In mid-October, the cautious government of Prince Konoye stood down, making way for the more belligerent General Hideki Tojo; even the new prime minister, though, was no great enthusiast for Nazi Germany.[4] His new foreign minister, Shigenori Togo, was a Goethe enthusiast who had served as ambassador to Berlin in 1937–1938. But Togo particularly disliked the bombastic Ribbentrop and was no friend to the Third Reich. Whatever their reservations about Hitler and the Führer's reliability, however, most of the Japanese elite, seeing only an all-or-nothing choice between war and continued inferiority, were ready to act. Tojo spoke for many when, alluding to an old Japanese proverb, he said that "there may be times in the life of a man when he has to close his eyes and jump."[5] Both Germany and Japan were preparing to take the plunge. The two worlds and the two wars were moving closer to becoming one world and one global conflict.

On November 3, 1941, the Japanese Navy approved Admiral Isoroku Yamamoto's attack plan for Pearl Harbor.[6] Concurrently, a senior diplomat, Saburo Kurusu, was sent to Washington to support Ambassador Kichisaburo Nomura's negotiations there. Kurusu was perhaps not the best choice, as his involvement in the signing of the Tripartite Pact rendered him suspect to the British and Americans. His journey went via the Philippines, Guam, Wake Island, and Midway Island, where he was detained because his plane had engine trouble. While waiting there, Kurusu was alarmed to hear on the wireless at Midway that Churchill had announced in the Mansion House in London that if the United States became involved in a war with Japan, Britain would weigh in on the American side within the hour.[7]

Roosevelt's military leaders painted a picture far different from Churchill's. Time was needed to establish an American air armada and ensure enough submarine strength in the Philippines to deter Japan. On November 5, Admiral Harold Stark and army chief of staff George Marshall advised against an "ultimatum" to Tokyo or any offensive moves in the Pacific unless Japan struck at American, British, or Dutch territory. Moreover, the army and navy continued to argue that a war with Japan would "greatly weaken the combined effort in the Atlantic against Germany, the most dangerous enemy."[8] While Churchill agreed that Germany was the priority, he feared that the United States would leave Britain to face Japan alone. As Churchill told the US ambassador John G. Winant in early November, his preference was that the United States enter the war against Germany without Japanese involvement. His second choice was American and Japanese belligerency, which was better than nonintervention by both. The "unthinkable," worst-case scenario was a new war with Japan but the United States still on the sidelines.[9]

On the same day that Roosevelt received Stark and Marshall's analysis, he was passed a MAGIC intercept of Tokyo's instructions to Ambassador Nomura that an agreement must be reached by November 25.[10] American diplomats in the region reported a growing buildup of Japanese forces in Indochina amid increasingly belligerent propaganda, with Tokyo's leading newspaper declaring that the United States had "the soul of a prostitute" and Domei, the official news agency, warning that the oil embargo was forcing Japan to "drastic action" for self-defense.[11] The mass of material generated by MAGIC was difficult to analyze, hardly helped by raw transcripts of diplomatic documents being delivered without a digest, but it increasingly pointed toward a Japanese drive south that threatened relations with the United States.[12] Roosevelt recognized that time was no longer on America's side. Tensions were rising in the Atlantic and Pacific, but the United States did not have "enough Navy to go round."[13] Supplying the anti-German coalition remained his priority.

Roosevelt was therefore ready to explore a temporary accommodation with Japan but waited for the Japanese to take the lead, seeking to maintain his bargaining position and avoid any hint of appeasement.[14]

The day after this intercept arrived, Wild Bill Donovan, director of the recently established Office of the Coordinator of Information, delivered a stark warning to the president in a memorandum. It reported that the German chargé Hans Thomsen had said privately to a US agent, Malcolm R. Lovell, a prominent American Quaker who had befriended the diplomat, that "if Japan goes to war with the United States, Germany will immediately follow suit." Thomsen also stated that because Japan "faced the threat of strangulation, now or later," it was "therefore forced to strike now, whether she wishes to or not." The president read this document and forwarded it to Secretary of State Cordell Hull on November 15.[15]

It would be tempting to infer, as a number of revisionist historians have, that Roosevelt now saw conflict with Japan as the back door to war with Hitler, and therefore pushed Tokyo into a corner knowing that it would lash out.[16] In fact, there is little evidence that he did so.[17] Indeed, by the end of the month, Donovan was reporting another comment from Thomsen to Lovell, that "as the strongest nation in the world, the United States has a perfect right to be interested in the future of Europe and Asia," and the Germans wanted to dispel Washington's "absurd fear that Germany would or could ever be able to cross the Atlantic Ocean for an attack on the United States." The intelligence picture was thus confused and, if anything, Thomsen's remarks tended to emphasize German concern to maintain relations amid fears that the United States was planning to declare war on them.[18]

On November 15, 1941, the Japanese leadership agreed on a strategy in the event that negotiations with Washington failed. This involved a "quick war" to secure "vital materials" and "thereby prepare for a protracted period of self-sufficiency." Japan would "endeavour to quickly destroy American, British and Dutch bases in the Far East," to "hasten the fall of the Chiang regime," to work "for the surrender of Great Britain in cooperation with Germany and Italy," and to "destroy the will of the United States to continue the war." In order to ensure these outcomes, it was desirable to try to mediate "a peace between Germany and the Soviets" and "necessary to strengthen immediately the alliance with Germany" and to get Italy and Germany to "agree not to sign a separate peace agreement."[19]

The Japanese were, in fact, far from certain that Hitler would support them. "There are many people," the notetaker at one of the liaison conferences wrote, "who believe that Germany cannot be trusted."[20] Some, such as Foreign Minister Togo, were worried that there would be another rapprochement between Hitler and Stalin, this time at Japan's expense.[21] Others feared "racial abandonment" by the Germans in favor of the Anglo-Saxons.[22] Speaking on behalf of the emperor, president of the privy council Yoshimichi Hara advised caution. Reminding his listeners that Hitler had described the Japanese as a "second-class" race, Hara warned that "once Japan launches a war against the United States, I fear that there would be an agreement between Germany, the United States and Britain to leave Japan behind." If that happened, Hara continued, "their hatred of the yellow race will immediately be transferred to Japan, overtaking their hatred of Germany." He suggested that the council should "consider the factors of race relations and make sure that the Japanese empire would not be left alone, encircled by the Aryan races."[23]

The Germans, in turn, could not be sure that they would not be left in the lurch by Japan. Some elements within the Japanese elite were indeed hoping to ditch Hitler in return for an accommodation with Roosevelt. On November 21, for example, diplomat Saburo Kurusu suggested privately to the Americans that if they intervened militarily in the war in Europe, Japan would abandon the Tripartite Pact.[24]

Meanwhile, Axis fears that they were losing the economic contest grew and grew. In late October 1941, the German Office for the War Economy and Armaments had warned that US Lend-Lease supplies could make up for the Soviet losses in industrial capacity during the summer and autumn.[25] In mid-November 1941, Italian military intelligence, perhaps already in receipt of leaks from Wedemeyer's Victory Program, reported that the United States was capable of producing at least fifty thousand planes and twenty-five thousand tanks a year by 1943.[26] A week later, Hitler conceded that wars were, at least initially, driven by "economic" rather than "racial" factors. Conflicts were decided by "the production of guns, tanks and ammunition," and for this reason the Führer said he would have to boost German armaments to such an extent as to "take away the breath of the enemy."[27] Six days later, though, Hitler was alarmed to hear from Fritz Todt, the armaments minister, and Walter Rohland, the head of tank production, that in their opinion the war could not be won; the industrial imbalance was just too great.[28]

Hitler and the Japanese had reached very similar strategies after pursuing very similar paths. Both initially wanted to avoid war with the United States and still hoped against hope that Roosevelt might be persuaded to lift the oil embargo, in the Japanese case, or be deterred from intervening, in the German one. Neither was under any illusion about the industrial might of America, which Hitler had stressed as far back as the 1920s, and which some of Tokyo's experts reckoned to be more than twenty times that of their own empire.[29] In September 1941, the president of the Japanese planning board stated that if the East Indies and Malaya were secured by early December 1941, or at least the New Year, the first consignments of oil and rubber could be off-loaded at the ports of Honshu, Japan's largest island, by March 1942.[30] In Germany, Hitler was making similar calculations about the oil of the Caucasus.[31] Both countries acted in the belief that time was running out, and that further delay only played into the hands of the Anglo-Americans.

HITLER'S ALL-OUT ATTACK on Moscow, which was designed to knock Stalin out of the war for good, started off strong.[32] On October 15, the evacuation of the Soviet government and foreign diplomats to the safety of Kuibyshev further east began; Stalin himself and his entourage remained in the Kremlin. In November 1941, the German spearheads moved closer to Leningrad, capturing Tikhvin, a railhead that gave access to a small port on Lake Ladoga vital to provisioning Leningrad. Severe rationing was introduced, and by the end of the month the inhabitants were in dire straits.[33] Meanwhile, German Army Group South took Rostov-on-Don, and looked set to move into the Caucasus. Then the advance slowed on all fronts, partly because the German supply lines were overextended; partly because the autumn rains turned the roads into swamps, followed by ice and snow, which caused machinery to seize up; partly because of Stalin's "scorched earth" order of mid-November 1941, which denied the Germans food, shelter, and infrastructure; and partly due to stiffening Russian resistance.

These moves were accompanied by an escalation of measures against the Jews, including the tightening of the camp system by Himmler and the chief of the Reichssicherheitshauptamt (RSHA), Reinhard Heydrich, in autumn 1941, the mass murder of Yugoslav Jews as "reprisals" for the Serbian uprising, and the wave of "evacuations" that swept whole communities of central European Jews. In early October, the local SS authorities were informed that Hitler wanted the establishment of a large camp for Jews in the greater Riga area, in Latvia.[34] On October 23, all emigration from the Reich was prohibited. The German Jews were now trapped. In Bucharest, the Romanian Jewish writer Mihail Sebastian observed the gradual tightening of the noose. "Everything is too calculated for effect," Sebastian wrote, "too obviously stage-managed, not to have a political significance." "What will follow?" he asked. "Our straightforward extermination."[35]

The deportation of German Jews began in late October 1941 and gathered pace over the next few months. Thousands of Berlin Jews were sent east in November 1941.[36] That same month, the Jews of Cologne, Düsseldorf, and Hamburg were ordered to supply contingents for further deportations to take place in early December.[37] Their property was carefully catalogued; only a small proportion could be taken with them, and the rest would be confiscated by the Reich. At around this time, too, the Erfurt-based company J. A. Topf and Sons was tasked with the construction of crematoria at Auschwitz for the disposal of bodies of Soviet prisoners of war. Later, these would be used to burn those of murdered Jews.

On November 29, the RSHA sent out invitations to a conference at a villa on the Wannsee in Berlin on December 9, where attendees would discuss the mechanics of deporting all Jews in the Nazi sphere of influence.[38] The intent at this point was not necessarily to murder the deportees.[39] The first German transport that went to Riga was not intended for "liquidation," and when Himmler learned that the local SS commander had murdered the Jews on board anyway, he was genuinely furious because the "guidelines" he had issued on the treatment of "Jews resettled to the Ostland [Baltic] area" had been violated. Although we do not know what Himmler's guidelines were, it is clear that the German Jews were not to be killed, at least not yet.[40] The systematic murder of the Jews of Riga, by contrast, began with a mass clearance of the ghetto and executions on November 29 and 30, 1941.[41] But unlike those of the Soviet Union, who had been classified and murdered as enemy belligerents, the Jews of central and western Europe were still regarded as hostages to constrain Roosevelt.[42]

Throughout the autumn of 1941, Hitler had made the connection between US policy and the fate of European Jewry more and more explicit. When Alfred Rosenberg, the Nazi chief ideologue and minister for the occupied territories in the east, demanded retaliation against German Jews for Stalin's deportation of the Volga Germans, Hitler refused.[43] The German Foreign Office was informed that the Führer was "holding back this measure for the event of an American entry into the war."[44] On October 25, 1941, Hitler privately repeated the "prophecy" he had made in January 1939, when he stated that the Jews of Europe would be held responsible for any new "[world] war."[45] Three weeks later, Goebbels made the same connection publicly, in a leading article in the journal *Das Reich* under the headline "The Jews Are to Blame." He added that "we are now experiencing the fulfillment of this prophecy and Jewry is experiencing a fate that, although hard, is still more than deserved," namely, a "gradual process of extermination."[46] Observing the escalation of Nazi policy, one South American diplomat in Prague reported to his government: "In proportion to the USA increasing its attacks on the Reich, Germany will expedite the destruction of Semitism, as she accuses international Judaism of all the calamities that have befallen the world."[47] These measures and the regime's public statements were also reported by other diplomats and widely discussed in the international press, so Hitler felt confident that the message was getting through to Washington.[48]

Hitler's perception that American Jews had an overbearing influence on Roosevelt and were pushing the United States toward war with Germany was a product of his conspiratorial mindset rather than reality. It was a claim also made by the aviator Charles Lindbergh, a prominent anti-interventionist, in a speech in Des Moines, Iowa, that September. Lindbergh claimed that "leaders of both the British and Jewish races . . . for reasons which are not American, wish to involve us in the war." Furthermore, he warned that America's "tolerance" of Jews would not "survive war," and that the Jews endangered the United States through "their large ownership in our motion pictures, our press, our radio and our government."[49] Lindbergh's overt anti-Semitism did much to discredit his foreign policy views among the wider American public, with polls showing that relatively few Americans shared his paranoia about Jews driving the United States into war.[50] In fact, Roosevelt and his closest advisers—such as Treasury secretary Henry Morgenthau and Supreme Court justice Felix Frankfurter, who were themselves Jewish—were determined not to offer any sign that the administration's pro-Allied policies were predicated on Nazi anti-Semitism over and above Hitler's other crimes.[51]

In any case, the Americans could not fully grasp the extent of Nazi barbarity, even as evidence mounted. When news reached the United States that autumn that the Nazis were perpetrating wholesale massacres of Jews behind the lines on the eastern front, many American Jewish political leaders were incredulous, as were newspaper publishers and editors, who consigned the reports to the back pages.[52] The *New York Times*, whose front page Roosevelt scanned each morning, only published one of these reports and gave it little prominence, reflecting the desire of its publisher, Arthur Sulzberger, himself Jewish but thoroughly assimilated, not to elicit charges from anti-Semites that the paper was too focused on Jewish causes.[53] The *Times* relegated to page eleven its coverage of Goebbels's November threat that "every Jew is our enemy, regardless of whether he is vegetating in a Polish ghetto or delays his parasitic existence in Berlin or Hamburg or blows the war trumpets in New York and Washington," and his pledge that the Nazis would "finally finish" them.[54] If Hitler thought that threatening European Jewry with destruction would deter American intervention, there is no evidence that the situation was understood in these terms in Washington.

Some European Jews clearly observed a link between a deterioration in US-Germany relations and their own collective fate. In the autumn of 1941, Jerzy Jurandot, a Polish Jew in the Warsaw ghetto, reported a revealing exchange concerning the rental of a piano for performances in a cafe. Beyond the usual safeguards, the owner of the instrument wanted to be indemnified for any damage consequent on "actions of a higher power." "For example," Jurandot writes, "if America entered the war and, as a result, the Germans staged a pogrom in the ghetto and the piano was damaged?" A clause to that effect was then added to the contract.[55]

Hitler found widespread support for his anti-Semitic program among European governments. In late November 1941, the signatories of the Anti-Comintern Pact—Bulgaria, Croatia, Finland, Hungary, Italy, Japan, Romania, Spain, and the puppet government of Denmark—were summoned to Berlin to renew their bond. Their union was now directed as much, if not more, against Anglo-American and Jewish international capitalism as it was against the Soviet Union and Communism.[56] On November 26, Ribbentrop gave the keynote speech of the conference at the opulent Hotel Kaiserhof, conveniently located close to the Reich Chancellery on Wilhelmplatz.[57] Reprising themes that Hitler himself had already elaborated on at length over the past years, Ribbentrop opened with an attack on "England," which had allegedly dominated the world in 1939, controlling a third of the globe's surface area with only forty-five million inhabitants. It was "Jewish forces" in England, Ribbentrop continued, who had ensured that London would only accept Germany as a "subordinate nation," which would be condemned to a lower "living standard." He praised Italy for joining the resulting "battle of the haves against the have-nots."

Ribbentrop, like Hitler, justified the continuing war with the Soviet Union not so much on an ideological basis but as a necessity for defeating

Britain and deterring Roosevelt. Announcing victory in the east, on the basis of early and, as it would turn out, premature reports, Ribbentrop claimed that "now this last hope of the Anglo-Saxons in Europe has been dashed." He reassured his listeners that Europe was now "economically no longer dependent on the rest of the world." Russian grain and raw materials were sufficient for all the continent's needs. "The organization of this vast space," he assured them, "is already in full swing." In the second half of his remarks, Ribbentrop warned that Roosevelt, the great "warmonger," had been threatening Germany and other countries with war for some time. Since the United States and the German Reich were not natural enemies, Ribbentrop could only explain Roosevelt's alleged forgeries and neutrality violations with reference to the machinations of a "Jewish-plutocratic" clique. There followed a long diatribe against the president and Churchill, which culminated in the prediction that the "young peoples" of the world would prevail over the "custodians of an international clique of Jewish deal-makers and political oppressors."

These days, in fact, the German capital was thronged with visitors from across Eurasia and what we today call the global south.[58] No sooner had the dignitaries from the Anti-Comintern powers left after the conference concluded on November 27 than the grand mufti of Jerusalem, Faisal Husseini, appeared. He was the recognized leader of the Arab national cause against the Zionist project of a Jewish homeland in Palestine. Husseini was received by the Führer in the Reich Chancellery on November 28—of this portentous meeting, more later.[59] The following day, Hitler met with the Italian foreign minister Count Galeazzo Ciano and the Slovak chief minister Vojtech Tuka; Ribbentrop received the Indian nationalist leader Subhas Chandra Bose.[60] The legendary Spanish Fascist defender of the Alcázar of Toledo, General José Moscardó Ituarte, was on his way to the Führer; Moscardó had been visiting the Spanish Legion stationed at Novgorod in northern Russia. The ousted Iraqi leader Rashid Ali al-Gailani, on the run since the British had suppressed his revolt back in May, was also beating a path to Hitler. As Count Ciano remarked, somewhat ambivalently, if Hitler was now master in Europe, the best thing to do was to sit on his "right hand."[61]

All this was observed with a mordant eye by the American press community in Berlin, represented by the Associated Press (AP), United Press International, the International News Service, the *New York Times*, and the *Chicago Tribune*. Many of the journalists—such as Frederick Oechsner, Louis Lochner, Angus Thuermer, Guido Enderis, Alvin Steinkopf, Glen Stadler, and Jack Fleischer—were (non-Jewish) German Americans. The Nazi authorities often spoke quite openly with them.[62] Very few of these journalists, though, were sympathetic to the Third Reich; one exception was Guido Enderis, the Berlin bureau chief of the *New York Times*. But the vast majority sent highly critical reports, which were regarded by the regime as part of the propaganda war waged by Washington against them. It was clear to most of these American correspondents that the hour of truth was fast approaching, and that they would soon have to leave Germany. The war of words, in which the US correspondents were major combatants, looked poised to escalate into a shooting war.

Across the British Empire, however, policy makers remained fearful that Roosevelt's rhetoric against Hitler would not lead to effective military action. After the Atlantic summit in August, Churchill informed his war cabinet that Roosevelt, given his "constitutional difficulties" with Congress, had told him that he would become "more and more provocative" with the Germans in the Atlantic, and "look for an 'incident' which would justify him in opening hostilities."[63] Yet, as one close confidant of Churchill, the South African leader Jan Christian Smuts, wrote to him in early November, the US president had "let slip so many opportunities for action including the sinking of American warships that I fail to see what stronger provocation is likely to be effective." Smuts lamented that "Roosevelt continues Hamlet-like to hesitate" and, as a result, the feeling was growing across the empire that "Roosevelt means to keep America out of the war in spite of his brave words."[64] Despite the growing provocations between the US and German navies in the Atlantic, the direct American military commitment to the struggle against Hitler remained restricted by its nonbelligerent status.[65] And without a formal declaration of war, the United States could not fully mobilize its economy on a war footing and its production could still only satisfy a portion of the Allied demand.

On November 18, Britain launched a major strategic initiative in North Africa that placed in stark relief its tremendous need for American war production, specifically tanks. This offensive, code-named Crusader, was Britain's principal operation of 1941 and the only opportunity for military breakthrough in the short term. Soon, Western Desert Force, now rechristened Eighth Army, had 750 tanks deployed in North Africa, which was probably more than either the Germans or the Russians had before Moscow.[66] Yet after initially surging deep behind German-Italian lines, the campaign descended into a "brutal slugging match" that wiped out most of the tanks on both sides.[67] Britain's fast cruiser tanks also endured severe mechanical breakdowns in the desert terrain.[68] When General Erwin Rommel and his Afrika Korps launched a counteroffensive toward the Egyptian frontier, they looked poised to break through. Deprived of so many tanks that British forces appeared outnumbered three to one, the British commander Sir Alan Cunningham feared the battle was lost. Facing disaster, the commander in chief of the Middle East theater, Sir Claude Auchinleck, replaced Cunningham with his deputy chief of general staff, General Neil Ritchie. The position eventually stabilized but for a while it was "touch and go."[69] If British casualties continued to mount and, in particular, if tank losses continued at such an alarming rate, then Egypt and the strategically vital Suez Canal were vulnerable to a German counterstrike.

This dire situation left Britain more desperate than ever to secure delivery of American medium tanks, on which, as the official historians of the Allied overseas supply effort later wrote, "more than on any other single factor, it seemed that the issue of the North African war would turn."[70] Roosevelt had already informed Churchill that US supply allocations to Britain would need to be cut back in order to sustain the Soviets in their life-or-death struggle.[71] Unable to offer the second front in the Balkans or France that Stalin argued was imperative to combat the "mortal peril" facing the USSR, Churchill also stretched himself by promising the Soviet leader 250 tanks a month from Britain's own production.[72] This met just half of Stalin's stated needs and, pressured to match the British offer, Roosevelt agreed to send the other half, but only by reducing the supplies to Britain further. The Americans placated the British by promising them a larger quota of tanks in the future. But in the meantime, with the US services protesting that their own requirements were being ignored, Britain was actually forced to make up the vast majority of Stalin's demand for five hundred tanks a month from its own stocks. Churchill, like Roosevelt, was committed to providing aid to the Soviets, not only to keep them in the fight but also to convince Stalin that he could rely on them as allies and so avoid the nightmare scenario of him again coming to terms with Hitler. Yet it was becoming increasingly clear that, without the United States on a war footing, American production was insufficient to meet the growing Allied needs, and Churchill feared that the Soviets would get the lion's share and Britain would lose out.[73]

In Moscow, Stalin was under no illusion about the magnitude of the immediate German threat. He candidly admitted as much in a speech on the occasion of the meeting of the Moscow Soviet on November 6, 1941, on the eve of the anniversary of the October Revolution.[74] He was also open about the disruption to the Soviet war economy caused by territorial losses and the evacuation of key industries beyond the Urals, not to mention the fact that "the Germans are producing considerably more tanks." Stalin consoled his listeners with the fact that the Soviet Union had now "acquired new allies in the shape of Great Britain, the United States [sic] and other countries occupied by the Germans." "Britain, the United States of America and the Soviet Union have united into a single camp," he claimed, even before the United States had entered the war. "The present war is a war of engines," he continued, and "the war will be won by the side that has an overwhelming preponderance in engine production." If the Germans, who he said had sunk to the level of "wild beasts," wanted a "war of extermination," they would "get it."

The key to Stalin's thinking was Lend-Lease. He said that on their recent visit to Moscow, the British minister of supply Lord Beaverbrook and American Lend-Lease coordinator Averell Harriman had "decided systematically to help our country with tanks and aircraft." "As is well known," Stalin remarked, "we have already begun to receive tanks and planes on the basis of that decision." It is likely that the dispatch of the former foreign minister Maxim Litvinov as Soviet ambassador to the United States on November 12, via Iran and India, was in part driven by the need to maintain these supplies. "Even prior to that," Stalin went on, "England arranged for supplies to our country of such materials in short supply as aluminium, lead, tin, nickel and rubber." The Soviet dictator also mentioned the huge loan that Roosevelt had advanced to him. The following day, the Soviet Union was formally incorporated into the Lend-Lease program—but what was striking throughout Stalin's remarks was his assumption not only that the United States was already a cobelligerent, but that its productive power would prove decisive in the struggle ahead.

BY THE END of November 1941, the Axis's strategic failure had become manifest. Militarily, the Third Reich was stalemated; the victory over the Red Army announced by the press chief, Otto Dietrich, shortly after the start of the offensive on Moscow had turned out to be premature. The southern flank of the Axis was in disarray. In Libya, Rommel had been surprised by Crusader. He had managed to rally, but then found himself pushed back again. He extended his supply lines too far and left his forces vulnerable to British air bombardment; the Luftwaffe was, at this point, too weak to do anything about it.[75] The Italian-German army was soon falling back across Libya, and there were mounting partisan attacks on Italian occupation forces in the Balkans.[76] In East Africa, the last Italian forces capitulated to the British at Gondar on November 27, 1941.[77] The Kriegsmarine was doing no better in the Atlantic, where British countermeasures and the shortage of U-boats led to increased losses and reduced sinkings.[78]

Things were even worse on the eastern front, where the autumn rains had been followed by intense snowfall and biting cold. In the north, the Red Army was prizing open the ring of encirclement around Leningrad and pushing back Wilhelm Ritter von Leeb's Army Group North. In southern Russia, the Wehrmacht was booted out of Rostov by a Soviet counterattack on November 28. On the central sector of the front, especially, German soldiers were now dying in large numbers. Given Soviet production shortfalls, the tanks and aircraft supplied by the British played—as the German Office for the War Economy and Armaments had feared—a not-unimportant role in these battles.[79] German fighters ran into a squadron of Curtiss P-40 planes that had come via the first Arctic convoys; German intercept stations claimed to pick up the voices of American instructors.[80] On November 26, German troops reported sighting their first British tanks.[81] In fact, British-supplied tanks, especially Valentines, played such an important role defending Moscow that Stalin specifically requested the dispatch of more of them.[82]

By the first days of December, the German advance on the Soviet capital had finally ground to a halt.[83] The commander of Army Group Center, Fedor von Bock, noted in his diary that "the hour at which the troops will be at the ends of their tether" was "fast approaching."[84] Hellmuth Stieff, a passionately anti-Nazi officer, wrote to his wife that he expected the eastern campaign to continue a good while longer.[85] Erich Hoepner, the commander of Panzer Group Four, stationed before Moscow, wrote to his wife that he "had achieved a great deal, but not the final objective." "We have insufficient forces," he continued, and "the men are worn out." It was "not a happy end to the year." Hoepner did not yet know, of course, that the year still had many further unpleasant surprises in store.[86]

Japan, too, had reached the end of the road. Apprised of Tokyo's stiff negotiating position and strict deadlines by MAGIC intercepts, and aware that Japan's forces were moving south, Roosevelt decided that concessions in the face of mounting Japanese aggression smacked of appeasement. This relieved Chiang Kai-shek, who had protested furiously against any accommodation that would come at China's expense. Churchill echoed Chiang's concerns, aware of the American popular "regard for the Chinese cause," but he was principally concerned that a US-Japan settlement, however temporary, could leave Japan free to attack the British Empire while the United States remained on the sidelines.[87] Sensitive to any suggestion that the United States was sacrificing China, and convinced by the movement of Japan's troop convoys into the South China Sea that Tokyo was negotiating in "bad faith," Roosevelt and Secretary of State Cordell Hull abandoned the idea of a modus vivendi.[88]

Negotiations effectively collapsed on November 26, 1941, when Hull handed Japanese diplomats Kichisaburo Nomura and Saburo Kurusu a list of demands. Japan, Hull insisted, must withdraw entirely from China and Indochina and abjure the Tripartite Pact.[89] There was no time limit specified, but in the fevered atmosphere in Tokyo, Hull's note was regarded as an "ultimatum." Nomura believed that it made war inevitable.[90] That same day, Kido Butai, the Japanese striking force of six aircraft carriers under the command of Admiral Chuichi Nagumo, left Hitokappu Bay in the Kuriles, bound for Pearl Harbor. Soon after, all Japanese forces were sent coded signals that were to be deciphered only on receipt of a subsequent dispatch. War was now not absolutely certain, but it was extremely likely.

On November 28, the Japanese informed the Germans that negotiations with the United States had failed. Ribbentrop assured the Japanese ambassador that Hitler would take a "very determined" line against the United States and that joint German-Japanese "resistance" against American attempts to dominate the world beyond the Western Hemisphere was "inevitable."[91] The United States, Hitler had told his foreign minister, was contesting Japan and Germany's right to exist. He regarded war with Roosevelt as inevitable, and he had already accepted that the campaign in the east would not be completed by the end of the year. "Should Japan become engaged in a war against the United States," Ribbentrop therefore told Japanese ambassador Hiroshi Oshima, "Germany, of course, would join the war immediately. There is absolutely no possibility of Germany's entering into a separate peace with the United States under such circumstances. The Führer is determined on that point."[92] The Japanese did not tell the Germans that the Combined Fleet had already put to sea. Berlin had, in effect, issued Tokyo with a blank check, which it could cash at a moment of its own choosing.[93] Indeed, Hitler had expressed a similarly broad assurance to then foreign minister

Matsuoka back in April. The question, though, was whether this verbal commitment from the Führer was worth the paper it wasn't written on.

Japanese anxieties were fueled by the dispatch of Maxim Litvinov to Washington, which they feared might lead to a US-USSR rapprochement at their expense.[94] On November 28, the Japanese foreign minister summoned the Soviet ambassador, Konstantin Smetanin, and demanded assurances that his country would remain neutral; he delivered them forty-eight hours later. The next day, the Imperial Conference met to discuss the American "ultimatum." None of the participants would accept Hull's conditions. Most said that war was now the only option. The decision to open hostilities was taken at the conference the following day. On November 30, 1941, Foreign Minister Togo reminded the German and Italian ambassadors that he expected their support in the event of war with the Western powers.[95]

Luckily for the Japanese, Stalin was not interested in attacking them. Indeed, with his eastern flank secure, the Soviet dictator had been steadily shifting men from the Far East and the Urals to the west, redeploying them at the front line near Moscow. On November 30, 1941, he instructed Georgy Zhukov, commander of the western front, to prepare a counterattack.[96] Zhukov was comparatively short of tanks—some of which were British made—but he had the "Siberians" transferred from the Far East to call on, and his men were better equipped for winter warfare than the Germans.[97]

At the same time, Stalin was seeking a firmer alliance with Britain, involving a British troop commitment on the Russian front and an agreement on war aims. Churchill initially balked at both of these requests. The prime minister told Britain's ambassador, Sir Stafford Cripps, that he would not send British divisions "into the heart of Russia" to be "cut to pieces as a symbolic sacrifice," particularly with Britain already committed in North Africa. Churchill also informed the Soviet ambassador in London, Ivan Maisky, that Britain's objectives were currently embodied in the Atlantic Charter. The British foreign secretary, Anthony Eden, was conscious, however, that Stalin was "very suspicious" that "we and the United States would get together and leave them out of the settlement of matters at Peace." Eager to enhance his own position in British-Soviet relations, Eden seized on a suggestion by Cripps to visit Moscow, together with military experts, and help allay Stalin's concerns. In order to strengthen relations at a critical time, Churchill agreed to Eden's mission and gave him permission to "discuss every question relating to the war," including sending British troops to fight alongside the Red Army on its southern front. But with the Libyan campaign still in the balance, Churchill almost immediately walked back this suggestion. Sending British soldiers to Russia would be "like taking coals to Newcastle," and it was far better to continue "giving the Russians as much equipment as possible," although he avoided telling Stalin ahead of Eden's trip. Churchill did bow to another Soviet demand and issued an ultimatum to Germany's allies Finland, Hungary, and Romania to end their war with the USSR within a week or face war with Britain.[98]

Across the globe, informed observers sensed that the world was on the brink. On November 26, the backbench member of Parliament Harold Nicolson, who had recently served in Churchill's coalition government, worried, "We may be faced with a very black week." As he surveyed the global scene, the dangers were innumerable: "Moscow may fall. Japan may come in against us. [Vichy] France may join the Axis. We may be beaten in Libya. I fear that all this will react very badly on Winston's prestige."[99] In Bucharest, writer Mihail Sebastian wrote four days later: "The German advance appears to have slowed or been checked." In Libya, he continued, "the British have superiority, but it is not completely clear cut." And "in Washington," he went on, "negotiations with the Japanese are on the point of collapsing. Will war break out in the Pacific?"[100] In Dresden, the Jewish retired professor Victor Klemperer, who lived in constant fear of deportation, wrote, "I have the impression that chaos and terror are getting stronger every day." "There are ever more battles in the east, although Russia is supposed to have been destroyed long ago," he noted, while "in Africa [there is] a big British offensive in the Cyrenaica." Klemperer also registered the fall of Gondar. "How long," he asked, "can Italy hold out?"[101] In Washington, on November 30 speechwriter Robert Sherwood advised Roosevelt to remind Americans that Japan's belligerent attitude stemmed from its relations with the "entire Axis." This was clearly demonstrated by the Anti-Comintern "conference in Berlin the previous week," which he said was "aimed primarily at the United States." Rather than focus on Japan specifically, Sherwood cautioned, Americans must recognize that this was a "whole world crisis."[102]

Britain's leaders, too, feared that American hesitance about getting involved in the war threatened to leave Britain isolated in Asia and Europe. Officials noted a sharp uptick in popular anti-British sentiment among the American public. Thomas Whitehead, a British professor at Harvard then serving in the Foreign Office as an expert on American opinion, told colleagues in November that "during all the years I have known America, I have never known her so actively suspicious and distrustful of our country."[103] Above all, this reflected the residual belief that British policy was narrowly self-interested and that its perfidious leaders were scheming to bring the United States into a war fought primarily to uphold the British Empire.

The principal force pushing this view was the America First Committee, which since its formation the previous year had devoted itself to campaigning against US aid to the Allies for fear that it would lead to American military involvement in the war. As tensions rose in the Atlantic and Pacific, supporters of America First played on distrust of Britain in their writings and speeches. A particular target was the new ambassador in Washington, Lord Halifax, who seemed to embody all that Americans found most suspect about Britain. A book published that year dismissed the former foreign secretary and viceroy of India as "a British Imperialist, an unrepentant old-school tie Tory, representing an outworn feudal system."[104] On a November visit to Detroit, a bastion of isolationism, the ambassador was splattered with tomatoes and eggs by America Firsters, who chanted, "Go home Halifax!"[105] Britain's embassy turned the incident to its advantage, with the country, and its much-maligned ambassador, receiving a raft of positive publicity after Halifax was quoted as saying, "How fortunate you Americans are, in Britain we only get one egg a week and we are glad of those."[106] Yet the latent mistrust of British motives lingered. As Churchill told the war cabinet on December 1, they "ought not to assume that the outbreak of war between England and Japan would necessarily precipitate the entry of the United States," as there remained a "strong party" who "would work up prejudice against being drawn into Britain's war."[107]

On the same day, Halifax met with Roosevelt to try and get him to publicly commit to standing with Britain against Japan, even if a Japanese attack bypassed the Philippines. The president assured him that, in case of a direct attack on British or Dutch possessions, "we should obviously be all together," but it would "take a short time" to manage the politics.[108] Unclear on the meaning of this vague comment, officials in London asked Halifax to clarify with the president when he met with him again two days later. Roosevelt confirmed that he did mean to provide armed support, but that he could not say whether Congress would concur.[109] He would also prefer that an American warning to Japan came first, so as to avoid public criticism that he was simply following Britain's lead. Moreover, he wished to hold off on a warning until Japan had responded to his November 26 demands and he had decided whether to follow up with a personal appeal to the emperor.[110] Halifax regarded Roosevelt as a "very adroit manipulator. . . . You never quite know when you've got him, or whether he will not slip through your fingers."[111] On this occasion, the ambassador was pretty convinced that Roosevelt had committed to issue a warning and, as a result, Churchill cautiously informed the war cabinet that he had "every confidence" that the Americans would stand with them if Malaya or the Dutch East Indies were attacked. Yet there is no evidence that Roosevelt said categorically he would ask Congress for a declaration of war if Japan attacked the British or Dutch colonies.[112] As a result, Churchill continued to fret that Britain would be left in the lurch.

The British hoped to deter Japanese aggression and defend the entrance of the Indian Ocean with the battle cruiser *Repulse* and the battleship *Prince of Wales*. On November 29, these two ships arrived at Ceylon (present-day Sri Lanka). Three days later, they reached Singapore.[113] Their commander, Admiral Tom Phillips, received what turned out to be remarkably accurate intelligence reports on the numbers and capacity of Japanese aircraft based within range in southern Indochina.[114] London was hopeful that the arrival in the theater of Force Z, as Phillips's command was soon to be christened—two state-of-the-art capital ships, bristling with anti-aircraft artillery and long-range guns in well-armored turrets—would make the Japanese think twice about landing in Malaya. That said, a good part of British confidence continued to rest on a racially driven underestimation of Japanese capabilities. Churchill was hardly immune to these sentiments, telling the American journalist John Gunther in an off-the-record remark at this time that if war came, then Japan would "fold up like the Italians" because they were the "wops of the Far East."[115] To make matters worse, Admiral Phillips had been notorious in the peacetime Royal Navy for his lack of understanding of the threat of air power. "One day Tom," RAF officer Arthur "Bomber" Harris predicted, "you'll be standing on a box on your bridge and your ship will be smashed to pieces by bombers and torpedo aircraft. As she sinks your last words will be 'That was a fucking great mine.'"[116]

It was evident that Japan was running out of time. The arrival of Force Z was spotted by Japanese agents in Singapore, and the increasingly hostile attitude of the United States was palpable. Seizing the resources of the Dutch East Indies was now imperative. General Hideki Tojo informed the Imperial Conference on December 1, 1941, that "our empire has no alternative but to begin war against the United States, Great Britain, and the Netherlands in order to resolve the present crisis and assure survival."[117] The chief of the Japanese naval general staff signaled to all ships at sea that the top-secret message received some days ago should now be opened. Commanders were informed that the empire would open hostilities against the three nations within the next ten days. They were not yet told exactly when and where this would happen. "Decision made," Admiral Matome Ugaki signaled each fleet commander in chief. "Day and time will be ordered later."[118] The following day, Ugaki and his staff struggled to come up with a suitably somber and dignified text to accompany the commander in chief's message at the start of war. They finally settled on the Nelsonian injunction that the empire expected everyone to do their duty. At 17:30 that afternoon, Ugaki sent the fateful signal to the Combined Fleet: "Climb Mt Nitaka 1208." They would attack in seven days' time on December 8. "At last," one diarist wrote, "the arrow leaves the bowstring."[119]

Some in the Japanese leadership were still daunted by the prospect of taking on the American colossus.[120] Throughout the late summer and autumn of 1941, the warnings piled up in Tokyo. "If I am told to fight regardless of consequence," Admiral Isoroku Yamamoto famously remarked, "I shall run wild for the first six months or a year, but I have utterly no confidence for the second and third years." "A war with so little chance of success," he said, "should not be fought." Yamamoto predicted that it would be a long conflict that would end in the exhaustion of Japan.[121] The head of the navy, Admiral Osami Nagano, pronounced himself "uncertain" of victory. Emperor Hirohito himself said it would be "a reckless war."[122] The Japanese ambassador in Washington was even blunter. "If I were to have a hand in choosing someone to fight," Ambassador Nomura said, "I'd make sure it was someone I could lick."[123] "We mustn't become utterly poor," the former prime minister Admiral Mitsumasa Yonai remarked, "in our quest to avoid becoming gradually poor."[124]

Both Nazi Germany and Imperial Japan had thus reached the same turning point—not so much in hubris, but in fear. Neither expected to defeat their enemy outright, but at best to seize the resources and a perimeter line behind which they could defend themselves until a compromise peace had been reached. The Axis and the Allies each had their anxieties and pathologies. If Hitler saw Roosevelt as the agent of the Jews, the president, as we shall see, portrayed the Japanese as a mere instrument of Hitler. All of the major actors had their private nightmare scenario. Hitler's was the prospect of fighting the United States without Japanese support. The Japanese feared that Hitler would double-cross them and leave them to fight the British and the Americans, and perhaps even the Soviet Union, on their own. Churchill fretted that the Japanese would attack the British Empire but not the United States, leaving him with an unwinnable two-front conflict. We do not know for sure what Stalin was thinking at this moment, but it is likely that he feared being left to face the Nazis, and perhaps even the Japanese, unsupported.

All sides were engaged in a racial struggle, though "race" meant different things to each. In his mind, Hitler was battling not only the Jews and Slavs but also the Anglo-Saxons; he was fighting Bolshevism, but even more he was struggling against international plutocratic capitalism. The Japanese were challenging white imperial rule in East Asia and articulating their vision of a Tokyo-dominated "Greater East Asia Co-prosperity Sphere," a stepping-stone toward a grand bargain with the Western powers.[125] Britain and the United States, by contrast, were battling Hitler on behalf of the balance of power, freedom, and democracy in Europe and—though this was less clearly articulated—Japan in defense of international law and the white position in Asia.[126] Yet, even while perceptions of these new threats were pulling each side's leaders and military officials closer together, older attitudes and historical antagonisms continued to keep the United States officially out of the war and formally apart from Britain.

THE NEXT WEEK was marked by two frenetic rounds of diplomacy unfolding simultaneously. One, the last-ditch discussions between the Japanese and the Americans, was essentially for show. The other—the scramble by Tokyo, Berlin, and Rome to agree a common diplomatic front in advance of the outbreak of war with the United States—was far more real.

Having decided on war and a surprise attack against the US fleet, the Japanese leaders were determined to disguise their intentions and movements. Some of them also wanted, if possible, to observe the niceties of international law by allowing a decent interval between the declaration of war and the firing of the first shots. Foreign minister Togo battled with the military commanders, who wanted to keep this period as short as possible in order to achieve surprise.[127] Either way, spinning out the discussions in Washington and Tokyo without arousing American suspicions was central to this strategy. For this reason, the Japanese leadership made a big show of engaging with various communications and initiatives coming from the United States.

The main focus of Japanese diplomacy was elsewhere. Axis diplomats were working overtime to agree on a common position against the United States, with drafts flying across the airwaves or being delivered, heavily annotated, in person. Everything needed to be nailed down. Who would promise what to whom? When would these commitments come into effect? When would any agreement be announced, by whom, and in what form? How long would the arrangement last? Would it supplement or supersede the Tripartite Pact? These were all thorny questions, but the biggest one of all was whether any of the putative contractants— Hitler, Mussolini, and the Japanese—could be taken at their word.

Convinced that war with the United States loomed, the Germans made one last attempt to win over Vichy France and ease the pressure in North Africa. On December 1, commander in chief of the Luftwaffe Hermann Göring met with the Vichy leaders Marshal Pétain and his prime minister, Admiral François Darlan, at Florentin-Vergigny in Burgundy. The old marshal obfuscated at length, and was in turn berated by Göring. The Luftwaffe commander criticized low industrial production in France in support of the German war effort, the unwillingness of the French Navy to take on the British, and the tendency of the French intelligentsia to hope for and believe in a British victory and the "fantastical idea that America was exercising a decisive influence." Darlan, for his part, warned that if France made the Tunisian port of Bizerta available to the Axis, "the British and Americans would then claim the right to attack Dakar, Martinique, and Guadeloupe."[128] In short, fear of the Anglo-Americans was having a chilling effect on any Vichy French desire to collaborate with the Axis.

That same day, the German representative at the Italian Comando Supremo met with Mussolini in the presence of the head of the Comando Supremo, Ugo Cavallero. The Duce spoke openly about his "powerful fears for the [outcome of] further battles in Libya." He worried that even the welcome dispatch of additional German submarines and aircraft would not be enough to guarantee a "transport solution" that would enable a long-term victory against the British. Only the use of Bizerta would ensure that, and Mussolini believed that if it could not be secured by bribing the French with "concessions," then it would have to be seized "by force." The Duce asked that his view be conveyed to the German Oberkommando der Wehrmacht (OKW), the Supreme Command of the Armed Forces.[129]

It was the twin crises in southern Russia and along his southern flank in the Mediterranean that most worried Hitler. On December 2, he flew to the Ukraine to sort things out. The commander of Army Group South, Gerd von Rundstedt, was scapegoated for the stalled advance and replaced by Walther von Reichenau. That same day, Hitler issued directive 38, announcing the transfer of a substantial number of aircraft to the Mediterranean. Field Marshal Albert Kesselring was appointed supreme commander south. Kesselring's overall mission was to change the dynamic not only in North Africa but in "the entire Mediterranean." His immediate task was to secure command of the air and sea between southern Italy and North Africa, so as to enable the continued supply of Axis forces in Libya.[130] He would be subject to the authority of the Duce and receive instructions from the Comando Supremo. This complicated arrangement was designed to spare feelings on the Italian side. A daily military consultation meeting of the two Axis powers was established at the Comando Supremo.[131] As far as Bizerta was concerned, though, the Germans remained fearful of pushing too hard, let alone seizing the port, lest this provoke the British to move against Vichy French colonies in North Africa.[132]

These shifts opened up opportunities for Vichy. Pétain and Darlan sought to defend their sovereignty through conditional collaboration with the Axis while avoiding direct confrontation with the Anglo-Saxons, using the French fleet, or what was left of it, as a bargaining chip.[133] Their relationship with the United States was—to Free French chagrin—relatively good; the US ambassador to Vichy, Admiral William Leahy, was a confidant of the president.[134] An American entry into the war held fewer terrors for Vichy France. Vichy also benefitted from the increasing Italian unease with German domination. Both sides began to talk of their "Latin" solidarity against Hitler and the despised Anglo-Saxons, against whom Darlan had particular animus.[135] There were even Italian calls for a "Latin Union."[136] Mussolini, who had formerly tried to bully Vichy, now sought accommodation. A meeting was scheduled between Darlan and Italian foreign minister Ciano in Turin to explore the possibilities.

De Gaulle, too, was trying to triangulate in order to restore French sovereignty. In his case, it was partly a matter of playing the British and the Americans against each other. Roosevelt was wary of de Gaulle, and so an American entry into the war, welcome from the military point of view, brought with it some political dangers for the Free French.[137] De Gaulle, though, was not daunted by the odds against him. Vichy might have all the assets—especially what remained of the fleet—but he had the brand.

De Gaulle had also positioned himself between the "Russians"—he avoided referring to the Soviet Union by its name—and the Anglo-Americans. He explained in the autumn of 1941 that Russia and France, "being continental powers, have other preoccupations from the Anglo-Saxon states." Moscow, he would later write, constituted a "counterweight" to the "Anglo-Saxons."[138] De Gaulle was therefore delighted when Stalin recognized him as the legitimate representative of France, just as Churchill had. He then demanded that the British arm and deploy a couple of Free French "divisions," recruited from France's garrisons in its territories in Syria and Lebanon, so that his men could participate in the war against the Axis in North Africa. When London hesitated, unwilling to alter its battle plans at this late stage, de Gaulle threatened to offer his men to fight with the Soviets on the eastern front. In the first week of December, the British military and political leadership was still wrestling with this question.

For the Soviets, desperately defending Moscow and Leningrad, the offer of French help would surely have been welcome, but more than anything what they needed were arms and munitions. Yet there was limited shipping capacity to transport the Lend-Lease matériel that the Soviets required to replenish their embattled forces. The Soviet merchant marine was too modest to shoulder the load. Although the United States and Britain had agreed to provide additional vessels, German U-boats had by now sunk around five million tons of shipping in the Atlantic that year, more than double the combined output of British and American shipyards, resulting in a shipping crisis. The long and dangerous supply routes to the Soviet Union, and the inadequate docking facilities at the ice-covered Archangel harbor, only exacerbated the issue.[139]

Despite the Roosevelt administration's best efforts, the United States lagged far behind its supply schedule, furnishing less than half of the promised tonnage in October and November. On December 3, the *New York Times* made this public, reporting that the administration had fallen "far, far short" of its commitments and that this threatened to "seriously affect" the Soviet struggle against the Nazis.[140] The bulk of the matériel the Soviets did receive continued to come from Britain, which remained largely on track to meet its obligations.[141] But with British aid derived partly from its own Lend-Lease allocations, and with American officials pressuring London to yield even more of these stocks to the Soviets, the complex system by which supplies circulated from the United States to the various members of the anti-Hitler coalition was under severe strain.

Meanwhile, the efforts to agree on an Axis text for the outbreak of hostilities with the United States continued apace. The Japanese also pressed the Italians to prepare for the breach. On December 3, the Japanese ambassador in Rome met with Mussolini and informed him that "the outbreak of a conflict between Japan and the United States and thus also with Great Britain" should now be regarded as "possible and imminent." Mussolini replied that the resulting war was the sole responsibility of Roosevelt and "American plutocracy," which "regarded Asia as its own zone of exploitation."[142] "So now we come to the war between continents," the Duce announced, "which I have predicted since September 1939."[143]

If the Duce was eager for war, the Italian Foreign Office was still divided, with the majority opposing conflict with the United States.[144] The chef de cabinet there, Marquess Lanza d'Ajeta, told the German embassy that there were some who believed that an American entry into the war would force Roosevelt to concentrate on the Pacific to such an extent that the supply of US war matériel to the European theaters would be reduced. That, of course, was Hitler's own calculation. There were others, though, including the marquess himself, who believed that an American entry into the war would considerably worsen the situation for the Axis.[145] It was perhaps no surprise that the Italian interpreter who took down the Japanese ambassador's requests for a common Axis front against the United States during the meeting with the Duce is reported to have been "shaking like a leaf."[146]

What Hitler would make of the coming breach was still unknown to the diplomats. That same afternoon in Berlin, Ribbentrop told Japanese ambassador Oshima that he had not yet been able to speak with Hitler face-to-face; the Führer was still in the Ukraine and it was not thought appropriate to discuss such a sensitive matter over the telephone. The German foreign minister repeated that he personally agreed with the Japanese request, but reiterated that he could only give an official answer once he had spoken with the Führer, which he hoped to do in Rasten-burg on Hitler's return the next day.[147] That evening, Ciano ruminated on the global significance of the Japanese move. "What does this new event mean?" he wondered. "For the moment," he suggested, "Roosevelt has succeeded in his maneuver," because though "unable to enter the war directly and immediately," he was now "doing so through an indirect route—forcing the Japanese to attack him."

The Italian foreign minister, no doubt conscious of his country's in-dustrial weakness, put his finger on the key issue. "To speak of a long war is a very easy forecast to make," Ciano concluded. "Who will have the most stamina?" he asked. "This is the way the question should be put."

This was also the question on Hitler's mind as he contemplated war with the greatest industrial power on earth. On December 3, 1941, he issued a decree on the "simplification and increased performance of our armaments production," which demanded the abandonment of tradi-tional German "technically and aesthetically accomplished equipment of high artisanal quality" in favor of "mass production." The danger, in effect, was that the war would be decided by American quantity rather than by German quality.

In addition to this "rationalization" of industry, Hitler called for the "additional deployment of prisoners of war."[148] There were also large numbers of "volunteer" workers in German factories, and the total number of foreign laborers had already reached three million by the summer of 1941. This, of course, created its own complications in the racially stratified society of the Third Reich. Hitler let it be known on December 3 that he didn't want a fuss made about sexual relations between Western workers and German women. Poles and Russians were another matter and continued to face heavy discrimination.[149] That same day, in fact, SS official Reinhard Heydrich chaired a meeting at the RSHA on how the presence of foreign workers in Germany was to be managed with respect to production, security, and "the danger of racial subversion."[150]

Hitler's most dire fears about American capacities and intentions were realized the very next day, December 4, 1941, when much of the world was transfixed by a report in the *Chicago Tribune*. The full details of Wedemeyer's Victory Program were published under a thick-type headline proclaiming "FDR War Plans."[151] The German Information Office duly slammed the "plan for a total war" against the Axis.[152] It was unclear who leaked the plan to the *Tribune*'s Washington correspondent, Chesly Manly, but the paper's anti-Roosevelt, anti-British, and anti-interventionist owner, Robert McCormick, relished publishing it. Most explosive was the suggestion that an American Expeditionary Force (AEF), comprising as many as five million soldiers, would participate in a massive offensive against Germany by the summer of 1943.

After initially refusing to answer questions, the administration admitted that the report was genuine but that its significance was vastly overstated. Secretary of War Stimson told the press that the report had "never constituted an authorized program of the government" and denounced those "so lacking in appreciation of the danger that confronts the country . . . that they would be willing to take and publish such papers." Roosevelt's opponents accused him of opposing intervention in public while privately preparing for war. The Montana senator Burton K. Wheeler, a Democrat and outspoken anti-interventionist, demanded a congressional investigation. New York congressman Hamilton Fish, leading Republican member of the House foreign affairs committee and "the Nation's No. 1 Isolationist" according to *Time* magazine, denounced it as a plan that would lead to the Soviets overrunning Germany, leave America "bankrupt and impoverished," and bring "communism" with all its associated "chaos and revolution."[153]

Meanwhile the German chargé d'affaires and head of mission in Washington, Hans Thomsen, reported to Berlin that "this secret report" in the *Chicago Tribune* had "undoubtedly been produced at the behest of Roosevelt." Thomsen noted that it confirmed the general view that the full extent of American fighting power would not be deployed before July 1943. In his opinion, the revelations also showed that the Anglo-Americans did not believe that a "war of starvation"—the blockade—would suffice to defeat Germany. Thomsen further drew attention to the largely "defensive" nature of the preparations against Japan, and that it was clear "that in the case of a two-ocean war, America would throw its weight behind an offensive in the direction of Europe and Africa."[154]

In fact, Thomsen opined that same day, the Roosevelt administration was seeking to intimidate Japan while it gained more time for its own preparations. War with Japan would also "most likely" mean war with Germany and thus a "two-front war" for which America, contrary to the bluster of navy secretary Frank Knox, was not prepared. Besides, Thomsen went on, Britain and Russia would be unable to cope "materially" with a US-Japan war. It would mean "a painful reduction of Lend-Lease support to both countries," partly because of the resulting demands of the American war effort and partly because of the closing of the supply routes via Vladivostok and the Persian Gulf.[155] Goebbels was also much preoccupied with the reports in the *Chicago Tribune* and with the flow of American supplies to the British and Russians. Both the propaganda minister and the diplomat lingered on how the global fronts were linked through Lend-Lease, a metaphor for the immense industrial power of the United States.

The Victory Program was Hitler's worst nightmare. If the Führer had not been aware of America's "Germany first" strategy, he was now. On the afternoon of December 4, Hitler returned by plane to Rastenburg. It was probably then that he confirmed to Ribbentrop that he would enter the war with the United States, in conjunction with Japan or shortly after.[156] The Führer would have been further exercised by the reports of the security service, the SD, on the mood of the German population, which had darkened over the past week. Reasons for dismay abounded—including the stalled advance in Russia, the loss of Rostov, the fall of Gondar, the British offensive in North Africa, and news of reduced U-boat successes in the Atlantic—even according to official Nazi claims.[157]

That same day, Japanese government officials agreed on the text of their lengthy reply to the American "ultimatum."[158] Over the next forty-eight hours, the diplomats and military men argued over when it should be delivered in Washington. Each passing hour brought the Kido Butai, Admiral Nagumo's strike force, closer to Hawaii undetected. His commanders spent their time familiarizing themselves with the layout of Pearl Harbor with the help of a scale model on the admiral's flagship, the *Akagi*. Strict radio silence was observed, in order to avoid detection by American listening stations at Midway and Hawaii.

At around the same time, elements of General Tomoyuki Yamashita's Twenty-Fifth Army sailed from Hainan island off southern China.[159] He was spearheading the Southern Operation, commanded by General Count Terauchi Hisaichi out of Saigon. Across the South China Sea and the Pacific, Japanese ships and aircraft were now on the move: toward Pearl Harbor; toward Thailand, Malaya, and British North Borneo; toward the American-garrisoned Philippines; and toward Guam and Wake Island. It was an operation unprecedented in size and complexity. Surprise and timing would be the key to its success.[160]

The Japanese soldiers and sailors aboard these ships received a pamphlet entitled *Read This Alone and the War Can Be Won*.[161] Millions of Asians in India, Malaya, and the Philippines, they were told, groaned under the oppression of a few hundred thousand Europeans. "Money squeezed from the blood of Asians," it said, "maintains these small white minorities in their luxurious mode of life" or disappears into the respective home countries. It was Japan's task, the soldiers and sailors were told, to "make men" of their emasculated fellow Asians and to "liberate East Asia from white invasion and oppression." This would be "a struggle between races," in which "destroy[ing] utterly" the white man would "lighten soldiers' hearts" of their "burden of brooding anger." It was also a battle for resources, as the empire secured vital oil, rubber, and tin, while denying critical supplies to the Americans. Securing these would end the slow US "strangulation" of Japan with "a soft cord of silken floss." The great war of annihilation and redistribution in East Asia was about to begin.

In Washington, Roosevelt remained wary of American public opinion. The reaction to the leak of the Victory Program demonstrated the residual strength of isolationist sentiment in Congress. Of even greater significance were a series of reports revealing just how many Americans continued to oppose full-scale involvement in the war. One survey of opinion in downstate Illinois, still a bellwether area for isolationist opinion, showed "tremendous fear of another A.E.F." and "no evidence" that "any large section demands more violent action." This was reinforced by a national poll from November that suggested roughly as many Americans opposed as supported sending a large American army to Europe, even if was required to defeat Hitler. While support for fighting Japan was more pronounced, all the evidence suggested opinion would be far more divided if Japan confined its attack to British or Dutch territories. On December 5, the president received a summary of national editorial opinion that stressed the media remained hopeful that war with Japan could be avoided and, moreover, "that the Axis can be defeated without full-scale American participation at the actual fighting fronts." This likely contributed to Roosevelt informing the British government that he was committed to "giving his warning to the Emperor and until he has done so, he doesn't want to act." In the British Foreign Office, one of Eden's principal aides, Oliver Harvey, feared that Roosevelt was "nibbling at this piece of time-wasting designed by the Japs to enable them to complete their preparations and to break the united front."[162]

Britain's diplomats were otherwise kept busy that day preparing declarations of war on Finland, Hungary, and Romania, as Churchill resentfully followed through on his pledge to Stalin. The prime minister also instructed the war cabinet to scrape together more supplies for the Soviets to make up for reversing his offer of troops.[163] At the same time, Churchill beseeched Averell Harriman for rifle ammunition and explained that, while he realized "the Russian requirements must be heavy," Britain required increased supplies from the United States as a matter of urgency.[164] The minister of supply, Lord Beaverbrook, also rejected American requests to send as much TNT as possible to the Soviets, telling Harriman that British stocks were almost depleted and his response was therefore "no, no, a thousand times, no."[165] Churchill's fears that the ravenous appetite of the new guest at the "hungry table" would leave little left over for Britain were starting to be realized.

To the consternation of the British press and the public, the situation in Libya remained precarious. The renowned Australian war correspondent Alan Moorehead, then covering the desert war for the *Daily Express*, recalled that ever since the start of Crusader a "myopic and confused propaganda" had ensured that "little or nothing had been allowed out about our losses or the German gains." By early December, with the battle still in the balance, all this had done was raise "a bogey of over-optimism," with "any setback made to appear doubly severe." Moorehead lamented that British propagandists failed to realize that people were "quite able to accept the news of defeats and delays; what the public disliked intensely was having its hopes raised high only to be plunged into the disappointment of reality later on."[166]

Sure enough, on December 5, Churchill heard from General John Kennedy, the director of military operations, that Britain had indeed suffered the dreaded "setback" in the desert. Kennedy assured Churchill that "our forces probably had another kick in them," which "might be sufficient to tip the balance and then the whole thing would slide quickly." Yet the prime minister was mindful that, if not, then Britain "would have to stage another offensive which might take some weeks." Despite the deteriorating position in the Pacific, Churchill was determined to divert resources to secure victory in the desert, even at the expense of other theaters.[167]

While Churchill struggled to hold the line in North Africa, Axis diplomats were drawing up terms for an alliance that they hoped would destroy him globally. That same December 5, Ribbentrop sent a draft of the proposed Axis agreement to the Italians. The preamble claimed that the British and Americans were trying to frustrate a "just reordering" of the world, to cut off the "lifelines of the Japanese, Italian, and German peoples" and thus to deny them their very "existence." In terms of substance, the Germans and Italians would agree that in the event of the outbreak of war between Japan and the United States, they would both immediately come to the aid of Tokyo and wage war against the Americans with all their might. Unlike the Tripartite Pact—which was defensive and only committed the contractants to come to each other's aid if attacked by the United States—this agreement was, implicitly, offensive in nature. Moreover, it was to be kept secret and only published in the event of war, and was thus not intended to deter Roosevelt.[168] Instead, the planned agreement was plainly intended to encourage a Japanese attack on the United States.

It did not take long for the Italians to approve Ribbentrop's draft. Ciano said that he wanted the German text to be the definitive version in order to "anticipate possible hairsplitting by the Japanese with respect to essentially trivial differences between the German and Italian texts."[169] Clearly, the Italians, too, were keen to avoid all unnecessary delay, and whatever Ciano's own private reservations about confronting the United States, he was happy to go along with this strategy. In fact, as the German ambassador, Eugen Ott, reported that day from Tokyo, the Japanese were determined "to move against the [US-British] encirclement" and were ready for a war that they thought could no longer be avoided. He expected a surprise attack on the Americans very soon. In line with his standing instructions, Ott told his interlocutors that they ought to do their best to make the United States responsible for the start of any conflict.[170]

That same day, Stalin unleashed a long-planned counterattack in hopes of turning back the forces menacing Moscow. It was originally conceived as a more limited operation, but over the next few days it would succeed beyond expectations.[171] The Soviet First Shock Army attacked Panzer Group Three, breaking through on such a wide front that General Georg-Hans Reinhardt called for a withdrawal. The Soviet Twenty-Ninth and Thirty-First Armies made big gains against the German Ninth Army. These operations were supported by heavy Soviet air attacks on Wehrmacht resupply and reinforcement columns.[172] "Masses of Russians were suddenly appearing," one German witness remembers. "The sheer number of them left us speechless . . . tanks, artillery units and countless motor vehicles. Where had they all come from?" Though the Soviet offensive was relatively tank light, many of the vehicles they did possess had been supplied from Britain.[173] All along the front, German commanders like Gotthard Heinrici of XXXXIII Army Corps were seized with anxiety about how they could hold the line with their weakened forces.[174]

The Soviet offensive caused havoc along much of the German line and has loomed large in historical consciousness since, but at first it did not alarm Hitler. Because of the phased nature of the Russian attacks, he did not take in the magnitude of the threat for about a week. Speaking to his generals on December 6, the day after the counterattack began, the Führer was instead profoundly depressed by the general state of the eastern campaign and the war as a whole. He was most concerned with the situation in the north—where he demanded the final capture of Leningrad—and the south. "We must secure the oil fields of Maikop," Hitler stressed, "so Rostov should not be written off for this winter." He specified repeatedly that there was to be "no [force] reductions" in the west, and that reinforcements should be sent to Norway to repel a possible American attack there.[175]

Hitler was also exercised by what he regarded as the shortcomings of the German high command. In particular, the Führer was fed up with the supreme commander of the army, Walther von Brauchitsch. "The relationship between Führer and supreme commander can no longer be patched up," Hitler's military adjutant Gerhard Engel noted in his diary. The tension between them made every military briefing meeting "unpleasant." Brauchitsch confided that evening that he could not "go on, not least for health reasons."[176] Dissatisfied with the war and dissatisfied with his commanders, Hitler was adrift as a seismic change in the course of the war lay directly ahead.

On the other side of the world, the Japanese Imperial Conference settled on their plan for communicating with the United States. Their reply to the American "ultimatum"—in effect a declaration of war—should be delivered to the US secretary of state, Cordell Hull, in person at 1 p.m. Washington time the following day. This would leave an hour before the attack on Pearl Harbor commenced. That afternoon, the Japanese embassy in Washington was told to stand by for a fourteen-part message. Once deciphered, it was to be handed to Hull. Ambassador Nomura and senior diplomat Kurusu duly made an appointment to meet the secretary at the State Department at the appointed time.

Already, word was circulating that Japanese forces were advancing across the Pacific, their destination unknown. Churchill had received intelligence reports that a Japanese flotilla—comprising thirty-five transports, eight cruisers, and twenty destroyers—was on the move, and he spent the day anxiously awaiting further news.[177] It was estimated the Japanese fleet was south of Cambodia, but the new chief of the British general staff Alan Brooke informed the permanent undersecretary for foreign affairs Alexander Cadogan that he could not be sure exactly where.[178] Desperately seeking information on Japan's intentions, an agitated Churchill made repeated calls to Bletchley Park, according to one cryptographer, at "all hours of the day and night, except for the four hours in each 24 (2 to 6 am) [in] which he sleeps."[179] As information emerged that the Japanese armada was heading across the Gulf of Siam from Indochina, Cadogan expressed hope that there might still be time for Britain and the United States to issue their "joint warning" to Japan.[180]

The importance that Churchill continued to attach to securing a common position with the Americans was evident in his invitation to Averell Harriman and his daughter Kathleen Harriman to join him that weekend at Chequers, his country retreat. It is not clear whether the prime minister was aware that the American envoy was embroiled in an affair with his daughter-in-law, Pamela Churchill, who also joined the group at Chequers while her husband Randolph was away serving in North Africa. On the night of December 6, the prime minister informed Harriman that "in the event of Japanese aggression" his policy would be to "postpone taking any action, even though this delay might involve some military sacrifice," until Roosevelt had decided what course to adopt.[181] Churchill clearly remained fearful that Britain would be left fighting a multifront war without an American ally.

Across mainland Europe, December 6, 1941, was a day of tension, anxiety, and terror. In Leningrad, the teacher Elena Skryabina contemplated her bombed-out apartment in the early hours of the morning and wondered how she would survive winter without any windowpanes.[182] In Rome, Ciano lamented further Italian disasters in Libya in his diary.[183] In Berlin, Goebbels worried about RAF bombing raids on Hamburg and pondered on how best to manage bad news from the front. He noted a general sense of exhaustion, that the war had become one of attrition.[184] Ribbentrop told the German ambassador in Tokyo, Ott, that, contrary to his previous instructions, he was not to give the Japanese advice on avoiding the opprobrium of starting hostilities but rather to let them get on with it.[185] Clearly, Berlin wanted Tokyo to attack the United States regardless of the political optics. Indeed, the war diary of the German naval leadership observed that the Reich was effectively already at war with the Americans.[186] The Germans need not have worried, though; the Japanese leadership was busy refining the text of their declaration of war on the United States.[187] That evening, Himmler boarded a train to see Hitler in Rastenburg.[188] In Russia, Ritter von Leeb, the commander of Army Group North, wrote in his diary that "the situation at Tikhvin is not sustainable with the current ratio of forces."[189]

For European Jewry, the nightmare continued. That morning, a train with 756 Jews from Hamburg departed for Minsk.[190] In the course of the day, the ghetto administration in Lodz halved the monthly expenditure on medicine.[191] Tadeusz Tomaszewski, a professor at the University of Lvov in occupied Poland, heard reports that the Jews of the city were being taken to a sandpit and shot.[192] That evening, on the banks of the Rhine, the Cologne Jews who had been selected for deportation assembled in the trade fair buildings of Deutz, on the Rhine, to await their "transport" in the morning. They were stripped of all papers and valuables, including jewelry, watches, and wedding rings, leaving them only ten Reichsmarks in cash. Then they were driven into the big trade fair hall, which had been ringed with barbed wire, and left to sleep as best they could on wet wood shavings.[193]

The linkage the regime and many Germans had made between the fate of the Jews and the confrontation with the United States was evident that day from a report from the office of the SD in Minden, a small town in Westphalia in western Germany. This noted the "grave concern" of the local population about the deportation of the Jewish population. First, from sympathy, because they thought that removing the Jews "in winter with all its attendant dangers" would lead to many deaths. This, better educated and wealthier Germans believed, was "too hard" a way of treating Jews, many of whom had lived in the region for a considerable period of time. Second, out of fear, because any mistreatment of the Jews would lead to "new suffering" for Germans in the outside world, "especially in America."[194]

In the Far East, there was a palpable holding of breath throughout the day. Nobody knew exactly what awaited them, and yet in Malaya, Hong Kong, and the Philippines, the authorities, and many ordinary people, were already bracing for impact. British reconnaissance planes spotted the large Japanese convoy in the South China Sea.[195] American scouts did not, however, detect the Kido Butai, which was now poised to strike to the northeast of Pearl Harbor. "Hawaii," Admiral Ugaki wrote in his diary that day, "is just like a rat in a trap."[196]

BY EARLY DECEMBER 1941, war and genocide had already changed Europe beyond recognition. Most of the continent had been occupied by the Germans and their allies; millions of soldiers and civilians had been killed. The Polish intelligentsia had been slaughtered, and in the Soviet

Union the majority of Jews living in the areas seized by the Nazis had been murdered. The deportations of central European Jews had just begun. Huge swaths of the continent had been physically devastated; cities such as Warsaw, Rotterdam, and Coventry had already been laid waste to. Some of the rest of the world had also been utterly transformed. China was a battleground where millions had already died. Southeast Asia and the Pacific were an armed camp.

Much of the old world, though, was still intact. The Jews of central and western Europe were in grave peril but mostly alive. The white man still dominated East Asia, not just in the embattled British Empire but also in the Dutch and Vichy French colonies. Mao was still a fringe communist leader in northwest China. German cities were still largely intact; those of Japan were as yet untouched. Above all, the greatest industrial power the world had yet seen, the United States, was still formally at peace. The outcome of the war seemed open.

3

SUNDAY, DECEMBER 7, 1941

O N THE EVENING OF DECEMBER 6, ROOSEVELT WAS TENSE. THE latest MAGIC decrypts had made the administration aware that Japan was stepping up its military preparations. Three Japanese convoys—including almost fifty troop transports, a battleship, and a flotilla of cruisers and destroyers—were steaming past Cambodia Point and had just entered the Gulf of Siam.[1] American officials were in the dark as to where, when, or against whom the strike would come, but it was clear that Japan was no longer interested in peace.

Although the president agreed to attend a dinner his wife was hosting at the White House for thirty people, he was in no mood for small talk. A fellow guest noted that he "looked tired and rather stern and he left after the meat course."[2] From the dining room, Roosevelt returned to his office for a conference with Harry Hopkins. Certain as the president was that Japan was poised to attack, he remained committed to placing his desire to avoid war on the record. He sent an urgent overture to the Japanese emperor, personally urging Hirohito "to give thought in this definite emergency to ways of dispelling the dark clouds."[3] After sending his appeal, Roosevelt ruefully remarked, "This son of Man has just sent his final message to the son of God," a reference to the Japanese nation-alist claim of the emperor's divinity.[4]

Soon after dispatching the message, Roosevelt received a visit from an aide, Commander Lester Schulz, who handed him a typewritten doc-ument. This contained the first thirteen parts of a fourteen-part message from Tokyo to the Japanese embassy in Washington, just deciphered and transcribed by cryptologists at the army intelligence service. The mes-sage completely rejected Secretary of State Hull's previous proposals, blamed the United States for the deterioration of relations, and finished by declaring that "because of American attitudes," there was no hope of resolving tensions. "This means war," Roosevelt told Hopkins.

It is likely that the president continued to believe that British and Dutch possessions remained the probable target—particularly given the intelligence on Japanese naval movements—rather than America's own forces or bases. Even so, Roosevelt and Hopkins remained convinced that even such limited attacks would inevitably draw the United States in, though domestic opposition would create new difficulties if Japan avoided striking the United States directly. When Hopkins bemoaned that the United States was not able to preempt an attack by striking first, Roosevelt responded: "No we can't do that. We are a democracy and a free people." Then, raising his voice, the president remarked, "But we have a good record."[5] This may have meant that America's reputation for rectitude prevented it from making the first move, or else that America's military record would ensure it emerged triumphant regardless. Either way, the president knew that night that war in the Pacific was almost certainly imminent. All he had left to do was wait to see between whom it would break out and where else it would spread.

Across the Atlantic, it was already December 7. In northern Russia, where the Red Army was battering at the gates of Tikhvin, the day was only fifteen minutes old when the owlish Franz Halder, chief of staff of the Supreme Command of the German Army, rang the chief of staff of Army Group North to demand that the town be held, as the Führer put it, "under all circumstances."[6] Army Group North's commander, Wilhelm Ritter von Leeb, was offered a fanciful range of reinforcements. Halder's interlocutor could be forgiven his skepticism. Even if the promised fresh panzer regiment—plus a hundred new tanks for two burned-out panzer divisions and 22,300 replacements—materialized, which was doubtful, it was not slated to appear until more than a fortnight or so later, by which time the Soviets would have long taken the position.[7] The Wehrmacht was also under pressure further south, where Army Group Center's Panzer Group Three was in the process of withdrawing in the face of Soviet breakthroughs on its northern flank. The Russians were on the move, too, against General Adolf Strauss's Ninth Army, General Günther von Kluge's Fourth Army, and General Heinz Guderian's Second Panzer Army.[8] Further south again, in the Crimea, the Germans and Romanians were still stalemated at Sevastopol, where the Soviets resupplied the city across the Black Sea.

For Romania, the situation was going from bad to worse. Britain—having seen its ultimatum to Finland, Hungary, and Romania to withdraw from the campaign against Russia ignored or rejected—declared war on all three powers.[9] For now, this was not a direct threat, but depending on the course of operations in the Mediterranean, the Romanian oil fields could, as Hitler feared, come within range of the RAF. One of those watching this development closely was Mihail Sebastian, who wrote in his diary shortly afterward that he was "very worried about the consequences" for Romania.[10] "After a few days of relative calm," he continued, "I fear there will be another outbreak of anti-semitism" as the local population blamed the Jews for manipulating Britain into a declaration of war.

In Berlin, Reich foreign minister Joachim von Ribbentrop was still awake. As arrogant and bullish as ever—the war had yet to take its toll on his outward appearance—Ribbentrop was no longer as influential as he had been in the late 1930s. But he remained an important figure, so long as diplomacy mattered in a world in which major powers like the United States and Japan, as well as many smaller ones, were not yet belligerent. Ribbentrop kept in touch with the Führer via his liaison at Rastenburg,

Walter Hewel. He himself was based in the heart of Berlin's governing quarter on Wilhelmstrasse.

Ribbentrop now cabled the German embassy in Rome with a message that was to be delivered immediately to the ambassador, Hans Georg von Mackensen. It concerned the thorny issue of the Tunisian port of Bizerta, controlled by the Vichy French, which the Italians wished to use to resupply their forces in North Africa. Hitler was holding back, because he feared that any pressure would drive the French African colonies into the arms of the British.[11] In three days' time, a scheduled meeting between Vichy French prime minister Admiral François Darlan and Italy's foreign minister Count Galeazzo Ciano in Turin was likely to bring matters to a head. Ribbentrop instructed Mackensen to tell Ciano that the French should only be tackled on Bizerta once the Axis had reestablished air superiority and command of the Mediterranean Sea.

On the banks of the Rhine in the historic city of Cologne, the early morning revealed a pitiful sight. Around a thousand Jews awoke in the trade fair exhibition halls in the suburb of Deutz. Despite the rumors swirling about them, these unfortunates were told only that they were heading "east." The "transport" left the station Deutz-Tief at 6 a.m., and their destination was to be the ghetto of Riga, where twenty-five thousand Latvian Jews had just been murdered to make way for them. The average age of the transport was forty years; sixty-four of the Jews were children below the age of ten.[12]

While diplomatic dispatches hummed across Europe and scenes of human misery played out along the rail lines, the day began at the Führer's headquarters at Rastenburg under a blanket of snow. Located deep in the heart of a primeval forest, the Wolf's Lair was a place of extremes, and not just politically. In the summer, it was hot and humid, and infested by mosquitos. Though his headquarters was far from the prying eyes of British aircraft, Hitler was obsessed with the security of the sprawling complex of 250 hectares of barracks, bunkers, and other installations.[13] There were three restricted areas, the most central of which was reserved for the Führer and his closest entourage. Hitler was in the habit of going to bed late and rising later in the day, but the complex worked through the night, and as the day began it was a hive of activity as reports came in from the various fronts.

The news from Russia was, as we have seen, grim. Things were no better in the Mediterranean, where the British were relentlessly pummeling the Italians. Italian convoys lived in fear of the RAF, Royal Navy submarines, and surface raiders. In the Cyrenaica, in Libya, the pendulum seemed to have swung back to the British Eighth Army, which now looked poised to finally relieve the city of Tobruk, besieged by General Erwin Rommel's Italian-German forces since April.[14] Mounting German casualties, the crushing British superiority in men and matériel, and the lack of promised Italian support forced Rommel to pull back to a defensive line further west. The Fascist elite in Rome was therefore seized by mounting panic throughout the day, no doubt fueled by the German commander's blame game. Despite Hitler's express instructions not to insult the Italians, Rommel tended, as one witness put it, "to lead by example" in criticizing them.[15] That day, Field Marshal Kesselring, the new commander in chief south, arrived at Rommel's headquarters to calm him down. Kesselring had little to offer, however, beyond a few more fighter aircraft.[16] There was no disguising the extent of the crisis. The news from Libya, Italian foreign minister Ciano wrote in his diary, was "dark." Soon, he said, the Italian-German forces on the coast would have to "break contact with the enemy" and prepare to defend the high ground of the Jebel Akhdar, a densely wooded upland area in the northeastern part of the country. All this made more urgent the demands from the Italian high command under General Ugo Cavallero that Mussolini should persuade or force Vichy to allow resupply through Bizerta.

German headlines reflected the concerns of the Reich leadership. For now, these focused on the southern front in Russia rather than Army Group Center. According to the Berlin daily *Der Westen*, the "massed attacks of the Soviets" there had "failed"; there had been "nowhere a breakthrough in the German lines." More generally, the paper once again attacked Roosevelt's "fantastical war plan," which had been leaked a few days earlier by the *Chicago Tribune*, and his alleged "dollar-imperialist aims." Far from Germany being isolated in the world, the paper claimed, it was the British Empire that stood alone. The rejection of the British ultimatum to Hungary was reported with a headline just below the fold on the front page claiming that it was now "Britain against the whole of Europe."[17]

In the Soviet high command, there was a mounting sense of excitement at the success of the attacks on the central front. Though some of the government had been evacuated, Stalin was following the situation from the Kremlin. The Soviet dictator had recovered his poise after the disasters of the summer, but he was still much diminished from his prewar ebullience. A few days earlier, one observer who had not seen him since 1933 was shocked to find "a short man with a tired haggard face." Stalin, he continued, "seemed to have aged twenty years in eight," his eyes had "lost their old steadiness," and "his voice lacked assurance."[18] That day, Stalin's ambassador to the United States, the former foreign minister Maxim Litvinov, would finally reach the American capital. The Kremlin, in turn, awaited the return of British diplomats evacuated to Kuibyshev, in advance of an expected visit by the British foreign secretary, Anthony Eden, in mid-December.

Ordinary Soviet citizens also followed developments closely. Behind the German lines, Nikolay Nikitovich Popudrenko, a party worker and partisan organizer in the Ukraine, heard on the radio that Britain had declared war on Finland, Hungary, and Romania. This, he believed, was "good" if true.[19] A gravely ill former Leningrad landlord, Anastasia Vladimirovna, by contrast, hoped for an end to the Soviet nightmare, through the defeat of Stalin if need be. As Vladimirovna lay dying, her roommate Elena Skryabina wrote that Vladimirovna was "most scared that we will somehow be able to evacuate, and she will be left alone." "After all," Skryabina went on, "while we are here, she receives her bowl of soup. I bring her a microscopic portion of bread, which I stand in line for." "Despite her seemingly doomed state," Skryabina concluded, "she nevertheless does not want to die. She awaits the end of the war," that is, a German victory.[20]

In the course of the morning, German ambassador Mackensen caught up with Ciano in Rome and informed him of Hitler's request that he should hold off raising the use of Bizerta with the Vichy French. The Italian parried by saying that Mussolini had not yet given him detailed instructions for the meeting, that he had been told that he should simply "listen" to Darlan, and that while the subject of the port and its importance to the Axis war effort might be mentioned, he was not to embark on any negotiations in this regard. It seems to have been a tricky conversation, which Ciano described to Mackensen's embarrassment as a "démarche" (a formal diplomatic step) because Hitler's demands were obviously an attempt to limit Italy's room to maneuver over a vital interest. That said, Ciano promised that he would proceed only in "lockstep" with Berlin on this issue, not least because of the "huge distances" between the port and the front line in Libya.[21]

Despite his show of confidence with Mackensen, Ciano's mood was grim. That morning, Mussolini brooded over the final humiliating collapse of the Italian East African empire at Gondar at the end of the previous month, where the garrison had numbered forty thousand. "The Duce," Ciano recorded, "was very much irritated by the small losses in Eastern Africa." "Those who fell at Gondar," he continued, "number 67; the prisoners are 10,000. One doesn't have to think very long to see what these numbers mean."[22] The Italian dictator was not stupid, but he was complicated, or, as General Ubaldo Soddu put it, "sometimes brilliant, sometimes catastrophic." Mussolini knew that his standing with the Germans was already low (though it would fall much further later), and he had been worrying for some time that Italy would become a mere "vassal" of Hitler. Yet the Duce's response was to clasp the Führer closer to him. Ciano knew that a breach with the United States, which Mussolini had enthusiastically agreed to in one of his "catastrophic" moments, was imminent. That day, Italian military intelligence reported that it would take six months to a year for the Americans to be ready for full-scale operations.[23] After that interval, it was clear, US superiority would be crushing. No wonder a visitor recalls Ciano looking out the window that day and remarking that one would soon be watching the American tanks go by.[24]

That morning, the British prime minister was still at his country residence. Churchill's usual routine was to wake at 8:30 a.m. He then took a colossal breakfast while clad in his multicolored dressing gown, during which he skimmed the newspapers before receiving Captain Richard Pim from the map room with the latest reports.[25] On this particular morning, after receiving news that the Japanese ships were continuing their voyage from Indochina apparently in the direction of Kota Bharu—on the east coast of Malaya near the border with Siam (modern-day Thailand)—Churchill dispatched a message to the Thai prime minister, Luang Phibunsongkhram.[26] He warned him of "the possibility of an imminent Japanese invasion of your country" and assured him that an attack on Thailand would be regarded as "an attack on ourselves."[27]

The British authorities in the Far East thus knew that something was afoot. Aircraft of the Royal and Dominion Air Forces were intermittently tracking Japanese convoys for some time. It was not clear, though, whether the convoys were bound for Malaya or Thailand, intended as provocations, or perhaps just part of an extended exercise. In Singapore, Churchill's special envoy Duff Cooper found himself in an "atmosphere full of rumours." If the military men knew any better, they didn't share it with him.[28] Prisoners of their racial misconceptions, the commanders in Singapore and Malaya played down Japanese capabilities and remained complacent about their own vulnerability. So did Major General C. M. Maltby, who was in charge of the colony of Hong Kong. That day, he told London to discount reports of Japanese concentrations in the Canton area. These, he wrote, had been "deliberately fostered by the Japanese who, to judge from the defensive preparations around Canton and in the frontier area, appeared distinctly nervous of being attacked."[29] The civilian populations in Hong Kong and Singapore, though conscious of the wider tensions, were still blissfully unaware of what was about to hit them. In the fashionable Peninsular Hotel in Hong Kong, the orchestra played "The Best Things in Life Are Free."[30]

Across Berlin, the ministries were now springing into life. The propaganda minister, Joseph Goebbels, was heading to his office on Wilhelmstrasse. Unlike Ribbentrop, his power and importance within the regime was increasing as the war escalated. A diminutive figure, Goebbels had always stood out with his crippled leg and sharp tongue. His legendary womanizing, though, was largely a thing of the past. Goebbels simply did not have time, as his activities (chronicled at increasing length in his diaries) multiplied. He preferred to spend more time with his family at his suburban villa in Schwanenwerder. On this Sunday, though, Goebbels was needed in central Berlin.

In a secret morning conclave in the Propaganda Ministry, located in the Palais Prinz Karl on Wilhelmsplatz at the heart of Berlin, Goebbels delivered the bad news to his staff. Drawing on his recent visit to Vienna, the minister warned that it had been wrong to spare the German people through "withholding of all unpleasant news." This, Goebbels continued, had made them "vulnerable to possible temporary reverses." People knew much more than they were told by the official media, he pointed out, and it would be much better to be open and honest with them. Churchill, Goebbels went on, had it "right" when he had promised the British "blood, sweat, and tears." Henceforth, German propaganda would have to be more "realistic," while remaining of course "justifiably optimistic" about final victory. For example, Goebbels suggested, the population could well be told that the "general situation" had made the giving of Christmas presents redundant, and that, for the same reason, there would be travel restrictions not merely for a few days but for the foreseeable future.[31] It was clear from all this that Goebbels knew that the war in Russia would not be over by Christmas, and that popular expectations would require careful management.

The Reichsführer-SS, Heinrich Himmler, was at his desk in the RSHA on Prinz-Albrecht-Strasse in Berlin's governing quarter. He spent part of the morning on the telephone and the rest in meetings. Like Goebbels, Himmler was ascendant in the regime. Despite the Reichsführer's unprepossessing exterior, his name struck terror into the hearts of millions. He had a large and growing complex of organizations under his control. The brutality of the already vast SS concentration camp system was demonstrated that day in Auschwitz, where twenty-one corpses were delivered that day to the morgue. Five of them, listed as numbers 23616, 15653, 19374, 21057, and 20254—all of them individual human beings with lives and prospects—were killed with phenol injections in the notorious Block 19.[32]

At 11 a.m., Himmler had a call with his trusted chief of staff, Obergruppenführer Karl Wolff, who was also serving as Himmler's liaison officer with Führer headquarters.[33] The conversation, which was scheduled for less than an hour, was probably a genial one. A tall, handsome man and serial philanderer, Wolff was popular with everybody. No overt anti-Semite himself, he was nevertheless an important facilitator and mediator for Himmler in many matters, including the murder of the Jews. We do not know what was said by either man—the "journey" mentioned in the record could refer to an inspection of SS units, or perhaps to Hitler's recent trip to Russia, which Wolff may have accompanied. Ten minutes before noon, Himmler spoke on the telephone with Obergruppenführer Gottlob Berger about "recruitment in the Germanic lands," the brochure *The Subhuman*, and Berger's holidays.[34]

By lunchtime, Hitler had risen and dressed with the help of his valet, Heinz Linge.[35] The Führer was still by far the most dominant figure in the Third Reich, and he enjoyed the continued loyalty of the German people, the institutions of state, and his entourage, but he was no longer quite the commanding presence he had been until the year before. The failure to subdue Britain, the stagnation of the Russian campaign, and the looming conflict with the United States had all taken their toll on his nerves and health. Hitler was already in thrall to his personal physician, Dr. Theo Morell, who pumped him full of stimulants and other drugs every day. The list exceeded eighty medications, more than a dozen of them consciousness altering. Though nominally a vegetarian, Hitler had various animal substances coursing through his blood, including derivatives of bull's testicles and Homoseran, which is a by-product of uterine blood. He complained of dizziness, tinnitus, and headaches, and there were also the first signs of a tremor.[36]

That very day, Fritz Lehmann, a doctor in the East Prussian city of Königsberg, reflected on Hitler's mental health. He found himself unable to judge whether the Führer was "normal" or "insane." Medically, Lehmann believed, Hitler should be reckoned a "schizoid psychopath" and "inflexible fanatic," on account of his "oscillation between inhibition and excitement," his "pronounced self-absorption," and his sense of "chosenness." That said, the doctor did not consider Hitler to be "an ordinary madman." For that, the Führer had too many "personal achievements" to his name, however "dangerous" one might consider these. Lehmann doubted that Hitler had a "detailed overall plan," but considered this typical for "creative people." Overall, he thought that the German dictator lacked "technical ability" and "critical understanding." For this reason, Lehmann concluded, sticking with his artistic metaphor, Hitler could not produce any "mature works," but was only capable of "ambitious, but hasty sketches" such as the invasions of "Norway, Crete, [North] Africa, and now probably also Russia."[37]

The Führer's first priority that day was the question of the army high command. After the setbacks on the eastern front, he had lost confidence in the incumbent, Field Marshal Walther von Brauchitsch. Shortly before the midday military briefing, Hitler's chief military adjutant, Oberstleutnant Rudolf Schmundt, summoned his junior colleague Major Gerhard Engel. Schmundt told Engel that because Hitler was stumped as to who to appoint to succeed Brauchitsch, the best solution would be for the Führer himself to take on the role to restore "confidence." Hitler, Schmundt remarked, had asked for time to reflect and consult with Wilhelm Keitel, the head of the OKW, and Luftwaffe chief Hermann Göring, whose opinion, despite his miserable failure to overawe Britain in 1940, obviously still counted. Engel, a doughty defender of the autonomy of the army, was aghast.[38]

At 1 p.m., Hitler met with General José Moscardó, the chief of Franco's military cabinet. He had been sent by the caudillo to check on the performance of the Spanish Blue Division in Russia, to find out how the war was going generally, and to raise the question of Gibraltar, which Franco hoped to take from Britain. The Führer briefed Moscardó on the performance of the division and its likely future deployment, but was careful, as the recordkeeper noted, not to reveal any militarily important information. Hitler also expressed his regret that Franco had not seized the opportunity to drive the British out of Gibraltar himself. The men continued their largely inconsequential conversation over lunch, during which the Führer expressed his astonishment at the intensity of the rivalry between Portugal and Spain.[39]

Churchill's principal concern that day revolved around whether a Japanese attack on Britain would be regarded by the Americans as sufficient incitement for them to join the war. He had invited the US ambassador, John Winant, to join him for lunch at Chequers. When Winant arrived, he found Churchill pacing up and down outside the dining room entrance. His other guests, the duchess of Marlborough and Lord Blandford, had already sat down to lunch twenty minutes before, but Churchill was anxious to pin down Winant on the American position in the Pacific. When Winant said that he thought war with Japan was imminent, Churchill responded with "unusual vehemence" that "if they declare war on you, we will declare war on them within the hour." Winant acknowledged that he understood this, as the prime minister had already stated it publicly, which led Churchill to press Winant: "If they declare war on us, will you declare war on them?" But the ambassador responded that only Congress could decide this. Winant was acutely aware that Churchill's fear was that Japan would push Britain into an "Asiatic war," with the Americans at war in neither the Atlantic nor the Pacific. Consequently, Britain would be "hanging on one turn of pitch and toss."[40]

In London, the British chiefs of staff spent almost three hours in conference discussing the Pacific situation. Together with a representative from the Foreign Office, they were painstakingly gaming out "all the various alternatives that might lead to war and trying to ensure that in every case the USA would not be left out." They reported to Churchill that Britain was prepared to "fire the first shot" against any Japanese force moving against Siam "before it reached its objective," but only if "US armed support" was guaranteed and, equally significantly, American noninterventionists could not present it "as a deliberate attempt on our part to drag them into a British war." The meeting concluded just after 2 p.m., with those questions unanswered and Britain's military leaders thus still unsure what they could do to preempt the seemingly inevitable Japanese attack.[41]

In Singapore, the British Malaya Command met that day in the war room of the naval base. Despite the news of Japanese ship movements, the supreme commander of all British forces in the Far East, Robert Brooke-Popham, decided to delay implementing the contingency plan in the event of a Japanese attack on Thailand and Malaya. Code-named Operation Matador, this plan would involve an advance northward to capture "the ledge," an area of high ground in southern Thailand. Thus ensconced, British forces would be able to seal off any Japanese landings on the east coast of Thailand. London had already authorized the British military leadership in Malaya to use its discretion in the matter, but the diplomatic costs of preempting the violation of Thai neutrality were deemed too high. Consequently, the colony remained highly vulnerable to attack.[42]

Back in Europe, in the early afternoon, Hitler would have had the first of two military briefings; the second was in the evening.[43] Afterward, the Führer probably turned to administrative matters. Much of his correspondence was now dealt with by the ever more influential head of the Nazi Party Chancellery, Martin Bormann. He had succeeded Rudolf Hess after the latter's dramatic flight to Scotland earlier in the year. Bormann also functioned as Hitler's chief private secretary and virtually controlled access to the Führer on non-private and nonmilitary business. That day, he sent a letter on Hitler's behalf to chief of the Reich Chancellery Hans Lammers, instructing him to pay the sculptor Josef Thorak five thousand Reichsmarks for a bust of Mussolini he had produced for the Palazzo Zuccari, located on Via Gregoriana in Rome and administered by a Professor Hoppenstedt.[44] It was but the latest example of Hitler's affection for the Duce, which persisted despite the intense exasperation he felt at the military and political unreliability of the Italians. Around the same time, Bormann sent Lammers a separate and rather plaintive missive stressing that the "stop-decree" halting most civilian construction must be obeyed, evidence that instructions from on high were not always followed.[45] It also suggests that the regime, which was not yet widely conscious of a crisis on the eastern front, was nevertheless settling in for the long haul.

More fatefully, Hitler signed draconian new guidelines on how to deal with "crimes" against the authorities in the occupied territories; this has gone down in history as the Night and Fog Decree.[46] It targeted the "Communist elements" that had been harassing the Wehrmacht since the start of Operation Barbarossa. The Führer demanded "the most severe measures" in order to "deter" future attacks. He decreed that those who committed offenses likely to endanger the security or effectiveness of the Reich or occupation authorities were to be sentenced to death "as a rule." The rest were to be deported to Germany forthwith, and no further information should be given as to their whereabouts. Such measures struck fear into the heart of Nazi-occupied Europe.

The head of the OKW, Keitel, mitigated the ferocity of this decree a little with regard to France. The supreme military commander there, Otto von Stülpnagel, had responded to the rising wave of resistance attacks by declaring that all French civilian prisoners, whether or not they had been convicted or acquitted, would be liable for reprisals. In the interest of maintaining the authority of the Reich's military courts, Keitel now instructed the army high command to exempt those French detainees who had been acquitted but were still in custody from this category.[47]

No such leniency was extended to the Jews, who were collectively considered to be either hostages, in the case of the western and central European Jews under Nazi rule, or enemy combatants, in the case of Soviet Jews. It was on this day that the murder of the Latvian Jews in the Riga ghetto, which had been paused a week earlier, was ordered to resume the following morning. It would be carried out by the relevant Einsatzkommando with the help of the SD, the Sicherheitspolizei, and local sympathizers in the notorious Arajs Kommando.[48] In the Crimea, the town commander at Kertsch reported that day that his men had murdered "about" 2,500 Jews over the past ten days, among them some suspected partisans but the vast majority evidently just civilians whose only "crime" was being Jewish. In a sign of the schizophrenia surrounding the language used in these documents, the phrase "execution" was crossed out and replaced with "resettlement," but was then followed in the very next sentence by the words "subsequent executions."[49] By the time these lines were written, most Crimean Jews had already been murdered, and, as the report stated, the killing of the few who remained was to follow shortly after.

The western and central European Jews, by contrast, were mostly still alive, and although the deportation of the German Jews had just begun, there was still no concrete plan for their wholesale murder. There were many reasons for this, including the fear of protests from non-Jewish spouses in mixed marriages, but the primary explanation was that Jews continued to be seen by Hitler as "hostages" to deter the United States from entry into the war on the Allied side. One of these pawns was the retired university professor Victor Klemperer, himself married to an "Aryan" woman, who were both still hanging on in Dresden. That day, he heard stories about Russian prisoners of war "searching dustbins for something to eat." Klemperer spoke again of his fear of "evacuations" and he remarked on receiving a postcard with the stamp "Litzmannstadt Getto," in which the "Elder of the Jews" let it be known that money could be sent to the evacuees there.[50] Unlike the murders in the east, the deportations were not secret. Indeed, the semipublic corralling of large numbers of living Jews was central to Hitler's "hostage" strategy.

Among these hostages were the residents of the Jewish ghetto of Litzmannstadt (Lodz) in the Warthegau (annexed Polish territory). One woman in the ghetto, Lotte Glücklich, who had been deported from Vienna, wrote that day to Otto Weill, who was still in the former Austrian capital. She missed her "very cozy and pleasant" home in the Sperlgasse district but tried to remain upbeat. Having traveled via a transit camp, she was now "in her own home, which is still rather primitive but quite cozy all the same." Lotte Glücklich was, of course, writing under the eyes of the censor, and an idea of her real feelings can be gained from her next sentence. "My impressions would fill volumes," she wrote. "It is completely, completely different than one imagined it in one's boldest dreams and only for people like me who are unfazed by everything." Others were completely unable to adapt to the loss of their comfortable life. By Glücklich's account, one woman had lost her mother the week before and she herself was "hardly recognizable."[51]

Throughout the afternoon, working from the Wolf's Lair, Hitler's principal focus was not on the fate of his millions of hostages but on the situation of Army Group North. He let it be known that the loss of the road and rail connections around Tikhvin would be a "fatal weakening" of the German position at Leningrad and could in fact lead to the breaking of the siege. It would also compromise joint operations with the Finns. The crisis in Army Group North, Hitler announced, was "currently the only critical point on the eastern front."[52]

The state secretary at the German Foreign Office, Ernst von Weizsäcker, was in a downbeat mood. That day, he gave his annual speech to the twenty-odd German air attachés in Europe. It was pointless, Weizsäcker mused, to discuss whether it had been right to attack Russia; the war there simply had to be won. "We must prepare for a long war," he told his audience. "[Just] sitting it out in possession of Europe is no strategy. We must wage war actively." After the speech, he ruminated, "I can't think of anything that my office can usefully contribute to the war. We are more and more on the path of violence. All our treaties are oriented towards war."[53]

ON THE OTHER side of the world, in Tokyo, where it was already evening, the US ambassador Joseph Grew "received a very brief, urgent message from Mr. Hull saying an important message for the Emperor was then being encoded" and to expect delivery soon. Grew was already on alert, as he had heard earlier that afternoon through a radio broadcast from San Francisco that a message from the president to the emperor was on the way, although "no information was given as to its substance or the channel of transmission."[54] A professional diplomat who had served in Berlin on the eve of American entry into World War I, Grew had worked doggedly during almost a decade as ambassador in Tokyo to prevent a US-Japan misunderstanding that might lead to another major conflict. Even as tensions between the two nations worsened, Grew remained convinced that reason could empower Japanese moderates at the expense of the military and bring Tokyo back from the brink.[55] Now, as he awaited instructions from Washington, Grew paced restlessly around his residence while drawing heavily on his pipe.[56]

Ninety minutes later, the US embassy received the telegram. American officials quickly realized that the initial message from the president was officially stamped as having arrived at noon. Therefore, although the telegram had been received at the Japanese post office at 12 p.m., just one hour after its dispatch from Washington, and had been labeled "triple priority," it had been held up for ten and a half hours. This, Grew assumed, was deliberate, because "the military authorities did not want this message to get to the Emperor."[57]

Shortly before receiving the telegram, an American embassy official had phoned the office of the secretary of the Japanese foreign minister, Shigenori Togo, to ask him to stand by. As soon as the message was decoded, Grew called Togo's secretary again to request a meeting with the minister, in order to deliver an urgent personal message from the president to the emperor. Togo had already heard from Ambassador Nomura in Washington that such a communication was on its way, but his secretary initially expressed reluctance and suggested meeting the following day instead. Ultimately, however, the secretary agreed to set up a meeting for Grew at quarter past midnight.[58] It was getting late in Tokyo, but in Washington the day was just beginning.

In the White House, after a restless night, President Roosevelt awoke at 9 a.m. local time and received breakfast in bed.[59] Around forty minutes later, the lead Japanese translator in navy intelligence, Captain Alwin D. Kramer, arrived at the White House with a packet containing the fourteenth and final part of the decrypted message from Tokyo. By 10 a.m., the president had received the material from his naval aide Captain John Beardall. Responding to Hull's appeal of November 26 for Japan to cease its military occupation of southern China and Indochina, the Japanese government had informed their representatives that because the United States would not accept "the creation of a New Order in Asia," it was "impossible to reach an agreement through further negotiations." An undaunted Roosevelt told Beardall that it "looked as though the Japs are going to sever negotiations."[60] The message had not categorically stated, however, that hostilities were imminent or where or when they might occur. What the Japanese intended to do next was still unknown.

Next, Kramer delivered a copy of Tokyo's message to his boss, Secretary of the Navy Frank Knox, who was at the State Department that morning for a meeting with Secretary of State Cordell Hull and Secretary of War Henry Stimson. Kramer then returned to his office at 10:20 a.m. to find more intercepted messages from Tokyo. In particular, one stipulated that the full fourteen-part message should be delivered to the State Department at exactly 1 p.m. that day. It was highly unusual for a Japanese dispatch to be so precise in demanding a specific time. In addition, there were "several other minor messages, one thanking the Ambassador for his services and another directing final destruction of codes." Kramer was thus convinced that there was a "crisis to take place at 1 o'clock." He ordered copies of the messages to be arranged into folders for Roosevelt and Knox for immediate delivery. This took a few minutes and, in the meantime, Kramer quickly calculated that the corresponding time in Kota Bharu, where the huge Japanese convoy was descending down the coast of French Indochina, was a couple of hours before dawn, "the normal time to institute amphibious operations."[61]

Kramer returned to the State Department to deliver the first folder, handing it over to one of Hull's private secretaries. He asked the secretary to impress on Knox—who, by then, was deep in discussions with Hull and Stimson—his conviction "that the Japanese intended to carry out their plans against Kota Bharu." He also mentioned "in passing" that 1 p.m. in Washington corresponded to 7:30 a.m. in Hawaii, more as a reminder of the "Fleet routine on a Sunday morning" than out of any sense that it was a target. Hull's secretary relayed the messages to Knox while Kramer dashed to the White House to deliver the other folder.[62]

Hull, Stimson, and Knox remained in conference at the State Department until lunchtime. Before his meeting with Ambassador Nomura and Saburo Kurusu, Hull had wanted to consult his two cabinet colleagues about "the situation created by the movement of the huge Japanese armada southward and westward of the southernmost point of Indochina." All three regarded the MAGIC intelligence intercepts as evidence that

Tokyo had delayed holding this meeting until now "in order to accomplish something hanging in the air." Hull was adamant that "the Japs are planning some deviltry," and each was left "wondering where the blow will strike." They agreed that the principal American policy goal must be to "hold the main people who are interested in the Far East together— the British, ourselves, the Dutch, the Australians, the Chinese"—and that the United States should fight even if Japan limited its attack to British or Dutch territories.[63]

Most significant, there was a joint recognition that events in East Asia were inseparable from the broader global struggle. Stimson noted that "if Britain were eliminated it might well result in the destruction or capture of the British fleet," which "would give the Nazi allies overwhelming power in the Atlantic ocean and would make the defense of the American Republics enormously difficult if not impossible."[64] Knox agreed that "we are tied up inextricably with Britain in the present world situation," while Hull noted that this was a "cohesive closely related world movement to conquer and destroy, with Hitler moving across one-half of the world and the Government of Japan under the military group moving across the other half of the world by closely synchronizing their efforts."[65] Just after the discussion concluded at noon, Hull received a phone call from Ambassador Nomura asking, as expected, for a meeting at 1 p.m., to which the secretary agreed.

While his cabinet principals were in conference, the president was undergoing his daily treatment for a chronic sinus problem from his personal physician, Rear Admiral Ross T. McIntire. While the president was "deeply concerned over the unsatisfactory nature" of Hull's exchanges with the Japanese emissaries, McIntire observed that he remained confident that "Japan's military masters would not risk a war with the United States." It was certainly feasible that Japan would "take advantage of Great Britain's extremity and strike at Singapore or some other point in the Far East, but an attack on any American possession did not enter his thought."[66]

Meanwhile, the Japanese embassy in Washington was abuzz. The naval attaché Ichiro Yokoyama called Kurusu at home to tell him that many messages had been delivered to the office during the night and throughout the morning. Then Secretary Shirozi Yuuki, the chief of the American section of the Japanese Foreign Office Commercial Bureau, informed Kurusu the "Imperial Government's Opinion," which he had been alerted to on November 28, had arrived.[67] Neither Nomura nor anyone else in the embassy knew, because the cable had not yet been fully deciphered, that it broke off of relations with the United States and amounted to a declaration of war. It was to be kept secret until delivered. The embassy was instructed to "hand the memorandum directly, if possible, to [US] Secretary of State [Cordell Hull] at 1pm on [December] 7th." At half past ten, the final part of the cable arrived. Two and half hours remained before Nomura and Kurusu were supposed to meet Hull. Unsurprisingly, the wireless room of the embassy dissolved into chaos as the cipher clerks rushed to decode the message. Because of the need to ensure secrecy, the job could not be left to an ordinary embassy typist. As a higher-grade secretary, Yuuki, struggled to type up a clean copy, erasing and correcting as he went along, with another, more senior embassy official standing over him as if willing him on. It was clear that time would be tight to meet the 1 p.m. deadline.[68]

In Tokyo, the new day of December 8, 1941, had already begun. As previously agreed, Togo met with Ambassador Grew, who proceeded to request a meeting with the emperor. The Japanese foreign minister informed him that he would need time to secure this. The American handed over the text of Roosevelt's message. Shortly afterward, Togo contacted Tsuneo Matsudaira, the minister for the royal house, with the request for an audience. He told him to get in touch with Koichi Kido, the lord privy seal. Togo then rang Kido, who said that he was always at his disposal, even in the middle of the night. Kido promised to be at court when Togo arrived. The foreign minister now had Roosevelt's message translated.

While Japanese and American diplomacy was almost exhausted, the military situation was deteriorating for the Germans on the eastern front. In Army Group South, the First SS Panzer Division, Leibstandarte SS Adolf Hitler, claimed to have seen "American"—more likely

British—tanks.[69] Things were much worse on the northern and central fronts, however. It was, as Fedor von Bock, the commander of Army Group Center, wrote, a "bad day."[70] The Red Army booted an advance party of the Tenth Motorized Division of General Guderian's Second Panzer Army out of Michailow. In the panic, a lot of material was abandoned, a portent of events to come. "It is unbelievable what we have destroyed," one German soldier wrote home that day, describing the task of blowing up field guns and disabling trucks as "dangerous and very depressing work."[71] Around Klin, General Georg-Hans Reinhardt tried to plug the gaps by sending radio operators, engineers, anti-aircraft gunners, truck drivers, staff officers, and even musicians to the front line.[72] His Panzer Group Three was, as its war diarist noted, "no longer operational." "Panic-like rumors" were swirling around.[73] The Soviet Operational Group Kostenko attacked the Second Army and pushed back the Forty-Fifth and Ninety-Fifth Infantry Divisions.[74] As they fell back, German troops created what Major General Walther Nehring, commander of Eighteenth Panzer Division, described as a "desert zone" of burned villages to deny the advancing Red Army any shelter.[75] Whole Russian families were simply thrown out into the freezing night.

In the area of Army Group North, the Red Army was also on the advance. The men of the Spanish Blue Division were on their last legs near Novgorod and awaiting the order to withdraw.[76] Then, just after 7 p.m., Hitler was told that Tikhvin, the same location that, as he had demanded only that morning, should be "held under all circumstances," would have to be given up.[77] He took the news very badly, shouting into the phone at Ritter von Leeb; Keitel, who was listening in, recalled the tension of the moment.[78] When the Führer finally put down the receiver, Ritter von Leeb's face was bathed in sweat.[79]

What all this meant for the men on the front line was described that day by Hellmuth Stieff in a long letter to his wife from army headquarters. He thanked her for her Christmas package, and agreed to her request not to open it until Christmas Eve. It was freezing cold that day, "only minus 18 degrees," he joked. The floors of Russian houses were so badly insulated, Stieff complained, that when seated the cold went from the floor to the head, no matter how much one heated the room. Everybody wore furs and boots even when indoors. Driving, Stieff continued, was "unimaginable." The windscreens were "constantly frozen over," the panels protecting them against frost were still far away on a train between Warsaw and Smolensk, and every three minutes one hand had to be used to thaw a "spy-hole" so that the driver could see "anything at all."

The most worrying news Stieff had for his wife, though, was that the offensive on Moscow, which he had written about so optimistically in his last letter, had "failed." "If the crisis is not dealt with," he warned, "the fate of the army is sealed." "The odds are slim," Stieff continued. "You should know that." It was a bleak message. "The worst thing," though, was "the sluggishness, bordering on apathy, of the troops who felt themselves to be abandoned in the terrible cold." Their officers were often dead, and Stieff was still "reproaching himself" for having supported an attack that had cost seven of nine company commanders their lives. After that failure, he went on, the men who came from "one of our best infantry regiments" could "only be driven forward under the submachine guns of the forward artillery spotters." In this brutal war, he confessed to his wife, he "unthinkingly gave the order for the shooting of so and so many commissars and partisans." It was "him or me," Stieff wrote. "That is damned simple."

Stieff, in fact, felt "betrayed" by the regime and by the blithe optimism and exhortations of a German public that was "*clueless* [emphasis in the original] about how things really are out here." "It is *completely different*," he wrote, "than the incredible [German] propaganda makes out." For this reason, Stieff was contemptuous of the slogans from home—"tellings-off" and "home patriotism"—including those of his wife and his father-in-law. "We could not care less about *any* crusade," he went on. "We are fighting for our lives, daily and hourly against an enemy who is superior on the ground and in the air in every respect." Exhausted, Stieff put his pen to one side. "I will stop now," he wrote, because "you don't understand me anyway." "Here in front of Moscow," Stieff concluded, "is the meeting place of the beau monde."[80]

Sunday, December 7, 1941

Unaware of the crisis on the eastern front, but conscious of the need to keep de Gaulle at bay and Axis forces in North Africa supplied, the German ambassador in Rome went to see Foreign Minister Ciano again in the course of the evening. Mackensen once more made clear Ribbentrop's view that the Italians should not, as they planned, try to persuade Vichy prime minister Darlan to allow the use of Bizerta to resupply the Axis forces in North Africa. Enno von Rintelen, German military attaché in Italy, conveyed a similar message from the Führer directly to the Duce. Ciano was inclined to agree with them. "Hitler is right," he wrote. "Tunisia is 101 percent Gaullist," and "any unwelcome pressure would . . . increase the separation that is developing between the French Empire" and Vichy. That said, the Italian military consensus, expressed most forcefully by General Ugo Cavallero, was that "without Bizerta Libya is lost."[81] There were no easy answers to this problem. Complicated though things were in the Mediterranean, they were about to become even more complicated thanks to Japanese moves on the other side of the globe.

To the northwest of Hawaii at 6 p.m. London time, the Japanese airmen assembled behind the shelter of the island of Admiral Nagumo's flagship, the *Akagi*. As the wind whistled around them, they stood facing the admiral and his staff, small glasses of sake in their hands. The two groups bowed and toasted each other. Some of the airmen had samurai scarves around their flight helmets.[82] Mitsuo Fuchida, the commander of the first wave, was presented with a specially made headband by his ground crew, and he wore red underclothes so as not to alarm his aircrew in case he was injured. The weather was bad and getting worse. The torpedo pilots, especially, worried about takeoff with their heavy "fish." Nagumo now ran up Admiral Togo's old and battered flag from the Battle of Tsushima, Imperial Japan's legendary victory over the tsarist navy. The launch of the strike force commenced to wild cheers from the crewmen lining the decks.[83] As the 183 fighters and bombers assumed formation, they looked to the observer-navigator Akamatsu Yuji "like a swarm of bees."[84]

While Nagumo's first wave was hurtling down the decks of the Kido Butai, the large Japanese force arrived off Kota Bharu on the northeast coast of Malaya and opened fire. Not long afterward, the first landing craft were on their way through the heavy seas carrying men from General Yamashita's Twenty-Fifth Army toward the beaches. Waiting for them were troops from the (British) Indian Army and the Royal Artillery. RAF aircraft were summoned. The British put up a bitter resistance, inflicting many Japanese casualties, not to mention those who drowned in the boiling surf.[85] Seventy minutes before the Japanese attacked Pearl Harbor, the war in the Pacific was already underway.[86]

At the very same moment as the first Japanese shells were falling on Kota Bharu, Tokyo issued an ultimatum to the Thai government in Bangkok demanding transit. Because the prime minister could not be reached, the Japanese received no reply.[87] Half an hour after the landing at Khota Bharu, the Japanese went ashore at Singora and Pattani in southern Thailand. The men of the assault force were briefly disconcerted by lights shining into the sea at Singora and feared they had been discovered, until they realized that it was just the local lighthouse. Nevertheless, in both places Thai resistance was initially tenacious; heavy shelling made the airfield unusable at first.[88]

Churchill was still unaware of what was unfolding in Thailand and Malaya as he reviewed the global strategic picture that evening before dinner. In an update on the wider war to his commander in chief in the Middle East, General Auchinleck, he began by telling him that, in order to "relieve a somewhat tense situation," he had acceded to de Gaulle's demand for his troops to be deployed in the desert war. The Free French leader's scheme to play London against Moscow had worked, and his men would soon have a chance to get "to grips with the Germans."[89] After informing Auchinleck that the "Russian news continues to be good," Churchill also told him that Roosevelt had definitely said that "United States will regard it as hostile act if Japanese invade Siam, Malaya, Burma or East Indies" and that he planned to warn Japan accordingly in the coming days. The prime minister expressed his "immense relief" at this, as he had "long dreaded being at war in the Pacific without or before United States." Yet Churchill's words remained cautious: "I think it is all right."[90] After all, Roosevelt had not categorically stated that he would declare war on Japan if it just invaded the colonies of Britain or the Netherlands. Despite Ambassador Halifax's probing, he had been unable to pin the president down on this crucial point. And, as US ambassador Winant had observed, Churchill, despite projecting an air of confidence to Auchinleck, remained fearful that Japanese aggression would be targeted in such a way as to leave the United States out of the war. Consequently, when Churchill sat down for dinner that evening with Winant and Harriman, the latter noted that he "seemed tired and depressed . . . didn't have much to say throughout dinner and was immersed in his thoughts, with his head in his hands part of the time."[91]

Around the same time, in his White House study, Roosevelt was reading aloud from his letter to the emperor, whom he called "the Mikado," alluding to the title of a famous Gilbert and Sullivan operetta. The president's audience that afternoon was Dr. Hu Shih, the Chinese ambassador, who had arrived to see him, as scheduled, at 12:30. The president's satisfaction was evident as he pointed to particular passages and declared, "I got him there; that was a fine telling phrase. That will be fine for the record." Roosevelt was content that the letter sufficed to prove that he had done everything in his power to honorably avert war. He told Hu that he now planned to publish the letter, with his own commentary, if he did not "hear from the Mikado by Monday evening, that is, Tuesday morning in Tokyo." He was adamant that there was "only one thing that can save the situation and avoid war, and that is for the Mikado to exercise his prerogative." Otherwise there was no escaping conflict. Roosevelt informed the ambassador that the Japanese envoys were hastily preparing a response to Hull's November notes and he had "just been told that those fellows have asked for an appointment to see Secretary Hull this noon." Nevertheless, the president was already concerned that the Japanese "have something very nasty under way," and he expected that it would "develop in Burma, or the Dutch East Indies, or possibly even in the Philippines."[92] An attack on Pearl Harbor does not seem to have crossed his mind.

Meanwhile, the emperor's lord privy seal, Marquess Kido, was on his way to meet Foreign Minister Togo at the palace. He was a fussy, formal, and bespectacled man with a receding hairline who looked not unlike a Japanese version of Heinrich Himmler. While Kido was climbing up the Akasaka slope, he saw the sun rising over one of the buildings. "I thought it was a symbol," he wrote in his diary, "of the destiny of this country, which had now entered the war against the USA and England, the two greatest powers in the world." Kido closed his eyes and prayed for the victory of the naval aviators, who were making their approaches to Pearl Harbor at that very moment.[93]

The clock struck 1 p.m. in Washington. Roosevelt was still in conversation with Hu. At the Japanese embassy, Ambassador Nomura nervously awaited the decoding of the long message from Tokyo. He "impatiently peeked into the office where the typing was being done, hurrying the men at work."[94] With the job not yet complete and the deadline already passed, Nomura telephoned Hull a few minutes after one to request that the meeting be postponed until 1:45 p.m. Hull agreed to the request after checking with Roosevelt, who had just finished his interview with Hu.[95] Neither the embassy nor the Americans knew it, but by that time the attack on Pearl Harbor would be in full swing.

In Tokyo, Foreign Minister Togo now hurried to see the prime minister and inform him of the American message. Prime Minister Tojo asked simply whether there were any "new concessions from them." Togo said there were not, and then began to take his leave. Just before parting, he remarked in jest—it was now around 3 a.m.—that "it is not pleasant to be running around and disturbing people in the middle of the night." Tojo replied, "It is good that the telegram arrived late." "Had it been received a day or two earlier," he continued, "then we would have had more difficulties." He meant that the attack on Pearl Harbor might have been paused to explore the American message. Togo rushed on to the palace for his meeting with Kido.[96]

Distracted by the deteriorating situation in the Pacific, Roosevelt informed his wife, Eleanor, that he would be unable to join the thirty-one-person luncheon that she had arranged at the White House that day. Mrs. Roosevelt was "disappointed but not surprised" and informed her guests that "she was sorry but the news from Japan was very bad." Furthermore, as Eleanor understood that, with such pressing matters hanging over the president, lunch was unlikely to be a relaxing proposition: "The fact that he carried so many secrets in his head made it necessary for him to watch everything he said, which in itself was exhausting."[97] Instead, Roosevelt took a quiet lunch of sandwiches and soup with his principal adviser, Harry Hopkins, in his study. Both men were in casual attire, the president wearing his son's turtleneck sweater, and they chatted informally about "things far removed from war."[98] Once the trays were cleared, Roosevelt busied himself with his stamp collection, while Hopkins "lounged on a couch."[99]

At 8 p.m., Hitler and Himmler sat down to dine and discuss the future of the Waffen-SS in the Wolf's Lair.[100] This was followed by tea. Together with the secretaries, liaison Walter Hewel, and a number of others, they talked about the impact of the winter crisis, especially the need to provide warm clothing for the men on the eastern front. Some were aware of the trouble brewing in East Asia. None had any idea of the magnitude of the storm that was just about to break.

When the Japanese foreign minister reached the imperial palace, he found Kido waiting for him. In the brief moment before the imperial audience, the two men spoke about Roosevelt's message. "There is no point in [exploring] this, is there?" the lord privy seal asked. "What is Tojo's opinion?" "The same as yours," Togo replied. They were then ushered in to see the emperor. Togo read him the full text of the message. He then handed him a draft reply he had prepared with Tojo. The emperor gave his approval.

At 3:15 a.m., Togo withdrew. He was deeply moved by the composure of his sovereign, but also by his "unbending attitude." Togo walked back through hundreds of meters of quiet corridor accompanied by a royal official. He was then driven out of the vehicle exit of the Sakashita Gate. Passing through the silent palace forecourt, the only sound the gravel crunching underneath, Togo reflected that a day of destiny was about to begin. Convinced that he had done the right thing, he awaited the judgment of heaven; his eyes filled with tears of emotion.[101]

Three minutes later—at 07:40 local time, 19:10 in London, and 13:10 in Washington, DC—Fuchida appeared over Pearl Harbor. He signaled Nagumo that complete surprise had been achieved: "Tora, Tora, Tora" (Tiger, Tiger, Tiger). The other planned operations across the Far East could now proceed. Fuchida fired a flare as a signal, and at 7:53 a.m. Hawaiian time, seven minutes ahead of schedule, the attack began.

Zero fighters swooped down on Wheeler Airfield. Two minutes later, Val dive-bombers attacked Kaneohe seaplane base. Simultaneously, dive-bombers and Zeros descended on Hickam air base, and the torpedo bombers began their runs on the battleships moored on "Battleship Row." About fifteen minutes into the attack, high-level Kate bombers hit the second line of battleships in Battleship Row. The USS *Oklahoma* was struck by nine torpedoes and sank with the loss of 429 men. The USS *Arizona* was also bombarded, and, within minutes, a bomb ignited its magazine. The chief of the US Pacific Fleet, Admiral Husband E. Kimmel, not yet fully dressed, could only watch, horrified, from just outside his house, "the Arizona lift out of the water, then sink back down—way down." Of its crew, 1,117 would perish, including twenty-three sets of brothers and an entire military band.[102]

Amid the carnage, there were many scenes of heroism. On the stricken *West Virginia*, for example, the African American mess attendant Doris Miller manned a machine gun under heavy Japanese fire before carrying his mortally wounded captain to cover.[103] With the runway under heavy fire, second lieutenants Kenneth M. Taylor and George Welch, still half dressed in tuxedos after a late-night party, managed to make it to their aircraft and get them off the ground, ultimately shooting down seven Japanese fighters.[104] They were among only five air force pilots who were able to engage the Japanese in the skies over Hawaii that morning; 188 US planes would be destroyed and 159 damaged, along with eight battleships. The only saving grace was that all three of the Pacific Fleet aircraft carriers were not at Pearl Harbor that morning and escaped unscathed. Fuchida and Admiral Yamamoto were aware that the carriers were absent, and ahead of the attack seemed more concerned about the possibility that land-based US planes might disrupt or even foil the Japanese assault.[105] They would come to bitterly regret missing these carriers, but at this time any disappointment was overtaken by exhilaration at the success of the operation.[106]

Japanese foreign minister Togo returned to his official apartment. At 4:30 a.m. local time he received a call from the navy ministry to tell him that the raid on Pearl Harbor had been carried out.[107] When he met with the German ambassador, Eugen Ott, not long after, Togo pretended to be surprised by the news. The German was completely deceived and cabled Berlin that the Japanese foreign minister had been "apparently not yet informed" about the dramatic events.[108]

Within half an hour of the bombs falling on Hawaii, the phone rang in Roosevelt's study. It was a White House telephone operator, insisting that Knox wished to speak with him urgently. When the navy secretary came on the line, his voice was quavering: "Mr. President, it looks as if the Japanese have bombed Pearl Harbor." At first, all the president could say was "No."[109] He then turned to Hopkins and told him that the message from Honolulu was, "We are being attacked. This is no drill."[110]

Hopkins was incredulous. His first thought was that "there must be some mistake and that surely Japan would not attack in Honolulu." His expectation, in line with all the principal military officials and civilian leaders in Washington, was that any Japanese attack would begin with a British or Dutch colony, and certainly not a core American territory on the other side of the Pacific. Yet Roosevelt recalled that Japan had initiated war with Russia in 1904 in a similar way by striking its naval base at Port Arthur, and he remarked that this was "just the kind of unexpected thing the Japanese would do, and that at the very time they were discussing peace in the Pacific they were plotting to overthrow it." He reminded Hopkins of "his earnest desire to complete his administration without war," but if the news from Hawaii was indeed accurate then "it would take the matter entirely out of his own hands, because the Japanese had made the decision for him."[111]

Roosevelt had indeed earnestly tried to keep the United States out of war in the Pacific, but this was less true with regard to the Atlantic. If Japan had in fact struck Hawaii and unambiguously brought the Americans into war, the unanswered question was: What did this mean for America's relations with Germany?

Shortly after 2 p.m., the president telephoned Hull to tell him there was "a report that the Japanese have attacked Pearl Harbor." While this was still unconfirmed, neither doubted the veracity. By this time, the Japanese embassy had finally transcribed the fourteen-part message, and the envoys had arrived at the State Department. It was over an hour after the initial 1 p.m. deadline, but they were as yet unaware of what their country had just done. As it was a Sunday, there were few reporters about.[112] Although Roosevelt instructed his secretary of state to "receive their replies formally and cooly and bow them out," Hull's initial inclination was to turn them away. Still, on "the one chance out of a hundred" that the report was untrue, he agreed to receive the Japanese emissaries.[113]

Simultaneously in Southeast Asia, when the Thai government did not respond to the ultimatum as requested by 8 p.m. London time, Japanese forces crossed the frontier and sped toward Bangkok, now largely unopposed. Within hours, they were in effective military control of the country.[114] The British, who had held off a preemptive invasion of Thailand because of the diplomatic costs and in the hope that Bangkok would invite them to Thailand's aid, were blindsided by this development. There was now no chance of securing "the ledge" in time. Northern Malaya, and perhaps the entire colony, was in mortal danger.

In Washington, Nomura and Kurusu were ushered into the secretary of state's office. He left them standing throughout the brief meeting. Hull began by looking at the clock in the room and announcing the time. It was 2:20 in the afternoon, a full hour after the original appointment and thirty minutes later than the rescheduled one.[115] After pressing the Japanese diplomats unsuccessfully to explain why the message was supposed to be delivered at precisely 1 p.m., Hull read the document, which, of course, he had already seen. Soon his hands were shaking with rage. He angrily dismissed the Japanese statement as "infamous falsehoods and distortions on a scale so huge that I never imagined until today that any Government on this planet was capable of uttering them."[116] "Throughout the nine months of negotiations," he continued, "I never did say a lie and in my fifty years of public service, I have never seen a document so full of fabrication and falsehood."[117] Using "some pretty strong Tennessee mountain language," the secretary berated the emissaries, rejected their protests, and showed them the door.[118]

As they left the State Department, Nomura and Kurusu were surprised to see a growing crowd of reporters. The press already knew, though the two Japanese diplomats did not, of the attack on Pearl Harbor.[119] Both men ignored the shouted questions and got into their car to bring them back to the embassy. When they arrived, the front gate was firmly shut, with police gathering to wave away the crowd that had gathered to protest.[120] Only then did Nomura and Kurusu learn of the dramatic events at Honolulu, and realized that Hull—who had treated them with a contempt bordering on hatred—must have heard the news just before their encounter.[121]

The entire Japanese embassy sank into a state of despair. On entering his office, Kurusu found the finance officer, Tsutomu Nishiyama, standing in shocked silence. The two men were old schoolmates and close friends. They stared at each other wordlessly as they contemplated the magnitude of what had just happened. The military attaché, Saburo Isoda, appeared and tearfully tried to console Kurusu on the failure of his mission. It was probably Nishiyama, though, who was most devastated. An economic expert who had lived and studied in the United States over many years, Kurusu recalled that "he knew better than anyone else that Japan would be no match for America in a protracted war."[122]

By now, Roosevelt had telephoned Henry Stimson at home, interrupting his lunch. In "a rather excited voice" the president asked his secretary of war whether he had "heard the news." Stimson had no idea what Roosevelt was talking about. "They have attacked Hawaii," the president responded. "They are now bombing Hawaii." Caught off guard, Stimson confided to his diary that night: "Well, that was an excitement indeed." The secretary had previously worried about convincing Americans that they, too, would need to fight if Japan attacked Britain in the Pacific. Now, his initial thought was that "the Japs have solved the whole thing by attacking us directly in Hawaii."[123] Of course, neither the president nor Stimson yet knew the full scale of the destruction that was unfolding at Pearl Harbor.

Besides notifying his cabinet principals, the US president also personally telephoned the ambassadors of the major Allied powers to inform them of the attack. The Chinese ambassador, Roosevelt's final visitor before he heard the news, was one of the first he spoke to afterward. Sounding "very much excited and very angry and worked up," according to Hu Shih, the president told him that "the Japanese have bombed Pearl Harbor and Manila" and it was "terrible, simply terrible."[124]

The Chinese nationalist leader Chiang Kai-shek had been asleep, but was woken by an aide bearing the news, either from Hu Shih or some other source, between one and two in the morning local time. Like many Chinese nationalists, he was deeply relieved, and perhaps even elated.[125] Chiang is said to have put on a record and danced at the news of Pearl Harbor, but this story is probably apocryphal.[126] We do know that he told the aide to summon a meeting of the Kuomintang's Central Standing Committee. Chiang then immediately dictated a letter to Roosevelt, which Madame Chiang translated into English. "To our new common battle," he wrote, "we offer all we are and all we have to stand with you until the Pacific and the world are free from the curse of brute force and endless perfidy."[127] In Chiang's capital, Chungking, reports of the attack on Pearl Harbor were greeted with delight. People went around congratulating each other.[128] It is not hard to understand why Chiang and his followers were so pleased. After a decade of facing Japan on its own, nationalist China now had the open support of the greatest power on earth. What could go wrong?

Not all Chinese saw it the same way. In Shanghai, Chiang's erstwhile comrade in arms Zhou Fohai, who had defected to the Japanese, heard gunfire as Japan's forces proceeded to seize control of the international settlements. "From now on," he predicted, "the Pacific becomes a killing ground."[129]

In Washington, Roosevelt also relayed the news to the British ambassador and asked him to tell Churchill as quickly as possible. The president informed Halifax at 2:15 p.m. local time that there was "pretty severe damage to ships and aeroplanes" but, at this time, he still believed that "most of the fleet was at sea already, and none of their newer ships in Harbor." The ambassador confided to his diary that Japan had made "the biggest mistake in their history" by uniting Americans in fury against them, and it would be "interesting to see whether Germany now follows suit."[130] For Halifax, scorned by American noninterventionists since his arrival as he worked to bring the United States into the war on Britain's side, this was a moment to savor. When Lady Halifax learned the news, she asked their American butler, Sidney Maddams, to open a bottle of champagne, claiming that there had been a birth in the family.[131]

The toast was premature, and not only because the destruction in the Pacific was far worse than initially thought. The British mission in Washington would now have to reckon with how the new war would impact American supplies to Britain and "other Lend-Lease problems."[132] Earlier that day, even before Pearl Harbor, Halifax had communicated to London that American shipping assistance was increasingly threatened by the transfer of Lend-Lease aid to other countries, particularly the Soviet Union; its own "preparation for possible Far East War"; and the "consequences of that war if peace efforts fail."[133] Consequently, Britain would need to constantly press its own case for supplies against stiff competition from these other claims. A "rising tide of anti-British feeling" in Congress, stoked by the America First Committee, made this situation even worse. Britain's diplomats, already fearful that the country's "unpopular" image would undermine the American "urge to assist us," cautiously waited to see how developments in the Pacific would affect their attempts to acquire desperately needed supplies.[134]

Soviet officials shared these fears. The new ambassador, Maxim Litvinov, had only arrived in Washington that morning—via Hawaii, where he had actually toured the military barracks at Pearl Harbor on December 4. After landing, Litvinov and his wife were met by the former US ambassador to the Soviet Union, Joseph E. Davies. The two men had become friendly in Moscow. Davies remained a confidant of the president after his return from the USSR and had also ingratiated himself with the Soviet authorities with the publication of his memoir, *Mission to Moscow*, earlier that year, which took a sympathetic line on Stalin's purges and his pre-1939 dealings with Hitler. It was during lunch at Davies's house that Litvinov took a call from Roosevelt asking him to notify Stalin of the attack on Pearl Harbor. Litvinov later suggested that the president sounded relieved and finished their conversation by declaring, "Praise God," a sentiment that Litvinov found "curious."[135]

After the call, the Soviet ambassador told Davies that he personally felt US intervention was probably too late to make a difference to the war with Hitler. When Davies asked about Stalin's likely reaction to Pearl Harbor, Litvinov responded that he had been out of contact for the past few weeks, but that the government "had been handling Japan gingerly, under the non-aggression pact, to avoid war on two fronts."[136] As Davies reported, Litvinov said that, when he had left Moscow, "the Germans were within 16 miles of the Kremlin" and their armies "had already taken over his own country house" in the city's suburbs. The ambassador "painted a bleak picture" and explained that the "military situation was desperate." Stalin had previously resisted attempts by the Japanese ambassador in Moscow to negotiate a separate, compromise peace between the Soviets and Hitler—"of course at Russia's expense," as it was based on the present battle line. Now, Soviet troops were being rushed from Siberia to defend Moscow and the south against Hitler's forces, and although this was a "desperate risk, facing a hostile Japan," Litvinov felt they had little choice. As a result, Davies reported back to the State Department that any tactical benefit for the United States from Stalin declaring war on Japan would be outweighed by the strategic cost of the "desperate plight" that the Soviets faced from a two-front war.[137] Of course, if Hitler influenced the Japanese forces to attack in the east, then "the problem becomes academic." But, if the administration had a choice, Davies's counsel was against encouraging the Soviets to join the fight with Japan, lest it "win the battle, but hazard the war."[138]

Of greatest concern to Litvinov was the fear that the American war in the Pacific would prevent the delivery of vital Lend-Lease supplies to Britain and the USSR.[139] Although the offer of Lend-Lease aid had been extended to the Soviets after Hitler's invasion, the setup had been slow and protracted, not helped by congressional opposition and the skepticism of the US military attaché in Moscow, who was convinced that the Soviet forces were in danger of imminent collapse.[140] Consequently, as we have seen, most of the initial aid allocations came through Britain, including British-manufactured tanks and planes, as well as aircraft that London had received from the United States. British-supplied armor had made up a crucial 30 to 40 percent of the heavy and medium tank strength in the Soviet defense of Moscow.[141]

When news of the Pearl Harbor attack arrived in the Soviet Union itself, Stalin's relief that the Japanese had not attacked him was offset by anxiety about this diversion of British and American resources. Territorial losses, enemy action, and the disruption caused by the evacuation program had slashed his own production, and he could not spare further support.[142] As Stafford Cripps, the astute British ambassador in Moscow, had already noted, there was a recognition on the Soviet side that "although the Germans will be very much weakened" by the Soviet counterattack, "they will still have a tremendous power of production to build up a mechanised force again during the winter and next spring."[143] There was now a real danger that Lend-Lease supplies would not be forthcoming by the time the Nazi offensive resumed.

In the Pacific, the Japanese onslaught continued. At 8:54 a.m. Hawaii time, Shigekazu Shimazaki, commander of the second wave of aircraft, gave the signal to attack. The base was now full of smoke and angry Americans. Pilots, some in pajamas, were running toward their planes. The anti-aircraft fire was intense, but Kaneohe air base was hit again and so was Hickam field. One American airman was illuminated hurrying along a front of burning hangars. As he was strafed by a swooping Zero, he appeared for a terrible moment to be running into the ground while his legs were cut away by Japanese machine-gun fire.[144] Dive-bombers caught the battleship USS *Nevada* attempting to make for the open sea and damaged it so badly that it had to be beached. As another battleship, the USS *Utah*, sank, Pharmacist's Mate Second Class Lee Soucy heard someone shout, "Where did those Germans come from?" Utterly fanciful sightings of German Messerschmitt Bf 109 fighters were reported, testament to the confusion of the moment, the ingrained belief that the Japanese were not capable of carrying out such an attack on their own, and the Americans' sense of also being under attack by the Third Reich.[145]

The full report of the destruction took time to reach Washington. At 2:28 p.m. local time, when the chief of naval operations, Harold Stark, telephoned the White House to confirm the earlier reports, he could only state that "it was a very severe attack and that some damage had already been done to the fleet and that there was some loss of life."[146] At the War Office, where "news of catastrophes" would filter in from Pearl Harbor throughout the day, Stimson's "dominant feeling" remained "of relief that the indecision was over and that a crisis had come in a way which would unite all our people." Yet for Stimson—the administration's principal proponent of intervention in the war in Europe—there remained what he called the "open question" of what this meant for the struggle with Germany. Even if the attack on Pearl Harbor would unify the country in fury against Japan, it remained unclear whether this would alter attitudes toward the war in Europe among those whom the secretary termed the "unpatriotic men."[147]

But the Pacific remained the immediate focus, and at 2:30 p.m. the president authorized Admiral Stark to implement War Plan 46—effectively empowering the US fleet to conduct unrestricted submarine and naval war in East Asia and the surrounding waters. He also telephoned his press secretary, Steve Early, to inform him about the Japanese attack on Pearl Harbor and Manila—the latter would, despite what Roosevelt had previously told Hu Shih, not occur until a few hours later—and to instruct him to tell the press immediately. Roosevelt then asked, "Have you any news?" to which Early responded, "None to compare with what you have just given me, sir."[148] Although the question struck Early as "funny," and historians have regarded it as an amusingly innocent inquiry, the president may have been wondering whether the Japanese assault was to be accompanied by an aggressive act or declaration from Hitler.

Although Thailand was on the verge of being lost, in Singapore, British leadership persisted in underestimating Japanese forces even after the strikes were known to them. Duff Cooper and his wife Diana were woken at 3 a.m. local time by Martin Russell, Duff's personal private secretary, poking his head into their bedroom. "The Japs have landed on the north-east coast of Malaya," he announced. Since there was nothing much they could do about this immediately, the Coopers—with considerable sangfroid—prepared to go back to sleep.[149] It was probably around the same time that the British military commander, General Arthur Percival, woke Singapore's civilian governor, Sir Shenton Thomas, and told him of the Japanese landing. "Well," the governor responded, "I suppose you'll shove the little men off."[150] The city was a sea of light, but nobody seems to have thought to call for a blackout, nor to man the headquarters of the civilian air-raid precaution center.

By the time Early had passed on Roosevelt's statement on the Japanese strikes to the three principal US press agencies (the Associated Press, United Press, and International News Service), the news had already filtered through to the guests at Eleanor Roosevelt's lunch. One of those present was Huybertie Hamlin, a longtime friend of the Roosevelts who had been staying as a guest at the White House since late November. Hamlin noted that "everyone stood around in stupefied knots—we almost whispered our amazement to one another." As guests dispersed, Hamlin found herself "standing alone by the portrait of President Wilson," who "seemed to say that all this might have been avoided . . . all the prophesies made by him that if some form of co-operation was not effected between nations that another war was inevitable for the next generation—and here it was."[151]

The American public was not yet generally aware of the attack. As Eleanor's guests were taking in the news that afternoon, the renowned conductor Artur Rodzinski was about to start the second of a series of guest concerts at the New York Philharmonic, broadcast by radio over the CBS network. The orchestra played Shostakovich's First Symphony followed by Brahms's Second Concerto. The latter featured a bravura solo performance by the Polish American pianist Artur Rubinstein.[152] The audience was spellbound, blissfully transported onto a higher plane.

News of Pearl Harbor reached the Free French leader Charles de Gaulle while he was having supper at home with his wife in London.[153] He immediately announced that "the war is now definitely won." "There will be two future phases," the general continued. "The first will be that the [Western] allies will save Germany [from dismemberment by Stalin]; the second will be a war between the Russians and the Americans." Though prescient, at that point these remarks must have seemed premature, if not far-fetched. After all, the main French interlocutor of the United States was Vichy, not the Free French, and the Americans and the Germans were not at war, and it was not clear when they would be.

At Chequers, Churchill had continued to look "unusually worried" throughout dinner and "hardly spoke."[154] Just before 9 p.m., as usual, the butler Frank Sawyers brought in a small radio so that the prime minister could hear the news. But Churchill was so "despondent" that "he did not seem to notice it was there." As the newsreader summarized the headlines, Churchill remained "immersed in his thoughts" and completely missed the special dispatch: "The Japanese have raided Pearl Harbor." While Churchill remained impassive and the summary moved on to a different item, a startled Averell Harriman burst out from across the table, "What's that about bombing Pearl Harbor?" The target seemed so implausible that Churchill's aide-de-camp Tommy Thompson thought the presenter had actually said "Pearl River," a major waterway in southern China.[155] However, Sawyers confirmed that the staff had just heard it on the radio in their quarters too. "The Japanese have attacked the Americans."[156]

Churchill was growing excited. Recalling that he'd promised to follow any Japanese attack on the United States with a British declaration within the hour, he announced, "We shall declare war on Japan" and headed for the door. US ambassador John Winant and Harriman talked him out of this, cautioning that he could not declare war on the basis of a radio announcement, "even from the B.B.C."[157] Consequently, Winant encouraged Churchill to first call the White House and find out the facts. When the prime minister got through, Roosevelt confirmed the report was "quite true": "They have attacked us at Pearl Harbor. We are all in the same boat now."[158]

This was more the case than Roosevelt knew. Churchill's principal private secretary, John Martin, informed the prime minister that the Admiralty had just called to say Japan had also attacked the British possession of Malaya.[159] The prime minister immediately issued orders for "all British units to take action against all Japanese formations wherever found."[160]

Churchill would later write in his history of the Second World War that news of Pearl Harbor brought America into the conflict directly and thus delivered him "the greatest joy." "So we had won after all," he wrote. "England would live; Britain would live; the Commonwealth of Nations and the Empire would live." "Hitler's fate," by contrast, "was sealed. Mussolini's fate was sealed." "As for the Japanese," Churchill continued, "they would be ground to powder." He remembered Foreign Secretary Edward Grey's remark to him thirty years earlier, comparing the United States to a "a gigantic boiler" that, once ignited, could produce unlimited power. The war, Churchill felt, or claimed to have felt, was now decided. "All the rest," he believed, "was merely the proper application of overwhelming force."[161]

But Britain was by no means out of the woods. Churchill's instinctive relief reflected the fact that Britain had avoided the worst-case scenario: fighting Japan and Germany across two oceans without the United States. But if the United States and Britain were "in the same boat" in the Pacific, then what about the Atlantic? After Churchill replaced the receiver and his initial excitement subsided, a new fear loomed: that the United States would focus entirely on Japan, devoting its resources to its own war and leaving Britain to face Hitler unaided.

Churchill's call had interrupted a meeting between the president and his principal advisers, including Hopkins, Stimson, Knox, Hull, Admiral Stark, and chief of staff General George Marshall. When the conference resumed, Hopkins observed that there was not "too tense an atmosphere" because there was a general agreement "that in the last analysis the enemy was Hitler and that he could never be defeated without force of arms; that sooner or later we were bound to be in the war and that Japan had given us an opportunity."[162] Yet as reports of greater casualties and further carnage continued to come in from the Pacific, the tension in the White House rose. For Roosevelt's secretary Grace Tully, who was fielding calls and transcribing them in shorthand, "the news was shattering," with "each report more terrible than the last." It was becoming increasingly apparent that "the Navy was dangerously crippled, that the Army and Air Force were not fully prepared to guarantee safety from further shattering setbacks in the Pacific." Over the course of the afternoon, the "anguish and near hysteria" continued to grow. In this febrile atmosphere, rumors abounded. There was speculation that "a Jap invasion force might be following their air strike at Hawaii—or that the West Coast might be marked for similar assault."[163]

Amid the "hysteria," the president continued to maintain a posture of studied composure, albeit one tempered by strain and exhaustion. Eleanor, who visited her husband in his study around this time, noted, "He was completely calm. . . . He just became almost like an iceberg, and there was never the slightest emotion that was allowed to show." Yet behind this mask lay immense anxiety. Roosevelt told his wife that he "never wanted to fight this war on two fronts. . . . We haven't got the Navy to fight in both the Atlantic and the Pacific."[164] Multiplying his worries, every telephone call brought news of his beloved navy's further devastation.

It was probably around this time that the after-dinner discussion at Hitler's bunker was dramatically interrupted.[165] Hearing the news of Pearl Harbor on Reuters East Asian radio, the press chief, Otto Dietrich, immediately raced to inform Hitler. As he waited to be admitted to the dictator's presence, Dietrich heard independent confirmation of the attack. Exercised by the bad news from Russia, the Führer received him coldly, obviously fearing tidings of another catastrophe. But when Dietrich cut him short by reading out the message, Hitler reacted with astonishment. Then his face brightened and he asked tensely, "Is the news true?"[166] Dietrich insisted that it was. Germany may have been Japan's closest ally, but their first inkling of the attack came not from a message from Foreign Minister Togo, Emperor Hirohito, or Ambassador Oshima, but from an intercepted enemy radio broadcast.

Grabbing the piece of paper from Dietrich, Hitler rushed out of the building, running about one hundred meters unaccompanied, without his usual cap and coat, to the OKW bunker to pass on the news in person.[167] He burst in excitedly, the only time Wilhelm Keitel remembered him doing so during the entire war. All accounts of his reaction agree that the Führer was surprised—he clearly had no foreknowledge of the date and time of the attack—and ecstatic.[168] "I had the impression," Keitel recalled, "that he felt as if freed from a heavy load." To be sure, Hitler was aware that Japan was about to strike, and hoped it would do so, but he had feared the Japanese might back out at the last moment.[169]

Throughout the coming hours and days, Hitler would express relief that Japan's actions would tie down substantial British and American resources in the Far East, accepting not merely that he would have to deliver on his draft treaty commitments to Tokyo, but that it was in his vital interest to prevent his ally from going down to defeat on its own. In any case, he was convinced that he was effectively already at war with America. And this time, unlike in 1917, the Reich would not wait to be openly attacked by the United States. Hitler would strike first.

The Führer would now try to get to Berlin as quickly as possible to complete the negotiations over the treaty with Japan, prepare his own declaration of war, and work out an overall strategy to deal with the new situation. As we shall see, as far as Hitler was concerned, the die was cast: he would take the plunge and go to war with the United States. There was no way, however, that the British, the Americans, or even the Japanese could be sure that he would actually do so.

News of Pearl Harbor seems to have taken slightly longer to reach Berlin. The press section of the Foreign Office picked up the news while monitoring the BBC. Its head, who was dubious about the veracity of the report, conferred quickly with Franz von Sonnleithner, a young diplomat on Ribbentrop's personal staff. It was decided to fetch the foreign minister from the "home cinema" of the Foreign Office.[170] Ribbentrop himself was not only surprised but initially skeptical. "It is probably another propaganda trick of the enemy," he remarked, "which has once again duped my press section."[171] While he was still reading the message, the phone rang. Hitler was on the line. Both men agreed that the news was good. But when Sonnleithner tried, on Ribbentrop's instructions, to claim Tokyo's actions as a victory for German diplomacy, Hitler bridled. "Tell the foreign minister," he retorted, "that such a great people as the Japanese do exactly that which they believe to be right and will not be influenced by us in the slightest."[172]

The new global dynamic was immediately obvious to the German leadership. Japan's entry into the war created a new urgency for Axis policy toward the British Empire, especially India. Within two hours of Pearl Harbor, and very shortly after hearing the news, the Germans and Italians scheduled a meeting on the subject in Berlin with the exiled Indian nationalist Subhas Chandra Bose.[173] Mohamed Shedai, the Indian nationalist sponsored by Italy, was summoned from Rome. After years of foot-dragging, it seemed as if there would now be some real movement in Axis anti-colonialism. It was probably around this time, too, that the decision was made to publicize Hitler's meeting with the grand mufti, which was potential dynamite in the Middle East, at an opportune moment over the next few days.

Shortly after 4 a.m. in Singapore, Duff and Diana Cooper were disturbed again, this time by falling bombs, anti-aircraft fire, and sirens. Seventeen Japanese aircraft struck the city, which still had not been blacked out. The planes did not make much of an impression on the docks or airfields, but the substantial damage to the city included hits to Raffles Place (one of the main squares in the city) and nearly two hundred civilian casualties, most of them Chinese.[174]

About two hours after Pearl Harbor, the British supreme commander in the Far East, Robert Brooke-Popham, issued a proclamation. "We have had plenty of warning," he announced, "and our preparations are made and tested." Pronouncing himself "confident," Brooke-Popham turned to the Japanese. "We see before us a Japan," he claimed, "drained for years by the exhausting claims of her wanton onslaught in China." From the local "civilian population, Malay, Chinese, Indian or Burmese," he expected only "that patience, endurance and serenity which is the great virtue of the east."[175] It was probably around this time that Admiral Phillips, commanding Force Z, received a signal from the Admiralty in London that he should do something about the Japanese landings in Malaya.[176]

Oshima, the Japanese ambassador to Berlin, heard the news of Pearl Harbor around 11 p.m., also via the BBC, and immediately made contact with Ribbentrop.[177] Despite or perhaps because of Hitler's remarks about Japanese autonomy, Oshima was worried that the Reich might no longer have any interest in concluding a no-separate-peace agreement now that Japan was firmly in the war and might renege on its promise to commence open hostilities with the United States.[178] To the Japanese ambassador's certain relief, the German foreign minister stated unequivocally that "Germany and Italy's immediate participation can be assumed to be a matter of course." At the same time, though, Ribbentrop would still need to confer with Hitler before anything was finally agreed. While Oshima was still in the room, Ribbentrop "immediately passed on the gist of our conversation by telephone to Ciano."[179]

Across Berlin, American diplomat George Kennan learned of the Pearl Harbor attack through his shortwave radio. He immediately telephoned Leland Morris, the US embassy's chargé d'affaires, who was home in bed, and as many of his colleagues as he could reach. The American diplomats met late that night at the embassy to "consider our course now that the end seemed near." It was immediately clear "that this situation might at any moment develop into war with Germany."[180]

In Washington, leading officials hurried to put the attack in its broader strategic context. When Hull returned to the State Department after the conference at the White House, he immediately convened his principal advisers. The secretary of state was keen to stress his belief that the Japanese would not act unilaterally, and that the United States must expect Germany and Italy to join them. Consequently, he told his subordinates that "every American merchant vessel in the world should be notified of the existence of hostilities as it was feared that these vessels anywhere would be prey for German, Italian or Japanese armed forces."[181] The War Department echoed Hull's concern that the Japanese assault on Pearl Harbor should not distract from the bigger picture. Stimson returned from the White House to find a memorandum from the Assistant Secretary John J. McCloy stressing that "any action taken by Congress and any statements made by the President should not be solely directed to the Japanese attacks." McCloy declared: "The note that this is part of the world-wide aggression of the Axis powers should be struck," for unless the administration was vigilant, "our energies may be hysterically directed to avenge this morning's attack and the country's opinion may lose sight of the world-wide significance of the move."[182]

Sensitive as the president was to the threat from Germany, he also remained attuned to the attack's likely impact on American public opinion. After taking some time alone to reflect, he called Grace Tully to his office shortly before 5 p.m. to dictate the address to Congress that he would deliver the following day. In between drags on a cigarette, the president composed a taut message of less than five hundred words. Once it was transcribed, the president called the secretary of state back to the White House for his comments.[183] Hull recommended a longer statement, based on one that the undersecretary of state Sumner Welles had already drafted. It not only included the long history of Japanese militarism in Asia but also linked it to the aggression by Hitler and Mussolini in Europe, with which "Japanese operations have been steadily interlocked."[184] Roosevelt declined to deliver a document that would "take half an hour to read" when the reality of Japan's aggression and duplicity was so obvious.[185] Moreover, the president remained concerned about the strength of anti-interventionist sentiment in Congress, aware that many of its members had denounced the administration's policies in Asia and dismissed arguments against greater American involvement in Europe.

At almost that exact moment, Senator Gerald Nye, one of the leading anti-interventionists, was attending an America First rally near Pittsburgh. He responded to a local journalist's report of the news from Pearl Harbor simply by saying, "It sounds terribly fishy" and remarking that he was "amazed that the President should announce an attack without giving details." The rally then carried on as if nothing had occurred, with each speaker "denouncing Roosevelt as a warmonger." An astonished military reserve officer in the audience called out: "Can this meeting be called after what has happened in the last few hours?" Were people aware "that Japan has attacked Hawaii"? The audience's response was to chant "Throw him out!" and "Warmonger!" while the reservist was escorted from the premises for his own safety.

As Nye was delivering his keynote address, at 5:20 p.m., over four hours after the start of the Pearl Harbor attack, the Associated Press reported that Japan had announced a state of war with the United States and Britain, effective as of dawn that morning (December 8) in the western Pacific. While covering the America First rally, local journalist Robert Hagy received the bulletin from his news desk and walked onto the platform to hand it to Nye. The senator "glanced at it, read it, never batted an eye, went on with his speech." After speaking for fifteen more minutes, Nye finally told the audience, "I have before me the worst news that I have encountered in the last 20 years." Even then Nye declared that he "can't somehow believe this" and "can't come to any conclusions until I know what this is all about," as "there have been too many funny things before."[186] Returning to his speech, he concluded with the declaration that "Christianity and intervention are as completely opposed as anything under God." After leaving the stage, Nye told reporters that the Pearl Harbor attack was "just what Britain had planned for us" and "Britain has been getting this ready since 1938."[187]

In light of sentiments like these, Roosevelt advised Churchill to avoid a British declaration of war until he had time to prepare American opinion himself. Anxious about anti-interventionist sentiment and conscious of the need for public unity, the president thought "it best on account of psychology here that Britain's declaration of war be withheld until after [his] speech."[188]

Nevertheless, as it became clear that Britain's own territory was under attack, Churchill reasoned that he had no choice but to call a session of Parliament for the following day. The prime minister had by now learned that Japanese forces had landed at Khota Bharu, on the east coast of Malaya near the border with Thailand, at 12:25 a.m. local time, two hours before the attack on Pearl Harbor had begun.[189] Information remained fragmentary at this point, and a fuller picture would not emerge until the morning.

Even as conditions worsened in the Pacific, the news from North Africa continued to improve for the British. At 11 p.m., General Auchinleck reported that it "looks as if enemy has decided to raise siege of Tobruk" and withdraw westward to Gazala on the Libyan coast. Finally, after 242 days, one of the longest sieges in British military history appeared to be over. Auchinleck continued to urge caution, however. Rommel was "evidently prepared" to continue fighting "to cover his withdrawal or possibly in hope of still dealing us a crippling blow." As a result, Auchinleck wrote, "do not think relief Tobruk should be claimed" until the situation was clearer.[190] In a battle in which fortunes seemed to change from hour to hour, this wariness was understandable.

Although the hour was growing late, Churchill's mind was racing, combing through the potential allies he would need as the war's next chapter commenced. Before retiring for the night, he sent a dramatic message to the British representative in Dublin, which appeared to offer Irish unity in return for that nation's support for the war effort against Hitler. At around the same time, Churchill also dispatched a telegram to the Chinese nationalist leader Chiang Kai-shek to tell him that Japan had attacked both Britain and the United States: "Always we have been friends: now we face a common enemy."

Yet Churchill's principal concern remained the United States. Late that night, he drafted a telegram to Harry Hopkins, whom he regarded as Britain's greatest advocate in the White House, to tell him that he was "thinking of you much at this historic moment."[191] Churchill headed to bed, but fears about how the Roosevelt administration would proceed meant that his night was far less restful than he later claimed.

Besides contacting foreign leaders, Churchill had also sent a message about Pearl Harbor to the naval commander's office at Invergordon, where his foreign secretary, Anthony Eden, would soon arrive ahead of setting sail for the Soviet Union for a meeting with Stalin.[192] Despite spending the entire day on the train from Euston to northern Scotland, Eden had, in fact, already heard the news. In the early evening, permanent undersecretary Alexander Cadogan, the deputy chief of the general staff, the Soviet ambassador Ivan Maisky, and two Foreign Office men, Oliver Harvey and Frank Roberts, had met with Eden in his carriage for a traditional English tea. Maisky found the conversation "general, social and uninteresting" and was about to leave for his own compartment when he noticed something "strange and incomprehensible." The train was nonstop, but when it passed through a small station Maisky saw people gathered in excitement on the platform, "running, gesticulating and clearly hotly debating something." It was the same at the next small station. Clearly something was going on. Eden ordered the train to stop at the next station. One of his men jumped onto the platform and soon returned with the momentous news that Japan had gone to war with the United States.[193]

Frustratingly, though the stationmaster had heard the report on the radio, he had no further details on how and where the attack had taken place. Still, Eden was very excited and immediately asked Maisky, "What do you think of this?" The Russian responded "that the war now essentially covered the whole globe, and the balance of power between the two camps had clearly changed in our favour." Eden then wanted to know whether he should press on to Moscow, or if it would not be better to return to London. "By no means," Maisky objected. "On the contrary, now your trip to Moscow is even more necessary."[194] The train continued on its way to Invergordon where, at 2 a.m., as well as receiving confirmation of the attack, Harvey would learn that the prime minister would call the following morning to discuss Eden's voyage to the east.[195]

On the East Coast of the United States, the New York Philharmonic concert was drawing to a close. The audience was so enthusiastic about what they had heard that they called back the conductor and orchestra again and again to receive ovations. The radio announcer Walter Sweeney, by contrast, had ceased to report on what was happening on stage, nor did he list the program of the forthcoming weekly concert, as he usually would have done. Instead, he signaled to the conductor, Rodzinski, and with trembling hands gave him an announcement to read. The conductor blenched and shook his head. The news had both upset him and struck him dumb. So it was Sweeney who told the audience that Pearl Harbor had just been attacked. Some gasped, others wept. At once, the orchestra rose to its feet and struck up the national anthem, thus vocalizing the intense feeling of patriotism that had gripped the hall.[196]

Just after 7 a.m. in Tokyo, many hours after the attacks, Japanese radio made a dramatic official announcement. The empire, Hirohito's subjects were told, had "entered into a situation of war with the United States and Britain in the Western Pacific before dawn."[197] The journalist Robert Guillain, who was working for the French Havas news agency in Tokyo, heard the news from a vendor in the biting morning air of the deserted Shimbashi intersection when he was heading to the railway station. "Senso! Senso!" the vendor called, ringing the bell used to announce special editions: "War! War!" Very soon the first commuters bought their copies. Guillain studied their reactions as they read. Most took a few steps, then "suddenly stopped to read more carefully." Looking up, their faces were, to him, "inscrutable." They said nothing, either to the vendor or to each other. Initially, Guillain recorded, the response of the Japanese public was one of "fear" and "consternation."[198]

The reaction from some elements of the Japanese elite was equally muted. "What on earth?" Prince Konoye exclaimed on hearing the news. "I really feel a miserable defeat coming." Unimpressed by the magnitude of the triumph at Pearl Harbor, he added that Japanese successes would "only last two or three months."[199] Former foreign minister Matsuoka, who was in bed recovering from a recurrence of his childhood tuberculosis, was also doubtful. "The Tripartite Pact," he lamented, "was the biggest blunder of my life." Toshikazu Kase, one of the Foreign Ministry's most senior American specialists, was equally aghast. Echoing British foreign secretary Edward Grey at the start of the First World War, Kase recalls feeling that "the lamps were going out."[200]

Despite the Japanese government's communiqué about the outbreak of hostilities, the American ambassador in Tokyo, Joseph Grew, was still in the dark about the attack. He was woken at seven that morning by a phone call from Togo's private secretary, who claimed to have called repeatedly for the past two hours. Grew replied that this was "surprising, because the telephone is right beside my bed and it has not rung." Togo wished to see the ambassador immediately and, within half an hour, Grew arrived at his official residence. Togo had just returned from an audience with Hirohito and wished to pass on the emperor's written response to Roosevelt's letter of the previous evening, which was actually just the fourteen-part message that the Japanese diplomats had already handed to Hull. When Grew protested that he had been instructed to see the emperor personally, Togo merely responded that, due to lack of progress, negotiations were now called off, and he thanked the ambassador for his "cooperation for peace." As discussions had broken down in the past, Grew was not unduly concerned and, after exchanging pleasantries with the minister, returned to the US embassy. Togo had said nothing about Pearl Harbor.

With US embassy officials still unaware of what was going on, Japan was being put on a war footing. Shortly after the Pearl Harbor attack, Prince Higashikuni was appointed supreme commander of defense, replacing the supposedly ill General Otozo Yamada. His remit was homeland defense. Higashikuni had been a dove, and though he was disappointed by the outbreak of hostilities, he felt that the nation should rally behind the flag. His main job, the prince was informed, would be to defend Japan against Allied air attacks.[201]

That night in the east of Europe, faced with escalating Soviet attacks, Hitler approved the "withdrawal" of Panzer Groups Three and Four to a line of observation on a "case-by-case basis."[202] The Führer clearly was prepared to countenance at least local retreats. He insisted, though, that key railway lines, such as that linking Stary Oskol with Yefremov, should be kept on the German side of the front.[203] One way or the other, there was, for now, with the exception perhaps of the position of Army Group North, no sign of acute anxiety on his side about the situation on the eastern front. As far as Hitler was concerned, he was simply winding down the Russian campaign for the winter in preparation for delivering the final blow in the spring. His main attention was on the extraordinary news coming in from the Pacific and the implications it had for his future conduct of the war.

The German high command received the news of Pearl Harbor with some satisfaction. They were delighted to see that the American president was now, in their view, getting his comeuppance. The naval leadership, for example, noted that Roosevelt "now has the war he has always wanted, but probably in circumstances and at a time which does not suit his calculations."[204] Many shared Hitler's assumption that the Japanese attack opened up a window of opportunity for the Reich before the United States could bring its full might to bear on them. A few hours after news of Pearl Harbor, Friedrich von Boetticher, the military attaché at the Washington embassy, predicted that while the Americans would respond to the outbreak of hostilities by introducing convoys, this would still not allow them to ship large quantities of rubber from Asia. The rapid expansion of US strategic stockpiles of that critical raw material had thus been brought to a sudden halt.[205]

The outbreak of hostilities in the Pacific was not yet widely registered on the eastern front.[206] In Army Group Center, Bock noted simply that Japan had attacked British and American sovereign territory.[207] One of those who did draw broader conclusions was Wolfram von Richthofen, whose Eighth Air Corps was bearing the brunt of the aerial operations on the central front. "With Japan," he wrote in his diary, "all British, American and Russian hopes are dashed for the next few years. It would be great." Then, Richthofen continued, "local setbacks (so long as they stay local!) here [in Russia] or in Africa can be contemplated."[208] It was clear that in his mind, as in the minds of the German military and political leadership generally, Japanese successes would compensate for recent German setbacks.

Yet in the very service that was supposed to benefit most from the relief brought by the Japanese entry into war with the United States, a note of caution was already evident. The war diarist of the Kriegsmarine spoke of the "painful" truth that while sea power would now be crucial to the outcome of the war, the German Navy would not be able to deal the "decisive blows" necessary. This was because the outbreak of war in 1939 had been "five years too early" for an utterly unprepared Kriegsmarine. In its current state, in fact, the navy was "not even in a position to take advantage in the Atlantic and the Mediterranean of the considerable relief which the Pacific [war] brought."[209]

THE GERMAN NAVY certainly had its work cut out, given the range and reach of the Allied supply network. The extent was demonstrated that night in Hvalfjordur on the west coast of Iceland. Normally a freezing backwater, this remote and deep inlet now witnessed a scene of world-historical importance. PQ6, the seventh British convoy carrying war matériel to the Soviet Union, was preparing to depart. Iceland was chosen as an assembly point partly for geographical reasons and partly because it was under American occupation, and Hitler was still trying to avoid clashes with Roosevelt, or so British planners believed. From Iceland, the convoy would be the responsibility of the Royal Navy. It operated from HMS *Baldur*, a "stone frigate" or naval shore establishment at Hvitanes, on a small peninsula jutting into the fjord. So far, none of the Arctic convoys had suffered losses en route, perhaps because of Hitler's restrictions against attacking American merchantmen.

There were nine merchant ships in the convoy. By far the oldest was *Dekabrist*, which had been completed in 1903 at Barrow-in-Furness. This ship already had a great deal of history behind it. As the *Anadyr*, it had served in the 1904–1905 Russo-Japanese War as an auxiliary cruiser in the tsarist navy at the disastrous Battle of Tsushima on the other side of the world. Rechristened *Dekabrist* after the Bolshevik Revolution, it had recently carted Polish prisoners of war to the gulag.[210] Now it was carrying a cargo of American bombers for Stalin.[211] Two other ships, the merchantmen *El Oceano* and the *Mount Evans*, were registered in Panama. Two were tankers, tasked with refueling the Royal Navy escorts already stationed at Murmansk. One, the *Mirlo*, was Norwegian. The other, the *Elona*, belonged to Anglo-Saxon Petroleum (part of Shell); the convoy commodore sailed in it. The vice commodore was in the *Empire*

Mavis, a cargo ship completed at Portland, Oregon, in 1918. Then there was the *Harmatris*, a merchantman carrying munitions and trucks, and the *Explorer*, a cargo ship built at Wallsend; two of its crew had suffered frostbitten hands while transshipping at Hvalfjordur.[212] The ninth vessel was the rescue ship, *Zamalek*.[213] Two other ships, the *Botavon* and the *Southgate*, had been too badly damaged on the way to Iceland to join PQ6 in time.[214] The meager escort consisted of three armed trawlers: the *Hugh Walpole*, the *Stella Capella*, and the *Cape Argona*. The cruiser HMS *Edinburgh* was only slated to join them from Scapa Flow in the Orkney Islands, Scotland, several days later.[215]

Though most of the crews were from the United Kingdom, some of the ships' officers and men hailed from around the world. For example, the captain of the *Stella Capella*, Walter Langdon Sadgrove, was a naval reservist from Queensland, Australia; Frank Roe on the *Elona* was a New Zealander; and the skipper of the *Mirlo*, Olav Reinertsen, was a Norwegian. What these three and the rest of the men made of the news from Pearl Harbor, which came through on the radio late that night and fundamentally changed the context of their voyage, is not known.[216] What they were all aware of was the immediate danger that awaited them once they left the safety of Hvalfjordur. "News today," gunner Leonard Chapman of the *Empire Mavis* wrote in his diary that evening, "that one ship, *Empire Wave*, was sunk going to Russia." Among the survivors, he continued, "several had to have limbs amputated—frostbite. Pleasant start."[217]

At the same time, another Allied convoy, WS-12X, was moving down the coast of West Africa. The WS convoys, nicknamed "Winston's Specials," transported large numbers of troops, as well as urgently needed strategic matériel, to reinforce British forces in the Middle East and India. With the Axis controlling the eastern Mediterranean and that approach to the Suez Canal closed off to Britain, the only route was the long voyage around Africa. With the Admiralty short of ships, Churchill had secured Roosevelt's approval in early September to loan Britain its most impressive escort vessels to carry over twenty thousand British troops to the Middle East.[218] British troopships initially carried the men of the Eighteenth Infantry Division across the North Atlantic to Halifax,

Canada, where they and all their equipment were transferred to American transport vessels in the dead of night. Convoy WS-12X, which had departed on November 10, was commanded by the US rear admiral Arthur B. Cook aboard the aircraft carrier *Ranger*, and included the USS *West Point*, the USS *Mount Vernon*, and USS *Wakefield*—each measuring over twenty-four thousand tons gross—as well as eight destroyers and a naval tanker, which joined at Trinidad.[219] Unlike previous transatlantic convoys, this was an entirely American mission, other than the passengers. Undertaken while the United States was still officially a neutral nation, this clandestine operation was still unknown to the American public as the convoy steamed toward Cape Town, South Africa.

British troops on board were required to adhere to American naval regulations, including the prohibition of alcohol on ships. On the other hand, there were significant perks. On the *West Point*, recently converted to a troop transport from the luxury liner USS *America*, one British soldier, Fergus Anckorn, was astonished to find marble staircases, mosaic floors, a complete gymnasium with gold fittings, a large swimming pool, and even shops selling everything from ice cream and chocolates to cigars and suits. What most astounded Anckorn and his colleagues was the food. They enjoyed luxuries like real eggs, barely seen in Britain for the past two years. The British troops were able to appreciate this "strange existence" relatively free from the attention of German U-boats.[220] A number of U-boats had been moving in their direction as they approached Africa, but the HMS *Dorsetshire*, aided by British naval intelligence, had subsequently forced the German supply ship *Python* to scuttle itself as it refueled those submarines south of Saint Helena.[221]

The weather slowed their progress, and on December 7 the ship was caught up in a violent storm. Anckorn and a couple of others were in the ship's library, perched on plush armchairs that "careered around the room of their own accord with the violent movement of the ship. It was just like being on the dodgems!" Suddenly, Anckorn noticed that the American sailor overseeing the library had turned somber. "We're one of you now," he told Anckorn, "they've bombed Pearl." Mistaking the seriousness, Anckorn quipped, "Who's Pearl?!" He was informed this was Pearl

Harbor, where America's Pacific Fleet was based, and "they" were Japan. His first reaction was puzzlement: "But they're not even in the war." After two months at sea, it is unlikely that Anckorn and his colleagues knew much about developments in the Pacific. Yet while the American sailors were shocked by the news, their British counterparts were less moved: "Our view was that we'd been at it for over two years, so 'welcome to the party.'"[222]

Many of Anckorn's compatriots back in Britain shared these sentiments. Since 1937, hundreds of Britons from across the country had been keeping diaries for Mass Observation, an initiative that was part social science, part anthropology, and part political project. Started by three socialist Cambridge University alumni, the project attempted to track the behavior and views of ordinary people, free from the filters of jobbing journalists. It offered unique insight into the opinions of diarists, and their neighbors, on the British home front. On the evening of December 7, one diarist, a thirty-one-year-old male artist in Bromley, recorded his sixty-five-year-old landlord's reaction to the Pearl Harbor attack: "Well let USA 'ave a taste of what we've 'ad—see how they like it! They ain't 'ad nothing to put up with." The artist himself was more concerned about the consequences for Britain: "I feel that this new theatre of war will prolong the European activity, since USA will not be able to supply Britain-Russia with so many—or any—arms to be used against Germany."[223] A housewife and voluntary worker in Maida Vale heard similar views from her colleagues: "People were asking each other whether they thought this would prevent the operation of the Lend-Lease bill, and if that was why Hitler had pushed the Japs into making war."[224] The prevailing suspicion seemed to be, as one Yorkshire woman engaged in domestic duties noted, that Japan had acted "at Hitler's request."[225]

In a small town in western Germany, Friedrich Kellner had not yet heard the news of Pearl Harbor. Instead, his diary entry that day contained another blistering attack on the Nazi regime. He condemned the widespread sentiment that the war had to be won to escape the revenge of the rest of the world. The only hope, Kellner mused, was a "palace revolution," but the problem was that there was no character of "substance" to carry one out. "The gentlemen financiers and industrialists," Kellner lamented, "all ran after the ratcatcher Hitler or at least misused him for their own purposes." He concluded his long diatribe against Germany's "so-called intellectual leadership class" with a final swipe at the regime. The Third Reich, Kellner wrote, was nothing more than an "El Dorado for thought-police and snitchers," governed by "sadists and bloodhounds."[226]

Hundreds of miles further east, in the Crimean capital of Simferopol, the eighty-one-year-old dentist Chrisanf Laskevic was pondering reports that the Germans would "shoot all Jews." Witnesses had heard them threatening to do so. "That is of course nonsense," the old man believed, "[because] however brutal the Germans may be, they will not decide to shoot civilians."[227]

On the other side of the Atlantic, in New York, Hertha Nathorff, one of the Jews who got away, heard the reports from Pearl Harbor. "Japan has attacked," she wrote. "The war is expanding more and more. More suffering, still more grieving and misery, how senseless all this is."[228] Charles Kikuchi, a Japanese American business student at University of California, Berkeley, who had gained some celebrity as the "young American with a Japanese face" in a recent collection of essays on American life, wrote of the news in his diary. "We are at war! Jesus Christ," he exclaimed. "I don't know what in hell is going to happen to us." His life, in fact, was about to take a dramatic turn for the worse. There were stories of riots in Los Angeles. The entire Japanese immigrant community, whether or not they had been born in the United States, would effectively be placed on trial.[229]

In Washington it was still early evening. Despite the AP report, the Roosevelt administration had still not received a declaration of war from official Japanese government channels. As a result, Hopkins noted that they still "did not know whether or not Japan has actually declared war on us."[230]

It was a fine morning in Tokyo. The Japanese lord keeper of the privy seal, the Marquess Kido, met with Prime Minister Tojo, the chief of the army general staff, and the chief of the navy general staff. They told him of the success of the strike on Pearl Harbor.[231]

In the White House, the telephone rang repeatedly with reports from the Pacific that grew ever more devastating. It was increasingly clear that damage to the fleet was enormous and many planes had been destroyed on the ground. All the while, the death toll continued to climb. Just before 6 p.m., Governor Joseph Poindexter telephoned from Honolulu. In the middle of the call, hearing planes and anti-aircraft fire in the background, the president's outer calm cracked and he exclaimed: "My God, there's another wave of Jap planes over Hawaii right this minute!"[232] Tragically, what Roosevelt heard was actually America's own gunners mistakenly shooting at a few remaining US planes, which were returning from an earlier pursuit of the Japanese raiders and fleet.[233]

Meanwhile, in the small White House press room, around one hundred journalists were packed into a space that normally held a dozen people to hear Early confirm "the report of heavy damages and loss of life."[234] Outside the building, people were gathering. Initially it was "mostly men with angry faces" standing in silence, but by the early evening choruses of "My Country, 'Tis of Thee" and "God Bless America" rang out from a one-thousand-strong crowd.[235] People were kept at a distance from the White House by the small Secret Service detail. Although the number of agents was doubled immediately after the Pearl Harbor attack, the man responsible for the president's protection, Treasury secretary Henry Morgenthau, still felt this was insufficient. Morgenthau recalled that Nazi agents had assassinated the Austrian chancellor, Engelbert Dollfuss, in 1934 and feared that Roosevelt might face a similar fate. He wanted at least one hundred soldiers permanently stationed outside the White House with machine guns and tanks, but Roosevelt rejected this. It was enough to block off the surrounding avenues while putting up barricades around the executive mansion.[236] He wished the White House to remain a symbol of democratic freedom rather than an armed camp in an increasingly militarized world.

As the evening was drawing to a close on the other side of the Atlantic, the German naval leadership was also taking stock of what had been a momentous day. "It remains to be seen," its diarist wrote, "what immediate impact these events will have." What was beyond doubt, he ventured, was that few states would be able to escape being caught up in a war that now embraced all the "global and great powers of the world." "The new order of things," the naval leadership continued, "could become a general one." December 7, 1941, in short, "marked not only a new phase in the military operations" but also opened a "global and pan-continental window onto the future order of the world."[237] The war of continents, which Mussolini had anticipated a few days earlier, was now at hand.

4

MONDAY, DECEMBER 8, 1941

I T WAS A TURBULENT NIGHT FOR THOSE IN AACHEN, THE WESTERN German city whose cathedral was graced by the throne of Emperor Charlemagne. RAF Bomber Command sent around 130 planes to strike the Nazi Party headquarters in the city center. Perhaps due to bad weather, just under half of these—sixty-four aircraft—claimed to have actually reached their target, some of them descending to four hundred meters to find it. The German authorities only recorded about sixteen attackers, who dropped five bombs, two of which failed to explode, on the city itself. Another three hit the railway station Aachen-West. There do not seem to have been any fatalities; a few houses were damaged, and two bombers were shot down. Yet the raid's importance was not physical but psychological, and subsequent Soviet propaganda leaflets to German soldiers on the eastern front would highlight the strike on Aachen.[1] That same night, Bomber Command also struck at Cologne, at German warships in Brest harbor, and at Calais, Ostend, and Boulogne. In all, there were 251 sorties by the RAF, at the cost of five aircraft.[2] It all served as a reminder of the continued ability of the British to strike at continental Europe.

As THE CLOCK struck midnight in London, planes from the Japanese Eleventh Air Fleet, which had been delayed by fog on Formosa (modern-day Taiwan), took off to strike at the Americans in the Philippines and the British in Hong Kong.[3] At Kota Bharu at the far northeast of Malaya, six hours after the start of the invasion, the Indian Army men on the beaches were still putting up a stout defense, and the operation was complicated by choppy seas. In desperation, an RAF pilot launched what may have been the first suicide attack of the war on an enemy transport ship in the bay.[4] Once ashore, however, the Japanese pushed inland and the British resistance soon began to collapse. Japanese columns raced along the coast toward Gong Kedah, and inland in the direction of Machang. The Japanese made further landings at Singora and Pattani on the southern coast of Thailand, pushing southwest toward the western coast of Malaya.[5] Both prongs targeted Singapore.

The Japanese leadership was by no means confident that these operations would succeed. Admiral Ugaki, chief of staff to the Combined Fleet, who was following the wireless reports in real time, noted that "it is quite dubious whether the landing at Khota Bharu, which is most important, was a success or not." "I understand that after the first landing, the rest apparently withdrew," he continued. "I am very worried about this issue."[6] Besides, there was also the problem of nearby Force Z, with *Prince of Wales* and *Repulse*, whose big guns would devastate the Japanese transports and smaller warships if Admiral Tom Phillips was able to get close to them. Eliminating this threat was a high priority.

In Tokyo, the British ambassador, Sir Robert Craigie, remained unaware his country was at war with Japan. Surprisingly, no one in London or Singapore seems to have reached him. He had been left to sleep through the night. Even more surprisingly, when he went to see the Japanese foreign minister at 8 a.m., Togo told him "a state of war existed between the United States and Japan but said nothing at that time that this was also the case with any part of the British Empire."[7] Perhaps it was too embarrassing for polite discussion. When Craigie complained of the omission months later to a senior member of the Japanese Foreign Office, his interlocutor remarked that the minister probably "assumed the ambassador had heard the radio announce the war at seven o'clock." Craigie laughed at this and replied, "My friend, you don't expect an Englishman to turn on the radio at seven o'clock on a Sunday morning."[8]

Like his British counterpart, the US ambassador had heard nothing in his meeting with Togo to suggest that his country was now at war with Japan. It was only after arriving back at the compound that Joseph Grew heard newsboys on the street calling, "Gogai! Gogai!"—an alert that they had important news. The ambassador dispatched an assistant to investigate, and he returned with a single-sheet special bulletin that declared that Japan had attacked the United States. Grew ordered his naval attaché to immediately head to the Japanese Navy Department for confirmation, where an official confirmed the report was true, assuring him that the Foreign Office would issue the declaration of war, though "he had no idea when it would be delivered."[9]

With the attack now verified, a group of American diplomats in Tokyo, directed by the second secretary Chip Bohlen, "started to burn the Embassy code books and classified files" in "metal waste baskets indoors and steel drums outdoors in the garage enclosure." The files were thick and numerous and, despite their best efforts, "whole or partial pages of unburned code or text would float up and away over Tokyo."[10] Meanwhile, the first secretary Edward S. Crocker received permission from Grew to drive to the Canadian legation and the British embassy to consult with their officials. Diplomats from the three missions had been scheduled to play a golf tournament that day. In an indication of "how slowly the true import of the situation really seeped into our consciousness," Crocker noted in his diary, the diplomats agreed that golf was off but expressed hope that the post-tournament dinner could still go ahead.[11]

Shortly after Crocker's arrival back at the US embassy, a car containing several Japanese officials and policemen drove into the compound. After Mrs. Grew informed them that her husband was busy, Crocker received the group, led by Mr. Ohno, a senior official in the Japanese Foreign Office. After Ohno, "his hands trembling," read out the declaration of war, Crocker remarked, "This is a very tragic moment," to which the Japanese diplomat responded, "It is, and my duty is most distasteful."[12]

The police then began to search the premises for radios. They showed no interest in the American diplomats destroying their cables, perhaps because Japan had already broken the US and British diplomatic codes earlier that year.[13] When the inspection was completed, the diplomats were instructed to remain within the compound, "as public feeling was running rather high throughout the city" and it would be unsafe for them to leave. Crocker doubted this account, claiming that he saw "no evidence of any hostile attitude" from the embassy windows, and the only report of aggression he had received was that of a "small contingent bearing swastika banners," which was easily dispersed.[14]

In Washington, it was still early evening of the previous day. While the president discussed his address to Congress with Hopkins, Eleanor Roosevelt became the first leading figure from the administration to address the nation since the attack. In her regular weekly radio broadcast at 6:30 p.m., the first lady began by incorrectly informing the nation that the "Japanese ambassador was talking to the president at the very time that Japan's airships were bombing our citizens."[15] In fact, the president had not seen Japan's ambassador that day, and Eleanor must have mistook him for the Chinese ambassador, who had met with the president shortly before the attack.[16] This was just the first instance of a phenomenon that would become widespread in the coming weeks, with angry Americans assailing their Chinese allies, whom they confused for their Japanese enemy. It happened so frequently that China's consulates began identifying their nationals with buttons and signs: "Chinese, not Japanese, please."[17]

Moving onto firmer ground, Eleanor preached unity. She rallied "the free and unconquerable people of the United States of America" to unite against the aggressor, drawing on her experience as the mother of "boys in the Services," including one who was at sea aboard a destroyer, and of two children who lived on the Pacific coast.[18] The safety of the Roosevelt family could not have been far from the president's mind either, particularly as he dined that evening with his other son, Marine captain James Roosevelt. They were joined by Hopkins and Tully for a light meal of scrambled eggs, cold cuts, and an apricot Bavarian cream pie in the oval study.[19] Roosevelt was scheduled to brief his cabinet at 8:30 p.m., followed by a meeting with congressional leaders, and he "wanted to relax a bit" beforehand. Over dinner, he "did not talk about Pearl Harbor and he did not complain."[20]

Downstairs, after returning from the studio, the first lady was herself scrambling eggs for a small group of guests, including Edward R. Murrow, the newsman who had captivated millions of Americans with his broadcasts from London during the Blitz.[21] Since returning to the United States a couple of weeks before, Murrow had grown increasingly concerned that his reporting had not convinced his countrymen that if Britain was to survive, and Hitler to be defeated, then the United States would need to enter the war. Just the day before, he had written to a friend in London that he feared Americans still did not appreciate what was at stake in the struggle. Murrow was sure that the Pearl Harbor attack—which had astounded him as much as the rest of the country when he had heard about it on the golf course that afternoon—made war with Japan a formality. But what about Germany? Perhaps conscious that Murrow's contacts in Britain might have given him some insight into that question, and eager to hear his thoughts on how the attack might affect American opinion on the broader conflict, the president sent word that he wanted to see the journalist that night after his meetings.[22]

Panic and rumors were beginning to spread. Huybertie Hamlin was also at Eleanor Roosevelt's evening gathering and heard "that in the next 24 hours we could expect Washington and New York to be bombed." Outside in the corridors, she spied "much coming and going in the outer hall" and spotted cabinet members, including Vice President Henry Wallace, and members of Congress, as well as "army and navy officers arriving hard and fast."[23]

For the moment, the Japanese had their hands full closer to home. At about 8 a.m. local time, Japanese bombers operating from Formosa struck Kai Tak airfield in Hong Kong, destroying all of the aircraft based there. A land invasion followed that same day. Astounded by the proficiency of the invading forces, Hong Kongers discussed unsubstantiated rumors that "German staff officers" were leading the offensive, as the Japanese were "little more than monkeys" who could not have cut through British defenses on their own. In reality, the Japanese required no such support.[24] The heavily outnumbered and outgunned British garrison defending the "gin-drinkers line" along the colony's northern border began to fall back. Even more worrying, the garrison commander received news from the British military mission in Chungking that Chiang's Chinese nationalist forces would not be ready to move before the start of January 1942 at the earliest. Much had depended on their support.[25]

While Hong Kong came under attack, Chiang opened an emergency meeting in Chungking on Pearl Harbor. He was dressed in a simple uniform modeled on that of the American First World War commander General John J. Pershing. After sounding out views, Chiang announced that he wanted a collective declaration of war by the United States, Britain, China, and the Soviet Union on Germany, Italy, and Japan, and a commitment not to enter into a separate peace until victory had been achieved. This was, in fact, equivalent to what the Axis diplomats were close to hammering out among themselves. Chiang laid particular stress on the need to bring the Soviet Union into the war against Japan. It was perhaps for this reason that he now showed a degree of ambivalence toward Pearl Harbor, because it made a Japanese attack on the Russians much less likely.[26]

Chiang's determination to declare war on the entire Axis was not so much driven by the desire to encourage US-British support against Japan. Both powers were already in that war, and in fact the outbreak of hostilities between Germany and the United States was likely to reduce the flow of American support to China. What Chiang wanted was a quid pro quo from Stalin. That day, he summoned the de facto Soviet ambassador in Chungking, Alexander S. Pnayushkin, to demand a Soviet declaration of war on Japan. Chiang was hopeful. "The Chief Soviet Military Advisor expresses his personal opinion," he cabled his ambassador in Washington afterward, "that the Soviet declaration of war against Japan is very much a matter of procedure."[27]

Nationalist China was greatly relieved by Pearl Harbor, to be sure, but a certain schadenfreude crept into its reaction to the humbling of the United States and Britain. One observer in Chungking, the writer Han

Suyin, recalled that it made the officers "almost delirious with pleasure," because it was "a big blow to White Power," at whose hands they had suffered even more than the Japanese had, and because the humiliating US criticisms of Chinese inefficiency could now be countered with the retort, "And what about you?"[28]

News of Pearl Harbor was also received with interest by Chiang's other great adversary, Chairman Mao Tse-Tung of the Chinese Communist Party (CCP). He, too, called a meeting of his party leaders, the Politburo. They met to thrash out a public statement that would be published in the official party organ *Liberation Daily* the next day. Mao was closely involved in crafting its wording. The statement he approved said that "this aggressive act by the Japanese fascists is . . . exactly like the acts of aggression of the German and Italian fascists against Europe and the Soviet Union." Despite this rhetoric, it is significant that Mao did not call upon the Soviet Union to go to war with Japan, mentioning only that "the great Soviet Red Army has moved to the phase of counter-attacking the Germans." Somewhat ironically in view of later developments, the CCP explicitly connected the fate of China to that of the United States and Britain in a "just war of liberation in defense of independence, freedom and democracy."[29]

Despite all the rumors flying around, there were no Japanese attacks on the continental United States. The offensive in the Pacific and Southeast Asia continued without slackening, and shortly before 9:30 in the morning, local time, Japanese Navy bombers operating from Saipan in the Mariana Islands launched the first of several air raids on Guam.[30] Three minutes later, a Japanese air strike hit American airfields in the northern Philippines. Even though the targets had had plenty of warning, the Japanese met little coordinated resistance.[31] There was, as one American commander recalled, "a grim thoughtful silence" after the raids, but no surprise. It had been a long-expected attack.[32]

The damage proved to be enduring, particularly for the Japanese immigrants who had built their lives in the Philippines. Long suspected by the American authorities and much of the population of being fifth columnists for Tokyo, these Japanese residents now faced wild rumors that some of the attacking pilots were the children of local settlers. The Davao provincial government responded by interning them. The resulting interethnic recrimination and suspicion did far more lasting damage to Philippine society than the bombs themselves.[33]

By now, the various diplomatic moves following news of Pearl Harbor were beginning to provoke dramatic responses. On receipt of Churchill's excited message about Irish unity, at 1:30 in the morning the British representative in Dublin, Sir John Maffey, contacted the secretary of the Irish Department of External Affairs, Joseph P. Walshe, and requested an urgent meeting. On hearing this, Irish taoiseach Éamon de Valera was convinced that he was about to be presented with a British ultimatum to join the war or hand over the treaty ports. He in turn called the chief of staff of the Free State Army, Lieutenant General Daniel McKenna, to mobilize the army.[34]

Half an hour later, at 2 a.m., Maffey delivered a "personal, private and secret" message from the prime minister to the taoiseach. "Now is your chance," Churchill announced in the message. "A nation once again. Am very ready to meet you at any time."[35] The reference to an evocative Republican ballad—"a nation once again"—and the context made de Valera think that he was being offered a united Ireland in return for Ireland's entrance into the war. "I indicated to Sir John Maffey," de Valera later recalled, "that I did not see the thing in that light." "I saw no opportunity at the moment of securing unity," he continued, and "our people were determined on their attitude of neutrality."[36] The best he could promise the British, with whom "his sympathies lay in this war," was to keep the Germans out of the Free State and enter the war if attacked.[37] The world might have changed after Pearl Harbor, but de Valera saw no reason to alter his stance on the war.

Around this time, at 8:20 p.m. in Washington, the US cabinet began filing into the oval study and "formed a ring completely around the President."[38] Roosevelt sat in silence with head bowed. When all members were present, the president "looked up for the first time." He told them "this was the most serious Cabinet meeting since the Spring of 1861."[39] The secretary of labor Frances Perkins noted that "his face and lips were pulled down, looking quite gray; his complexion did not have that pink and white look that it had when he was himself."[40] Perkins, like a number of those present, had just flown back to Washington that afternoon. Many had only heard "a scare headline: Japs attack Pearl Harbor" and now pressed the president for more information.[41] Roosevelt summarized the situation to the best of his ability: Japanese bombers had struck Pearl Harbor and its airfields, inflicting "extremely heavy" casualties, including sinking three, possibly four, battleships, potentially irreparably damaging two more, and also wrecking other smaller vessels.[42] In addition, Japan had attacked Guam, Wake Island, and possibly Midway too. Roosevelt, whose "pride in the Navy was so terrific," could barely bring himself to recount the depth of the destruction or how badly the fleet "could be caught off guard." As they all received this horrifying news, Perkins thought that her colleagues, while defiant and resolute, shared the same fear: "Where in the world is the rest of the American navy? Have we got any navy left?"[43]

Though the aircraft that had inflicted the devastation were Japanese, the president told his cabinet that "there was no question that this was a concerted effort running over several weeks with Germany and that he expected the possibility of war with Germany and Italy."[44] Indeed, he claimed that Japan had acted "under pressure from Berlin," which wished "to divert the American mind, and the British mind from the European field."[45] Critically, the president claimed, Hitler wanted to "divert American supplies from the European theatre to the defense of the East Asian theatre," but Roosevelt was adamant that any war in the Pacific "should not interfere with the flow of our supplies to Britain and Russia."[46] Despite his emphasis on German responsibility, however, when Roosevelt read aloud the address he planned to give to Congress the following day there was no mention of Germany. Secretary of War Stimson was disappointed to learn that "it was based wholly upon the treachery of the present attack" and only asked for a declaration against Japan. Not only did the statement overlook Japan's long record of lawlessness, it did nothing to "connect her in any way with Germany." After Roosevelt finished reading, Stimson pressed him to request "a declaration of war against Germany also," stressing that he "knew from the interceptions and other evidence that Germany had pushed Japan into this and that Germany was the real actor."[47]

Only a few members of the cabinet had access to these MAGIC intercepts. Those who did knew that the Japanese ambassador Oshima had had a meeting with Ribbentrop on November 28, during which the German foreign secretary suggested that now was the time to establish "Japan's New Order in East Asia," and that if this led to conflict with the Americans then Germany would join Japan in declaring war on the United States.[48] Neither this intercept, nor indeed anything else in MAGIC, necessarily verified the claim that Berlin had instigated Tokyo's ruthless assault. Stimson and Roosevelt's statements were consistent, however, with a wider and erroneous perception in Washington that Japan was itself incapable of initiating such swift and sophisticated strikes. That afternoon, when Admiral Stark had received word from Hawaii of a reported sinking of an enemy submarine, he enquired, "Is it German?"[49]

Though the president agreed with Stimson that Germany was the driving force behind Japan's actions, he rejected his counsel to request a declaration against Hitler at this time. None of the other cabinet members supported Stimson either. Attorney General Francis Biddle noted in his diary that night: "Our information is that Italy has said she would declare war and von Ribbentrop is now waiting to see Hitler and will also urge a declaration of war."[50] As a result, there was general agreement that the United States should wait and see how Hitler and Mussolini responded. Meanwhile, the United States would proceed "on the assumption that we were at war with the European section of the Axis as well," and its fleet in the Atlantic would act accordingly.[51] Having long advocated American intervention in the European conflict, even as the majority of the public had consistently opposed it, Stimson remained concerned that the moment might pass, leaving the United States fighting in the Pacific but still not legally at war in the Atlantic. After the cabinet meeting wrapped up, he again privately urged Roosevelt to act against Germany "before the indignation of the people was over." The president would only state "that he intended to present the full matter two days later."[52]

Although Secretary of State Hull was content to wait for Hitler to move, he believed the president should at least make the connection with Germany when he went before Congress. Others in the cabinet agreed that this "should be done even at the first presentation tomorrow."[53] Roosevelt held his ground, maintaining that his address would be brief and to the point.[54] He intended to do nothing that would fuel criticism from noninterventionists in Congress; he would not expose the administration to criticism that it had mishandled the negotiations with Japan or that it was exploiting the crisis to bring the United States into the European conflict. Roosevelt's concern was evident in his confession to the cabinet that he "didn't want to tell the Congressional leaders who were waiting to come into his study all the things he had told us." The fact that the president prefaced this last remark by suggesting the attack was designed to "bring about the transfer of American naval vessels from the Atlantic to the Pacific," and he was determined "to avoid this if at all possible," indicated that this was exactly what he feared many in Congress, and probably the country at large, would demand once they knew the full scale of the disaster.[55]

Even if Roosevelt did not plan to mention Germany by name in his speech requesting a declaration of war on Japan, the administration was determined to imprint Nazi responsibility for Pearl Harbor on the American public consciousness. That evening, the director of the Supply Priorities and Allocations Board, Donald Nelson, had been scheduled to give a nationwide radio address. After consulting with the White House, he proceeded with a revised text. "We must keep in mind," Nelson told the country, "that though the attack has been made by the Japanese it is in reality an attack upon us by the Axis powers. . . . We are face to face with an attack directed primarily from Berlin."[56] The New York mayor Fiorello La Guardia, appointed by Roosevelt as director of the Office of Civilian Defense, also broadcast a press conference over WNYC public radio in which he claimed "Nazi thugs and gangsters" were "the masterminds" of the Pearl Harbor attack.[57]

It was now midmorning in Tokyo. At 10:45 the Japanese privy council issued its formal declaration of war against Britain and the United States. This was a full seven hours after the first aircraft had appeared over Pearl Harbor and some time after the news of the attack had become widely known in the country after earlier radio broadcasts. Later that day, the Japanese leadership approved the "Plan for the Prosecution of the War against the United States, Britain, Holland, China." There were to be two stages to the planned operations. The first would involve the elimination of the enemy navies in the western and southwestern Pacific, in particular the US Asiatic Fleet in Manila, the Royal Navy forces in Hong Kong and Singapore, and the occupation forces in much of Southeast Asia. This would lead to the establishment of a defensive perimeter across the middle of the Pacific, running from the Kuril Islands in the north—via Wake Island, the Marshall Islands, and the Gilbert Islands— to the Bismarck Islands in the south. The second phase would involve the consolidation and exploitation of the territory gained to defend against enemy counterattacks.[58] This conception, a Blitzkrieg followed by a war of attrition, was very similar to the one that Hitler had already carried out in Europe.

As soon as the cabinet session wrapped up in Washington at around 9 p.m., ten congressional leaders—a mixture of Democrats and Republicans, interventionists and noninterventionists—joined the group. For the benefit of the newcomers, the president recounted the backstory leading up to Japan's offensive, again reiterating that "the German government was pressing Japan for action under the Tripartite Pact."[59] After Roosevelt's account of that day's brutal assault, Stimson recorded, "the effect on the Congressmen was tremendous. They sat in dead silence."[60] Eventually, one asked whether Japan had also sustained losses. Roosevelt responded that he had no reliable figures, but that he did know that "the principal defense of the whole west coast of this country and the whole west coast of the Americas had been very seriously damaged today."[61] Roosevelt also shared a "rumor" that "two of the planes were seen with swastikas on them." While stating that he could not say "whether that is true or not," he said that he would take it as "news until something more definite comes in."[62] Clearly determined to imprint on his audience the link between the war in the Pacific and that in the Atlantic, the president added: "We have reason to believe that the Germans have told the Japanese that if Japan declares war, they will too."[63] This, as we now know, was absolutely correct.

The congressional leaders' questions now came thick and fast, and focused very much on Japan rather than Germany. As the president explained how the Japanese forces likely avoided detection, a couple of the legislators became "very red and flushed, muttering profanities to express their distaste and their revulsion at the whole episode."[64] One in particular, the Texas Democrat Tom Connally, chairman of the Senate Foreign Relations Committee, finally exploded: "Hell's fire, we didn't do anything!" and slammed his fist on Roosevelt's desk. He then turned on the navy secretary, Knox: "Didn't you say last month that we could lick the Japs in two weeks? Didn't you say that our navy was so well prepared and located that the Japanese couldn't hope to hurt us at all?" Neither Knox nor the president was able to satisfactorily answer Connally as to why the navy "were all asleep" and why they were so utterly unprepared for the attack, despite knowing that "these negotiations were going on."[65] An exasperated Connally exclaimed, "How can we go to war without anything to fight with?"[66]

IN TOKYO, PRIME Minister Tojo now read out the declaration of war on the radio at 11:30 a.m. and finished by citing a famous poem, "Umi Yukaba" ("Across the Sea"). "Across the sea," he intoned, "corpses soaking in the water, across the mountains, corpses heaped upon the grass, we shall die by the side of our lord, we shall never look back." These lines were also the lyrics to a navy song that would be sung often during these heady times. They were rebroadcast, together with the declaration of war, on several occasions throughout the day. One student at a girls' high school in central Japan wrote that she had heard the news before going to school, where she heard it again at morning assembly, which was followed by numerous broadcasts during classes, including the imperial announcement, and then a lunchbreak assembly and visit to a nearby shrine. The excitement continued after she got home. It is little wonder that, as she complained, there was no time to study for her examinations.[67]

As the Japanese public overcame the initial shock of the success at Pearl Harbor, elation set in. After years of interminable struggle with fellow Asian nations, food shortages, and the disappearance of luxury goods from stores, the people of Japan could now celebrate a successful and daring assault against the mighty Anglo-Saxon powers. Where previous celebratory ceremonies had been stage-managed by the government, now Tokyo witnessed a genuine public eruption of joy.

On the streets of Tokyo, crowds spontaneously gathered. As one French journalist observed, they manifested "intense satisfaction," exhibiting "no trace" of "that morning's worried astonishment."[68] Across the country people rushed to pray for victory at local shrines.[69] Some of these expressions of patriotism were officially sponsored, but most seem to have been unprompted, driven by relief that the uncertainty of the past months was over. "At long last," a woman from a provincial port wrote, "the war has started."[70] It is no surprise that there was a surge in demand to repair home radio receivers, which had been damaged by the constant twisting and turning of knobs, as owners strained to get better reception on their crackly sets.[71]

The Japanese population had long groaned under American sanctions, living in fear of further harsh measures. Now they believed, as Foreign Minister Togo recorded, that the days of want were over.[72] People congratulated each other; some made bombastic impromptu speeches on the train.[73] The long war in China was recast as the prelude to an "Asian Mission" to free the continent from white imperialism.[74] This was a sentiment conservatives and progressives alike could rally behind.

This widespread sense of humiliation avenged was admixed with a surge of chauvinist exuberance.[75] "Britain and America should be afraid," one middle school student wrote in his diary. A university student spoke of a "delightful day."[76] After decades of racial humiliation, as the Japanese saw it, the Western powers had finally got their comeuppance. "If

I may say in one word what I felt on that morning," the Japanese writer Tatsuno Yutaka recalled, it would be "serves you right!"[77]

These effusions became known as "the philosophy of December 8," much as similar outpourings by German intellectuals at the start of the First World War were dubbed "the ideas of 1914."[78] The philosophy hinged on the notion that the material advantage of the West would be compensated by the cultural superiority of the samurai. Colonel Masanobu Tsuji, the architect of the attack on Singapore, later recalled that "our candid idea at the time was that the Americans, being merchants, would not continue for long with an unprofitable war, whereas we ourselves if we fought only the Anglo-Saxon nations [i.e., not the Russians as well] could carry on a protracted war."[79]

Many of the ordinary Japanese soldiers who had been in the army for a long time found their future plans dashed by this new war. That morning, Lance Corporal Koji Kawamata of Third Company, First Battalion, 214th Infantry Regiment, Thirty-Third Division was looking forward to his discharge after nearly three years of service. He went to the railway station hoping to apply for a job with the Japanese-run North China Railway Company. "Your discharge is most unlikely," the astonished railway employee told him. "Look at this!" He handed Kawamata a newspaper whose headline announced war with the British Empire and the United States. The shocked lance corporal ran back to his comrades and told them that "discharge is out of the question. It's war with white people!"[80]

If many Japanese saw themselves struggling against the entire white race, the Anglo-Saxons were set aside for particular hostility as the shared racial enemy of all the Axis powers, including the European ones. The well-known poet Takamura Kotaro summed this up in his poem "December 8." "Remember December 8," he wrote, "the day world history changed. The day Anglo-Saxon power was denied across the land and sea of East Asia." Besides lambasting the Anglo-Saxons, Kotaro's poem took aim at the "powerful clan of Anglo-America, monopolists of global wealth," who had battened on the "exploitation" of Asians—a description that tapped into ideologies bearing a striking resemblance to the ideas of

Hitler and his European propagandists.[81] Support for the attack on the British Empire and the United States was perhaps most vividly expressed that day by the poet and novelist Ito Sei, who later went on translate James Joyce's *Ulysses* into Japanese. "Our destiny is such," he wrote, "that we cannot realize our qualifications as first-class people of the world, unless we have fought with the top-ranking white men."[82]

There were some who did not share in the general consensus. One worker at the Mitsubishi aircraft plant in Nagoya was enthused by the skill of the Japanese pilots, but his knowledge of the strength of the American economy gave him pause.[83] In northern Japan, a fifteen-year-old farm boy similarly feared for the future. That day he wrote of his "unease" that the government, which was struggling in the war in China, would have difficulty defeating the British and the Americans as well.[84] "With the China incident still unresolved," a twenty-four-year-old man from Osaka lamented, "Japan must do battle with a strong enemy."[85] "What do they think they are doing," a middle-aged insurance salesman asked, "going to war with America? Don't they know how rich and powerful it is and how strong American industry is? Japan can't hope to defeat a country like that." This sentiment was particularly marked among those who knew the United States firsthand, such as Aiko Takahashi, a Tokyo housewife, who had lived many years in Los Angeles. She remarked simply that going to war with America "was like a child challenging an adult to a fight."[86]

This sense of anxiety found expression in the rush to prepare for the expected Allied air raids. Shops selling helmets and books about air-raid protection saw a lively trade. One young man, who was studying for college entrance, made a beeline for the nearest shop and bought strong rice paper and glue. He then spent the whole morning covering the windows to prevent bomb blasts from shattering the glass and causing serious injury.[87] There was also a marked drop in the number of cinema-goers that day, as ordinary Japanese awaited the Anglo-Saxon response with trepidation.[88]

While the declaration of war was being broadcast, Marquess Kido went to see Hirohito. He was "very much impressed by the self-possessed attitude of the emperor this day."[89] Hirohito's written message to the nation on the declaration of war claimed that he had been forced to act to "secure the stability of East Asia" and to promote the establishment of "world peace." He accused the British Empire and the United States of inciting China against Japan and of seeking to "dominate the Orient." Their alleged provocations and attacks on Japanese trade had been intended to "subjugate" Japan. For all these reasons, the emperor appealed to his subjects to think of their ancestors in the struggle ahead.[90] What this declaration did not contain, remarkably, was any reference to the Axis alliance, or the fact that Japan's war might be part of a larger global conflagration.

Twenty minutes after Kido appeared at the palace, the Twenty-Fourth Japanese Air Flotilla, operating from the Marshall Islands, attacked Wake Island, an important American air base in the central Pacific.[91] Several planes were destroyed on the ground, and the airfield and the Pan American flying-boat installations were damaged. Despite knowing about the attack on Pearl Harbor, the garrison lacked radar and was taken by surprise when the Japanese aircraft appeared out of the dense clouds. Meanwhile, a smallish invasion force of cruisers, destroyers, and transports had sailed from Kwajalein Atoll with a view to capturing the island. They were not expecting serious resistance.[92]

Just as the attack on Wake was beginning, the leading Japanese aeronautical engineer Kiyoshi Tomizuka was finishing a lecture to the Tokyo Municipal Officials' Institute in Sendagaya. Having hurried from home, he had missed news of the outbreak of war. A longtime critic of confrontation with the Anglo-Americans on account of the industrial imbalance, Tomizuka told his audience that "because Japan was poor in resources and scientific technique was lacking, no matter how much we persevered, there would be no victory in a modern war." Perhaps surprisingly, there were no objections to this analysis from the audience. Even more extraordinarily, neither his listeners nor his hosts mentioned that the government had in fact just declared war. Perhaps they considered it bad form to embarrass him, or perhaps they, too, were unaware. Still ignorant of developments, Tomizuka set off for his next appointment, which was a meeting of the central cooperation assembly of the Imperial Rule Assistance Association.[93]

It was still December 7 in Washington. By the time the congressional delegation departed around 11 p.m., some of the tension had dissipated, but questions remained. The leaders had invited the president to address a joint session of Congress at 12:30 p.m. the next day, but Roosevelt could not yet tell them "what he was going to say because the events of the next fourteen hours would be numerous and all important."[94] The president did ask congressman Sol Bloom, a New York Democrat and chairman of the House Foreign Affairs Committee, how soon he could have a war resolution ready to introduce. Bloom was "troubled" by this responsibility and "shrank," as he later recalled, "from exposing the Jews of a future generation to the possible charge that this war had been set in motion by a Jew." He feared "the followers of some unborn Hitler killing and torturing because the name of a Jew had been found on the declaration." Therefore, he worked out a plan with the House parliamentarian to suspend the rules and have a clerk read the resolution instead.[95]

As midnight approached, it remained unclear whether Japan's attack had brought about the national unity that Roosevelt sought. Among the hopeful signs were the fact that the recriminations expressed in the meeting with congressional leaders did not leak to the press, and that Republican House minority leader Joseph W. Martin Jr. told the waiting reporters outside the White House that "there is no politics here. There is only one party when it comes to the integrity and honor of the country." This was echoed by the Republican minority leader on the House Committee on Foreign Affairs, Hamilton Fish, who was not even invited to the briefing that evening because "the President will not have him in the White House." Even so, he told the noninterventionist *Chicago Tribune* that Japan's "unwarranted, brazen and senseless attack . . . forces us into a war in defense of our own possessions."[96]

Others, however, remained unshakably skeptical. Like his Republican colleague Gerald Nye, the North Carolina Democrat Robert R. Reynolds, chair of the influential Senate Military Affairs Committee, publicly affirmed that he was still "100 percent against war" and he wanted "to know all about what has happened" before saying anything further. Above all, the conspiratorially minded Reynolds remained suspicious of Britain, claiming it benefitted most from American intervention in the Pacific and thus had engineered the situation to "get us to protect their $3,000,000,000 investments in China and to relieve forces that can be sent elsewhere to fight."[97] For years, Reynolds and other noninterventionists had railed against British attempts to co-opt the United States in its European war. Now, he suspected it had found a way to achieve that end through more circuitous means, dragging the United States into East Asia so Britain could free up its own forces for the fight against Hitler.

Even if Nye and Reynolds were outliers—a broad congressional consensus was forming around a response to Japan's assault—the idea of war against Germany and Italy was another story. The colossal national effort such a conflict would require, the potentially huge casualties, and the uncertain outcome were objectively intimidating. This continuing divide on any intervention in Europe was brought home to the president during the meeting with congressional leaders by the steadfastly anti-interventionist California Republican Hiram Johnson, a leading member of the Senate Foreign Relations Committee. Johnson maintained that "the worst part of this Japanese War" was that it increased the risk of sliding "very easily into the European war."[98] Indeed, some noninterventionists charged that Roosevelt's meddling in Europe, particularly the defense aid that he had provided to the Allies, had left the United States even more exposed in East Asia. Senator Burton K. Wheeler, a Democrat from Montana, told a journalist that the United States would have its hands full fighting Japan: "Because we have been giving away so much of our equipment [to Britain and the USSR] we haven't got as much as we should have."[99]

Wheeler's views were echoed by the America First Committee's most famous spokesman, Charles Lindbergh, in his journal that day. Lindbergh was at his home on Martha's Vineyard, preparing his address for a large America First rally in Boston on the tenth of December. On hearing news of the Pearl Harbor attack on the radio, Lindbergh had plenty of questions: "How did the Japs get close enough, and where is our Navy?" More hopefully, he wondered, "Is it just a hit-and-run raid of a few planes, exaggerated by radio commentators into a major attack?" But the foremost question in Lindbergh's mind: How much of the US Navy "has been sent to the Atlantic to aid Britain?"[100]

As it became clear that this was indeed "a major attack," Lindbergh spoke on the telephone to the head of the America First Committee, General Robert Wood, who bitterly said of Roosevelt, "Well, he's got us in through the back door."[101] While both agreed that the Boston rally would need to be canceled, the America First Committee was not yet ready to give up hope of barring US entry into the European war. That evening, it issued a statement committing itself to full support of the war effort against Japan but pointedly made no reference to its attitude in connection with the war in Europe. Furthermore, the committee's founder, R. Douglas Stuart Jr., sent a circular to all chapter chairmen stating that "the facts and arguments against intervention in Europe remain the same as they were before the Japanese issue arose" and informing them that the national committee would meet in Chicago that Thursday, December 11, to decide its policy.[102] Clearly, Pearl Harbor had failed to bring about the instantaneous collapse of isolationism.

That night, Canada became the first of the English-speaking nations to declare a state of war with Japan. As part of the Commonwealth war effort, the Canadian Parliament had previously given Prime Minister Mackenzie King and his government the authorization to stand at the side of Britain if it was attacked. Having declared in 1937 that Canadians would "swim the Atlantic" to come to Britain's aid, King now plunged into the Pacific fight.[103] Canada had its own Pacific coast to defend and, of the fourteen thousand men in the Hong Kong garrison, two thousand were Canadians. Like Churchill, King initially felt "immense relief" on hearing news of the Pearl Harbor attack. As yet unaware that the attack on Malaya had begun earlier, the deeply religious King told his cabinet "that Providence had certainly been on our side in that the attack by Japan was upon the U.S. in the first instance." Shortly after the decision was made to ask King George VI to approve a declaration of war, news arrived from London that Britain would not declare war until tomorrow and might even hold off until Congress had acted. While Canada's prime minister recognized it was "a little disconcerting" to move ahead of both London and Washington, he also saw political benefits, both among independence-minded Canadians and Anglophobic Americans, in demonstrating that Canada was acting autonomously of Britain. By 11 p.m. in Ottawa and Washington, the news that Canada had recognized a state of war was being reported across North America.[104]

While this was happening, on the far side of the Atlantic, the inhabitants of Cologne had been kept awake by a British air attack and the resulting intense anti-aircraft fire. The all clear was sounded at 6:15 a.m. local time. As the Swiss consul noted that day, the city authorities were frantically engaged in constructing public shelters, especially in the vicinity of the city's legendary cathedral. Private shelters were also under construction "everywhere."[105] It was not merely the bombing, though, that depressed the people of Cologne. The consul went on to describe how the reduction in food rations and the ubiquitous lack of goods in the shops had caused the "general mood" to be "exceptionally grim." As Christmas approached, he noted the complete lack of children's toys, leather goods, and other presents.[106] All this illustrated not only Britain's capacity to hit deep inside Europe, but also the precarious state of German civilian morale.

Although the hour was late in Washington, a number of Roosevelt's cabinet returned to their offices to continue working into the night. Before leaving the White House, Attorney General Francis Biddle had the president sign a proclamation for immediate detainment of all suspected Japanese citizens and, back at the Justice Department, he prepared "similar proclamations for the Germans and Italians," in case their declarations of war were forthcoming by morning. In the meantime, the Japanese telephones were "plugged," and Biddle noted that "probably the Germans and Italians will follow." He also advised Roosevelt to instruct the FBI director, J. Edgar Hoover, to "take charge of all censorship pending some permanent arrangement."[107] Finally, before heading to bed, the attorney general took a call from the Treasury Department, where officials wanted his input on a proclamation preventing "Japanese aliens" from leaving the country and Americans from trading with Japan "or any ally." The vagueness of this last clause had surprised the Treasury secretary when his staff had presented the draft to him. "Isn't Germany an ally [of Japan]?" Morgenthau enquired. He had to be reminded that it was "not yet officially," and at this time these restrictions would apply to the "Japanese alone."[108]

Morgenthau's more pressing concern revolved around the president's personal security. He had returned to the Treasury via the rear of the White House and was furious to find only three guards there. He fumed to his subordinates that "anybody could take a five ton truck with 20 men and they could take the White House without any trouble." This fear was symptomatic of the unpreparedness that had already cost the country so dearly in the Pacific. For the Treasury secretary, it was "just unexplainable" how Japan had "walked in just as easily as they [the Nazis] did in Norway." He confided to his staff that Roosevelt had not given congressional leaders the "full story," which was "much worse than anybody realizes." The attack had left the United States exposed: "We have always been led to believe that the Navy was our first line of defense and Hawaii was impregnable. I mean that was [what was] sold to us." When the entire account became public, which Morgenthau did not expect to occur for a few days, "it is going to be the most terrific shock this country has ever had."[109] By that time, maybe the situation would be clearer with regard to Germany.

At the War Department, while Stimson was at the White House, officials had continued work on the "necessity for including Germany" in the war declaration. When Stimson returned, though, he informed officials that, until further notice, the United States would remain technically a nonbelligerent in the European conflict, and that the priority for now was to supply the embattled American forces in the Pacific.[110] As a result, and despite the president's earlier commitment not to interrupt aid to those fighting Hitler, that night the US Army suspended the transfer of Lend-Lease aid to Europe. This was an "emergency action" to ensure that the US military's needs were met amid the unfolding crisis in the Pacific. With 180 US cargo vessels then employed in transporting Lend-Lease material to the Allies, the War Department could not afford to forego the ships or matériel aboard until the situation was clearer.[111] Yet it also meant that the government department most committed to US intervention in the European war had cut, at least temporarily, the lifeline on which the Allied war effort depended.

At the White House, journalist Edward R. Murrow was waiting in Harry Hopkins's bedroom in the Lincoln suite until the president was ready to see him. Hopkins had only recently returned to the White House, where he had lived for over a year, after spending the past month in the hospital receiving blood transfusions and nutrients for a mystery illness that had long plagued him.[112] His health remained fragile, and that evening Grace Tully noted that he resembled a "walking cadaver, just skin and bones."[113] The day's events had clearly taken a heavy toll on him. As Hopkins lay in the large bed, Murrow thought he "looked like a tired, broken child" and was murmuring to himself, "Oh God, if only I had more strength."[114] That the man who had done so much to imprint the seriousness of Britain's plight on the president's mind and to ensure the transfer of defense aid as the first Lend-Lease administrator was so severely debilitated just as a new struggle over supplies loomed would no doubt have alarmed Churchill.

Finally, just after midnight, Murrow was shown into the oval study for beer and sandwiches. While the journalist observed that the president was "so calm and steady," the grayness of Roosevelt's face betrayed his real feelings. He pressed Murrow for information about Britain's morale before switching to that day's shocking events. He gave Murrow a candid account of the devastating losses, and as he discussed the destroyed US planes, he suddenly smashed his fist down on the table and exclaimed: "On the ground, by God, on the ground!"

At this point, the two men were joined by Wild Bill Donovan, the intelligence director, whom the president had summoned back to Washington that afternoon from New York, where he had been watching a football game. Clearly still uncertain about the popular response, Roosevelt asked his guests about the likely impact on American public opinion. Both were confident that the country would wholeheartedly support a declaration of war. What the president most wanted to know was how Hitler would respond. Had Japan coordinated its attack with Germany? Donovan had no evidence of this. He suspected Hitler was as surprised as they were.[115] Nor was it clear that the Nazi leader would approve of Tokyo's actions. Two days before, the German chargé d'affaires Thomsen had told Donovan's agent, Malcolm R. Lovell, that it was "not to Germany's advantage to have Japan go to war with the United States," as this risked involving "Germany in formal war with the United States." Thomsen felt "Germany's purpose is just as well served by a state of high tension in the Pacific."[116] Now that a US-Japan war had come, American intelligence offered little certainty as to how Hitler would respond.

In Tokyo too, a nagging sense of unease prevailed about German intentions. Would Hitler keep his word? Nobody could be sure. The Japanese general staff pondered the possibility that the empire would have to fight the Americans alone. They also began to draw up ambitious plans for military cooperation at a global level, and for an air bridge to connect the two poles of the Axis.[117] At around 2 p.m. Tokyo time, Togo received the German and Italian ambassadors, and the main topic of their conversation was the text of the joint agreement that would announce the military alliance of the Axis to the world at large. Admiral Ugaki, for his part, expressed his belief that Germany and Italy would soon declare war on the United States, but clearly he, too, had concerns.[118]

Some members of the Japanese establishment, in fact, were already questioning the entire rationale behind the war. "I knew," the emperor's uncle wrote in his diary that day, "that Japan had taken the first step to ruin and I was disheartened." Prince Konoye, who had resigned in protest against the confrontation, mooched around the Peers Club in despair for the entire day. The political scientist Shigeru Nanbara vented his fears in poetry. "Beyond common sense, beyond any learning," he wrote. "It has happened. Japan at war against the world."[119]

Meanwhile, engineer Kiyoshi Tomizuka had reached Tokyo Hall in the early afternoon, where he was due to attend a meeting of the Imperial Rule Assistance Association. To his astonishment, the building was completely empty. A bystander told him the meeting had been called off. "Really, why?" Tomizuka asked. "We started a war with America and England," his interlocutor replied. "There was a radio broadcast this morning. Didn't you hear it?" Tomizuka was astonished. In that case, he said to himself, "my lecture this morning was inappropriate."[120]

It was still early morning in eastern Europe, where the killing of the Soviet Jews proceeded apace. Friedrich Jeckeln, the supreme SS commander in northern Russia, ordered the extermination of the Riga ghetto, suspended in late November, to be resumed. When his men moved in, they found the inhabitants much less cooperative than they had been a week earlier; everybody now knew what fate awaited them. Some hid, many others refused to come out of their buildings. The distinguished historian Simon Dubnow was shot on the spot. Many of the security forces were drunk, adding to the terror. About nine hundred Jews were murdered that day within the ghetto itself. The rest were marched in columns to the forest of Rumbula outside the city and massacred there in pits previously dug under the eyes of the SS, the police, and the civil authorities. The killing went on all day and until the following morning. Only three Jews are known to have escaped.[121]

One of them was the seamstress Frida Michelson. She threw herself into the snow just before the shooting began and played dead. The other Jews were forced to take off their shoes before the murders, and these were thrown on top of her. Thus hidden, she overheard a macabre conversation between two of the Latvian auxiliary policemen. Over a cigarette, they deemed the killings "a fine performance" that was "very efficiently organised." This was, the Latvians opined, because the Germans "have experience": "Just leave it to the Germans, they are good at it." The talk then turned to hopes of getting their "cut of the booty." "The Germans" they said, "have the first choice," but "there is enough for everybody."[122]

Elsewhere, Europeans awoke to newspaper headlines about Pearl Harbor. Throughout the day, new editions would bring regular updates. The *Hamburger Fremdenblatt*, for example, announced in bold letters that

Japan had "broken the [ring of] encirclement," adding proudly that Singapore, Hong Kong, Hawaii, and the Philippines had been bombarded and Shanghai occupied.[123] Maps showed the advance of Japanese forces. It was, as Goebbels cynically noted, a good moment to bury bad news—worrying reports from North Africa and Russia, for instance.[124]

In the Axis and pro-Axis press, the Japanese attack was interpreted as part of a wider struggle of the have-nots against the Western haves, and of the Japanese and German peoples against the Anglo-Saxons. The German news service reported that the Spanish paper *Arriba* had proclaimed that "the slavery of the rich peoples and the patience of the poor ones have their limits." "The so-called poor peoples," it continued, "have a soul, a courage and a history which count for more than [mere] earthly goods."[125] Jakob Sprenger, the gauleiter and *Reichsstatthalter* of Hesse-Nassau, greeted delegates to the "European Artisans" in Frankfurt am Main by hailing the "common struggle of peoples suppressed by the plutocracies for their right to life and their freedom."[126] Other reports spoke of a "war of the Jews and the plutocrats," which had been launched by the "warmonger Roosevelt."[127] "Dollar Imperialism," it was claimed, "has prevailed over the good sense of broad circles of the North American people."[128] German radio pronounced Europe united against "Roosevelt's Jewish-controlled robber barons." The Spanish daily *Informaciones*, a mouthpiece for the Franco regime, claimed that "Roosevelt and his clique of American millionaire bankers [were out] to attack and destroy the continent [of Europe]."[129]

There was a distinct racial tinge to this rhetoric, which pitted the United States and Britain against much of the rest of the world. Later that day, the German evening press featured articles analyzing the impact of the Japanese moves on the alleged "domination plans of the Anglo-Saxon powers."[130] This language was echoed in confidential documents and exchanges. The German naval leadership, for example, stressed the importance of Asia for the economic interests of the Anglo-Saxons.[131] Likewise, the president of the Italian Armistice Commission with France, Arturo Vacca Maggiolini, referred that day to the Vichy regime's hostility toward the "Anglo-Saxon powers."[132]

The vital question of whether Hitler and Mussolini would respond to the Japanese move by joining the war on the United States was left unanswered. German radio was silent on the topic, but a broadcast from Rome showed the direction of travel. The Japanese attack, it argued, was actually motivated by Tokyo's obligations to the Axis powers under the Tripartite Pact. Although the United States had not "openly declared war on Germany and Italy, it is in reality at war with these two states."[133]

In Russia, news of Pearl Harbor was slowly percolating through to the public. The eminent Moscow scientist Vladimir Ivanovich Vernadsky heard about it that morning over the radio.[134] Poet Vera Inber heard of the attacks in Leningrad.[135] Pavel Luknitskiy, a special war correspondent for the Soviet news agency TASS, got the news from his colleague, Major Filippenkov, at 9 a.m. Japan and the United States were at war. The two men immediately wondered whether "we will also enter the war with Japan now." "After all," Luknitskiy observed, "35 Japanese divisions are concentrated on our borders!"[136]

This was probably the question going through the mind of the Soviet ambassador to Japan, Konstantin Smetanin, who was summoned that morning by the Japanese foreign minister. Somewhat to Smetanin's relief, perhaps, Togo did not greet him with news of a declaration of war on the Soviet Union. Instead, he listed all of Japan's grievances against the Western powers. Most importantly, Togo stressed that "the Japanese side in its turn will observe the Neutrality pact" and that he assumed the Soviet Union would do the same.[137] This reassuring picture was confirmed by the Allied intercepts of Japanese cables, copies of which were made by the Soviet Cambridge Five spy network.[138] These arrived on Stalin and Molotov's desks that day and confirmed that Tokyo had no immediate intention of breaking the neutrality pact.[139] Clearly, their spy Richard Sorge had been right. The Japanese were striking south and east, not west. Stalin could rest easy, as there would be no second front in Mongolia and Siberia.

In Britain, after only a few hours' sleep, Churchill departed Chequers for London to prepare for a cabinet meeting, scheduled for midday, after which he was to address both houses of Parliament on the new situation.

He sent word to the naval commander's office at Invergordon that he wanted to speak to Foreign Secretary Eden at 9:30.[140]

By then, Eden's train had reached Invergordon. Although Eden had caught gastric flu on the journey and was feeling awful, he immediately rang Churchill, now arrived back at Downing Street.[141] On receiving the full story of the attack on Pearl Harbor, Eden felt no need to conceal his relief at the turn of events, even though he was in the presence of the Soviet ambassador, Maisky.[142] The British foreign secretary later claimed that, at that moment, he knew that whatever happened "it was merely a question of time," because while previously "we had believed in the end but never seen the means, now both were clear."[143]

Contrary to these later recollections, however, at the time Eden was not quite so serene. After asking Churchill how he should now proceed, Eden found the prime minister not just buoyant that the United States was engaged in the Pacific but also insistent that he needed to get himself across the Atlantic to meet with Roosevelt as soon as "next Thursday." Eden and his principal diplomatic advisers, Alexander Cadogan and Oliver Harvey, all expressed alarm at this idea. With the American position still uncertain, all three were convinced that Churchill would be "unwanted in America at such a moment." Nor was there anything that Churchill could do in Washington until the overall situation became clearer. Eden and his advisers agreed that if the prime minister and foreign secretary were both absent at the same time, then this would disturb the British public, who would think "quite rightly that they are mad."[144]

For this reason, Eden rang US ambassador Winant, who had not appreciated that Churchill intended to depart for North America so soon. Winant shared Eden's fears about the trip while events remained so unsettled and agreed to try to dissuade Churchill. Both also concurred that under no circumstances should Eden postpone his visit to Stalin in order to accommodate Churchill's visit to Roosevelt, as this would only confirm the Soviet dictator's "worst suspicions."[145] Eden also called the deputy prime minister, Clement Attlee, who was completely unaware of Churchill's planned trip, and encouraged him to rally the cabinet against the idea.

While Eden was confident that the cabinet, or if necessary the king, would prevent Churchill from leaving for Washington, he decided to make another personal attempt to dissuade the prime minister. Yet Churchill would hear nothing of Eden's fears, declaring that "the emphasis of the war had shifted" and that, as "what now mattered was the intentions of our two great allies," they should each go to them. The prime minister told Eden that his trip to Moscow was now "even more necessary" than before and to embark on his journey.[146]

Eden's advisers remained concerned about Churchill's prospective trip, however. Harvey lamented in his diary that the "PM is a lunatic" who "gets in such a state of excitement that the wildest schemes seem reasonable." While he and Cadogan hoped that Churchill could be talked out of it, they agreed that the members of cabinet were a "poor lot for stopping anything."[147] Eden's delegation to Stalin departed on destroyers for Scapa Flow at 11:30 a.m., where they would join their ship, but the British officials resolved to make one final call to Churchill before heading east.

In rural China, the Kempeitai, the feared Japanese military police, began rounding up foreigners, just as they were doing in the international settlements in Shanghai.[148] After years of special treatment, Europeans and Americans were now placed on the same level as the Chinese. In Asia, war was already proving a great leveler.

If the Axis and friendly neutral press welcomed the news from the Far East, the Italian foreign minister was, as he put it, "not so sure about the advantage." He met with King Victor Emmanuel III of Italy in the morning, who was supposedly pleased at the turn of events. "One thing is now certain," Ciano warned his monarch, "America will enter the conflict, and the conflict itself will last long enough to allow all her potential strength to come into play." After some discussion, the king, who was in fact far from eager to take on the United States, said that "in the long run," the foreign minister "might be right." Ciano found Mussolini "also happy." He had been in favor of "clarifying" the position between America and the Axis powers.[149] The Duce was, after all, already committed to bringing Italy into the war against the United States. Perhaps he was buoyed by the news from North Africa, which was a bit better than it had been for some time, or so it was believed. Mussolini thought that "the gloom of the last forty-eight hours" had passed. His naval leadership was planning a major operation against the British naval presence in the Mediterranean. "All the ships and all the admirals at sea," Ciano noted. "May God help us!"[150]

Some of the king and Ciano's skepticism about the value of the Japanese attack on Pearl Harbor for the Axis was shared by the head of the German Foreign Office, Ernst von Weizsäcker. That morning, he was still wrestling with its implications. When all the "plusses and minuses" were taken into account, Weizsäcker thought that there was still a plus left over."[151] It is against the background of this grudging assessment that his subsequent uneasiness about Hitler's declaration of war on the United States needs to be understood.

On the eastern front, the day opened with the German evacuation of Tikhvin in the north, which appeared to be proceeding smoothly. At 10:15 that morning, the commander of Army Group North, Field Marshal Ritter von Leeb, spoke with the commander of the Eighteenth Army, who explained with some "vigor" that he could not carry out any further attacks.[152] There were no reserves, and the men were exhausted. Further south, the Red Army smashed through Army Group Center positions near Moscow and cut the Klin-Kalinin road. In places, the German withdrawal became a rout, with hasty retreats to escape encirclement and the abandonment of large quantities of heavy equipment. The commander of the Second Army, General Rudolf Schmidt, reported to the commander of Army Group Center, Fedor von Bock, that he planned to begin that evening with the destruction of all militarily significant installations at Jelez, and that he would commence withdrawal to a "winter position." He warned, though, that he would need another two or three divisions to hold that line against a major enemy attack.[153]

In Japan, the day was already drawing to a close. It had been dominated by the dramatic news of Pearl Harbor. That evening, cinema and theater performances were interrupted by rebroadcasts of the announcement from General Tojo.[154]

At 1 p.m. in Berlin, Ambassador Oshima called on Ribbentrop to convey the Japanese government's demand that Germany and Italy immediately declare war on the United States.[155] The two men spent much of the afternoon working on the draft text of an Axis "no separate peace" agreement.[156] Ribbentrop also met with the Italian ambassador, Dino Alfieri, an old Fascist, and told him that he would clarify Germany's position later that day or the next. The German foreign minister asked Alfieri to be granted "plenipotentiary" powers to agree upon a common statement.[157]

At the same time, the two Axis powers were trying to coordinate their policy on India, which was given fresh urgency by Pearl Harbor and the looming war with the United States. That day, Mohamed Shedai, the Italian government's principal interlocutor on Indian affairs, flew to Berlin from Rome to attend a conference that was called immediately after the attacks. Representatives from the Italian embassy sat with him on one side of the table, while Indian nationalist Subhas Chandra Bose and men from the German Special India Bureau, the intelligence services, and the German high command sat on the other. Both Bose and Shedai called for an immediate Italian-German and Japanese declaration on India, while Berlin stalled on the grounds that it was not yet warranted by the military situation.[158]

About half an hour later, Churchill convened the war cabinet in Downing Street, with all the principal ministers other than Eden present, as well as the military leadership. He informed the group that, after receiving news of the air attacks on Hawaii and Singapore and the attempted landing at Kota Bharu, he had telephoned President Roosevelt, who had asked Britain to hold off on its declaration of war until he had addressed Congress. However, having received news in the early hours of the morning that Japan—through its high command rather than its government—had issued its formal declaration of war on the United States and Great Britain, Churchill had arranged to address the houses of Parliament at 3 p.m. The cabinet authorized the declaration of war against Japan and a letter was dispatched to the Japanese chargé d'affaires. Churchill later noted that some people resented the "ceremonial style" of the letter, which concluded, "I have the honour to be, with high consideration, Sir, your obedient servant." But he was adamant that "after all when you have to kill a man it costs nothing to be polite."[159]

Next on the cabinet's agenda was the most urgent question: What did a US-Japan war mean for US relations with the other Axis powers? For his own part, Churchill claimed to have believed for some time that if Japan went to war with the United States then it would do so "as part of an arrangement whereby Germany and Italy would at the same time declare war" on Washington and that they should expect this development in the near future.[160] He also revealed his intention to "start this week for America to see Roosevelt to ensure that American help to this country does not dry up" and received the cabinet's approval.[161]

After reading a draft of his speech and agreeing to make a short radio broadcast to the country that evening, Churchill moved on to the question of Ireland. While discussing the message he had delivered to Irish prime minister de Valera during the night—that now was the time for the Free State to enter the war on the Allied side, and that he would meet de Valera whenever he was available—a telegram arrived from the high commissioner in Dublin. Sir John Maffey reported that neither de Valera "nor anybody else would have a mandate for entering the war on a deal over partition." Churchill now wrote in an internal communication that he had "certainly contemplated no deal over partition." "That," he claimed, "could only come by consent arising out of war comradeship between North and South."[162] Churchill's suggestion was not in itself completely ridiculous—there are examples in history of unity coming about in that way—but it was not to be.

Of more pressing concern, the chiefs of staff informed the cabinet that, despite the fact that sinkings were down overall in the second half of the year, the U-boats were continuing to wreak havoc. Twenty-four thousand metric tons of merchant shipping had been sunk during the past week, and losses from mines were "heavier than usual." This would only exacerbate the already acute shipping crisis. More positively, in the desert, very few of Rommel's forces remained in the region between

Tobruk, Libya, and the Egyptian frontier, as they continued to withdraw westward. Over the past week, the RAF had also destroyed a confirmed sixty-six enemy aircraft in Libya, as well as probably forty-one more, and damaged seventy, while losing thirty-three of its own and an additional five damaged. Nevertheless, as Churchill informed the group, Britain had few additional forces to spare for when battle recommenced, particularly given the new war in the Pacific, while aircraft and tanks suitable for the desert terrain remained at a premium.[163] "The position on the Russian front was satisfactory," however, with the chiefs reporting that German pincer movements against Moscow were gaining little ground.[164]

Indeed, that afternoon the situation would worsen further for Hitler on the eastern front. A crisis erupted in Russia in Army Group Center, where Soviet cavalry breached the lines of General Schmidt's widely stretched Second Army and headed toward Liwny, a town between Orel and Voronezh in southwestern Russia. A motorized SS brigade, which had been told by Hitler to move south, was diverted to support the hard-pressed defenders, but its arrival was not expected for several days. General Guderian's Second Panzer Army was also under pressure. His left wing began to fall back. General Reinhardt's Panzer Group Three buckled, too, as the Red Army broke through the center of his front and reached the railway between Klin and Kalinin. Everybody was thrown into the fight: headquarters staff, mechanics, construction units, and anti-aircraft formations—whatever was to hand. The roads were iced over and congested. Bock planned to fly some five hundred machine gunners to Klin to plug the gaps.[165] In Panzer Group Four, Gotthard Heinrici's corps was assailed by the Soviet Fiftieth Army at the joint between the Thirty-First and 296th Infantry Divisions.[166] Along much of the northern and southern fronts, the German line was crumbling.

Learning of these developments at his compound in Rastenburg, Hitler was more angry than anxious. He endorsed the withdrawal from Tikhvin, albeit without grace.[167] "There is helplessness everywhere," one witness in the headquarters observed. "Scapegoats are being sought for the stalled advance on Moscow." The chief of the operations staff of the OKW, Alfred Jodl, argued strongly that the exposed tank spearheads needed to be withdrawn. Rejecting this analysis, the Führer expounded at length that the supposed Russian reinforcements were just "bluff." The reports from the generals, Hitler claimed, were "exaggerated" and "deliberately negative." It would not be the first time, he thundered, that the Germans lost their nerve in the hour of destiny. He himself, the Führer made clear, did not want to hear the word "withdrawal." Despite these pressures, Hitler took time out to demand that no damage be done to the estate of the writer Leo Tolstoy, on which Guderian had his command post and which Hitler considered a "national treasure" of the Russians. The great writer's tomb and manor house, he decreed, should be left untouched.[168]

It was perhaps no coincidence that it was on this day that Gustav Hilger, one of Hitler's "eastern experts," penned a gloomy memorandum entitled "How Can and Will the Soviet Union Continue the War in the Year 1942?" Its premise was heretical, as until recently Russia was supposed to have been crushed before Christmas. Hilger, who had lost his son on the central front just over a week earlier, saw no chance of a popular uprising against Stalin and stated that so long as he was in charge there would be neither a Soviet capitulation nor a separate peace. The Russians, Hilger predicted, would trade space for time and evacuate more key industries behind the Volga and even the Urals. Drawing on Stalin's speech from the previous month, Hilger noted that the Soviet dictator rested his case for ultimate victory on the "invincible world coalition [of] the United States, Great Britain, and the Soviet Union." He hardly needed to add that their joint combined productive capacity far exceeded that of the German Reich. Stalin had characterized the war in his last speech as a war of "engines," Hilger continued, ramming the point home, "which will be won by those who dispose of the most engines."[169]

Hitler knew all this perfectly well. Indeed, it was precisely the reason he welcomed the Japanese entry into the conflict, which would divert the attention and efforts of the world's greatest producer of engines, the United States. "We cannot lose the war," he remarked that day to Ribbentrop's liaison officer Walter Hewel. "We now have an ally who has not been beaten in 3,000 years and always stood on the right side."[170] This was, of course, a poorly concealed dig at the Italians, whose pathetic performance so far threatened to allow the British into Europe via the Mediterranean back door.

Hitler reacted to the new situation with a multipronged strategy. First, he now formally accepted that the war in Russia would not end that year. The Führer issued directive 39, which was prefaced by the claim that the "surprisingly early" severe winter weather, and the "consequent difficulties of bringing up supplies, compel us to abandon completely all major offensive operations and to go over to the defensive."[171] This would "establish conditions suitable for the resumption of large-scale offensive operations in 1942." By this stage, of course, the Wehrmacht had been on the defensive for several days. Hitler's directive should therefore primarily be understood as a reaction not to the worsening situation on the eastern front, which he had not yet fully registered, but to the changing global strategic picture.

The directive also demonstrated Hitler's four immediate priorities. His focus was no longer Moscow and the central front, but the northern and, especially, the southern sector. First, he wanted the capture or destruction of Leningrad to be "finally" completed. Hitler also demanded that Army Group South should, "in spite of all difficulties," try to capture the lower Don-Donets river line during the winter. This would provide a springboard for operations against the Caucasus in the spring. To these ends, aircraft could be withdrawn from Moscow, and Hitler authorized the transfer of forces from west to the east, but only as a "purely temporary measure during the winter." Clearly, he was expecting trouble from the west quite soon. Indeed, the Führer insisted that the forces in France be strong enough to carry out the occupation of Vichy should that prove necessary, evidence that Prime Minister Darlan's maneuvers had not gone unnoticed.

Second, the Führer decided to let the German Navy off the leash against American shipping in the Atlantic and Caribbean. The Kriegsmarine had long been operating under severe restrictions, for fear of giving Roosevelt a pretext to declare war on the Reich. Now it could prepare to defend itself against US destroyers and launch an all-out attack on American merchant shipping. That day, the German Navy instructed that all American ships were to be attacked without warning and that no account was to be taken of the "pan-American security zone."[172] The Kriegsmarine was already exchanging intelligence with the Japanese, but there was—as was pointed out that day—a limit to actual military cooperation due to a shortage of transport capacity; the distances were simply too large.[173]

Third, Hitler made preparations that indicated he was resigned to a long war. It was now to be expected that the hundreds of thousands of foreign workers in German factories, and the millions of foreign prisoners of war, would be in the Reich for some time. Foreign laborers were in fact already part of the cityscape of many larger German cities. To Hitler, their presence conjured up the danger of the "contamination" of the German population. Presumably acting on his Führer's behalf, Martin Bormann warned the party chancellery that day that these "partly racially foreign workers" represented a "danger" to the "racial health and spiritual strength of our people." He lamented the general lack of consciousness of this in the population at large, and called upon the party to inform them of the "necessity of the maintenance of the purity of German blood and German honor" and the "safeguarding of the biological growth of our people."[174]

The imminence of war with the United States also had important implications for naval armaments. It had not escaped the German naval high command that the document leaked in the *Chicago Tribune* the previous week was based on the assumption that the United States had the industrial capacity to carry on the struggle against Germany even after the defeat of the British Empire and the Soviet Union.[175] That day, the leadership of the Kriegsmarine was informed that Hitler had called for the conservation of nonferrous metals "in consequence of the unavoidable lengthening of the war." In particular, the Führer accepted Admiral Erich Raeder's suggestion that construction should be resumed on the aircraft carrier *Graf Zeppelin*. The Luftwaffe should help out with modified planes until suitable bespoke carrier aircraft were developed, which was not expected before 1944.[176] Clearly, the war with the United States was expected to last at least until then. The obvious futility of relying on the belated completion of a single aircraft carrier to defeat or repel the United States was not remarked upon by any of the protagonists.

Fourth and finally, Hitler began to craft a rhetorical strategy in hopes of flanking the impending outbreak of open war with the United States. During the afternoon—while Ribbentrop, Oshima, and Alfieri wrestled with the text of the Axis agreement in Berlin—Hitler was in a conclave at the Wolf's Lair.[177] He decided that the Reichstag was to be summoned to meet on December 10. There, the Nazi elite and the German people would hear why Hitler had decided to plunge them into an even larger and longer conflagration by taking on the greatest power the world had ever seen.

Key to German thinking remained the calculus around Lend-Lease. "The USA will hardly be in a position," Goebbels crowed that day, "to send significant amounts of material to England, let alone the Soviet Union." He mused, "They will need it themselves in the next weeks and months. . . . The British seem to see that very clearly."[178]

The new situation also had implications for the Nazi war against the Jews. Since the end of the previous month, well before Pearl Harbor, the head of the Section for Jewish Affairs at the Foreign Office, Franz Rademacher, had been preparing his submission in support of the meeting planned for noon the next day in Wannsee to discuss the logistical aspects of the deportation of the Jews to the east. Now, on December 8, the day before the planned conference, he presented his memorandum on "Wishes and Ideas of the Foreign Office with Respect to the Envisaged General Solution of the Jewish Question in Europe" to State Secretary Hans Luther, one of the invitees.[179] Rademacher called for the "deportation" of all German, Croatian, Romanian, Serbian, and Slovak Jews in the Reich "to the east." He also demanded that the friendly governments in Bulgaria, Croatia, Hungary, Romania, and Slovakia deport the Jews living in those states, and that the Bulgarian and Hungarian regimes be put under pressure to introduce anti-Semitic legislation along the lines of the Nuremberg laws.

That same day, Rademacher received a call from Felix Benzler, the imperial plenipotentiary of the Foreign Office to the military commander in Serbia. His main task was the economic exploitation of Serbia and the struggle against "anti-German" elements there. In this connection, he was closely involved in the destruction of Serbian Jews, many of whom had already been murdered as supposed Communist partisans or Allied agents, primarily by the Wehrmacht.[180] Now Benzler was anxious to ensure the deportation of the survivors and asked his interlocutor to ensure that "the Jews were taken to the east as soon as possible."[181] There was thus, from the point of view of Rademacher, and indeed of the entire anti-Semitic apparatus, a newfound urgency about solving the "Jewish problem."

In the course of the day, however, chief of the RSHA Reinhard Heydrich postponed the planned meeting at Wannsee. The reason for this "last minute" delay, he explained, was "because of suddenly announced events" and the resulting "demands on [the attendance of] some of the invited gentlemen"—in other words, the consequences of the attack on Pearl Harbor.[182] The event to which Heydrich was giving way was none other than the session of the Reichstag at which Hitler planned to declare war on the United States. Several attendees of the planned meeting were also members of parliament, such as Dr. Alfred Meyer, the state secretary at the Reich Ministry for the Occupied Eastern Territories, and Heydrich himself.[183] Obviously, the Führer's Reichstag appearance took precedence over the Wannsee conference. The meeting was now rescheduled for January 20, 1942, the date under which it has gone down in history.

All Jews in occupied Europe were now in mortal danger, but they were still experiencing a range of possible fates, depending on whether they were in eastern or central and western Europe. As we have seen, the shootings in the Soviet Union continued. That same day, the first Jews were gassed to death at the Chelmno camp in Poland.[184] This did not mark a shift in policy, for these murders had been decided on sometime earlier, but it was a change in the usual method from shooting. By January 1945, more than 153,000 Jews would be murdered there.

By contrast, most Jews in central and western Europe, who served as Hitler's hostages to deter Roosevelt, were still alive. Many of those who had already been deported to the east were still in contact with friends and relatives in the west. Indeed, that day, the secretary of the Cologne section of the Imperial Association of Jews wrote to the Jewish Religious Association of Luxemburg that, while it was forbidden to send cash or food by mail to the Litzmannstadt ghetto, postal orders were permitted.[185] He would have been well aware, of course, that there had been a "transport" of Cologne Jews en route to the east since the day before.

The fate of the deported Jews was no secret in Cologne. The Swiss consul wrote that day that he heard from several sources of the terrible conditions in the ghettos of the east. Adults and children were dying "literally like flies" from hunger and disease. Corpses were hastily wrapped in paper and left by the side of the road, where they were picked up the next day by the rubbish collection. As yet, though, there were no reports of deportees being murdered en masse—though rumors of the Einsatzgruppen killings in the Soviet Union had been circulating since the autumn—and the idea that the German Jews would simply be annihilated had not yet entered the consul's mind.[186]

To be sure, conditions for these Jews remained horrifying. On this same day, the Jewish car mechanic and former socialist activist Berthold Rudner, who had been deported from Berlin in November 1941, described his latest experiences in the Minsk ghetto in his diary. The local Jews had already been murdered to make way for the German arrivals. He spoke of the threats of being "shot in the back of the neck" from the guards, the beatings administered, and the "wheezing" of the sick at night. Rudner noted the large number of Austrians among the guards, with whom he conversed in dialect. There was, he added wistfully in English, "no place like home."[187] Still, the deported German Jews, unlike the Soviet ones, had not yet been systematically targeted for extermination. Their future was still unclear.

The Nazis saw "world Jewry" as the directing mind behind partisan activity in occupied Europe, but in fact the mounting resistance the Nazis faced was driven by a combination of local factors and British subversion. There was a spate of attacks on German personnel in Paris, which led to the imposition of a curfew on that day from 6 p.m.[188] That day, too, the representative of the German Foreign Office at the office of the Reichsprotektor in Prague reported that, although tribunals in that city and in Brünn (Brno) were continuing to sentence and execute "pests," the "civil state of emergency" had recently been lifted in several districts thanks to the "continuing pacification of the Protectorate."[189] The picture was perhaps not quite as rosy as described, because that same day the RSHA reported that in Kladno, one of the districts in which the state of emergency had been lifted, unknown figures had thrown a stone wrapped in a threatening message through the windows of the local administration. "We will show you what we are capable of," the letter warned. "We will give you no rest."[190]

In the far north of occupied Europe, the SD in Oslo reported the sentencing of five men to death for alleged espionage and support of an enemy power. Another was sentenced for espionage and partisan activities, four were to die just on account of alleged espionage, and one man was marked for execution on account of having maintained a secret store of weapons. Many others were given lesser sentences for complicity, for the possession of firearms, and for having listened to enemy broadcasts on illegally held radio sets. Another dozen or so arrests were reported. Despite these measures, Norway remained restive. There were reports of a list in a Narvik cinema with the names of fifteen women, four of them married, condemned as "German whores" who associated with German troops. Three men were taken into custody for spitting at a pro-German girl in their workplace.[191]

Most of the partisan activity was centered in the eastern front, and it was there that the German "countermeasures" were the most brutal. That day, the SD reported suspected poisoning of the civilian population by the "Bolsheviks" as well as the usual partisan attacks on German forces. Nazi retaliation, which was directed as much against the "Jewish enemy" in general as against actual partisan operatives, was staggering in scale. The resulting report spoke of shootings of "Jews and partisans," and stated that Sonderkommando 4a had executed 57,243 people by the start of November. The report described the Ukrainian-nationalist Bandera rebels, whom they perceived as "clearly opposed to the Reich," and stated that they "did not believe in a victory of Germany over the Soviet Union and Britain."[192] For all the killing, there was a palpable sense on the eastern front that German authority hung in the balance.

IN WASHINGTON, THE president woke at 7:30 a.m. and spent the morning finalizing his speech with the aid of Hopkins. As further news of Japan's onslaught against American and British territories across Southeast Asia filtered in, Roosevelt continued to update his draft text.[193] At the War Department, American officials confronted a stark new reality. Japan's lightning offensive left the United States exposed, still three months away from completing its rearmament program. Now it faced having to fight a two-front war. Consequently, a priority for the War and Navy Departments' beleaguered officials that morning was to change the supply priorities put in place before Pearl Harbor, when the emphasis had been on providing the tools for the Allied forces to wage war against the Axis. With the Japanese dominating the Pacific and US outposts across the ocean at their mercy, the army and navy were determined to get hold of as many aircraft, tanks, and ships and as much ammunition as possible. In the weeks before Pearl Harbor, these officials had grown increasingly frustrated with the bureaucratic inefficiencies that characterized the Lend-Lease program.[194] With the onset of war, they moved to bring Lend-Lease allocation under their control, streamlining the process but, more importantly, ensuring that they could retain any Lend-Lease material "for their own use at their discretion" and allowing them "at the last moment or at any time during production to retain articles finally needed for the defence of the United States."[195]

That morning, the Lend-Lease administrator Edward Stettinius was told by the director of defense aid at the War Department, Colonel

Henry Aurand, that "we are suspending for the time being all defense aid transfers." When Stettinius protested, he was told bluntly: "We are suspending the whole works. We have got to sort the thing out. Some of them we can use desperately."[196] Just hours before the Pearl Harbor attack, Stettinius had finally received assurances that sufficient ships had been allocated for the United States to make up its Lend-Lease shortfalls by the end of the month.[197] But the Japanese assault had immediately rendered that null and void. With the United States now at war itself, Stettinius had little choice but to acquiesce to the War Department's embargo. Still, he remained wary and asked his subordinates to "work out some procedure by which we get reimbursed in kind, if the circumstances permit."[198] Yet with the Soviets and British desperately in need of supplies, any recompense risked coming too late. As a result, Stettinius urged Harry Hopkins to encourage the president to "say something about the continuance of Lend-Lease aid." Stettinius recommended that he say: "We will get our equipment to the places and people where it can do the best job in licking the aggressors."[199] As well as an important propaganda tool to demoralize the Germans and boost the Allies, Stettinius regarded this as a critical intervention in his bureaucratic battle with the army and navy to prevent them hoovering up any material destined for Europe and the Middle East.

US war secretary Henry Stimson awoke shortly before 9 a.m. to a barrage of "very bad news" from the Pacific. The Japanese were attacking the Philippines and, although General Douglas MacArthur's forces were manfully defending the archipelago, Stimson was aware that they were rapidly losing aircraft. The destruction of the fleet at Pearl Harbor meant that Japan controlled the sea lanes, leaving little chance of resupplying MacArthur "in time to save the islands." Stimson was nevertheless determined to get "everything started going that we could" and, at the same time, to ensure that Hawaii was adequately defended against the expected Japanese naval assault. As a result, his first priority on arrival at the War Department that morning was to call the British air marshal, Sir Arthur Harris, into his office to request that Britain release as many of the American-built four-engine B-24 long-range heavy bombers as it could back to the United States as quickly as possible.[200]

Harris had been dispatched to Washington in July 1941 as part of a purchasing mission to secure American aircraft for the RAF. Over the following five months, he regularly complained to London that the Americans were engaging in a "plain double cross" by scaling back the number of aircraft that they had initially agreed to supply to Britain in the aftermath of the Lend-Lease Act. While Harris appreciated that Roosevelt and Harry Hopkins "leant over backwards to help us . . . within the limitations," his private assessment of the Americans was scathing.[201] He regarded them as "a people so arrogant as to their own ability and infallibility as to be comparable only to the Jews and the Roman Catholics," and he resented their "conviction of their own superiority and super efficiency—and of our mental, physical and moral decrepitude."[202] Harris bemoaned that British officials had been "living in a fool's paradise where expectations of quality and quantity in American production and releases are concerned." He had become convinced that "these people are not going to fight. . . . They have nothing to fight with," and, as he reported back to a colleague at the Air Ministry, "if they come in under any other circumstances, short of being kicked in, I'll stand you a dinner and eat, as my share, a pink elephant, trunk, tail and toenails—and raw at that."[203]

In the wake of the news about Pearl Harbor the previous day, Harris found the US War Department panic-stricken. The assistant secretary for the air, Robert Lovett, with whom Harris was on good terms, confided with horror that the Japanese assault had devastated the whole Pacific Fleet. Harris later noted that the department was "dazed and Stimson himself hardly able to speak." What they did get across to Harris, however, was that the United States found itself in a "very serious position" and, as a result, had "put a total embargo on the export of munitions to the allies." Moreover, the United States needed 250 aircraft, previously provided to the RAF, back immediately in order to defend Hawaii. This would "nullify" all the efforts that Harris and the RAF delegation had made in Washington. The "serious" impact was particularly calamitous for the bomber forces. Britain was currently "sending large quantities of aircraft to Russia, the situation in the Middle East required every possible aircraft that could be sent to give support to the army whose plans were based on American deliveries," and Britain now faced "an entirely new and vast sphere of operations in the Far East."[204] A shocked Harris urgently telegrammed the chief of the air staff Charles Portal requesting instructions as to what to "save from the wreck if wreck is unavoidable."[205]

In London, although Parliament had been summoned on short notice, the chamber and the gallery were packed. Shortly before 3 p.m., Churchill, accompanied by his wife Clementine and adviser George Harvie-Watt, pushed his way through the crowd into the chamber. The backbench member of Parliament Harold Nicolson noted that "Winston [entered] the Chamber with bowed shoulders and expression of grim determination on his face." As the members had expected "jubilation at the entry of America into the war," Nicolson noted that his colleagues were a "trifle disconcerted." Churchill declared war on Japan in what Nicolson described as a "dull matter-of-fact speech." He outlined the events of the last twenty-four hours and emphasized that, in declaring war, he was living up to the spirit of his commitment "that should the United States be involved in war with Japan, a British declaration of war would follow," even if the attack on Britain's territories meant it was necessary to preempt the US Congress. Churchill also publicly reiterated his private statement to Chiang Kai-shek that China and the English-speaking powers now faced a common foe and would wage war in concert. Furthermore, he announced that Britain would fight alongside the forces of the Dutch government-in-exile in the East Indies, which that morning had also declared war on Japan in solidarity with Britain and the United States, even though Tokyo had not yet attacked the Dutch territories.

Churchill's most significant rhetorical flourish was to tie Japan's actions to those of Nazi Germany. "When we think of the insane ambition and insatiable appetite which have caused this vast and melancholy extension of the war," he said, "we can only feel that Hitler's madness has infected the Japanese mind, and that the root of the evil and its branch must be extirpated." Aware that his words would also be relayed to the United States, this appeal for treating the Axis powers as one was as much for American ears as for his immediate audience.

Churchill urged the members not to underestimate the "gravity of the new dangers we have to meet" and to appreciate that "the ordeal to which the English-speaking world and our heroic Russian Allies are being exposed will certainly be hard, especially at the outset, and will probably be long."[206] While he concluded his speech on a hopeful note that "in the future there will be a light which shines over all the land and sea," parliamentarians were nevertheless left with a deep sense of uncertainty. As the Conservative member Sir Henry "Chips" Channon observed, "Nobody seems to know whether this recent and dramatic development is helpful to the Allied cause or not."[207]

Later that evening, Channon confided to his diary that the Japanese attacks brought "immense complications," and he could only say that it "will probably bring about America's immediate entry into the war" (against Hitler). Just a few hours earlier, on hearing the news of Pearl Harbor, Channon had written that "America's participation of course ensures final victory for the Allies." He no longer seemed so sure.[208]

In Washington, the German embassy noted the continuing deterioration of relations with the United States. Two days earlier, beginning on the Saturday before Pearl Harbor, the American censors had stopped letting through telegrams of the Deutsches Nachrichtenbüro (DNB) and the German press correspondents. The telephone connection with Berlin was also interrupted. Embassy telegrams had been held up for twenty-four hours, though recently released. At 10:29 a.m. local time, chargé d'affaires Hans Thomsen cabled Berlin demanding "appropriate countermeasures" against American news agencies and correspondents in Berlin until the situation in Washington had been clarified.[209]

Although Eden was due to telephone Churchill from Scapa Flow on his way to Russia, his health had worsened on the journey. So Cadogan put him to bed and contacted Churchill himself at 5 p.m. As he had expected, the cabinet had failed to dissuade Churchill from his plan to visit Washington. When Cadogan explained that Eden was "distressed" at the idea of both the prime minister and foreign secretary being away at the same time, Churchill responded, "That's all right, that'll work very well: I shall have Anthony where I want him!" Cadogan took this to mean that Churchill was now determined to coordinate strategy in close concert with the leaders of Britain's two powerful cobelligerents. Cadogan scribbled in his diary, "Does this mean that we shall have to stay indefinitely in Moscow, to conduct 3-cornered conversations?"[210] Still concerned that Churchill's trip across the Atlantic was a mistake but at least relieved that it had not prevented their visit to Moscow—even if they were uncertain how long they would be detained there—Cadogan and the Foreign Office party sailed from Scapa Flow at 6 p.m. on the HMS *Kent*.

Around the same time, in western Iceland, convoy PQ6 for Archangel was ready to depart. "Cheers we're off," a gunner on the *Empire Mavis* wrote in his diary. "Off to Russia and a warm time." It is unclear whether he was referring to the warmth of the Russian welcome in Archangel or the heat of the likely reception by the Luftwaffe and the Kriegsmarine. As the convoy left port, the gunner "watched the lights disappear" and noted that it was "a pitch black night."[211] That was what the Admiralty wanted, because the darkness would hide the convoy not only from the prying eyes of possible spies onshore but also from those of U-boat wolf packs, long-range Condor reconnaissance bombers, and German surface raiders. Their goal was to intercept convoys like PQ6 and to send as much of their lethal cargo to the bottom as possible, thus stopping them from reaching the eastern front where the matériel would be used against the Wehrmacht. In the German capital, Axis diplomats had no idea, of course, about PQ6, but they were well aware of the pressure Lend-Lease was putting on their forces in Russia and North Africa. This made it even more imperative to prepare for the breach with the United States. At 6 p.m., Ribbentrop, assisted by a German Foreign Office adviser, and Oshima, assisted by two of his embassy staff, sat down in Berlin to thrash out the text of the joint agreement.[212] It would take them nearly two hours.

Across the Atlantic, just before noon on a warm sunny day in Washington, motor cars began lining up outside the southern entrance of the

White House. The time had come for Roosevelt to make his way to the Capitol to address the nation. As the procession swept down Constitution Avenue, escorted by motorcycles, and toward the Capitol building, Huybertie Hamlin observed that "crowds stood everywhere—for the most part rather silent as if they understood how serious the situation was."[213] The president rode to the Capitol in an open, semi-armored 1938 V16 Cadillac. Soldiers lined the route, and the secret service team, anxious about an assassination attempt, was "draped" over the car to protect him. Outside the Capitol, security had also been stepped up. Bayonet-wielding marines patrolled the premises and everyone, even members of Congress, was now required to present a pass before going into the building.

Upon Roosevelt's entrance into the House of Representatives chamber, supported by his son James, a joint session of Congress gave him a standing ovation. Across the nation, people waited by their radios in rapt attention.[214] At 12:30, a grave-faced president, stiffened by his steel braces, grasped the podium and began his twenty-five-sentence address. Focusing on Japan's "surprise offensive throughout the Pacific area" on December 7—"a date that will live in infamy"—Roosevelt let "the facts of yesterday speak for themselves."[215]

Halfway through the speech, a "queer crackling noise" broke the tense silence in the chamber. According to a terrified Hamlin, "everyone thought their last hour had come." In fact, as she discovered later from the president's son Franklin, the sound was caused by a member of the secret service running across the Capitol's roof after he "thought he saw a shadow."[216] It was an indication of the tension gripping the nation. Throughout this disturbance, Roosevelt continued undaunted, declaring that "with confidence in our armed forces—and with the unbounding determination of our people—we will gain the inevitable triumph—so help us God." He closed by asking Congress to recognize that since "the unprovoked and dastardly attack" of yesterday "a state of war has existed between the United States and the Japanese Empire."[217] After Roosevelt's recital, Congress rose again in acclaim.

Secretary of War Stimson was less impressed. While acknowledging that the president's message was "a very effective document," he confided to his diary that it was "not one of broad statesmanship." Because Roosevelt's address was based "on the just indignation of the country at Japan's treachery in this surprise attack," Stimson feared that the grounds for America's entry into the war were too narrow and, in particular, the statement did nothing to connect Japan's "lawless conduct" in "any way with Germany." Nevertheless, he recognized that the president had successfully gauged the mood in Congress and the pace at which the resolution "was carried through was very impressive of the unity of the country."[218]

Both chambers passed the resolution for war with Japan with only one voice in opposition: Republican representative Jeanette Rankin of Montana, the first woman to hold federal office and a committed pacifist who had also voted against the US declaration of war against Germany in 1917. Memory of the First World War was at the forefront of Roosevelt's mind as well. He had asked the widow of Woodrow Wilson, the US president during that previous conflagration, to accompany him on his appearance at the Capitol.[219] Like Wilson, Roosevelt was determined that, if he was going to bring the United States into a major international conflict, he must have a united country behind him. He recognized that, despite Pearl Harbor, there was still considerable opposition to the United States again dispatching its young men to die in a European war. This explained his decision to refrain from including any of the other Axis powers in his declaration of war, or indeed making any mention of Germany or Italy in the speech. One of the leading dissenters, former president Herbert Hoover, confirmed the accuracy of Roosevelt's analysis in a letter that day to another leading anti-interventionist, the Republican senator Robert Taft: "I thought the President was very wise in limiting his declaration of war to Japan. I know he was strongly urged to declare it on the whole world. I am in hopes that we can even yet limit the area of the war."[220]

Shortly after the president's speech, a meeting of the Supply Priorities and Allocations Board—chaired by Vice President Henry Wallace—was held in the vice president's room in the Capitol building. Stimson took the lead in calling for a change in priorities now that the United States was engaged in war in the Pacific. In outlining the War Department's demand to take over appropriations for Lend-Lease, he "pointed out the change which this declaration of war would make in the sentiment of the people." Rather than merely "subsidising and arming outside nations," the American public would "insist that our own forces should be responsible for defense much more than in the past."[221]

This position was perfectly understandable. Given the gravity of the situation in the Pacific, there were fears of a potential Japanese assault on the continental United States. At this critical juncture, the United States military, which had sacrificed a significant proportion of the American arms produced over the past eighteen months to strengthen the Allied forces, was ill-equipped to wage war immediately. Throughout 1941, and particularly since the passage of the Lend-Lease bill, the Roosevelt administration had striven to balance the buildup of its own forces with its role as the "arsenal of democracy" for the Allies. Now that the United States was a combatant in East Asia, it was only natural that the emphasis would shift to supplying America's own war effort. The danger for Britain and the Soviet Union, however, was that their immediate defense needs would be completely overshadowed.

The fact that it was Stimson and the War Department that was responsible for dramatically curtailing Lend-Lease supplies in the twenty-four hours after Pearl Harbor was particularly ominous for British and Soviet interests. Stimson was the administration's leading advocate of American intervention to aid the Allies prior to December 7. While the United States was a nonbelligerent, he and his aides had argued passionately for sending munitions to those forces who could use them directly against the principal Axis power, Nazi Germany. Yet now, the US forces needed to fight in the Pacific, and they required planes, tanks, and guns, even if this deprived the Allied forces. Undoubtedly, Stimson and his cohort were convinced that establishing a powerful, supremely well-supplied American military machine was best for Britain and the broader war effort.[222] But many British officials feared that if too many vital supplies were redirected to American forces in the Pacific and the flow to Britain and Russia dried up, then there were several dangerous possibilities: Germany could emerge victorious in Libya and drive on to the Suez Canal, the Red Army might be forced back into Siberia, or the German Navy could emerge victorious in the Battle of the Atlantic or even successfully invade Britain itself.[223] This was perhaps an unduly pessimistic scenario, which credited German forces with greater reach than they actually possessed, but the anxiety was no less real for all that.

In the Soviet Union, there was also some concern that Stalin's hope that the Japanese would strike east rather than south would backfire on the war effort.[224] The importance of Western military aid was visible that very day on the eastern front. Lieutenant general of aviation Alexander Novikov, commander of the Soviet Air Force on the Leningrad front, ordered the deployment of twenty Tomahawk fighter aircraft of the 159th Fighter Air Regiment to cover one of the routes into the beleaguered city.[225] These were American-built airplanes that had been supplied to Stalin and shipped to the Soviet Union, most likely through the Arctic route. They constituted about 14 percent of the aircraft under Novikov's command at this time. Clearly, fending off Hitler's forces in Leningrad, particularly given the Führer's new emphasis on the city in his directive from that same day, would be considerably more difficult if Lend-Lease were cut off.

The potential impact of the American entry into the war on Britain's Lend-Lease supplies was becoming ever clearer. At the Ministry of Supply, the second secretary Sir William Palmer drafted a memorandum summarizing the situation. Britain's "total shipping programme was likely to be cut because the U.S. may want to divert ships" that it had previously lent to London and now needed for resupplying its troops in the Pacific. There was also the strong likelihood that the United States would now require a large cut of Britain's own vital supplies, such as rubber imported from Malaya, Burma, and Ceylon and tin ore sourced from Bolivia. Most critical was the probability that the need to supply the American services with more munitions would mean significantly less for British forces at a time when they could ill afford to go without.

On top of this, Britain's war effort depended on the supply of vital commodities from the United States. A quarter of Britain's carbon steel and even more of its alloy steel came from the United States, as did 40 percent of its zinc and a tenth of its copper, or sixty thousand tons annually (at a time when Britain was supplying the Soviet Union with thirty-six thousand tons a year). Britain was also dependent on American imports in textiles, particularly silk and manila hemp. And then there were essential chemicals, such as acetone (required for the production of propellants) and glycerin, phenol, and alcohol (all of which were needed for explosives).[226]

As the supply agreements between the Allies threatened to unravel, the Axis powers were finalizing their own pacts. Shortly before 8 p.m. in Berlin, Ribbentrop and Oshima agreed to their text. It was immediately sent to Rome. A few minutes later, the German ambassador there, Mackensen, called on Ciano and presented him with the revised draft agreement. Ciano, in turn, rang Mussolini at once. He instantly approved the agreement. The Italian foreign minister immediately called Ribbentrop with the good news.[227] It was agreed that the treaty would be accompanied by three separate explanatory narratives, each representing that of the individual contractants. The diplomatic and military alignment of the Axis was nearly complete—the ball was now in Tokyo's court.

Roosevelt continued to work toward unifying the American public behind the war effort. Arriving back at the White House after his speech, the president had lunch with Hopkins, Tully, and his two speechwriters, Robert Sherwood and Samuel Rosenman. There was "no small talk." Instead, the president set out his plan to address the nation in a fireside chat the following evening. Most Americans were now completely focused on Japan, and Roosevelt wanted to impress on the country that Hitler was the main enemy, even though the United States was not officially at war with Germany. He recognized the administration would face criticism for neglecting the Japanese threat. He therefore told Sherwood and Rosenman to emphasize that, although "for more than a year we have been trying to prevent war in the Pacific," this was not about "appeasing the Japanese, but that the longer we could prevent war with Japan the stronger we could become and the more help we could send to the people fighting Hitler."[228]

After lunch, Roosevelt met with the Soviet ambassador Litvinov, who described the president as "fatigued and preoccupied," which he assumed was due to the casualties in the Pacific being far graver than initially reported. When Roosevelt asked if the Soviets intended to open a "second front" in the Pacific, Litvinov responded that this was unlikely and expressed confidence that Tokyo would not declare war, as it was not in its interest to do so. Litvinov also informed Moscow that Roosevelt had asked if American bombers could use the Soviet port of Vladivostok as a resupply point for missions from Manila to Japan and asked for a formal response.[229] From the Soviets' perspective, however—as Litvinov had already informed former US ambassador to Moscow Joseph E. Davies—the top priority was avoiding a two-front war, and they were unwilling to do anything that would threaten their neutrality pact with Japan.

Another, more cynical reason, which Litvinov did not share with the Americans but later confided to the Polish ambassador to Washington, was the Soviets' belief that if they declared war on Japan then this would "relieve the United States of the need to incur losses itself."[230] This was a sentiment that the Soviet military attaché in Chungking also shared with his Chinese interlocutors, stating that if the Soviets declared war then "the United States would not be willing to concentrate its full war effort upon Japan and thus hold Japan in check."[231] With Stalin already scarred by Hitler's violation of a neutrality pact, he was eager to see Japanese forces tied down in the Pacific while he concentrated his resources in the west. It was significant that Litvinov had only one question in his meeting with the president. "Will the new development of events affect the supply promised to us?" he asked.[232] Roosevelt's reply was not entirely reassuring. No, he said, before adding the qualification that while tanks would not be needed for the war with Japan, he was not sure about aircraft. It was thus already clear to the Soviets that, far from making life easier, the uncertainty created by the attack at Pearl Harbor was threatening to reverse the rally their forces had mounted before Moscow.

This fear was shared by Professor Tadeusz Tomaszewski in German-occupied Lvov. News of Pearl Harbor, he noted, had "unsettled" his strongly anti-Nazi friends and acquaintances. People were not sure,

Tomaszewski continued, whether the new war was "a good or a bad thing." On the one hand, the Japanese attack was a positive development because the United States was "finally" intervening directly in the armed conflict. On the other hand, there was concern that the outbreak of war in the Pacific was bad for the anti-Hitler cause because American forces would be tied down "elsewhere"—that is, in the Far East—and Lend-Lease supplies to Russia would be "reduced."[233]

Tomaszewski's fear was Germany's hope. On the eastern front, Lieutenant Georg Kreuter saw the outbreak of war in the Pacific as a relief. "Japan has declared war on America!" he wrote. "That helps shorten the war," especially if their "successes continue."[234] The global connections between the theaters of war were thus widely understood at all levels on both sides.

That said, while the president was well aware that the conflicts in the Pacific and in Europe were inextricably linked, he remained acutely conscious that many of his fellow citizens were unconvinced. Eager to redirect public opinion back to the principal enemy, Roosevelt released a statement to the press claiming that "obviously Germany did all it could to push Japan into the war as it hoped that such a conflict would put an end to the Lend-Lease program." The administration was aware that German propaganda was already gleefully claiming that war in the Pacific would deprive Britain of Lend-Lease supplies. As a result, the Roosevelt administration informed the press that "the Lend-Lease program is and will continue in full operation" but did not mention that distribution had, in fact, been suspended the night before.[235]

In Russia, as the German situation continued to deteriorate throughout the day, for the first time there was a general sense of crisis across the eastern front, though this had not yet entirely communicated itself to Hitler and the OKW.[236] In Army Group North, the Spaniards of the Blue Division near Novgorod were at the end of their tether. Their commander, Agustín Muñoz Grandes, was forced to withdraw most of his men across the Volkhov river in biting cold temperatures of minus-forty degrees Celsius.[237] But the real crisis was in Army Group Center, where the front was buckling in many places. At Moscow, another foreign volunteer formation of anti-Bolshevik warriors, the Légion des Volontaires Français Contre le Bolchévisme, was so crippled by enemy action, frostbite, bronchitis, and various nasal infections that it had to be taken out of the line that day and replaced with German forces.[238] Rudolf Schmidt's Second Army was on the verge of disintegration. The many withdrawals along primitive highways meant that the roads were, as the tank commander Heinrich Engel wrote, "continuously jammed." It took his assault gun nineteen hours to cover only fifteen kilometers.[239] Hoepner, commanding Panzer Groups Three and Four, summed it up in a letter to his wife that day. He wrote of a "day of great tension" in which "everyone was screaming for help."[240]

In the evening, the commander of the German Second Panzer Army, Guderian, rang Bock in a panic. He painted his situation "in the blackest colors" and said that he could not deny that there was now a growing "crisis of trust." Guderian asked Bock "for the hundredth time" if this was known to the high command. Bock challenged him to specify against whom his crisis of confidence was directed, offering that if Guderian did not trust he was being heard, he should fly himself to the high command to deliver the warning. Guderian did not take the bait. He ignored both the question and the suggestion. Bock told him that there was no point in complaining, as he had no reinforcements to give him. Everyone would just have to hold their ground as best they could. Afterward, Bock reported the situation to chief of staff of the high command Halder, and warned that his forces were nowhere prepared to resist a Soviet attack in any strength. Halder replied that the army high command had no control over the transfer of reinforcements from the west.[241]

Withdrawal would not be easy. Bock told the OKW that if the decision was made to embark on a large-scale retreat, then that would "cost a lot of matériel, guns, and equipment." No matter how much he prepared, the army group commander went on, these losses could not be avoided and would amount to a "defeat."[242]

Running short on options, German leadership tried to compensate for military weakness through ideological coherence. That day, the commander in chief of the army, Walther von Brauchitsch, instructed officers across the entire Wehrmacht that the "inner mental attitude of every individual" was critical to the outcome of the war. Officers needed to remember that the conflict was a "decisive struggle for an ideology." This would have to suffice to overcome Soviet numerical and material superiority.[243]

It was against this background that General Gotthard Heinrici, whose corps had just been hit by the Soviet Fiftieth Army, sat down to write to his wife and daughter, who lived in the Westphalian city of Münster. He had to send his letter early to be sure that they would receive his Christmas greetings in time. Heinrici confessed that he did not "dare" to predict whether it would be a "merry" one. His expectation was that "the Russians will do everything to spoil it for us," and that his "Silent Night" would be broken by the "thunder of guns." Heinrici apologized for having no presents to send, not even a fur coat, as all of these had been confiscated by the Reich. He lamented that the offensive had not ended before the start of winter, so that the troops would have been "halfway functioning," been in positions from which they could defend themselves, and had "billets" in which they could sit out the winter. Finally, Heinrici expressed his regret that "our Münster has suffered so badly," but explained that he wanted to keep their apartment there because he wanted to "at least have a sense that one has a home somewhere." This was a reference to the damage caused by British air attacks on the city five months earlier, evidence that the bombing campaign was taking its toll not merely on civilian but also military morale.[244]

The regime was particularly sensitive to the situation in Münster, where Bishop von Galen's public attacks on the euthanasia program, British bombing, and an intensive RAF leafleting campaign had created a perfect storm. That very day, the local Gestapo arrested the Münster cleric Kaplan Heinrich Hennen. His crime had been to complain that thousands of children went without catechisms, while indecent books attacking the church had no problems finding a publisher. This Hennen blamed on the "current situation," which is to say the Third Reich.[245]

This incident was just the tip of the iceberg. The regime's profound concern with the Catholic threat was underlined by a report of the SD also released that same day. The section entitled "Political Catholicism" told its own tale of supposed Catholic subversion. The Stuttgart Gestapo reported the arrest of a widowed cleaning woman and a carpenter, both known as "fanatical adherents of the Catholic Church," for having spread "a rabble-rousing rumor directed against the Führer." In Karlsruhe, in the neighboring region of Baden, the police broke up an illegal Catholic group called "New Germany." One of the nuns involved, "Sister Liberta"—born Elisabeth Schoch—had not only said that "we are to blame for the war" but claimed that the Wehrmacht had already suffered two million dead and that the badly wounded were being put down. But perhaps the greatest heresy was spoken by the Bavarian priest Rupert Reiter. "The Russians are people just like us," he had allegedly said. "The Germans will bleed to death there and afterward America will come [into the war] and Germany will be finished."[246]

The general mood among the Germans was downbeat. That day, the internal surveillance services report from the SD told of continued widespread popular worries about the "unbroken" Russian resistance.[247] Reading between the lines of the increasingly vague Wehrmacht reports and unsettled by often graphic descriptions of the situation in letters from the front, the German people could intuit that things were not going according to plan. There was quite a lot of anxiety about North Africa, too, where further British offensives were expected. To add to the general gloom, there was unhappiness about the continuing shortage of tobacco, shoes, and everything else, which led to queues forming in front of shops many hours before they actually opened. The report was based, of course, on information gathered before Pearl Harbor, and thus did not yet reflect the widespread euphoria generated by the Japanese successes. Hitler paid little heed either way, as he was preoccupied with writing his speech for the Reichstag meeting and deliberating on how to best to frame his forthcoming declaration of war on the United States. Later, he got on the overnight train from Rastenburg to Berlin.[248]

Churchill, too, busied himself with reframing the conflict for popular consumption. In a radio address that evening, he repeated much of what he had told Parliament, but there was one crucial addition. He emphasized the need for workers to step up munitions production, now that deliveries from the United States could no longer be guaranteed. Above all, this applied to tanks and aircraft, as it was "quite certain that some of the supplies on which we had counted, which had been diverted to Russia, will have to be made good by us."[249] Churchill's exhaustion was evident to the British public. A UK Ministry of Information survey noted the general impression was that it was "the speech of a very tired man."[250]

In private, Churchill's anxiety over the production situation was growing ever more acute. While Harry Hopkins had expressed hope that enhanced production of merchant ships would ensure that more shipping and imports would be available for Britain in 1942, that dispatch had arrived before the attack on Pearl Harbor.[251] With the United States engaged in the Pacific, Britain's needs were no longer top priority. As Churchill wrote to King George VI that day, "We have to be careful that our share of munitions and other aid which we are receiving from the United States does not suffer more than is, I fear, inevitable." Consequently, he must set sail for Washington to meet with Roosevelt as soon as possible, in order to coordinate the "whole plan of Anglo-American defence and attack."

The prime minister informed the king that he was "expecting that Germany and Italy will both declare war on the United States, as they have bound themselves by treaty to do so."[252] Churchill's apparent confidence stemmed primarily from the interception by British intelligence of two cables from the Japanese ambassador Oshima regarding meetings that he had held with the German foreign minister Ribbentrop. These revealed that on November 28, Ribbentrop had pressed Japan to go to war with the United States and suggested that if it did then "Germany would, of course, join in immediately" and that there was no possibility of Hitler entering into a separate peace.[253] That was clear enough.

But the second cable from a meeting between the two on December 2, after Oshima had been instructed by Tokyo to get a German signature on the new Tripartite Pact, seemed less conclusive.[254] The Allies read only that Oshima had reported back to Tokyo that Ribbentrop expressed his personal support for Germany joining Japan in a declaration of war against the United States but would need the approval of Hitler, who was currently in the east. As a result, the foreign minister cautioned that this message should not be wired to Japan.[255] It was by no means clear to British and American leaders reading this exchange that a German declaration of war was necessarily imminent. Perhaps it was this uncertainty that led Churchill to tell the king, "I shall defer proposing my visit to the President until this situation is more clear."[256]

The intelligence that Roosevelt gleaned from the German embassy was also inconclusive. Wild Bill Donovan's agent, Malcolm R. Lovell, spent an hour with Thomsen that afternoon and was told that the "severance of diplomatic relations now probably depended on Germany." The German chargé "saw no reason for the United States to break relations, as they would gain nothing by it." He suspected that "he will not be here very long," but Lovell could discover nothing more definite as Thomsen "did not know how his government would act."[257]

Though the British and Americans could not be sure, for Berlin, the die was cast. Now that war with the United States was inevitable, Ribbentrop sent a personal message to the chargé at the Washington embassy. "I request with respect to the situation," it ran, "that all secret material of the embassy and other agencies based there be immediately destroyed." "Continued cipher traffic" was to be ensured "for the time being."[258]

At around 11 p.m. in Rome, Ciano got on the overnight train to Turin, where he was scheduled to meet the Vichy leader, Admiral Darlan. It was an important encounter for the Italian foreign minister. Though France had been comprehensively beaten in 1940, the country still enjoyed some diplomatic leverage. Both the French and the Italians were anxious about Hitler's dominance of Europe. As the president of the Italian Armistice Commission, Vacca Maggiolini, wrote that day, Darlan was expected to seek "the beginning of a cooperation between

Mediterranean powers that could counterbalance German power in the future." At the same time, Italy—whose colonial ambitions were diametrically opposed to those of France—was determined not to give too much away.

Hanging over everything, as Maggiolini remarked toward the close of his memorandum, was Pearl Harbor. This added "new unknowns" to what was already a very "complex problem." On the one hand, Britain might be able to pass off many of its Atlantic obligations to the United States and concentrate more on the Mediterranean, which would obviously be bad news. On the other hand, it was possible that "the United States may instead be forced to concentrate a large part of its resources in the Pacific and therefore to mitigate their present notable contribution to British war operations." This would reduce the chances of a US-Britain attack on Dakar, which Vichy France so feared, and meant that there was less reason for Darlan to fear reprisals for allowing the Axis to use French facilities in North Africa.[259] The whole dynamic of the war was changing before their eyes.

As NIGHT FELL, mainland Europe was, for many, a place of acute anxiety and perplexity. The roundup of Jews in Lvov continued. Professor Tadeusz Tomaszewski hid one of them for six months. Many others were shot, as Jews were brought to a sandpit to be murdered.[260] Further west, in the small town of Szczebrzeszyn near Zamosc, the Gestapo broke up the wedding dinner of a Miss Rajewska and Mr. Kozlowski. They were searching for the brother of the bride, a member of the Polish underground. The groom escaped in the confusion. All other guests were arrested but soon released, with the exception of the bride, who was taken to the local police station for a night of beatings.[261] This was, of course, just one of thousands of similar experiences the Poles had to endure during the war. In Germany, the deportation of Jews continued apace. That night, the feeder trains from the length and breadth of the Hesse region arrived in Kassel station. The deportees on them were taken to the gymnasium of a city-center school, where they were stripped of their papers and all their valuables. They would begin the fateful journey to Riga in the morning.[262]

In Bucharest, Mihail Sebastian contemplated the Japanese moves against Malaysia, Borneo, and Thailand and the air attacks on Singapore, Hong Kong, the Philippines, and Pearl Harbor with astonishment. "The war is spreading to the whole planet," he wrote. "The old reasoning that held until yesterday has become redundant. . . . Everything is more serious, more complex and more obscure."[263]

For others, Pearl Harbor was a welcome moment of clarity. In Germany, the anti-Nazi diarist Friedrich Kellner wrote that Japan had "revealed itself to the world in its low, devious nature." In this respect, he continued, "Japan is an avid pupil of Germany. . . . Finally, finally, there are clear front lines. . . . Now it will hail declarations of war." Kellner asked, "Will the isolationist gentlemen in the United States finally have their eyes opened?" He continued, "How could they" remain neutral in this "gigantic struggle for human dignity and freedom?" This would be tantamount, Kellner believed, to siding with the Axis "tyrant states." "Now Japan and Italy will not escape their well-deserved fates," he concluded. "The harsh judgment of history will be 99% guilty in Germany!!!"[264]

Across Britain, opinion was split on whether the new Pacific war was good or bad news. A thirty-year-old medical health officer in Staffordshire received news of Pearl Harbor with "excitement and almost jubilation. I thought, now we are all in it." Yet his wife was "very depressed about it," lamenting "now it will go on for twenty years."[265] In Belmont, Surrey, a thirtysomething food-packing manager, after listening to Roosevelt's speech on the BBC, "was disappointed that the other Axis villains were not included, as of course Germany is the moving spirit of the Japanese action."[266] In Wales, a Newport insurance clerk in his sixties was more concerned with Churchill's radio address that night, labeling it "his worst broadcast so far," as the prime minister "seemed pre-occupied." For his own part, the clerk just hoped "our side don't make a few silly blunders and lose a couple of big ships before we have got the proper measure of Japanese naval strength."[267]

On the other side of the Atlantic, the implications of Pearl Harbor were still sinking in. Even the naturally exuberant Japanese American college student Charles Kikuchi began to realize that things would never be the same. That evening, he left Berkeley and headed to San Francisco in order to "chase girls." "Holy Christ!" he wrote in his diary afterward. "San Francisco was like nothing I ever saw before and everybody was saying that the Japs are going to get it in the ass." It was clear that the Japanese community in the United States was now under intense suspicion.[268]

Among other observers, there was grim determination and a confidence that the country would finish what Japan had started. This was vividly expressed by John B. Chevalier, the secretary of the American Asiatic Association, to his old friend Stanley Hornbeck, formerly of the State Department Division of Far Eastern Affairs and now a special adviser to Secretary of State Cordell Hull. "It will be a long hard war," he wrote, "but after it is over Uncle Sam will do the talking in the world."[269]

5

TUESDAY, DECEMBER 9, 1941

THE SKIES OVER EUROPE WERE QUIET DURING THE NIGHT. RAF Bomber Command sent only four planes to Germany, all of which returned safely after doing no significant damage.[1] The seas off Malaya, by contrast, were busy. Force Z, the British squadron headed by the battleship *Prince of Wales* and battle cruiser *Repulse*, was on the move, ordered to engage the Japanese landings in the north of the peninsula. Thanks to faulty reconnaissance of the harbor, naval high command in Tokyo was under the impression that the two British ships remained in port. Elsewhere, the Japanese offensive proceeded apace. Amid heavy air attacks on the US garrison at Guam, an invasion force from Saipan prepared to disembark there. The air attacks on Wake Island continued, and a force was landed on the central Pacific atoll of Tarawa.[2] In Hong Kong, the "gin-drinkers line" was buckling under the Japanese onslaught. Only in the Philippines was there a brief respite. While the situation in Europe was still shrouded in uncertainty, the battle lines in Asia were now clear.

Through the hours of darkness in Europe, the airwaves had been humming. The day was just fifteen minutes old in Berlin when Ribbentrop sent a personal message to Ambassador Ott in Tokyo. He asked him to personally present the text of the Axis agreement that he had discussed with Oshima. Ribbentrop wanted him to "make every effort" to ensure that Oshima was authorized to sign along with the other Axis representatives, as planned, on the next morning, Wednesday, December 10.[3] The message indicated that the agreement was to be "made public in a special way," referring to Hitler's plan to stage the event at the Reichstag.[4]

In Washington, it was still early evening of the previous day. The German embassy was closely following the connection the Roosevelt administration had made between Hitler, Japan, and the Lend-Lease strategy. Thomsen now sent Berlin the full text of the White House statement accusing Germany of pushing Japan into the war in order to disrupt the Lend-Lease program.[5] It was evident that Roosevelt recognized Hitler's strategy very clearly. The flow of American matériel was going to be critical to the outcome of the war. The Americans knew that the Germans knew it, and the Germans knew that the Americans knew that the Germans knew it.

For the American security services it had also been a busy night. The rising tensions between the United States and the German Reich led to the targeting of the press corps, which each side regarded as central to the other's armory. Thomsen reported that the FBI had arrested the local DNB representative, as well as August W. Halfeld, the local representative for Scherl, which was part of the vast Nazi publishing empire Eher-Verlag. Thomsen demanded "countermeasures" be taken against American journalists.[6] Later, someone from the German embassy went to the State Department to protest, but the diplomats there did not seem to know anything about the matter.[7]

Throughout the day, American interventionists in Congress and the press reiterated the argument already made by some administration officials that Japan had attacked the United States at Hitler's behest. That day's *Washington Post* carried an article from its foreign policy reporter, Barnet Nover, declaring that Japan was "acting as Hitler's puppets; in running amok the Japanese militarists are obeying the promptings of Nazi wirepullers."[8] Regional newspapers, including some in the more traditionally noninterventionist Midwest, echoed this theme. Interventionists in the Senate used these articles to imprint the image of Hitler as puppet master. The New Hampshire Republican Styles Bridges quoted the *Washington (DC) Daily News* as stating, "Hitler is attacking, indeed, but through the Japanese as he had long tried to do." The Illinois Democrat and administration loyalist Scott W. Lucas referred to the *Chicago Times* speaking of a "mad military clique in Tokyo that has made war against us on orders of a madder military clique in Berlin."[9]

The argument that Japan was merely Hitler's cat's-paw in Asia had long been common among advocates of intervention, particularly since the signing of the Tripartite Pact.[10] But in the immediate aftermath of Pearl Harbor, some went even further to suggest that German planes, and even Nazi pilots, had led the Japanese assault. This partly reflected the long-standing racially charged insinuations that the Japanese were incapable of perpetrating such sophisticated operations.[11] The source for many of the stories about German planes over Hawaii were "well informed legislators," perhaps repeating early reports conveyed by the president himself to the congressional delegation, of planes with swastikas involved in the Pearl Harbor attack. Even a reporter in the leading noninterventionist newspaper, the *Chicago Tribune*, noted that "conjecture spread in congressional circles today that German pilots carried out the damaging blitzkrieg on the navy's Pearl Harbor base."[12] Yet a note of caution was sounded by the *New York Times*, which before the Pearl Harbor attack had repeatedly argued that Tokyo was a mere satellite of Hitler. On December 8, however, its lead editorial suggested that it was "more credible" that "this is primarily and essentially an independent Japanese adventure." This was because "Hitler, much as he may wish to direct our attention to the Pacific," could "scarcely desire" to provoke the open and formal entrance of the United States into a war, which the *Times* editors were convinced would eventually precipitate war with Germany too.[13]

Speculation as to Germany's responsibility for the attack on Pearl Harbor was also rife among the public. Across ten different American cities that evening, the Library of Congress began conducting a series of "Man on the Street" interviews to record the opinion of ordinary Americans on the new war and what might come next. In Washington, outside the Palace Theater on 9th Street, one nineteen-year-old man told the interviewer that "like everyone else" he "didn't want us to go to war." Yet now the United States was involved, he hoped "we go to work on them." That meant the Nazis too, as he was convinced Japan was "kind of forced in it by Germany." The Pearl Harbor strike was "part of a prearranged plan sort of that too many supplies were going to England and it was hurting Germany," and Japan's attack was intended to "try to divert some of them." Another unidentified man, who was "behind Mr. Roosevelt one hundred percent," reported that he and his friends were certain that the Japanese "were forced into it by Mr. Hitler."[14] This view was also relayed to another "Man on the Street" interviewer in Burlington, North Carolina, by a man who claimed the Japanese "aren't anything more but a mouthpiece for Hitler."[15]

There were some who voiced criticism of the president. One man interviewed in Washington maintained that "they could have easily stayed out of this" and felt the country had done the "wrong thing by electing President Roosevelt."[16] Prominent noninterventionists felt similarly. In the privacy of his diary, Charles Lindbergh wrote that Japan had only adopted a course that it "in national honor was bound to take in the face of our conduct," suggesting Tokyo had "simply beaten us to the gun."[17] Publicly, Lindbergh was more conciliatory. That day he released a statement through the America First Committee, charging the Roosevelt administration with "stepping closer to war for many months" but stating that, "whether or not that policy has been wise, our country has been attacked by force of arms, and by force of arms we must retaliate."[18]

This emphasis on fighting a defensive war, focused on retaliating against the country that had directly attacked the United States, was picked up by others. The *New York Daily News*, whose owner and publisher Captain Joe Patterson was a virulent critic of the president's foreign policy, adopted a similar position. The paper's editorial that day declared, "When you are attacked there is nothing to do but fight," while also urging an "America first" war strategy and arguing against venturing too far from America's shores.[19] This view was heard in the US House of Representatives, prior to the vote on declaring war against Japan. The Irish American Democratic congressman Martin L. Sweeney of Ohio, a steadfast opponent of intervention in Europe and critic of Lend-Lease, warned, "Our war with Japan must not be construed as a war to protect the material interest of any other nation in the Orient," a thinly veiled dig at the British Empire. Moreover, he reminded his more intervention-ist colleagues who were urging action against Hitler, "this is the only war in which we are now officially engaged."[20]

Similar sentiments were expressed even within the American foreign service. From a US consulate in Ontario, Canada, H. T. Goodier, who had previously served in Japan, wrote to the president that he thought his address to Congress "was grand; just enough and without heroics." But just because the United States was now at war with Japan, "that does not mean that we should become involved in war with any other country that does not declare war against us." For Roosevelt, who closely moni-tored the White House mail after any major speech, it would have been evident that the vast majority of letters dated December 8 applauded his address without necessarily pushing for him to extend America's war to Europe.[21]

Across Washington, British embassy officials' concerns were mul-tiplying. It was becoming impossible to ignore the potential "problem arising from the Japanese war as regards demands for realization of mil-itary supplies from the United States previously destined for us." After consulting with the Supply Council and the Joint Staff Mission, Am-bassador Halifax wrote to Churchill of the "obvious dangers of supplies from United States of America which may be equally or more needed by us being diverted through the natural preoccupation of the United States with the Pacific situation and the tendency to equip all forces regardless of the prospect of their immediate employment." With the Pacific war in its infancy, and particularly due to the "uncertainty caused by the disaster at Hawaii," the ambassador warned, there was a "special danger of unilateral decisions being taken without being sufficiently re-lated to a general strategic conception." The British position was "diffi-cult" and would "quickly become more so."

As a result, Halifax urged Churchill to cable the president about the "difficulties involved on our side in [the] reallocation of supplies previously intended for us and on which we have been counting for our immediate and future operations." In order to develop a concerted strategy, it would be necessary for the current ad-hoc discussions between the British Joint Staff Mission and the US services in Washington to be formalized. Halifax confided that there had been "for political and other reasons reluctance on the United States side hitherto to have such combined Staff discussions." While there was hope from the British team in Washington that the "psychological moment has come to suggest them," it was clear that there still existed in some quarters clear opposition to the idea that the two countries were united in a "single cause."[22]

Though Washington was traditionally a town where people went to bed early, activity continued into the night. Just before 10:30 p.m., Stimson was awoken by a call from Assistant Secretary McCloy at the War Department to warn him of reports that an enemy fleet was approaching San Francisco. Planes had been sighted off the California coast heading north. Still reeling from the attack on Pearl Harbor, a helpless Stimson informed his subordinate that there was nothing that he "could do to prevent it."[23]

The story spread quickly across the nation. Eleanor Roosevelt was on her way to Los Angeles with New York mayor Fiorello La Guardia to bolster civilian-defense organization and morale on the West Coast. Flying over Tennessee, they received a "flash from AP" that "San Francisco was being bombed." On hearing the news, the first lady "paled." Even so, she and LaGuardia decided that if the news was true, they would "go direct to San Francisco."[24]

Almost as quickly as the story emerged, it was revealed to be a false alarm. McCloy informed Stimson that the planes detected were actually the United States' own big bombers returning from convoy duty.[25] Still, the mix-up demonstrated Americans' mounting confusion and anxiety. As Eleanor Roosevelt's aide Joseph Lash, who accompanied her on the trip, confided to his diary, "No one on plane believed it impossible that SF should be bombed tonight."[26] Crossing the Pacific had previously been dismissed as beyond Japanese capabilities, but in light of the shock two days previous, an attack on the California coast had become all too conceivable.

Arriving in Los Angeles, Eleanor witnessed the fevered panic descending on California, where there was a great deal of antagonism being whipped up against Japanese Americans.[27] The focus along the West Coast was entirely on the Pacific, and little if any thought was given by most people to the war in Europe at this time. That night in Seattle, where a blackout was in place to guard against a potential air raid, a mob rioted and smashed store windows that radiated light, including one downtown shop with red-and-green Christmas bulbs. For two hours the rioters rampaged through city streets, only stopping to sing "God Bless America" before resuming their destruction.[28]

In Japan, after the success of Pearl Harbor, the appetite for daring initiatives had only grown. That Tuesday, Admiral Yamamoto ordered Admiral Ugaki, chief of staff of the Combined Fleet, to devise a plan for the wholesale capture of Hawaii. Previously, Ugaki had thought it could not be done. Now he became an enthusiastic protagonist of the Eastern Operation, a landing on the islands. The plan would rely partly on support from the substantial ethnic Japanese population there but mainly on the supposed weakness of the American defenses.[29]

It was already midafternoon locally when a Japanese I-65 submarine spotted Force Z, the *Prince of Wales* and the *Repulse*, as it passed through the Anambas Islands on the way to attack the Japanese landing forces further up the coast of Malaya. The news came as an unpleasant surprise, but it also suggested an opportunity. The operations room of Admiral Ugaki's Combined Fleet suddenly became a hive of activity. The submarine was ordered to "keep contact with these enemy ships." The Southern Expeditionary Fleet and the Second Fleet were diverted to deal with the threat. Ugaki was aquiver. Would the Japanese aircraft catch them before nightfall? Would there be a surface action? Or would the submarine be left to handle the problem on its own?[30]

The mood on the Japanese side on the second day of the war remained buoyant. Two minutes after Force Z was spotted, the emperor, who received a number of senior politicians throughout the day, met former foreign minister Matsuoka "in high spirits."[31] His good cheer was shared by much of the population, which was still celebrating the success of the Pearl Harbor raid. Yabe Teiji, a prominent political scientist at Tokyo Imperial University, wrote that "the Navy's Hawaiian operation is one of the greatest triumphs in the history of war."[32] All this was good for the stability of the empire. The Ministry of the Interior reported that day that "there is a deep sense that the system of national unity is strengthening more and more."[33]

Underpinning these shared public sentiments was a strong sense of racial pride and animosity against the Anglo-Saxons, somewhat tempered by a nagging sense of inferiority. The respected poet Saito Mokichi demanded that day that the empire "destroy those animal-like, redheaded, blue-eyed, spineless nations."[34] His colleague, Ito Sei, wrote that "the vindication of our sense of superiority of the [Japanese] race is driving us forward." War, he said, was necessary in order "to believe firmly that the Yamato [Japanese] race is the most superior on the globe." This meant taking on the Anglo-Americans "because the races who use English possess the finest culture, the greatest strength and riches of any country in the world." So far, Sei continued, "they had been the supreme rulers of the world." This fact had "seeped into the bowels of the Japanese people," "the so-called 'Yellow Race,'" and only war could ensure "the superiority of a race that has been discriminated against." The way in which the Japanese imperial project was both a colonizing and anti-colonial enterprise could not have been more neatly expressed.[35]

Throughout these action-packed days, ordinary Japanese remained glued to their radio sets awaiting further news from the battlefronts. That Tuesday, the radio the Takahashi family had brought back from their time living in Los Angeles finally gave in under the strain of overuse. It burst into flames, burning the ceiling. As Aiko Takahashi remarked with humor, the "American radio" had obviously found broadcasting Japan's war news "distasteful."[36]

Ugaki's high hopes following the sightings of the *Prince of Wales* and *Repulse* were dashed when contact with Force Z was lost. "What a pity," he lamented. "What were we doing to lose such a chance?" Ugaki was plunged into depression as he wondered about British intentions. Were their big ships going to attack the landing at Kota Bharu or attempt some kind of cat-and-mouse game to wear out the enemy? One way or the other, Ugaki profoundly regretted "that we could not send them to the bottom of the Pacific."[37] It seemed as if a historic opportunity had been lost.

While all this was going on, an officer on the *Repulse*, oblivious to the danger he had just escaped, was boasting to the American war correspondent Cecil Brown. When warned that there had been reports of a substantial enemy naval force approaching, he simply laughed. "Oh but they are Japanese," the officer replied. "There is nothing to worry about."[38]

This sort of misplaced confidence was common among white men in the Far East, but it was not confined to them. The Indian nationalist newspaper the *Bombay Chronicle*, which had been a steadfast critic of Japanese militarism and expansionism, also seriously underestimated the enemy. "It is one thing," the newspaper wrote that day, "to harass an impoverished, ill-equipped and defenceless China, or to make surprise air-raids, and quite a different matter to challenge the might of Britain, the USA and Russia."[39]

That morning's British newspapers contained much speculation about the consequences of Japan's gambit in the Pacific. Of pressing concern was the question of American supplies to Europe. The country's most popular paper—with daily nationwide sales of over two million—was the *Daily Express*, owned by the Canadian-born media magnate and Churchill's minister of supply Lord Beaverbrook.[40] Unsurprisingly, its editorial reiterated the prime minister's message from the previous day that, to make up the shortfall in American supplies, "a new burden will be upon the war workers of Britain and new burdens on our sea power." While America's immense productive potential offered hope for the future, in the short term it was inescapable "that there will be less aid for her allies while America is collecting her war senses."[41] This sentiment was echoed in the *Times*, which warned of "the necessary diversion of war supplies—including that most strained and least elastic supply, shipping—from the assistance of Great Britain and Russia to the maintenance of America's own campaign in the Pacific."[42]

Journalists signaled confidence that Hitler had ordered Japan to attack the United States in order to interrupt this flow of American supplies. Among members of Parliament and government officials, the *Guardian* reported that it was "largely accepted that Hitler demanded the attack."[43] The paper's US correspondent heard the same view expressed in Washington, where "it is widely believed that Tokyo's strategy is being directed from Berlin."[44] These observers were, of course, unaware that Hitler had had little advance warning of an attack on the United States and had been happily surprised when informed of the news. As a result, British journalists also largely took at face value reports from Tokyo that the government was "confident about their treaty relationships with the Axis."[45] At 8 a.m., a BBC broadcast reported that Tokyo had said it "naturally expects" Germany to join the war.[46] The *Guardian*'s diplomatic correspondent also relayed a Japanese wireless announcement that it was "expecting Germany to declare war upon the United States within 24 hours."[47]

This certainty was not universal, however. "Up to a late hour last night," the *Express* political correspondent told readers, neither Germany nor Italy had declared war on the United States. Nor was this by any means inevitable: "The Tripartite Pact gave them a loophole. They were pledged to go to Japan's assistance only if she were attacked."[48] As a result, the writer wondered whether "war with Japan may be interpreted by the United States Government as involving war with the whole of the Axis." The *Express*'s editorial was clearly designed to impress this upon the US president, urging him to recognize that the "only way to be certain—to kill the root of this infamy which has spread its branch to the Pacific"—was to target Nazi Germany, "the power that shows the way in infamy and promises safety to infamy." This theme was echoed across the empire. For example, the *Sydney Morning Herald* in Australia wrote of the "folly" of Japan's decision, which had allegedly not been driven by real national interest but by "Germany's sore need for help."[49]

At Kassel station, in central Germany, dawn brought only misery, as more than a thousand Jews, among them ninety children, were jammed into trains for deportation.[50] Further east, the earlier transport from Cologne was wending its way toward Riga. In order to make way for these German Jews, the Jews of the Riga ghetto were being massacred all morning in the forest of Rumbula. The transport from Hamburg, originally bound for Minsk, was also on its way to the Riga area. In the ghetto of Litzmannstadt, Poland, Antonia Kimel was barely surviving. She wrote that all of her children had been in the hospital, and that she was "completely broke and close to despair." She therefore asked for a "collection" to be made on her behalf among her remaining friends and family in Vienna.[51] Arthur Lorch, who was interned at Noé-Mauzac just south of Toulouse in Vichy France, wrote that day about the "cold" and the "shortage of coal and firewood." He had just heard of the outbreak of war between Japan and the United States, which for him meant that he would get less mail from America.[52] Unlike the Latvian Jews of Rumbula, however, it was not yet clear whether Antonia Kimel, Arthur Lorch, or any of those deported from Kassel, Cologne, and other parts of Germany were yet slated for extermination.

In Dresden, Victor Klemperer was brooding that morning on the "big news" of Pearl Harbor, which he had heard the night before. "Everything about it," he thought, "is inexplicable and unpredictable." "Why" had the Japanese attacked, Klemperer wondered, and "why now?" "What effect," he asked, "will this have on the relationship between Germany and the United States," and what on that "between Russia and Japan?" One of his interlocutors, Paul Kreidl, was convinced that "now all US public opinion will be for war with Germany." Either way, Klemperer could be sure of one thing, at least: the German advance had stalled. The OKW, he noted, had announced that the eastern front would now be quieter on account of the weather. Klemperer interpreted this as an admission that the attack on Moscow had been a "failure." He also noted that the British offensive in North Africa seemed to be gaining ground.[53]

Writing from Stuttgart, Grete Doelker-Rehder saw things differently. "So far," she wrote that day, the war had been a "European conflict," but now it was "a world war." If the struggle had previously been about "the complete reorganization of Europe," it was now the "whole world" that was being ordered anew. Germany, she believed, was "fighting for survival," but things were looking up. "If one considers," Doelker-Rehder argued, "how long we have been waiting for a declaration of war by the United States and that we were sometimes concerned whether in that event Japan would actually actively join in on our side," then one could only be "happy and relieved" by Pearl Harbor. Listing all the Japanese achievements of the past two days, she said they simply had to "take the pressure off" the Reich.[54]

In occupied Poland, the new Mrs. Kozlowski, whose wedding had been broken up by the Gestapo the day before, enjoyed a brief respite. She had spent the night being beaten at the local police station, but after being released at around 9 a.m. she returned home, traumatized. She had hardly an hour to catch her breath before the authorities were knocking at her door again. Gestapo and police from the regional capital of Zamosc arrived to arrest her and took her away to an unknown destination. The apartment of the newlyweds was searched in a particularly brutal manner. An elderly neighbor, the mother of several grown-up children, was struck in the face with considerable force by a Gestapo officer. The whole town was in an uproar for several hours.[55] While his policies turned communities upside down, Hitler was almost certainly still sleeping, en route from Rastenburg to the Reich capital on his private train

People in Axis nations awoke to exultant headlines celebrating further Japanese successes. Italian broadcasters hailed the Japanese entrance into the war as "the moral adherence" of a "comparatively poor nation with the common cause of the young proletarian nations fighting for their won existence against plutocratic powers," meaning the United States and the British Empire.[56] The DNB reported that Wake and Guam had been occupied, and that Midway Island was being bombarded.[57] There was particular satisfaction in the fact that British newspapers were resigning themselves to a long war. Both the London *Times* and the *News*

Chronicle, it was noted, had warned the day before that there would now be less Lend-Lease material for Britain and the Soviet Union because the United States was tied down in the Pacific. Indeed, the British would have to produce more weapons just to fulfill their obligations to Stalin.[58]

Goebbels reprised this theme once again in his diary. "It is certainly good for now," he wrote that day, "that the United States have their hands full and can deliver significant amount of war material to neither England nor the Soviet Union." "London has gradually become aware of this," the propaganda minister continued. He diagnosed "a palpable unease about this on the enemy side."[59] He had listened to Churchill's radio broadcast of the previous night and was "under the impression that he is drunk" because he "stutters and constantly interrupts himself." Goebbels exulted once again in the prime minister's admission that "Britain would now have to work harder because it would likely not expect to receive weapons and aircraft from the United States." This theme was stressed in German radio broadcasts, which gloated that "Churchill has admitted that US shipments have actually been decreasing in volume and now will decrease further."[60] The German naval leadership also noted with satisfaction Churchill's speech to the House of Commons, warning "that some of the war material which was supposed to go to Russia [from the US] would now have to be produced in Britain."[61]

At the Ministry of Supply in London, fears were growing about the impact that America's entrance into the Pacific war might have on exports to Britain. Officials were busy compiling lists of commodities and chemicals for which Britain was "wholly or partly dependent on USA."[62] It soon became apparent just how many materials there were for which "any delay in sending supplies would be fatal to us." These included propeller veneers, steel bars for armor-piercing shell, ball-bearing steel, drop forgings for crankshafts, steel bars for 7.2 shell, steel tubes for axles for wheeled vehicles, carbonized nickel strip for wireless valves in aircraft, and nickel-alloy wires for thermocouples.[63] Then there were the supplies of vital chemicals for which "no delay can be contemplated." Second Secretary Palmer was informed by a subordinate that "aeroplanes will be grounded" if supplies of ethylene glycol, an antifreeze and engine coolant, were held up for any time. Aircraft production would be suspended unless Halowax, required for radio equipment, arrived immediately. In order to bulletproof aircraft tanks, Britain desperately needed shipments of butyl zimate, and unless Ty-Ply bonding rubber arrived in sufficient quantities, further airplane and tank production was impossible. This was just the material that was needed immediately. The list of urgent materials for which "we need not worry the Americans before the end of December" but would have to arrive by early 1942 if Britain was "to keep going" was even longer.

Even if an item was not on either list, that did not mean "we are free of anxieties." It merely demonstrated the "immediate stock position" was such that British officials did "not feel that we can make a case for worrying the Americans over the next few weeks."[64] To make matters worse, there was also the acute problem of shipping capacity. Palmer noted that even prior to the events of December 7, "we have had twenty-seven ships diverted from the North Atlantic run to ship US supplies to Russia." Now it was unavoidable that the United States would begin a "heavy trooping and supply programme in the Pacific," leading to the withdrawal of even more ships on which Britain relied for its imports. This would have serious implications for Britain's essential supply of iron, steel, and textiles.[65]

It was also a hectic day at the British Foreign Office, which received constant reports relaying Japan's continued onslaught across the Pacific. The principal private secretary Valentine Lawford confided to his diary that the "office was hell, and the telephone never stopped ringing." News arrived that Japan was "landing reinforcements in Malaya and may have taken Guam and Wake." In Hong Kong, the Japanese had taken the Shing Mun Redoubt, breaching the northern defensive line.[66] At this point, it seemed to Lawford that while the situation was bad for Britain, "the Americans have been doing still worse, poor dears." It was now apparent that the "Japs have done tremendous damage to US aircraft, and the American Pacific Fleet looks rather silly." With the California coast now seemingly vulnerable to attack, Lawford noted that the American-born Lady Leslie Doverdale, a family acquaintance then working for the Red Cross, was returning home, as "Beverly Hills is now in the front line!"

Lawford's slightly sneering tone at the American predicament reflected a feeling, shared by other Britons, that the United States had sat on the sidelines too long and was now experiencing a taste of what Britain had faced over the past two years.[67]

With Britain so reliant on US aid, however, the most pressing concern for Lawford and his colleagues remained how American attitudes toward Britain might affect the supply question. One US watcher in the Foreign Office suggested that an "inability to open a second front and our freedom from German bombing no doubt contributed largely" to an upsurge in anti-British sentiments in the United States over the past few months. Yet Britons would be "deluding" themselves if they thought these factors alone explained the hostility or "believed that now that the U.S. is at war all is going to be lovely in the garden for us." The analyst thought "it was significant that in addressing Congress yesterday, President Roosevelt made no allusion whatsoever to the British Empire having already declared—or being about to declare—its solidarity with the US." In his view, this reflected Roosevelt's political prudence. The president was "a politician to his finger-tips and knows what will and will not go down with Congress." It was revealing that "he preferred the solely American note." The observer was surprised that Halifax "seems to take comfort" that Britain's difficulties in securing greater support in Congress was "due not to the organized propaganda of America First but to a more deep-rooted isolationism." Either way, British officials in Washington would "need to watch their step with Congress." The decline in Britain's standing in the United States, at least among congressmen, did not bode well for the "highly technical but important questions" that its diplomats confronted now that the United States was at war in the Pacific, above all those surrounding the provision of Lend-Lease aid.[68]

WHEN THE BRITISH Chiefs of Staff Committee met at 10:30 that morning, the first item on the agenda was the question of a Soviet declaration of war on Japan. They had before them a Joint Intelligence Committee report from December 5 that, as Japanese belligerence became increasingly apparent, had weighed up the advantages and disadvantages of the Soviets joining any potential Pacific conflict. There were clear benefits to forcing Japan to fight on another front, which would strain its resources and undermine its morale. The presence of one hundred Soviet submarines in the Pacific would also force Japan to maintain many of its destroyers and small craft north of Taiwan in order to protect its military and trade convoys. Moreover, it was only from Vladivostok that sustained air attacks could target Japan's naval bases and industries.

But there were also clear strategic drawbacks to a Japan-Soviet Union conflict. Most critical was the impact that this would likely have on the war with Germany. Maintaining the USSR's western front was of "paramount importance" to Britain. If the Soviet Union was forced into a war on two fronts, this would "strain still further her reserves of men and material, and would face her with the necessity of dividing a diminished war production" and could precipitate Soviet "collapse." Any war with Japan would also inevitably result in the closure of the Vladivostok supply route, by which the Soviets were receiving vital raw materials. For now, Japan would have little interest in disrupting these shipments if it wished to avoid provoking Moscow into war. At the same time, however, Tokyo would need to guard against the possibility of such a war, forcing it to retain substantial forces that would otherwise be thrown into the struggle against the ABCD (America, Britain, China, Dutch) combination. Ultimately, while intelligence on Moscow's full defense capabilities remained sketchy and British analysts were thus not "in possession of sufficient information to assess Russia's abilities to fight on two fronts," it was advised that nothing should be done to weaken "the Russian effort in the West."

The events of the intervening four days had fundamentally changed the strategic picture, however. The chair of the Joint Intelligence Committee, Victor Cavendish-Bentinck, a career diplomat, informed the chiefs that a telegram from Washington had emphasized the importance of the air bases at Vladivostok to American strategy. He expected the Soviets to strike a hard bargain if the United States pushed them for use of these facilities. The chief of the imperial general staff, Alan Brooke, now argued that while the Soviets should remain on the defensive in any land conflict in Asia, Britain and the United States should pressure the Soviet Union "to strike at Japan with her submarines and air forces." Others remained unsure, and it was agreed that a revised intelligence report was required immediately for the chiefs of staff to review the following day before any recommendation was made to Eden ahead of his meeting with Stalin.[69]

There was in fact some debate among the Soviet elite on how best to deal with Japan. Litvinov, who was under pressure from Roosevelt to deliver a declaration of war against Tokyo, cabled that same day from Washington. He recommended that Stalin openly condemn Japanese aggression and declare his support for the British and American cause in the Pacific. Litvinov did not, despite the president's entreaties, suggest that the Soviet Union actually go to war in the Far East. But even this relatively weak gesture of solidarity with Washington and London was refused by Foreign Minister Vyacheslav Molotov, who feared provoking the Japanese.[70]

In Leningrad, the desperate plight of the city showed no signs of abating, even though the imminent recapture of Tikhvin would in time lead to an easing of the blockade once the supply route over the lake was reopened. Workers were receiving two hundred grams of bread a day, the rest of the population one hundred grams. There was no other food. Some residents were eating cats, dogs, and horses to survive; at least twenty-five cases of cannibalism were reported during the month of December. That day, the headmaster of a school was riding along a road when his horse collapsed from emaciation. While the rider was away looking for a new mount, the local population hacked the cadaver into pieces and took them away to eat.[71] German shelling and air attacks also took their toll on the civilian population. Between December 1 and 15, 1941, the Leningrad air defense forces reported 446 killed and 1,015 wounded in the city.[72] In these circumstances, it is not surprising that rumors spread quickly. That day, for example, German intelligence reported that anti-Semitism was rife among Leningrad's inhabitants, with allegations that influential Jews were being flown out to safety.[73] These accounts, of course, reflected Nazi preoccupations rather than the actual situation on the ground.

Despite the hunger and the cold, some Russians followed the news on the other side of the world with intense interest. The Leningrad resident Pjotr Samarin had to put aside his copy of Tolstoy's *War and Peace* because there was no electricity for lamps to read by, but he was still able to hear radio reports—perhaps on a communal set—of the "treacherous" Japanese attacks. "Events are piling up," he wrote that day, "and passing with lightning speed." "What an era we live in!" he mused. "Lucky are those who survive it all!"[74] In Moscow, the literary scholar Leonid Ivanovich Timofeev wrote that things were now "going alright," although the inhabitants of the surrounding countryside and towns were suffering badly from the Soviet "scorched earth" policy. He, too, grappled with the implications of Pearl Harbor. "Japan has entered the war," if not "with us" then "with America." "The whole world," Timofeev wrote, "is fighting. This complicates the situation." It was, he admitted, "difficult to figure out." The Japanese move, Timofeev speculated, might be "an indicator of Germany's crisis."[75]

The Soviet press was rather muted in its response to the outbreak of the Pacific War, perhaps because they were unsure of the implications for relations with Japan.[76] That said, the *Soldatenzeitung*, a Soviet-sponsored German-language paper, ran a front-page proclamation from the exiled German communist leaders Wilhelm Pieck, Wilhelm Florin, and Walter Ulbricht. "Hitler," they said, was waging a "hopeless" war against the Soviet Union, the greatest land power, Britain, the greatest naval power, and the United States, the "greatest industrial power in the world." Below the proclamation there was a photograph of an American Flying Fortress bomber with a caption stating that the United States would produce fifty thousand planes in the course of the next year.[77] What was striking here was the emphasis on American industrial power, which was portrayed as being the largest in the world, greater even than the USSR, and the assumption of American belligerency, even before the United States' formal entry into the war.

Unlike for the Anglo-Americans, who collected copious public-opinion material, and the Third Reich, whose internal surveillance reports give a good idea of popular views, it is very difficult to assess how the Soviet public reacted to the news of Pearl Harbor. It is clear, however, that there was widespread concern about its impact on Western arms supplies for the Red Army. For example, among the questions asked of a propaganda unit working with the Soviet Forty-Ninth Army was the following: "Won't the war in the Pacific have an effect on military deliveries to us?" The response is not recorded.[78]

One German woman, an evacuee from Düsseldorf who was billeted with a family in Laubach, could scarcely contain her joy at the news of Japanese successes. "Is it not wonderful this new war?" she announced. Friedrich Kellner responded, in the privacy of his secret diary, by calling her a "brutal Aryan" who was wrongly convinced that the war in the Far East would relieve the pressure on Germany. There had been similar hubris in the First World War, he remarked. "We need the war to impact much more strongly," Kellner concluded, "until all Germans have had their fill of war."[79]

Taking advantage of the widespread euphoria over Pearl Harbor, the Nazi Propaganda Ministry buried some bad news, just as Goebbels had suggested. It announced that the German economy was under such pressure due to the war that the production of "presents of any sort" would have to be considered "of secondary importance." Workers who had previously made children's toys, the announcement ran, were now producing shells. Workers who had once sewn handbags, it continued, were now busy making fur coats for the soldiers on the eastern front. Besides, whatever transport was available was needed to supply the men in the east and for the shipment of coal and potatoes. The delivery of mail to the military alone, it was pointed out, involved fifteen million letters and packages a day. "There is therefore an acute lack of presents in Germany," the ministry explained, and for this reason "the Christmas table cannot be as richly laid this year as it would usually be." Many "People's Comrades," in fact, had been able to buy only modest or no presents. The ministry thus appealed for restraint in the purchase of Christmas presents this year. It did so in the name of "our soldiers in the field" for whom every "People's Comrade" would surely "happily make this modest sacrifice."[80]

The Japanese triumphs also made the setbacks on the eastern front, whose dimensions were not yet widely appreciated, less painful for the German public. This was of little help to the Wehrmacht on the ground, however. In Russia, the Soviet Thirteenth Army so comprehensively smashed open the front of the Second Army that the two divisions taking the brunt of the attack were falling back in some disorder. There were also Soviet breakthroughs against Panzer Group Three and the Ninth Army. There was a distinct danger that the Soviet Operational Group Kostenko would now thrust forward as far as Kursk and Orel.[81] The Soviet Thirtieth Army struck north of Moscow at the Third Panzer Army, capturing many guns and trucks left behind by the fleeing Germans. South of Moscow, the Red Army took Venev and Yelets.

Of course, the Red Army did not have it all its own way. The Germans retained their capacity for improvised instant ripostes. That day, Zhukov, commander of the western front, sent a directive warning of the danger. "Protect forces' operations with anti-tank defenses reconnaissance and constant security," he ordered, "bearing in mind that, when withdrawing, the enemy will search for opportunities to counter-attack."[82] In late morning a platoon of the German Thirty-Sixth Motorized Infantry Division realized Zhukov's worst fears when it counterattacked a Soviet force holding the village of Arkhangelskoe. "About 150 Russians lie in heaps," commander Ludwig Freiherr von Heyl wrote afterward. "Our soldiers immediately pull the boots and fur coats off the dead bodies." Zhukov also cautioned his men against wasteful "frontal" attacks on "fortified positions." Again, his warnings were not always heeded. Another German regiment claimed to have killed more than six hundred Russians that day at a cost of only three dead and twenty wounded.[83]

These tactical successes, though, were small consolation. Operationally, Army Group Center was now on the back foot, and withdrawal would not be easy, as Bock had warned the day before. There was not enough fuel for all the tanks and trucks. The war diary of Hoepner's panzer group saw a "supply crisis" coming.[84] When Hermann Breith's Third Panzer Division fell back that day, many vehicles had to be abandoned or destroyed. Those that got away usually had to tow another. "Everything which is left is being blown up," a crewman from the Seventeenth Panzer Division wrote in his diary, "so that nothing falls into Russian hands."[85] To make matters worse, the weather warmed somewhat during the day, causing sleet showers, which resulted in more ice and further chaos on the roads.

At Army Group Center, Bock was now seriously worried. The SS brigade detailed to help the Second Army would not be ready for another five days. Hopes of flying in reinforcements to Panzer Group Three were dashed by bad weather. A battalion rushed to the front in trucks was unable to get through on the congested and icy roads. Bock gave orders that "everybody who was trained and capable of bearing arms" was to be brought in by rail the following day. In the meantime, he began to plan for a difficult withdrawal.[86]

Yet in the midst of this escalating crisis, Bock's headquarters received the army high command's "Instructions for the Tasks of the Ostheer [Eastern Army] During the Winter of 1941/42."[87] It read like a document from another planet. The Russians, they were told, were not yet "finally beaten," and instead of reinforcements, Army Group Center was offered unrealistic advice on how to prepare for the winter and to safeguard the mechanized forces for the resumption of operations in the spring. Clearly, there was as yet no real consciousness in the German Army high command, still less in the OKW, of how rapidly the situation in Russia had gotten out of control.

The Führer's mind was firmly on America. In the morning, Hitler issued a politically and operationally fateful instruction to the Kriegsmarine. The gloves were to come off. Hitler declared that all restrictions on the sinking of ships in the Atlantic, Mediterranean, Black Sea, and the Arctic "are lifted." The United States and all those Central and South American states who associated themselves with Washington's policy toward Germany and its allies, such as Costa Rica, the Dominican Republic, Haiti, Honduras, Nicaragua, Panama, "San Salvador [*sic*]," and

Uruguay, Hitler continued, were to be "regarded as hostile." Their war and merchant ships were to be treated the same as British ones. The so-called pan-American security zone was no longer to be recognized. Hitler also extended all these measures to cover newly cobelligerent nationalist China.[88] Admiral Karl Dönitz wasted no time. That same day, he told the naval leadership to release twelve submarines to attack shipping along the American coastline.[89]

Hitler arrived in Berlin's Anhalter Bahnhof at 11 a.m. For security reasons, the Führer's trains were not announced, and so ordinary travelers were told over the loudspeakers that they should clear the platform as soon as possible.[90] Hitler was soon plunged into a cycle of meetings. He spoke at length with Goebbels over lunch. Hitler was exultant about developments, which he claimed to have long predicted. Japan, the Führer believed, had had no choice but to act if it did not want to lose its great-power status. He was convinced that the Japanese fleet was now superior to the US-British naval forces in the Pacific. Hitler, Goebbels noted, had not known of the impending Japanese strike and had at first not believed the news.

Hitler was conscious of America's economic potential, which would reveal itself over time. This is why he was so pleased with Japan's audacity. Roosevelt, he told Goebbels, had made a mistake in exposing himself. "A boxer who saves his most crushing blows for the fifth or sixth round," he continued, "can experience what Max Schmeling experienced in his last encounter with Joe Louis, which is that he is knocked out in the first round." This was a remarkable insight into Hitler's own strategic conception, which was based on defeating or at least deterring a heavyweight opponent by front-loading a series of devastating blows to keep him off balance.

The Führer made clear to Goebbels his determination to "make public" the German declaration of war on the United States, but explained that hostilities had already begun with the order to pursue unrestricted submarine warfare against American shipping. Hitler also hoped to induce his other allies—meaning states like Bulgaria, Finland, and Romania—to make their own declarations of war on the United States, mobilizing a more impressive list of supporters than the Latin American states traveling in Roosevelt's slipstream. Overall, Hitler and Goebbels were delighted to have secured so powerful and reliable an ally as the Japanese, whom they regarded as "the Prussians of the Far East."[91]

It was clear that Russia was very much a second-order issue for Hitler at this time. "The Führer," Goebbels noted, "is not too worried about events on the eastern front." Hitler conceded the strength of Russian heavy tanks, his surprise at the appearance of ever more Russian armor, and the resilience of the Red Army soldier and the Russian people, who could put up with much greater hardships than he would dare to impose on the German *Volk*. He blamed the pause in operations on the "weather" and "the problem of supply." No doubt Hitler was more anxious than he let on, but the exchange is consistent with his relative lack of concern about the eastern front during the days following Pearl Harbor, and the priority he attached to the contest with the United States.

The "most pressing matter" now, Goebbels concluded, was Hitler's upcoming speech to the Reichstag, at which the war with the United States was to be announced. The Führer wanted to devote particular care to this address and therefore delayed the convening of the Reichstag by another day. Goebbels vowed not to trouble Hitler with any more minor matters until the great set piece was out of the way. He was struck by how much Pearl Harbor had rejuvenated the jaded Hitler. "The Führer," he noted, "once again radiates a wave of optimism and confidence in victory."[92]

As global war loomed, there was increased concern in the Nazi elite about Soviet prisoners of war. Millions of them languished in German camps, malnourished and poorly, often murderously, treated. Nazi Party leader Martin Bormann's anxiety was not for their welfare, but that of the German people, as he understood it. That day, he circulated a secret directive, which had been drawn up four days earlier, warning about how Soviet prisoners were being left unguarded or had committed various alleged "crimes." He insisted that the population be "informed again and again" of this matter. There was no actual shift in policy, but it seems likely that the lengthening of the war implied by the impending conflict with the United States led to an awareness of the fact that Germany would have to reckon with a large captive Slav population for the foreseeable future.[93]

In the German Army high command, the true extent of the disaster on the central sector of the eastern front had not yet sunk in. When Bock telephoned Franz Halder at 11:15 a.m. local time, the chief of the general staff was unworried. Halder remarked toward the end of their conversation that "the pressure exerted by us until a few days ago must have forced the enemy to deploy his remaining veteran troops he had originally intended to husband for the spring campaign, plus some newly established units, in order to meet our offensive head on." Halder "presumed" that "this level of activity will last till the middle or the end of the month and then ebb away."[94] It was, given what was widely known even then, an astonishingly optimistic prediction, but yet more evidence that the Soviet offensive was not the first thing on the mind of the German leadership.

Off Malaya, it was now dinnertime on the *Repulse*, where overconfidence also prevailed. While Halder reassured Bock, journalist Cecil Brown was sitting in the wardroom with a dozen or so officers listening to BBC radio and commenting dismissively on Japanese capabilities. One condemned their "pinpricks at widely separated points," another claimed that the enemy "can't fly [and] can't see at night" and was "not well-trained," yet another said "they can't shoot," and one simply laughed them off as "bloody fools." After Brown wondered aloud whether they were not being overconfident, the men pondered briefly but stood by their views. "We are not overconfident," he was told. "We just don't think the enemy is much good."[95]

In London, there was growing alarm as the suspension of Lend-Lease material became apparent. Just before 11 a.m., the Foreign Office received Halifax's telegram of the previous night warning of urgent problems posed by the "Japanese war" for the reallocation of supplies previously destined for Britain to US forces in the Pacific. The message was rushed to the prime minister. It was soon followed by another from the British Supply Council in Washington, reporting that "on Monday

8th December, the U.S. authorities had issued an order freezing the movement of all military supplies."[96] By then, Churchill had also heard from the chief of the air staff that the US War Department had requested the urgent transfer of 250 aircraft from British allocations.[97]

An anxious Churchill was now even more convinced that he needed to see Roosevelt personally as soon as possible. He pressed the president for "another conference" so that they could "review the whole war plan in the light of reality and new facts, as well as the problems of production and distribution." Churchill confided that these issues were "causing me concern" and could "best be settled on the highest executive level . . . the sooner the better." With as yet no declaration of war between Germany and the United States, American attention firmly fixed on the Pacific after the humiliating devastation at Pearl Harbor, and the disruption to the American supplies on which Britain relied, it is little wonder Churchill was concerned. As a result, he proposed departing "in a day or two" for a weeklong visit to Baltimore or Annapolis, accompanied by the chiefs of staff, and requested Roosevelt inform him "at earliest what you feel about this."[98] A message to that effect was sent to Halifax, who was instructed to deliver it to the White House that morning.[99]

All this would have alarmed Eden, then in the midst of a "very rough" journey to Murmansk, in far northwest Russia. From aboard the *Kent*, he continued to urge Churchill to rethink his trip to Washington, telegramming the prime minister that day to express his "wish you could postpone a fortnight till my return."[100] Churchill had no intention of delaying, if only he could convince Roosevelt to permit a meeting. At his lunch with the prime minister that day, King George VI noted that "W told me he is anxious to go to Washington to arrange various matters with F.D.R."[101] By then, Churchill had already told his chief military assistant, General Hastings Ismay, to arrange for his cipher staff to accompany him on a potential trip across the Atlantic and also ensure that he could keep in touch with the war fronts, "especially in regard to Libyan telegrams."[102]

Positive reports were continuing to arrive from North Africa, though it was unclear whether the government would benefit politically from the victory. General Auchinleck's latest dispatch from the desert, which reached London just after midday, contained the best news yet: "Consider tide turned."[103] Even so, press reports of the battle naturally lagged slightly behind events on the ground, and so considerable public criticism of the campaign persisted. As the editor of the *Sunday Express*, John Gordon, noted in his latest column, "There is no use blinking the fact that the Libyan developments of the past week have not been very palatable news to the people of this country."[104] The authorities' previous poor handling of public expectations about the campaign and its challenges meant that the victory would not necessarily receive the reaction it deserved. As Alan Moorehead, embedded with the troops in the desert, noted, "So now, when the Eight Army, by a moral triumph of its general and by the fighting stamina of its men, was about to move forward to a victory, there were few to applaud, still fewer to understand how it was done." Instead, "the earlier glowing heroics had soured into cynicism and boredom."

Even if it was not yet fully appreciated at home, it was clear to Moorehead "that the shape of the battle had altered." As the men advanced, they "came on the wreckage of many Nazi planes" and it became apparent that, "worn out, short of supplies, badly short of armour, Rommel was clearing out."[105] Indeed, that day Rommel wrote to his wife, "I've had to break off the action outside Tobruk on account of the Italian formations and also the badly exhausted German troops." His dejection was evident: "You can imagine what I'm going through and what anxieties I have. It doesn't look as though we'll get any Christmas this year." At the same time, the struggle was not yet over, and Rommel had no plans to surrender the desert: "I'm hoping we'll succeed in escaping enemy encirclement and holding on to Cyrenaica."[106]

In eastern Europe, the horrors perpetrated by the Nazis and their allies continued to grow. In the forest of Rumbula outside Riga, Friedrich Jeckeln called off the shootings between noon and 1 p.m. local time.[107] This was because he had to prepare for the next transport, which was of Jews from Hamburg. The remaining Latvian Jews were given a stay of execution and sent back to the ghetto. Their state of mind can only be guessed at. The bodies of those already murdered—which numbered twenty-five thousand—lay, for now, in shallow graves. Their possessions had either been confiscated by the murder squads or lay strewn across a devastated ghetto; the last meals they cooked were still on the tables, long gone cold. The Hamburg Jews arrived that day at the freight station in Skirotava, a suburb of Riga, and were bound for the nearby Jungfern-hof, a country estate that had been converted into an improvised concentration camp.

In the Crimean town of Simferopol, it was the turn of the Krymchaks, a community of Turkic-speaking Jews who had lived on the peninsula for centuries. The staff of Einsatzgruppe D and the men of Sonderkommando 11b murdered more than 1,500 of them that day. Then, the commander, Otto Ohlendorf, ordered the killing to be paused. He probably did so due to unease among the men, who did not object to the murders as such but found them onerous and now requested to be assigned to other tasks. Ohlendorf looked for replacements so that he could resume his mission as soon as possible.[108]

The murders of the Soviet Jews were not publicized, but the Nazi war against "world Jewry" was no secret. That day, the governing council of the Jewish religious communities in eastern Upper Silesia (in today's Poland) met to mark their second anniversary. One of their members, Hugo Kunz, said that "if you follow the newspapers, you will see that one is driving forward the destruction of the European Jews." "War," he added, "has been declared on Jewry as a whole." Kunz hoped that the following generation of Jews would survive and be able to continue the struggle.[109]

Very few Germans protested against these heinous crimes. One of the few who did was the Protestant *Landesbischof* of Württemberg, Theophil Wurm. He had managed to preserve much of the independence of his church in the face of Nazi encroachments and had been an open critic of what the regime was doing. That day he spoke out again, penning a memorandum to Hitler pointing out, among other things, that the treatment of the mentally ill and "non-Aryans" could be exploited by "enemy propaganda," which was indeed the case. Wurm also penned a letter to the Nazi minister in charge of relations with the churches,

Hans Kehrl, in which he not only condemned the "doing with of the mentally ill and the feeble-minded" but also spoke of "rumors of mass killings in the east."[110]

The former Austrian chancellor, Dr. Kurt Schuschnigg, was a different sort of resister. Hitler considered him the embodiment of clerical Catholic and conservative opposition to the regime. That day, Schuschnigg was transferred from the Gestapo prison in Munich to the concentration camp at Sachsenhausen near Berlin, where he was classified as a VIP prisoner. He was accompanied by his wife, enjoyed privileges unheard of by the rest of the inmates, and was in no immediate physical danger. All the same, the former chancellor was cast down by the sheer size, grayness, and menace of the complex. The camp, he wrote on arrival, was set in a wilderness of sand and pine trees. It was a place of "gray nameless misery," in which "ashen faced" and "haggard figures" dragged themselves between the barracks. The guards in the observation towers could practically see through the windows of their huts.[111]

Meanwhile, another resister, the Free French leader Charles de Gaulle, was lunching at the Connaught Hotel in London with Harold Nicolson, then working for the British Ministry of Information. The Briton was repelled by the Frenchman's "arrogance and fascism" but attracted by his "fine retriever dog" eyes. De Gaulle wanted Nicolson to say that all the French elements in England should rally around him. The Englishman retorted, to de Gaulle's irritation and the blushes of his aide-de-camp, that he "was cross at having one Frenchman tell me that de Gaulle was surrounded by Jews and Freemasons, another that he was surrounded by Jesuits and [extreme right-wing] Cagoulards." This tetchy exchange was typical of what the French leader had experienced in London. This time, though, talk turned to the new global situation. Nicolson bet that Germany would declare war on the United States. "Not on your life," de Gaulle responded, adding, though, that he would not take the bet, "since you may be right."[112]

Free French anxiety about the new situation was evident in the broadcast of de Gaulle's propaganda station out of Brazzaville, in central Africa, that day. "The world war predicted in June 1940 by General de Gaulle," it claimed, "has now become a reality." Pearl Harbor, the broadcast continued, had been instigated by Hitler and was a "mere incident." The main enemy, it insisted, was Germany, which had set Japan against the United States after suffering reverses on the Russian front. The station therefore concluded that de Gaulle would lead the French contingent in the reformed "victorious bloc of 1917."[113] As for what would happen if Germany did not declare war on the United States—as de Gaulle had feared during his conversation with Nicolson—and the Americans instead were sucked into a war with Japan alone, this alternative was not discussed.

In the afternoon, Hitler met with Ribbentrop. There was no discussion about the decision to declare war on the United States. Indeed, Minister of State Otto Meissner recalls that the Führer told the foreign minister and his entourage "that the state of war between Germany and the United States was already de facto in existence since Roosevelt's shoot-on-sight order of the previous September."[114] Instead, the subject of their discussion was the text of the Axis declaration and treaty, which Hitler wanted in place before he stood up to make his great speech. That same day, in accordance with the previous agreement to provide a narrative justifying the breach with the United States, the Foreign Office produced a memorandum containing a list of "unneutral, insulting, and provocative speeches of President Roosevelt," beginning with the Quarantine Speech of October 1937 and ending with the president's Armistice Day speech on November 11, 1941. This list was clearly designed to serve as fodder for Hitler's fulminations.[115]

On hearing that the Führer had returned, Nicolaus von Below, his Luftwaffe adjutant, hastened to Hitler's apartment in the Imperial Chancellery, which was already full of people. It was so loud that Below's greeting went unheard. Like Goebbels, Below found Hitler convinced that Pearl Harbor was a "signal to declare war on America." The adjutant later recalled that he was shocked at "Hitler's ignorance about America's potential, which had in the end decided the First World War." He saw this as evidence of Hitler's "foreign-political dilettantism" and his "lack of knowledge of the outside world." But the Führer, as we know, was in no doubt about what he was facing. His expectation, as Below went on to say, was that the United States would for the foreseeable future be distracted by Japan and kept from interfering in the European theater of operations.[116] This had been Hitler's strategy all along—a catastrophically mistaken one, as it turned out, but one that made sense to him given the information available and the lens through which he interpreted that knowledge.

Strikingly, there was no opposition to the prospect of a new war in the German Foreign Office, the armed services, or the Nazi Party. They had been conditioned by Hitler's rhetoric and Roosevelt's actions to believe that they were already at war with the United States. Ribbentrop's principal concern was to nail down the treaty text with Tokyo and Rome. This was partly in order to ensure that the Japanese would not be able to conclude a separate peace with the Allies and partly to agree upon a common ideological front against the United States and Britain. The agreement was designed as a rhetorical and ideological counter to the Atlantic Charter, which had sent such a collective shudder down Axis spines four months earlier. It was not, however, a program for military cooperation. There were plans for extensive sharing of intelligence, but that was about it.[117] Ambassador Oshima told Goebbels that the Japanese were planning a strike at Singapore, which they expected to capture soon, but the Germans were skeptical. "He is already forging plans for a joint attack on India," the propaganda minister wrote, "but we are not yet at that stage."[118] Besides, as the German naval leadership noted that day, there was simply not enough fuel oil for joint operations.[119]

On the other side of the Atlantic, the Americans were trying to peel the Italians away from the Axis. The former US ambassador to Rome, William Phillips, told the Italian ambassador to Washington, Don Ascanio dei Principi Colonna, that even if attacked by the Reich, "any decision which could be taken with respect to Germany would not necessarily also affect Italy."[120] Mussolini would ignore this gambit, which seems to have reached Rome with some delay. In fact, he was determined to prosecute the war more vigorously. Mussolini and General Ugo Cavallero agreed that day that, contrary to Rommel, who wanted to evacuate the whole

Cyrenaica region in Libya, Agedabia must be held to cover Benghazi to ensure the resupply of the forces in North Africa.[121] Ribbentrop did not know all this, but he was well aware that the Italians were the weak link in the chain. For this reason, he was keen to impress on them the need to rise to the new situation. "This was a heavy blow for America," Ribbentrop told Dino Alfieri, the Duce's man in Berlin, that same day, "and even more so for Britain." "It was," he continued, "the most important event since the start of the war."[122]

As the new day broke in Washington, Edward Stettinius, the Lend-Lease director, was awoken at dawn by a call from London. On the line was an extremely "perturbed" Averell Harriman. Was the White House aware, he wanted to know, that there was a "complete embargo" on Lend-Lease shipments? This had caused a "most embarrassing situation" for Harriman, as British officials beseeched him for desperately needed materials. The aid was urgently required for the campaign against the Axis forces in the Middle East, and delay in releasing the supplies could prove disastrous. It is not clear whether the Soviets were yet aware of the suspension, but, at a time when their resources were badly stretched, the possible consequences for them were potentially even more dire.

The Lend-Lease director assured Harriman that the suspension was temporary as "the Army and Navy desired to take a 48 hour look at the situation." But Stettinius was himself privately furious about the state of affairs, which "has been created without consultation with any member of the Lend-Lease Administration."[123] He told Hopkins that the United States must get "guns and tanks and planes," as well as vital raw materials, into the "hands of the people who can use them most effectively." With "questions of high military, naval and political strategy now arising with greatest speed," it was imperative that decisions were connected to a broader grand strategy, not made "in a makeshift way in too low a level." It was vital "in the light of the present critical situation" that American military hardware reached "countries such as the United Kingdom" immediately.[124] He resolved to take up the issue with the president at a meeting of the Supply Priorities and Allocations Board, which coordinated the distribution of militarily critical commodities and materials, that morning.

A power struggle between agencies was already underway. At the War Department, officials were working to ensure "the merger of Lend-Lease with the War Department appropriations." Assistant Secretary McCloy was adamant that it was "illogical and foolish to differentiate the Lend-Lease program from our over-all defence program now that we are at war."[125]

The Japanese assault on Hawaii had knocked out the nation's Pacific bulwark, and it was not clear that the United States could currently afford the luxury of exporting aircraft to other countries. After consulting with the chief of staff, Secretary of War Stimson was determined to impress this on the president and arranged to see him ten minutes before the Supply Priorities and Allocations Board meeting. He reminded Roosevelt that "the defense of the west coast has always been dependent upon Navy reconnaissance and the fortress at Hawaii," but that was now "practically gone." The insecurity of the West Coast therefore called into question America's capacity "to fulfil the Lend Lease program." Only if the air force was "free to take all the Lend Lease production and possibly some of the British production" could the administration "fill out our original 54 group program for defense of continental United States by the end of the year, December 31st." Despite his previous commitment to continue Lend-Lease in "full operation," the president now recognized the force of Stimson's argument and agreed it was "reasonable." Consequently, during the board meeting he "referred to it as something the Government would have to do."[126]

At the meeting, Stimson also received Roosevelt's approval to merge all appropriations of Lend-Lease into the respective army and navy production. He reassured Stettinius that this would be restricted to military matériel and that other supplies, such as agricultural production, would be untouched. This did little to allay Stettinius's fears about the immediate consequences for the fighting capabilities of America's allies. After the meeting, he reported his discussion with Harriman that morning to Roosevelt and received confirmation that the embargo would only last forty-eight hours. Still concerned, however, he wrote to Hopkins after arriving back at his office: "I am rushing this note to you by hand as I think a situation exists which you and the President should know about immediately. Lend-Lease shipments have been virtually stopped." Ships were being held at the docks and goods in transit were now backed up under orders from the War Department. In some instances, shipments from suppliers had been stopped altogether. An anxious Stettinius urged that those goods "already loaded, in transit and ready for delivery" be released as quickly as possible "to avoid the cumulative effects of even a short delay."[127]

The US Foreign Broadcast Intelligence Service's daily report made for interesting reading that day. Unsurprisingly, German newsmen continued to claim that the "only one to blame in the Far Eastern conflict is Roosevelt," quoting the Berlin-based *Lokal-Anzeiger* that the US president had "carefully planned and worked out the spreading of the war conflagration." Little concern was evinced about the US Army affecting the balance in Europe if its troops entered the fray there, with one commentator suggesting they were "even more poorly equipped than the English army was in 1937-9" and, as a result, an Allied "attack on Western Europe would not be feasible for some time."

To American intelligence analysts, though, the emphasis by both German and Italian commentators on the disruption to Lend-Lease was notable. Radio Berlin crowed that "at a moment of most fateful importance to the British World Empire, Churchill has admitted that U.S. war shipments have actually been decreasing in volume and now will decrease further." This was regarded as a clear "admission of growing German successes in the Atlantic." The same note was struck by Radio Roma, which claimed that Lend-Lease was "now a scrap of paper in the hands of the White House Jews." Of most concern to the president and his advisers on receiving this digest was likely a "last minute reception" relayed by the Italian propaganda outlet that morning. "From a reliable source," Rome declared, "it is learned that all U.S. ships on their way from the west coast of the U.S. to the Siberian coast of the U.S.S.R. have been recalled."[128] It was clear that, despite the White House press release claiming Lend-Lease was continuing as usual, the truth could not remain hidden for much longer.

This was also the day that the Germans chose to release news of Hitler's meeting with the grand mufti of Palestine, Amin al-Husseini, about ten days earlier. The DNB announced that the Führer had received him in the company of Ribbentrop and that their conversation had been not merely "cordial" but "important for the future of the Arab lands."[129] The news bureau also let it be known that the former Iraqi prime minister Rashid Ali al-Gailani was on his way to Germany. The timing of both announcements was significant, because they suggested that the Third Reich was going to use the opportunity created by Pearl Harbor to increase the pressure on the British Empire.

The grand mufti and the Führer were linked not merely by their joint hatred of Britain, but also by their anti-Semitic worldview. We know from the confidential record of the meeting that Hitler had told the mufti that he opposed a Jewish homeland in Palestine, because it would be "nothing more than a state focus for the destructive influence of Jewish interests." Germany, the Führer continued, was determined to demand that all European countries undertake measures to deal with the "Jewish problem" and would make a similar appeal to the wider world at the "appropriate time." His only interest in Palestine, Hitler insisted, was "the destruction of the Jews living in the Arab lands under British protection." The mufti listened to all this and declared himself "completely reassured and satisfied."[130] There is no evidence that Amin al-Husseini originated the idea of murdering "world Jewry," but there is no doubt that he welcomed the measure as beneficial for the Arab interest in Palestine, as he understood it, and more generally.

Shortly after 3 p.m., the German Foreign Office received a report from the ambassador to Tokyo, Ott, on his negotiations with the Japanese. Two days into the new war, there was still no consensus on the Axis text. Ott had been summoned to the Japanese Foreign Ministry, where Togo told him that his legal section wanted article 3 to be removed from the draft treaty. The cooperation stipulated therein, the foreign minister continued, was already guaranteed by the Tripartite Pact, and the proposed new article seemed to limit the length of the relationship to the end of the war, rather than the ten years envisaged in the pact. Togo also asked that he be sent the Italian text as soon as possible.[131] Even with due dispatch and goodwill on both sides, it seemed, agreeing and signing the statement Hitler wanted before he declared war on the United States would take time. What the Führer did not know, of course, was that thanks to their intercept service, the Americans and British already had copies of the draft text being discussed.[132]

At around the same time, a report arrived from the German embassy in Washington. Thomsen wrote that while the conflict with Japan enjoyed massive popular support, "the American people were not yet ripe for a war on European soil." In other words, it might still be possible to avoid direct military confrontation with the United States. "Whether Roosevelt will also call for a declaration of a state of war with Germany and Italy," the envoy continued, "is unclear." That said, Thomsen suggested that though it might make little sense to become entangled with Germany while the United States was under assault in the Pacific, the president might "attempt" to anticipate Germany and Italy's decisions, if only to compensate for his lack of preparedness against Japan.[133]

Here, Thomsen, wittingly or unwittingly, was feeding Hitler and Ribbentrop's narrative that it was psychologically important to seize the initiative and declare war on the United States, rather than passively waiting to be attacked. He also affirmed Nazi strategy in another important respect. "War with Japan means redirecting all energy toward one's own armaments," he wrote, "and a corresponding limitation of Lend-Lease." He expected a "shift of all activities to the Pacific and the closing of Vladivostok for supplies to the Soviet Union." Thomsen further predicted "a threat to raw material imports, especially of rubber."[134] At almost exactly the same time as this report arrived, Thomsen sent a short additional message confirming that he had "carried out the instructions he had been given," meaning that he had destroyed the embassy's secret files as ordered by Ribbentrop.[135]

In occupied Paris it was now late afternoon, and the new German curfew was already showing its consequences for city life. Two hours before it was due to come into effect, Parisians began to rush for the metro and the train stations to make it home in time. Bakeries were sold out; shops and restaurants were shut. Within an hour, there were police patrols on the streets while the last commuters scrambled to get clear. By the time the curfew was in force at 6 p.m., the city was deserted. For the Americans still left in Paris, it was a time of great uncertainty.[136] They did not know what their status would be now that Germany's ally Japan was at war with their country, and whether or when Hitler and Roosevelt's duel would erupt into open hostilities.

Just after midday in Washington, Dr. T. V. Soong, Chiang Kai-shek's personal emissary to the United States, arrived at the Treasury. He wanted Morgenthau to transmit a message to the president from the generalissimo: China was now ready to declare war on Japan. Despite Japan's aggression over the past decade, war had never been technically declared. More recently, Chiang had delayed "in the hope of getting Russia to join in the declaration of war against Japan," enabling the two countries to deploy their armies against Japan's forces on the "Asiatic Continent." As Stalin had not yet responded to this suggestion, Chiang wished to know whether Roosevelt would prefer an immediate Chinese declaration or a postponement in the hope of a favorable Soviet response. When Morgenthau called the White House, Grace Tully informed him that the president was tied up for the rest of the day with meetings and drafting his radio address for that evening.[137] Soong was directed to the State Department instead, where Sumner Welles, speaking on behalf of Roosevelt, suggested that China go ahead and declare war on all three nations, as "Russia was getting its troops in shape to go to war with Japan shortly."[138] Ultimately, even before hearing Roosevelt's response, China would declare war on Japan, Germany, and Italy that day and therefore become a full Allied cobelligerent. It is not clear why Welles expressed such confidence that the Soviets would soon be at war in the Pacific. Litvinov had given no such indication in his meetings with the president or other Americans during the preceding two days. In fact, Stalin's perspective on the new situation in Asia remained a mystery to all sides.

Shortly after Morgenthau's call, Lord Halifax arrived at the White House with his message from Churchill. He found the president in "good resolute shape" and "pretty confident that Germany and Italy would declare war almost immediately."[139] Halifax was seemingly unaware that Roosevelt now had knowledge, through MAGIC decrypts, of Ribbentrop's personal assurance to Oshima that Germany and Italy would enter the conflict against the United States. Yet could Roosevelt really be certain how Hitler would respond? As Robert Sherwood, then busy revising the text for the president's fireside chat that night, later noted, the Nazis "were in honour bound by their pledges to the Japanese, but they had not previously shown much inclination to let such bourgeois-democratic considerations interfere with their own concepts on self-interest."[140]

Despite Roosevelt's apparent air of confidence, Halifax noted a sense of uncertainty below the surface. When he relayed Churchill's request for a meeting, Roosevelt demurred. Although the president emphasized concerns for Churchill's safety in taking a transatlantic voyage, particularly as "publicity could not be avoided," the ambassador had a "slight feeling" there was more to it. He reported back to London that Roosevelt had given the impression a visit was "rather too strong medicine in the immediate future for some of his public opinion that he still feels he has to educate up to the complete conviction of the oneness of the struggle against both Germany and Japan." It was clear to Halifax that Japan's attack had perhaps not been sufficient to convince America's still considerable swathe of isolationist opinion that the United States should go to war with Nazi Germany.

The president thus remained reliant on Hitler to act. He was also acutely conscious of the political dangers from any perception that US foreign policy was not wholly independent. As the US analyst at the Foreign Office had noted, Roosevelt had scrupulously avoided connecting America's entrance into the Pacific war too closely with Britain's. Now, he clearly feared that a visit by the British prime minister would antagonize American public opinion, fueling accusations that Britain was seeking to draw the United States into a European war too. Roosevelt hoped that Hitler would resolve his conundrum, with a "possible crystallisation of the position vis-à-vis Germany very close," but at least until then a meeting with Churchill was out of the question. Consequently, the president informed Halifax that no meeting was possible before the New Year.

To soften the blow, Halifax told Churchill that Roosevelt had "perfectly genuine" pressures on his time over the coming weeks, with the upcoming annual budget, his State of the Union address, and, above all, addressing the "immediate position on the defence side." The ambassador could see the administration was "terribly shaken here, as you can well suppose, and fully realize that they have been caught napping."[141] This did not mollify Churchill, who felt that Halifax, a former foreign secretary and his erstwhile rival for the premiership, had been too craven and accommodating. He had long regarded Halifax as a "man compounded of charm" and certainly "no coward; no gentleman is." Nevertheless, there was "something that runs through him like a yellow streak; grovel, grovel, grovel." As viceroy, "grovel to the Indians"—for offering India dominion status, much to the arch-imperialist Churchill's horror—as foreign secretary, "grovel to the Germans"—for his consistent support of appeasement—and now, "grovel to the Americans."[142]

Whatever the validity of Churchill's general assessment, on this occasion Halifax was merely relaying Roosevelt's remarks faithfully while also astutely assessing the pressures on the president. It is hard to fault his evaluation "of a still lingering distinction in some quarters of the public mind between war with Japan and war with Germany."[143]

That day, the head of MI6 passed Churchill the intercepted message from Oshima to Tokyo reporting his meeting with Ribbentrop in the immediate aftermath of the Pearl Harbor attack. The prime minister now knew that although Ribbentrop "had not yet secured Hitler's sanction," he had assured Japan that "the immediate participation in the war by Germany and Italy was a matter of course." A date was not set, but Oshima was asked to call again on December 8 to discuss "the time of publication of this declaration."[144]

From other intelligence that Churchill received that day, however, it would have been evident how little trust there was between the two governments. It was clear that the Nazis had been unaware that the Japanese attack on the United States was imminent. In a cable dispatched in the hours before Japan struck, Togo had informed Oshima, then in the process of negotiating the revised Tripartite Pact, that "the situation may take a sudden turn and we cannot tell whether a collision may not occur in the interval before the formal signing is performed." As a result, the ambassador was urged to impress on the Nazis that even "if war breaks out between Japan and America before the formal signature of the agreement," Tokyo still expected that "Germany and Italy will immediately participate."[145] Even though Ribbentrop had pledged this to Oshima on the night of December 7, the Japanese ambassador was clearly not completely convinced and continued to keep the pressure up. Thus, when he had met with Ribbentrop on December 8, he had again pressed for a "formal declaration of war against America without delay." The German foreign secretary promised to transmit this request "as quickly as possible" to Hitler, who was then discussing the matter with advisers at his headquarters. Ribbentrop was convinced that "a formal declaration of war would likely make a good impression on the German people." He informed the ambassador that Hitler had already told the navy that "American ships were to be attacked wherever and whenever encountered."[146] Undeclared hostilities with the United States had clearly begun, and Churchill now had confirmation that Ribbentrop had pledged that Germany would make war official, although it was not clear when that might be or even whether he definitely spoke for Hitler.

The Italians were preoccupied by the situation in the Mediterranean, and so was the German naval high command.[147] Britain's Eighth Army continued to advance in Libya. A number of British submarines were sunk, but resupply of Italian forces in North Africa remained precarious. The use of the port facilities at Bizerta would certainly have eased the situation, as would more cooperation from the Vichy authorities across the board. This was why the meeting scheduled for the following day between Foreign Minister Ciano and Admiral Darlan in Turin, where the Italian foreign minister had now arrived, was so important.

Hitler hoped to turn the new global scenario to Axis advantage in the Mediterranean. "The Führer expects," Franz Halder noted that day, "that the entry of America into the war will put France under pressure." "He wants to draw France over to our side," he continued, "and deploy it in Africa and the Mediterranean against England-America."[148] Göring had met with Admiral Darlan, and there were hopes the Italians would come to an arrangement with him when he met with Ciano.

The widening of the war not only put Vichy France on the spot; it also placed further pressure on other neutrals. It was hard enough to remain aloof in a war involving the British Empire, the Soviet Union, and the German Reich, but after Pearl Harbor, the situation became even more complicated. "The situation of Switzerland has become delicate," the chief of the Swiss intelligence service wrote that day, because "the entry of the United States poses the problem of a world war." "It is," he continued, echoing Mussolini's rhetoric, "a struggle between two continents and our country finds itself completely isolated in the middle of one of them [Europe]." "Switzerland's economic situation," which was "already precarious," could worsen. That said, the country now needed "more than ever" to show its will to defend itself and maintain its neutrality.[149]

In Washington, where it was now just after 2 p.m., Thomsen was penning another dispatch. Federal, state, and local authorities, he reported, were making numerous arrests of German citizens. In New York alone, Thomsen went on, there had been three hundred arrests on suspicion of endangering the peace and security of the United States. Detainees were apparently being brought to immigration offices, which suggested that speedy deportation was being planned.[150]

Sir Arthur Harris noted that across the country "Americans were very raid conscious after Pearl Harbor." As he and his wife listened to the radio in their Washington apartment that lunchtime, they "heard a running commentary of a most terrible air raid on New York." Utterly alarmed, they got "quite worked up about it," as it was reported "that casualties were not negligible."[151] At the Treasury Department, Morgenthau received the same reports on the "news ticker" and immediately called Undersecretary of War Robert Patterson "about enemy planes over New York and New Jersey." Patterson had just returned from lunch and had heard nothing about it but rushed to investigate. Within five minutes, he called back to say that "there's nothing at all to that rumour" and that the air force had been "trying to kill it for half an hour." Patterson breathed a sigh of relief: "You don't know what to believe these days, do you?"[152]

Throughout the day, the president continued to work on the text of that evening's fireside chat. He drafted and redrafted the address with the help of Robert Sherwood, Samuel Rosenman, and Archibald MacLeish, the librarian of Congress and director of the recently established Office of Facts and Figures.[153] To strike the correct balance between informing the public about the scale of the destruction in the Pacific and avoiding giving too much away to the enemy, MacLeish consulted with McCloy at the War Department and Adlai Stevenson, Knox's aide at the Navy Department.[154] It was also vital for the president to justify why the administration had been correct to furnish aid to the Allies fighting Nazi Germany and why, even as it geared up for the struggle with the Japanese aggressors, the United States must continue to maintain that logistical lifeline to Europe. Above all, it was essential that the indivisibility of Imperial Japan and Nazi Germany was impressed on the American mind, even while the president remained alive to the continued political risks of requesting a formal declaration of war against Hitler. With those goals in mind, White House secretary Steve Early informed the press that the president's sixty-minute radio address, which would air at 10 p.m., would deal more with "the Nazi pattern of this overall situation" than with the specific details of the Japanese attack.

If the "Man on the Street" survey is any guide, Roosevelt's message was getting through. On this day a Mrs. Whitaker was stopped on the streets of Austin, Texas, and asked whether the Japanese were "in any way justified" in attacking Pearl Harbor. "Well," she answered, "I think they were influenced by Hitler in every way." The German dictator, Mrs. Whitaker continued, "knew" that he could not make any headway against Moscow that winter, so he had encouraged the Japanese to "start war with the United States" and thus "get the whole world involved." That, she believed, was what Hitler "intended in the first [place] and he's now climaxed it all by getting us all mixed up."[155]

Though there was widespread consensus that Hitler was primarily to blame, there was no agreement among Mrs. Whitaker's fellow Texans as to what should be done about Germany. On the one hand, the Reverend John Espey Watts wanted "a peace . . . that will look at the countries we have defeated as human beings and not as a bunch of people or a nation of people that we want to enslave as our servants." "Versailles," he said, "should not be repeated."[156] Sixty-seven-year-old J. C. Brodie, on the other hand, favored a much harder line. "The only way to keep out of war with Germany," he argued, "is to do away with Germany entirely and put them under other governments and have no Germany at all." "As long as there is a Germany," Brodie insisted, "there'll be wars."[157] All this, it should be noted, was being said when the two countries were not officially at war.

What America's contribution to that war would be still remained uncertain. That day's *Chicago Tribune* reported that "according to the White House the President is not considering a declaration of war on Germany and Italy." It was clear that "the United States is now engaged in an undeclared war" with those two countries, "but whether it becomes formalized appears to be up to Hitler, for the time being at least." As the *Tribune*'s reporter pointed out, Germany and Italy were only obligated to go to war under the Tripartite Pact if the United States had attacked Japan: "Unless it suits his purpose for ulterior reasons, however, not even Hitler would attempt to construe the events of yesterday as an American attack on Japan."[158] While the *Tribune*, previously the country's preeminent noninterventionist newspaper, focused its editorial exclusively on "Japan's perfidy," supporters of intervention in Europe urged Americans not to be blind to the bigger picture.[159] Walter Lippmann, whose "Today and Tomorrow" column was syndicated to over one hundred newspapers, warned that the United States must fight the conflict "not as an isolationist's isolated war with Japan, but as a war of our coalition against the Axis coalition."[160] The fact that Lippmann felt it necessary to make this argument was an indication of the continued concern about the potential persuasive power of the limited-war advocates.

One prominent anti-war activist, Norman Thomas, the Socialist Party presidential candidate in the past four elections and a frequent speaker at America First events, told a rally in Baltimore that day he was "pleased" the president had not extended America's war to Europe. "Insofar as it is possible to control, I believe that the smaller the area of American troops the better," Thomas maintained.[161] The Montana senator Burton K. Wheeler also told a reporter that, given "the facts that are in my possession now," there was no reason for the United States to immediately declare war on Germany and Italy. Wheeler remained adamant "that what we ought to do was build our defenses, and to save the best planes and guns for ourselves instead of giving them to other countries."[162] In an attempt to combat this sort of rhetoric, the assistant secretary of state Breckinridge Long told the annual convention of the American Farm Bureau Federation in Chicago that evening not to become so obsessed with the Pacific that they forgot Hitler. Long warned the group that Hitler's first step in his bid to "gain control of the Atlantic" was to "prevent supplies from reaching the British Isles and thus make easier an invasion of England." From there, "he would proceed to blast a way for himself toward the conquest of the Western Hemisphere."[163] The American debate over the nation's role in the war against Hitler remained a live one.

While this intense campaign of persuasion was being waged in the United States, the Wehrmacht was in more and more trouble in the east. Reinhardt's Panzer Group Three saw off a Soviet thrust at Klin with a vigorous counterstroke, but Guderian's forces were falling back from the salient around Tula. It was clear that the Soviet offensive was much bigger and more sustained than at first realized. Bock ordered Army Group Center to prepare a rearward position along the line of Kursk-Orel and Medyn-Rzhev, creating a straighter front line that would enable him to release forces for use elsewhere.[164] The Germans were also falling back to the north, where army group commander Ritter von Leeb was forced to admit that Tikhvin could no longer be held, and that therefore Hitler's order that it should only be evacuated with his permission was redundant. All the same, Ritter von Leeb put through a call to army high command at 6 p.m. local time to seek authorization for the withdrawal.[165]

The sense of crisis on the Russian front was now unavoidable. "The soldiers are no longer able to offer resistance," it was reported from General Walther Fischer von Weikersthal's LII Army Corps. "They don't fight anymore."[166] An increasingly frantic Guderian spoke of a serious "crisis of confidence" among the men and said that he did not know how he was supposed to repel the next attack. The question of whom the troops had lost confidence in—their local commanders, the theater commanders, the high command, or the Führer himself—was left open.[167] Halder once again dismissed these concerns and claimed that Soviet attacks would run out of steam by the end of the month at the latest. Bock responded to this by saying that by then Germany would be *kaputt*, to which Halder replied grandiosely down the telephone that "the German soldier does not go kaputt." That was about all he could offer, because when Bock requested more troops, Halder had to confess that he had "nothing left" to send him.[168]

When the commander of Army Group North, Ritter von Leeb, spoke to the German Army high command about Tikhvin, much more drama ensued. That day, the Red Army had cut the road between the town and the rest of the German line, and extraction became imperative.[169] At around 9:30 p.m., Ritter von Leeb gave orders to the Sixteenth Army to conduct a fighting withdrawal. Two hours later, OKW official Alfred Jodl rang to give him freedom of action. Fifty minutes after that, Keitel was on the line, revoking the previous authorization. "The Führer," he reported, "is very unhappy about the request to build up a position to the west of Tikhvin because that would mean giving up Leningrad"—that is, abandoning all hopes of linking the Finns and effectively lifting the siege. Despite this, Ritter von Leeb ordered the withdrawal. "Let them shoot me," he exclaimed. "What does it matter, I am an old man [and] I will bear the responsibility."[170]

Withdrawal, though, was by no means a panacea. As plans were made to fall back, General Kluge of the Fourth Army warned that the resulting equipment losses would be multiples of those already sustained. Besides, he pointed out, the Red Army would probably be attacking the new positions within a few days. It would be much better, Kluge argued, to hold out and make do.[171] This, in due course, would also be Hitler's strategy.

The sheer awfulness of the situation was summed up that day by Hellmuth Stieff in a letter to his wife. He spoke of the "critical" situation of Hoepner's panzer group, which had been forced to withdraw because Reinhardt had given way to his north. Stieff did not welcome that Reinhardt's two corps had been placed under him. "It is a Greek gift," he wrote, "because [Reinhardt] brings with him nothing but beaten fragments [literally, rubble]." Stieff went on to say that he was spending his entire time "plugging one hole with another," in effect robbing Peter to pay Paul. He openly accused the "supreme leadership" of being "so drunk with their own propaganda" that they had withdrawn substantial forces for future tasks before the matter had been decided on the ground. Stieff lamented that he was short of everything, because three-quarters of his trucks were out of action, and all new vehicles were being held back for use by new formations. "We feel terribly abandoned," he concluded, warning that "if there is no miracle then we await an 1812 moment," alluding to Napoleon's legendary retreat from Moscow.[172] The official Europe-wide Wehrmacht report, by contrast, spoke of "only local fighting" in the east. Most of the communiqué was taken up with claims of successes against British shipping and aircraft in the North Sea, English Channel, and Mediterranean.[173]

Meanwhile, the diplomatic wheels continued to turn toward unity. At 9:30 p.m., Ambassador Mackensen in Rome reported that he had had just handed the text of the proposed Axis declaration to the Italian chef de cabinet, Marquess d'Ajeta. The marquess had been given full plenipotentiary powers by Ciano, who was now in Turin to sort out the Vichy French the following morning. D'Ajeta promised to draw up a similar Italian declaration. He said that the Duce wanted to know whether the Japanese government had already approved the treaty text, and whether a time had been set for its publication. Mackensen told the Italian that he had no instructions yet on these matters.[174]

There was still some way to go on the Axis treaty text. Shortly after 10 p.m. in Berlin, Ott's second dispatch of the day from Tokyo was received. He reported that "the Japanese government [was] very anxious to sign and make public the agreement."[175] Foreign Minister Togo finally asked Ott "when the German declaration of war on the United States was to be expected." He repeated his demand for "a formal [German] declaration of war with subsequent announcement of the Axis treaty." Ott's message made clear that the agreement would not be ready for the following day, and so Hitler would not be able to declare war until the day after.[176] The Japanese leadership, clearly, remained nervous that they would be left to face the Americans alone.

It was still midafternoon in Washington. Just after 4 p.m., Roosevelt welcomed journalists into the executive office for his first press conference since the war had begun in the Pacific. The president had "little darn news, except that I haven't finished my speech," although a fifth draft was close to completion. After bantering with the reporters about the added security around the White House and joking with journalist May Craig that he would "have to hire a female Secret Service agent around here to do the frisking" of her, he reported that he had little to say on operations, other than that Japan had continued its sweep across Asia with an attack on Clark Field in the Philippines that morning. Now that the country was at war, the administration was committed to sharing information with the public once it had verified the accuracy and as long as it did "not give aid and comfort to the enemy."[177]

Yet the president could not avoid leaks altogether. That same day, Secretary Knox and Admiral Stark appeared before a secret session of the Senate Naval Affairs Committee to explain the full extent of the losses in the Pacific. Before long, an anti-interventionist passed the information to America First's Senate lobbyist, Ruth Sarles. Writing to General Robert Wood, America First's national chairman, she reported that it was "difficult to describe the profound sense of shock experienced by the men on the Hill at the enormity of the catastrophe that has literally overwhelmed us in the Pacific." While the "powers that be will sit on the lid as long as possible," Sarles wrote, it was "doubtful that the facts can be concealed for long," as the news was already circulating freely around Congress. The destruction and damage to the eight US battleships had left the Japanese Navy unrivaled in the region. "We have 5 left in the Pacific, as against Japan's 15. We would not have parity even in our own waters."[178] Once this information filtered out to the general public, the America First leaders believed, many Americans would react by joining them in opposing any administration attempt to precipitate a two-ocean war with Germany as well.

Most Americans were unaware just how engaged the US Navy already was in the war with Germany. That day, a flotilla of the country's best transport ships arrived at Cape Town, having sailed 8,132 miles from Halifax, Canada. Given the secrecy around the WS-12X convoy, the crowds that greeted its arrival were astonished to see the group composed entirely of US vessels, just two days after Pearl Harbor. As one British private, John Farmer, noted, "The local people were amazed at the rapid response of the Americans in bringing troops so soon after the declaration of war!"[179] As the men began their shore leave, dressed in their khaki kits for the desert campaign, they had no way of knowing that their fates would soon be transformed by events on the other side of the world.

Meanwhile, convoy PQ6, laden with war material, was making good progress toward Russia. After leaving Hvalfjordur, the convoy turned right and then right again. It spent the day steaming up the west coast of Iceland. Once it had cleared the northern tip of the island, it would swing right once more into the Arctic Sea. In the summer months, the convoys would stay as close to Greenland, and as far away from the German bases in Norway, as possible, leaving Jan Mayen and the Svalbard Islands to their right. In the winter, though, the encroaching ice edge meant they had to keep further east, leaving Jan Mayen and Bear Island to their left. This brought them much closer to the German bases in Norway and the moment when they would be in range not only of Luftwaffe reconnaissance aircraft but also of attack planes. Luckily, at this time of year, there was very little daylight to see the convoy in.

It was always cold in the Arctic, but in December the chill was truly punishing. The gunner on the *Empire Mavis*, luckily, was well wrapped up in his "arctic kit" (cost: £16) and passed the day without incident. When night fell, those on deck could admire the "magnificent effects by the northern lights" and the "moonlight."[180] Hampered by a heavy storm that further reduced visibility, the *Harmatris* fell behind the convoy, as its skipper slowed the vessel to prevent damage to the eight thousand tons of cargo, including vehicles and ammunition for the Red Army.[181] At exactly midnight, the *Empire Mavis* stopped dead in the water. Something was wrong. Part of the convoy had been lost in the darkness.

In London, Churchill's focus that night was on another sea altogether. At 10 p.m. he chaired an emergency chiefs of staff meeting in the cabinet war room at Downing Street. As General Alan Brooke recorded in his diary, the prime minister's principal concern was the "naval situation in the Pacific due to result of Japanese action on USA fleet in Honolulu in which 3 battleships were sunk and 3 badly damaged out of 8!" As a result, this had "entirely upset the balance in the Pacific and leaves Japs masters of the ocean until we can assemble forces there."[182] As well as exploring whether Britain had the capacity to send battleships to redress the balance, the group discussed the future movements of the now terribly isolated *Prince of Wales* and *Repulse*. One suggestion was that the ships "should vanish into the ocean wastes and exercise a vague menace," serving as "rogue elephants." Another option was for them to cross the Pacific "and join the remnants of the American fleet." At midnight, the meeting broke up with no decision reached, other than to "reconsider the problem in the morning light."[183]

ACROSS EUROPE, EVEN those who knew little of the diplomatic machinations sensed that the world was in flux, though there was not much consensus on what to make of it. The German writer Ernst Jünger, stationed in Paris, was confused. He wrote that day that he caught himself "mixing up the alliances." Sometimes Jünger thought that Japan had declared war on Germany rather than the United States. Everything, he felt, was "inextricably snarled up like snakes in a sack."[184] In Romania, Mihail Sebastian spoke of "a new type of war" in the Pacific "unlike anything we have seen since August 1939." He was stunned by the Japanese "Blitz technique" and found it "most disturbing to see America taken by surprise like any old Belgium or Yugoslavia."[185] Word of Pearl Harbor had finally penetrated to the heart of the Polish region of Zamosc, deep in Nazi-occupied territory. "News of the outbreak of the Japanese-American War arrived," Zygmunt Klukowski wrote, which "provoked great excitement—everybody is speaking only about this."[186] In the village of Rhöndorf by the Rhine, where he was living in internal exile, the former mayor of Cologne Konrad Adenauer reflected to an old friend how the world had changed. Referring obliquely to the despised Third Reich, he added that he thought "this period will also come to an end one day, perhaps earlier than we now think."[187]

Opinion was divided on what the Pacific War would mean for the European theater. Even the expectation that the Soviet Union would no longer receive Lend-Lease equipment did not cheer up Hellmuth Stieff on the eastern front. "On the contrary," he wrote to his wife, "I now have the feeling that the Russians will stake everything on one last throw because they will not be getting any more aid in future." This would cause the Red Army to throw everything at the Wehrmacht while they still could. "And their prospects are good," Stieff concluded bleakly, "because we are exhausted and the winter is against us."[188]

In Lvov, Professor Tadeusz Tomaszewski and his friends made the same calculation but came to a radically different conclusion. Having thought over the implications of Pearl Harbor, they were no longer so optimistic. The "preponderant" view now was, he recorded in his diary, that the Japanese attack was "bad" and could "prolong" the hostilities by distracting the United States from Europe and reducing the flow of equipment across the Atlantic to Britain.[189] Lend-Lease clearly loomed as large in his mind as it did in the minds of Roosevelt, Churchill, Hitler, and Goebbels.

In England, too, the Mass Observation diarists worried over the fate of American aid. The Maida Vale housewife noted that "opinion has now become general that the reason for Japan's entry into the war was primarily at Hitler's instigation to prevent the operation of Lend-Lease."[190]

The Newport insurance clerk concurred, fearing the worst: "Just when we were getting the measure of the war and were relaxing in the luxury of unlimited lease-lend from America, anarchy and confusion breaks loose again."[191] From Lvov in the belly of the Nazi beast to the British industrial harbor of Newport at the western edge of war-ravaged Europe, people were having the same pipedreams or nightmares. The connections between events in the Pacific, the power of American industry, and the war in Europe were well understood. But the implications of the new war for the vital supply line from the United States and the resulting impact on the struggle against Hitler remained unclear.

6

WEDNESDAY, DECEMBER 10, 1941

As the clock struck midnight in London, and the evening still stretched ahead in Washington, tensions between the White House and the Reich continued to rise. While most of his compatriots slept, Hans Thomsen awaited the president's fireside chat that evening, aware that the focus would be on Germany. In the meantime, the German diplomat sent an open telegram to Berlin reporting that Roosevelt had issued no fewer than three proclamations warning of "an invasion or predatory incursion" by Nazi Germany, despite the fact that the two countries were not at war. The president had also designated German and Italian nationals as "alien enemies." The Justice Department and FBI were empowered, Thomsen reported, to detain German and Italians considered "dangerous" to US security.[1]

A few minutes after Thomsen sent that cable, Churchill received the news from Lord Halifax that Roosevelt was unable to commit to a meeting until early January and would prefer that it take place in Bermuda, rather than the United States, "on security grounds."[2] Clearly, the president was trying to put some distance between himself and the prime minister, at least until relations with Hitler had been sorted out. It was already evident that Pearl Harbor alone was not enough to cement the US-Britain partnership.

In Rome, American diplomats closely monitored the Italian political scene for clues of Germany's next move. The chargé d'affaires George Wadsworth had been overseeing the American mission in Italy since the resignation of the ambassador, William Phillips, in October. A career diplomat, Wadsworth was dismissed by Ciano as a "good but rather timid man, with whom I have had little to do."[3] Nevertheless, as an efficient and professional foreign service officer, he had quickly responded to the Pearl Harbor attack by sizing up "opinion in well-informed Rome circles" on the "crying question of the day, whether Germany will declare war on the United States." He found it "divided." Those who doubted a German declaration stressed that the Axis powers were free to assist "Japan with all political, economic and military means" without actually declaring war. The assumption was that if any break did come, then Hitler would gain greater propaganda benefit within Germany if the declaration came from the United States. On the other hand, those who believed a German declaration was coming argued that America's whole Pacific policy meant Japan's response was simply "legitimate defense and that the only reply is world war."

Wadsworth's dispatch, which reached Washington just before the new day began in Rome, provided copious evidence to support the latter view, suggesting that he found it more convincing. For a start, an American intelligence analyst, Harold Tittman, had heard from the cardinal secretary of state in the Vatican the previous day that he expected the Axis nations to sever relations with the United States shortly. Wadsworth himself had heard from the exiled queen of Spain that her son Don Juan "had received information which persuaded him Germany would declare war on United States in very immediate future." More opaquely, Wadsworth mentioned that a "German Embassy source" was "reliably reported to have said yesterday that Ribbentrop had promised Japan that if it would declare war on United States Germany would also do so." For those leading US officials in Washington who had access to MAGIC, this would simply have confirmed what the decrypted Oshima telegram to

Tokyo had already shown. Interestingly, the rationale that the German diplomat in Rome gave for this commitment to Japan was that, as the United States was now moving to a "full war footing," there was "no longer any good reason for 'postponing' open war."

Wadsworth also heard from American journalists in Rome that their German counterparts were "strongly arguing" that "Berlin had been taken unawares by and was displeased with Japan's action." They were, of course, right on the former but not the latter. The American correspondents were certain, however, that these claims that "a break with the United States is not intended" were designed "to pull the wool over their eyes." That said, Wadsworth noted that Italian journalists had been instructed by Mussolini's government to emphasize "Rooseveltian war mongering," to make no reference to "Americans being surprised" by the attack, and not to "touch for the time being on the implications of the Tripartite Pact," presumably because it currently only covered instances where the signatories were the victims of an attack rather than the aggressors. Either way, one thing was clear to the American diplomat: whatever decision was made by Berlin, there was little doubt that Italy would simply follow without question.[4]

At 2 a.m., the German ambassador to Rome, Hans Georg von Mackensen, sent Ciano the latest draft of the Axis agreement. It committed the three contractants to pursue the war against the United States and Britain with "all the means at their disposal" to "a victorious conclusion." They undertook not to conclude an armistice or separate peace with either Britain or the United States without the full agreement of the others. Furthermore, the Axis powers committed themselves to work closely in the spirit of the Tripartite Pact, "even after the victorious end of the war," "in order to achieve a just new order." The agreement would enter into force immediately upon its signature and remain for the entire duration of the Tripartite Pact, after which they would agree on a further form of collaboration.[5]

Meanwhile, wave after wave of Japanese Navy bombers were taking off from their bases in southern Indochina on their way to intercept the *Prince of Wales* and the *Repulse* of Force Z. At 8 a.m. local time, the

Henzan Air Group took off. A few minutes later, the British ships appeared off Kuantan, Malaya. The destroyer *Express* was sent to investigate the harbor. There was no sign of the reported Japanese landing; the report had been mistaken. Not long after, the Kanoya Air Group was aloft. Six minutes later, the Mihoro Air Group was on its way. At around this time, *Express* rejoined Admiral Tom Phillips and the rest of Force Z, reporting "complete peace" in the harbor of Kuantan. The British admiral was relaxed, having refused the offer of RAF air cover so long as he stuck reasonably close to the shoreline.[6]

About an hour after sending his last message, Thomsen followed up with a confidential dispatch reporting that the American public was still in a state of "shock and dismay" about the losses in the Pacific. "The air is full," Thomsen continued, "of wild rumors of threatened enemy aerial incursions" not only on the West Coast but also New England and New York. He spoke of the continued "blackouts and air-raid precautions and practice alarms" in several big cities in expectation of an "imminent German declaration of war." Reports of the summoning of the Reichstag and of an important announcement to be made by the Reich government, Thomsen said, had caused people in Washington to assume that a formal declaration of war from Germany, or at least a break off of diplomatic relations, was to be expected within twenty-four hours.[7]

Over the course of the day, Roosevelt received additional intelligence that supported this inference. Wild Bill Donovan told the president that all German journalists in the United States were preparing to either return to Germany or head to South America, and those departing for Europe would travel on the "same boat as the [German] Embassy staff." American journalists were being told by their bureau chiefs in Berlin to make a decision "promptly," with the expectation that "Germany is to declare war within a few days." Donovan's source, who worked in the United States for a German newspaper, had said "that Germany would rather declare war on the United States than wait for the United States to declare war on her—this for the reason that she wishes to show her own people her internal strength."[8] For Roosevelt, this insight into Hitler's reasoning, if accurate, must have been welcome. He had always regarded Germany as the greatest threat of the Axis powers and thus had no intention of waging war against only Japan, but he also remained conscious of the political difficulties of preempting Hitler with an American declaration of war.

In mainland Europe, there was little aerial activity during the night.[9] The diplomatic wires, however, were once again humming. In the early hours of the morning, Mackensen was called by the Italian Foreign Office and told that Mussolini's government had agreed to Ribbentrop's version of articles 3 and 4 of the new Axis treaty. Not to be outdone by the Germans, they wanted to include some additional grievances against the United States in an accompanying declaration. The Italians also requested that the moment when the Americans were presented with the declaration should be coordinated and not take place before 10 a.m. on December 11, by which time the Italian foreign minister would have returned from Turin. Ciano, Mackensen was told, wished to deliver it personally. At 3 a.m., the ambassador reported all this to Berlin.[10]

In Singapore and Malaya, the British were still confident that they could contain the Japanese thrust. That morning, Duff Cooper received a telegram from London appointing him resident cabinet minister for Far Eastern affairs at Singapore, to "assist the successful conduct of operations in the Far East" by providing political advice to the military commander and relieving him of all civilian matters.[11] To do this, Cooper was authorized to form a war council. London, it seemed, was finally getting serious about coming to grips with the Far East. The first meeting of the war council was to be at half past five that same afternoon. Cooper got in his car to drive to the commander in chief of the Far East, Robert Brooke-Popham, to pass on the news.[12] Nevertheless, complacency continued to leave the British vulnerable to disaster.

ADMIRAL PHILLIPS'S FIRST sign of trouble came at 10 a.m. local time when the destroyer *Tenedos*, part of the screen of smaller vessels shielding *Prince of Wales* and *Repulse*, reported that it was under attack from enemy aircraft to the southeast. A quarter of an hour later, Force Z was sighted by a Japanese scout plane. Not long after that, it was discovered by land-based aircraft. This time, the Royal Navy lookouts in turn spotted the Japanese. Phillips put Force Z on first degree of readiness. Then British radar picked up large numbers of enemy aircraft. It was clear that Force Z would soon be under heavy attack.

While Japanese forces were on the move, their principal ally was monitoring the British and American media. The listening service of the German Foreign Office reported that Roosevelt had dubbed Germany "the main driver" of "Japan's war against the United States." They also noted that the BBC had announced that the Reichstag had been summoned for a meeting on December 10, and that the evening's performance at the Kroll Opera House, in which the German parliament had been meeting since the fire in the old Reichstag building nine years earlier, had been canceled.[13] Intentionally or not, the BBC was suggesting that one operatic performance was being replaced by another.

In Washington, where it was still 10 p.m. on December 9, Roosevelt addressed the American people in his first fireside chat since the Pearl Harbor attack. The focus in this address was as much on Hitler's Germany as it was on Japan. The president argued that Japan was only following the German example in its preemptive attack on the United States and Britain and that the Japanese were in "actual collaboration" with the Nazis. The United States, Roosevelt said, was "now in this war. We are all in it—all the way," and the administration would step up production on a seven-days-per-week basis to support America's allies as well as its own war effort. In order to end all "sources of international brutality" and to prevent the establishment of a "world ruled by the principles of gangsterism," the United States could no longer afford to remain just within its own hemisphere. Roosevelt accused Germany of instructing Tokyo to attack the United States in order to share the spoils of war, informing his audience that Germany and Italy considered themselves at war with the United States, even without a formal declaration. It would therefore not be sufficient, he continued, to defeat Japan if Americans "found that the rest of the world was [still] dominated by Hitler and Mussolini." This was a massive escalation in Roosevelt's rhetorical warfare with Hitler as he sought to educate Americans on the global situation. But, crucially, he stopped short of asking Congress for a declaration of war. In order to overcome his anti-interventionist opponents and bring the country into the war in Europe united, he was still reliant on Hitler making the decisive move.

If the intelligence was incorrect or Hitler reversed himself, as he had done so many times before, the Anglo-Americans would face difficult choices. Roosevelt was far from confident that he could continue to support his allies with arms, at least in the short term. As the president was speaking, Halifax cabled Churchill to the effect that Roosevelt had confided "they would have to make certain demands on us from Lease-Lend during the next three weeks."[14] Roosevelt hoped to resume full deliveries by the new year, as he moved American industry onto a twenty-four-hour, seven-day schedule. Still, the interruption might have grave consequences for British forces in North Africa and the Soviet defenses against Hitler. But for now, British problems were multiplying off Malaya.

Within a quarter of an hour of being spotted on radar, the Japanese air groups began to catch up with Admiral Phillips's Force Z. Immediately, the entire British force, with the exception of the outranged destroyer *Vampire*, opened fire. Eight Nell bombers from the Mihoro Air Group peeled off to attack *Repulse*. One bomb struck the ship, exploding just below the mess deck of the marines. It started a fire on the catapult deck and fractured a steam pipe. No damage was done to the engine or boiler rooms, and the fire was rapidly brought under control, but there would be no respite. Twenty minutes after the first attack, nine torpedo bombers bore down on the *Prince of Wales*. It took one hit just to the aft of the port bow, resulting in flooding to the engine room, a boiler room, and a machinery room. The port propeller shafts stopped turning; the ship's speed was reduced to fifteen knots. Most worrying of all, the steering gear was badly damaged. The entire ship soon began to list thirteen degrees to port. The anti-aircraft crews fought back courageously, but they were simply overwhelmed by the skill and numbers of the enemy. The *Prince of Wales* was in deep trouble.

The next wave of attackers concentrated on the *Repulse*. Nine torpedo bombers approached its port side. Captain William Tennant skillfully "combed" all the torpedoes, all of which missed. Simultaneously, just as the playbook stipulated, the bombers attacked overhead. Again, they all failed to hit their target, though one achieved a near miss to starboard. Captain Tennant signaled to Phillips that he had avoided all torpedoes, and that the fires started by the previous bomb hit had been brought under control.

While this desperate struggle was reaching its climax, Japanese foreign minister Togo went to see the emperor at 1 p.m. Tokyo time. He reported that Japan, Germany, and Italy had signed a treaty committing not to sign a separate peace with the Western powers.[15] Tokyo was still anxious that Hitler might not follow through with his promise to join their war. A Japanese government spokesman nonetheless announced pointedly that Germany would "of course" declare war against the United States, which was a demand as much as statement.[16]

By now, the *Prince of Wales* was stricken. A signal was hoisted to report that the ship was "not under control." *Repulse* began to steam in its direction. In the process, *Repulse* took a torpedo amidships on its port side but remained maneuverable after the hit. The port side of the *Prince of Wales* was awash, however, and within a few minutes it was hit by another two torpedoes, this time on the starboard side. The paradoxical result was to reduce its list to port to three degrees as it shipped water on the other side. The *Prince of Wales* gunners managed to shoot down one of the Japanese aircraft, but by now its starboard outer propeller had stopped, and the ship was down to eight knots.

Then it was the turn of the *Repulse* again. A fresh wave of aircraft attacked on both sides. Two of them were shot down. Four torpedoes hit their mark. One struck the steering gear, two simultaneously went into the port side, and a fourth hit the starboard side. The *Repulse* was clearly doomed. Captain Tennant ordered his men on deck and called on them to "abandon ship." There was, as Cecil Brown recalled, "no alarm, no confusion [and] no panic."[17] The life rafts were cast loose. At 5:44 a.m. London time, the *Repulse* capsized and sank. The escorting destroyers succeeded in rescuing forty-two out of sixty-nine officers and 754 of 1,240 sailors, including the captain; Admiral Phillips drowned. The Japanese aircraft were still, as Brown wrote, "winging around like vultures" and swooped on the remaining battleship. Eleven minutes later, the *Prince of Wales* was struck by another bomb, causing more fires. Within about half an hour, it, too, had rolled over and sunk. Force Z had been annihilated. It was one of the biggest disasters the Royal Navy has ever suffered, emblematic for some of Britain's decline as a maritime and colonial power.[18]

Just before the *Prince of Wales* sank, British fighter aircraft finally arrived at the scene. Though they were much too late to make any difference, their commander, Flight Lieutenant Tim Vigors, was impressed by what he took to be the sangfroid of the survivors. They were, he recalled, "waving, cheering and joking as if they were holidaymakers at Brighton, waving at low-flying aircraft." It is equally possible, though, that the men were actually shaking their fists at what they would have taken to be the delayed arrival of fighter cover (they had no way of knowing that Phillips had requested none). Or perhaps they were simply engaged in a desperate attempt to attract the attention of the British pilots to facilitate their own rescue.[19]

As yet unaware of the destruction in the Pacific, Churchill dispatched an early morning cipher message to Eden, updating him on all that had happened since he had embarked for Russia. First and foremost was the "major disaster at Hawaii" that had left the United States with only two battleships against ten Japanese vessels in the Pacific. Consequently, the Americans were recalling all their warships from the Atlantic and had "laid embargo on all exports of munitions for the time being," information that Eden was told to keep strictly secret. The ramifications of the Japanese assault were already evident throughout East Asia, where Britain's territories were under attack or faced imminent invasion now that Japan enjoyed naval supremacy in the region. Additional intelligence intercepts, including instructions from Rome to its embassy in Washington to destroy secret material and prepare to burn ciphers, meant Churchill was now certain that Germany and Italy were poised to declare war on the United States.[20] He expected a "tripartite declaration of implacable war against British Empire and United States" later that day or on the eleventh. On the Russian front, he reported "magnificent Russian successes at Leningrad, on the whole Moscow front, at Kursk and in south," and that the Germans were now in retreat in the face of Russian counterattacks and the brutal weather. On Britain's own "second front" in Libya, Churchill reported that the "tide [had] turned" but the battle was actually far from won, not least as aircraft from the Middle East were now needed to reinforce Malaya.

All this meant that Eden was instructed "not, repeat not" to offer ten squadrons of British aircraft to Stalin. The most critical immediate consequence of the new global situation was that "everything is in flux with United States supplies." Only by getting to Washington as soon as possible could Churchill address this, which is why he would "start Thursday if invited."[21] With Roosevelt still concerned about anti-British political currents in America, this remained a big "if."

By now, it was early afternoon in Tokyo, and news of the destruction of *Prince of Wales* and *Repulse* was already circulating. The Marquess Kido heard at 3 p.m. and "rejoiced."[22] Half an hour later, the Japanese imperial navy headquarters in Tokyo officially announced the sinkings, making much of the huge enemy losses. In Downing Street, after a large breakfast, Churchill was in bed working when the telephone rang. It was the first sea lord, admiral Sir Dudley Pound. His "voice sounded odd" and was barely audible. After "a sort of cough and gulp," Pound delivered the devastating news: "The *Prince of Wales* and the *Repulse* have both been sunk by the Japanese—we think by aircraft. Tom Phillips is drowned." A dumbfounded Churchill asked if the report could be mistaken, but Pound confirmed there was "no doubt at all." Churchill would recall in his memoirs that he "was thankful to be alone" when he received this terrible news. In fact, his secretary was sitting "silently and unobtrusively in the corner," and noted, as the prime minister got off the phone, that he murmured, more to himself than her, "Poor Tom Phillips."[23]

It was nothing short of a catastrophe. Churchill later declared that he "never received a more direct shock" during the whole war as when he learned of the sinking of Force Z. So many "efforts, hopes, and plans foundered with these two ships." Before their departure for the Pacific, Churchill had assured Stalin with bravado that the *Prince of Wales* could "catch and kill any Japanese ships" and would be the centerpiece of a "powerful battle squadron."[24] Now, as the prime minister "turned over and twisted in bed, the full horror of the news sank in." The strategic consequences were dire: "There were no British or American capital ships in the Indian Ocean or the Pacific except the American survivors of Pearl Harbor, who were hastening back to California. Over all this vast expanse of waters Japan was supreme, and we everywhere were weak and naked."[25]

After hearing the news on arriving at the War Office that morning, General Alan Brooke's reaction was equally stark: "It means that from Africa eastwards to America through the Indian Ocean and Pacific we have lost command of the sea."[26]

News spread across the British Empire in the hours that followed. In the Australian Parliament, Prime Minister John Curtin announced that "the loss of these two ships is a bad blow. It illustrates the gravity of our position."[27] In Singapore, Duff Cooper had by now reached Brooke-Popham, who patiently listened to Cooper's message about the war council and then dropped the bombshell. "I have also something to tell you," he said. "The *Prince of Wales* and the *Repulse* have been sunk." "This was," Cooper later wrote, "the worst single piece of news I have ever received."[28] The shock of it was compounded by the fact that nobody had thought the Japanese capable of sinking such well-armed and enormous ships.

This disbelief was not confined to the British. Stalin, who of course had repeatedly bested the Japanese in Manchuria, later wrote to Churchill that he thought the *Prince of Wales* and the *Repulse* had been sunk by German aircraft, or at least by German pilots in Japanese planes.[29] The Soviet leader clearly was no less susceptible to Western condescension than the British or indeed the Americans, some of whom not only believed they saw Messerschmitts at Pearl Harbor but claimed to see "German" planes over the Pacific right up until the Battle of Midway six months later.

It was around 9 a.m. in Berlin when the Nazi leadership first heard of the sinkings.[30] After an initial period of astonishment, once the Japanese announcement was confirmed by Reuters Berlin was exultant. Goebbels welcomed the news as "the greatest sensation of the war at sea so far." Japan, he believed, now enjoyed "absolute supremacy" in the Pacific. The German public was also lifted by the destruction of the two warships, though there were many who now compared the Japanese achievement with the pathetic performance of their Italian allies in the Mediterranean. The fact that the dreaded Atlantic Charter had been devised on the *Prince of Wales* by the two "war-mongers" Churchill and Roosevelt was not lost on the DNB in its crowing announcement of the sinkings. "The destruction of the *Prince of Wales* right at the start of their [Roosevelt and Churchill's] activities," it claimed, was "a symbol of the fact that the manipulations and deviousness of these two graspers cannot withstand the sword of a determined people."[31]

The German naval high command immediately recognized the military significance of the news. It was not just that the British had lost two badly needed capital ships, or that the Japanese had shown exceptional skill in sending them to the bottom. The engagement was in fact a watershed in the history of naval warfare, an "event of particular importance." "It is particularly remarkable," the German naval war diary explained, that the success had been achieved by "naval aviation." This, the Kriegsmarine argued with typical *campanilismo*, should be "an integral part" of the navy, rather than a separate service. It noted pointedly that the "independent Luftwaffe"—Göring was not specifically named, but his failure was implied—had, over the course of two years of combat operations against the Royal Navy, achieved less than the Japanese had in just two days.[32]

On the other side of the world, Admiral Ugaki was thinking exactly the same thing. "As a result of this action," he believed, "the opinion that battleships are nothing and airplanes are everything will become active." "I cannot," Ugaki conceded, "but recognize the remarkable power of airplanes, seeing the results since last night." Like the DNB, he, too, saw the sinkings as a settling of scores, though in his case they were framed as revenge for the destruction of the German battleship *Bismarck* earlier in the year, in which *Prince of Wales* had participated. "Tokyo is a long way from Nagasaki," Ugaki wrote, citing an old Japanese saying, "but vengeance may be exacted far from the scene of the original offence."[33]

Word of the sinking of the two British ships poured fuel on Japan's war frenzy. Where Pearl Harbor had been a surprise attack on an unprepared enemy cooped up at port, these two British ships had been underway on the high seas and ready for action. To have inflicted such a blow on the redoubtable Royal Navy, which ranked higher than the American one in the popular mind, gave particular satisfaction.[34] "Navy Banzai!" Professor Yabe Teiji wrote in his diary.[35] The news probably helped to swell attendance at official rallies in support of the war. Seventy thousand people came to the "Great Assembly of the Prefectoral Population for Certain Victory Against America and England" in Hiroshima. The governor spoke of the "annihilation of the Americans and British." In the city of Kumamoto, on Kyushu, the authorities that afternoon convened a "Grand Assembly for the Annihilation of the Americans and British." There were further events calling for the "the annihilation of America and England" in other cities, such as Kanazawa, on Honshu.[36]

The news dashed Anglo-American hopes for an immediate turning point in the war's course. In London, the writer and Conservative member of Parliament Harold Nicolson was returning from visiting his doctor when he saw a poster in Oxford Circus announcing, "Prince of Wales and Repulse sunk." Shocked, he felt the whole circus "revolve" in the air. Nicolson suddenly felt sick and short of breath. He made for the exclusive Beefsteak private members' club as quickly as he could to take a reviving glass of sherry. "When disaster comes," Nicolson explained, "we always flock to the Beefsteak to comfort each other."[37] On the other side of the world, in Pacific Palisades, California, his fellow writer Thomas Mann, who had escaped Germany at the outset of Hitler's regime, found the sinkings "very disturbing [literally, creepy]." To him, they were evidence of the fact that the Japanese were a "very wild and enterprising enemy," to whose "uncompromising" nature the United States would struggle to adapt.[38]

News of the loss of the *Prince of Wales* and *Repulse* spread as far as convoy PQ6 in the Arctic.[39] It can only have added to the anxiety caused by the temporary loss of contact with some of the ships. By daybreak, though, the original convoy was together again and doing seven knots. The weather was awful, with intermittent blizzards all day. Luckily, as the gunner on the *Empire Mavis* reported, the "new [Arctic] gear was very warm indeed."

Lurking in the gloom, though, was another danger: German submarines, surface ships, and aircraft. For this reason, the gunner noted, "everyone now sleeps clothed," with their "life belt on top." It would be "no fun," he explained, "having to run to the boats scantily clad," thus risking "frostbite—a terrible danger." The convoy had only three armed trawlers to defend it. These were not at this stage equipped with sonar or radar, but their high-frequency direction-finding sets could locate a U-boat on the surface if it used its radio. The trawlers could attack a submarine above water with their solitary four-inch gun, hit a submerged one with their depth charges, and engage aircraft with their machine guns. But if attacked by a German surface ship of destroyer size or larger—and there were five German destroyers on standby in Westfjord near Narvik, Norway—it would be game over. Then the only option was to "scatter," with every ship for itself.

The best defense for the convoy, paradoxically, was the foul weather. If the Germans were going to attack PQ6, they would have to find it first. The Germans tended not to conduct large sweeps over the Arctic Sea unless they had specific intelligence. To the despair of the Kriegsmarine, which lacked a dedicated naval air service, the Luftwaffe, despite the courage of its pilots, was never really comfortable over water. In bad weather like this, there was too great a chance of getting lost, and if the crew was forced to "ditch" in the Arctic, the chances of survival were close to zero. In any case, searching for a convoy in the December blizzards was akin to finding a needle in the proverbial haystack. None of this, of course, was much comfort to the lookouts on PQ6, as they continued to scan the Arctic gloom for signs of enemy activity, four hours on and eight hours off.

Meanwhile, in Cape Town, Fergus Anckorn and the rest of the Eighteenth Infantry Division were astonished to find that, across the city, shopkeepers "simply wouldn't let us pay for anything," instead showering complimentary gifts on the soldiers. Only when they returned to the ships did they find out that these were acts of sympathy for the sinking of the British ships in the Pacific, particularly the *Prince of Wales*, which had stopped in Cape Town on its route east and whose crew had left quite an impression on the city.[40] Little did Anckorn and his colleagues realize that, as a consequence of this disaster, they, too, would soon be heading to the Far, rather than Middle, East.

Throughout the day, German diplomats continued to monitor the American political scene for clues as to whether Washington might be preparing to open formal hostilities with Berlin. At around the same time as the momentous news was coming in from the Pacific about the British vessels, the German Foreign Office received another dispatch from Hans Thomsen in Washington. He reported that the US State Department had pronounced the temporary interruption of telegraph and telephone connections between the embassy and Berlin to be the result of a "mistake." Communication could thus be resumed. Given that the Americans were being as good as their word in this respect, Thomsen suggested that any reprisals that were already underway in response to the previous restrictions should be terminated.[41] The messages coming from Washington were thus very mixed. There was still no inexorable sense that hostilities with the German Reich would be opened on the American side.

Stalin's immediate response to the string of Allied defeats in East Asia and the Pacific is not recorded. He had known for some time through Richard Sorge that Tokyo had the British and Americans in its sights rather than the Soviet Union, but he received further confirmation that morning in the form of a copy of a revealing Japanese cable from his agents in Britain. This was the dispatch from Foreign Minister Togo to Ambassador Oshima in Berlin, in which he announced that war with the Western powers was imminent, but that while the Soviet Union should be contained, the main Japanese effort was to be made in the south and

271

east against the Western powers, rather than in the northwest against the Russians—at least for now. Stalin must have felt relief that this intelligence had proved true.[42]

Despite this, Stalin was under strong American pressure to declare war on Japan, which would make the president's task of selling continued support to the Soviets much easier. The dictator refused. He let it be known, with remarkable chutzpah given the recent record of Soviet aggression, that the Soviet Union did "not consider it possible to take the initiative in violating the pact, for we ourselves have always condemned governments that violated treaties."[43] Soviet radio announced that Tokyo had reiterated its policy of neutrality in the Germany-USSR conflict and that there was therefore "no fundamental change in Soviet-Japanese relations, which are regulated by the pact of April 15."[44] Stalin even refused to mount a military demonstration on the border to distract Tokyo, because he feared that this would provoke a Japanese preemptive strike.[45]

Besides, Foreign Minister Molotov pointed out, "almost all our forces are concentrated against Germany, including half the troops from the Far East." War with Japan would mean "war on two fronts." Soviet public opinion, he continued, in what must have been a rare argument in Stalinist Russia, "would not understand and would not approve" of any new conflict at a time "when the enemy has not yet been expelled from the territory of the USSR" and the economy was under such "stress." "We think," Molotov concluded, "that Hitler's Germany is our main enemy." Taking on Japan at this stage, he warned, would be bad not only for the Soviet Union but also for "all of our allies."[46]

As we have seen, there was ambivalence on the Anglo-American side about any Soviet entry into the war with Japan, because it might distract Stalin from concentrating on Hitler. Worse still was the possibility that the Soviet dictator might take advantage of Pearl Harbor and the looming US-Germany conflict to come to terms with Hitler. He had, after all, done so once before. That day, Bruce Hopper, the eastern Europe analyst for the US Office of the Coordinator of Information, raised exactly that scenario, only to dismiss it. Hitler would never give up the Ukraine, Hopper predicted, and Stalin would never trust him again. Nor did he think that Stalin would break his neutrality pact with Japan. That said, Hopper warned that in this war for "the re-division of the earth," the "friend of yesterday may be the foe of tomorrow and vice versa."[47] Nothing could be taken for granted in these changing times.

The dramatic news from Malaya arrived too late for the morning newspapers in Britain, which focused on the ways in which the two conflicts, in Europe and Asia, seemed to be converging. The *Daily Express* led with Roosevelt's warning from his fireside chat that the United States was "under threat of German-Italian invasion" and discussed his decision to treat Germans and Italians, as well as Japanese, as enemy aliens. The paper reported that Hitler had "called the Reichstag for today" (which had indeed been his original intention) and that it was "believed he will make speech declaring war on America."[48] The *Times*' Washington correspondent also revealed that "rumours ran thick and fast to-day of a German declaration of hostilities," but there was a feeling that Hitler might "confine his declaration to an assertion of the solidarity of the Axis and a pledge of moral support for Japan." The journalist also suggested that American officials believed Japan's assault on Hawaii had "not pleased the Germans." By bringing the United States in as a belligerent in the Pacific, the attack had "shifted the onus of Axis obligation from Tokyo to Berlin and it brought nearer the day when Hitler must announce that Germany is at war with the United States—tidings which will fall heavily on the ears of the people who have never forgotten that the year 1917 made their defeat inevitable."[49]

The British press exhibited an awareness of the enormity of the task ahead. The *Guardian* focused on pressing home Churchill's message that "the extension of the war to the Pacific throws new burdens on us." Above all, it threatened to impose an intolerable strain on Britain's supply lines. The war now engulfed two more great oceans, the Pacific and Indian. Furthermore, the United States was now "less free than before to throw her growing weight into the Atlantic battle," as US vessels and aircraft were needed for its own defenses in the Pacific. "Most serious" was the "inevitable diversion of American supplies to the new war." Britain would have to continue diverting supplies to Russia, with little hope of immediate replenishment from American stocks. Moreover, in the coming months it would receive far fewer American planes, particularly long-range bombers, undermining its ability to launch offensive campaigns. Even worse could follow if Japan succeeded in capturing Singapore, "the key to the East, [thus] controlling the important sources of American and British war supply, dominating the lines of American aid to China and to Russia, and menacing India."[50] Whatever happened, Britain would have to adapt to a radical new global situation, without many of the supplies on which it had previously depended.

On the other side of the world, the Australian press would echo the positions taken in London. The *Sydney Morning Herald* argued that Japan's infamous and treacherous actions had transformed the European war into a global conflagration that must be prosecuted "until the linked aggressor [Axis] powers have been utterly overthrown." Japan was described dismissively as "Germany's Asian accomplice" and "Hitler's oriental imitator." Without victory, the paper continued, there would be "no future for civilisation." Given the speed of the Japanese advance, there were some newspapers, such as the *Age*, that warned that an underestimation of the enemy and a belief in the "invincibility" of as-yet-uncaptured fortresses such as Singapore had "served to promote a predominant mood of complacency."[51] Nevertheless, the *Herald* predicted that Japan would now face in the United States "the concentrated and cumulative force of a mighty industrial nation roused to cold fury by the injuries treacherously inflicted upon it."[52]

Despite all the bad news from across the Pacific, determination rather than despair prevailed across the British Empire. Australian prime minister Curtin stressed that there could now "no longer be 'business as usual' but an absolute concentration on war production and war necessities" in Australia. His minister for the navy and munitions, Norman Makin, echoed these sentiments. "Wherever it may prove necessary for increased efficiency," he announced, "the government will not hesitate to take powers over any, or all, industries so as to concentrate our war production on such work as may be deemed most vital."[53] Enlistment among ordinary Australians surged, with five hundred signing up that day just in Martin Place in the center of Sydney.[54]

The Axis and pro-Axis press, inevitably, saw the conflict instead as a struggle between the established powers and their hungry challengers. "The Anglo-Saxons," one Spanish paper wrote, "encircled Japan in order to force Japan to capitulate." It explained—consciously or not, adapting German chancellor Leo von Caprivi's famous statement about the choices facing late-nineteenth-century Germany—that "Japan must import rice or export people. . . . The plutocracies denied her both options." The paper explained, "Australia was closed [to Japanese immigrants], the same was the case with California. . . . Now Japan is determined to solve the problems heroically."[55] The Nazi press also slammed Allied "plutocrats," among whom they included even the Australian Labor Party prime minister, John Curtin.[56] In the same vein, Japanese radio broadcast not only crowing accounts of the sinking of the *Prince of Wales* and the *Repulse*, but also a statement of war aims from the government's chief spokesman Tomokazu Hori. "We have resorted to arms," he announced, because "the Anglo-Saxon powers" had used "dollar diplomacy" and "intimidation by armed force" in order to "place East Asia in a state of permanent bondage."[57]

The growing tension between Washington and the Berlin-Rome alliance was also evident in German and Italian radio broadcasts. German radio reported that Japan had joined the "Axis powers in a front against the democracies." In rhetoric matching that of the Japanese spokesman, Italian broadcasters "saluted" their "new brother in arms against plutocracy"—Japan—which was "a victim of the same intolerable methods with which the Anglo-Saxons tried to throttle other nations and to keep them in ever-lasting bondage." They also lambasted Roosevelt for his alleged campaign of "public defamation against the Italian, German and Japanese regimes" so that "he harvests now in the Pacific what he sowed in the Atlantic and the Mediterranean." Japanese radio reported hopefully that the Italian embassy in Washington was burning official papers in anticipation of the imminent rupture of diplomatic relations with the United States.[58]

Around midmorning, Admiral Darlan arrived in Turin—on a special train that the Italians had organized for him—to a ceremonial welcome at the station.[59] At 10 a.m., Ciano and Darlan met in Turin's opulent Palazzo Madama. The Frenchman was full of bile against Britain and America and especially Roosevelt, whom he described as "a madman." Darlan also exulted in the Japanese victories, which he regarded as "sensational and depressing defeats for the Anglo-Saxon world," a term he used at least twice during the encounter. That said, Darlan was apparently unyielding on the key points. He refused to allow the Axis use of ports in Tunisia for fear that British would respond by treating Vichy France as a belligerent and attack Dakar or some other part of the French colonial empire. Darlan wanted France to take an "active part in the reconstruction of the new European order." The real reason for the meeting was that Darlan wanted to "break the ice" with Ciano, and to open a channel for communication outside the Joint German-Italian Armistice Commission—in other words, without the Germans listening in.[60]

In addition to their mutual disdain for the British, Americans, and (sotto voce) Germans, Darlan and Ciano also took a dislike to each other. The Frenchman dismissed the Italian as an "amateur diplomat" and—no doubt an allusion to his notorious philandering—a "gigolo." The Italian, in turn, saw in the Frenchman not a "real admiral" but a "faux politician."[61] Despite this, and despite Ciano's belief that he had achieved nothing beyond a "clearing of the air," the meeting did have two significant results.[62] First, the two men agreed to establish a direct connection via an Italian embassy in Paris and a representative in Vichy. Second, Darlan secretly permitted the Italians to transport food, clothing, and trucks via Tunisia, something he had repeatedly denied the Germans.[63] This was risky as far as London and Berlin were concerned but was intended to gain some room to maneuver for Vichy while Germany was not only bogged down in Russia but on a confrontation course with Washington. If Darlan could improve relations with Italy and maintain his so-far-cordial connection with the United States, then the prospects for unoccupied France were better than they had been for some time.

In London, when the Chiefs of Staff Committee met that morning at 10:30, discussion centered on the US War Department's request for Britain to transfer back 250 aircraft from its allocation. Chief of the Air Staff Charles Portal found the American rationale unconvincing. He had already advised Churchill that "Staff conversations should take place before any large releases of equipment should be made" and informed his colleagues that he had relayed the same message to General of the US Air Force Henry "Hap" Arnold. The chiefs agreed with Halifax that the Roosevelt administration must be told that decisions should be "properly related to our joint needs" and made "on the basis of regular staff discussions" between the two countries. However, it was acknowledged that there was little that Britain could do "if the U.S. arbitrarily diverted the allocation."[64]

There was still some hesitation in Berlin about how to deal with the Americans. At 11:45 a.m. local time, a German Foreign Office official rang Ribbentrop's office to ask whether the restrictions on communications by diplomats should be lifted. Shortly after noon the US chargé d'affaires, Leland Morris, was told that he was permitted once again to send coded telegrams from his embassy, now that the same privilege had been restored to his German counterparts in Washington. The American diplomat, in turn, asked the State Department to release the German journalists held in New York.[65] And so the game of cat and mouse continued, with each step carefully calibrated.

That morning the Nazi regime gave a clear signal of intent at its daily foreign press conference. Right at the start, the interpreter Dr. Paul Schmidt told all American journalists to leave the room, and the rest of the foreign press corps was instructed to no longer regard them as colleagues. The Americans rose to leave without complaint. Schmidt then stood at the door to shake hands with them, starting with the doyen of the American press corps, Louis Lochner, head of the Associated Press bureau in Berlin. The conference then resumed in what the Swedish journalist Arvid Fredborg recalled as "a heavily charged atmosphere." Afterward, those in the know claimed that a Reichstag session had been called for 3 p.m., at which Hitler—"acting on pressure from

Japan"—would declare war on the United States.[66] That had indeed been Hitler's original plan, but the meeting had already been postponed to the following day.

All this diplomatic and propagandistic activity was flanked by secret military preparations for the breach. At a meeting of the naval high command, Admiral Raeder agreed to the release of six large submarines "for a decisive deployment on the American coastline," christened Operation Drumbeat. This was half the number Admiral Dönitz had requested. The German intercept service also reported that the obsolete code hitherto used by the US Navy had been replaced by a new system, which was "uncrackable by us for now."[67]

Hitler may have been buoyed by Japanese successes, but most of the news from his own battlefronts, especially in Russia, was not good. To be sure, the situation around Kalinin seemed to be easing. The commander of the Ninth Army, General Adolf Strauss, opined that the Soviet attacks to the southeast of that city had "peaked."[68] But an attempt by the elite *Grossdeutschland* Infantry Regiment to close the breach in the lines of XXXXIII Army Corps failed.[69] A twenty-kilometer gap was opened by the Red Army, which pushed west and threatened the Second Panzer Army from the rear. The counterattacks mounted by Bock and Guderian failed. Heavy snow drifts hampered the mobility of the German columns.[70] Three whole divisions were encircled by the Soviets at Livny, south of Moscow. Guderian summed up the catastrophe in a letter to his wife that day. "The enemy," he wrote, "the size of the country and the foulness of the weather were all grossly underestimated."[71]

In the course of the morning, Bock spoke with Kluge, the commander of the Fourth Army. The latter was still keen to hold on as long as he could, to deal with each breakthrough as it occurred, and to delay a general retreat "as long as at all possible." Despite Kluge's bullishness, Bock then drafted a telegram to Brauchitsch at army high command. He repeated his view that Army Group Center would not be able to hold the line with the available forces for much longer. Even if the current breakthroughs could be sealed off, this effort would involve the "exhaustion" of "last available strength." Despite the difficulty of moving in the cold weather on terrible roads, the entire army group was in flux as a result of withdrawing men from quieter sectors and throwing them into the crisis areas. Bock went on to say that with the exception of some sectors of the Fourth and Ninth Armies, few winter shelters and fortifications had been prepared. There was thus nowhere to retreat to, and even if it were possible to withdraw to a shorter line along Kursk-Orel-Rzhev-Lake Volgo, the condition of the vehicles and the transportation network meant that that this would be "synonymous with very high losses of weapons and equipment."[72] The only solution, Bock concluded, was "to defend every square foot of ground with determination and only to retreat locally where there is no other choice." To do that, however, he needed reinforcements.

Hitler had still not yet realized the full extent of the crisis in the east, but by now it was dawning on him that he had, at minimum, a problem on his hands. The Führer met with Goebbels around noon and admitted "that things are not going too well in the east at the moment." Hitler agreed with his propaganda minister's suggestion that the German people needed to be prepared for blows that could not be avoided. Hitler lamented the "complete lack of winter equipment," which meant "the men there are confronted with physical and psychological stresses to which they had not been exposed in earlier campaigns."[73] It was probably for this reason that Hitler that day authorized the transfer of two or three divisions from the west to the eastern front.[74]

Even if the military pressure on Leningrad had eased somewhat, conditions within the beleaguered city remained grim. In a cramped apartment on 41 Furshtatskaya Street, for example, four women tried to cook and keep warm over a single stove. "They argue, and constantly groan and talk about food," the diarist Elena Skryabina wrote that day. "The children, whom it is impossible to escort out of the warm kitchen, are also here." One of them was "always trying to steal something from her neighbours." As a result, the women were reluctant to leave their "pathetic" meals unattended or the stove unwatched. Tempers flared. Then the electricity went out, and the kitchen was plunged into a "half darkness" in which it was difficult to prevent theft.[75]

Meanwhile, Reichstag members were arriving in Berlin for the scheduled meeting. One of them was Hans Frank, the governor of the Generalgouvernement in Poland.[76] It had been Hitler's intention that the Reichstag should meet this day, but he was not ready. He had been so taken up with meetings that he had only just started drafting his speech. Despite the entreaties of the Japanese to hold the session earlier, the meeting of the Reichstag was delayed again, and scheduled for 3 p.m. on the next day (December 11). The timing was dictated not so much by the need to reach a German audience, but by the necessities of global messaging. This way, Goebbels explained, the Japanese could "still" hear the speech before they went to bed, and the Americans could "already" hear it in the midmorning.[77] Clearly, the Führer would be addressing not just the Reich but the world.

Hitler spent much of the day preparing his speech, assisted mainly by Goebbels.[78] He also consulted Hans-Heinrich Dieckhoff, the former ambassador to Washington, who concealed his own opposition to what he regarded as the Führer's mistaken policy toward the United States.[79] The reason Hitler took so much trouble was that this speech was in many ways the most important of his career. The themes he was planning to address in it—the supposed power of international Jewry, the evil of plutocracy, the hostility of Roosevelt, the centrality of race and space—were those that had dominated his thinking for more than twenty years, and in the case of the American president for the last four (since the Quarantine Speech). Hitler also adopted a suggestion that he should use the occasion to convene a meeting of the gauleiters, the regional party chiefs. After assembling in Berlin to attend the speech, they would now meet with the Führer on the day after.

Ribbentrop, too, was preparing for the confrontation with the United States. That morning, he sent an urgent telegram to Ott in Tokyo instructing him to tell the Japanese "immediately" that the German government agreed with all their suggested changes to the text of the agreement; not long after, he added that the Italians concurred. Ribbentrop now pressed Ott to instruct Oshima to sign the final text "without any further delay" and certainly no later than midday German time.[80] Ott replied that he would do what he could.

The German foreign minister was also closely involved in the rhetorical flanking of the impending war. He received a memorandum from Dieckhoff entitled "The Anti-German Policy of President Roosevelt." The two men did not see eye to eye on the subject of America, but on this occasion Dieckhoff entered into the spirit of his brief, which was to provide the minister with ammunition against Roosevelt. The very first grievance he listed was the Quarantine Speech of October 5, 1937, when—at least in German eyes—the president had first shown his hand against the Reich. The last item came from the previous day (December 9), when Roosevelt had used a radio speech to describe Japan, Germany, and Italy as "bandits." The trajectory was clear: from 1937 to 1941, the United States had framed the Third Reich first as contagious and then as downright criminal.[81]

State Secretary Ernst von Weizsäcker, the most senior professional diplomat in the German Foreign Service, had considerable doubts about the wisdom of taking on the United States. "We value the fact," he wrote that day in the privacy of his diary, "that the United States are not declaring war on us, but that we are declaring war on them." He had unsuccessfully argued that one should "take the opposite approach." In other words, the reason why Hitler was determined to take the first step had nothing to do with braggadocio or underestimation of the United States—still less a death wish—but rather the Führer's desire to show Japan that he was actively keeping his promises. Weizsäcker was not convinced, though. He wondered "whether this gesture is so important to Japan." "In general and especially in the Western Hemisphere," Weizsäcker concluded, "we are thereby doing the enemy a favor."[82] Hitler, in other words, was simply falling into the trap Roosevelt had set for him.

Meanwhile, the Reich authorities prepared to move against the American press corps, ostensibly in retaliation for the arrest of about three hundred German journalists in the United States, but primarily because they were now regarded as combatants in a vital theater of the war: namely, propaganda and information management. A list of eighteen was drawn up with addresses.[83] Ribbentrop instructed that—with the exception of Guido Enderis, on account of his "proven pro-German sentiments"—all US journalists were to be detained. In fact, there were plans to arrest "all reachable" Americans, again with exceptions for "pro-German Americans." If the United States went on to arrest women and children, the German Foreign Office warned, then Germany would do the same. That said, Ribbentrop let it be known that he wanted the Gestapo to treat "all detainees well for the time being."[84] They were, in effect, to be hostages, though of a very different type than central and western European Jewry.

This sentiment was evident in a memorandum penned that day by a German Foreign Office official. Reichsführer-SS Heinrich Himmler, it stated, had been tasked with drawing up a list of 150 male US citizens between the ages of twenty and sixty who could be detained in Germany. The Paris embassy was asked to do the same for occupied France. In the same spirit, German diplomats in Belgium, Greece, Holland, Norway, and Serbia were asked to locate all American citizens and identify how many could be detained using these criteria.[85]

The disaster in the Pacific that had occurred that morning had ramifications for Churchill's position in Parliament. At eleven, Churchill "stalked"—as one witness put it—into the House of Commons. From his seat behind Churchill, Chips Channon could see that the prime minister seemed particularly "anxious to speak." After the usual preliminary customs were observed, Churchill rose to inform the House that he had "bad news" and wanted to relay it "at the earliest possible moment." When he announced the sinking of both the *Prince of Wales* and *Repulse*, "a wave of gloom spread everywhere; the House was restive, the Government suddenly unpopular," according to Channon. Churchill had little information beyond the official Japanese communiqué but promised to discuss the "general war situation" tomorrow and how it had, "from many points of view, both favourable and adverse, undergone important changes in the last few days." Despite Churchill's attempt to put the crippling losses in perspective, it did little to lift the despondency and depression. As Channon noted, it was "a most shattering blow for our Pacific fleet and Naval prestige." It was also devastating for Churchill personally, after he had told the House just two days earlier that some of Britain's "finest ships" had reached their Pacific stations "at a very convenient moment." In light of those unfortunate remarks, Channon's dinner guest that evening, the society hostess Dame Margaret Greville, snarkily remarked that "if only the Prime Minister could have permanent laryngitis we might win the war."[86]

Churchill channeled his despair into again pressing for an immediate visit to the United States when he met with Ambassador Winant immediately after his appearance in Parliament. The dire news from the Pacific was yet further evidence of the vital need "for reconsideration of planning" and a meeting between the two leaders to address it. The US ambassador reported back to Washington that "discouragement seems only to give him new courage and add to his determination."[87] Meeting with the chiefs of staff at noon in Downing Street, however, the prime minister revealed his anxiety. Despite the dire naval situation in the Pacific, Alan Brooke noted that Churchill "had stood [the] shock well." But in light of Roosevelt's determination to postpone any visit until January, the general observed the "PM fretting a bit at this delay."[88] It was America's role, and the question of whether it would become a full belligerent in every theater, that continued to cause Churchill the most alarm.

There was no better news from the rest of the world. In Hong Kong, the garrison was preparing to evacuate the entire mainland. Soon, only Hong Kong Island itself would remain under British control, and it was clear that the entire colony was on its last legs.[89] That day, too, Churchill received a private message from Irish prime minister Éamon de Valera that showed his gambit had failed. Pearl Harbor would not bounce the Free State into the war. Instead, the taoiseach invited Lord Cranborne—who, as secretary of state for Dominion affairs, was responsible for relations with independent Ireland—for talks in Dublin as "the best way towards a fuller understanding of our position here."[90]

While Churchill met with the chiefs of staff in Downing Street, the BBC was rebroadcasting Roosevelt's fireside chat, which they had originally aired live in the early hours of the morning. Winant reported back to Roosevelt that his stirring words "gave people great confidence here," as they "assume that we are in the total war together."[91] This sentiment was echoed in the UK Ministry of Information's survey of British opinion, which found that the speech "was received with unanimous praise and has been compared with some of Lincoln's speeches." Roosevelt's commitment "for 100% war effort" made a particularly strong impression.

Nevertheless, the ministry's analysts noted that these pro-American feelings were mixed with a good deal of antipathy toward the United States for having to be pushed into the war rather than entering it willingly. Resentment was expressed at the "remarkable unanimity of the Americans in going to war when they are directly threatened, after the years in which they appeared content to let other people do their fighting for democracy." These sentiments were reported to be "strongest among working people, who most admire the Russian resistance." The public was willing to make "immense sacrifices to assist the Russians, even giving up food and materials that are badly wanted here," but the American entrance provoked indignation at "the possibility of diminished supplies of food and tobacco."[92] Of particular concern was the seemingly inevitable immediate decline in military supplies, with fears repeatedly expressed that Lend-Lease would "dry up."[93] While there was hope that "America's well-nigh inexhaustible material resources, and her vast man-power" would ensure that "before long they will assume greater proportions than ever," rumors that the British government had offered the US government shells from Canada were "considered to reveal a state of unpreparedness even worse than had been anticipated." Coupled with the "lack of foresight indicated by the grouping of ships at Pearl Harbor, and the poor defences of her island bases," there was a great deal of anger, even contempt, at what was regarded as a lack of American preparedness.[94]

Speaking on the BBC, the journalist and independent member of Parliament Vernon Bartlett acknowledged that Britain would have a "fairly grim time ahead" because of the new demands imposed on shipping by the American entry into the Pacific war. Bartlett noted that most of his political colleagues agreed that "we may have to continue for a little longer in the depressing phase of the war when we have generally to be on the defensive because our armies are not yet well enough equipped to take the initiative on a large scale." Everything would ultimately come down to two crucial questions: "What will the U.S. do about Germany? And what will the Soviets do about Japan?" On the former, Bartlett urged Americans not to become preoccupied with the Pacific theater to the detriment of the other fronts and to recognize that Hitler was "the chief executive in the Axis firm" who had pushed Japan to attack the United States. On the latter, only time would tell whether Stalin would decide to attack Japan to safeguard his eastern possessions or would prove unwilling to risk anything that would weaken his western front.

In the Arctic, where the waters were "very rough indeed" and it was "almost perpetual night outside," Foreign Secretary Eden and his party were pondering the same questions. Oliver Harvey confided to his diary that they had received Churchill's "perturbing" early morning telegram. The principal concern among these British officials remained Churchill's continued determination to depart for the United States "if invited." They could "only hope that Roosevelt will refuse to have him now." Their sense seemed to be that if Churchill crossed the Atlantic to implore Roosevelt to focus America's war effort on Hitler—while a new war raged in the Pacific and the US-German relationship was still unresolved—this would antagonize the American public, go down badly at home because the prime minister was away just as a new struggle began, and perhaps also arouse suspicion in Moscow. Eden and his advisers implicitly understood Churchill's concern about Roosevelt prioritizing the Pacific but considered it "a poor look-out if the Americans get into a flat spin and concentrate entirely on Japan." Having also received word that the US State Department "has even suggested that Russia should join in war against Japan," Harvey considered this "a bit stiff when America isn't yet fighting Germany."

When news of the sinking of the *Prince of Wales* and *Repulse* reached Harvey and his fellow passengers, they found it "almost incredible," as "*Prince of Wales* supposed to be proof against anything." They of course recognized that "it alters the whole balance in the Far East and will put us definitely on defensive there." The only slight positive they could see was that "surely P.M. can't leave now."[95]

On top of the tragedy in the Pacific, December 10 was also the date of another heavy British naval loss, this time in the Atlantic. The convoy SC-57, comprising slower, older vessels, was in the midst of an eastbound transatlantic voyage when it was attacked by a German U-boat (U130) off the northwest coast of Donegal, in the Irish Free State. Three merchant ships, the *Kirnwood*, *Kurdistan*, and *State of Luxor*, were torpedoed and sunk within minutes. Twelve crewmen died on the *Kirnwood*, with 5,500 tons of grain lost; ten men were lost from the *Kurdistan*, as well as 4,256 tons of foodstuffs and 2,100 tons of metal; and four men from the *Star of Luxor* drowned, along with 7,094 tons of general cargo and military stores. Thanks to the work of British rescue ships, over one hundred survivors were saved from the waters.[96] It was further proof, if any was needed, of the continued devastation that the German submarines could inflict on British convoys and the vital supplies that they carried.

The Royal Navy was now being pushed to its very limits. The Japanese raids across the Pacific were forcing the Dominion governments to request the return to their home waters of ships they had previously lent to Admiral Andrew Cunningham, commander of the Mediterranean station. That day, the first sea lord wrote to Cunningham and Sir James Somerville, commander of Force H at Gibraltar, to ask about the likely consequences if all heavy ships were withdrawn from either or both of their fleets. While Cunningham was eager to help with the crisis that had overtaken other theaters, he knew that with the Eighth Army looking to press home its advantage over Rommel in Cyrenaica, any withdrawal would be a gamble. Without sufficient naval forces in the Mediterranean to guarantee supplies or the air power to protect them and support troops on the ground, it was highly doubtful that the army could exploit the momentum in the desert. Cunningham was already operating without an aircraft carrier and had beseeched London to dispatch one as soon as possible to prevent his fleet having to operate without the carrier-borne fighters necessary for air coverage against the Luftwaffe. Yet the shipping crisis was so severe that none could be found. As the official historian of the British naval war would later write, "Never since the evacuation of the Mediterranean in 1796," at the height of the French Revolutionary Wars, "had the Royal Navy been so hard pressed; it even seemed possible that a similar withdrawal might now have to be carried out."[97] Much British public sentiment was growing desperate. One London-based chemist in his midthirties, after hearing about the *Repulse* and *Prince of Wales*, declared for Mass Observation, "Today is another day when all there is left to say is 'Thank God for the Russians.'"[98]

As if to vindicate this declaration, over the course of that afternoon, the situation on the eastern front grew ever worse for Hitler. At 3 p.m., Himmler received a report from SS-Brigadeführer Karl Gebhardt on the state of the embattled SS division Leibstandarte.[99] The crisis at Army Group Center continued. Strong Russian troop deployments were observed. Gaps were opening up all along the line, and further attacks seemed likely.[100] The supply situation was dire. Army Group Center reported that the temperatures of minus-fifteen degrees Celsius had led to a loss of about half the railway transportation capacity as engines seized up and snow drifts blocked lines. The army group warned that it "would have to reckon with the temporary loss of all rail connections."[101] The tone of the OKW war diary darkened. It now spoke candidly of enemy "breakthroughs" and of the "tirelessly continuing attack" of the Red Army. There was now also talk of "a new defensive line" in places where the Wehrmacht had already begun to retreat.[102] Brauchitsch felt obliged to send a telegram to the troops that "he was fully aware as was our Supreme Commander [Hitler] of the difficult situation at the front."[103] This was a direct response to Guderian's repeated charge that the army leadership did not understand what was happening in the east.

If all this was not bad enough, the SD sent a bleak situation report that day about the situation behind the lines in Russia. A typhus epidemic loomed in Minsk and other parts of White Russia. Suspicions of "calculated bacteriological measures by the Soviets" had not been substantiated. That said, the authorities were doing "everything to prevent the spread of typhus to the men of the Einsatzkommandos." In the more recently occupied areas, the Jews, who had evidently heard rumors of their impending fate, had largely fled. The food supply of the civilian population was not secure, a situation aggravated, as the SD openly admitted, by the "pointless plundering" of German soldiers. There had been extensive damage to property due to the ripping out of wood fittings for fuel to keep warm. The worst offenders, apparently, were "the Spaniards . . . who have taken everything with them that was not nailed down."[104]

The real problem, though, was not individual theft or sadism but the systematic brutality and criminality of the German occupation itself. Goebbels was at least honest enough to admit it. "The situation in the occupied areas of the Ukraine," he wrote that day, "is extraordinarily tense." Goebbels made Gauleiter Erich Koch, the chief of the Imperial Commissariat for the Ukraine, responsible for this, as his "rigorous" policies paid no heed to those of the German Foreign Office, which sought to win over the local population with the prospect of some sort of statehood. Not only had the Ukrainian intelligentsia been "eliminated," but "it was to be expected that as a result of the poor treatment the Ukrainians generally receive from us, a tough resistance [movement] will gradually develop there." This would be a direct threat to the German supply lines. Goebbels was not the only man to ask whether it was right to let a brute like Koch "let rip according to his general disposition."[105] In this connection the Foreign Office noted that day the alarming news that the Soviet Union was abandoning "domestic and party-political slogans" in favor of "appealing to Slavic solidarity against anything German."[106] The Foreign Office was also anxious about Ukrainian nationalists, who had launched an unsuccessful rising in Lvov. "The activities of the Bandera group," Ribbentrop was told, "are an acute threat to German interest."[107]

Resistance was stirring not only in Russia and the Ukraine but in other parts of occupied Europe. That day, the Nazi security service in Oslo reported that a class of schoolchildren in Halden, a southern Norwegian town close to the Swedish border, had gathered in a corner of the schoolyard to sing the Communist "Internationale." It also announced various arrests of people on suspicion of listening to the BBC and other crimes. One woman was locked up for saying that "I hope it will be minus

50 degrees today so that this German scum freezes."[108] There were also reports from the police authorities in the Moravian city of Brünn of a Czechoslovak subversive organization that planned the "establishment of a revolutionary Czechoslovak state"; thirty-six functionaries had been arrested so far.[109] In Paris, there were assassinations of German personnel. Partisan activity in Yugoslavia, though not as high as during the autumn, was still significant. There were even acts of sabotage in the Reich itself.[110]

The Nazis generally responded to any opposition, real or imagined, with ferocity. That day, the Wehrmacht completed the "cleansing and securing" of the western Morava Valley in Yugoslavia. The target here were the forces of the royalist resistance leader Dragoljub Mihailovic; the man himself escaped but his chief of staff, Major Misic, was captured. In nearby Cacak, eighteen "Communists," who may simply have been random civilians, were shot.[111] The most brutal actions, however, were always directed against the Jews, who were held responsible both for local resistance and for the global coalition against the Third Reich (which Hitler had in fact brought down on his own head).[112] The reports of the SD spoke openly that day of how the alleged Jewish activities as "saboteurs, plunderers, spies, terrorists, and snipers" had "caused" the security police to "liquidate" more than eleven thousand Jews in the north Ukrainian district of Radomyschl "alone."[113]

For now, most Jews to the west of the German-occupied Soviet Union were still alive, but their existence was desperately precarious. In the ghetto of Lodz, Fanny Werner was still hanging on. She bitterly regretted taking her pearls with her, because nobody had enough money to buy them. It would have been better, she continued, if she had brought some more cloth with her, as she would have been able to do work for one of the local textile factories. The directorate there had liked her samples. "I am too old for factory work there," she concluded, "and there is no other way of earning money."[114] If she could not work, Fanny Werner would starve.

Even so, she was still better off than the deportees who had left Cologne on December 7. On December 10, their train arrived at Riga. The journey had been terrible, because although there had been enough food, they had soon run out of water, not to speak of the cold and the overcrowding. Now these unfortunates were in for another shock. The largely empty ghetto was in complete shambles after the Latvian Jews had been dragged out by SS commander Friedrich Jeckeln's men. There was smashed furniture and blood in the streets. Many stairwells and apartments were wrecked. The precipitate manner in which the previous inhabitants had been torn from the ghetto was evident from the frozen meals on tables and in kitchens. It was an utterly desolate scene, and a grim portent of what was to come. All the same, the Cologne Jews had no choice but to get to work and try to make themselves as comfortable as possible.[115]

For many Crimean Jews, December 10, 1941, was the end. In Kara-subarsar (now Belogorsk), Sonderkommando 11b stripped the Jewish population of all their valuables, took them to a crossroads in the sur-rounding countryside, and murdered them nearby.[116] In Feodossija, 1,052 Jews, who had already been imprisoned for more than three weeks, were taken to a tank trap outside the city, forced to strip despite the bitter cold, and shot by Sonderkommando 10b under the command of SS-Obersturmbannführer Alois Persterer. Some of the executioners were volunteers from the local army post who had specifically asked to participate in the killing—whether this was out of innate anti-Semitism or in the belief that they were exterminating "partisans" is not clear. Whatever their motivation, these men not only mowed down their frightened, naked, and freezing victims but also forced the bigger Jews to "stack" the dead "properly" before shooting them in turn. Afterward, Persterer organized a big drinking session, either to reward or to anaes-thetize his fellow murderers.[117]

Worse yet was on the horizon. The responsible military commander, Count Sponeck, issued a brutal order that day demanding that all Jews were to be registered, tagged with the Star of David, and conscripted for forced labor. "Partisans" were to be killed outright. In the context of this time and place, where Jews and partisans were largely interchange-able categories, it was clear that both were marked for annihilation.[118]

That same day, reinforcements for Einsatzgruppe D arrived in Crimea via Odessa. These policemen were to be deployed in the mass murder of the Jews of Simferopol planned for the following day.[119]

There were as yet relatively few Jews in the concentration camp at Auschwitz; the extermination camp at Birkenau was still under construction.[120] The first big wave of transports there was about to begin, however, and the authorities were preparing themselves. That day, the commandant Rudolf Höss, along with all other camp administrations, received an instruction from the Inspectorate of the Concentration Camps.[121] Höss was ordered to help commissions of doctors tasked with selecting those prisoners who were capable of working. The rest were to be subjected to "Special Treatment 14f13"—that is, "euthanasia," or rather, murder. Auschwitz was not yet an extermination camp on an industrial scale, though nine inmates were killed that day through "Phenol injections" in the prisoner's hospital, with numbers 22366, 24470, 18853, 20873, 13534, 7966, 22584, 22148, and 20417. It was also on this day that J. A. Topf sent its second reminder to the SS Construction Directorate at the camp demanding payment for the construction of an "incinerator," probably to dispose of the bodies of Soviet prisoners of war, at the cost of 3,650 Reichsmarks.

The murder of the Jews involved large parts of the German military and state apparatus. There were few open protests, but there was some unease. This was articulated that day by Admiral Wilhelm Canaris, the head of the Abwehr, the German military intelligence service. In a lecture to the heads of his field offices, he stressed that "the Abwehr has nothing to do with persecution of the Jews." Canaris demanded that his men carry out their duties in a "humane, respectable, correct and soldierly manner." "Activity against the Jews," he repeated, "is no concern of ours." "We have nothing to do with it," Canaris insisted, but rather than try to stop it, he ordered the Abwehr to remain "aloof" and not to "criticize." There was no doubting Canaris's commitment to a German victory as he told his men to work together with the Gestapo and SD on all military and intelligence matters and to "stick to [their] guns for victory."[122]

But victory appeared increasingly distant for German forces in North Africa. That day, the German Afrika Korps and the Italians continued their retreat in Libya, as the British advanced west from Tobruk. The Royal Navy shelled Derna. In fact, Rommel probably still faced more British tanks in North Africa than Guderian did Soviet ones in front of Army Group Center.[123] At sea, in the air, and even on land, the British Empire remained a formidable foe for Hitler. As Alan Moorehead wrote from the headquarters of Eighth Army for publication in the next day's *Daily Express*, "It seems that we have done better than we thought." Moorehead informed those back at home that progress was so rapid "it is getting more and more difficult to keep pace with the advancing British front." Most impressive was what he called "the best tank scoop of the war," with British troops capturing almost thirty German tanks, battered though not beyond repair. It was a demonstration, in particular, of the capacity of the new American-supplied tanks to inflict damage on their German counterparts. Under the headline "Libya Panzers Are Being Smashed Westwards," Moorehead signed off his piece positively, if still cautiously: "Rommel is not beaten yet. But today's news is good."[124]

The British advance in North Africa and the impending war with the United States now made an alliance with Vichy France even more urgent for the German Reich. First, because Rommel's retreat made the use of Bizerta imperative, and a total collapse of the Axis position in Libya would soon bring British tanks into Tunisia. Second, because American belligerence would both increase the vulnerability of Morocco and Algeria to a US-British landing, and because that space now acquired new significance as a potential base for long-range Anglo-American bombing raids on mainland Europe. For this reason, Hitler decided to continue the negotiations begun between Göring and Pétain. He hoped that these could be deepened through discussions between the former and the supreme commander of Vichy forces in North Africa, General Alphonse Juin. That day, Hitler let it be known that "the French should be requested to submit plans particularly on how they envisage a military cooperation for the defense of [their] African colonies."[125]

The German public was aware of the ferocity of the battle in North Africa. If the mood with respect to Russia had darkened, so did that of the reporting from Libya. The official OKW report spoke merely of "local attacks" in the east but of "heavy fighting" in North Africa.[126] "The battle [in Libya] rages with great bitterness," the war reporter R. W. Billhardt wrote from the front line. "The British have deployed much greater forces in comparison to their earlier attacks." He warned that "the battles we have to endure here are tough," as the Afrika Korps faced large quantities of British anti-aircraft guns and "swarms of Australian, New Zealand, South African and British fighters."[127] The report gave a vivid sense of a Reich already at war with much of the globe.

For German propaganda, the situation posed a severe challenge at home and abroad. Goebbels, who had always advised caution in claiming victory in Russia, lamented that the Reich had announced back in October "that the eastern campaign was already decided." That left the Germans at the mercy of every new Soviet triumph.[128] This explains the relief of the Nazi leadership at the Japanese successes, especially the dramatic sinkings off Malaya. "Thanks be to God," Goebbels wrote that day, "that the world public has plenty to discuss about these themes so that events in the east and in Libya hardly feature in the news."[129]

The disjunction between domestic perceptions and military realities was stressed that day by the commander of Army Group North. Ritter von Leeb noted the "insufficient winter equipment" issued to his forces, which was epitomized for him by the fact that some of the gloves sent lacked fingers. He contrasted this with the films showed at home, where soldiers were shown wearing thick fur coats. "Thus," he wrote, "appearances and reality differ."[130]

That morning in Washington, confusion continued over the holdup in Lend-Lease supplies. Following the alarmed messages that he had received from Lend-Lease administrator Stettinius the previous day, Harry Hopkins spoke to Assistant Secretary McCloy at the War Department to clarify the situation. McCloy confirmed to the president's chief aide that, immediately after the Japanese attack on the seventh, all shipments of "Lend-Lease materials were stopped for a look-see." Within twenty-four hours, the department had released any material already signed for at the ship's side "except aircraft, ammunition and armament," all of which had been repossessed.[131] Other standard material, including trucks and signal equipment, was scheduled for release that day, but no aircraft and ammunition would be released for the remainder of December.

To reinforce this measure, collectors of customs were ordered not to clear "exportation of aircraft, aircraft parts, accessories or equipment of any nature whatever, unless consigned to military or naval forces of the United States Government."[132] The War Department was categorical about the need for this blanket suspension, and when Stettinius continued to press for the supplies, he was brusquely advised by an army general to stop badgering: "We have got to go slow, and we just can't be bothered with people demanding this and that."[133] With US forces under siege in the Pacific, the priority was on reinforcing their own men rather than exporting supplies overseas. As General Hap Arnold told his staff that day, "We must run a rake through the United States, gathering up every combat plane and fill up every pursuit group."[134]

The quandary of whether to concentrate on Japan or Germany, and how to proceed on Lend-Lease, was known to and discussed by the wider public. That day, the "Man on the Street" project recorded a lively exchange on the matter at Indiana University in Bloomington. "I believe that as a military standpoint it is far better to fight on one front than two," said one student, Mike Fox. "By concentrating our efforts on Japan," he continued, "I am of the opinion that we can knock her out of the war much more rapidly than we can if our efforts are split by an AEF [American Expeditionary Force], for example, in Africa and an Atlantic Fleet which must see action in the Atlantic." His interlocutor, a Mr. Russell, disagreed. "Don't forget," he argued, "that is exactly what Hitler wants us to do." "If we concentrate entirely upon Japan," Russell went on, "then we must stop our flow of goods to Great Britain and Russia. And evidently, the grand strategy pact of the Axis powers is to divert the flow of our materials."[135]

Suspending Lend-Lease shipments had implications for Britain's North African campaign, where American planes and particularly tanks were playing an important role in Operation Crusader. As Morgenthau told his staff that morning, "It is perfectly amazing how our M-3 tank mechanically is so far superior to the English that there is just no comparison between them." Basing his analysis on an aide's report on the Libyan campaign that he had received the previous evening, the Treasury secretary confided that the American light tanks had stood up to the rigors of desert warfare better than their British equivalents, a number of which had suffered mechanical failure traversing the terrain.

The Treasury secretary was therefore aware that the War Department's suspension of Lend-Lease export licenses on American military supplies had "great significance," not only for Britain but also, even more seriously, for the Soviets. He was scheduled to meet that afternoon with the Soviet ambassador, at the latter's request, to discuss the supply situation. Morgenthau told his staff not to inform the press about the conference, perhaps conscious that any suggestion that the Soviets were lobbying for American supplies for the fight with Hitler might antagonize those who wanted the administration to keep its focus on arming its own forces for the fight with Japan.[136]

Morgenthau's meeting with Litvinov might also enable the administration to learn more about Stalin's intentions in the Pacific. That morning, Secretary of War Stimson had heard from a besieged General Douglas MacArthur in the Philippines that, as the Japanese forces were now widely extended, this "offered a golden opportunity by cooperation with the Russians to attack from the North."[137] Consequently, Stimson had arranged to meet with Secretary of State Hull to explore the likelihood of a Soviet intervention.

Overnight, the secretary of state had received a telegram from the American chargé in Moscow, Walter Thurston, that there was as yet "no official indication of the reaction of the Soviet Government to the Japanese attack upon the United States." Thurston had met with Andrey Vyshinsky, the deputy commissar of foreign affairs, who had "made no comment other than to indicate his very cordial good will." While the local paper in Kuibyshev devoted roughly two-thirds of its external-affairs coverage to the war in the Pacific, this was exclusively based on foreign news outlets and there was no Soviet perspective given on the hostilities. Thurston was encouraged that the press largely based their dispatches on American and British, rather than Japanese, sources and also learned from American journalists in the city that the feeling among their contacts was "hostile to Japanese, entirely favourable to ourselves." Nevertheless, from these fragments, the chargé surmised that the United States should expect Stalin to "continue at least for the present to be guided by the Soviet-Japanese pact of neutrality."[138] This was also the conclusion drawn by Hull and Stimson. Both agreed "that the chances of getting the Russians to do much is small."[139] The principal Soviet concern, Thurston concluded, echoing what Roosevelt had earlier heard from Litvinov, was "the possibility that our involvement in actual hostilities might result in the curtailment of the flow of American war supplies to the Soviet Union."[140]

This situation was unlikely to improve in the short term. In the immediate aftermath of the Pearl Harbor attack, Roosevelt had established a strategic munitions board to enable the Joint Chiefs of Staff to institute programs for allocating munitions to the United States and the nations receiving defense aid. The agenda for the board's first meeting, drawn up on December 10, understandably gave precedence to US forces to the "extent necessary to meet their immediate probable consumption of munitions and build up and maintain reserves."[141] The urgent priority was to strengthen US continental defenses, develop emergency task forces, and step up training for new recruits. Consequently, many critical items that were previously destined for Britain and the Soviet Union were canceled. Rather than following the schedules agreed to before Pearl Harbor, allocations would now be made on an ad-hoc, day-by-day basis. While the president had made clear his intention to maintain Lend-Lease shipments, in reality, the emphasis had now shifted from the United States as the "arsenal of democracy" to America as a besieged wartime belligerent with its own vital munitions needs.

Meanwhile, in the Arctic, some of the munitions being shipped to Russia were in deep peril. The *Harmatris* was underway again, but now out of sight of the convoy. It was noticed that, despite the intense cold, water on one of the hatches on deck was vaporizing into steam. The hatch was carefully lifted to reveal that a burning truck had come loose and was careering around the hold, breaking open and setting alight bales of cargo. This was alarming, not least because there were ten tons of cordite and some small-arms ammunition stowed underneath. If these exploded, the ship would surely sink or burn out. An attempt to put out the fire with steam failed. The ship's mate then courageously descended the hatch wearing the only smoke helmet and trailing a hose. When he was overcome by the smoke, another seaman joined him, but neither was able to put out the fire. In these circumstances, the skipper, Captain R. W. Brundle, had no choice to break radio silence and request help. The rescue ship *Zamalek* turned back to come to his aid. Eventually, the fire was put out. Meanwhile, more and more cargo broke open and began to crash around the hold. *Zamalek* returned to the convoy, but the battered *Harmatris* had had enough. As Iceland lacked the necessary facilities, the convoy commodore instructed Brundle to make for the safety of the Clyde estuary in Scotland.[142] The war matériel on the *Harmatris* would not help Stalin, at least not yet.

Throughout the afternoon, Berlin remained a hive of activity. At 4 p.m., Himmler went to the hairdresser, presumably to be presentable for the Reichstag meeting.[143] Later he went to the Imperial Chancellery, one assumes, to confer with Hitler about the day to come.[144] Meanwhile, German Foreign Office officials conferred on the practicalities of the reprisals against American journalists in response to the arrests of their German counterparts across the Atlantic. The meeting was attended by the ministerial councillor Dr. Ernst Brauweiler, head of the Foreign Press Section of the Foreign Office, by representatives from the press service of the Foreign Office, and by a contingent from the RSHA, who would have to do the dirty work. It was agreed that the Americans would be arrested the following morning between 5 and 6 a.m. by the Gestapo in one of their feared dawn raids. They would be interned in the residency of the former French ambassador on the Little Wannsee in eight heated rooms, an important privilege in the dead of winter. Guido Enderis was exempted. The officers were to be instructed to treat their captives "correctly."[145]

At 4:30 p.m. Ribbentrop rang Mackensen in Rome to communicate Hitler's intention to declare war during a Reichstag speech beginning at 3 p.m. the next day.[146] An hour later, the German ambassador went to inform the Duce, who interrupted a meeting of his ministerial council. Mussolini assured him that he would not put on a similar event himself, but that he would "listen to the speech of the Führer on the radio, as he always did." Mackensen worried, though, that the Italian plan to make its declaration of war public at 3 p.m. might distract from the start of Hitler's speech. They agreed that the Italians could notify the press at 3 p.m., but the radio only at 3:30, so that it would only be able to broadcast the news toward the end of Hitler's speech or shortly afterward. Mackensen promised to consult with Berlin on the matter, and while he was unable to reach Ribbentrop in person, the German foreign minister let it be known that he did not want the Italians to announce anything anywhere before 4 p.m., to make quite sure that the Führer would have a clear run. Later that afternoon, the Italian foreign minister agreed to this arrangement.[147]

For the Roosevelt administration, after Pearl Harbor, mobilizing the population against Japan was not difficult. A cartoon published that day in the isolationist *Chicago Tribune* summed up the depth of hatred among the American people. Titled "Throwing in an Extra Charge," it featured a US gunner loading a gun with a charge labeled "war without mercy on a treacherous foe." The gun was pointed over a smoking Hawaii toward a rising sun with a skull at its center.[148] Selling war with Germany, by contrast, was not so straightforward.

In this context, the continued reports of German involvement in the Japanese offensive across the Pacific took on heightened significance. That day, an AP story appeared in newspapers across the United States: "Rumors were afloat that some Germans had been shot down in Japanese planes" during attacks on the Philippines. "A United States Army spokesman" in Manila was quoted as stating, "The Japanese ground tactics . . . indicated German tutelage if not actual German participation." One newspaper, the *Minneapolis Morning Tribune*, carried the story under the headline "Japanazis: Tokyo Air Force Is Equipped by Nazis."[149]

These unsubstantiated reports, and others, were seized on by those who had long warned about the German threat. The *Atlanta Journal* reported that Carl Vinson, chairman of the House's naval committee, was "confident that the attacking planes and ships were Japanese in name only." The Democratic chair of the Senate Finance Committee, Walter F. George, was quoted by the same paper as saying that many Germans planes "have been overhauled and flown to Japan . . . and there can be no question that the attack [on Pearl Harbor] was arranged and engineered, as to time, by the Germans."[150] Not everyone believed the Germans were complicit in Japan's actions. In a nationally syndicated column that day, the long-time anti-interventionist Paul Mallon argued, "The theory that they [the Japanese] might have been inspired by a desire to help Hitler is not forceful. Hitler is too far away to do the Japs either harm or good."[151]

If disagreement remained over Germany, the war also poured salt into old political wounds, especially racial ones. Despite the heroism of African American sailor Doris Miller at Pearl Harbor, the Democratic Texas representative W. R. Poage, a fellow Wacoan, wrote that day to Secretary of the Navy Frank Knox with a message of division. He demanded nothing less than the "complete segregation of the races" in the military, which Poage, himself a World War I navy veteran, claimed was vital to secure the "full-hearted cooperation" of white southerners with the war effort. "To assign a Negro doctor to treat some southern white boy," he concluded, "would be a crushing insult and in my opinion, an outrage against the patriotism of our southern people."[152] Interestingly, Poage was a critic of isolationism and had explicitly endorsed Roosevelt's anti-Nazi policy.

Another critic of isolationism, Arthur W. Mitchell, a Democratic representative from Illinois and the only Black American in Congress, instead argued that the new struggle was an opportunity to secure full civil rights at home. Speaking in the House on the Japan war resolution two days earlier, Mitchell had declared that, rather than a conflict with Tokyo alone, this "bloody struggle engaged in by Germany, Italy and now Japan is a challenge to civilization itself," threatening to "wipe out the possibilities of democratic government and to establish in its stead

abject slavery." Mitchell followed that up with a written statement pledg-
ing "the unbroken and continued loyalty not only of the First Congressional District, which I represent, but that of the 15,000,000 Negroes
in America," who would give everything, including their lives, "for the
success of our effort to withstand Hitlerism." In view of those sacrifices,
which Black Americans had made previously for their country and were
now prepared to make again, Mitchell declared that "the Negro expects
the same treatment under our so-called democratic form of government
that is accorded all other citizens." Not only would a Black American "be
unworthy of citizenship in this country if he contended for less," but "if
he is good enough to die for his country, he should be given the largest
and fullest opportunity to live for his country without any type of racial
discrimination."[153] Mitchell had worked to promote Roosevelt's New
Deal after his election in 1935, doing so in a manner that downplayed
"race matters" and led to criticism from African Americans that he was
an "Uncle Tom." He now urged the president, and Congress, to live up
to the democratic rhetoric that they had employed to distinguish the
United States from its despotic enemies.[154]

At the White House that morning, the president was immersed in
a two-hour conference with his military advisers from 11 a.m. Stimson
observed that "in spite of the terrific pressure that had been upon him, he
was businesslike, clear and effective."[155] The focus of the meeting was on
the situation in the Pacific. The previous day, army and navy leaders had
stopped a convoy heading for the Philippines and ordered it to return to
Hawaii. The navy, in particular, was adamant that reinforcing America's
western defenses was the priority and "pointed to the catastrophe that
would develop if Hawaii should become a Japanese base."[156] Yet Stimson and army chief of staff George Marshall were determined that the
United States could not afford a strategic withdrawal from the western
Pacific and that General McArthur should be provided with reinforcements to defend the American position. The president agreed, and the
decision was reversed, with the convoy proceeding to Australia, from
where the supplies would be transferred to the Philippines. As a result,
it was agreed by the general staff that Hawaii would be supplied from

the continental United States. Stimson was also adamant that the islands should be defended by long-distance bombers, which would probably add to the pressure on Britain to forego its allocation of that type of aircraft.[157]

Morgenthau's aide Harry Dexter White would hear similar sentiments that morning when he met at 10:40 with Andrei Gromyko, Litvinov's deputy at the Soviet embassy. Gromyko informed White that while on December 8, Stettinius had assured him that "Lend-Lease arrangements would be continued," in fact, "on December 9, ship loadings were stopped by U.S. authorities."[158] Hitler's calculation that war with Japan would divert US resources away from Britain and the Soviet Union was, it seemed, being vindicated.

In London, Churchill was drafting his response to Roosevelt's request to delay their meeting until January. Brushing off Roosevelt's concern for his personal safety, the prime minister assured him that there was no "serious danger about [the] return journey." Far more perilous was the risk of "not having a full discussion on the highest level about the extreme gravity of the naval position as well as upon all the production and allocation issues involved." Churchill was prepared to meet in Bermuda or Washington but was convinced that it "would be disastrous to wait for another month before we settled common action in face of new adverse situation particularly in Pacific." He was prepared to leave as early as the following night but would delay departure until the president had confirmed the "rendezvous." The prize of US entrance into the war as a full belligerent against all the Axis powers seemed so close, but an interruption in the continued flow of American supplies threatened to undermine Britain's war effort, particularly the defense of its territories in East Asia and Australasia. Churchill had "never felt so sure about the final victory, but only concerted action will achieve it." The message was dispatched from the US embassy at 6 p.m., just as the prime minister sat down for a meeting of the extended war cabinet at 10 Downing Street.[159]

Churchill began by discussing the strategic implications of the tragic loss of the *Prince of Wales* and *Repulse*, which, coupled with the devastation at Pearl Harbor, had "entirely changed the balance of naval forces in the Pacific." Churchill hoped that the situation could be "brought round," but until then Britain would "have to suffer considerable inconveniences," with its shipping exposed to punishing enemy attacks. Just as in Parliament earlier, however, he was keen to stress the positive recent developments, which he maintained "far outweighed the immediate consequences of the position in the Far East, serious as they were." The Germans had suffered a serious setback in Russia and the situation had greatly improved in Libya, with Tobruk relieved and Britain poised to take the initiative in North Africa. Above all, the United States "was now in the war with us."

Yet, as Churchill had just told the US president, the full benefits of American belligerence required a coordinated strategy against all the Axis powers. The prime minister informed the war cabinet that Roosevelt was insisting their personal meeting be delayed until January and that he was "not satisfied" with this. While he was pressing Roosevelt for a meeting much sooner, all he could say at this point was that "he was hoping that his visit would take place in the near future."[160] That Roosevelt was not expected to reverse his decision and extend an offer for an immediate visit was apparent from a message that Churchill received from the king that day. George VI was "deeply" affected by the loss of the two great vessels, describing it as a "national disaster" that would "create consternation in Australia." The sovereign was therefore "very thankful" that, as he understood it, Churchill was "not undertaking your journey just now."[161]

Returning to the situation in the Pacific, Churchill told the war cabinet that even though the United States was now transferring its Atlantic Fleet to the Pacific, the two powers could not presently compete with the Japanese Navy. Sir Earle Page, the Australian government's special envoy, relayed his country's anxiety and urged the use of aircraft and submarines to ensure Japan was deprived of access to the Indian Ocean. Page also proposed appealing to Stalin to enter the war against Japan, stressing that Vladivostok offered an invaluable base for striking Japan from the air and that the Soviets possessed numerous submarines in Pacific waters that could target the Japanese Navy. Churchill remained ambivalent. The Soviets were already providing an "enormous service" by "hammering" the German Army and needed divisions from Siberia for the struggle against Hitler. If Roosevelt wished to urge a Soviet declaration of war again Japan, that was another matter, but Churchill's concern was with the situation in Europe. He did assure Page, however, that Eden had been instructed not to offer Stalin ten squadrons to defend his southern front, as originally planned, due to the "changed situation" caused by American entrance into the war and the consequent impact on supplies.[162]

While the cabinet was in session, the Lend-Lease coordinator Averell Harriman was cabling Hopkins to update him on how British officials in London were reacting to the "changed supply picture." Clearly aware of the need to placate American officials and perhaps conscious that this would be well received by American public opinion, cabinet ministers had told Harriman of their desire to "cooperate," and Beaverbrook was "ready to release any British production in America asked for." The Royal Navy was also amenable, but the other services faced "immediate problems" and were "not ready to give up their urgently needed supplies and equipment without a fight."[163] The RAF's resistance to American attempts to secure its allocation of aircraft was evidence that this was producing tension between the two countries. Unlike in the United States, Harriman explained, in Britain these types of decisions were made on the political level rather than by the services. Nevertheless, it still remained difficult for Churchill and the cabinet if the chiefs of staff advised against releasing these supplies and then they did it anyway. As a result, Harriman urged Hopkins to update him daily on the status of Lend-Lease shipments, as there was currently "confusion caused by different reports to different ministries" and he wanted to ensure that there were no nasty surprises for British ministers.[164]

Back in Washington, Halifax convened a meeting of the British Supply Council to update them on his conversation with the president the previous day and the likely impact of the war with Japan on Britain's allocations. The ambassador relayed Roosevelt's admission that "it might unfortunately be necessary to cut into war supplies intended for the UK" but had expressed hope that this would be limited and, in any case, that increased American production would lead to the full resumption of the Lend-Lease program "by the end of January." This was even later than the previous estimate, which had said that the schedule would be back on track by the first weeks of 1942. But even the revised date was regarded by Halifax as "rather optimistic."

As a result, the head of the British Supply Council, Edward Plunkett Taylor, stressed that it was essential for Britain to immediately register its most pressing requirements with the Roosevelt administration. It was clear that the president would soon move to "a total war-effort," leading to major requests to Congress for new military appropriations. All of Britain's most important matériel, chemicals, and components for producing its own munitions "would only be obtained in the US through Lend-Lease, and there was a danger of being left at the post if British requirements were not quickly tabled."[165] The list of supplies that Britain desperately needed from the United States had continued to grow since yesterday. Among the commodities for which "immediate delivery from U.S.A. is essential," one of the most critical was copper, with British officials warning that provisions were "very tight and we cannot afford to let our supplies fall." Any delay in securing aircraft veneers and plywood would also "injure vitally our aircraft production programme."

On top of this, stocks were low for Port Orford cedar veneers (the "only wood which can be used for submarine battery separators"), for pitch pine (required for shipbuilding), and for a whole range of chemicals that were needed for aircraft manufacture, explosives, and cable making. Of added concern were the dwindling supplies of pulp and papermaking material, which would lead to the curtailment of shell production and deprive Britain of such basic items as maps, blueprints for building munitions, and even the packaging for products, especially food. With the stakes so high, members of the Supply Council and the Purchasing Commission made repeated calls to the War Department, aware that it now possessed the authority to decide whether to release Britain's Lend-Lease requirements.[166]

One member of the Supply Council decided to take his case right to the top. Jean Monnet, who would later become famous as a founding father of the European Union, had previously served as the French negotiator for war material from the United States and, after France's collapse in 1940, had stayed on in Washington to help Britain take over these contracts and secure fresh supplies. By 1941, the supremely well-connected Monnet was critical to the British supply operation. Yet, as lieutenant general Sir Ian Jacob, military assistant secretary to the British war cabinet, noted around this time, Monnet was "regarded with suspicion by our Military Mission." The military leaders were "doubtful of the loyalty of a man who has no particular allegiance to anybody," a "real cosmopolitan" who had kept his distance from de Gaulle's Free French "and seems to have contacts with everyone of any importance." The civilians on the Supply Council, however, "regard him with respect, as he is a man of great brainpower, very clever in negotiation, persistent and determined, and with clear and far-sighted views." Jacob himself found Monnet "very acute, and with a grasp of the American situation and of how we should act to get the most out of it, which was unequalled by anyone else."[167]

Even before the United States entered the war, Monnet had urged American officials to recognize that the Victory Program was insufficient and required more effective institutions to coordinate the overall strategy of the anti-Hitler coalition.[168] Now, three days after the Pearl Harbor attack, Monnet met with the Supreme Court justice Felix Frankfurter, a key adviser to Roosevelt and staunch supporter of the British cause. Through Frankfurter, Monnet put a proposal to the president to expand munitions production by 50 percent more than the US military chiefs were currently proposing under the Victory Program. The Frenchman was concerned the US military's conception of America's war effort was "defensive," too "narrow," and did not provide, immediately in 1942, for the "overwhelming superiority which was the only way to overcome the enemy's material strength and morale."[169] Monnet advised Roosevelt to centralize America's strategic planning and combine its production pool with Britain's, including the principal raw materials, so as to ensure that munitions and commodities went to the forces, regardless of nationality, who could most effectively deploy them. Monnet recognized that America's immense manpower and resources would be decisive, but only if its munitions reached the armies that could do the greatest damage to the Axis, particularly its principal power, Germany, as quickly as possible.[170] Otherwise, Monnet and the Supply Council feared that supplies to Britain would continue to be cut drastically in favor of America's war with Japan.[171]

That afternoon, the Soviets were also putting forward their case for supplies to the Roosevelt administration. At the Treasury, Litvinov expressed alarm to Morgenthau at the suspension of Lend-Lease, telling him, "Unfortunately all shipments had been stopped and that they were, in fact, unloading the fighter planes and tanks from the ships that had already been loaded." The Soviet ambassador was aware that this was a consequence of the "unfortunate effectiveness" of the Japanese attack, but he also reminded Morgenthau that, "as the President pointed out in his speech, it was all one fight and each country had to do whatever it could to defeat the common enemy."[172]

Yet Roosevelt was acutely aware that, even after his radio address, this was not a view shared by all Americans. There remained considerable congressional opposition to greater American engagement in the war with Germany. The continued strength and influence of the noninterventionist lobby was illustrated by Senator Hiram Johnson, who prevented discussion that day in the Senate of a bill that would prepare an American Expeditionary Force for potential action in Europe. Johnson privately informed his son that he had at least ten Senators who supported his stance on the issue.[173] His erstwhile isolationist comrade, Arthur Vandenberg, also asked on the Senate floor for assurance that the congressional approval for war with the Japanese would not be used as cover for deploying US forces against any another country.[174]

Among the leading figures in America First, differences of opinion were emerging over the group's position now that the nation was at war. One member of its national committee, former US ambassador to Japan William R. Castle, had reluctantly come to the conclusion that America First could not "any longer oppose war against Germany and Italy, much as I hate to say this." Not only were those nations "allies of Japan," but

Castle was "inclined to believe, in any case, that the matter will be taken out of our hands by a German declaration of war on this country; that would, perhaps, be the best way out of it." Others, like Hiram Johnson, continued to oppose entry into the European war. The prevailing opinion among America First's leading figures in Congress was that the group should wait a "week or two" before deciding how to proceed. So much remained in flux. According to America First's lobbyist on Capitol Hill, Ruth Sarles, after Japan's sinking of the *Repulse* and *Prince of Wales* it was now dawning on lawmakers that there had been a change in the "whole military picture—the balance is completely shifted." Sarles heard rumors that "Britain may be forced to make peace with Germany and combine with us to lick Japan." In any case, America First's national chairman Robert Wood, its most famous advocate Charles Lindbergh, and the vast majority of local chapter chairmen all continued to believe that the committee's work should ultimately go on. Most important, as one congressional staffer put it to Sarles, America First must "urge, for instance, that no more materials can be lease-loaned to Britain since we now need them ourselves."[175]

This lingering anti-interventionist and anti-British sentiment continued to worry Roosevelt. With that in mind, he drafted a response to Churchill's message stating that, with the situation still unclear, any discussion of a visit should be delayed for at least a couple of weeks. For the moment, the president was content for his naval officials to liaise with their British counterparts over radio to shore up "your and our defensive position in the Pacific," and he felt that "our joint Atlantic position is good." The president offered to revisit the decision in a week when the early stages of American mobilization were complete and the Allied position in the "Pacific more clarified."[176] Perhaps concerned that the tone was too harsh, however, he decided to sit on the message.

Sensing the British and Soviet predicament, German propagandists continued to bombard the airwaves with gloating accounts of the impact that American fighting in the Pacific would have on Lend-Lease supplies and shipping capacity in the Atlantic. One German commentator reported with relish that the BBC had suggested that "war supplies to

England will naturally have to be reduced because America has to concentrate its whole power elsewhere, and it is for this reason that England is now preparing for an effort that must be greater than the one made after Dunkirk."[177]

The German public was getting the message. In Königsberg, the anti-Nazi doctor Fritz Lehmann wrote that day of the "general happiness" over Pearl Harbor. It was hoped, he continued, that "the distraction of the Americans in the Far East would hinder the supply of their western and Russian allies." Lehmann was not so sure. This might be true "initially," he argued, but now the United States was "fully involved in the conflict" and "nobody could doubt" that it would become militarily active not only in the Far East but "after a while" in "the west as well." This, Lehmann predicted, would lead to a "conflagration of the entire world."[178]

It was thus becoming increasingly clear to Roosevelt administration officials that they could no longer maintain the facade that the Lend-Lease program had continued uninterrupted. Consequently, the British Supply Council was informed that Roosevelt would announce at his next press conference that, "as a precautionary measure, immediate shipments of Lend-Lease materials to the British Empire were temporarily suspended pending a rapid examination of our most pressing requirements in the light of the Japanese attack." In order to demonstrate to the administration's isolationist opponents that Britain was making every effort to be helpful, the president would also publicize that Churchill "was fully aware of the advisability of such a step" and that his government "had already issued instructions to prepare a list of British War materials which could be made immediately available to us in the event we desired them."[179]

In the Far East, the Japanese kept up the military pressure throughout the day. Their relentless advance in Malaya continued. In the Philippines, General Masaharu Homma's Fourteenth Army began to land in northern Luzon and made quick progress capturing key airfields. At around 9 p.m. London time—which was already early the following day in the Pacific—the Japanese Navy began its approach to Wake Island. After their earlier swift victories, the Japanese were confident in taking the island in short order. Instead, the landing force was subjected to intense and accurate fire by American shore batteries and aircraft. Two Japanese destroyers were sunk, one with all hands. Not long before mid-night London time, the entire Wake invasion force turned back.[180] It was the first Japanese defeat, and one that the US press would soon exploit at length.

As THE DAY drew to a close, across the globe there was a general sense that the war was spreading and the world was being fundamentally trans-formed. Nikolay Nikitovich Popudrenko, a Communist Party worker and partisan activist in Nazi-occupied Ukraine, noted this with great ex-citement. "Events are heating up," he wrote in his diary. "Yesterday New Zealand, Australia declared war on Japan. Today it was reported on radio that America declared war on Japan." Even the Japanese puppet state of Manchukuo, he noted, had declared war on the United States. "I think," Popudrenko added, "that this is not the end."[181] Italian foreign minister Ciano, for his part, was struck by the sense of new possibilities. "News of the amazing Japanese victories continues to arrive," he wrote in his diary. "Against this the land fighting in Libya and in Russia is not going well." "Such," Ciano concluded, "are the incredible surprises of this war."[182]

In Bucharest, Mihail Sebastian was left "thunderstruck" by the "cata-strophic" news about the *Prince of Wales* and the *Repulse*. Frustrated that he could not "follow the situation because I don't know the map," Sebas-tian believed that it was "a moment equal to the French collapse" and that "the other fronts now move to the back of the stage." "Even the war in Russia," he wrote, "has become less important." Sebastian noted that the Russians had retaken Tikhvin and that "the Germans are talking of a winter lull as if it were an established fact." "It is the Japanese," Sebastian concluded, "who have sensationally captured the notice boards."[183]

Across Britain, headlines on chalked news placards had given many people "the first inkling of the tragic news that the *Prince of Wales* and the *Repulse* had been sunk."[184] In Wales, the Newport insurance clerk's initial reaction was to recall his earlier premonition: "My foreboding about losing a couple of battleships have been duly fulfilled. . . . I shall have to take up astrology and make money."[185] In Surrey, the food-packing manager recorded in his Mass Observation diary that "December 10th will remain for a long time as one of the blakest [*sic*] days of the democracies." Visiting the barber that day, he found "the staff here were most depressed too. A lot of defeatism was heard." Yet the food-packing manager countered that, seen in perspective, the loss of these ships "becomes an incident in this war." He consoled himself by reasoning that "every sunrise means that the Axis has consumed goods which cannot be replaced, and in that lies the crux of this world war." As a result, there could be only "one ultimate conclusion—the destruction and the grovelling of the aggressor nations."[186]

The Canadian prime minister, Mackenzie King, was far less sanguine. He was "perfectly stunned when the word came" of the sinkings, almost certain this would "sweep away the last hopes of the British being able to protect effectively any of their possessions in the Orient." Of even greater concern was "the effect on the French," with King convinced this would cause Vichy to fully throw in its lot with the Germans by handing over its fleet. Consequently, "the English-speaking world may be faced by a predominance of power at sea on the part of its enemies," which would also have a dire effect "upon Russian morale." While most people, particularly in North America, were distracted by the Pacific, King maintained that "Europe is blotted out but the greatest danger is still there." Fearing that the war would now "be greatly prolonged," King was bleak: "It verily is the time of Armageddon."[187]

In western Germany, the anti-Nazi diarist Friedrich Kellner, by contrast, maintained an Olympian detachment. "It is delicious," he wrote in his diary, "how the party members draw fresh courage from the early victories of the Japanese," especially Goebbels. "What advantage is there for Germany," Kellner asked, "if Japan attacks the Hawaiian Islands, the Philippines, and the Peninsula of Malacca? . . . It would be different," he continued, "if Japan had drawn the sword against Russia, then one could speak of a relief for Germany in the east." But, Kellner added, "so far Japan haven't done us that favor." He was of the opinion that the "spread of hostilities" would "under all circumstances" be negative for the Reich. Trade via neutrals would now be virtually impossible. "The future," he predicted, "will show even the stupid and unteachable National Socialists what it means to make the entire world one's enemy."[188]

The day still had fifteen minutes left in Germany when Franz Halder received an urgent telephone call from Fedor von Bock. Soviet forces had broken through the German Second Army on the central front. Two divisions, the Ninety-Fifth and the 134th, had been "overrun" and a "large gap had opened up." Bock was frantically "calling for help." Halder scrabbled around. Dropping airborne forces at Orel was considered. Support from the SS and a motorized division was not to be expected for two days.[189] A quarter of an hour later, Halder was on the phone to General Georg von Sodenstern, chief of staff of Army Group South, with "a plea for help." He managed to extract some forces to be sent to help the embattled Second Army, but, again, none of these would actually arrive for a few days.[190]

While this conversation was taking place, Ribbentrop was completing his preparations in Berlin. A dispatch was sent to the embassies in South America. Ribbentrop had given up on Central America and the Caribbean, which were completely dominated by Washington. The governments in Buenos Aires, Lima, Rio de Janeiro, and Santiago de Chile, by contrast, were to be told that Germany's conflict with the United States did not mean that their relationships with Berlin should change.[191]

Ribbentrop also sent a dispatch to Thomsen, instructing him to hand a declaration of war to Cordell Hull or his representative at 15:30 German time the following day, that is, when Hitler's speech to the Reichstag was already underway. Before then, no contact with the State Department should be initiated, and no communications from the American side should be accepted, probably in order to avoid muddying the waters or giving the game away. Thomsen should then ask for his passports and ensure the safe return of the embassy staff to Europe, leaving the handling of German interests to the Swiss envoy Charles Bruggmann. The remaining encoding apparatus, codebooks, and all related material were to be destroyed.[192] The die was cast.

Meanwhile in Berlin, despite the foreign minister's instructions to wait until the following morning, the Gestapo late that evening rounded up all the American journalists and took them to their headquarters at Alexanderplatz. The Americans were informed by a Propaganda Ministry official that their arrest was to ensure their protection from the "outraged masses."[193] The German Foreign Office wired the Associated Press with an ominous warning: "American journalists no longer exist for you."[194] American embassy officials had already discovered that the German Foreign Office was now refusing to accept any memoranda from them and declining to explain why. With the situation clearly on a knife's edge, diplomat George Kennan's prevarication over whether to burn the US codes and cables was at an end and, as the fire roared in the embassy, ashes began drifting over the surrounding neighborhood.[195]

At around this time, newspaper bureaus in New York received reports that Berlin and Rome had both cut communications between the Associated Press and its base in Bern. The bureau chief in Berlin, Louis Lochner, had managed to inform the office in Switzerland that he and his colleagues were ordered out of the daily press conference and confined to their homes, ostensibly in retaliation for the arrest of German correspondents in the United States.[196] In a final telegram to Bern, Lochner's staffer Angus Thuermer made light of the situation: "Bye-bye. We are heading to jail now."[197]

Unpleasant though their situation was, the American journalists could be reasonably certain that they would survive. The worst they could expect was a spell in the cells, a period of internment, and then deportation to the United States. Not so the 1,007 Jews of all ages corralled at this very moment in the old city slaughterhouse of Düsseldorf, in preparation for their deportation east.[198] They would spend a miserable night in a place intended only for animals, not humans.

Just before midnight, the DNB made an important announcement. The Reichstag would meet at 3 p.m. the following day, Thursday, December 11. It would then receive a declaration from the Reich government, which would be broadcast at 8:15 that evening.[199] Wednesday, December 10 had been a very important day, but Thursday, December 11 was shaping up to be epochal.

7

THURSDAY, DECEMBER 11, 1941

T HE DAY STARTED EARLY FOR THE KRIEGSMARINE. IT HAD BEEN DE facto at war with the United States since December 9, and even though Hitler's formal declaration was not scheduled until 3 p.m., the navy's orders made the war official starting at midnight. Additional submarines were released to attack American shipping in the Atlantic and along the East and Gulf Coasts. This was done by stripping other theaters such as the Mediterranean, but the grand total envisaged was still only twelve boats, not nearly enough to do any lasting damage to US commerce.[1] At the same time, in accordance with Hitler's directive 39, the German Navy was instructed to "immediately halt all large-scale offensive operations" in the east and to "go over to the defensive" there.[2] The Kriegsmarine's main enemy had always lain in the west; now this was to be even more the case.

In London, at twenty-five minutes past midnight, Churchill heard from General Auchinleck about the continued British advance in North Africa as they pushed the enemy forces back past El-Adem. Britain's commander in chief of Middle East forces deduced that the Germans and Italians had "suffered heavily" and were "much disorganized." While Auchinleck expected the Germans to "reorganize further resistance on

313

a new line," he expressed confidence that the British troops were prepared for this contingency.[3] Things continued to go well for Britain in North Africa, but American supplies would be crucial to drive home the advantage.

At roughly the same time in Washington, where it was around 6:30 p.m., Roosevelt took up his pen again. He had initially written in his draft response to Churchill's request for an immediate meeting that the crucial questions of production and allocation "are being worked out with complete understanding and accord." Now, clearly conscious of the ongoing supply problems, he amended this to "can and will be." Where his first draft optimistically suggested that he expected "to resume regular schedule of shipments to you and Russia by January first," his revisions tempered the new draft with realism, replacing "expect" with "hope," in line with the caution that he had expressed to Halifax. A reference to the positive situation in the Atlantic was removed. The president continued to believe that "full discussion would be more useful a few weeks hence than immediately," but now deferred to Churchill, stating that he would "wholeheartedly and gladly accept your opinion on timing."

While it is not clear exactly what led to Roosevelt's change of heart, the reports from Germany, especially the official announcement of the Führer's forthcoming statement to the Reichstag, now suggested that Hitler was poised to make his move.[4] A visit from the British prime minister would be less likely to antagonize majority opinion if the United States was already at war with all the Axis powers than if it was suspected that Britain was scheming to have the United States formally intervene in Europe. Consequently, Roosevelt accepted Churchill's assessment that the "naval situation and other matters of strategy require discussion." In a final flourish, he stated unequivocally: "Delighted to have you here at the White House." And he signed off by assuring Churchill, "The news is bad but it will be better."[5] Grace Tully sent the message to the Navy Department for immediate dispatch.

The president spent the rest of the evening relaxing with Crown Princess Martha of Norway. After the German invasion in 1940, Roosevelt had invited Martha and her children to take refuge in the United

States, initially as live-in guests at the White House. Over the past year, she had spent more time with Roosevelt than any other figure outside of his immediate White House circle, leading his aides to refer to her as "the president's girlfriend" and Roosevelt's own son to suspect that "a true romantic relationship developed between the president and the princess."[6] On this particular night, with Eleanor still away on the West Coast, the president mixed cocktails and had dinner alone with Martha, before "parting just after midnight." As the crown princess told her chief aide, "There was no talk of policy!"[7]

Though it was long past midnight in central Europe, Axis diplomats were still hard at work preparing for the coming day's momentous announcement. At 3:15 a.m. local time, the German ambassador to Rome, Mackensen, received a copy of the dispatch to be sent to Thomsen in Washington. This he was to pass to the Italians as part of a coordinated sequence of moves that would lead to the final Axis declaration of war on the United States.

At exactly the same moment in Singapore—8:45 a.m. local time—the British war council convened. It consisted of Duff Cooper (the resident cabinet minister), the governor of Singapore, General Arthur Percival (the general officer commanding), air vice marshal Conway Pulford (the air officer commanding), and Admiral Geoffrey Layton (the supreme naval commander in the region). These men now tried to address the worsening situation in northern Malaya, where Japanese forces were pushing back British forces with alarming speed.[8] They would meet every morning until Cooper left the city.[9] Though the group was deeply depressed by the loss of the two ships, they had as yet no inkling of the much greater catastrophe that would soon befall the colony.

Further north, Thailand was concluding its treaty of alliance with Japan. The Thai premier Luang Phibunsongkhram had admired Fascism and revered Mussolini in particular since his student days in France twenty years previously. After a brief show of Thai resistance, Phibunsongkhram folded, agreeing to terms with the Japanese ambassador Teiji Tsubogami. Thailand now vowed to join the "the establishment of a New Order in East Asia as the only road to the prosperity of Eastern Asia."

Both parties would help the other by "every kind of political, military and economic means" if involved in "military dissension" with another power. Neither would make a separate peace without the approval of the other.[10] Ten days later, the agreement was formally signed and announced in Bangkok, and Thailand would declare war on the British Empire and the United States. The British Empire had acquired another enemy. Meanwhile, Japanese troops raced toward the border with the British colony of Burma. The eastern gate to India was now wide open.

That morning, the British newspapers were unanimous in urging Americans to understand that the Axis powers were inseparable and only a unified war effort against all of them could reverse the devastating losses of the past few days. The *Times* saluted President Roosevelt's "noble address" of December 9 for recognizing that the "cause of liberty in the modern world has become indivisible, and its grand strategy is planned over five continents and seven seas." The editorial advised the president to act on his rhetoric that this was a "single universal war," throw off America's "isolation," and "take up her share of responsibility—for the maintenance of human freedom."[11] The *Express* was blunter: "We ask the people of America to follow the lead of their President and declare the Axis chief [i.e., Hitler] their open enemy." The paper's editors clearly recognized that, however eloquent Roosevelt's rhetoric, under the American constitution only Congress could sanction a declaration of war and raise the appropriations necessary to fight it. They warned those representatives "to declare war on Hitler now and begin blockading him, before he gets to Dakar and begins to blockade America."[12]

Other papers put it more brusquely still. The *Sketch* was baffled by the American response: "Can anyone in the country understand why America, in [the] face of Japan's attack on her, does not declare total war against Germany and Italy?" The *Mirror* believed it was "because like ourselves in days of Munich she wished to be deceived" and, as a result, the United States was unwilling "to abandon her ancient dream of an impossible isolationism drenched with Lindbergian drivel." For too long, the country had "fed on far western chaff" and while it was "slowly, cautiously awaked by her President," it was now playing catch up.[13]

Nor did the British press spare its own government from condemnation. Reflecting on the destruction of the *Repulse* and *Prince of Wales*, the *Times* in particular could not understand why Britain's commanders had not "learned the lesson" that unified air-sea command was essential to protect the fleet from enemy bombers. Almost every newspaper led with the Japanese onslaught, with news of the Soviet-German struggle and Britain's own campaign in Libya pushed to the periphery.[14]

In naval circles, recriminations over the loss of the ships continued. That day, retired admiral Reginald "Blinker" Hall, the legendary head of British naval intelligence during the First World War, wrote privately that "if we won't learn the lessons we paid for so dearly at Crete and [in] Greece we shall go on losing ships." "We do pay dearly for our lessons," he continued, "and the fools who will not learn them." "I refer to the powers at the top," Hall went on, "though I shall never understand how Tom Phillips came to go out into air-controlled waters without air support."[15]

The Australian newspapers, too, were full of the naval disaster off Malaya. In the *Herald*, the paper's war correspondent Geoffrey Tebbutt wrote that the only good news was on the Russian front, calling the loss of the *Prince of Wales* and *Repulse* the "most breathtaking, single blow to our naval prestige that has been struck in the whole world." Tebbutt was incredulous that the Japanese had sunk these ships. "It is a calamity that cannot be explained away," he wrote. "It is hateful to concede any thing to the brown-skinned people," he continued, "but it has to be acknowledged that they have achieved something without parallel."[16] A report from Melbourne in another paper said that "the belief is growing in federal circles that Australia must be prepared for raids by Japanese bombing planes."[17]

Though mostly preoccupied with American travails, the US papers found space to cover the sinking of the two ships. Once again, as with Pearl Harbor, some observers made sense of the magnitude of the loss by pointing to alleged German involvement. "In Washington," the *New York Times* reported, "it was suggested unofficially that the giant German battleship *Tirpitz* [the sister ship of the vanquished *Bismarck*] might be in Far Eastern waters."[18]

Even with the announcement of Hitler's Reichstag address that day, there remained considerable uncertainty in the American press as to whether this would lead to a declaration of war. The *Washington Post*'s correspondent in London suggested that the "Führer may not declare war" but instead "will restate his policy" and might limit himself to a "declaration reaffirming German-Japanese solidarity under the Tripartite Pact." Reports from Berlin the previous day, including the cutting of US newswires, suggested "that Germany might step over the borderline between undeclared and declared war with the United States," but this was "still only a possibility."[19] The *New York Times* suggested that "opponents of a declaration of war—mainly of the 'conservative' group in the party hierarchy and some of the military—hold it far better to wait and 'finish one thing' at a time," a reference to the war in Russia and the now "defensive character of the operations" there. The *Times* also referenced a "Swedish informant" who "reports the German public's opposition to further extension of the war in a ratio of about 60 to 40." Of course, "Herr Hitler," as this informant made clear, "does not necessarily listen to public murmuring. He commands and the public follows."[20]

In Berlin, American journalists' free movement was coming to an end as the Gestapo continued their roundup throughout the early hours of the morning. The Foreign Office had intended to confine the journalists at home until the declaration of war, after which they would have been taken to the police station for registration prior to internment, but the RSHA had jumped the gun. "No-one seemed to know what to do with us," Louis Lochner later wrote, "either the guards or the dozens of officials who peered at us as they came on duty. We felt like monkeys."[21] On Goebbels's orders, the journalists were finally brought to a hotel in Grünau.[22]

As the day proceeded, the German authorities also tightened the noose on the American embassy in Berlin and Americans in occupied Europe generally. Altogether, they conducted reprisal arrests of more than three hundred US citizens in Paris and throughout the Reich.[23] These were in retaliation for the detention of German journalists and nationals in the United States. The OKW asked whether the US embassy should be allowed to send coded telegrams. After consultations with Weizsäcker at the Foreign Office, it was agreed that the American diplomats should only be permitted to send one or two, at most, during the next few hours. There should be no more telephone conversations.[24] "I am looking forward," Goebbels wrote in his diary, "to the winding up of the American embassy, because it is in fact nothing more than a center of espionage."[25]

Unlike the journalist hostages, German Jewry could have no expectation of lawful or ethical treatment. In Düsseldorf, just over a thousand Jews were herded in the rain out of the slaughterhouse where they had spent the night. They were assembled at 4 a.m. in what must have been the freezing cold for their deportation from Düsseldorf-Derendorf station.[26] On the way, one Jewish man tried to commit suicide by jumping under a tram, but he suffered only minor injuries and was forced to rejoin the rest of the deportees. An older woman took advantage of the darkness to escape into a nearby house. There, she undressed but was discovered at a public bath by a cleaning woman and returned to the station. The transport was not scheduled to leave for another five and a half hours. During that time, regular German police searched the deportees' luggage and made sure they actually boarded the train. The operation was conducted by Captain Paul Salitter of the Schutzpolizei. This was all observed by the railway workers.[27] So far as we know, none of Düsseldorf's non-Jewish population protested against the deportation of their fellow citizens, and some, like the cleaning lady at the public baths, actively collaborated with it.

That is not to say that there were none who spoke up, at least in other parts of Europe. That day, an anonymous Czech woman from the small southern Bohemian town of Trhove Sviny (Schweinitz) wrote to Emil Hácha, the puppet president of the Protectorate of Bohemia and Moravia, to express her outrage at the deportation of Jews to Poland. This she had witnessed by chance during her last visit to Prague. One of the "evacuees" was a three-and-a-half-year-old orphan girl whose father had been taken to a work camp two and half years earlier. She had been sent on the voyage unescorted and was completely dependent on help from others. "I will never forget the sad eyes of the little girl," the woman wrote, "when she asked one of those escorting the transport 'Are you the good man who will bring me to my father?'"

Appealing to the national and Christian sentiment of the president, this good Samaritan argued that in these "festive days" ahead of Christmas, everybody was "obliged to do some sort of good deed." She called upon the "noble father of the Czech people" to help by making a radio broadcast and appealing to "Mr. Protector Heydrich" whether it would be possible to send at least a small Christmas present to these children. "He is very strict," the woman went on, "but surely also has a good heart." After all, whatever was going on—an allusion to the Nazi war on the Jews—"the little ones are not to blame." Besides, the author added pointedly, "our Führer likes children so much."[28]

At around 9 a.m., the delayed deportation train arrived in the station at Düsseldorf. Captain Salitter and his fifteen-man escort oversaw the "loading," as he later described it, and carriages were shunted back and forth. Salitter was dissatisfied with the location of the escort, which was placed between the twenty passenger carriages and the seven luggage wagons, instead of the usual position in the middle of the train, which would have made patrolling it much easier. He was unable, however, to persuade the Reichsbahn to rearrange the transport, as this would have resulted in further delays. In the confusion, some carriages were crammed with more than sixty people, while others had scarcely more than half that number. Groups were separated, and mothers were divided from their children.[29]

While Jewish families were being separated in Germany, Axis diplomats were completing their preparations for the afternoon's announcement. Ambassador Mackensen made his way to Rome's main railway station of Termini, where Ciano was slated to arrive soon on return from his meeting with Darlan in Turin the day before. At 9:15 a.m., Mackensen handed the Marquess d'Ajeta the draft dispatch to Thomsen in Washington for passing on to Ciano. Both men confirmed that all was now "sorted out" for the "order of things today." When Ciano arrived, he was assured that the choreography of the afternoon's performances had been carefully prepared.[30] In fact, the Italian foreign minister found that the Duce showed "very little interest" in his discussions with Darlan, being instead totally focused on the impending war with the United States.[31]

In Tokyo, the Japanese leadership basked in the successes of the past few days. On December 11, the chief of staff of the navy, Admiral Nagano, briefed the German naval attaché in person on the sinking of the *Prince of Wales* and the *Repulse*. He ended his detailed description with a flourish: "The *Bismarck* has been avenged," but "there is still a lot to do. Give my wishes to the Grand Admiral [Raeder]."[32] At 6 p.m.—it was still only 9 a.m. in London—the influential "Juichi-kai" circle of senior statesmen held a party that was attended by nine of its eleven members: Count Oda, Viscount Uramatsu, Viscount Sasaki, Count Matsudaira, Viscount Kuroki, Baron Harada, Viscount Okabe, Viscount Yanagiasawa, and Viscount Sakai. "The Chief subject of conversation," one of those present noted, was unsurprisingly "the war with the USA and England."[33]

A quarter of an hour later, the last Jews had been "loaded" in Düsseldorf-Derendorf. Almost an hour behind schedule, the train finally left the station. Conditions on board were terrible. Initially, according to Salitter's report, the guards were not shielded from the inclement weather, because the faulty heating prevented steam from reaching them at the rear. It had rained during most of the operation, and they were unable to dry their clothes. The atmosphere among the deportees was one of extreme anxiety. At each stop, many of them tried to attract the attention of travelers on the platforms, to beg for water or ask them to post letters on their behalf. At first, Salitter found it difficult to stop this because his guards had to jump down and run to the front of the train to check the carriages, then run back to their guard carriage before the train left the station again. He therefore transferred two men to a compartment near the locomotive.[34]

There was no mention, of course, of all this in German newspapers. Rather, for the fourth day running, the German papers were full of Japanese victories. The report from the internal surveillance agency spoke of great popular enthusiasm for the Japanese victories, which had pushed the stalemate in Russia and the retreat in North Africa into the background.[35] Across Germany, people pored over maps supplied by the regime to follow the Japanese advance vicariously. In a closed meeting with his team in the Propaganda Ministry, however, Goebbels warned against making too much of the resulting gloom in Britain. He feared stoking unrealistic expectations among the German population, which would then be dashed, as after Dunkirk. The other danger, Goebbels continued, was that the German public was drawing "a comparison between the Japanese and the Italian [military] achievements," to the detriment of the latter. For this reason, he instructed that Italian voices should be given less prominence in reporting.[36] This was the paradox of the German media effort. On the one hand, it was keen to stress that Germany was not alone in the world. On the other, the Reich's closest ally was so pitiful that it could not be mentioned without embarrassment.

This had been a busy week for Italian diplomats as they scrambled to maintain alignment with the vastly more powerful Germans, but this had now been achieved. In order to avoid crossing their wires and alerting the Americans before time, Ciano instructed Ambassador Colonna in Washington to "refrain from any contact" with the US State Department and not to accept any official communication from the Americans until he received further instructions.[37] Five minutes later, the chef de cabinet at the Italian Foreign Office, Marquess d'Ajeta, informed Mackensen that the Italian ambassador in Washington had given identical instructions to Thomsen.

At 11 a.m. local time, Ribbentrop met with the Italian and Japanese ambassadors in Ribbentrop's study in the Foreign Office for a ceremonial signing of the Axis agreement. The mood was optimistic. Alfieri congratulated Oshima on the "magnificent successes" of his navy in sinking the *Prince of Wales* and the *Repulse* (the confirmation by London had now been received). The Italian also chatted with a "satisfied" and jovial Ribbentrop. The German foreign minister had just read Roosevelt's speech to Congress and pronounced it "very weak." "Roosevelt," he said, was like "a drunken sailor who enters a bar and bullies" until "someone knocks him to the ground with a single blow." After a few minutes of banter, the three men signed the German text of the agreement only, because the protocol office had not yet had time to prepare the Italian and Japanese translations.[38]

The common front against the Anglo-Saxons was now complete.[39] Germany, Italy, and Japan all agreed to wage war against the British Empire and the United States to a successful conclusion. They also promised not to enter into separate peace negotiations without the agreement of their allies. Finally, all three committed themselves "to collaborate closely also after the end of the war for the purpose of establishing a just new order" in the world. This was their answer to the Atlantic Charter.[40] The Axis powers, it seemed, were in lockstep at last.

It did not take long before the day's careful choreography threatened to unravel. Despite having agreed everything the day before, the Duce was already having second thoughts about the sequencing. At half past eleven, the Italian ambassador in Berlin, Alfieri, was instructed to tell Hitler that Mussolini had now decided "in the interest of dealing with the question in collaboration" to make a speech at the Piazza Venezia at 2:45 p.m., that is, fifteen minutes before Hitler was due to speak to the Reichstag.

At the very moment that the Italians were trying to rewrite the Axis plans, the British chiefs of staff met in London to improve alignment with their ally. "Strategic co-ordination in Washington" was the first item on the agenda. The chiefs wholeheartedly endorsed Halifax's recommendation that an inter-staff committee was required to ensure that Britain's supply needs were not disregarded in the American scramble to furnish their own forces. As a result, they drafted a minute to the prime minister urging him to impress this on the president and encourage the administration to "weigh the re-allocation of supplies in relation to the general strategy in the war."[41] By this time, Roosevelt's message had arrived at Downing Street. The chiefs were thus informed that the "PM's trip to USA had been put forward again and that he proposed to start tomorrow night," providing the opportunity to hammer home this vital message in person.

While united in their concern about the supply situation, the prime minister and the chiefs disagreed somewhat on where Britain should concentrate its forces. With the British position under severe strain in East Asia, and emboldened by Auchinleck's reports from North Africa, Churchill wanted to divert troops from the Mediterranean theater to block the rampant Japanese forces at the strategically vital Kra Isthmus, the narrowest part of the Malay Peninsula, which separates the Gulf of Siam from the Indian Ocean. Specifically, the prime minister wanted to send the Eighteenth Division, just over forty-eight hours after it had arrived in Cape Town. Alan Brooke was alarmed at this idea, regarding it as evidence of Churchill's lack of strategic forethought and propensity to "work by intuition and impulse." While Churchill was apparently "now convinced that we had enough troops for this North African business," the chief of the imperial general staff feared that the situation there remained uncertain.[42] Alan Brooke wanted to wait for the joint planning staff to review the British position, fearing that otherwise Britain would simply be "denuding the Middle East for the Far East." He was particularly concerned that troops were needed "for the support of Turkey," amid fears that Germany might invade as part of a drive to the Persian Gulf and Indian Ocean or toward Egypt; Britain currently lacked the capabilities to offer any credible contribution to Turkey's defense.[43] Above all, this strategic dilemma demonstrated just how stretched Britain's resources were and the precariousness of its position in the new global struggle.

The potential impact of American entry into the Pacific conflict on Britain's supplies was becoming even more alarming. The services continued to compile lists of their priorities in light of the American embargo and amid fears of future restrictions on exports. At the Admiralty, the list of absolutely essential items was extensive, and included auxiliary aircraft carriers, tugs, salvage vessels, Oerlikon guns, shells, machine guns, Bofors guns, torpedo components, and motorboat engines.[44] The Ministry for Aircraft Production collated an inventory of chemicals, commodities, and raw materials for which "early and continuous delivery" from the United States was required for Britain to "keep going" in 1942.[45] These included the Fibestos needed for aircraft, tanks, and bulletproof glass. There was a whole range of alcohols that were required for aircraft hydraulic fluids, and it was "essential that quantities destined for UK should not be consumed in USA." Also nearly depleted were stocks of a vast array of other materials, including nonferrous metals, such as the nickel and copper products required for aircraft and tank production. Due to Lend-Lease, Britain had only maintained a couple of months' supplies of these vital commodities, and it was "essential that exports from USA should not be held up," otherwise production would grind to a halt. At the Ministry of Supply, officials were adamant that Britain could not afford "to acquiesce in the degrading of these in order of American priorities." If shipments remained interrupted beyond January, the consequences for Britain's war effort could be disastrous.[46]

The Germans continued to worry that the Italians would upset the careful choreography of the Führer's appearance that afternoon. In Rome, Ciano sent along his final instructions to Colonna at 11:45 a.m. local time. He informed his ambassador in Washington that at 2:30 p.m., he would tell the US chargé that Italy considered itself at war with his country. Colonna was told to go to the State Department an hour later to communicate this decision to the Americans formally and to request his passports—that is, permission to leave. He was instructed to ensure not only his own safe return but that of all the embassy staff and as many Italian teachers and others as possible. He should try to "ensure reciprocity," in other words, to trade the good treatment of Americans in Italy for that of Italian nationals in the United States.[47] But the timing of the speeches was still at issue. Mackensen asked for more information, evidently concerned by "the clash with the Hitler speech." There was clearly a danger that the Duce's performance might preempt or distract from Hitler's. D'Ajeta reassured the German ambassador that Mussolini planned only to make a few short remarks from the balcony and that there would be no clash with the Reichstag speech.[48] The spotlight would be entirely on Hitler.

SHORTLY AFTER 11:30 a.m. in London, a visibly exhausted Churchill entered a restless House of Commons. Chips Channon observed that the prime minister looked "worn," while Harold Nicolson could see that his colleagues were "depressed."[49] Nicolson noted that "our nerves are not as good as they were in July 1940," during the Battle of Britain, and that the country had become "tired of defeat."[50] Faced with a "touchy and irritable" chamber, Churchill was frank in his assessment and reviewed Britain's global position with the "coldest form of factual narration."[51]

The prime minister began by surveying the situation in North Africa, admitting that progress was slower than initially hoped. He implored his audience to recognize that "victory is traditionally elusive," that "accidents happen, mistakes are made," and that "war is very difficult, especially to those who are taking part in it or conducting it." Nevertheless, Churchill was confident that Auchinleck would ultimately defeat his enemy by maintaining "an absolutely unrelenting spirit of the offensive," particularly as this was the first campaign in which Britain was "fighting the Germans on equal terms in modern weapons." In the Battle of the Atlantic, Churchill reported a "great recovery" in Britain's shipping capacity, "the foundations upon which we live and carry forward our cause." On the Russian front, Churchill confessed that just weeks before he had feared that Hitler's armies would capture Moscow, Leningrad, and the oil fields of Baku, leaving Britain in peril "on the long line from the Caspian Sea to the Mediterranean." Now, thanks to the "glorious steadfastness and energy" of the Russian armies and people, the Germans had suffered a "body blow, almost unequalled in the history of war." Yet Churchill reminded them that the Soviets had lost huge supplies of munitions in their campaign. Although Britain's own position had been transformed, "not all in a favourable direction," it must continue to fulfill its "pledges to the Russians for the heavy monthly quotas of tanks, aeroplanes and vital raw materials." All three of these commitments, of course, were to some extent predicated on continued American supplies.

Just a week earlier, Churchill declared, these "three great spheres" of Libya, the Atlantic, and Russia "would almost have covered the scene of war with which we were concerned." Now Japan's "treacherous attack" had led to an "enormous and very grave expansion" of the struggle to the Pacific. And it would "not stop here." It seemed to Churchill "quite certain" that Japan, in striking its "dastardly blow at the United States," counted on the active support of the German Nazis and of the Italian Fascists." It was thus "very likely that the United States will be faced with the open hostility of Germany, Italy and Japan." Of course, Churchill could not share that he knew of Ribbentrop's pledges to Oshima or the advance negotiations for a new pact between the three powers, as it would reveal that Britain had broken the Japanese diplomatic codes. Nevertheless, as Britain's morning newspapers had reported that Hitler would address the Reichstag that day, those present would now strongly suspect that a declaration of war was imminent. Proclaiming that their common foes were aiming at "the destruction of the English-speaking world and all it stands for," Churchill maintained that the United States and the British Empire "would all rather perish than be conquered. And on this basis, putting it at its worst, there are quite a lot of us to be killed."[52]

Continuing in this "very grim" tone, he told the House that Britain must prepare for "heavy punishment." This brutal honesty was embraced by members of Parliament, with Channon remarking that it had an "exhilarating effect on the House."[53] It also appealed to the general public when the speech was broadcast that evening. The Ministry of Information reported that people appreciated the "candid admission that the loss of these vessels was the severest naval blow ever suffered by Britain," as "the public prefers such frankness to attempts to gloss over unpleasant facts."[54] After conveying the extent of the disaster in East Asia, however, the prime minister concluded on a hopeful note that Britain's war effort would ultimately be bolstered by a flow of American "munitions and aid of every kind [that] will vastly exceed anything that had been expected on the peace-time basis that had ruled up to the present."[55]

Yet, at the same time, Averell Harriman was reporting to Washington that the supplies desperately needed for Britain's Middle Eastern campaign and to fortify the Soviets were still being "held up."[56] Harriman urged that they be released urgently to prevent disaster. Despite Churchill's bravado, his government remained fearful that American aid would continue to dwindle and that this would have dire short-term consequences for the war against Hitler.

In Australia, the war cabinet met to discuss the deteriorating situation.[57] The chiefs of staff assessed that an attack on Malaya "might well be a first step in the Japanese plan for a major attack on Australia. . . . The possibility of a direct move on Australia via the islands to the north and north-east must now be considered."[58] Such a move would begin with attacks and attempts to occupy Rabaul, Port Moresby, and New Caledonia, which, along with the occupation of Singapore and the Dutch East Indies, would put the Japanese in a position to invade Australia.[59] In a telegram to the Dominions Office, Australia contended that it was time to "make an earnest attempt to obtain Russia's intervention" in order to divert Japan's attention from the Pacific, asking that the British war cabinet and United States government promptly considered this.[60]

From lunchtime, the Nazi elite began to congregate around the Brandenburg Gate in advance of the Reichstag meeting in the Kroll Opera House later that afternoon. At 1 p.m., Himmler met with the *Reichskommissar* for Norway, Gauleiter Josef "Jupp" Terboven; the collaborationist prime minister of Norway, Vidkun Quisling; and the Dutch Nazi leader Anton Mussert at the Hotel Adlon on the Pariser Platz.[61] They, too, had been invited to hear the Führer. The presence of the Norwegian and the Dutchman was surely intended to show a wide level of support among "Nordic" Europeans for Hitler's decision to declare war on the United States.

News of the impending hostilities was already seeping out across the world. In the course of the morning, the German ambassador in Buenos Aires, Edmund von Thermann, met with the Argentine foreign minister, Enrique Ruiz Guiñazú. He briefed him verbally about the impending breach with Washington. The foreign minister was clearly alarmed and declined to express a view on either US policy in general or President Roosevelt in particular. Thermann predicted that Argentina would press for a continuation of the neutrality policy of the Pan-American Conference, but he was not certain how the next meeting, which was scheduled to take place in Rio de Janeiro, would react to the outbreak of war between the German Reich and the United States.[62]

While the Nazi leaders assembled for the great set piece at the Reichstag, the German ambassador to the neutral state of Sweden, Prince Viktor zu Wied, was sending a dispatch to his Foreign Office. He had just come from a meeting with the king, Gustav V. Wied handed him Hitler's personal letter, written December 7, which thanked the king for his supposed "understanding" for Germany's struggle in Russia on behalf of "the whole of Europe." The Führer lamented, however, that "large parts of society" in Sweden were not so well disposed. It was a shot across Stockholm's bow.[63] Choosing not to engage directly with the letter, the king instead refused to support further German troop transports across the country. The reason for this was partly Britain's recent declaration of war on Finland, but mainly "the state of war between Germany and the USA." Gustav V feared that London and Washington would now see any Swedish assistance as a hostile act. Even before it had been formally declared, Hitler's war with the United States was changing the global dynamic.[64]

By now, the area around the Brandenburg Gate and the Reichstag was abuzz, as delegates, dignitaries, and journalists converged for the Führer's speech. Foreign reporters noted that their invitations had the previous day's date hastily crossed out (the Reichstag had originally been summoned for December 10).[65] Even before 2 p.m., the approaches to the Reichstag from Wilhelmstrasse via Unter den Linden and the Brandenburg Gate were blocked. Thousands lined the barriers in anticipation. A steady stream of cars from the state, party, and military institutions, as well as the remaining foreign legations, arrived. The Swedish journalist Arvid Fredborg noted, though, that the shortage of petrol meant that there were fewer vehicles "than usual." An honor guard of the Leibstandarte SS Adolf Hitler, the Führer's bodyguard division, assembled outside.

Meanwhile, Ribbentrop had summoned the American chargé d'affaires, Leland Morris, to his office at Wilhelmstrasse 74. A Foreign Office car was sent to collect him. While Morris got ready to depart, Kennan was left alone with the Foreign Office escort. "A stiffer conversation," he later recalled, "has never transpired." On Morris's arrival, Ribbentrop kept the American standing, and at a quarter past two read him a prepared text accusing the United States of intervening "to an ever greater extent in favor of Germany's enemies" and finally of engaging in "open military attacks." Ribbentrop then provided several examples, most of them attacks on German submarines in the Atlantic, before concluding that "from this day on Germany considers herself as being in a state of war with the United States." When he was finished, Ribbentrop handed over his statement with a flourish, saying, "Your President wanted war, now he has it." Morris listened quietly, and then asked for permission to telegraph his government immediately; this was granted. Ribbentrop bowed stiffly to indicate that the audience was over, and the American took his leave. The meeting lasted exactly three minutes.[66]

The translator, Dr. Paul Schmidt, who, like many others in the German Foreign Office, liked Morris very much, accompanied him to the door and shook hands smilingly. Schmidt left the building in a state of depression. He realized that Germany had acquired another huge enemy. "The war will now drag on forever," he said to himself. Later, Schmidt admitted that even he had no idea at the time just how quickly and catastrophically the fortunes of war would turn against the Reich on account of this disastrous decision.[67]

Just over ten minutes later, in the Italian Foreign Ministry in Rome, Ciano received the American chargé George Wadsworth. Confronted with the Italian declaration of war on the United States, Wadsworth reportedly "turned pale." "It is very tragic," the American responded. He passed on a message from Ambassador Phillips, by then back in the United States, expressing his "gratitude and good wishes." "Phillips is an honest man," Ciano noted, "and he loves Italy. I know that for him this is a day of mourning."[68] That day, Ciano received the cable from the Italian embassy in Washington informing him of Phillips's visit two days earlier and his message that he was planning to return to Italy and wished to receive a brief audience with Mussolini. Phillips's approval to return had clearly come from the US president, with whom he had met on the morning of the eighth before the declaration of war on Japan. Phillips had told the Italian ambassador that Roosevelt's attitude was that "the United States are determined to fight even for thirty years [against] Japan." With regard to the rest of the Axis, however, Phillips "did not think Washington had made any move." Even if it did, however, he suggested that whatever was decided for Germany did not have to apply to Italy.[69] For Ciano, privately opposed to the expansion of the war, this suggestion that Roosevelt had not been preparing to act—at least against Italy—was doubtless a bitter pill to swallow.

In Berlin, Göring, Goebbels, and Brauchitsch arrived in front of the Reichstag ten minutes before Hitler was due to speak. The band played the "Präsentiermarsch," followed by the German national anthem.[70] At exactly the same moment, in faraway Auschwitz, another drama was unfolding. The prisoner Feliks Nakielski (number 16004) was seized trying to pass a line of sentries near tower 21. It was his second attempted escape (the first had been on November 23, 1941), this time from the punishment company to which he had been sent after the first attempt had failed. Nakielski was thrown into the notorious punishment "bunker," where he later died.[71] That same day, the former camp doctor of Gross-Rosen concentration camp, Friedrich Entress, arrived to take over the same role at Auschwitz. He was not a qualified doctor. In due course, Entress would carry out "selections" of sick prisoners for the gas chambers and conduct experiments on them for typhus.[72] All this was a harbinger of the fate awaiting the Jews of western and central Europe after Hitler's announcement.

In the Crimean capital of Simferopol, the "execution" suspended on December 9 was resumed with the help of the police reinforcements who had arrived from Germany. All members of the unit were told that they had to participate, even the medics. The Jews were told that they would be registered for "work," ordered to leave their baggage for subsequent delivery, and hastily driven in army trucks, buses, and smaller confiscated vehicles to a tank ditch in the snow-covered countryside. It was not visible from the city. According to their murderers, some of the younger and fitter men jumped into the ditch and sang the Communist "Internationale" before they were mowed down. The killing lasted three days. Sorting the stolen possessions of the victims took another fortnight.[73]

Just before 3 p.m., Hitler and Himmler arrived in front of the Reichstag. They inspected the guard of honor. The band played the "Horst-Wessel-Lied," the Nazi Party anthem. Then, at exactly 3 p.m., the Führer entered the Reichstag building, flanked by Göring and Wilhelm Frick, the head of the Nazi Party Reichstag delegation. The delegates rose quietly at first, and then erupted in loud heils. Some of the detained American journalists heard the fanfare announcing the Führer's speech on the radio in the police station where they were being held.[74]

Hitler took his seat. So did the deputies, with the *Reichsleiter*, those who reported directly to the Führer, in the front row. Many were in field gray, wearing their decorations, such as the Iron Cross and Knight's Cross. In the circles sat representatives of the three services: army, navy, and Luftwaffe. The diplomatic corps was in the central box, with the friendly nations of Italy and Japan in the front. So were prominent foreign sympathizers, such as the grand mufti of Jerusalem in full Arab dress, the Dutch Nazi leader Anton Mussert, and the Norwegian puppet, Vidkun Quisling, described by one witness as looking "like an errand boy who for the first time in his life had been invited to travel first class."[75] To the right and left of the rostrum sat the Reich and regional governments and the state secretaries. Ribbentrop, Raeder, Brauchitsch, Keitel, Lammers, and Dietrich sat beside the lectern. They were about to witness a performance. It was an opera house that they were sitting in, after all.[76]

In contrast to the hubbub outside, the atmosphere inside the chamber was somber. There had been much speculation about what was to come, but no one could be certain. The Reichstag president, Hermann Göring, opened the meeting. Behind him was a huge golden swastika in the claws of a giant eagle on a white background, the only decoration in the entire chamber. He gave a remarkably downbeat introduction, prefaced by a call for a moment's silence for the dead. Outside, the crowd listened to the proceedings via loudspeaker.[77] Then Göring called upon Hitler to speak.

Hitler's tone was measured and grim, even funereal.[78] He began by stressing the costs of the Russian campaign, which, he told the Reichstag, had so far resulted in 162,314 dead, 571,767 wounded, and 33,334 missing from the Wehrmacht. The huge figure caused a massive stir in the audience.[79] Hitler argued that the conflict was being fought not merely for Germany, but on behalf of the entire European continent, which he defined not in geographic but racial and cultural terms. Hitler then moved to attack his main target, Roosevelt. The Führer cast the war as a generational struggle that had been forced upon him by the perfidy of Roosevelt and the manipulation of the Jews. On the basis of the reports of the Polish ambassador to Washington, Count Jerzy Potocki, which German intelligence had obtained, Hitler accused the American president of encouraging Warsaw to resist justified German demands and thus precipitating the war. The Führer explained this perfidy with reference to the workings of US capitalism, which, he claimed, the Nye Committee had blamed for the American entry into the First World War. All this, Hitler asserted, was happening at the behest of the "eternal Jew," the "power" behind Roosevelt, which sought to reduce Germany to the same chaos and subjection as the Soviet Union. They were prominent, so he claimed, in the "brain trust" informing Roosevelt's policies.

Meanwhile, Mussolini, contrary to earlier promises, was already issuing his own public declaration of war. It would appear that he did indeed beat Hitler to the punch by a few minutes, just as the Germans had feared. The Duce gave, as Ciano noted, a "brief and cutting" speech from the balcony of the Palazzo Venezia.[80] Some sources estimate the crowd at about one hundred thousand people. At fifteen minutes, the Duce's remarks were indeed uncharacteristically short. Mussolini emphasized the international character of the war. Given that the recent Japanese victories had created a pro-Tokyo fervor in Rome, Mussolini was repeatedly interrupted by applause from some listeners. Even so, most of the crowd was, as the foreign minister conceded, "not very enthusiastic." It was cold, and people were hungry.[81]

Even though Mussolini had jumped the gun, the rest of the joint performance proceeded according to schedule. The same time Hitler began to speak, the German chargé d'affaires, Hans Thomsen, arrived at the State Department to deliver a message. It was 8 a.m. local time. As Thomsen and the first secretary of the embassy, Heribert von Strempel, entered the building, three newspaper photographers suddenly appeared. Thomsen muttered to his colleague, "This is not very dignified."[82] America's diplomats were not prepared to accommodate them. Secretary Hull refused to receive them, and no one else, apparently, did either. The Germans were left cooling their heels in an outer office for ninety minutes.

Back in Berlin, Hitler was still in full flow before the Reichstag. He elaborated the contrast between himself and the American president, and that between the United States of the New Deal and the Third Reich. Both men had taken power in 1933, and yet they had come from very different backgrounds and had led their countries in very different directions. Roosevelt came from a "very rich" family, while Hitler's background was modest. Both countries had been on the verge of economic collapse, but whereas the Third Reich was now prosperous, Roosevelt, "the candidate of a thoroughly capitalist party," had failed to reduce unemployment, run up a massive debt, and devalued the dollar. This explained the president's "hatred against the social Germany."

In order to distract from his failure, Hitler continued, Roosevelt was bent on "diverting public opinion from his domestic policy to his foreign policy." This is why he had begun "from the year 1937" to attack Hitler in a series of speeches, "among them a particularly base one on 5 October 1937 in Chicago," in which he had threatened to place the Reich in "quarantine." The Führer traced the president's escalating rhetoric and measures—especially Lend-lease and the "shoot on sight order"— over the following years, bewailing Roosevelt's refusal to acknowledge a German "Monroe Doctrine for the central European space." He described Roosevelt's envoy, William "Wild Bill" Donovan (one of the few Americans singled out by name), as "a completely inferior person" and accused him of trying to stir up opposition to the Reich in the Balkans in early 1941.

Reprising themes that had formed part of his stock rhetoric over the past couple of years, the Führer framed the struggle as a "battle for the defense and therefore the preservation of the freedom" of Japan and the German Reich against the president's "ever greater expansion of a policy intended to achieve an unlimited world domination," which the United States was pursuing "in collaboration" with Britain. It was, Hitler claimed, the revolt of the "have-nots" against "the American president and his plutocratic clique."[83] The Reich was not deceived by the promises of the Atlantic Charter, which Hitler alluded to near the end of his speech. "If Mr. Churchill or Mr. Roosevelt declare," he thundered, "that they later want to erect a new social order then that is roughly as if a bald barber would recommend a fail-safe hair-restoring potion." The Führer suggested that instead of criticizing the Axis, the two men should rather sort out the social problems and hunger in their own lands.

As Goebbels noted, the purpose of these arguments and the new Axis treaty was to present an alternative to "similar agreements"—that is, the Atlantic Charter—on the Allied side. Hitler was signaling that Germany, Italy, and Japan would offer the world a different form of coexistence and international justice. The resources of the world would be redistributed more equitably, or at least away from the "old" Western democracies toward the "younger" rising powers in Europe and the Far East. Even after the end of the war, Goebbels claimed, the new alliance would cooperate in "the reordering of the continents."[84]

Finally, Hitler framed the war as a racial struggle between two "fragments" of "Germanic ethnicity." "England did not develop the continent," he claimed, "but rather fragments of Germanic ethnicity from our continent moved as Anglo-Saxons and Normans to that island and enabled a development there which is surely unique." "In the same way," Hitler continued, "America did not discover Europe, but [it was] the other way around," and whatever value the United States possessed it had drawn from the old continent—even though, in his view, it had since been corrupted by Jewish and Black influence. Hitler reminded his listeners of "the emigration of many millions of Germans . . . from which the American continent had benefitted immensely."[85] Indeed, the Führer stressed, Germany had "helped to defend the United States with the blood of many of its sons." In that sense, the new conflict was also a

Germanic civil war. Summarizing toward the end of his speech, Hitler spoke of the clash between the Reich and an alliance of the "Anglo-Saxon-Jewish-capitalist world with Bolshevism," which was trying to "exterminate" Germany.[86]

The same themes that had driven Hitler since the 1920s had now led him to their logical conclusion: a war of extermination against the Anglo-Saxons, the Jews, and their Bolshevik puppets. With his remarks completed, it was now official. The Third Reich was openly at war with the United States.

Frequent ovations and approving laughter interrupted Hitler's ninety-minute speech.[87] Mentions of the Japanese and their courage received particular applause; a contemporary photograph shows Oshima, the ambassador, taking a bow during the speech. The announcement of a state of war was applauded by the audience for several minutes. All the same, there was a palpable sense of unease. Members of the audience shifted in their seats and looked at each other with questioning eyes. One observer recalls that some clapped "only with hesitation," especially among the long row of field marshals and admirals, where journalist Fredborg "saw not a single hand move." It is possible, as the Swede speculated, that they were discomfited by the tone of Hitler's rhetoric against Roosevelt, but it is more likely that they were aghast at the thought of adding the United States to their already long list of enemies. Be that as it may, at the end of the performance, Göring thanked Hitler for his speech.[88] There was a moment of silence. Then the German national anthem was struck up. Göring led those present in another round of "Sieg heil!" And then Hitler left the building.[89]

Declaring war on the United States was the culmination of Hitler's career, both ideologically and strategically. Neither ignorance nor insouciance led him into conflict with the most powerful state on earth, but rather the conviction that war was inevitable. The speech was thus the climax of his long rhetorical duel with Roosevelt, which had begun in October 1937. The cold war had turned hot.

But if December 11, 1941, saw the climax of Hitler's worldview, it also signaled a deeper failure. In the 1920s and 1930s, Hitler had initially sought accommodation with the United States and Britain, albeit on his own terms. He deeply respected Anglo-Saxon power and racial qualities, and he had been determined to avoid a repetition of the Reich's fatal isolation during the First World War. Now he found himself in a very similar place. The only way that Hitler could explain this failure, to himself and to the world, was through the malignity of the Jews. The complete destruction of the western and central European Jews still held hostage by the Nazis was thus the logical consequence of the outbreak of open conflict with the United States.

News of the formal declaration of war was greeted with relief by the Japanese leadership. Hitler's speech was broadcast in Japanese translation, after which Tokyo radio announced that "Japan's military might cannot [now] be stopped by [Anglo-American] economic pressure."[90] There was no longer any danger that Hitler would leave the empire in the lurch and conclude a white man's peace. Instead, there would be a worldwide common front against the Anglo-Saxons. That day, Admiral Ugaki reflected on the new conflict. "Now it has really turned out to be the Second World War," he mused. "Everything connected with the future operations and leadership of the new world order rests upon the shoulders of our empire." "The whole world," Ugaki continued, "will revolve around our empire, which forms an axis. We must stress this idea."[91]

The Kriegsmarine also welcomed the declaration of war against the United States. As far as the German Navy was concerned, it had already been fighting the Americans for some time, but with one hand tied behind its back. The move to open war, the diary of the naval high command recorded that day, simply "confirmed in international law a situation which already pertained for months in a more or less one-sided form to the disadvantage of the Axis powers."[92] The Kriegsmarine also expressed satisfaction that "all the premises of the war plan" published by the *Chicago Tribune* had been "overturned by recent developments." In other words, in the mind of the German Navy, as in that of the Nazi elite, the war against the United States was a preemptive one, launched to forestall an American attack in the near future.[93]

Beyond this, the Kriegsmarine—and the German leadership more generally—expected that the outbreak of open war between Germany and the United States would bring the Axis some relief in Europe. First, it would reduce the flow of Lend-Lease supplies to the British and Russians even further than Pearl Harbor had. The navy noted with satisfaction a report from the German ambassador in Turkey that "one knew very well in Ankara that the end of the supply of war material to Russia would decisively affect their situation both with respect to morale and in real terms."[94] Second, they believed—not without justice—that the heavy Anglo-Saxon losses in the Pacific were causing public opinion to demand the dispatch of much larger naval units to the Far East in order to "knock out" the Japanese.[95]

Shortly after Hitler finished his address, the head of the European Division of the US State Department in Washington, Ray Atherton, finally received Thomsen and his message, which was identical to the one given to the chargé d'affaires in Berlin. Ribbentrop's claim that US actions had "created a state of war in practice" echoed the main narrative framing for Hitler's speech. From the Nazi perspective, this was not so much a declaration of war as a recognition of a conflict that was already long underway. What is striking is that, in contrast with Hull's genuine anger at the Japanese declaration, the German one was received in a matter-of-fact and almost offhand way. Thomsen affected a nonchalant air on leaving the department. Turning to the reporters who had by now gathered outside the building, he opened the door of his black Buick and genially asked, "Anybody want to buy a nice car?"[96]

For at least one of the president's closest advisers, Secretary Morgenthau, Hitler's move came as a surprise. At the Treasury that morning, the undersecretary, Daniel Bell, offhandedly asked what impact "these two additional declarations of war" would have on the bond market. "What declarations? Have they declared war on us?" Morgenthau demanded to know. When Bell confirmed this, Morgenthau repeated again, "On us?" Apparently, the news "came over the ticker" at around "ten minutes after nine," twenty minutes before Thomsen was finally received at the State Department.[97] Another aide said that even before Thomsen was admitted, the chargé had announced "that he was waiting at the State Department to hand the notice to Hull as soon as he got in." Suspecting a run on German and Italian banks, Morgenthau was advised by his staff that they be taken over and liquidated. When he hesitated, asking for confirmation that the news was accurate, one staffer responded, "I wouldn't let it turn on that, Mr. Secretary. We were prepared to do it . . . before the declaration of war."

Assured that the news was genuine, Morgenthau moved to close a whole range of German and Italian firms. Edward Foley, the department's general counsel, suggested the administration should go further and imprison Axis nationals en masse, stating that it was "no time to be thinking about civil liberties when the country is in danger." Morgenthau dismissed the idea of "suddenly mopping up a hundred and fifty thousand Japanese and putting them behind barbed wire, irrespective of their status, and considering doing the same with Germans." The secretary declared that "anybody that wants to hurt this country or injure us, put him where he can't do it, but irrespective—indiscriminately, no."[98]

Meanwhile, the Americans hoped that they could succeed where Britain had failed by bringing the Irish Free State into the war on the Allied side, or at least bullying it into granting them the use of bases in twenty-six counties. Shortly after Hitler had finished speaking—it was 9:47 a.m. in Washington—Wild Bill Donovan rang Morgenthau about the bases. "It seems to me," he argued, "that instead of trying to do any conciliating there or any appeal, that we ought to consider the further reduction of our assistance to them." Donovan continued, "So if you have over there any place, data on specific commodities"—this was probably oil supplied to the Irish Free State by Allied convoys, as the country was largely dependent on this for its energy needs and for which, in return, Dublin provided foodstuffs to Britain—"and how they might be reduced, I'd appreciate having it." In other words, Donovan (who was Irish American) and perhaps the president himself were planning to use the threat of reducing the flow of supplies to Dublin to get their way.[99]

It was probably around this time, after hearing Hitler's speech in the Reichstag, that Ribbentrop received Alfieri and Oshima for the second time that day. They met in a more formal setting to now sign the Japanese and Italian versions of the Axis treaty. Germany was represented by Ribbentrop himself, undersecretary of state and international legal expert Friedrich Gaus, Baron Dörnberg (the head of ceremonial), Paul Schmidt, and various assistants and secretaries. Oshima and Alfieri were each accompanied by a secretary. Afterward, Ribbentrop spent a long time chatting with the two ambassadors, once again expressing his "satisfaction" at the turn of events. Perhaps as a consequence, Alfieri took a more positive view of the new war than Ciano. He agreed with the German analysis that the formal breach with the United States had brought the Axis valuable help "in the fight against the Anglo-Saxon democracies," which had now moved in both Europe and the Far East from the "position of the besieger to that of the besieged."[100]

At the White House, where it was now 10:10 a.m., Steve Early was informing the press that "the long expected is now a reality." Hull had received the German declaration of war and notified the president. The State Department had also heard from Rome that "Italy has goose-stepped apparently in compliance with orders." The president would dispatch a message to Congress around noon, with the Senate leader and Speaker of the House having already "advised that resolutions will be promptly introduced and passed."

In his office, Roosevelt worked on his response. Initially, he began his message by condemning the "international brigands led by Hitler" of "enslavement, barbaric lawlessness, general destruction and fiendish cruelty, without parallel." He ultimately decided, however, not to mention Hitler by name at all. Where the German dictator had framed his whole speech around a personal duel with Roosevelt, the president clearly decided that the most effective riposte was to ignore Hitler altogether.[101]

Between revising drafts of his message, Roosevelt met with one of his close confidants, the former South Carolina senator and current Supreme Court justice James F. Byrnes, and his attorney general Francis Biddle to begin crafting the laws and executive orders that would mobilize the whole government and economy for total war. Byrnes, in particular, had been instrumental in the late 1930s in helping Roosevelt establish the modern presidential bureaucracy, centered on the West Wing and encompassing an array of departments and agencies. He was now tasked with establishing executive control over the federal bureaucracy and shaping this administrative institution to overcome all "serious interferences with our war effort."[102] With Hitler's intervention and the American entrance into the war as a full belligerent, the stage was set for the emergence of the "imperial presidency."[103]

With his anti-interventionist opponents silenced by the week's events, Roosevelt felt vindicated. That morning he met with Captain Joe Patterson, whose *New York Daily News* had relentlessly attacked his foreign policy. Roosevelt lambasted Patterson for doing "untold harm to this country" and having "tried to lull the nation into an inertia from which it might never have awakened." In the face of the president's attack on his patriotism, Patterson "broke down and cried like a baby." The president dismissed the newspaper baron from his office with an "assignment" to "go back home and read your editorials for the past six months—read every one and then think over what you have done!"[104]

The two Frances reacted to the news of the American entry into the war against Germany in different ways. Unsurprisingly, Vichy—which had always cultivated good relations with Washington—became more reserved toward Hitler. It was now clear to many at Vichy that the Axis could not win. At 6 p.m., the US ambassador Admiral Leahy informed Pétain and Darlan that "America's formal involvement in war with Axis Powers may change the entire picture from the point of view of the United States." The Vichy leaders expressed regret that the United States had become involved in the "World War" and wanted to maintain "friendly relations" with the Americans. Marshal Pétain particularly hoped that the United States would continue its "economic relief in Africa" and pledged to keep France's warships disarmed in "French colonial ports in the Western Hemisphere," unless the British engaged in "hostile action" first. Nevertheless, Leahy was aware that Vichy would make no "effective effort" to challenge Hitler if he demanded that it sever relations with the United States. Pétain had already pitifully lamented that "if Germany should make such a demand, they can starve our civilian population and we are helpless."[105] Even so, the marshal was happy to give a written guarantee of his determination to stay out of the fighting.[106] All hopes in Berlin and Rome that he might come in on the Axis side were dashed.

De Gaulle, of course, was delighted at the news of Hitler's declaration of war against the United States. "Well then," he remarked, "this war is over." "Of course," the general continued, "there will be military operations, battles, conflicts, but the war is finished since the outcome is known from now on." "In this industrial war," he prophesied, "nothing can resist the power of American industry."[107]

Throughout the day, the Jewish transport from Düsseldorf traveled eastward via Wuppertal, Hagen, Schwerte, and Hamm. At around 6 p.m., it reached Hannover-Linden for a stopover lasting nearly an hour. The escort commander, Captain Salitter, ordered that the deportees be given water and demanded to have the carriages rearranged. Despite having been promised this at Düsseldorf, the shunting turned out to be "technically impossible." Salitter was assured that one of the next stations on his route, Stendal, would be briefed in good time to carry out the adjustments to the carriage order he required.[108] This was all due to the preference being given to troop transports on the main route, so that the deportation trains had to stop at smaller stations for fuel and water. These German Jews did not know it, but as of that afternoon, they had lost any value to Hitler as hostages for the good behavior of the American president.

At 12:30 p.m. Washington time, Roosevelt responded to the dictators with a short message to Congress and simultaneous press release. Strikingly, he did not bother to berate Hitler in person, instead having the text read out by Irving Swanson, the reading clerk. Declaring that the "long known and long expected has thus taken place," the statement urged Americans to rise to this unprecedented "challenge to life, liberty and civilization."[109] Even now, the president requested a recognition of the state of war with Germany and Italy, rather than a declaration like the one issued against Japan, perhaps fearing an open debate in Congress over whether Europe or Asia should be the focus of America's war effort.[110]

After five days of apprehension and uncertainty, Hitler had followed Japan in solving Roosevelt's "sorest problems," in the words of Robert Sherwood.[111] It was only with the German declaration of war that the anti-interventionist resistance was completely broken. Meeting in Chicago at noon local time, just half an hour after Roosevelt responded to Hitler's gambit, the America First Committee dissolved itself, issuing a final salvo that "their principles were right" and, if followed, "war could have been avoided," but the German declaration had now settled that debate.[112] In the Senate, one of the anti-interventionists' leading supporters, Hiram Johnson, expressed his shock at Hitler's conduct and lamented to his son that the votes he had gathered against the American Expeditionary Force the previous day had now disappeared.[113]

As the America First declaration demonstrated, the anti-interventionists did not feel discredited. In fact, some felt vindicated. Herbert Hoover wrote to a fellow noninterventionist that afternoon: "The day will come when this war will be put in the scale of judgement, and when this time comes you and I will be found to have been right." Norman Thomas told a colleague, "I am surer than ever that we have been right; the mammoth calamity could have been averted." Even after Pearl Harbor, Thomas "was for localizing the conflict as far as possible," but Germany and Italy had settled the matter.[114] Writing in his diary, Senator Arthur Vandenberg ruefully remarked, "The interventionist says today—as the president virtually did in his address to the nation—'See! This proves we were right and this war was *sure* to involve us.' The non-interventionist says (and I say)—'See! We have insisted that this course would lead to war and it has done exactly that!'"[115]

Now that the war was here, however, even the most resolute noninterventionists in Congress could no longer stand in the way. The Senate voted unanimously to recognize the state of war with Germany and Italy, while in the House it was endorsed by all except the pacifist Republican representative from Montana, Jeanette Rankin. Even she, on this occasion, simply answered "present" rather than voting against. Just after 3 p.m., a congressional delegation arrived at the White House to deliver the declarations. At the signing ceremony in the Oval Office, noting that the United States was now at war with all the Axis powers, Roosevelt quipped, "I've always heard things came in threes!"[116] Hitler had resolved Roosevelt's dilemma for him. By some readings, the German dictator had fallen into the trap the president had set for him. In Pacific Palisades, Thomas Mann shared in the relief. After listening to Hitler's speech and hearing of the congressional declarations of war, the writer remarked, "Roosevelt's stratagem has worked. Hitler attacked him in his speech." The president, Mann continued "is certainly [Hitler's] great adversary. What he [Roosevelt] did, had to be," he concluded. "May it all turn out well."[117]

Surely the biggest sigh of relief, though, was that breathed in Moscow. Since Pearl Harbor, Stalin had resisted entering the war against Japan, even if he would thereby have brought about a US declaration of war on Hitler. Now he was off the hook. Hitler's declaration of war deprived Roosevelt of important leverage. That day, the Soviet ambassador in Washington, Litvinov, received a cable from Molotov communicating a definitive refusal to enter the conflict in the Far East. This was because the Japanese had given them no cause to abrogate their neutrality pact, and because they were engaged in a mortal struggle with Nazi Germany, which admitted of no distraction. In short, Molotov explained, it was policy "to maintain neutrality so long as Japan observes the Soviet-Japanese Neutrality Pact."[118]

Later, Litvinov visited the White House to meet Hopkins and discuss the United States carrying out its full Lend-Lease military allocations to the Soviets. During Litvinov's visit, "he came in contact with [the] President" and gave him the bad news that the Soviet government had decided not to enter the Pacific war.[119] Roosevelt admitted that he would have done the same in the Soviet situation. The president asked, though, that the decision not be publicized, in order to tie down as many Japanese forces as possible. His request that the Soviet Union announce that it was open to changing its stance was firmly rejected, for fear of provoking a preemptive Japanese attack. The president's parting shot was that the Soviet decision "would inevitably prolong the war with Japan but there was nothing to be done about it."[120]

After leaving the White House, Litvinov went to the State Department to see Hull. The secretary of state recalled that he had warned the Soviets in January, on the basis of American intelligence, that Hitler would invade around May and that this was disregarded. He now revealed that he had new information that Japan would violate their neutrality agreement with the Soviets as soon as Hitler demanded it. Hull noted that while "the Ambassador seemed very much interested in this," he did "not seriously attempt to discuss it, although indicating that he did not doubt the truth of it." Hull continued to impress on Litvinov that they were confronted with a "world movement" of "international desperadoes, operating together in all mutually desirable respects," who must be combated in concert. If the Allies did not fully unite in fighting all of the Axis powers, then the consequences could "be terrible for all of us, including Russia." In effect, Hull was making a similar case to the Soviets about declaring war on Japan that British figures had put to the Americans with regard to Germany over the past few days. In response to Hull's arguments, though, Litvinov "nodded his head and spoke in the affirmative but did not discuss these views." When Hull urged the Soviets to allow American aircraft access to its bases on the Kamchatka Peninsula and Vladivostok to target Japan's bases, fleets, and cities, the ambassador again demurred.

Hull warned that there would be consequences. He repeatedly cautioned that if "Russia should refrain from cooperation with us in the East while we continue to aid her; there will be a constant flow of criticism about why we are aiding Russia in a world movement involving all alike and Russia in turn is not cooperating with us in the Far East." Earlier that day, Hull had been forced to issue a statement "to allay some of this very kind of rising criticism," and he told Litvinov that unless the Soviets changed their position "it will become an increasingly serious matter for both governments." While Litvinov recognized this, there was clearly little that he could offer in return.

The two men concluded with a vague agreement that it was "highly important for some kind of formula to be worked out in regard to what each government is doing and should do" to advance the broader campaign against the Axis.[121] The Soviets had, in principle, secured the supply of munitions without conceding belligerence against Japan, but whether that would hold if opposition in the United States to maintaining levels of military aid to the Allies continued to grow remained uncertain.

Following Hitler's declaration of war, Hopkins also moved to reassure British officials that "shipments to the United Kingdom and Middle East were rapidly clarifying." Harriman was informed that "tanks [were] released this afternoon" and "ships [were] leaving regularly." Over the past few days, the administration "of necessity had to make some moves which you must understand." But Hopkins told Harriman that Britain should be "greatly encouraged" by the day's events: "If Hitler thought he could stop materials going to Russia and British Empire by striking us he will be greatly mistaken."[122] That afternoon, in fact, convoy PQ6 was making good progress in the Arctic and fell in with the cruiser *Edinburgh* and the destroyers *Echo* and *Escapade*.[123] Now the merchantmen would no longer be dependent on the puny trawlers for protection.

Hitler had always been sensitive to the suggestion that Germany was at war with "the world," and so great emphasis was placed on bringing the rest of Europe into line against the United States. Ribbentrop now turned to the task of lining up the Reich's allies in support. He told the German missions in Bratislava, Bucharest, Budapest, Sofia, and Zagreb that it was essential that the governments there not merely break off diplomatic relations with Washington but formally declare war as well. Even if the military implications of such a move would be minimal, it was "politically of the greatest importance, that all signatory powers of the Tripartite Pact expressed their solidarity unhesitatingly in an unambiguous way."[124]

Ribbentrop urged the Italians to help in this exercise, which they were happy to do, but with a distinctive slant. Ciano saw Italy as the representative of "Latin" and "Catholic" power in the Axis and the natural focal point of the Latin world against American domination. In the early evening, the Italian foreign minister cabled his ambassadors in Argentina, Brazil, Chile, and Peru in this spirit.[125] It was also in these terms—that of Latin solidarity—that Ciano had appealed to Vichy France's Admiral

Darlan in Turin. He even wondered whether Spain could be persuaded to declare war on the United States.[126]

The danger of pushing the Vichy colonies into the hands of de Gaulle was one that Hitler had been concerned about for some time, and so Vichy France was singled out for special attention. That day, the chief of staff of the German Armistice Commission with France requested that the OKW be consulted on any plans to demand that Vichy France break off relations with the United States. Any such move, it was pointed out, would affect the supply of neutral Vichy-held colonies in West Africa, which depended on toleration of convoys by the British and the Americans.[127] This mattered, because the loss of those colonies would not only bolster the Free French but also weaken the already shaky Axis position in North Africa.

While all eyes were on the Reichstag and the new war that had just broken out, the situation on the eastern front continued to deteriorate. The onslaught on Army Group Center showed no sign of abating. That day, the Soviet Kalinin front, under pressure from Soviet high command, resumed its offensive. Things were no better in the south. The First SS Brigade, which Himmler had instructed to support the embattled Leibstandarte at Rostov with the "greatest dispatch," was still stuck at Orel hundreds of miles away on the central front.[128]

The days of quick victories over the Red Army were long past, but there were still millions of Soviet prisoners of war in German hands from the great encirclement battles of the summer and autumn. Their fate was a particularly grim one. The Nazis had initially intended to let them starve to death, in order to use saved foodstuffs to feed the Reich in the face of the British blockade. When it became clear that the war in the east would not end soon and that the entry of the United States into the war would prolong the conflict for a considerable period of time, this policy was reversed. Now the prisoners were to be deployed in the German war economy. For many, this came too late. That day, Goebbels noted that nine hundred thousand of them had "already" died of hunger, weakness, and sickness. There would, he continued, at best be 350,000 workers available from the pool. This meant, Goebbels went on, that the Reich would continue to have to rely on foreign labor from other parts of Europe, which brought with it a set of associated problems.[129] Unlike the Soviet prisoners of war, these workers could not necessarily be completely separated from the German population, leading to all kinds of issues.

At around 9 p.m., the Düsseldorf transport drew into Miesterhorst, a village between Wolfsburg and Gardelegen in northern Germany. There it was noticed that the axle of carriage number 12 was on fire. Unsurprisingly, there was no replacement available at the tiny station. The unfortunate deportees in that carriage were thus distributed among the rest of the train. It was another awful scene, as the sleeping Jews initially refused to budge and were then brutally driven out under the spotlights of the guards into the pouring rain. The train was too long for the small platform, so there was no shelter. Eventually, the damaged carriage was shunted out of the way, and the transport was on the move again.[130]

On the eastern front, there was still no consensus among commanders on how best to react to increasing Soviet pressure. In the north, the German situation had eased slightly. "Today is the first day for some time," Ritter von Leeb noted, "which has not brought any particular problems."[131] In Army Group Center, though, the situation was getting worse and worse. The Russian breakthrough against Rudolf Schmidt's Second Army, Bock opined, "is to be attributed less to the greater strength of the Russians than to the failure of our completely exhausted troops." One division, which had been tasked with a counterattack, was too short of men and ammunition; another "had lost a shocking amount of its fighting capacity." Likewise, Strauss's Ninth Army was under heavy pressure from the Soviet force attacking Kalinin.[132] From across Army Group Center, Bock was receiving reports of smaller tactical withdrawals, which he approved. "A large-scale withdrawal under enemy pressure," Bock wrote in his diary, "would have incalculable consequences."[133]

How all this looked to the men on the front line was graphically described by the soldier Jackl Hirschbold in a letter to the Reverend

Stephan Wellenhofer, a Catholic priest. Wishing him a happy Christmas and New Year in advance, Hirschbold apologized for not having had time to write earlier. "The last few days were the most terrible in my life," he explained. "So far I had always said the fighting in the east was the worst I had ever experienced [but] I don't know how to describe the past fortnight." "It is spitting fire from all barrels and bomb bays," Hirschbold continued. "In one night we endured a fifteen-minute artillery bombardment in one stretch." All around him, he said, shells were exploding. On one occasion, Hirschbold described, it was "as if a voice was saying run another fifteen meters and I ran." When he returned to where he had been a moment earlier, he found that his comrades were dead. "I know it was the Mother of Andechs [that is, Mary, the mother of God]," he wrote, "who spoke to me," and "again I felt the heat of the explosion in my face and remained in one piece." "These are the days," he believed, "I will not forget for the rest of one's life."[134]

Hirschbold then went on to describe the terrible weather conditions. Everything was frozen: "Bread, sausage, coffee, everything." They kept going, he reported, on chocolate and cigarettes. Now, Hirschbold continued, they were at least out of immediate danger and resting in a farmhouse. He was now pathetically grateful for things "which would regard as the bare minimum of civilization at home." This would be his first Christmas "in the field," though one of several far from home. "For how many Christmases have I been away from my loved ones," he lamented, "[but] I am confident all the same that this Christmas Eve will be a very fine one, without anything external, only the core of the feast." "How often," Hirschbold reflected, "has the war revealed the most inner, the most deep in our religion," because "there is nobody at home who is as close to God as the soldier in the field, no one." "It is a great gift," he concluded, "to be able to experience such hours. I greet you from the front of the wild east."[135]

This was just one of the many horror stories that were making their way west from the front line, back to homes across Germany. That same day, Goebbels despaired of "the effect of the military mail," whose exuberance had at first been such a boon to morale, but whose effects were now largely "negative." "The soldiers," he explained, "give a pretty un-varnished account of the difficulties with which they have to cope." These could be complaints either about the "lack of winter equipment" or "the lack of food and ammunition." Goebbels knew all this because it was picked up by the military censors, who read mail to prevent soldiers from revealing military secrets.

With so much bad news from the east, it was not clear how the German public would react to the outbreak of a new conflict, whose dimensions meant that any thought of an imminent end to the war had to be abandoned. Goebbels, in fact, was nervous about popular opinion. "The German people," he lamented, were "too easily prone to an illusory optimism," which would be dashed by the onset of bad news. "The British," by contrast, were "masters of dealing with the psychology of the people" and knew how to prepare their population for defeats and the need for perseverance. As a result, they had "an exemplary toughness in leadership and people," and Goebbels believed that "we should really take a leaf out of the British book." "We Germans," he continued, "are by no means yet as used as the British to taking hard blows quietly and without complaining."[136] For this reason, Goebbels once again regretted the "illusionary predictions" of his rival Otto Dietrich back in October that the eastern campaign was all but over.[137]

The official OKW report of the day, oddly, made no mention of the new war with the United States. Instead, it claimed that "local attacks" by the Red Army had been repelled with heavy losses. The Luftwaffe was credited with "successful attacks" on Soviet columns, tank concentrations, fortified positions, and lines of communication. The OKW also reported that there had been "no major fighting" in North Africa. British tanks and vehicle concentrations, it was claimed, had been dispersed by German aircraft. In the Mediterranean, the Luftwaffe and the Italians had allegedly caused heavy damage to a British cruiser and destroyer. Finally, the OKW announced that the Luftwaffe ace Joachim Müncheberg had shot down his sixtieth enemy aircraft.[138] Whatever the veracity of the individual claims, the report bore no relation to the actual situation on either front. If Goebbels hoped to practice what is today called the "expectation management" of popular opinion, this is what he was up against.

In the absence of reliable polling, it is impossible to know for sure what the German people made of the turn of events. The surveillance report of the SD submitted that day, which did not cover Hitler's speech or any other event on December 11, spoke of widespread elation at Japanese victories, "especially" the sinking of the *Prince of Wales* and the *Repulse*. Interest in the Russian front was considerably reduced, just as Goebbels had hoped it would be. Unaware of the Japan-Soviet Union neutrality pact, some parts of the German population expected the Japanese to attack the Soviet Union, or at least to tie down Soviet forces in the Far East, relieving the eastern front. They also expected that the Afrika Korps would benefit from Britain being distracted by Japanese attacks. Finally, there was a widespread hope "that America would no longer be able to support the British and Soviets with supplies of war material as it would now need all its war material for its own defense."[139]

Even in the regime's own reporting, though, signs of popular anxiety were visible. It was feared that the Russians would use the lull in the east to prepare for the spring campaign in the year to come. There was "anxiety" among many Germans about whether the Axis forces in North Africa would be able to contain the British attacks for much longer. There were the usual grumbles about the supply of foodstuffs in the cities. Above all, "many parts of the population" still entertained an "exaggerated impression" of the US Navy and Air Force, and "the word 'America' was instinctively associated with the idea of irresistible strength."[140]

Foreign observers told a still more somber story. "The German people," Arvid Fredborg recalled, "received this new declaration of war with resigned calm and without the least trace of enthusiasm." Many had "dire forebodings" and began to speak of the First World War, when, of course, US intervention had tipped the scales against the Reich. There was also anxiety about British advances in North Africa, but especially about the situation on the eastern front. If nothing else, Fredborg explained, people were now convinced that the war, even if victorious, would be a "long one."[141] The Hamburg diarist Erich W. summed this sentiment up that same day. Hitler's declaration of war with the United States, he wrote, "probably means war for the rest of our lives."[142]

At about 11 p.m., the Düsseldorf transport arrived at Stendal in the Altmark region to the west of Berlin. The locomotive was changed, and a third-class carriage was added, presumably to make up for the one left behind at Miesterhorst. Salitter was wary of "loading" it during the hours of darkness, in case any of his prisoners tried to escape. He was also unable to carry out the desired shift of the escort carriage, because the station was on the main line and he was told to depart forthwith. For whatever reason, the Reichsbahn had once again ensured that the train spent the minimum amount of time in Germany en route.[143]

The experience of the Düsseldorf transport was being repeated in other parts of Germany. That day, preparations for the deportation of the Jews of Bielefeld were in full swing. Despite the fact that it was kept quiet by the authorities, the operation was—as the report of the local SD *Hauptaussenstelle* put it—"widely known" by the rest of the population. It was largely welcomed by them, the SD report suggested. One worker remarked that "if this had been done to the Jews 50 years ago," then Germany would have had to endure neither "the world war [that is, the First World War] nor the current war."[144]

In the Polish ghettos, the Jews were not yet explicitly marked for destruction, but conditions were very bad. That day, Arthur Kimel wrote to Renee Uhrmann in Vienna to thank her for the *Doppelkarte* she had sent nine days earlier.[145] He claimed to be "well" and "healthy," though that was probably just to reassure the recipient. Kimel went on to say that he had spent five weeks in the hospital with pneumonia. He then, confessing his embarrassment, asked for news and money, the two most precious commodities in the ghetto, because they kept up hope and enabled bare survival. They were especially important for those who were unable to work, or to find work, because they would otherwise have no means of support.

Even this slender basis for continued Jewish life was being closed off. That day, the police president of Sosnowitz in the newly German region of Upper Silesia, Alexander von Woedtke, protested against the large number of Jews still in employment. Despite the general policy of "Germanisation" and "pushing back of Jewish influence," he complained, there were still seventy thousand Jews resident in his bailiwick. Woedtke accepted that the "lack of tradesmen" made it necessary to leave Jewish plumbers, electricians, painters, decorators, and roofers in place. But he regarded the "removal" of Jews from the commercial enterprises as "absolutely necessary." Woedtke rejected the notion that these Jews were "indispensable." As a case in point, he advanced the alleged fact of the "complete separation of the Jews in Litzmannstadt without damaging the local economy." "The Jews cannot work in the productive economy," he claimed, because "profiteering is the basis of their livelihoods."[146] Here, Woedtke was reflecting the supposed link between capitalism and Jewry, which was also at the heart of Hitler's anti-Semitism.

If Hitler's declaration of war marked the start of a new and even darker chapter for his genocidal regime, it would also secure the alliance that would bring about his downfall. In London, Churchill's relief that the United States was now officially at war with Germany was captured by one of his private secretaries, John Martin, in his diary that night: "The stars in their courses are fighting for us," a biblical allusion drawn from the book of Judges.[147] Six months earlier, the prime minister had made a similar reference in a radio broadcast to the United States, shortly before the German invasion of the Soviet Union, when Britain stood alone: "The stars in their courses proclaim the deliverance of mankind. . . . Not so easily shall the lights of freedom die. But time is short. . . . United we stand. Divided we fall. Divided, the dark age returns. United, we can save and guide the world!"[148]

At last, on December 11, Churchill had the unity with the United States against Hitler that he had so long craved. That united effort still needed to be made a practical reality, however. Despite Hopkins's earlier message, the British government continued to fear that any continuation of the American embargo would have dire consequences, particularly for the next stage of the Libyan campaign. Beaverbrook told Harriman that in American harbors "about thirty ships ready to sail or scheduled shortly destined for Middle East are being held up" and the cargo was "vitally needed for the successful completion of campaign." Shortly before midnight in London, Beaverbrook and Harriman telephoned Hopkins at the White House to ask for urgent help. Hopkins reassured them that "in order to make it really tough for Hitler we will undoubtedly greatly increase our amounts." The Americans would soon increase production to previously inconceivable levels. "They made another mistake, by God," Hopkins roared. American aid would now be stepped up, not stood down: "If Hitler thought he could start a war and do that he is going be greatly mistaken."[149]

IT HAD BEEN a momentous day, and arguably the most important twenty-four hours in history. In the morning, the future had seemed open; it was still theoretically possible that Nazi Germany might not go to war with the United States. By the end of the day, there was no going back. "Germany and Italy have declared war on the United States," Mihail Sebastian wrote in his diary. "The sensation of the first Japanese successes," he went on, "the Anglo-Saxon consternation, the general stupefaction—all this adds an aspect of pomp and theatricality to the events." He concluded, "It will take several days for heads to clear."[150]

General Gotthard Heinrici, writing from just behind the front line in central Russia, "welcomed" the Japanese entry into the war. "I am not assuming," he wrote, "that it will turn against Russia in the foreseeable future," but "it prevents" or "at least makes more difficult the transport of material from America and Britain to Russia and that is a big gain for us." The continued salience of Lend-Lease in German thinking even in the heart of the Russian countryside—or perhaps especially there—is remarkable. Heinrici also saw Pearl Harbor as "a very great relief" for the Italians. They had been in danger of being expelled from North Africa, enabling an enemy landing in southern France. "I hope," Heinrici declared, "that all such chimeras have been dispelled by the entry of Japan into the war."[151] The sense of the global interconnectedness of events in his mind was thus very acute.

In Britain, Harold Nicolson was "full of faith." "We simply can't be beaten with America in," he wrote. He could not understand, however, why his fellow countrymen were not more exultant. Of course, the sinking of the *Prince of Wales* and *Repulse* the previous day had "numbed our nerves." Yet Nicolson reflected "how strange it is that this great event should be recorded and welcomed here without any jubilation," without even "an American flag flying in the whole of London. How odd we are!"[152]

The curiously downbeat manner in which the British received news of the American entry into the war against Hitler was also noted by the food-packing manager in Belmont, Surrey. "Not much notice," he remarked, "has been taken of the fact that Italy and Germany to-day declared war on America." This was attributed to the fact that it would have "little immediate effect." In due course, he expected the arrival of American troops in Europe, the Middle East, and even Russia, if necessary. The manager was also intrigued to note that Mussolini was the first to mention the declaration: "Did he steal Hitler's thunder?" Reflecting that it had taken twelve months for US troops to reach the front lines in the last war, but "within six months Germany asked for an armistice," he now wondered, "Will history be repeated?" However long it took, he was now certain "this joint action of the dictators will ultimately bring such retribution over their heads that December 11th 1941 will be a day which is cursed wherever German and Italian is spoken."[153]

In Canada, too, Prime Minister Mackenzie King found it "remarkable that a declaration of war against the U.S. by Germany and Italy seems to be almost an incidental matter." His colleagues had made "no particular comment other than the relief it was to have all countries where they could co-operate freely and be rid of restrictions." But King realized just how significant a moment this was. His understanding of American politics meant he knew to whom the Allies should be grateful: "We have to thank Germany and Italy, not the people of the U.S. themselves for the U.S. coming into the war."[154]

In the White House, Roosevelt's advisers were well aware of the magnitude of what had occurred and the tragedy that had been averted.

"When Pearl Harbor happened," the president's economic adviser John Kenneth Galbraith recalled, "we were desperate. . . . We were all in agony." This was because he and like-minded British sympathizers feared that the administration would be "forced" by the public "to concentrate all our efforts on the Pacific, unable from then on to give more than purely peripheral help to Britain." To the amazement of the president and his advisers, Hitler made the "truly astounding" and "totally irrational" decision to declare war on the United States. Galbraith remembered an indescribable "feeling of triumph" upon hearing the news from Berlin: "I think it saved Europe."[155]

8

THE WORLD OF DECEMBER 12, 1941

I<small>T WAS</small> H<small>ITLER'S DECLARATION OF WAR ON THE</small> U<small>NITED</small> S<small>TATES</small>, much more than Pearl Harbor, that created a new global strategic reality and, ultimately, a new world. America did not enter "the war"—the conflict with Hitler—on December 7, 1941. Rather, the United States was plunged that day into a new and initially separate struggle against Japan. America did not truly join the war until December 11, 1941, and unlike the First World War, the United States did not take the initiative. It was, as British air marshal Arthur Harris had predicted, "kicked into the [European] war." Harris was therefore spared the ordeal of eating, as he had vowed to do if the Americans entered the war of their own accord, "a pink elephant, trunk, tail and toenails—and raw at that." In short, the global significance currently attached to December 7 should really be attributed to December 11, 1941.

Both Hitler and Roosevelt explained the escalating hostility that led to this dramatic turn of events through conspiracy theory. The Führer was convinced that "the Jews" had suborned Roosevelt, who in turn had manipulated the United States into such a hostile attitude toward the Reich that Germany had no choice but to declare a preemptive war. The president, for his part, intimated that it was Hitler who pulled the strings in Tokyo. He did not credit the Japanese with agency of their own, even though they had indeed planned to attack regardless of the Führer's intentions and promises. But the comparison ends there. On December 11, having plunged his country into an unwinnable war against the greatest industrial power on earth—and a racially kindred one to boot—Hitler had landed exactly where he did not want to be. Roosevelt, by contrast, would soon have the German dictator exactly where he wanted him.

Whether Roosevelt had wanted to enter the war against Hitler as a full-scale belligerent before December 7, 1941, remains unclear. The president, in the words of Rexford G. Tugwell, one of his advisers and subsequently one of his most perceptive biographers, "deliberately concealed the processes of his mind. He would rather have posterity believe that for him everything was always plain and easy . . . than ever to admit to any agony of indecision."[1] The president did not frankly confide his innermost thoughts to even his closest confidants, while his political skill enabled him to convince others that he completely shared their views even while scrupulously avoiding commitments to do what they wanted.[2]

As a result, there is no conclusive evidence either way on whether Roosevelt regarded American intervention in Europe as inevitable. Some analysts emphasize that he stretched executive authority to the limit—infuriating congressional opponents, risking a constitutional crisis, and flouting international law in order to aid the Allies—with the intention of provoking Hitler into attacking American vessels and precipitating a crisis that would unite the country in support of war. Others, however, argue that even when US warships were sunk in the Atlantic and Americans died, Roosevelt did not fully exploit these incidents, aware that a request for war would encounter serious opposition in Congress and among the wider public even as late as the first week of December 1941.[3]

So while the president implied to British contacts that "he would not be sorry to see the United States in the war," he evaded any pledge to request a declaration of war from Congress.[4] Surveying the American political scene for Britain's Ministry of Information, the philosopher Isaiah Berlin later recalled that "Roosevelt thought he would win the war without actually fighting it . . . by supplying the British, but not actually declar[ing war], so no American boys would actually get killed," eventually leaving him "in the neutral position of being able to dictate the kind of world he wanted."[5] The debate over when, and if, Roosevelt would have directly intervened in the war of his own accord still continues today, but the president's internal deliberations remain as elusive as ever.

His private considerations notwithstanding, it is clear that Roosevelt was committed to the total and utter defeat of Hitler, even if his method for achieving this before December 1941 was uncertain. As Tugwell astutely observed, Roosevelt "was apt to see the importance of immediate ends more readily than the consequence of doubtful means."[6] By 1941, Roosevelt had decided that Hitler should be vanquished, but he was flexible as to how. While the president hoped to secure victory by aiding Britain and the Soviets as a noncombatant if possible, he was increasingly open to formal intervention if necessary, but only if he could do so with the support of a united nation at home. But he remained doubtful about this unity even after Japan's attack on Pearl Harbor, which was why Hitler declaring war neatly solved his most urgent problem. The Nazi dictator ultimately did so out of fear that, if he did not, the United States would overwhelm Germany at a time of its choosing, even though the American president was convinced that only a fait accompli would ensure the congressional and national unity necessary for another war in Europe.

On the morning of December 12, an aide reported to the president that "the country's newspapers give expression to a thrilling and uplifting sense of union. . . . The United States has again become a community."[7] The president refused to be complacent, however. Over the following weeks, he worked to cement this unity wherever he could. In response to the Republican commitment to cooperate with the administration, Roosevelt announced that partisan politics were now over, for in wartime there was "only a determined intent of a united people to carry on the struggle for human liberty."[8] On December 15, to mark the 150th anniversary of the Bill of Rights, the president issued a public declaration rallying the country to destroy Nazi "barbarism" and defend the principles of liberty. Reversing his strategy of just a few days before, he now focused almost exclusively on Germany, referring to Hitler frequently and explicitly while barely mentioning Japan.[9] This was clearly designed to ensure that public opinion was not distracted from the broader struggle, and it largely succeeded, with an administration official approvingly noting that press coverage of the speech "subordinated the early narrow sense of outrage against Japan and stressed the need for destroying totalitarianism as a whole."[10]

All the same, the official warned that "despite the large measure of unity, the press reveals certain fissures which persist among the American public." In the early days of the war, there was "almost unanimous endorsement of forceful action against Japan; but the minority groups which opposed the Administration prior to the attack on Hawaii give evidence that they will continue to resist the larger purpose of the Administration on the war as a whole." Clearly, he concluded, even "if isolationism, as the commentators insist, is dead, a parochial spirit still exists."[11] Perhaps that is why, when Roosevelt received news that Germany's allies Bulgaria, Hungary, and Romania had declared war on the United States, he "told Cordell [Hull] to take no notice of it and I will not send word to Congress." Conscious that congressional and public opinion remained potentially volatile, Roosevelt wanted to avoid anything that might provoke disunity. America's diplomats were even instructed to get the three governments to withdraw their declarations.[12]

The impact of Hitler's declaration of war was immediate. The envoys, the attachés, and the journalists departed. US officials and pressmen in Berlin were sent to a freezing hotel in the suburbs, then to the spa town of Bad Nauheim, and then were finally shipped home via Lisbon on a chartered Swedish ship.[13] In Washington, the German embassy was closed down. Thomsen and his staff were eventually repatriated to Germany. The Japanese embassy was cut off from all outside contact. After Christmas, Saburo Kurusu was moved with the rest of its staff to Hot Springs, Virginia. Six months later, Kurusu and Ambassador Nomura boarded another Swedish ship for Yokohama.[14] Diplomacy and journalism, after playing such a large part in our story, would wait in the wings until the end of the war. As Cordell Hull observed, after December 11, "the voices of diplomacy were now submerged by the roar of the cannon."[15]

THE UNITED STATES was now the Third Reich's open enemy. In the Nazi view, which Goebbels articulated the day after the declaration of war, the conflict pitted "hungry" Germany against the "satiated" and "plutocratic" United States. This inequality, he claimed, was "the true origin of the war." It had to be resolved. That same day, Hitler met with the gauleiters in a hastily convened conference. He explained that "even if Japan had not entered the conflict," he would still "have had to declare war on the Americans sooner or later." In that context, the Führer continued, "East Asian conflict was like a present from heaven." The opening of formal hostilities with the United States would also enable him to wage unrestricted submarine warfare against Allied commerce. Whether or not the "plutocratic powers"—that is, the United States and Britain—would withdraw entirely from East Asia was unclear, Hitler said, but he believed that they would divide their strength across the various theaters of war. This, he explained, would lead to them "dispersing their forces to such an extent that they would be incapable of concerted action on any one front." "That," the Führer concluded, voicing the rationale behind the declaration of war on the United States, "would be the best thing they could do from our point of view."[16]

Hitler also told the gauleiters of his intention to "make a clean sweep" in the "Jewish question." He was referring to central and western European Jewry, the hostages who were now held responsible for the behavior of the United States, as the Führer had long threatened they would be.[17] He reminded the gauleiters of his threat in 1939 to retaliate against Jewry in the event of their "plunging" Europe into war. "The world war is here," Hitler continued, "[and] the extermination of the Jews must be the necessary consequence."[18] "The Führer," the Nazi chief ideologue Alfred Rosenberg recorded two days later, "said that they [the Jews] had burdened us with this war," with all its "destruction," so that "it was no wonder if the consequences should strike them first."[19]

In Russia, the Nazis had long treated Jews of both sexes and all ages, in or out of uniform, as enemy combatants or partisans to be systematically killed. Now the Jews of Germany and central and western Europe were to be murdered as well. Whether the entry of the United States into the war was the decisive factor here or merely an accelerant, it is clear that a primary motivation and context for Hitler's war of annihilation against western and central European Jewry was his relationship with the United States.[20] After December 11, 1941, this entered a new and more deadly phase. The murder of the remaining Jews under Nazi control was now a settled matter; all that remained were questions of definition and methods of execution.

At least some of the German population were aware of the radicalization of regime policy toward the Jews and its connection to the United States. On December 12, 1941, the same day that Hitler spoke to the gauleiters, the SD *Aussenstelle* in Minden reported on public opinion in the area. People were "talking a lot," the report explains, about the deportations "to Russia" in "cattle trucks," and about the sight of Jews trudging through the streets with their household belongings. The SD disapproved of the fact that some Christians showed "strong sympathy" for the victims. These Christians "could not understand" how anybody could be treated "so brutally" because they were all, in the end, "God's creation." The SD also noted that people were speaking "a lot" about the way in which Germans in America were allegedly forced "for purposes of identification" to wear a swastika on their left breasts, just like the Jews had to wear the Star of David. The Germans in America, it was felt, would have to "suffer a lot" for the fact that the Jews in Germany were being treated "so badly."[21]

Goebbels was also concerned with the situation of the German Americans after the outbreak of war, but in a different way. On the same day the Aussenstelle Minden reported on the views of the city's inhabitants, Goebbels wrote that "the German Americans are putting themselves at Roosevelt's disposal." "I expected no less," he continued, adding that "the American continent has a strange power of assimilation." "German elements are particularly susceptible to it," Goebbels went on, noting that "we saw a very similar process during the first world war."[22]

Goebbels threw himself into the new propaganda war with gusto. On the one hand, he affected to be unimpressed by American claims "that Germany was a starving country while America was well-fed." He promised to make that phrase, of a starving Germany and a satiated America, into a "slogan" and *"Leitmotiv* of the whole war." It certainly supported Hitler's "have-not" rhetoric.[23] On the other hand, it was obviously risky to let the image of an all-powerful United States go unchallenged. Goebbels told the Propaganda Ministry that the American responsibility for the outbreak of war should be relentlessly hammered home, as should the need to expand the theater of operations. Alleged parallels with the situation in 1917–1918 should be countered by referring to the fact that Germany now controlled "the entire continent" and had reliable allies. A few days later, the ministry was instructed to prepare material that would explain US cultural inferiority to the wider population. Without it, Goebbels feared, the German people—"with the German tendency toward objectivity"—would default to a positive view of the United States.[24]

While the German press dutifully reported that Hitler's speech declaring war on the United States had been received with "satisfied relief and deep solemnity" by the German people, in the absence of reliable polls, it is impossible to know what German society actually made of the new war.[25] Some Germans affected indifference. When Victor Klemperer asked a Dresden shopkeeper the day after whether war had been declared, the latter simply responded, "I don't know, I am busy here."[26] The report of the SD on December 15 showed a mixed picture. There were those who were happy that Hitler had seized the initiative and who applauded his speech. They were surprised and elated at the quality of their Japanese allies. There was widespread agreement that Roosevelt was now "world enemy no. 1," perhaps the first time a US president has been so described. But there were also those who were anxious about the acquisition of another enemy. They now expected a much longer war.[27]

Among those expecting a drawn-out conflict were men on the eastern front. On December 12, the day after Hitler's declaration of war, General Heinrici wrote to his wife, "How nice it would be if one could once again be in one's own flat which now stands cold and empty." "Now that we really have a war," he continued, "it is almost impossible to foresee when one might once again be able to use it."[28] That same day, and in the same vein, the soldier Ludwig Bumke wrote from Russia that "hopefully that is the last surprise. The Japanese have won some big victories, which pleases us." "Hopefully they will continue to do so," he went on, "and it will not become a Thirty Years' War."[29]

In Italy, Mussolini seemed unconcerned by the fact that a colossal new enemy, the United States, had entered the war against him. On December 12, the day after his declaration of war, the Duce argued that things were looking up in North Africa because the Americans and British were now distracted in the Pacific.[30] As for American productive power, Mussolini preferred to rely on the advice of Count Giuseppe Volpi, the most important industrialist in the country and head of the Fascist confederation of industry. Volpi, who should have known better, told the Duce that Italian industry was more efficient than that of the Anglo-Americans and would be able to sustain two or three more years of war without difficulty. Mussolini claimed not to think of the Americans as a serious military threat and dismissed reports of their armaments production as mere propaganda. He affected to be much more concerned about the growth of German power, which was causing Italy to be marginalized in Europe.[31]

The Duce, like the Führer, may just have been putting a brave face on things. Both were perfectly aware of the United States' immense industrial potential. And Mussolini, like Hitler, had rational grounds not only to fear that Roosevelt intended to join the conflict anyway but also to believe that the outbreak of war with the United States would give him some short-term relief. The Duce had been worried for months that the Americans might land in French North Africa and engage the Italo-German force in a two-front war.[32] That threat now receded, at least for the moment, as the Americans were distracted by the Pacific and the British were expected to withdraw men and matériel to deal with the Japanese in Malaya.

For the Axis powers and their sympathizers, the war was not merely a geopolitical conflict but also an ideological and racial one. The Third Reich believed it was locked in deadly combat not merely with the Jews and the Slavs but also with the Anglo-Saxon powers, Britain and the United States. From now until the end, whether privately or in formal documents, Hitler spoke of "the Anglo-Saxon powers," "Anglo-Saxon statesmen," "Anglo-Saxon forces," or simply of "the Anglo-Saxons."[33] This was now also the official view from Rome, whose press claimed that "240 million people stand united in their struggle against the Anglo-Saxon powers."[34]

The conflict was also, as we have seen, an ideological one against Western "plutocracy." According to the Nazi narrative, "the Jews" had manipulated the "Anglo-Saxons" into war with the racially kindred Reich. This created some obvious dissonances in German messaging. It was for this reason that Goebbels instructed the Propaganda Ministry on January 13, 1942, that the word "Anglo-Saxons," which suggested a tribal kinship, should be replaced with the phrase "Anglo-American plutocracy."[35] It was no use. Almost everybody, from the Führer down, continued to refer to them as Anglo-Saxons.

In Japan, the conflict continued to be widely perceived as a "war with white people" in general.[36] It was also more specifically referred to as a contest with the "Anglo-Saxons." The Japanese therefore appealed to the racial solidarity of the rest of the world, and to the anti-colonialism of the Indian and Asian nationalists resisting Western imperialism. When Prime Minister Tojo proclaimed the creation of a "New World order" on December 13, 1941, the crowd responded with a "rousing and thunderous banzai for the humiliation of the haughty Anglo-Saxons."[37] As in Germany, the naming of the enemy was important, but Japanese priorities were reversed. General imprecations against white people threatened to offend their European allies and result in mixed messaging. To that end, five days after Hitler's declaration of war on the United States, Japanese intellectuals were instructed to drop references to "whites" and "the yellow race" and write instead of "Britain and America" or, simply, "the Anglo-Saxons."[38]

The Japanese also launched what they called "Negro Propaganda Operations" to exploit historic discrimination against African Americans. Most of this fell on deaf ears. People like Leonard Robert Jordan—dubbed the "Harlem Hitler," he looked forward to "President Roosevelt picking cotton and Secretaries Knox and Stimson riding me around in rickshaws"—were very much the minority in the United States. There was no great upsurge of African American support for the Japanese cause.[39] Still, enough Black Americans were receptive to Japanese blandishments that the National Association for the Advancement of Colored People felt obliged to publish a statement in support of the US war effort in response.[40]

The Roosevelt administration's Office of Facts and Figures informed the president in mid-to-late December that Black American newspapers "reveal an intense and widespread resentment against the treatment accorded Negroes in the defense activities of the United States." In particular, there was vehement protest "against flagrant racial discrimination in the armed forces," where the administration had bowed to the pressure of W. R. Poage and other southern segregationists to keep Black and white servicemen separate. Roosevelt was told clearly that there was "a strong sentiment among Negroes that democracy, as it is practiced in the United States, has no real meaning for them, that the liberties granted to them here are scarcely worth defending."[41]

Within a fortnight, however, the Office of Facts and Figures reported that, "while complaints are still frequent and bitter, the trend seems to be to view the war as an opportunity for Negroes to become a welded, instead of a segregated, part of American society."[42] This report described the green shoots of what would become the "Double V Campaign," announced by America's most widely read Black newspaper, the *Pittsburgh Courier*, on the two-month anniversary of Pearl Harbor (February 7, 1942).[43] Echoing the rhetoric of US representative Arthur W. Mitchell, the campaign urged Black Americans to give everything for the war effort while simultaneously pressuring the government to make the prose of the Declaration of Independence and the Reconstruction-era amendments to the Constitution a practical reality for all Americans, regardless of race.

In Japanese-occupied Asia, particularly in the detention camps holding European prisoners, the traditional racial hierarchy was subverted not just rhetorically but in practice.[44] This was widely noted, often with approval. "Although my reason utterly rebelled against it," a Malay civil servant of Indian origin recalled, "my sympathies instinctively ranged themselves with the Japanese in their fight with the Anglo-Saxons." In the Philippines, prominent collaborators hailed Japanese advances as a blow to "Anglo-Saxon imperialism" and a "vindication of the prestige of all Asiatic nations."[45] The myth of European invincibility, and with it the legitimacy of colonial rule, had been shattered beyond repair.

The irony of supporting the end of white rule in the Far East was not lost on Hitler. He was conscious, he told the gauleiters on December 12, that one might accuse him of acting against "the interests of the white race in East Asia."[46] "Strange," he remarked shortly afterward, "that we are destroying the bastions of the white race in East Asia with the help of Japan," while Britain was supporting the "Bolshevik pigs" in their struggle against "Europe."[47] Hitler claimed that he had "not wanted" the end of the British Empire in Asia and Australia, but this was the inevitable result of British policies, beginning with the Western alliance with Japan to exclude Germany from the Far East in World War I and culminating with Britain's refusal to accept Hitler's hegemony in Europe.[48] He predicted that "the white race" would "disappear" from that "space." Contrary to myth, however, it was a price the Führer was very happy to pay for the defeat of the Anglo-Saxons; he saw it as a deserved punishment for the British failing to heed his warnings and spurning his hand of friendship. "The interests of the white race," he insisted, "must take second place to the interests of the German people" and its need for "living space." "We would ally with anybody," Hitler continued, "if we could thereby weaken the Anglo-Saxon position."[49] In short, the alignments of December 12, 1941, did not reflect the "global color lines" but transcended them.

For the Axis and its fellow travelers, the war remained both a colonizing and a decolonizing project. As the global have-nots, Germany, Italy, and Japan, as they saw it, sought to escape enslavement by the international Anglo-Saxon and Jewish plutocratic ruling class and their Bolshevik auxiliaries. America and Britain, Hitler explained in a speech on January 30, 1942, had "the world at their disposal," with everything they needed. Not so for what he called the "three great have-nots."[50] The Japanese, as we have seen, echoed this rhetoric. In order to survive, the have-nots argued, the Axis powers would have to establish their own empires. This was a self-serving narrative, of course, but it was accepted by enough of what was then the global south to make it plausible. In fact, nationalist leaders such as Subhas Chandra Bose in India, Sukarno in Indonesia, and the grand mufti of Jerusalem all lined up behind the Axis.[51] For some, such as Sukarno, the move did not much harm their postwar careers, but for others, like Bose, the association would prove fatal.

WITH HITLER'S DECLARATION of war on the United States, Churchill could finally begin to relax. "I am enormously relieved at the turn world events have taken," he wrote to Roosevelt on December 12.[52] To Eden, still at sea en route to Moscow, the prime minister declared, "The accession of the United States makes amends for all, and with time and patience will give certain victory."[53] Since assuming the premiership, Churchill's strategy had been based on holding out long enough against Hitler until—as he phrased it in his famous "We Shall Fight on the Beaches" speech—"in God's good time, the New World, with all its power and might, steps forth to the rescue and the liberation of the old."[54] In the dark days of 1940, it was the expectation of future American intervention in the war that had encouraged his determination to fight on.[55] In pursuit of American participation, he had felt compelled to concede British bases and overseas assets for weapons and warships, to compromise his imperial ideals to sign a charter committed to "the right of all peoples to choose the form of government under which they live," and to call on the president with increasing urgency to intervene.[56] Now, an exultant

Churchill told Clement Attlee, "We have no longer any need to strike attitudes to win United States' sympathy, we are all in it together."[57] When one of the chiefs of staff urged continued caution in Britain's dealings with America, a "wicked leer" came into Churchill's eye. "Oh that is the way we talked to her while we were wooing her," he said. "Now that she is in the harem, we talk to her quite differently!"[58]

Yet, amid Churchill's jubilation, there still remained a lingering concern: that Americans' simmering fury at Pearl Harbor, and their increased sense of vulnerability now that the Japanese Navy dominated the Pacific, would force Roosevelt to concentrate on Japan, despite his previous commitment to a "Germany first" strategy. At lunch with King George VI on December 12, Churchill reported that he was departing for the Clyde estuary in Scotland that evening and would sail for Washington in the morning. He would take Harriman, Beaverbrook, and the chiefs of staff with him. The king recorded that Churchill was confident the "Libyan situation is going well" and "he can do more good going to talk to F.D.R. at this moment." The prime minister would tell the US president that "we must have our food and armaments." With the US Atlantic Fleet now moving to the Pacific to replace losses, Churchill was adamant that he and Roosevelt "must make a plan for the future as they are the only two people who can."

The king also noted, with satisfaction, that "the Germans are in a mess in Russia."[59] The American entry into the war closely coincided with the end of the German advance and the success of the Soviet counteroffensive before Moscow. Contrary to widespread belief, the German high command did not perceive any serious sense of crisis at the start of the offensive on December 5–6.[60] It was only in the middle of the month, a week after Pearl Harbor, that Hitler and the supreme military leadership finally registered the true state of affairs. First, as we have seen, the Führer admitted the casualties the Wehrmacht had sustained so far in his speech to the Reichstag on December 11. Second, Hitler was forced to intervene personally, this time not to restart the advance, but to prevent what threatened to be a chaotic retreat. In the Soviet Union, victory was made "official" by a Kremlin announcement on December 13 that the

Germans were in retreat from Moscow.[61] The extent of their disaster on the central front was now clear for all to see.

In Germany, the anti-Nazi Friedrich Kellner exulted. "Those whom God wishes to destroy," he wrote in his diary on December 12, "he has in all ages first made blind." At best, Kellner thought, the move could only "prolong the war." The "final result," he was sure, could only be "the total defeat" of Germany, Italy, and Japan. It was, Kellner continued, "a harsh punishment to be born in Germany. These people have gone completely insane." He was upset by the loss of the *Prince of Wales* and *Repulse*. "Where were the aircraft carriers to protect these battleships," Kellner wondered, "and where were the fighter aircraft on the island of Malacca?" Kellner demanded that the Allies should "chop the Japs to pieces." There should be large-scale air attacks on Germany and Japan. Japanese houses, he pointed out, were made of wood and should be burned.[62]

Pavel Luknitskiy, the special TASS correspondent in Leningrad, was equally ecstatic. That day, he heard the "wonderful news" on the radio. The Germans had been "crushed" near Moscow, Hitler had given a "hysterical speech" on December 11, and the United States had entered the war with Germany and Italy. "This is a big development," Luknitskiy wrote. "It will speed up the defeat of Hitler and the full destruction of the Fascist empire." "The start of victory," he said with pride, "is laid here, in Russia." "All else now is a question of time," he concluded, because he could "see victory."[63] In occupied Poland, the news reached Zygmunt Klukowski a day later. "America is at war with Germany!" he wrote in his diary on December 13. "The mood is brilliant," he continued. "All have taken courage and are full of hope that this will hasten the end of the war, which must result in a complete defeat for Germany."[64]

There was some speculation about whether Tokyo and Moscow would commence hostilities and close the circle. It seemed logical after Pearl Harbor and Hitler's declaration of war on the United States. "One of these days," Luknitskiy wrote, "there will be war with Japan," before adding the qualifier "probably."[65] That was certainly the hope of the Americans and of the Chinese nationalists, both of whom demanded that the Soviets take on the Japanese. Stalin, though, had no intention of adding to his burdens until he had sorted out the Germans. "Russia today," he explained to Chiang, "has the principal burden of the war against Germany" and should "not divert its strength to the Far East." "I beg you therefore not to insist," he implored the Chinese nationalist leader, "that Soviet Russia at once declare war against Japan." Stalin did add, though, that "Soviet Russia must fight Japan" eventually, "for Japan will surely unconditionally break the Neutrality Pact."[66] The Soviet dictator also told Eden, on December 16 after his arrival in Moscow, that while he could not help against Japan yet, "he might be able to in the Spring." Like Roosevelt, Stalin doubted that Tokyo was truly the master of its own fate, suggesting that "the Germans were running the Japs' airforce and campaign for them." Despite Stalin's conviction that Hitler was reorganizing for a fresh offensive on Moscow in early 1942, Eden noted that he did not "press at all for our airforce or men to be sent to Russia but he would still like more tanks."[67]

"Hitler's failures and losses in Russia are the prime fact in the war at this time," Churchill observed that same day aboard the HMS *Duke of York* on his way to the United States. He was adamant that the United States and Britain must send "without fail and punctually, the supplies we have promised," as this was the only way "we hold our influence over Stalin and be able to weave the mighty Russian effort into the general texture of the war."[68] Despite the dangerous voyage, as the *Duke of York* dodged detection by German U-boats and bomber squadrons, "the P.M. was in constant high spirits and never turned a hair," noted Sublieutenant Vivian Cox, a Churchill aide who was responsible for setting up a floating map room belowdecks for him. After nineteen months as the solitary leader of an empire fighting for survival, Churchill spent the journey strategizing how Britain would soon take the fight to the Axis alongside its powerful allies. Churchill's personal physician, Lord Moran, reflected that "he is a different man since America came into the war." Moran recalled that "the Winston I knew in London frightened me. . . . He was carrying the weight of the world," but now "the tired, dull look has gone from his eye; his face lights up as you enter the cabin."[69]

Surveying the new international picture, the prime minister declared, "This is a new war, with Russia victorious, Japan in and the Americans in up to the neck."[70]

Churchill's fellow countrymen, still in the dark about his clandestine trip, were also struggling to make sense of the new global conflict. That week's *Economist* noted that some were baffled by "Hitler's greatest blunder." Yet its editors cautioned that "it would be wise to assume that Hitler and his General Staff do not commit blunders—they seldom make ordinary mistakes." Instead, "if Hitler thinks that a Japanese attack on America serves his purpose, it is more probable that he is right than wrong." Too many Britons had made the simple assumption that the United States, previously out, was now in the war. In reality, the United States had already been engaged in Europe "with nearly all the weapons she has presently ready," and Hitler saw Japan's intervention as a way "to pull her out of the war in Europe and Africa by engaging her attention elsewhere." Stressing the limited American munitions currently available, the *Economist* argued that the balance of supplies had altered over the past week "in Hitler's favour and the democracies' disfavour." Despite Roosevelt's pledge to continue Lend-Lease, "hard strategic facts and the shock sustained by the American peoples will give 'America First' a new and very real meaning." The claims of the United States and its Pacific front would inevitably take precedence over those of the Allies and the Atlantic. Rather than blundering, therefore, Hitler was "gambling—gambling on time, short-term against long-term, immediate results against future hazards." It would be "folly" to underestimate the Axis, given its past record. In time, the vast productive potential of the United States could supply the armaments to sweep the dictators away, but it was imperative that immediate plans were established for "countering the world-wide plan of the Axis with a grand design for the grand alliance."[71] As the words went to press, the prime minister was already on his way to Washington to do just that.

Establishing a concerted grand strategy with the Americans, now that it could be done openly, was a priority for British officials. The day after Hitler's declaration of war, after months of secret liaisons, the Roosevelt administration was finally prepared to publicly recognize the existence of the British Joint Staff Mission in Washington.[72] The most urgent question to address remained that of supplies. Shortly after Hitler's declaration of war, the British Ministry of Supply cabled its consolidated list of orders, emphasizing those whose "non-fulfilment would seriously impair our fighting effort or gravely interrupt vital production here." The army required tanks, tank transporters, heavy trucks, and ammunition to immediately reinforce British forces in the North African campaign. Equally, the RAF needed aircraft and component tools for Britain's own production in order to step up its bombing raids against German industry while the Luftwaffe was engaged on the eastern front. And with Britain's shipping losses intensifying, the Admiralty was demanding carriers, torpedoes, and engines. On December 14, a member of the British Purchasing Commission in Washington wrote back to London that "the events of the week have made a tremendous difference in the atmosphere here, but it is too early yet to say precisely how our operations are going to be affected." It was essential, however, for there to be "a pretty rapid development in the way of closer cooperation, if the joint effort is to be properly conducted."[73]

These sentiments were shared by Edward Stettinius. On December 16, the Lend-Lease administrator expressed alarm at the "considerable uncertainty" caused by the War Department still holding up shipments in order to repossess materials urgently needed for "our war with Japan." In New York Harbor, twelve thousand railway carriages of material were backed up, awaiting loading onto ships, with 1,600 additional carloads arriving every day.[74] Nazi propaganda continued to exploit this. Among the enemy broadcasts "designed to spread defeatism," an aide informed Roosevelt, "most significantly of all, perhaps, the Berlin broadcasts declare that Lend-Lease aid must now be decreased."[75] Stimson was forced to issue a statement admitting that there had been a temporary embargo but that "very substantial quantities of Lend-Lease material" would be released soon.[76]

Ultimately, the actual "repossessions" of British goods were not as bad as initially feared. They principally consisted of small-arms ammunition and aircraft that the Americans urgently needed in the Pacific. Of the 1,200 aircraft that the US War Department demanded of Arthur Harris immediately after Pearl Harbor, less than half were eventually requisitioned. Nevertheless, British officials remained fearful that the bill would yet come due, at a time when Britain's resources remained dangerously stretched. As the British official history put it, "If the inroads made by the American Services went too far, if the flow of the really vital supplies to Britain and to Russia were not maintained," then "defeat in 1942 was a distinct possibility." Of course, the American services in the Pacific required immediate reinforcement and, in general, US forces needed to receive a far greater proportion of American production than during the period of neutrality. Yet, "if Suez was lost, if the Red Army were driven into Siberia, if India and Australia fell to the Japanese, if the Battle of the Atlantic were lost or Great Britain successfully invaded, it would be poor consolation to see the American Army emerge a mighty force in 1943."[77] Even if these fears seem overblown in retrospect, they were very real at the time.

The only way to ensure a coordinated approach, as Jean Monnet proposed in the British Supply Council on December 17, was for Churchill to press for the establishment of a "Joint Anglo-American (and possibly Russian) Military Board charged with the responsibility of deciding upon allocations . . . in accordance with strategic needs."[78] As British officials knew, the Americans had already set up their own strategic munitions board and, unless Britain's representatives were added, much of the British share risked being swallowed by the American services. With West Coast aircraft factories vulnerable to air raids, fears of a second Japanese assault on Hawaii's naval installations, and reports of Axis task forces lurking off the coast from Alaska to the Panama Canal, the overriding priority of the US generals was to consolidate their own forces. Furthermore, the situation in the Pacific was growing worse by the day, as Japanese forces surged with brutal efficiency through Malaya and the Philippines.

In mid-December, General George Marshall told Roosevelt that a temporary redistribution of military supplies from Lend-Lease programs to meet America's needs was "imperative."[79] In particular, the availability of cargo shipping was so restricted that Marshall had been advised by a subordinate that deploying American forces at the level previously envisaged by the Victory Program was incompatible with the country also being the "arsenal of democracy."[80] As a result, the chief of staff told the president that foreign aid allocations must be revised "in light of the vastly expanded requirements of the U.S Military Establishment."[81] It remained to be seen whether Lend-Lease, designed to enable Roosevelt to wage economic warfare while the United States was a nonbelligerent, could be converted into an instrument of coalition warfare, or if it would be radically revised in order to prioritize supplies for America's own armed services.

All this had serious implications for the Soviet Union, at least in the short term. On December 20, 1941, the British PQ6 convoy reached Murmansk, somewhat delayed but without further incident or loss. Its precious cargo would help the Red Army hold the line against Hitler. The problem, as the people's commissar for foreign trade Anastas Mikoyan wrote to Stalin in early January 1942, was not Britain, which was "fulfilling her obligations more or less accurately and carefully." "The same," he cautioned, could "not be said of the USA." Of nearly four hundred aircraft promised by Washington for October to December 1941, "only 204" had been shipped, and ninety-five had so far arrived in the Soviet Union. Between December 13 and 17, Mikoyan continued, the Roosevelt administration had "recalled almost all aircraft supplied from those situated in US ports at the time." In some cases, he stated, the Americans had "actually unloaded" aircraft already stowed in transports. It was much the same story with tanks.[82] Clearly, Pearl Harbor, by diverting US resources to fight Japan in the Pacific, was taking its toll.

THE UNITED STATES was transformed by its entrance into the war. Returning to Washington from the West Coast on December 15, Eleanor Roosevelt wistfully noted that "it seems like a completely changed world."[83] It was now no longer possible for visitors to wander around the

White House lawn. There were Secret Service and White House guards at all external gates, and blackout curtains were fitted on all the windows. A special air-raid shelter was hurriedly dug in the vault of the Treasury, although Roosevelt joked to Morgenthau that he would only use it if he could play poker with the secretary's gold reserves. Huybertie Hamlin, still living with the Roosevelts as a houseguest, noted that each room had a metal pail filled with sand and a scoop shovel, "ready to use when an incendiary bomb drops through the roof."[84] Gas masks were handed out to residents. Security conditions in the capital had changed forever, and life in the United States would never be the same again.

For Churchill's party, used to the far more stringent blackout restrictions of wartime London, their impression on arrival was nevertheless of "the amazing spectacle of a whole city lighted up." Churchill's aide de camp, Commander Tommy Thompson, declared that "Washington represented something immensely precious. Freedom, hope, strength. We had not seen an illuminated city for five years. My heart filled."[85] The view was made even more spectacular as the British first saw it from the air, having taken the last leg of their journey by plane after anchoring at Chesapeake Bay. The initial plan had been to sail up the Potomac River, but Churchill, according to Moran, "was like a child in his impatience to meet the President. He spoke as if every minute counted. It was absurd to waste time; he must fly."[86]

The British prime minister remained alive to the "serious danger that the United States might pursue the war against Japan in the Pacific and leave us to fight Germany and Italy in Europe, Africa and in the Middle East."[87] His mind was put at ease during the first session of the conference, when Roosevelt reaffirmed the administration's commitment to deal with Germany first. Marshall recorded after this initial session that "the President considered it very important to morale, to give the country a feeling that they are in the war, to give the Germans the reverse effect, to have American troops somewhere in active fighting across the Atlantic."[88] Churchill was aware, however, that the president's strategy remained susceptible to shifts in American public opinion. Therefore, on the second day of his visit he stressed to reporters that, while the remarkable resources of the United States would ensure that soon there would be more than enough supplies for every theater, the most pressing issue now was the allocation of scarce supplies to the fight against Hitler.[89]

Churchill followed this up on December 26 in his address to a joint meeting of Congress. He frankly told his audience that it would be "a long and hard war," but the productive power of the "English-speaking world" would ultimately eclipse "anything that has been seen or forseen in the dictator states." His voice rising to a crescendo, he thundered, "What sort of people do they think we are? Is it not possible they do not realize that we shall never cease to persevere against them until they have been taught a lesson which they and the world will never forget?"[90] Roars of approval rang around the chamber, with one Roosevelt administration official describing it as "the first sound of blood lust I have yet heard in the war."[91] The drama of Churchill's arrival and appearance before Congress captured the broader public imagination. His "presence and actions here seem to have made real for the first time a sense of alliance between the United States and Britain," Roosevelt was informed by his administration's Office of Facts and Figures. "The need for overall planning of grand strategy is now generally recognized," and, "more than anything else, Mr. Churchill's words have fostered an awareness that the war is on a planetary scale."[92]

Five days after Churchill's speech, on the very last day of the year, the British and US chiefs of staff agreed on an Allied "grand strategy." "Notwithstanding the entry of Japan into the war," they declared, "our view remains that Germany is still the prime enemy and her defeat is the key to victory." Once that had been achieved, the collapse of Italy and Japan would quickly follow. For this reason, the chiefs suggested that "only the minimum of force necessary for the safeguarding of vital interest in other theatres should be diverted from operations against Germany."[93] In other words, the "Germany first" strategy articulated back in February 1941, well before the open belligerency of the United States, was reaffirmed not long after Pearl Harbor.

Roosevelt and Churchill now moved to formalize the principles for which they were fighting by issuing a joint declaration signed by all the anti-Axis nations. Roosevelt's continued concern about preserving domestic unity meant he was unwilling to term this an alliance, fearing that it would force him to put a treaty before the Senate, where it was sure to arouse great controversy. For all Churchill's popular appeal, he remained the embodiment of the British Empire. As Roosevelt privately noted to one adviser during Churchill's visit, "As a people, as a country, we're opposed to imperialism—we can't stomach it." As a result, "this distrust, this dislike and even hatred of Britain" that Americans traditionally felt "make for all kinds of difficulties" in forging closer Anglo-American relations.[94] Combined with the anxiety, particularly prevalent among conservative Republicans, that a Soviet victory over Germany would lead to the spread of Communism and the historic American aversion to "entangling alliances" in general, this left Roosevelt searching for a different title for the anti-Axis forces. Ultimately, he hit on "United Nations." According to Hopkins, on coining this phrase the president had himself wheeled into Churchill's guest room to share his idea, only to find him in the bath. Churchill laughed off Roosevelt's embarrassment by standing, fully naked, and declaring, "The Prime Minister of Great Britain has nothing to hide from the President of the United States!"[95] The story would come to symbolize the growing intimacy of the wartime partnership between their two nations.

The "Declaration by United Nations" was issued on New Year's Day 1942. Recalling the Atlantic Charter of August 14, 1941, the signatories committed themselves to "employ the full resources, military or economic" against the members of the Axis with which they were already at war, to cooperate with the other Allied powers, and not to make a separate peace. The declaration was initially signed by Roosevelt, Churchill, Litvinov on behalf of the Soviets, and Hu Shih for China. It was then countersigned by twenty-two other nations the following day to demonstrate that the war "was being waged for freedom of small nations as well as great."[96] The signatories expressed the hope that their declaration "may be adhered to by other nations which are, or which may be rendering material assistance and contributions in the struggle for victory over Hitlerism."[97] Roosevelt managed to convince the atheist

Soviets to sign up to a document committed to "religious freedom" by pointing out that this "meant freedom to have a religion or not to, as one saw fit." The US president's appeal for India to be included among the signatories, principally to placate American domestic opinion, was accepted by Churchill, although he angrily resisted the president's additional appeals to go further in the direction of Indian independence.[98] American anti-imperialism was a major obstacle for Churchill. His was a "vision of the ultimate conjunction of the English-speaking peoples," joining together to control global affairs after the conflict.[99] But this did not prevent an unparalleled integration of the British and American war efforts, in a manner matched by no other two combatants.

The personal rapport between Roosevelt and Churchill was central to this new arrangement. During the three weeks of Churchill's stay at the White House, the two men dined together with Hopkins on most days and stayed up to the early hours drinking, smoking, and strategizing most nights. While the principals bonded, their political advisers and the generals formalized the "common-law marriage" established before America's intervention. In an unprecedented step for two great powers at war, a Combined Chiefs of Staff in Washington was established to coordinate their grand strategy. An agreement was also reached to cooperate closely on intelligence gathering, and joint committees were set up on shipping and munitions production. Crucially, the British secured American agreement that combined wartime production would be treated as a common pool, with supplies allocated to the forces best placed to advance the overall strategic priorities of the United Nations. Assignments would be decided by a new Joint Munitions Assignment Board, headed up on each side of the Atlantic by Hopkins and Beaverbrook.

It was by now clear that Lend-Lease would not only continue but be greatly expanded. Roosevelt told the army that foreign aid shipments must resume without restrictions on January 1 and everything possible done to fill the gaps caused by the temporary embargo. In particular, supply commitments to the Soviet Union, which were already in arrears before Pearl Harbor, must be prioritized and deficits made up as soon as practicable.[100] To ensure that the United States could maximize its own military commitment and also serve as the "arsenal of the democracy," Roosevelt, encouraged by Beaverbrook and Monnet, ordered a massive expansion of American industry and production targets.[101] In his State of the Union on January 6, 1942, the president told Americans that victory was "a task not only of shooting and fighting, but an even more urgent one of working and producing," because "the superiority of the United Nations in munitions and ships must be overwhelming—so overwhelming that the Axis Nations can never hope to catch up with it." While "Germany, Italy and Japan are very close to their maximum output of planes, guns, tanks, and ships, the United Nations are not—especially the United States of America."[102]

The production figures announced by Roosevelt were so "astronomical," according to the *US News*, that "only by symbols could they be understood: a plane every four minutes in 1943; a tank every seven minutes; two seagoing ships a day."[103] Aware of the impact this looming onslaught of American power would have on the country's enemies, Roosevelt hoped "that all these figures which I have given will become common knowledge in Germany and Japan."[104] Returning to London "drunk with the figures" and having agreed on a coordinated grand strategy with the Americans that would focus on Germany first, Churchill informed his cabinet that now "nothing would get in the way of defeating Hitler."[105] As the prime minister, the president, and their advisers had agreed that winter in Washington, and as Churchill would later declare in another address to Congress, "It was evident that, while the defeat of Japan would not mean the defeat of Germany, the defeat of Germany would infallibly mean the ruin of Japan."[106]

HITLER'S GLOBAL WAR required a global strategy. On December 13, 1941, he met with the Japanese ambassador, Oshima, to discuss the new situation.[107] The Führer stressed the relief that the US entry into the war represented for the Kriegsmarine, which would now be able to attack American shipping at will. Presenting his strategic conception for 1942, he said that major operations in Russia would be resumed in the New

Year. In the meantime, Hitler planned to concentrate his attention on the Mediterranean, where he had deployed large numbers of submarines and aircraft. He stated that his "principal aim" was "first the destruction of Russia," then an "advance cross the Caucasus towards the south" and the "torpedoing of the Anglo-Saxon navies and merchant marine." His first blow in Russia would be in the south, partly "because of the oil," to be followed by the strike into Iraq and Iran against the British Empire. On several occasions during this briefing, Oshima suggested that Japan and the Reich coordinate their operations, but Hitler showed little interest. The only thing he specifically asked of the Japanese was that they cut off the supply of American war material to the Soviet Union via Vladivostok, which they never did.

In practice, Hitler struggled to develop a coherent strategy in early 1942. As Walter Warlimont, the deputy chief of the operations staff of the OKW from December 1941, recalls, no thought had been given to the likely American strategy either.[108] Hitler did not even issue a fresh directive addressing the new situation. This was because the Führer had no viable strategy for defeating the Americans. They were the world's greatest economic power, and he was quite simply stumped. "I am not yet sure," Hitler admitted to Oshima with disarming honesty on January 3, 1942, "how to defeat the United States."[109]

In Russia, Hitler confronted a rapidly deteriorating situation. Until December 12–13, 1941, the Wehrmacht was just about holding its own on the central front; thereafter, it began to give way.[110] In a report to Stalin on December 12, Zhukov, as commander of the Soviet western front, would claim that his forces had inflicted significant damage on German forces from December 6 to 10, with ground forces alone destroying 271 and capturing 386 tanks, for example. He would go on to claim that more than eighty-five thousand German troops had been killed according to incomplete figures. Zhukov concluded with the statement, "The pursuit and destruction of the retreating German forces continues."[111] "There is only bad news," panzer group commander Erich Hoepner wrote on December 12, 1941, as the telephone announced one Russian breakthrough after the other. He compared Germany's situation with that of Napoleon in 1812.[112] "The catastrophe," officer Hellmuth Stieff wrote to his wife the following day, "is at the door," a deserved punishment, in his view, for Nazi crimes.[113] That same day, the mighty Sixth Panzer Division reported a strength of just 350 riflemen and no tanks.[114] There were no reserves. All leave was canceled.

A change of course was clearly needed. On December 16, Hitler issued his legendary "halt order." To avoid a general rout and the loss of irreplaceable equipment, all units were to stand fast, showing "fanatical resistance," until reinforcements had arrived from Germany and new positions had been prepared to the rear.[115] The following day, on December 19, 1941, Hitler sacked Brauchitsch and took over supreme command of the army himself. The winter crisis was not over; on the contrary, it was only just beginning.[116]

Hitler saw the new conflict as primarily one of attrition. The key to victory therefore lay in production and destruction, with shipping a critical front. Hitler saw the "tonnage problem" as "the decisive question of the conduct of the war." Whoever solved it would "probably win the war."[117] Either the U-boats would sink enough shipping to cut Britain off from its "lifelines," or they themselves would be sunk in sufficient number to render the destruction of the Reich inevitable. The same logic applied in the air, on the ground, and in all theaters. The fronts were closely connected in Hitler's mind, not least because of the vast quantities of matériel being supplied to the Russians through Lend-Lease. Right at the end of December 1941, he remarked to Admiral Raeder that he would rather see the sinking in the Arctic of "four ships bringing tanks to the Russian front" than the destruction of much larger tonnage in the south Atlantic.[118]

Despite the nasty shock he had received in 1941 regarding the quantity and quality of Russian equipment, Hitler's main focus was on matching not the output of the Soviets, but that of Britain and, especially, the United States. On January 10, 1942, as the winter crisis raged in the east, Hitler set out his priorities. "The long-term aim," he decreed, "remains the expansion of the Luftwaffe and the Navy to fight the Anglo-Saxon powers."[119] These goals had not shifted since 1940–1941; all that had changed was the timing. Now, in a concession to the unexpectedly strong resistance put up by the Red Army and the imperative to capture the Soviet resources necessary to outlast the United States and Britain, Hitler ordered that production should concentrate "initially" on the "increased needs" of the army; the other two services were to take a step back, for now.[120] Particular attention was paid to the production of ammunition, which was deemed more urgent than tanks.[121]

To meet the new production requirements, the Reich needed millions more workers. Hitler proposed to make up the shortfall by drafting Russian prisoners. On Christmas Eve, he issued a formal decree determining that the "decisive" issue for the German war economy was now the question of how to integrate the Soviet prisoners of war into the system of production. This required, he continued, "the provision of adequate rations and banishing the danger of a typhus epidemic."[122] The racial hierarchy at the start of Barbarossa had thus been reversed. Then, Hitler had planned to starve the Slavs of the Soviet Union to death but keep the Jews of central and western Europe alive as hostages. Now the Soviet Slavs would live, if only to work, and the Jews would die.

THERE WERE SOME Axis attempts to formalize their collaboration. Ribbentrop and Oshima quickly agreed that they would not consult the Italians. Despite its title—"Military Agreement Between Germany, Italy, and Japan"—the document signed on January 18, 1942, was effectively a Germany-Japan agreement.[123] It was decided that everything to the west of seventy degrees east meridian—that is, roughly a line drawn north-south through Karachi—would be the German and Italian area of operations. Everything to the east of it would fall into the Japanese sphere. The agreement specifically permitted both sides to operate across the boundary line in the Indian Ocean, an exemption that was clearly intended to authorize such endeavors by the much larger and more capable Japanese Navy.[124]

Operationally, the plan was for the Japanese to attack British and American bases in the greater East Asian space and to secure command of the sea in the western Pacific. If the Allies concentrated a large part of their naval forces in the Atlantic, then Japan should detach some of its own units to deal with them, thereafter stepping up its commerce raiding in the Pacific and Indian Ocean. The powerful Japanese Navy would thereby compensate somewhat for the global inadequacy of the Kriegsmarine. For their part, the Germans and the Italians would focus on control of the Middle East, the Mediterranean, and the Atlantic. If the Allies concentrated their fleets in the Pacific, then the Germans and Italians would send some of their ships there to support Japan. Above and beyond that, the three Axis powers committed to sharing information and collaborating in the war on Allied shipping.

Unlike the United States and Britain, though, the Third Reich never developed a worked-out strategy with its partners.[125] The Japanese constantly pressed for closer coordination, but Hitler showed little interest. The reasons for this were simple. Hitler hesitated to support Tokyo's demand for an all-out attack on British India because he still hoped for a negotiated settlement with London.[126] Hitler also largely ignored Japanese suggestions of a compromise peace between him and Stalin in order to focus on the Anglo-Americans, because he did not think that one could be had without giving up the Ukraine, which in his eyes was a vital counterbalance to Britain and the United States. The Japanese, for their part, did not respond to Hitler's attempt to mediate between Tokyo and Chiang Kai-shek, for the related reason that control of China was central to their conception of an empire large enough to stand up to the Anglo-Saxons.[127]

Axis strategic military coordination was thus very limited. In mid-February 1942, the Führer did not respond to the demands of the Japanese military attachés, Vice Admiral Nomura and Lieutenant General Ichiro Banzai, and of his own naval leadership to link up.[128] Hitler never really intended to join hands with the Japanese in the Indian Ocean, primarily because he didn't think he had the capacity to do so in the near future.[129] The Führer also believed that he didn't know enough about Japanese capabilities to make useful suggestions to their high command.[130] This may well have been the right decision, because—unlike

Britain and the United States, who in many respects had a shared strategic culture—Germany and Japan had no experience of military cooperation or joint values to fall back on. No summits, no hymn singing, hardly any statements, no staff talks worth the name, none of the whole panoply of grand alliance. The planned air bridge between the two halves of the Axis petered out after two flights, both Italian.[131]

The geo-ideological alignment between the two main Axis powers, by contrast, was close.[132] They envisaged the establishment of a new world order in which the German Reich dominated Europe and the Japanese Empire the "Greater East Asia Co-prosperity Sphere." Together, they would claim their fair share of the world's resources and global recognition. The United States and the British Empire would not be broken up entirely, but rather confined to a much smaller global zone of influence. There would not necessarily be Axis world domination as such, but rather—from their point of view—a more equitable distribution of global power and global goods. Anglo-Saxon hegemony would give way to Axis-led multipolarity. The agreement of January 18, 1942, should therefore not be seen as a worked-out plan for victory, but rather as a partitioning of the globe between Germany and Japan.

THE AXIS JOINT strategy got off to a mixed start. Imperial Japan enjoyed a run of victories after Pearl Harbor. Wake Island was soon subdued and so was Guam. Hong Kong fell before the end of 1941. Although the Japanese met stiff American resistance on the Philippines under General MacArthur, he was soon forced to withdraw from Manila to Bataan. Not long after, the Japanese invaded the Dutch East Indies and Dutch Borneo. An attempt by Allied naval forces to intervene was crushed in the Java Sea. The Japanese also pushed into Burma and the Solomon Islands in the South Pacific. In mid-February 1942, the British surrendered at Singapore. Among those captured by the Japanese forces were Fergus Anckorn and thousands of his Eighteenth Infantry Division colleagues. Their convoy had ultimately been diverted from the Middle East, first sailing to Bombay. Then, after a brigade was split off to defend Malaya, the full division was sent in installments to Singapore to reinforce its beleaguered garrison. After sailing almost eighteen thousand miles and having spent around three months virtually uninterrupted at sea, the Eighteenth Infantry Division reassembled in Singapore just days before the fortress fell. They would soon experience the brutality of Japan's prisoner of war camps; many, including Anckorn, were forced to work on the notorious Burma railway.[133] Three weeks after the fall of Singapore, the Dutch gave up in Java. All this, as the British anti-colonialist historian Margery Perham wrote in March 1942, wrought "a very practical revolution in race relationships."[134] Old hierarchies were suddenly inverted; the "white man" was cast down. Militarily, the Japanese tide seemed unstoppable, and the agreed Allied focus on Europe increasingly unsustainable.

Germany, by contrast, was already in crisis. To be sure, the U-boats enjoyed a brief, happy time slaughtering American shipping before a convoy system was introduced. Elsewhere, though, the news was grim. Rommel was on the back foot in North Africa. Worse still, the whole eastern front was in danger of collapsing. Despite Hitler's "halt order," the German line broke in several places. Whole divisions were cut off and had to be supplied from the air. The magnitude of the disaster could no longer be concealed from an anxious German public. Throughout the first three months of the year, the fighting raged in Army Group Center. Stalin hoped, and many Germans feared, that war might end there and then. It took until the end of March 1942 before the Russian front was completely stabilized.

Meanwhile, the radicalization of policy toward the Jews, announced immediately after the declaration of war on the United States, proceeded apace. On January 20, 1942, Reinhard Heydrich finally held his long-planned conference in the villa on the Wannsee.[135] The assembled bureaucrats discussed definitions of who was a Jew and the modalities of "deportation," which by this stage meant mass murder. The lists included not merely numbers of Jews in the areas under German control or countries presumably still to be conquered or coerced, such as Sweden. Hitler was clearly determined to eliminate the Jewish presence in Europe—the whole of Europe—for all time. A Rubicon had been crossed. Despite the slaughter of Soviet and Serbian Jewry in 1941, most European Jews were still alive at the start of 1942; by the end of the year, most of them would be dead.[136]

On December 12, 1941, the day after Hitler's declaration of war on the United States, the train with Jewish deportees from Kassel had reached the Riga ghetto. The following day, the transport from Düsseldorf arrived.[137] They enjoyed a brief respite in terrible conditions, but the vast majority soon met the same fate as the Latvian Jews who had been murdered to make way for them. During the summer of 1942, the scope of the killing was widened to the entire Jewish population of the Generalgouvernement in Poland. They were deported to, and for the most part murdered in, camps such as Belzec, Treblinka, and, of course, Auschwitz, which became an extermination camp. The corpses were burned in the crematoria that the company of J. A. Topf and Sons had been erecting in December 1941. Over the next three and half years or so, the vast majority of Jews under Nazi control were murdered, a crime primarily, though not exclusively, driven by Hitler's anti-Semitic antagonism toward the "plutocratic" powers, which culminated in his declaration of war on the United States.

In March–June 1942, the Axis moved to the next stage of its joint strategy, such as it was. The Japanese carrier strike force, Kido Butai, swept into the Indian Ocean, sank an old British aircraft carrier and two cruisers, and bombarded Ceylon. Further operations were planned south toward the Coral Sea, to cut Australia off from the United States, and east against Midway, to lure the American carrier force out to its destruction. In North Africa, Rommel surged forward and appeared within striking distance of Egypt and Palestine. In the Arctic, the Luftwaffe and the Kriegsmarine largely destroyed PQ17, an Allied convoy bringing military aid to Stalin. In Russia, the Wehrmacht captured Sevastopol, and German tanks raced toward the Caucasus. Their target was the oil fields of Maikop and Baku, and ultimately those of Iraq and Persia. It seemed possible that the Axis powers might link up in the Persian Gulf or the Indian Ocean.

Meanwhile, Hitler escalated his foreign propaganda. Within Europe, Nazi agitators targeted Bolshevism, international capitalism, and the Jews. In the rest of the world, they primarily took aim at the British Empire, the United States, international capitalism, and the Jews. As the Germans prepared to attack the Middle East, the Caucasus, and Persia—with Afghanistan apparently in contention—much of the focus was on the area east of Libya and west of India. For this reason, Nazi propagandists bombarded Arab audiences throughout the summer of 1942 with stories about the "Jewish" White House of President Roosevelt.[138]

In Britain, the bleak strategic picture, particularly in the Pacific, led to a parliamentary challenge to Churchill. The prime minister had returned from Washington to find "an embarrassed, unhappy, baffled public opinion . . . swelling and mounting about me on every side."[139] In a closed session of the House of Commons during his absence, Chips Channon noted that "there was continued criticism of the Government, a barrage of questions, bickering and obvious dislike. . . . No Government could survive such unpopularity for long."[140] At the end of January, amid growing disapproval of his government's conduct of the war, the prime minister effectively told his critics to put up or shut up, demanding a "declaration of confidence of the House of Commons as an additional weapon in the armoury of the United Nations."[141] After a three-day debate, he secured a resounding victory by 464 votes to 1. Yet, with the loss of Singapore in February, which Churchill called the "greatest disaster to British arms" in history, the criticism resumed with a vengeance.[142]

The ferocious Japanese offensive across the Pacific also put serious pressure on the Roosevelt administration to switch to a Pacific-first strategy. While in late December, polling had shown roughly 60 percent of Americans accepted the administration's argument that Hitler was the main enemy, by February the majority opinion was reversed, with more than twice as many respondents wanting to concentrate America's war effort against Japan as against Germany.[143] "Only by an intellectual effort had the Americans been convinced that Germany and not Japan was the most dangerous enemy," Stimson later told Churchill. "The enemy whom the American people really hated," the war secretary continued, "was Japan which had dealt them a foul blow."[144]

Animosity was particularly pronounced on the Pacific Coast, home to the vast majority of Japanese immigrants. After a government report found extensive espionage by Japanese nationals before the Pearl Harbor attack, this exacerbated existing racial antagonism and fueled further claims, this time false, that Japanese American citizens were engaged in sabotage, presenting a substantial threat to national security. Facing widespread public appeals to act, Roosevelt accepted the War Department's argument that it was a "military necessity" that 110,000 Japanese be forcibly "relocated" in February to what the president himself called "concentration camps." Roosevelt only requested that it be conducted as reasonably as possible, and he evinced little concern at the suffering that resulted.[145] He was aware that this order violated the Bill of Rights, which he had so publicly invoked just two months previously to justify America's war effort. It also singled out the Japanese while failing to take similar action against Germans and Italians, provoking inevitable charges of racial discrimination. Yet, as his attorney general Francis Biddle, who alone opposed the policy in cabinet, later wrote, Roosevelt was "never theoretical about things." With the military claiming it was necessary and the public on their side, "there was no question of any substantial opposition, which might tend toward the disunity that at all costs he must avoid."[146] In fact, there was little real military justification for the policy, and the incarceration would be described by the American Civil Liberties Union as the "worst single wholescale violation of civil rights of American citizens in our history."[147] It was an illustration, above all else, of just how far Roosevelt was willing to go to prevent substantial domestic dissension that he felt might undermine the prospect of winning the war.

As Japanese successes continued to mount, so did public pressure for complete American preoccupation with the Pacific, particularly after a valiant stand at the Bataan Peninsula was followed by the capture of thirty-five thousand Americans and Filipinos on April 9, the largest surrender in American history. Roosevelt responded by ordering the dispatch of such a large proportion of American forces to the Pacific that the balance of America's war effort was slightly tilted toward the region for the rest of the year. With the loss of Singapore signaling the demise of Britain's status as a major power in East Asia—leading Britain to a renewed concentration on propping up its position in the Middle East and India—the American role in the Pacific became more import- ant than ever, particularly for the protection of Australia. At the same time, Roosevelt remained determined to get US ground forces swiftly into battle against the European Axis, overcoming opposition from his service chiefs to press for a North African offensive that would begin in November 1942 and laying the foundations for an overwhelming shift to a "Germany first" approach from 1943.[148] It was the anticipation of the impending arrival of American troops and matériel to bolster both theaters that enabled Churchill to again face down his critics during an- other secret session of the Commons on April 23. As Chips Channon recorded: "We left the Chamber confident that the war would, after all, be won, thanks chiefly to the stupendous American production."[149]

For the rest of that spring, however, as General Alan Brooke recalled, the British were "literally hanging on by our eyelids! Australia and India were threatened by the Japanese, we had temporarily lost control of the Indian Ocean, the Germans were threatening Persia and our oil, Auchin- leck was in precarious straits in the desert, and the submarine sinkings were heavy."[150] Churchill dubbed the Japanese Indian Ocean raid "the most dangerous moment of the war."[151] Despite the overwhelming Allied industrial superiority, the outcome still seemed uncertain.

In reality, though, the Germans and the Japanese were running on engine fumes, their industrial and raw-material tanks far too empty to deliver the decisive victory they so desperately needed. By early sum- mer, the Axis advance was faltering, and by the autumn it had completely ground to a halt. In the Battle of the Coral Sea in May 1942, the first car- rier battle in history, the Japanese were forced to turn back. The Japanese advance toward Port Moresby was halted. A month later, Kido Butai was surprised by American dive-bombers at Midway and annihilated. Four Japanese carriers were sunk. The *Prince of Wales* and the *Repulse* had been avenged. Shortly after, the Americans counterattacked at Guadalcanal.

The Royal Navy returned in strength to the Indian Ocean and remained dominant there until the end of the war.[152] The Pacific war turned into a war of attrition in the Solomons: on land, at sea, and in the air. This was a conflict that only the United States, with its vast industrial base, would win. Admiral Yamamoto's prediction had been vindicated.

In Hitler's area of operations, things were no better. A British raid on Dieppe, France, in August 1942 suffered heavy casualties but was a portent of the Anglo-American intention to return to mainland Europe. The thrust into the Caucasus was halted well short of Baku in the late summer of 1942. The Wehrmacht now concentrated on trying to capture Stalingrad, itself a poor substitute for Moscow. Plans to finish off Leningrad had to be shelved. In North Africa, Rommel was first checked, and then thrown back at the Battle of El-Alamein. Then the Russians counterattacked at Stalingrad, with the help of vital Allied supplies, cutting off the entire Sixth Army.[153] There were still hopes in Berlin that the British could be starved out through the U-boat campaign, but by the following Easter, the tide had turned there too.

THE REST OF the conflict consisted of what Churchill later declared in his memoirs as the application of overwhelming Allied force.[154] The "war of motors," which Stalin had spoken of, was won by American production, just as he had said it would be. The American industrial "cauldron," as Churchill had once described it, bubbled and hissed. It already massively outproduced the combined German and Japanese war economies.[155] Despite the millions of slave laborers pressed into service—who, just as the RSHA had feared, made Germany more ethnically diverse than it had ever been before—the Reich could never hope to win this race. Hitler himself was only too conscious of the disparity, and he came back repeatedly to the enormous productive power of the United States until the end of the war.[156]

This determined the outcome of the conflict in two ways. First of all, directly, through the US armed forces. After a mixed debut in the Pacific and North Africa, American armies increasingly stamped their authority on the war. Together with their British and Commonwealth allies, they cleared the Axis out of Sicily and southern Italy in 1943, knocking Italy out of the conflict. American tanks paraded through the streets of Rome, just as Ciano had said they would. Allied warships and merchant marine had won the battle for the Atlantic by March 1943. British and American bombers then took the war to the enemy, opening up a second front over the Reich, attacking both industrial targets and (especially in the case of the RAF) the civilian population. In 1944, the Allies landed in Normandy and eventually pushed all the way into Germany.

Second, the American war economy had a huge indirect impact through the supply of Lend-Lease equipment to the Soviet Union. The importance of Lend-Lease actually grew as the war continued. This aid came via the Arctic, Iran, and Vladivostok. Unlike 1941, the Red Army now had plenty of home-produced tanks and aircraft. What Lend-Lease gave them was a critical mobility that the Wehrmacht lacked. The speed of the Soviet advances from 1943 to 1945 would have been unthinkable without the American trucks and jeeps that transported men and supplies, the popular ration packs that fed them, or the radios that enabled communication between the spearheads and the generals.[157] When reviewing the totals shipped on the Arctic route alone, the naval historian Friedrich Ruge, who had served in the Kriegsmarine throughout the war, was in no doubt that "Anglo-American sea-power exerted a decisive influence on the land operations in Eastern Europe."[158]

As we have seen, Stalin was profoundly conscious of the value of Lend-Lease support during the conflict, especially in 1941. For the rest of the war, though, he said little to nothing about Lend-Lease, instead bitterly complaining about the absence of a "second front" until D-Day. During the Cold War, Anglo-American help was downplayed by the Soviet Union.[159] "Disagreements over Lend-Lease arose after the war," Molotov candidly recalled. "We hadn't noted them before."[160] In fact, Russian president Vladimir Putin recently emphasized that the Western Allies had rendered substantial help to the Soviet Union, which he estimated at about 7 percent of total Soviet military production.[161] But the United States didn't aid the Soviets with munitions alone. By the end of the war, it is estimated that over half of the vehicles in the Red Army were originally American produced. The oil to fuel them also came overwhelmingly from the United States, which produced around 65 percent of the world's petroleum at this time. By 1944, the country was refining 90 percent of the Allies' aviation fuel, with oil ultimately making up two-thirds of Lend-Lease supplies.[162] "This is a war of engines and octanes," Stalin again proclaimed, this time while proposing a toast at the 1943 Tehran Conference in the presence of Churchill and Roosevelt. "I drink to the American auto industry and the American oil industry."[163]

In late 1942, the Soviet Union went over to the attack. The German Sixth Army at Stalingrad capitulated in February 1943, and a major German offensive was halted at Kursk in July. By the end of the year, the Nazis had been driven out of most of the Ukraine. In the course of 1944, the Red Army surged forward again. Leningrad was relieved, after a siege that had lasted more than nine hundred days. The Crimea, site of the murder of the Jews of Simferopol, was liberated. In July 1944, the Russians tore the heart out of Army Group Center in Operation Bagration. The Red Army first reached German soil that autumn. In early 1945, the Russians began their final offensive on the Reich, which ended in the siege and capture of the imperial capital by early May 1945.

On the other side of the world, American industry sustained another epic contest. The Pacific Fleet was reconstituted. A veritable armada of aircraft carriers and landing craft was fitted out. The Japanese were driven out of the Solomons; Admiral Yamamoto was shot down during an inspection of the area in April 1943. Slowly but surely, the Americans hopped from island to island. Soon, mainland Japan was in range of the American bomber fleets. In Burma and northeast India, the Japanese were checked and thrown back by the British. The Royal Navy returned in strength to the Far East, this time with a substantial force of aircraft carriers. One Japanese capital ship after the other was sent to the bottom of the sea. The end of the battleship era, which Japanese naval aviators had inaugurated at Pearl Harbor and through the sinking of the *Prince of Wales* and the *Repulse*, was now completed by the US Navy.

As the tide turned, the cities of the Axis were subjected to a terrible retribution. In the early summer of 1942, Cologne, from which a transport of Jews had departed on December 7, 1941, was hit by a devastating RAF "thousand-bomber raid." By the end of the war, most of the city center had been leveled; only the iconic cathedral loomed out of the rubble, apparently undamaged. A year later, Hamburg, from which the transport arriving in Riga had originated, was struck by a blizzard of RAF incendiaries. Düsseldorf, from which another transport had departed on December 11, 1941, was also badly hit by Allied bombing. General Heinrici's Münster, already badly damaged when he was writing in December 1941, was wrecked by the end of the war; half the city and nine out of ten houses in the old city had been leveled. The imperial capital, Berlin, was struck on many occasions; in October 1943, one of the raids heavily damaged the new Japanese embassy.[164] Japan, too, was mercilessly firebombed, in this case by the Americans. The wooden houses of Japan burned intensely, just as Friedrich Kellner had suggested they would. In March 1945, for example, the writer Kafu Nagai's home was incinerated in a US air raid.[165] Japan was not just "ground to powder," as Churchill had predicted, but burned to ashes.

Slowly, resistance to Hitler mounted. Count Sponeck, who had played such a baleful role in the murder of the Crimean Jews, shortly afterward defied an order that would have led to the destruction of his division and was jailed in 1942. He was then killed in the aftermath of the abortive July 1944 assassination attempt on Hitler, and history has been kind to him as a consequence. Hellmuth Stieff, who had suffered so much at Moscow, was closely involved in the July plot. Despite sustained Gestapo torture, he refused to betray any of his comrades before he was executed. The clerical opposition that the security services had grappled with in December 1941 was treated with some circumspection; Hitler vowed to settle the account after the war had been won. None of these efforts, however, came close to dislodging the German dictator.

At the end of April 1945, as the Russians closed in on his bunker, Hitler committed suicide. In his "Political Testament," the Führer returned to the themes he had elaborated upon on December 11, 1941 (and, of course, on many occasions before and after). Hitler reiterated his view that the war was "desired and provoked solely by those international statesmen who were either of Jewish origin or who worked for Jewish interests." "I never wanted," Hitler continued, "that the first unholy world war" should have been followed by "a second one against Britain or even America." He lamented that German cities and cultural treasures had been reduced to "ruins," that millions of adult males had died at the front, and that hundreds of thousands of women and children had been burned in their cities, but he reminded his readers that he "left no one in any doubt" that the "real guilty party"—the Jews—"would have to pay for his guilt," if "by more humane means." This was an oblique, but unmistakable reference to his mass murder of the Jews in the gas chambers. Strikingly, this last will and testament made no direct mention of either Communism or the Soviet Union but inveighed instead against those Hitler saw as the real villains, "international money and finance conspirators" who treated the "peoples of Europe" like "blocks of shares."

Four months later, the United States dropped two atomic bombs on Japan. "Tokyo is a long way from Nagasaki," Admiral Ugaki had written back in December 1941 about the sinking of the *Prince of Wales* and the *Repulse*, "but vengeance may be exacted far from the scene of the original offence."[166] Now the United States had exacted its revenge at Nagasaki, far from the original site at Pearl Harbor. A few days after that, the Red Army attacked and defeated the Japanese Kwantung Army in Manchuria. Stalin had finally broken his agreement with Tokyo, honoring the spirit of his commitment to Chiang in late 1941 and the letter of his promise to the Allies at Yalta that he would declare war on Japan the moment Germany had been defeated. By the middle of the month, Japan had surrendered. On hearing the news, Admiral Ugaki embarked on a final fatal suicide mission. A fortnight later, a Japanese delegation—including Toshikazu Kase and the new foreign minister, Mamoru Shigemitsu—signed the official document of surrender on the USS *Missouri* in Tokyo Bay.

By the autumn of 1945, the world had been partitioned, but not in the way the Axis alliance of December 1941 had envisaged. The new dispensation both reflected and created new global realities. Most European Jews had been murdered. Germany had been utterly vanquished and partitioned into four zones of occupation; the anti-Nazi diarist Friedrich Kellner's son Fred, now a US citizen, served in the American one. The European center had collapsed. The western half of the continent was dominated by the Anglo-Saxons, the eastern half by the Soviet Union. If the Germans and Japanese had previously reckoned themselves leaders of the global have-nots, then the little they had had now been taken from them. Western colonialism was briefly reinstated in East Asia, but its nimbus had been destroyed forever, shattered by the fall of Singapore and the other military humiliations inflicted by Japan on the white man in 1941 and 1942. The Anglo-Saxons still dominated most of the world, but the balance between the British Empire and the United States had shifted decisively toward the latter.

Most of this was inevitable after Hitler declared war on the United States on December 11, 1941. It was by no means a forgone conclusion on December 6, or even on December 8, just after Pearl Harbor. As we have seen, many alternative outcomes were discussed at the time. The world of August 1945 was only one of several that seemed possible in early December 1941. Japan might have attacked the Soviet Union to avenge the defeats of 1938–1939. Russia might have declared war on Japan in solidarity with the Western Allies. Hitler might have backed out of declaring war on the United States.[167] Japan could have attacked the British Empire only, and not the Americans. Each of these alternatives, and their permutations, would have produced a substantially different world in 1945.

If Japan had attacked Britain but not the United States—Churchill's nightmare scenario and one that Hitler had promoted in 1940 and early 1941—it would have been an even greater disaster than British planners had expected. Roosevelt would have struggled to persuade the US public to join the war. India might have fallen. A linkup of the Axis partners in the Indian Ocean and Persian Gulf would have been quite feasible. British resources would have been stretched to the breaking point, damaging Britain's capacity to fight Hitler. This was why Roosevelt feared any such Japanese move and did his best to deter it. This option was considered but rejected by Tokyo out of fear that the United States would intervene on Britain's behalf. Roosevelt's bluff had worked.

Though Pearl Harbor clarified the relationship between Japan and the Anglo-Saxon powers, the future still appeared open in other respects. Churchill's other nightmare—and the two were not mutually exclusive—was that the United States would not formally enter the European conflict after Pearl Harbor, unless Hitler did him the favor of declaring war. In that event, the confrontation between the US Navy and the Kriegsmarine in the Atlantic could have been wound down as Congress and public opinion forced Roosevelt to concentrate on defeating the Japanese. The resulting diversion of American industrial capacity would have either ended or seriously reduced the Lend-Lease program. If that had happened, the British would have struggled in the Atlantic, they would have been much weaker in the skies over Europe, and they would have had fewer tanks and guns to deploy in North Africa. In that event, Stalin might have been able to hold the line in 1942–1943, but offensives of the kind he actually mounted in the last two and half years of the war would have been impossible. The course of military operations would have been completely different.

Nobody can be sure how European Jewry would have fared if Hitler had not declared war on the United States on December 11, or on some later date. The Soviet Jews under Nazi control had already been murdered, and so had many others. But most European Jews were still alive, and Hitler's plans for them were closely connected to his relationship with the United States. The deportation of the central and western European Jews had been planned some time before December 11, 1941, but as Hitler's remarks on December 12 show, their situation deteriorated markedly from that day.

For Stalin, the threat of a Japanese attack receded after December 7, 1941, but it was still a possibility. He also had to deal with initial American pressure to declare war on Japan in solidarity. Given that Stalin had bested the Japanese twice in the 1930s, any such war would probably have ended in a Soviet victory, but its impact in late 1941 and early 1942 would nevertheless have been substantial. Conflict would certainly have led to the closing of the Vladivostok aid route from the United States. It would have forced Stalin to transfer forces back east when he was grappling with Hitler in the west.

Of course, the future was not actually as open as it seemed on December 6, 1941. Hitler believed that war with the United States was inevitable, and he had promised the Japanese that he would support them. Thanks to their intelligence reports, Churchill and Roosevelt strongly suspected this. Likewise, Stalin knew that the Japanese were not planning to attack him in the east. But neither the two Western leaders nor the Soviet dictator could be entirely sure. Churchill did not sleep as soundly the night of Pearl Harbor as he subsequently claimed, and he had good reason not to do so. The United States had long stood on the cusp of world power, but it was Hitler's December 11 declaration that supplied the final push. It was only then that the United States became fully engaged in the war, against every Axis power and in every theater, and could deploy its preeminent economic power to create the most powerful military machine in global history.

It is often claimed that Hitler attacked the United States in ignorance or in spite of its immense power. This is not so. As we have seen, he declared war on the United States *because* of its colossal industrial and demographic potential. In late 1941, the Führer saw a narrow window of opportunity not to defeat the United States outright but to create a self-sufficient Axis bloc strong enough to withstand it. Otherwise, he risked gradual strangulation. Thanks not least to Roosevelt's skillful messaging, Hitler committed suicide for fear of dying. It was he, and not the president, who had ultimately brought the United States into the war, dooming the Third Reich. Likewise, the Japanese felt the only alternative to accepting American hegemony was a desperate and probably doomed attempt to secure the economic basis for an independent existence. Like the Germans, they saw a choice, as one Japanese statesman had put it before Pearl Harbor, between becoming "gradually poor" and becoming "utterly poor." That has been the fate of the have-nots down the ages.

Conflict between the Axis powers and the United States was inescapable for geopolitical, economic, and ideological reasons. Their defeat was also inevitable, but Germany and Japan could still choose the manner of their destruction, and they chose the most terrible.

ACKNOWLEDGMENTS

WRITING A BOOK is a monumental task in normal times but even more amid a global pandemic. We are glad to have the opportunity to acknowledge all those who have helped make this book possible.

At a time when we have largely been confined to our homes, we are grateful to the librarians and archivists who have helped us to locate particular sources and documents in their collections. Where possible, we have thanked them individually in the relevant endnotes.

Our editors at Basic Books, Lara Heimert, Claire Potter, Brandon Proia, Abigail Mohr, Kelly Lenkevich, and Elizabeth Dana, Simon Winder at Penguin, and our agent, Bill Hamilton, have made innumerable suggestions that have helped make this a better book.

We would like to thank all those who kindly commented on earlier drafts of this book or helped in other ways: Josh Abbey, Chris Andrew, Karri Aston, Triffie Axworthy, John Barber, Keisha N. Blain, Sam Clements, Alan Donohue, Nele Glang, Christian Goeschel, Edwina Goodwin, Daniel Hedinger, Suzanne Heim, Chris Helmecke, Alexander Hill, Eri Hotta, Bruce Hudson, Stefan Huebner, William Inboden, Julian Jackson, Gerhard Keiper, Paul Kennedy, Gerhard Krebs, Christoph Kreutzmüller, Barak Kushner, Daniel Laderman, Rhonda Laderman, Sheila

Lawlor, Francesco Lefebvre, Peter Lieb, Mina Markovic, Bernd Martin, Evan Mawdsley, Steven McGregor, Sean McMeekin, Jay Mens, Aaron Moore, Sönke Neitzel, Federico Niglia, Mikael Nilsson, Phil O'Brien, Allen Packwood, Alessio Patalano, John Pollard, Andrew Preston, Anja Reuss, Sven Saaler, Klaus Schmider, Bastian Matteo Scianna, Jason Sharman, Constance Simms, Hugh Simms, Katherine Simms, Danny Snyder, Sarah Snyder, Monika Sommerer, David Stahel, Enrico Syring, Sylvia Taschka, Geraint Thomas, John Thompson, Chika Tonooka, Karine Varley, James Vitali, Chris Wadibia, Liz Wake, Gerhard Weinberg, and Andrew Williams. Kristina Nazariyan and Nora Topor-Kalinskij kindly located and translated Russian sources for us. While Eliza Charnock-Laderman is far too young to have read the manuscript, she was a source of joy and inspiration for her father throughout the writing process.

Charlie Laderman is very grateful to the support of colleagues at the War Studies Department, King's College, London, and for the opportunity provided by Peterhouse, University of Cambridge, to be a senior research associate for the 2019–2020 academic year. He would also like to acknowledge the generous support of the Harrington Faculty Fellowship, which enabled him to spend a year as a visiting professor at the University of Texas, Austin, based at the Clements Center for National Security, at the outset of this project. Brendan Simms would like to thank his colleagues at the Centre for Geopolitics, at Peterhouse, and at the Department of Politics and International Studies, all at the University of Cambridge.

Our families have offered advice, encouragement, and support, without which this book simply would not have been completed. The greatest debt is owed to our wives, Drs. Anita Bunyan and Emily Charnock, who made very helpful suggestions on the text and put up with our prolonged absence in December 1941. This book is for them.

ABBREVIATIONS

AA	Auswärtiges Amt
ADAP	Akten zur Auswärtigen Politik
ADM	Admiralty
AK	Armeekorps
Anckorn	Anckorn, Fergus Gordon (Oral History), Imperial War Museums
AOK	Armeeoberkommando
AVIA 12/123	Ministry of Supply and Ministry of Aviation: Second World War and Miscellaneous Unregistered Papers, UK National Archives
BA	Bundesarchiv
Biddle Papers	Francis Biddle Papers, Franklin D. Roosevelt Library
Bock diary	Generalfeldmarschal Fedor von Bock Das Kriegstagebuch
CAB 65	Cabinet Conclusions, UK National Archives
CAB 79	War Cabinet and Cabinet: Chiefs of Staff Committee: Minutes, UK National Archives
CAB 121	Cabinet Office: Special Secret Information Centre: Files, UK National Archives

Abbreviations

CAB 122	War Cabinet and Cabinet Office: British Joint Staff Mission and British Joint Services: Washington Office Records, UK National Archives
CHAR	Chartwell Papers, Papers of Winston Churchill, Churchill Archives Centre
CHOH	Churchill Oral History, Churchill Archives Centre, Churchill College, Cambridge
CHUR	Churchill Papers, Papers of Winston Churchill, Churchill Archives Centre, Churchill College, Cambridge
Ciano diary	Diaries of Count Galeazzo Ciano, Italian Minister for Foreign Affairs
Cox Papers	Oscar Cox Papers, Franklin D. Roosevelt Library
Crocker diary	The Edward S. Crocker II and Lispenard Seabury Crocker Papers, Library of Congress
Davies Papers	Joseph E. Davies Papers, Library of Congress
DDI	Documenti Diplomatici Italiani (Ministero Degli Allani Esterni, I documenti diplomatici Italiani, Nona Serie 1939–1943, Vol. III, 24 Aprile–11 Diciembre 1944, Rome, 1987)
Diaries of Mackenzie King	Diaries of William Lyon Mackenzie King, Library and Archives Canada
DNB	Deutsches Nachrichtenbüro
ED	Einzeldokumente, Institut für Zeitgeschichte
Eleanor Roosevelt Papers	Eleanor Roosevelt Papers, Franklin D. Roosevelt Library
FDRL	Franklin D. Roosevelt Library
FHQ	Führerhauptquartier (Hitler's headquarters)
FO 954	Sir Anthony Eden's Private Office Papers, 1935–46, UK National Archives
FRUS	Foreign Relations of the United States
Goebbels diary	Joseph Goebbels, Die Tagebuecher
Halder diary	Franz Halder, Kriegstagebuch
Halifax Papers	Papers of Lord Halifax, Hickleton Papers, Borthwick Institute for Archives, York University

Hamlin Papers	Huybertie Hamlin, "Visit at the White House November 1941–January 1942," Charles Hamlin Papers, box 358, folder 15, Library of Congress
Harriman Papers	W. Averell Harriman Papers, Library of Congress
Hopkins Papers	Harry Hopkins Papers, Franklin D. Roosevelt Library
IFZ	Institut für Zeitgeschichte
Jacob Papers	Ian Jacob Papers, Churchill College, University of Cambridge
JMDS-13	Jean Monnet Duchêne Sources, British Supply Council Minutes, 10/07/1940 – 21/01/1942, Historical Archives of the European Union, European University Institute
Kellner diary	Friedrich Kellner, Tagebuecher 1939–1945
Kido diary	Diary of Marquis Kido
King George VI diary	King George VI Private diary, Royal Archives, Windsor Castle
Klemperer diary	Victor Klemperer, Tagebuecher, 1933–1945
Koeppen	Werner Koeppen, Herbst 1941, im Führerhauptquartier
KTB	Kriegstagebuch des Oberkommandos der Wehrmacht
Lash Papers	Joseph P. Lash Papers, Franklin D. Roosevelt Library
Lawford Papers	Valentine Lawford Papers, Churchill Archives
Long Papers	Breckinridge Long Papers, Library of Congress
"Man on the Street"	After the Day of Infamy: "Man on the Street" Interviews Following the Attack on Pearl Harbor, Library of Congress
McCloy diary	John J. McCloy diary, John J. McCloy Papers, Amherst Library
MK, IFZ	Mein Kampf, Institut für Zeitgeschichte
MOA	Mass Observation Archive, University of Sussex
MOI Digital	A History of the Ministry of Information, 1939–46, moidigital.ac.uk
Morgenthau Papers	Henry Morgenthau Jr. Papers, Franklin D. Roosevelt Library
OF	Official Files, Franklin Roosevelt Papers, Franklin D. Roosevelt Library
OKW	Oberkommando der Wehrmacht
Patterson Papers	Robert Patterson Papers, Library of Congress

Perkins Interview	Research Offices: Notable New Yorkers, Frances Perkins Interview, Columbia University Library
Pol Arch AA	Politisches Archiv Auswärtiges Amt
Popudrenko diary	Diary of Nikolay Nikitovich Popudrenko
PPA	Franklin D. Roosevelt and Samuel I. Rosenman, *Public Papers and Addresses of the Presidents of the United States: Franklin Roosevelt*
PREM	Prime Minister's Office records
PSF	President's Secretary's File, Franklin Roosevelt Papers, Franklin D. Roosevelt Library
Roosevelt Papers	Franklin D. Roosevelt Papers, Franklin D. Roosevelt Library
Rosenberg diary	Alfred Rosenberg, Die Tagebuecher von 1934 bis 1944
RSHA	Reichssicherheitshauptamt
SD	Sicherheitsdienst
Sebastian diary	Mihail Sebastian, Journal 1935–1944
Secret Files from World War to Cold War	secretintelligencefiles.com
SKL	Kriegstagebuch der Seekriegsleitung 1939–1945
Skryabina diary	Diary of Elena Aleksandrovna Skryabina
SS	Schutzstaffel
Stark Papers	Harold Stark Papers, Operational Archives, Washington, DC
Stettinius Papers	Edward Stettinius Papers, Special Collections Library, University of Virginia
Stimson MSS	Henry Stimson Papers, Yale University, Sterling Memorial Library
Taft Papers	Robert Taft Papers, Library of Congress
Thomas Papers	Norman Thomas Papers, New York Public Library
Toland Papers	John Toland Papers, Franklin D. Roosevelt Library
Ugaki diary	Diary of Admiral Matome Ugaki, 1941–1945
VJZG	Vierteljahrshefte fuer Zeitgeschichte
Welles Papers	Sumner Welles Papers, Franklin D. Roosevelt Library
Wickard Papers	Claude Wickard Papers, Franklin D. Roosevelt Library

NOTES

PREFACE

1. Arthur H. Vandenberg Jr., ed., *The Private Papers of Senator Vandenberg* (London, 1953), 1. For recent, important accounts that include similar statements, see Doris Kearns Goodwin's remark that "isolationism collapsed overnight," in her *No Ordinary Time: Franklin and Eleanor Roosevelt: The Home Front in World War II* (New York, 1994), 295; Robert Kagan's comment that "long-held assumptions about American security in a troubled world collapsed in a single day" in his "Superpowers Don't Get to Retire," *New Republic*, May 26, 2014; and, in the same vein, Marc Wortman describes Pearl Harbor as ending the debate on isolationism in his *1941: Fighting the Shadow War: How Britain and America Came Together for Victory* (London, 2017), 335–336.

2. Winston Churchill, *The Second World War*, vol. 3, *The Grand Alliance* (London, 1950), 539.

3. Our watershed is eighteen months later than that proposed by David Reynolds, "1940: Fulcrum of the Twentieth Century?," *International Affairs* 66 (1990): 325–350.

4. Winston Churchill to King George VI, Churchill Papers 20/20, December 8, 1941, in *The Churchill War Papers*, vol. 3, *The Ever-Widening War, 1941*, Martin Gilbert (London, 2000), 1585.

5. Vandenberg, *Private Papers of Senator Vandenberg*, 16.

6. Robert Sherwood, *Roosevelt and Hopkins: An Intimate History* (New York, 1950), 441.

7. Eri Hotta, *Japan 1941: Countdown to Infamy* (New York, 2013), 277.

8. George F. Kennan, *Memoirs*, vol. 1, *1925–1950* (Boston, 1967), 134–136.

9. Laurence Rees, "Pearl Harbor and Hitler's Devastating Conclusions: Why December 1941 Was the Most Important Month of the Second World War," December 11, 2019, HistoryExtra, www.historyextra.com/period/second-world-war/pearl-harbor-hitler-america-most-important-decisive-month-ww2/.

10. This is a "cognitive trap" that humans in general are susceptible to, as demonstrated by the psychologist and Nobel Prize winner Daniel Kahneman. See Daniel Kahneman, "The Riddle of Experience vs. Memory," February 2010, TED video, 19:50, www.ted.com/talks/daniel_kahneman_the_riddle_of_experience_vs_memory?language=en; and Daniel Kahneman, "How do Memories Become Experience?," May 24, 2013, *TED Radio Hour*, www.npr.org/2013/11/29/182676143/how-do-experiences-become-memories.

11. Hadley Cantril, ed., *Public Opinion, 1935–46* (Princeton, NJ, 1951), 1173.

12. For examples, see Richard F. Hill, *Hitler Attacks Pearl Harbor: Why the United States Declared War on Germany* (London, 2002), 209; John M. Schuessler, "The Deception Dividend: FDR's Undeclared War," *International Security* 34, no. 4 (Spring 2010): 162; and Marc Trachtenberg, *The Craft of International History: A Guide to Method* (Princeton, NJ, 2006), 127.

13. Gallup Organization, Gallup Poll # 1941-0255: World War II/Employment, Question 7 [USGALLUP.41-255.Q03] (Cornell University, Ithaca, NY: Roper Center for Public Opinion Research, 1941). We are grateful to the Roper Center's data archivist, Kathleen Joyce Weldon, for verifying this dataset and confirming this discrepancy.

14. Hitler's decision to declare war on the United States was, in the words of Martin Gilbert, "arguably his single greatest mistake of the war" (*Descent into Barbarism: The History of the 20th Century, 1933–1951* [London, 1998], 408). Yet the reasons why Hitler made such a monumental error have largely remained a mystery to historians, and the period between December 7 and 11 has been little studied. Ian Kershaw's absorbing and stimulating *Fateful Choices: Ten Decisions that Changed the World* (London, 2007), is mainly on the long lead-up, concentrating on the period before September 1941 rather than the December days themselves. It is also avowedly deterministic, suggesting at the end that America's entry into the war against Nazi Germany was inevitable even without Hitler's declaration, something we dispute. Klaus Schmider's brilliant *Hitler's Fatal Miscalculation: Why Germany Declared War on the United States* (Cambridge, 2021) likewise concentrates on the Reich and the deeper background, rather than the five days between Pearl Harbor and Hitler's declaration of war on the United States. Evan Mawdsley's *December 1941: Twelve Days that Began a World War* (New Haven, CT, 2011) covers some of the same time period as our book but from a very different angle. About half of his work deals with the period prior to December 7. It is an excellent grand strategic history with detailed coverage of the individual battlefronts, but the author's ap-

proach differs from our in several respects. In our view, Mawdsley is too inclined to take Churchill at his word and does not capture the richness of the debate in the United States over involvement in the European war. As a result, he claims that war with Germany was "inevitable" from an early stage after Pearl Harbor, which downplays the sense of uncertainty that gripped Washington right up to the moment that the die was finally cast by Hitler on December 11. We also argue that Mawdsley misunderstands Hitler. Far from underestimating America's strength, as Mawdsley contends, the Führer was driven by Roosevelt into declaring war, eventually doing so out of fear that, if he did not, the United States would overwhelm Germany at a time of its choosing. Finally, we think that Mawdsley, like all other writers on this period, does not give enough attention to the threat posed by Pearl Harbor to vital American Lend-Lease support the Allied powers. David Downing's *Sealing Their Fate: Twenty-Two Days that Decided the Second World War* (London and New York, 2009), takes the story from November to Pearl Harbor and thus leaves off more or less when our detailed account begins. Stanley Weintraub's absorbing *Long Day's Journey into War: December 7, 1941* (New York, 1991) is a blow-by-blow account of December 7, and only briefly touches on the four subsequent critical days leading up to Hitler's declaration of war.

CHAPTER 1: ORIGINS

1. Brendan Simms, "Against a 'World of Enemies': The Impact of the First World War on the Development of Hitler's Ideology," *International Affairs* 90, no. 2 (March 2014): 317–336.

2. Speech, December 11, 1941, in Max Domarus, *Hitler: Reden und Proklamationen, 1932–1945. Kommentiert von einem deutschen Zeitgenossen Teil I. Untergang. Vierter Band, 1941–1945*, 1802.

3. Charlie Laderman, *Sharing the Burden: The Armenian Question, Humanitarian Intervention, and Anglo-American Visions of Global Order* (New York, 2019), 111–114.

4. Paul Kennedy, *The Rise and Fall of the Great Powers: Economic Change and Military Conflict from 1500 to 2000* (London, 1988), 242–249; James A. Huston, *The Sinews of War: Army Logistics, 1775–1953* (Washington, 1970), 273. For a discussion of America's remarkable manufacturing expansion in this period, see Douglas A. Irwin, "Explaining America's Surge in Manufactured Exports, 1880–1913," *Review of Economics and Statistics* 85, no. 2 (May 2003): 364–376; and Edward B. Barbier, *Scarcity and Frontiers: How Economies Have Developed Through Natural Resource Exploitation* (Cambridge, 2010), 392.

5. Churchill, *Second World War*, 3:540.

6. Kennedy, *Rise and Fall of the Great Powers*, 327.

7. American economic output had overtaken Europe as a whole by 1919. See Kennedy, *Rise and Fall of the Great Powers*, 248. For an excellent recent discussion

of this transition, see Adam Tooze, *The Deluge: The Great War and the Remaking of Global Order* (London, 2014).

8. *Oxford Research Encyclopedia of American History*, s.v. "The League of Nations and the United States," by Charlie Laderman, accessed August 26, 2020, https://doi.org/10.1093/acrefore/9780199329175.013.314.

9. Charlie Laderman, "Conservative Internationalism: An Overview," *Orbis* 62, no. 1 (Winter 2018): 11–13.

10. John Thompson, *A Sense of Power: The Roots of America's Global Role* (Ithaca, 2015), 156.

11. Before the war Britain was America's principal creditor, but by 1918 it owed the US government over $4 billion. See Charles Kindleberger, *A Financial History of Western Europe* (London, 1984), 296.

12. John R. Ferris, "'The Greatest Power on Earth': Great Britain in the 1920s," *International History Review* 13, no. 4 (November 1991): 726–750.

13. The rivalry should not be exaggerated: see P. P. O'Brien, *British and American Naval Power: Politics and Policy, 1900–1936* (Westport, CT, 1998). For the transition, see Kori Schake, *Safe Passage: The Transition from British to American Hegemony* (Cambridge, MA, 2017); and Kathleen Burk, *The Lion and the Eagle: The Interaction of the British and American Empires, 1783–1972* (London, 2019).

14. Andrew Williams, *Failed Imagination?: The Anglo-American New World Order from Wilson to Bush* (Manchester, UK, 2007). For the intellectual roots, see Duncan Bell, *Dreamworlds of Race: Empire and the Utopian Destiny of Anglo-America* (Princeton, NJ, 2020). For the economic side, see Michael J. Hogan, *Informal Entente: The Private Structure of Cooperation in Anglo-American Economic Diplomacy, 1918–1926* (Columbia, MO, and London, 1977). How it all looked at the receiving end is described in Paul A. Kramer, *The Blood of Government: Race, Empire, the United States, and the Philippines* (Chapel Hill, NC, 2006).

15. Charlie Laderman, "Sharing the Burden? The American Solution to the Armenian Question, 1918–1920," *Diplomatic History* 40, no. 4 (September 2016): 664–694. For more on the British vision of using the League of Nations to establish an US-Britain alliance after World War I, see William Roger Louis, *Imperialism at Bay: The United States and the Decolonization of the British Empire, 1941–1945* (New York, 1978), 5; Mark Mazower, *Governing the World: The History of an Idea* (New York, 2012), 135–136; and Susan Pedersen, *The Guardians: The League of Nations and the Crisis of Empire* (New York, 2015), 19.

16. Quoted in Christopher Thorne, "Racial Aspects of the Far Eastern War of 1941–1945," *Proceedings of the British Academy* (1981): 339. For more on American attitudes toward British dominance elsewhere in Asia, see Charlie Laderman, "The Rise of the Modern Middle East," in *The Cambridge History of America and the World*, vol. 3, *1900–1945*, eds. Brooke Blower and Andrew Preston (New York, 2021), chap. 9. For the ambivalent relationship between the United States and Britain during the interwar years, see John Moser, *Twisting the Lion's Tail: American*

Anglophobia Between the Wars (New York, 1999). For pro-British sentiments among East Coast elites, see Mark Lincoln Chadwin, *The Warhawks: American Interventionists Before Pearl Harbor* (New York, 1970), 19–20.

17. Brendan Simms, *Hitler: Only the World Was Enough* (London, 2019), 77, 119, 156 (with quotations).

18. See Simms, *Hitler*, 39–40, 90–93 passim.

19. Antony Best, "'The Great Question of the World Today': Britain, the Dominions, East Asian Immigration and the Threat of Race War, 1905–1911," in *Race and Racism in Modern East Asia: Interactions, Nationalism, Gender and Lineage*, eds. Rotem Kowner and Walter Demel (Leiden, Netherlands, and Boston, 2015), 184–187, 194–195 passim; Hotta, *Japan 1941*, 41.

20. Naoko Shimazu, *Japan, Race and Equality: The Racial Equality Proposal of 1919* (London, 1998), 2–3, 17, 165 (regarding equality with Anglo-Saxons), 166 passim.

21. Hotta, *Japan 1941*, 34–37 (quote on 37).

22. Marilyn Lake and Henry Reynolds, *Drawing the Global Colour Line: White Men's Countries and the International Challenge of Racial Equality* (Cambridge, 2008), 303.

23. Reginald Kearney, "Japan: Ally in the Struggle Against Racism, 1919–1927," *Contributions in Black Studies* 12 (1994): 117–128 (quote on 119). See also Ernest Allen Jr., "When Japan Was 'Champion of the Darker Races': Satokata Takahashi and the Flowering of Black Messianic Nationalism," *Black Scholar* 24 (1994): 23–46. The dark side of African American support for Japanese imperialism is discussed in Seok-Won Lee, "The Paradox of Racial Liberation: W. E. B. Du Bois and Pan-Asianism in Wartime Japan, 1931–1945," *Inter-Asia Cultural Studies* 16 (2015): 519.

24. Douglas T. Shinsato and Tadanori Urabe, trans., *For that One Day: The Memoirs of Mitsuo Fuchida, Commander of the Attack on Pearl Harbour* (Kamuela, HI, 2011), 27.

25. Kearney, "Japan: Ally in the Struggle Against Racism," 121.

26. Sven Saaler, "Pan-Asianism in Modern Japanese History: Overcoming the Nation, Creating a Region, Forging an Empire," in *Pan-Asianism in Modern Japanese History: Colonialism, Regionalism and Borders*, eds. Sven Saaler and J. Victor Koschmann (London, 2007), 1–18.

27. Quoted in Hotta, *Japan 1941*, 62.

28. Steven Ward, "Race, Status, and Japanese Revisionism in the Early 1930s," *Security Studies* 22 (2013): 607–639 (especially 631–632, regarding "Anglo-Saxons").

29. See Michael A. Barnhart, *Japan Prepares for Total War: The Search for Economic Security, 1919–1941* (Ithaca and London, 1987), 62, 267. See Chika Tonooka, "'Have-Nots' or Neobarbarians?: Narrating the Manchurian Crisis," in *British Eurocentrism and the Challenge of Japanese Civilisation, c.1880–1945* (forthcoming).

30. See generally: Stefan Huebner, "Hitler und Ostasien, 1904 bis 1933. Die Entwicklung von Hitlers Japan- und Chinabild vom Russisch-Japanischen Krieg bis zur 'Machtergreifung,'" *OAG-Notizen* 9 (2009): 22–41.

31. Adolf Hitler, *Mein Kampf: Eine kritische Edition*, eds. Christian Hartmann, Thomas Vordermayer, Othmar Plöckinger, and Roman Töppel (Munich and Berlin, 2016) (hereafter MK IFZ), 1:405, 445, 715.

32. MK IFZ, 2:1621.

33. MK IFZ, 1:757.

34. MK IFZ, 1:757.

35. Donald Sassoon, *Mussolini and the Rise of Fascism* (London, 2007), 22.

36. Quoted in Charles Floyd Delzell, ed., *Mediterranean Fascism 1919–1945: Selected Documents* (New York, 1970), 189.

37. Joseph Goebbels, November 27, 1936, in *Die Tagebücher von Joseph Goebbels*, ed. Elke Froehlich (Munich, 1993–2006) (hereafter Goebbels diary) I/3/II:266.

38. William L. Langer and S. Everett Gleason, *The Challenge to Isolation, 1917–1940* (New York, 1952), 14.

39. For an insightful discussion of this enduring theme, see Cushing Strout, *The American Image of the Old World* (New York, 1963).

40. Thompson, *A Sense of Power*, 133–137.

41. Sherwood, *Roosevelt and Hopkins*, 227.

42. "I Have Seen War . . . I Hate War," Speech at Chautauqua, New York, August 14, 1936, in *Public Papers and Addresses of the Presidents of the United States: Franklin Roosevelt* (New York, 1938) (hereafter PPA), 5:285–292.

43. Waldo Heinrichs, *Threshold of War: Franklin D. Roosevelt and American Entry into World War II* (New York, 1988), 6–7.

44. Franklin Delano Roosevelt, *Development of U.S. Foreign Policy: Addresses and Messages of FDR* (Washington, DC, 1942), 22–23.

45. Robert Dallek, *Franklin D. Roosevelt and American Foreign Policy, 1932–1945* (New York, 1979), 76–77.

46. G. Bruce Strang, "'The Worst of All Worlds:' Oil Sanctions and Italy's Invasion of Abyssinia, 1935–1936," *Diplomacy and Statecraft* 19, no. 2 (2008): 210–235.

47. Heinrichs, *Threshold of War*, 7–8.

48. Kennedy, *Rise and Fall of the Great Powers*, 331. See also Quincy Wright, *A Study of War* (Chicago, 1942), 672; and H. C. Hillmann, "Comparative Strength of the Great Powers," in *The World in March 1939*, eds. Arnold J. Toynbee and F. T. Ashton-Gwatkin (London, 1952), 446.

49. Quoted in John Morton Blum, ed., *From the Morgenthau Diaries*, vol. 1, *Years of Crisis, 1928–1938* (Boston, 1949), 489.

50. David Reynolds, *The Creation of the Anglo-American Alliance: A Study in Competitive Co-operation* (London, 1981), 10–23.

51. Chamberlain to his sister Hilda, December 17, 1937, quoted in Reynolds, *Creation of the Anglo-American Alliance*, 297.

52. Quoted in Paul Haggie, *Britannia at Bay: The Defence of the British Empire Against Japan, 1931–41* (Oxford, 1981), 73.

53. Quoted in John Lamberton Harper, *American Visions of Europe: Franklin D. Roosevelt, George F. Kennan, and Dean G. Acheson* (Cambridge, 1996), 62–63.

54. Daniel Todman, *Britain's War: Into Battle, 1937–1941* (London, 2016), 149, 154.

55. Mark Skinner Watson, *Chief of Staff: Prewar Plans and Preparations* (Washington, DC, 1950), 136–143.

56. Reynolds, *Creation of the Anglo-American Alliance*, chap. 1.

57. Jonathan Haslam, *The Soviet Union and the Threat from the East, 1933–41: Moscow, Tokyo and the Prelude to the Pacific War* (Basingstoke, 1992).

58. Rana Mitter, *Forgotten Ally: China's World War II, 1937–1945* (Boston and New York, 2013), 214.

59. See Herbert Sirois, *Zwischen Illusion und Krieg: Deutschland und die USA 1933–1941* (Paderborn, 2000), 105–110.

60. Sylvia Taschka, *Diplomat ohne Eigenschaften?: Die Karriere des Hans-Heinrich Dieckhoff (1884–1952)* (Stuttgart, 2006).

61. Wolfram Pyta, "Weltanschauliche und strategische Schicksalsgemeinschaft. Die Bedeutung Japans für das weltpolitische Kalkül Hitlers," in *Naziverbrechen: Täter, Taten, Bewältigungsversuche*, eds. Martin Cüppers, Jürgen Matthäus, and Andrej Angrick (Darmstadt, 2013) 31–37; Alfred M. Beck, *Hitler's Ambivalent Attaché: Lt. Gen. Friedrich von Boetticher in America, 1933–1941* (Washington, 2005).

62. Simms, *Hitler*, 347–394.

63. Quoted in Simms, *Hitler*, 332. See also Saul Friedländer, *Das Dritte Reich und die Juden: Die Jahre der Verfolgung, 1933–1939* (Munich, 2007), 335; and L. J. Hartog, *Der Befehl zum Judenmord: Hitler, Amerika und die Juden* (Bodenheim, 1997).

64. The idea that Hitler considered the Jews "hostages" whose fate depended on American behavior is well established in the literature. See Shlomo Aronson, *Hitler, the Allies, and the Jews* (Cambridge, 2006), 5, 127. See also Hans Mommsen, "Hitler's Reichstag Speech of 30 January 1939," *History and Memory* 9 (1997): 147–161. As Mommsen notes, even before Hitler deployed it, "the notion of using the Jews as hostages in order to prevent the Western powers from inflicting damage on Germany was familiar to the fanatical anti-Semites of the era" (p. 151).

65. Simms, *Hitler*, 329–330.

66. Rana Mitter, *China's War with Japan, 1937–1945: The Struggle for Survival* (Oxford, 2013); Hans van de Ven, *China at War: Triumph and Tragedy in the Emergence of the New China, 1937–1945* (London, 2017).

67. See Mark R. Peattie, *Sunburst: The Rise of Japanese Naval Air Power* (Annapolis, 2001).

68. Eri Hotta, *Pan-Asianism and Japan's War: 1931–1945* (New York, 2007), 49, 104.

69. Hartmut Bloß, "Die zweigleisigkeit der deutschen Fernostpolitik und Hitlers Option für Japan 1938," *Militärgeschichtliche Zeitschrift* 27, no. 1 (1967): 55–105.

70. Tajima Nobuo, "Die japanische Botschaft in Berlin in nationalsozialistischer Zeit," in *Formierung und Fall der Achse Berlin-Tokyo*, eds. Gerhard Krebs and Bernd Martin (Munich, 1994), 57; and Jost Dülffer, "Die japanische Botschaft im Tiergarten im Rahmen der nationalsozialistischen Umgestaltung der Reichshauptstadt Berlin," in *Formierung und Fall der Achse Berlin-Tokyo*, 75–92.

71. Quoted in Owen Matthews, *An Impeccable Spy: Richard Sorge, Stalin's Master Agent* (London, 2019), 209.

72. "The President Urges the Extraordinary Session to Repeal the Embargo Provisions of the Neutrality Law, September 21, 1939," PPA, 8:520.

73. Quoted in Thompson, *A Sense of Power*, 166.

74. Quoted in Simms, *Hitler*, 369.

75. Ernest May, *Strange Victory: Hitler's Conquest of France* (London, 2009); Julian Jackson, *France: The Dark Years, 1940–1944* (Oxford, 2001).

76. Julian Jackson, *A Certain Idea of France: The Life of Charles de Gaulle* (London, 2018), 128.

77. Thompson, *A Sense of Power*, 166–167.

78. "Address at University of Virginia, Charlottesville, Virginia, June 10, 1940," PPA, 9:259–264.

79. Thompson, *A Sense of Power*, 168–169.

80. Harper, *American Visions of Europe*, 72–73.

81. See Christian Gerlach, *The Extermination of the European Jews* (Cambridge, 2016), 59–65.

82. Alvin D. Coox, *Nomonhan: Japan Against Russia, 1939* (Stanford, CA, 1985).

83. Malte König, *Kooperation als Machtkampf: Das faschistische Achsenbündnis Berlin-Rom im Krieg, 1940/41* (Cologne, 2007).

84. W. E. Crosskill, *The Two Thousand Mile War* (London, 1980), 105–182.

85. Roger Moorhouse, *The Devils' Alliance: Hitler's Pact with Stalin, 1939–1941* (New York, 2014).

86. See Bianka Pietrow-Ennker, "Das Feindbild im Wandel: Die Sowjetunion in den nationalsozialistischen Wochenschauen, 1935–1941," *Geschichte in Wissenschaft und Unterricht* 41 (1990): 341–344; and Willi A. Boelcke, ed., *Kriegspropaganda 1939–1941: Geheime Ministerkonferenzen im Reichspropagandaministerium* (Stuttgart, 1966), 475 (referring to a meeting on August 23, 1940).

87. Quoted in Moorhouse, *The Devils' Alliance*, 51.

88. See Simms, *Hitler*, and Sean McMeekin, *Stalin's War: A New History of the Second World War* (London, 2021). For Stalin's preoccupation with Britain in 1939–1941, see Gabriel Gorodetsky, *Grand Delusion: Stalin and the German Invasion of Russia* (New Haven, 1999).

89. Toshikazu Kase, *Journey to the Missouri* (New Haven, 1950), 38.

90. For example, Masanobu Tsuji, *Singapore: The Japanese Version* (London, 1962), 17.

91. Jeremy Yellen, "'Into the Tiger's Den': Japan and the Tripartite Pact, 1940," *Journal of Contemporary History* 5 (2016): 569. See also Jeremy Yellen, *The Greater East Asia Co-prosperity Sphere: When Total Empire Met Total War* (Ithaca, NY, 2019).

92. Claims that Japan intended conquests as far afield as California or South America have been debunked by Gerhard Krebs, "Was Fidel Castro's Cuba Rescued by the Yankees from Japanese Aggression? A Very Special View of the Pacific War," *Contemporary Japan* 10 (2020). Japanese aims, though grandiose, were nonetheless limited.

93. Heinrichs, *Threshold of War*, 10–11.

94. Quoted in David Kennedy, *Freedom from Fear: The American People in Depression and War, 1929–1945* (New York, 1999), 504.

95. Leahy to Roosevelt, July 28, 1941, France 1941, box 29, president's secretary's file, Franklin Roosevelt Papers. For more on Leahy and Roosevelt's shared conception of Japan and Germany acting in lockstep at this time, see Phillips Payson O'Brien, *The Second Most Powerful Man in the World: The Life of Admiral William D. Leahy, Roosevelt's Chief of Staff* (New York, 2019), 143–161.

96. Mao Tse-Tung, "On How to Prepare for Any Dark Circumstances Given the Present International Circumstances," October 25, 1940, in *Mao's Road to Power: Revolutionary Writings, 1912–1949*, vol. 7, *New Democracy, 1939–1941*, ed. Stuart R. Schram (Armonk, NY, 2005), 529.

97. Kase, *Missouri*, 58.

98. Mitsuo Fuchida and Masatake Okumiya, *Midway: The Battle that Doomed Japan* (London, 1961), 40.

99. See Theo Sommer, *Deutschland und Japan zwischen den Mächten, 1935–1940: Vom Antikominternpakt Zum Dreimächtepakt* (Tübingen, 1962).

100. Yellen, "'Into the Tiger's Den,'" 555–576.

101. David Reynolds, *From World War to Cold War: Churchill, Roosevelt, and the International History of the 1940s* (New York, 2006), 19–20.

102. "Plan Dog Memorandum 12 Nov 1940 with accompanying personal letters of Admiral Stark—October-Dec 1940," series 3, box 5, Anglo-American relations, Harold Stark Papers, Operational Archives, Washington, DC.

103. Heinrichs, *Threshold of War*, 10.

104. This approach was discussed in "Annual Message to Congress," January 4, 1939, in PPA, *1939 Volume: War and Neutrality*, ed. Samuel I. Rosenman (New York, 1941), 3.

105. David Edgerton, *Britain's War Machine: Weapons, Resources, and Experts in the Second World War* (London, 2011), 75–76.

106. Todman, *Britain's War*, 417–419; H. Duncan Hall and G. C. Wrigley, *Studies of Overseas Supply* (London, 1956), 2–3.

107. Quoted in Louis Allen, "Setting Europe Ablaze," *New Blackfriars* 48 (1966): 35. See also M. R. D. Foot, *SOE: An Outline History of the Special Operations Executive, 1940–46* (London, 1985), 20–21.

108. Wolfgang Michalka, *Ribbentrop und die deutsche Weltpolitik, 1933–1940. Aussenpolitische Konzeptionen und Entscheidungsprozesse im Dritten Reich* (Munich, 1980).

109. Robert A. Divine, *Foreign Policy and U.S. Presidential Elections: 1940–1948* (New York, 1974), 34–35.

110. See David Reynolds, "Lord Lothian and Anglo-American Relations, 1939–1940," *Transactions of the American Philosophical Society* 73, no. 2 (1983).

111. "Fireside Chat," radio broadcast, December 29, 1940, in PPA, 9:635.

112. *To Promote the Defense of the United States: Hearings Before the Committee on Foreign Relations, United States Senate*, Seventy-Seventh Cong. (1941), 1–2.

113. William L. Shirer, "December 1, 1940," in *Berlin Diary: The Journal of a Foreign Correspondent, 1934–1941*, rev. ed. (London, 1942), 463–464. This book was first published in September 1941, before Pearl Harbor.

114. Aufzeichnung betreffend Kriegserklärung durch die Vereinigten Staaten, [Freytag] 13.8.1940, Berlin, AA Pol Arch, R29937, Vereinigte Staaten, August 1940–February 1943.

115. See Sirois, *Zwischen Illusion und Krieg*, 230.

116. Simms, *Hitler*, 389–390. This resonant phrase achieved renown after Ernest Hemingway's novel *To Have and Have Not*, which was published in 1937, and Hitler certainly used it repeatedly long before the appearance of the famous film version with Humphrey Bogart in 1944.

117. Simms, *Hitler*. For the strategic side, see Andreas Hillgruber, *Hitlers Strategie: Politik und Kriegführung, 1940–1941* (Bonn, 1993), and Gerhard Weinberg, "22 June 1941: The German View," *War in History* 3, no. 2 (1996): 228–229.

118. See Andreas Hillgruber, "Die 'Endlösung' und das deutsche Ostimperium als Kernstück des Rassenideologischen Programms des Nationalsozialismus," *VJZG* 20 (1972):144, and the record of a meeting between Göring and Heydrich, March 26, 1941, in Bert Hoppe and Hildrun Glass, eds., *Die Verfolgung und Ermordung der europäischen Juden durch das nationalsozialistische Deutschland 1933–1945, Band 7, Sowjetunion mit annektierten Gebieten I. Besetzte Gebiete unter deutscher Militärverwaltung, Baltikum und Transnistrien* (Munich, 2011), 113–117, especially 116.

119. Thus, Ulrich Herbert, "Vernichtungspolitik. Neue Antworten und Fragen zur Geschichte des 'Holocaust,'" in *Nationalsozialistische Vernichtungspolitik 1939–1945: Neue Forschungen und Kontroversen* (Frankfurt, 1998), 49.

120. Halder diary, March 31, 1941, in Franz Halder, *Kriegstagebuch: Tägliche Aufzeichnungen des Chefs des Generalstabes des Heeres, 1939–1942*, ed. Hans-Adolf Jacobsen (Stuttgart, 1962–1964), 2:336–337.

121. "Erlass über die Ausübung der Kriegsgerichtsbarkeit im Gebiet 'Barbarossa' und über besondere Massnahmen der Truppe," May 13, 1941, FHQ, in *Führer-Erlasse, 1939–1945*, ed. Martin Moll (Stuttgart, 1997), 172–173.

122. Quoted in Reynolds, *From World War to Cold War*, 19.

123. Andrew Preston, "Monsters Everywhere: A Genealogy of National Security," *Diplomatic History*, 38 (2014): 477–500.

124. For more on the background to the passage of the Lend-Lease bill, see Warren Kimball, *Most Unsordid Act: Lend-Lease, 1939–1941* (Baltimore, 1969).

125. Quoted in Schmider, *Hitler's Fatal Miscalculation*, 107.

126. For a concise overview of Roosevelt's policy as he began "enlisting the nation" for war see David Kaiser, *No End Save Victory: How FDR Led the Nation into War* (New York, 2014), chap. 6.

127. Timothy P. Mulligan, "'According to Colonel Donovan': A Document from the Records of German Military Intelligence," *Historian* 46 (1983): 78–86, especially 82.

128. Heinrichs, *Threshold of War*, 48.

129. Sherwood, *Roosevelt and Hopkins*, 264–275.

130. "The cords that bound the two countries were becoming thicker, more tangled and more secure," as noted in Reynolds, *Creation of the Anglo-American Alliance*, 182.

131. Henry R. Luce, "The American Century," *Life*, February 17, 1941, 64.

132. We take the phrase from Stephen Wertheim, *Tomorrow the World: The Birth of US Global Supremacy* (Cambridge, MA, 2020).

133. "Give us the tools," broadcast, February 9, 1941, London, in Winston S. Churchill, *Never Give In! The Best of Winston Churchill's Speeches* (London, 2013), 214–217. He would later, of course, famously describe Lend-Lease as the "most unsordid act in the history of any nation" in his speech at the Guildhall in November 1941. See Churchill, *Never Give In!*, 259.

134. Churchill to Wood, March 20, 1941, PREM 4, 17/2. Nevertheless, Churchill continued to believe that Britain retained leverage because "the power of the debtor is in the ascendant, especially when he is doing all the fighting."

135. John Colville, *The Fringes of Power: Downing Street Diaries, 1939–1955* (London, 1986), 327.

136. For a broader discussion of Roosevelt's evolving perspective on Britain see Harper, *American Visions of Europe*, 7–47.

137. September 6, 1941, Joseph Lash Papers, box 31, folder—Journal, 1939–1942, FDR Library. Lash, a close friend of the first lady, heard this directly from the president. In this journal, he also records Dorothy Overlock, one of Eleanor Roosevelt's principal assistants, expressing "fears" on March 22, 1941, that "President's motivating idea may be Luce's conception of a rampant American imperialism running the world with Britain as a junior partner."

138. "The Light of Democracy Must Be Kept Burning," address at Annual Dinner of White House Correspondents' Association, March 15, 1941, PPA, *1941 Volume: The Call to Battle Stations*, ed. Samuel I. Rosenman (New York, 1950), 69.

139. King George VI private diary, Friday, March 4, 1941, Royal Archives, Windsor Castle.

140. Averell Harriman, "Foreword," in Gerald Pawle, *The War and Colonel Warden: Based on the Recollections of C. R. Thompson, Personal Assistant to the Prime Minister,*

1940–45 (London, 1963). For more on the role of potential American intervention in Churchill's strategy, see David Reynolds, "Churchill and the British 'Decision' to Fight on in 1940: Right Policy, Wrong Reasons," in *Diplomacy and Intelligence During the Second World War: Essays in Honour of F.H. Hinsley*, ed. Richard Langhorne (Cambridge, 1985), 147–167.

141. Churchill to Anthony Eden, May 2, 1941, in Reynolds, *Creation of the Anglo-American Alliance*, 199.

142. Churchill to Roosevelt, May 3, 1941, C-84x in *Churchill and Roosevelt: The Complete Correspondence*, ed. Warren Kimball (Princeton, NJ, 1984), 1:181–182. The same point was also being made by the joint planning staff in London: Christopher G. Thorne, *The Issue of War: States, Societies, and the Far Eastern Conflict, 1941–1945* (Oxford, 1985), 16.

143. George H. Gallup, *The Gallup Poll: Public Opinion, 1935–1971* (New York, 1972), 1:270–275.

144. Cantril, *Public Opinion*, 976.

145. On Roosevelt's emphasis on hemispheric security, see Heinrichs, *Threshold of War*, 82, and Harper, *American Visions of Europe*, 68–69.

146. Hall and Wrigley, *Studies of Overseas Supply*, 23–28.

147. Heinrichs, *Threshold of War*, 90.

148. Hall and Wrigley, *Studies of Overseas Supply*, 21; Richard M. Leighton and Robert W. Coakley, *Global Logistics and Strategy, 1940–1943* (Washington, DC, 1955), 115.

149. John J. McLaughlin, *General Albert C. Wedemeyer: America's Unsung Strategist in World War II* (Philadelphia and Oxford, 2012), 33, 37, 39.

150. The most systematic account of Hitler's perception of Lend-Lease in the first half of 1941, and that of the German leadership more generally, is in Schmider, *Hitler's Fatal Miscalculation*, 105–115.

151. Thus, Adam Tooze, *The Wages of Destruction: The Making and Breaking of the Nazi Economy* (London, 2007), 440–443.

152. Speech, May 4, 1941, in *Hitler: Reden und Proklamationen*, 1708.

153. See Tooze, *Wages of Destruction*, 383–384, for figures.

154. Thus, Pyta, "Weltanschauliche und strategische Schicksalsgemeinschaft," 21–44, especially 21–22, 31; and Peter Herde, *Die Achsenmächte, Japan und die Sowjetunion: Japanische Quellen zum Zweiten Weltkrieg* (Berlin and Boston, 2018), 36–37 passim.

155. "Die Judenfrage als Weltproblem," March 28, 1941, in *Der Kampf gegen den Osten*, ed. Hans Vilz (Berlin, 1944), 2:567–582.

156. Quoted in Hotta, *Japan 1941*, 59. Konoye (p. 52), also spoke of Japan as one of the "have-nots."

157. "Aufzeichnung über die Unterredung zwischen dem Führer und dem japanischen Außenminister Matsuoka am 27 März 1941, Berlin," and "Aufzeichnung über die Unterredung zwischen dem Führer und dem japanischen Außenminister

Matsuoka am 4 April 1941, Berlin," in *Staatsmänner und Diplomaten bei Hitler. Vertrauliche Aufzeichnungen über Unterredungen mit Vertretern des Auslandes, 1939–1941*, ed. Andreas Hillgruber (Frankfurt am Main, 1967), 1:503–514, 518–5242.

158. McMeekin, *Stalin's War*, 254, 257.

159. See also Andreas Hillgruber, "Japan und der Fall 'Barbarossa': Japanische Dokumente zu den Gesprächen Hitlers und Ribbentrops mit Botschafter Oshima von Februar bis Juni 1941," *Wehr-wissenschaftliche Rundschau* 18 (June 1968): 312–336.

160. Stalin's remarks were made in March 1941 during his first meeting with Matsuoka. See McMeekin, *Stalin's War*, 54.

161. Peter Herde, *Italien, Deutschland und der Weg in den Krieg im Pazifik* (Wiesbaden, 1983), 34; Richard J. B. Bosworth, *Mussolini* (London, 2002), 381 (for Mussolini quote).

162. David Stahel, *Operation Barbarossa and Germany's Defeat in the East* (Cambridge, 2009).

163. Christian Streit, *Keine Kameraden: Die Wehrmacht und die Sowjetischen Kriegsgefangenen, 1941–1945* (Stuttgart, 1978).

164. X. M. Nunez Seixas, "Wishful Thinking in Wartime? Spanish Blue Division's Soldiers and Their Views on Nazi Germany, 1941–44," *Journal of War and Culture Studies* 11, no. 2 (2018): 99–116; J. Dafinger, "Show Solidarity, Live Solidarity: The Nazi 'New Europe' as a 'Family of Peoples,'" *European Review of History* 24, no. 6 (2017): 905–917; Reto Hofmann, "The Fascist New-Old Order," *Journal of Global History* 12, no. 2 (2017): 166–183.

165. Hannes Heer and Klaus Naumann, eds., *Vernichtungskrieg: Verbrechen der Wehrmacht, 1941–1944* (Hamburg, 1995).

166. Rudolf Höss, *Kommandant in Auschwitz: Autobiographische Aufzeichnungen*, ed. Martin Broszat (Munich, 2018).

167. For example, October 28, 1941, in Friedrich Kellner, *"Vernebelt, verdunkelt sind alle Hirne": Tagebücher, 1939–1945* (Goettingen, 2011) (hereafter Kellner diary), 1:191–192.

168. Hotta, *Japan 1941*, 110.

169. Quoted in Churchill, *Second World War*, 3:331. See also Joan Beaumont, *Comrades in Arms: British Aid to Russia, 1941–1945* (London, 1980), 23–60, and Alexander Hill, "British Lend-Lease Aid and the Soviet War Effort, June 1941–June 1942," *Journal of Military History* 71 (2007): 773–808.

170. Morgenthau, as quoted in John Morton Blum, ed., *From the Morgenthau Diaries: Years of Urgency, 1938–1941* (Boston, 1959), 265.

171. Both quotes in David Reynolds and Vladimir Pechatnov, *The Kremlin Letters: Stalin's Wartime Correspondence with Churchill and Roosevelt* (London, 2019), 32.

172. First quote in Harry Hopkins, "The Inside Story of My Meeting with Stalin," *American Magazine* 35 (December 1941): 14–15, 114–17. Additional quotations in "The Ambassador in the Soviet Union (Steinhardt) to the Secretary of State,"

August 1, 1941, 740.0011 European War 1930/13601: Telegram, in *Foreign Relations of the United States* (hereafter FRUS) *1941*, vol. 1, *General: The Soviet Union* (Washington DC, 1958).

173. Quoted in Heinrichs, *Threshold of War*, 140.

174. Quoted in Steven J. Zaloga, *Soviet Lend-Lease Tanks of World War II* (Oxford, 2017), 4.

175. See Bogdan Musial, ed., *Sowjetische Partisanen in Weißrussland: Innenansichten aus dem Gebiet Baranovici, 1941–1944. Eine Dokumentation* (Munich, 2004), 18–20.

176. For U-boat losses during this period, see Werner Rahn, "Einsatzbereitschaft und Kampfkraft deutscher U-Boote 1942. Eine Dokumentation zu den materiellen Voraussetzungen und Problemen des U-Boots-Krieges nach dem Kriegseintritt der USA," *Militärgeschichtliche Mitteilungen* 1 (1990): 92–94 (this article reaches back before 1942).

177. Heinrichs, *Threshold of War*, 159.

178. Thus, Nicolaus von Below, *Als Hitlers Adjutant, 1937–45* (Selent, 1999), 287. The importance of the charter for Hitler's thinking has been shown by Tobias Jersak, "Die Interaktion von Kriegsverlauf und Judenvernichtung. Ein Blick auf Hitlers Strategie im Spätsommer 1941," *Historische Zeitschrift* 268 (1999): 311–374.

179. See Pyta, "Weltanschauliche und strategische Schicksalsgemeinschaft," 36–37.

180. "September 11, 1941: The Greer Incident: Quasi-War in the Atlantic," in *FDR's Fireside Chats*, ed. Russell D. Buhite and David W. Levy (Norman, OK, 1992), 188–197.

181. J. R. Beardall to FDR, September 9, 1941, President's Secretary's File (PSF), box 4, folder—Navy Department, 1934–February 1942, Franklin Roosevelt Papers, FDR Library.

182. "September 11, 1941: The Greer Incident," 188–197; Gallup, *Gallup Poll*, 1:299.

183. See his directive 36, September 22, 1941, in *Hitler Weisungen für die Kriegsführung 1939–1945*, ed. Walther Hubatsch (Frankfurt am Main, 1962).

184. See the reports extracted in Joachim Kuropka, ed., *Meldungen aus Münster, 1924–1944. Geheime und vertrauliche Berichte von Polizei, Gestapo, NSDAP und ihren Gliederungen, staatlicher Verwaltung, Gerichtsbarkeit und Wehrmacht über die politische und gesellschaftliche Situation in Münster* (Münster, 1992), 556–557.

185. Norman Ohler, *Blitzed: Drugs in Nazi Germany* (London, 2016), 137–141.

186. Mamoru Shigemitsu, *Japan and Her Destiny* (London, 1958), 238–240. See also, Antony Best, "Shigemitsu Mamoru: Critical Times in a Long Ambivalent Career [London, 1938–41]," *Japanese Envoys in Britain, 1862–1964: A Century of Diplomatic Exchange*, ed. Ian Nish (Folkestone, 2007), 173–184.

187. See Bernd Martin, *Deutschland und Japan im Zweiten Weltkrieg: Vom Angriff auf Pearl Harbor bis zur deutschen Kapitulation* (Göttingen, 1969), 26–27.

188. Thus, Martin, *Deutschland und Japan*, 28.

189. Quoted in Carl Boyd, *Hitler's Japanese Confidant: General Oshima Hiroshi and Magic Intelligence, 1941–1945* (Lawrence, KS, 1993), 31.

190. Clandestine contacts between Berlin and Chungking actually continued over the next few years. See Nele Friederike Glang, "Germany and Chonqing: Secret Communication During World War II," *Intelligence and National Security* 30 (2015): 871–889.

191. Mitter, *Forgotten Ally*, 232–235.

192. Harper, *American Visions of Europe*, 76n107; Akira Iriye, *The Origins of the Second World War in Asia and the Pacific* (London, 1987).

193. Christopher Capozzola, "The Philippines and the Politics of Anticipation," in *Beyond Pearl Harbor: A Pacific History*, eds. Beth Bailey and David Farber (Lawrence, KS, 2019), 158–172.

194. Heinrichs, *Threshold of War*, 131–136.

195. Thus, Hotta, *Japan 1941*.

196. Jonathan Marshall, *To Have and to Have Not: Southeast Asian Raw Materials and the Origins of the Pacific War* (Berkeley, CA, 1995).

197. See John W. Dower, *War Without Mercy: Race and Power in the Pacific War* (London and Boston, 1987), 24.

198. Heinrichs, *Threshold of War*, 152–163.

199. Welles, Memo of Conversation, August 11, 1941, in FRUS 1941, 1:363. See also Dallek, *Roosevelt and American Foreign Policy*, 299.

200. Quoted in Heinrichs, *Threshold of War*, 163.

201. Telegram of August 28, 1941, Churchill Papers, 20/42 in *Churchill War Papers*, 3:1125.

202. David Macri, "Canadians Under Fire: C Force and the Battle for Hong Kong, December 1941," *Journal of the Royal Asiatic Society Hong Kong Branch* 51, (2011): 237–256; Terry Copp, "The Defence of Hong Kong. December 1941," *Canadian Military History* 10 (2001): 5–20.

203. Christopher M. Bell, "The 'Singapore Strategy,' and the Deterrence of Japan: Winston Churchill, the Admiralty and the Dispatch of Force Z," *English Historical Review* (2001): 604–634.

204. Thus, Barry Gough, "*Prince of Wales* and *Repulse*: Churchill's 'Veiled Threat' Reconsidered," *Churchill Proceedings*, 2007, 1–23 (quote 4).

205. Churchill to Roosevelt, November 2, 1941, C-125x, in *Churchill and Roosevelt*, 1:265.

206. Quoted in Dower, *War Without Mercy*, 99. That said, naval intelligence in the Far East did a good job, and there were many who had a clear sense of Japanese capabilities: Andrew Boyd, *The Royal Navy in Eastern Waters: Linchpin of Victory, 1935–1942* (Barnsley, 2017), 401.

207. All quotes in Dower, *War Without Mercy*, 109.

208. Matthews, *An Impeccable Spy*, 314–317.

209. Quoted in Martin Gilbert, *Churchill and America* (New York, 2005), 233.

210. October 26, 1941, in *A Delicate Mission: The Washington Diaries of R. G. Casey, 1940–42*, ed. Carl Bridge (Canberra, 2008), 193.

211. McLaughlin, *General Albert C. Wedemeyer*, 42.

212. Quoted in Thompson, *A Sense of Power*, 187.

213. Thompson, *A Sense of Power*, 155. See also "Gallup and Fortune Polls," *Public Opinion Quarterly* 5, no. 4 (Winter 1941): 680; and Hadley Cantril, *Public Opinion*, 971–977.

214. Quoted in Maurice Matloff and Edwin Snell, *Strategic Planning for Coalition Warfare* (Washington, DC, 1980), 55.

215. Leighton and Coakley, *Global Logistics and Strategy*, 140.

216. Quoted in George Herring, *Aid to Russia, 1941–1946* (New York, 1973), 35–36.

CHAPTER 2: THE WORLDS OF DECEMBER 6, 1941

1. See Simms, *Hitler*, 437–438.

2. Nobutaka Ike, ed., *Japan's Decision for War: Records of the 1941 Policy Conferences* (Stanford, CA, 1967), 152.

3. Fuchida, *For That One Day: The Memoirs of Mitsuo Fushida, Commander of the Attack on Pearl Harbor*, trans. Douglas T. Shinsato and Tadarori Urabe (Kamuela, HI, 2011), 61.

4. Martin, *Deutschland und Japan*, 29–31.

5. Quoted in Hotta, *Japan 1941*, 201. Specifically, in this instance, Tojo referred to a leap off the platform of the Buddhist Kiyomizu temple in eastern Kyoto.

6. Fuchida and Okumiya, *Midway*, 51.

7. J. Garry Clifford and Masako R. Okura, eds., *The Desperate Diplomat Saburo Kurusu's Memoir of the Weeks Before Pearl Harbor* (Columbia, MO, 2016), 66–67.

8. Quoted in Dallek, *Roosevelt and American Foreign Policy*, 304–305.

9. "Confidential for William J. Donovan for Whitney," London, November 12, 1941, Coordinator of Information, 1941, Franklin Roosevelt, Papers as President, PSF, box 128, FDR Library. See also Joseph E. Persico, *Roosevelt's Secret War: FDR and World War II Espionage* (New York, 2001), 154.

10. Tokyo to Washington, November 5, 1941, tr. same date, #44, "Magic" Background, 4A:22.

11. Quoted in Heinrichs, *Threshold of War*, 202.

12. Persico, *Roosevelt's Secret War*, 103, 150.

13. Quoted in Harold L. Ickes, *The Secret Diary of Harold Ickes*, vol. 3, *The Lowering Clouds, 1939–1941* (London, 1955), 567.

14. Heinrichs, *Threshold of War*, 206.

15. Franklin Delano Roosevelt, Memorandum to the Secretary of State, White House, November 15, 1941, with enclosed memorandum by William J. Donovan, November 13, 1941, Coordinator of Information, 1941, Franklin Roosevelt, Papers as President, PSF, box 128, FDR Library.

16. This argument is made by Harry Elmer Barnes, *Pearl Harbor After a Quarter of a Century* (Torrance, CA, 1980), 19. For similar sentiments, see Robert A. Theobald, *The Final Secret of Pearl Harbor* (New York, 1954), 4. For a more recent revisionist account that argues the United States and Britain knew of a Japanese attack in advance and allowed it to happen to precipitate an US-Germany war, see Robert B. Stinnett, *Day of Deceit: The Truth About FDR and Pearl Harbor* (New York, 1999). For an excellent textual analysis of the primary and secondary sources on the back-door-to-war thesis, see Trachtenberg, *Craft of International History*, 115–131.

17. For comprehensive refutations of the revisionist argument on Pearl Harbor see Persico, *Roosevelt's Secret War*, 134–157, and Gordon W. Prange, Donald M. Goldstein, and Katherine V. Dillon, "Revisionists Revisited," in *At Dawn We Slept: The Untold Story of Pearl Harbor* (London, 1982), 839–850.

18. Malcolm R. Lowell to Donovan, November 24, 1941, Coordinator of Information, 1941, Franklin Roosevelt, Papers as President, PSF, box 128, FDR Library.

19. Ike, *Japan's Decision for War*, 247–249.

20. Ike, *Japan's Decision for War*, 190.

21. Ike, *Japan's Decision for War*, 194.

22. We take the phrase "racial abandonment" from a paper given by Eri Hotta in Cambridge, September 2019. See also Hotta, *Japan 1941*, 277.

23. Ike, *Japan's Decision for War*, 237.

24. See Hotta, *Japan 1941*, 261–262.

25. Schmider, *Hitler's Fatal Miscalculation*, 147–148, 405–407.

26. John Gooch, *Mussolini's War: Fascist Italy from Triumph to Collapse, 1935–1943* (London, 2020), 278.

27. Quoted in Simms, *Hitler*, 440.

28. Franz W. Seidler, *Fritz Todt: Baumeister des Dritten Reichs* (Frankfurt and Berlin,1988), 356.

29. Hotta, *Japan 1941*, 167.

30. Barnhart, *Japan Prepares for Total War*, 246.

31. Joel Hayward, "Hitler's Quest for Oil: The Impact of Economic Considerations on Military Strategy, 1941–1942," *Journal of Strategic Studies* 18 (1995): 94–135.

32. David Stahel, *Operation Typhoon: Hitler's March on Moscow, October 1941* (Cambridge, 2013).

33. John Barber and Andrei Dzeniskevich, eds., *Life and Death in Besieged Leningrad, 1941–44* (Basingstoke and New York, 2005); Richard Overy, *Russia's War* (London, 2010), 99–110.

34. Wolfgang Scheffler and Diana Schulle, *Buch der Erinnerung: Die ins Baltikum deportierten deutschen, österreichischen und tschechoslowakischen Juden* (Munich, 2003), 1:3.

35. Mihail Sebastian, "October 29, 1941," *Journal 1935–1944* (London, 2001) (hereafter Sebastian diary), 436.

36. One of these was the leftist mechanic Berthold Rudner: Susanne Heim, ed., *Die Verfolgung und Ermordung der europäischen Juden durch das nationalsozialistische Deutschland, 1933–1945*, vol. 6, *Deutsches Reich und Protektorat Böhmen und Mähren Oktober 1941–März 1943* (Berlin, 2019), 244–246. We thank Susanne Heim for letting us have sight of the edition in draft form, and Dr. Anja Reuss of the Sinti und Roma Council for background information on Rudner.

37. For Cologne, see Dieter Corbach, *6.00 Uhr ab Messe Köln-Deutz. Deportationen 1938–1945* (Cologne, 1999), 113–115.

38. See Johannes Tuchel, *Am Großen Wannsee, 56–58. Von der Villa Minoux zum Haus der Wannsee-Konferenz*, 110, 112–113.

39. Thus, Peter Longerich, *The Unwritten Order: Hitler's Role in the Final Solution* (Stroud, 2001), 148.

40. Peter Longerich, *Heinrich Himmler* (Oxford, 2012), 550.

41. Katrin Reichelt, *Lettland unter deutscher Besatzung, 1941–1944. Der lettische Anteil am Holocaust* (Berlin, 2011), 162–165; Frida Michelson, *I Survived Rumbuli* (New York, 1979), 74–78.

42. Thus, Longerich, *Unwritten Order*, 130 and 148.

43. Rosenberg diary, September 12, 1941, in Alfred Rosenberg, *Die Tagebücher von 1934 bis 1944*, ed. Jürgen Matthäus and Frank Bajohr (Frankfurt am Main, 2015), 408.

44. Reported in Werner Koeppen, September 21, 1941, in *Herbst 1941 im Führerhauptquartier, Berichte Werner Koppens an seinen Minister Alfred Rosenberg*, ed. Werner Jochmann (Munich, 1982), 35.

45. October 24, 1941, in Adolf Hitler, *Monologe im Führerhauptquartier, 1941–1944. Die Aufzeichnungen Heinrich Heims*, ed. Werner Jochmann (Munich, 1982), 106.

46. Quoted in Longerich, *Unwritten Order*, 148–149.

47. Quoted from the summary by the Chilean consul in Prague in Richard Breitman et al., *US Intelligence and the Nazis* (Cambridge, 2005), 17. This ordinance was noted by the diplomat in a message to Santiago and eventually picked up by British intelligence, but was not decrypted and read in London and Washington until early 1942.

48. Thus, Longerich, *Himmler*, 543.

49. For a transcript of Lindbergh's Des Moines speech, see Jeffrey A. Engel, Andrew Preston, and Mark A. Lawrence, *America in the World: A History in Documents from the War with Spain to the War on Terror* (Princeton, NJ, 2014), 124–125.

50. For a sample of the reaction, see "Jews Listed Fifth in Pro-War Groups: Gallup Poll Finds Only One in 16 Voters Agrees with the Views of Lindbergh," *New York Times*, October 25, 1941. For the broader outrage at Lindbergh's speech, see Richard Breitman and Allan J. Lichtman, *FDR and the Jews* (Cambridge, MA, 2013), 187–189.

51. Robert Shogan, *Prelude to Catastrophe: FDR's Jews and the Menace of Nazism* (Chicago, 2010), xi, 76, 83–84, 112, 221 passim.

52. Michael Oren, *Power, Faith and Fantasy: America in the Middle East, 1776 to the Present* (New York, 2011), 443.

53. For a detailed discussion of the *New York Times* and the Holocaust see Laurel Leff, *Buried by the Times: The Holocaust and America's Most Important Newspaper* (New York, 2005), particularly 107–135 for the period leading up to American entry into the war. For Roosevelt's daily perusal of the paper, see Heinrichs, *Threshold of War*, 21.

54. "Goebbels Spurs Abuse for Jews," *New York Times*, November 14, 1941, 11.

55. Jerzy Jurandot, *City of the Damned: Two Years in the Warsaw Ghetto*, trans. Jolanta Scicinska (Warsaw, 2015), 123.

56. *Memoirs of Ernst von Weizsäcker*, trans. John Andrews (London, 1951), 265–266.

57. Ribbentrop speech, November 26, 1941, Berlin, in *Der Kampf gegen den Osten*, 473–495.

58. Following the classification in David Motadel, "The Global Authoritarian Moment and the Revolt Against Empire," in *American Historical Review* (2019): 852 and 874.

59. Motadel, "Global Authoritarian Moment," and Klaus Gensicke, *Der Mufti von Jerusalem und die Nationalsozialisten* (Frankfurt am Main, Bern, New York, and Paris, 2007), 86–89.

60. Romain Hayes, *Subhas Chandra Bose in Nazi Germany: Politics, Intelligence and Propaganda, 1941–1943* (London, 2011), 69, 183–188.

61. Quoted in Ray Moseley, *Mussolini's Shadow: The Double Life of Count Galeazzo Ciano* (New Haven and London, 1999), 137.

62. See the memoirs by Frederick Oechsner, *This Is the Enemy* (London and Toronto), 4–7, 292–293, and the list in Pol Arch AA, R29891, fol. 25102.

63. "Secretary's File, Only," CAB 65, 84 (41), August 19, 1941, UK National Archives. See also Churchill to Smuts, November 9, 1941, CHAR 20/44/132-133, Churchill Papers.

64. Smuts to Churchill, November 4, 1941, CHAR 20/44/115-116, Churchill Papers.

65. In mid-November, Roosevelt finally convinced Congress to amend the Neutrality Act to allow US merchant ships to be armed for self-defense but, as Martin Gilbert has pointed out, Roosevelt received less support from his own Democrats

on this than he had previously on the Lend-Lease bill. See Martin Gilbert, *Winston S. Churchill: Finest Hour, 1939–41* (London, 1991), 6:1238n1.

66. Thus, Mawdsley, *December 1941*, 52.

67. Quoted in Heinrichs, *Threshold of War*, 212.

68. Todman, *Britain's War*, 708.

69. Pawle, *War and Colonel Warden*, 141.

70. Hall and Wrigley, *Studies of Overseas Supplies*, 27.

71. Roosevelt to Churchill, September 8, 1941, R-56x, draft, not sent, and editorial note in *Roosevelt and Churchill*, 1:239–240. As Kimball notes, Roosevelt preferred to have this message sent over Hopkins's signature, his go-between on these supply questions.

72. Stalin to Churchill, September 3, 1941, and Churchill to Stalin, September 5, 1941, in Reynolds and Pechatnov, *Kremlin Letters*, 40–44.

73. Heinrichs, *Threshold of War*, 171–175. For more on fears of Stalin again coming to terms with Hitler see Herring, *Aid to Russia*, 33.

74. "Speech on the Eve of the 24th Anniversary of the October Revolution," in *The Great Patriotic War of the Soviet Union, 1941–1945: A Documentary Reader*, ed. Alexander Hill (Abingdon, 2007), 75–76.

75. Walter Baum and Eberhard Weichold, *Der Krieg der "Achsenmächte" im Mittelmeer-Raum. Die "Strategie" der Diktatoren* (Zurich and Frankfurt, 1973), 185–187.

76. Gooch, *Mussolini's War*, 242.

77. Gooch, *Mussolini's War*, 192–193; Andrew Stewart, *The First Victory: The Second World War and the East Africa Campaign* (New Haven, 2016), 330–331.

78. Werner Rahn, "Der Seekrieg im Atlantik und Nordmeer," in *Das Deutsche Reich und der Zweite Weltkrieg*, vol. 6, *Der globale Krieg: Die Ausweitung zum Weltkrieg und der Wechsel der Initiative 1941 bis 1943*, ed. Horst Boog et al. (Stuttgart, 1990), 335–336.

79. Alexander Hill, "British Lend-Lease Tanks and the Battle of Moscow, November–December 1941—Revisited," *Journal of Slavic Military Studies* 22 (2009): 574–587; Alexander Hill, *The Red Army and the Second World War* (Cambridge, 2017), 288–292.

80. Thus, Schmider, *Hitler's Fatal Miscalculation*, 405. See also Vladimir Kotelnikov, *Lend-Lease and Soviet Aviation in the Second World War* (Solihull, 2017), 165–190, especially 103 and 166.

81. See Hill, *Red Army and the Second World War*, 289.

82. Beaumont, *Comrades in Arms*, 66.

83. Klaus Reinhardt, *Die Wende vor Moskau. Das Scheitern der Strategie Hitlers im Winter 1941/2* (Stuttgart, 1972), 204–205.

84. December 3, 1941, in *Generalfeldmarschall Fedor von Bock, Zwischen Pflicht und Verweigerung Das Kriegstagebuch*, ed. Klaus Gerbert (Munich, 1995) (hereafter Bock diary), 337.

85. Hellmuth Stieff to wife, November 24, 1941, in *Hellmuth Stieff: Briefe*, ed. Horst Mühleisen (Berlin, 1991), 137–138.

86. Letter of December 4, quoted in Heinrich Bücheler, *Hoepner: Ein deutsches Soldatenschicksal des zwanzigsten Jahrhunderts* (Herford, 1980), 160.

87. Churchill to Roosevelt, November 26, 1941, C-133x, in *Churchill and Roosevelt*, 1:275–278. For a brief, but detailed, overview of the complex negotiations over the modus vivendi see Heinrichs, *Threshold of War*, 206–214.

88. Dallek, *Roosevelt and American Foreign Policy*, 308.

89. Memorandum regarding a conversation between the secretary of state, the Japanese ambassador (Nomura), and Mr. Kurusu, Washington, November 26, 1941, in *Peace and War: United States Foreign Policy* (Washington, 1943), 807–810.

90. Peter Mauch, "Revisiting Nomura's Diplomacy: Ambassador Nomura's Role in the Japanese-American Negotiations, 1941," *Diplomatic History* 28 (2004), 381–382.

91. Gerhard Krebs, "Deutschland und Pearl Harbor," *Historische Zeitschrift* 253 (1991), 313–369, especially 344–347; the text of Oshima's message, with quotes, is on 368–369.

92. Oshima report, November 29, 1941 (intercepted document), in *Der Prozess gegen die Hauptkriegsverbrecher vor dem internationalen Militärgerichtshof* (Nuremberg, 1949), 320–323.

93. Thus, Martin, *Deutschland und Japan*, 41, dates the "blank check" a few days later.

94. Thus, Ike, *Japan's Decision for War*, 256.

95. Indelli to Ciano, November 30, 1941, DDI, IX, VII, 795; Ott, November 30, 1941 (we thank Francesco Lefebvre and Bastian Scianna for drawing our attention to the Italian documents).

96. Overy, *Russia's War*, 117.

97. Overy, *Russia's War*, 118–119.

98. All quotes in Reynolds and Pechatnov, *Kremlin Letters*, 64–74.

99. Nigel Nicolson, ed., *Harold Nicolson: The War Years 1939–1945* (London, 1967), 191.

100. Sebastian diary, November 30, 1941, p. 446.

101. November 30, 1941, in Victor Klemperer, *Ich will Zeugnis ablegen bis zum letzten Tagebücher 1933–1941* (Berlin, 1995) (hereafter Klemperer diary), 691.

102. Germany, folder 1941–43, Franklin Roosevelt Papers, box 198, Office Files (hereafter OF), FDR Library.

103. Quoted in Christopher Thorne, *Allies of a Kind: The United States, Britain, and the War Against Japan, 1941–1945* (New York, 1978), 106.

104. Rene Kraus, *The Men Around Churchill* (Philadelphia, 1941), 13.

105. "Women Hurl Eggs and Tomatoes at Lord Halifax on Detroit Tour," *New York Times*, November 5, 1941, p. 25.

106. Quoted in Andrew Roberts, *The Holy Fox: The Life of Lord Halifax* (London, 2019), 382.

107. War Cabinet: Confidential Annex (Cabinet Papers, 65/24), December 1, 1941, in *Churchill War Papers*, 3:1538.

108. Halifax to Foreign Office, December 1, 1941, PREM. 3 156/5.

109. Halifax to Foreign Office, December 4, 1941, PREM. 3 156/5.

110. Dallek, *Roosevelt and American Foreign Policy*, 309.

111. Quoted in Roberts, *Holy Fox*, 384.

112. Warren Kimball, *Forged in War: Roosevelt, Churchill, and the Second World War* (Chicago, 2003), 119.

113. We have hugely benefitted from reading Samuel Clements, "The Sinking of Force Z and the End of the Battleship Era" (BA dissertation, University of Cambridge, 2020), 14.

114. Boyd, *Royal Navy in Eastern Waters*.

115. Quoted in Andrew Roberts, *Churchill: Walking with Destiny* (London, 2018), 693.

116. Quoted in Cameron Forbes, *Hellfire: The Story of Australia, Japan, and the Prisoners of War* (Sydney, 2005), 118.

117. Imperial Conference, December 1, 1941, in Ike, *Japan's Decision for War*, 263.

118. December 1, 1941, in *Fading Victory: Admiral Matome Ugaki, 1941–1945*, eds. Donald M. Goldstein and Katherine V. Dillon (Annapolis, MD, 2008) (hereafter Ugaki diary), 32.

119. Quoted in Barnhart, *Japan Prepares for Total War*, 262.

120. See Ike, *Japan's Decision for War*, xxv.

121. Quoted in Hotta, *Japan 1941*, 20, 192.

122. Quoted in Hotta, *Japan 1941*, 178.

123. Quoted in Peter Mauch, "Revisiting Nomura's Diplomacy: Ambassador Nomura's Role in the Japanese-American Negotiations, 1941," *Diplomatic History* 28 (2004): 383.

124. Quoted in Hotta, *Japan 1941*, 275.

125. Thus, Jeremy Yellen, *The Greater East Asia Co-prosperity Sphere: When Total Empire Met Total War* (Ithaca, 2019), 2, 58–59.

126. Thus, Christopher Thorne, "Racial Aspects of the Far Eastern War of 1941–1945," *Proceedings of the British Academy* (1981): 332–333, 347. See also Gerald Horne, *Race War! White Supremacy and the Japanese Attack on the British Empire* (New York and London, 2004).

127. See Shigenori Togo, *Japan im Zweiten Weltkrieg: Erinnerungen des japanischen Außenministers 1941–42 und 1945* (Bonn, 1958), 172–174.

128. "Aufzeichnung über die Unterredung zwischen dem Reichsmarschall Göring und Marschall Petain," December 1, 1941, in *Akten zur Deutschen Auswärtigen Politik 1918–1945. Aus dem Archiv des Auswärtigen Amtes, Serie D. 1937–1941.*

Volume XIII.2 Die Kriegsjahre. Sechster Band. Zweiter Halbband 15. September bis 11. Dezember 1941 (Göttingen, 1970) (hereafter ADAP), 744–754 (quotes 750–751).

129. See the account of the meeting in Rintelen to OKW, December 2, 1941, Rome, ADAP, 760–761.

130. Directive 38, December 2, 1941, in *Hitlers Weisungen für die Kriegführung, 1939–1945: Dokumente des Oberkommandos der Wehrmacht*, ed. Walther Hubatsch (Frankfurt, 1962), 169–170.

131. See Enno von Rintelen, *Mussolini als Bundesgenosse: Erinnerungen des deutschen Militärattachés in Rom 1936–1943* (Tübingen and Stuttgart, 1951), 158.

132. See Keitel to Rintelen, December 4, 1941, ADAP, 761.

133. Thus, Karine Varley, "Defending Sovereignty Without Collaboration: Vichy and the Italian Fascist Threats of 1940–1942," *French History* 33 (2019): 422–443, especially 422–423.

134. Andrew J. Williams, *France, Britain, and the United States in the Twentieth Century*, vol. 2, *1940–1961: A Reappraisal* (London, 2020), 39–40; Julian G. Hurstfield, *America and the French Nation, 1939–1945* (London and Chapel Hill, 1986), 9–12, 52; O'Brien, *Second Most Powerful Man in the World*.

135. Robert L. Melka, "Darlan Between Britain and Germany, 1940–41," *Journal of Contemporary History* 8 (1973): 57–80 (64 re: "Anglo-Saxons"). See more broadly on this theme: Williams, *France, Britain, and the United States*, 49, 53, 77 passim.

136. Karine Varley, *Vichy's Double Bind: French Axis Entanglements and Relations with Fascist Italy, 1940–1943*, forthcoming, 90. We thank Dr. Varley for letting us have sight of her manuscript in advance of publication.

137. The tensions between de Gaulle and Roosevelt are described in Jackson, *A Certain Idea of France*, 204–205. For the general's own account, see Charles de Gaulle, *The Call to Honour, 1940–1942: War Memoirs Volume One* (London, 1955), 214, 236.

138. Quoted in Jackson, *A Certain Idea of France*, 202.

139. Herring, *Aid to Russia*, 42–45.

140. Arthur Krock, "U.S. Aid to Soviet Is Found Wanting," *New York Times*, December 3, 1941, pp. 1–2.

141. In December, Harriman would tell colleagues in Washington that "Britain was 100 percent on schedule in meeting its commitments while the United States had shipped only 25 percent of scheduled quantities." Quoted in Leighton and Coakley, *Global Logistics and Strategy*, 1:115.

142. "Aufzeichnung des Gesandten von Bismarck," December 4, 1941, ADAP, vol. 13.2, 776. See also DDI, IX, VII, 808.

143. December 3, 1941, in *The Complete, Unabridged Diaries of Count Galeazzo Ciano, Italian Minister for Foreign Affairs, 1936–1943* (London, 2002) (hereafter Ciano diary), 470.

144. Herde, *Italien, Deutschland*, 86.

145. Mackensen report, December 3, 1941, Rome, ADAP, 765–768 (quotes 766–767).

146. Thus, Ciano diary, December 3, 1941, p. 470.

147. Krebs, "Deutschland und Pearl Harbor," 351.

148. "Vereinfachung und Leistungssteigerung unserer Rüstungsproduktion," December 3, 1941, in *Führer-Erlasse*, 210–221.

149. Ulrich Herbert, *Fremdarbeiter: Politik und Praxis des "Ausländer-Einsatzes" in der Kriegswirtschaft des Dritten Reiches* (Bonn, 1999), 150–152.

150. *In der Gestapo-Zentrale Prinz-Albrecht Straße 8. Berichte ehemaliger Häftlinge: Eine Dokumentation der Evangelischen Akademie Berlin (West) im Evangelischen Bildungswerk* (Berlin, 1989), 216.

151. McLaughlin, *Wedemeyer*, 43.

152. Deutsches Nachrichtenbüro (DNB) report, New York, 5/6/12/1941, R106102, Politisches Archiv Auswärtiges Amt, [192155-192167]. This is a summary of the December 4, 1941, report on the Victory Program in the *Washington Times Herald*.

153. Quotes in H. W. Brands, *Traitor to His Class: The Privileged Life and Radical Presidency of Franklin Delano Roosevelt* (New York, 2008), 625–626. For the statement on Fish, see "U.S. at War: Sloppy Citizenship," *Time*, November 16, 1942.

154. Thomsen report, December 4, 1941, Washington, ADAP, 773–774.

155. Thomsen report, December 4, 1941, Washington, ADAP, 771–772 (quotes 771).

156. Thus, Martin, *Deutschland und Japan*, 40. See also Alfieri to Ciano, December 4, 1941, DDI, IX, VII, 514.

157. December 4, 1941, in *Meldungen aus dem Reich: Die geheimen Lageberichte des Sicherheitsdienstes der SS, 1938—1945*, ed. Heinz Boberach (Herrsching, 1984), 8:3059–3060. See Marie-Helene Benoit-Otis and Cecile Quesney, "A Nazi Pilgrimage to Vienna? The French delegation at the 1941 'Mozart Week of the German Reich,'" *Musical Quarterly* (2017): 6–59, especially 8–9.

158. Togo, *Japan im Zweiten Weltkrieg*, 172–181.

159. Paul S. Dull, *A Battle History of the Imperial Japanese Navy, 1941–1945* (Annapolis, MD, 1978), 36–37.

160. Thus, David C. Evans and Mark R. Peattie, *Kaigun: Strategy, Tactics, and Technology in the Imperial Japanese Navy, 1887–1941* (Annapolis, MD, 1997), 479.

161. Text in Masanobu Tsuji, *Singapore: The Japanese Version* (London, 1962), 295–349 (quotes 301–302, 304, 306, 347).

162. December 6, 1941, in John Harvey, ed., *The War Diaries of Oliver Harvey* (London, 1978), 69.

163. Reynolds and Pechatnov, *Kremlin Letters*, 73–74.

164. Churchill to Harriman, November 27, 1941, folder: Chron File November 25–30, box 161, W. Averell Harriman Papers, Library of Congress.

165. Harriman to Beaverbrook and Beaverbrook to Harriman, December 4, 1941, folder: Chron File December 1–19 1941, box 161, Harriman Papers.

166. Alan Moorehead, *The Desert War: The North African Campaign 1940/1943* (London, 1965), 105–106.

167. "Friday 5 December 1941, General John Kennedy, Director of Military Operations, Discusses the Middle East with Churchill," in Richard J. Aldrich, *Witness to War: Diaries of the Second World War in Europe and the Middle East* (London, 2004), 367–368.

168. Ribbentrop to Rome embassy, Berlin, December 5, 1941, ADAP, 779.

169. Mackensen report, December 5, 1941, Rome, ADAP, 781.

170. Ott report, December 5, 1941, ADAP, 778.

171. Thus, David Stahel, *Retreat from Moscow: A New History of Germany's Winter Campaign, 1941–1942* (New York, 2019), 75.

172. Reinhardt, *Moskau*, 206.

173. Stahel, *Retreat from Moscow*, 21, 139.

174. Reinhardt, *Moskau*, 209.

175. "Notizen aus der Führerbesprechung vom 6 Dezember 1941," in Halder, *Kriegstagebuch*, 3:329–331.

176. December 6, 1941, in *Heeresadjutant bei Hitler, 1938-1943: Aufzeichnungen des Majors Engel*, ed. Hildegard von Kotze (Stuttgart, 1974) (hereafter Engel diary), 117.

177. Churchill, *Grand Alliance*, 535.

178. "The Diaries of Sir Alexander Cadogan OM, 1938–1945" (hereafter Cadogan diary), December 6, 1941, in *Churchill War Papers*, 3:1570.

179. Malcolm Kennedy, diary entry for December 6, 1941, quoted in David Stafford, *Churchill and Secret Service* (London, 1997), 234.

180. Cadogan diary, December 6, 1941, in *Churchill War Papers*, 3:1570.

181. Harriman to Hopkins, December 6, 1941, Harriman Papers, Library of Congress.

182. Skryabina diary, December 6, 1941, Elena Aleksandorvna Skryabina, Godi skitaniy: Iz dnevnika odnoy leni Skryabina diary, December 6, 1941, Elena Aleksandrovna Skryabina, "Godi skitaniy. Iz dnevnika odnoy leningradki," Militera (Voyennaya Literatura), Oleg Rubetsky, http://militera.lib.ru/db/skryabina_ea/index.html (there are no page numbers). We thank Kristina Nazariyan for locating this source.

183. Ciano diary, December 6, 1941, p. 471.

184. Goebbels diary, 477.

185. Ribbentrop to Ott, December 6, 1941, ADAP, 786.

186. December 6, 1941, in *Kriegstagebuch der Seekriegsleitung, 1939–1945 Teil A. Band 28 Dezember 1941*, eds. Werner Rahn and Gerhard Schreiber (Herford and Bonn, 1991) (hereafter SKL diary).

187. December 6, 1941, in *The Diary of Marquis Kido, 1931–45: Selected Translations into English* (Frederick, MD, 1984) (hereafter Kido diary), 322.

188. Heinrich Himmler, *Der Dienstkalender Heinrich Himmlers, 1941/42*, ed. Peter Witte et al. (Hamburg, 1999), 285.

189. December 6, 1941, in *Generalfeldmarschall Wilhelm Ritter von Leeb: Tagebuchaufzeichnungen und Lagebeurteilungen aus zwei Weltkriegen*, ed. Georg Meyer (Stuttgart, 1976) (hereafter Ritter von Leeb diary), 405.

190. Alfred Gottwaldt and Diana Schulle, *Die "Judendeportationen" aus dem deutschen Reich, 1941–1945: Eine kommentierte Chronologie* (Wiesbaden, 2005), 125–126.

191. Gettoverwaltung Litzmannstadt, December 6, 1941, in *Die Verfolgung und Ermordung der europäischen Juden durch das nationalsozialistische Deutschland, 1933–1945. Vol 10. Polen. Die eingegliederten Gebiete. August 1941–1945*, ed. Ingo Loose (Berlin, 2020), 208–209.

192. Tomaszewski diary, December 9, 1941 (looking back on events of the previous three days), in *Polen: Generalgouvernement, August 1941–1945*, ed. Klaus-Peter Friedrich (Munich, 2014), 147. For the wider context in Lvov, see Philippe Sands, *East-West Street: On the Origins of Genocide and Crimes Against Humanity* (London, 2016), 219–221.

193. Thus, the eyewitness account of the survivor Hans Baermann in Walter Kempowski, ed., *Das Echolot Barbarossa '41: Ein kollektives Tagebuch* (Munich, 2014), 323–324.

194. SD Report Aussenstelle Minden, December 6, 1941, in *Die Juden in den geheimen NS-Stimmungsberichten 1933–1945*, eds. Otto Dov Kulka and Eberhard Jaeckel (Düsseldorf, 2004), 476–477.

195. See Christopher Shores and Brian Cull, *Bloody Shambles: The First Comprehensive Account of Air Operations over South-East Asia. December 1941–April 1942*, vol. 1, *The Drift to War to the Fall of Singapore* (London, 1992), 74.

196. Ugaki diary, December 6, 1941, p. 35.

CHAPTER 3: SUNDAY, DECEMBER 7, 1941

1. Kenneth S. Davis, *FDR: The War President, 1940–1943* (New York, 2000), 336.

2. Huybertie Hamlin, December 6, 1941, "Visit at the White House November 1941–January 1942," Charles Hamlin Papers, box 358, folder 15, Library of Congress.

3. PPA, 1941, 512–513.

4. James Roosevelt and Sidney Shalett, *Affectionately, FDR: A Son's Story of a Courageous Man* (London, 1960), 646.

5. *Hearings Before the Joint Committee on the Investigation of the Pearl Harbor Attack, Congress of the United States*, Seventy-Ninth Cong. (1946) (hereafter PHA), part 9, 4663.

6. Quoted in Ritter von Leeb diary, December 7, 1941, p. 406. David Glantz, *The Battle of Leningrad, 1941–1944* (Lawrence, KS, 2004), 103–109. For Halder's

general lack of urgency that day, see Christian Hartmann, *Halder: Generalstabchef, 1938–1942*, 2nd ed. (Paderborn, Munich, Vienna, Zurich, 2010), 299.

7. See Schmider, *Hitler's Fatal Miscalculation*, 347.

8. See Bock diary, December 7, 1941, p. 341.

9. As later described in the circular from the Hungarian Foreign Ministry, Budapest, December 18, 1941, in *Allianz, Hitler-Horthy-Mussolini. Dockumente zur ungarischen Aussenpolitik (1933–1944)*, eds. Magda Adam, Gyula Juhasz, and Lajos Kerekes (Budapest, 1966), 327–328. In Budapest, the news was conveyed by the American embassy, which looked after Britain's interests.

10. Sebastian diary, December 7, 1941, p. 449.

11. Ribbentrop to Mackensen, December 7, 1941, Berlin, ADAP, 786–787. We are hugely indebted for our understanding of the Italian side of the story to Francesco Lefebvre and Bastian Scianna.

12. Dieter Corbach, *6.00 Uhr ab Messe Köln-Deutz. Deportationen, 1938–1945* (Cologne, 1994), 113–132; Gottwaldt and Schulle, *Judendeportationen*, 126; Horst Matzerath, "Die Deportation aus Köln am 7 Dezember 1941," in *Buch der Erinnerung* (Munich, 2003), 2:627–629.

13. Uwe Neumaerker, Robert Conrad, and Cord Woyrodt, *Wolfsschanze: Hitlers Machtzentrale im zweiten Weltkrieg* (Berlin, 2007), 52.

14. Major-General I. S. O. Playfair et al., *The Mediterranean and Middle East: British Fortunes Reach Their Lowest Ebb (September 1941 to September 1942)* (London, 1960), 77.

15. Quoted in Juergen Foerster, "Die Wehrmacht und die Probleme der Koalitionskriegführung," in *Die "Achse" im Krieg. Politik, Ideologie und Kriegführung, 1939–1945*, eds. Lutz Klinkhammer, Amedeo Osti Guerrazzi, and Thomas Schlemmer (Paderborn, 2010), 108–121 (quote 117).

16. Martin Kitchen, *Rommel's Desert War: Waging World War II in North Africa, 1941–1943* (Cambridge, 2009), 174.

17. *Der Westen: Berliner Tageszeitung*, December 7, 1941, p. 1.

18. Quoted in Overy, *Russia's War*, 118.

19. Popudrenko diary, December 7, 1941, p. 30, 34, www.litmir.me/br/?b =139947&p=30#section_5. We thank Kristina Nazariyan for drawing our attention to this source.

20. Popudrenko diary, December 7, 1941, Nikolay Nikitovich Popudrenko, "Dnevnik N.N. Popudrenko (23 avgusta 1941 g.-19 yanvarya 1943 g.)," LitMir: Elektronnaya Biblioteka, 30, 34, www.litmir.me/br/?b=139947&p=30#section_5. We thank Kristina Nazariyan for drawing our attention to this source.

21. Machenson to Auswärtiges Amt, December 7, 1941, Rome, ADAP, 792–793.

22. Ciano diary, December 7, 1941, p. 472. See also Bastian Matteo Scianna, "Forging an Italian Hero? The Late Commemoration of Amedeo Guillet 1909–2010," *European Review of History* (2018): 1–17.

23. Gooch, *Mussolini's War*, 278.

24. Quoted in Moseley, *Mussolini's Shadow*, 138.

25. For more on Churchill's morning routine, see Patrick Peter Kinna, "Winston Churchill: Personal Reminiscences," 1941–45, Confidential Assistant to the Prime Minister, Date Recorded—17 June 1986, in Interviews with former staff of Winston Churchill, 1979–1986, CHOH, Churchill Archives Centre, Cambridge University. See also John Potter, *Pim and Churchill's Map Room: Based on the Papers of Captain Richard Pim RNVR Supervisor of Churchill's Map Room 1939–1945* (Belfast, 2014).

26. See Peter Calvocoressi, Guy Wint, and John Pritchard, *The Penguin History of the Second World War* (London, 1999) for confirmed numbers.

27. Winston Churchill to the prime minister of Thailand (Hansard), December 7, 1941, quoted in *Churchill War Papers*, 3:1573.

28. Duff Cooper, *Old Men Forget* (London, 1953), 300.

29. Quoted in Copp, "Defence of Hong Kong," 4.

30. See the evocative description of the last day of the old Hong Kong in Horne, *Race War!*, 62 (the given date of December 8 should be December 7, because the Japanese invasion began in the early hours of the following day).

31. Meeting December 7, 1941, in *Wollt ihr den totalen Krieg?: Die geheimen Goebbels-Konferenzen 1939–43*, ed. Willi A. Boelcke (Stuttgart, 1989), 196–197.

32. Danuta Czech, *Kalendarium der Ereignisse im Konzentrationslager Auschwitz-Birkenau 1939–1945* (Hamburg, 1989), 151.

33. See Brendan Simms, "Karl Wolff—Der Schlichter," in *Die SS. Elite unter dem Totenkopf. 30 Lebensläufe*, eds. Ronald Smelser and Enrico Syring (Paderborn, Munich, Vienna, Zurich, 2000), 441–456.

34. Himmler, *Dienstkalender*, 286.

35. Linge's recollections are in Henrik Eberle and Matthias Uhl, eds., *The Hitler Book: The Secret Dossier Prepared for Stalin* (London, 2005).

36. Ohler, *Blitzed*; and Ellen Gibbels, "Hitler's Nervenkrankheit. Eine neurologisch-psychiatrische Studie," *Vierteljahrshefte fuer Zeitgeschichte* 42 (1994): 167.

37. Quoted in Kempowski, *Das Echolot*, 319–321.

38. Engel diary, December 7, 1941, 117. It is assumed from the context that the midday rather than evening briefing is meant. The "midday briefing" was a movable feast and could take place in the midafternoon.

39. Memorandum on Moscardó visit to Führer headquarters, December 7, 1941, in *Staatsmänner und Diplomaten bei Hitler*, 680–681.

40. John G. Winant, "A Letter from Grosvenor Square," in *Churchill War Papers*, 3:1573; John G. Winant, *A Letter from Grosvenor Square: An Account of a Stewardship* (London, 1947), 197.

41. COS (41) 411th meeting, War Cabinet, Chiefs of Staff Committee, December 7, 1941, CAB-79-16-11, UK National Archives.

42. Mawdsley, *December 1941*, 54–55, 155–156.

43. At this point in the war, no records were kept of these meetings, but they were later taken down verbatim at Hitler's request.

44. Bormann to Lammers, December 7, 1941, FHQ, IFZ, Berlin, fol. 60.

45. Bormann to Lammers, December 7, 1941, FHQ, IFZ, Berlin, fol. 128–129.

46. Decree, December 7, 1941, FHQ, in *Führer-Erlasse*, 213. See also Lothar Gruchmann, "Nacht und Nebel-Justiz," VJZG, 1981, 342–396, especially 344–345.

47. Keitel to supreme commander army, December 7, 1941, Berlin, in *Attentate und Repressionen: Ausgewählte Dokumente zur zyklischen Eskalation des NS-Terrors im besetzten Frankreich 1941/42*, ed. Regina Delacor (Stuttgart, 2000), 195.

48. Reichelt, *Lettland unter deutscher Besatzung*.

49. Report Ortskommandantur Kertsch, December 7, 1941, in Marcel Stein, *Die 11 Armee und die "Endlösung" 1941/42: Eine Dokumentensammlung mit Kommentaren* (Bissendorf, 2006), 110. See also Andrej Angrick, *Besatzungspolitik und Massenmord: Die Einsatzgruppe D in der südlichen Sowjetunion 1941–1943* (Hamburg, 2003), 356–358.

50. Klemperer diary, December 7, 1941, pp. 92–93.

51. Lotte Glücklich to Otto Weill, December 7, 1941, in *Post41: Bericht aus dem Getto Litzmannstadt. Ein Gedenkbuch*, eds. Angelika Brechelmacher, Bertrand Perz, and Regina Winisch (Vienna, 2015), 211.

52. Quoted in Ritter von Leeb diary, December 7, 1941, p. 407.

53. Leonidas E. Hill, ed., *Die Weizsäcker-Papiere, 1933–1950* (Frankfurt, Berlin, and Vienna, 1974), 279.

54. Affidavit of Joseph Clark Grew, PHA, part 2, 569–570.

55. For more on Grew's diplomatic background and experience in Tokyo, see Waldo Heinrich, *American Ambassador: Joseph Grew and the Development of the United States Diplomatic Tradition* (New York, 1966)

56. Weintraub, *Long Day's Journey*, 188.

57. PHA, part 2, 569–570. In fact, this was due to an arrangement between Lieutenant Colonel Morio Tomura, a member of the army general staff's communications section, and Tateki Shirao, chief of the Ministry of Communications' censorship office, that all incoming and outgoing cables, other than those from Japan's government, would be delayed. This was initially put in place on November 29, with a five-hour delay, and then from December 6 switched to five hours one day and ten hours the next. December 7 was the first ten-hour day. See Gordon W. Prange, *December 7, 1941: The Day the Japanese Attacked Pearl Harbor* (New York, 1991), 59–60.

58. Togo, *Japan im Zweiten Weltkrieg*, 192; Grew affidavit, PHA, part 2, 570, 693.

59. Nigel Hamilton, *The Mantle of Command: FDR at War, 1941–42* (London, 2016), 44.

60. PHA, part 11, 485, 5273–5274.

61. All quotes in Prange, *December 7, 1941*, 61–64.

62. Prange, *At Dawn We Slept*, 489. (Beardall had no recollection of receiving this folder or of delivering it to the president. See David Kahn, *Codebreakers* [London, 1973], 56–57.)

63. Henry Stimson diary, December 7, Stimson Papers (hereafter Stimson MSS), Reel 7, Yale University, Sterling Memorial Library.

64. PHA, part 11, 5427–5428; Stimson statement to joint committee.

65. Stimson diary, December 7, Stimson MSS.

66. Ross T. McIntire, *White House Physician* (New York, 1946), 136–137.

67. Clifford and Okura, *Desperate Diplomat*, 121–122.

68. Clifford and Okura, *Desperate Diplomat*, 122. See also, Robert J. C. Butow, "Marching Off on the Wrong Foot: The Final Note Tokyo Did Not Send to Washington," *Pacific Historical Review* 62 (February 1994): 67–79.

69. Schmider, *Hitler's Fatal Miscalculation*, 409.

70. Bock diary, December 7, 1941, p. 341.

71. Quoted in Stahel, *Retreat from Moscow*, 39.

72. We take this list from Stahel, *Retreat from Moscow*, 37.

73. Quoted in Reinhardt, *Moskau*, 205.

74. See Reinhardt, *Moskau*, 211.

75. Quoted in Stahel, *Retreat from Moscow*, 56.

76. Xavier Moreno Julia, "Spain," in *Joining Hitler's Crusade: European Nations and the Invasion of the Soviet Union, 1941*, ed. David Stahel (Cambridge, 2018), 208–209.

77. Ritter von Leeb diary, December 7, 1941, p. 405.

78. Wilhelm Keitel, *Mein Leben: Pflichterfüllung bis zum Untergang*, ed. Werner Maser (Berlin, 1998), 343.

79. Ritter von Leeb diary, 409 (information in editor's footnote).

80. Hellmuth Stieff to his wife, December 7, 1941, in *Briefe*, 138–141.

81. Ciano diary, December 7, 1941, p. 471.

82. Dan van der Vat, *Pearl Harbor: An Illustrated History* (London, 2001), 56.

83. Fuchida, *That One Day*, 86–87.

84. Quoted in Takuma Melber, *Pearl Harbor: Japan's Attack and America's Entry into World War II* (Cambridge, 2021), 1.

85. Masanobu, *Singapore*, 93–95.

86. Beth Bailey, "The Attacks of December 7/8," in *Beyond Pearl Harbor*, 9–10; Bert Kossen, "'Seventy Minutes Before Pearl Harbor': The Landing at Kota Bharu, Malaya, on December 7th, 1941," https://dutcheastindies.webs.com/kota_bharu.html.

87. Bailey, "The Attacks of December 7/8," 10–11.

88. Masanobu, *Singapore*, 79–87, 92, and 104.

89. First quote in Winston S. Churchill to General Auchinleck (Churchill Papers 20/46), December 7, 1941, in *Churchill War Papers*, 1574. Second quote in

Winston S. Churchill to General de Gaulle (Churchill Papers 20/22), December 7, 1941, in *Churchill War Papers*, 1572.

90. Winston S. Churchill to General Auchinleck (Churchill papers, 20/46), December 7, 1941, in *Churchill War Papers*, 3:1575.

91. W. Averell Harriman and Elie Abel, *Special Envoy to Churchill and Stalin, 1941–1946* (New York, 1975), 111.

92. Quoted in David Lilienthal, *The Journals of David E. Lilienthal*, vol. 1, *The TVA Years* (New York, 1964), 506–507.

93. Kido diary, December 8, 1941, pp. 322–323. Kido's imagination may have run away with him at that point, as it was surely pitch dark at that time.

94. Quoted in Prange, *At Dawn We Slept*, 98.

95. Cordell Hull, *The Memoirs of Cordell Hull* (New York, 1948), 2:1095.

96. Togo, *Japan im Zweiten Weltkrieg*, 193.

97. First quote in Eleanor Roosevelt, *This I Remember* (New York, 1950), 232–233, and second quote in Huybertie Hamlin, December 7, 1941, "Visit at the White House," Hamlin Papers, box 358, folder 15, Library of Congress.

98. Hopkins memorandum of day's events, December 7, 1941, in *Roosevelt and Hopkins*, 430.

99. David Brinkley, *Washington Goes to War* (London, 1989), 86.

100. Himmler, *Dienstkalender*, 286.

101. Togo, *Japan im Zweiten Weltkrieg*, 193–196.

102. For an account of this first wave of attacks see Prange, *December 7, 1941*, 113–163. Kimmel's quote is on 119 from December 1, 1963, interview with the author.

103. Robert K. Chester, "'Negroes Number One Hero': Doris Miller, Pearl Harbor, and Retroactive Multiculturalism in World War II Remembrance," *American Quarterly* (2013): 31–32.

104. "Tribute to Retired Brigadier General Kenneth M. Taylor," August 1, 2008, *Congressional Record*, Senate, vol. 54, part 13, 17825–17826. See also Prange, *December 7, 1941*, 199–201, 242, 287, 289, 296.

105. Alan D. Zimm, *Attack on Pearl Harbor: Strategy, Combat, Myths, Deceptions* (Philadelphia, 2011), 21–23, 362.

106. Prange, *December 7, 1941*, 109. See also Katherine V. Dillon, Donald M. Goldstein, and Gordon W. Prange, *God's Samurai: Lead Pilot at Pearl Harbor* (Dulles, 2003), 43. For later regrets, see Jon Pearshall, "Reflecting on Fuchida, or a Tale of Three Whoppers," *Naval War College Review* 63, no. 2 (Spring 2010): 128–130.

107. Togo, *Japan im Zweiten Weltkrieg*, 193.

108. Ott report, December 8, 1941, Tokio, Pol Arch AA, R29891, fol. 25055.

109. Quoted in David L. Roll, *The Hopkins Touch: Harry Hopkins and the Forging of the Alliance to Defeat Hitler* (New York, 2013), 160.

110. Prange, *December 7, 1941*, 247.

111. Hopkins memorandum of day's events, December 7, 1941, in *Roosevelt and Hopkins*, 430–431.

112. Clifford and Okura, *Desperate Diplomat*, 123.

113. Hull, *Memoirs*, 2:1095.

114. Bailey, "The Attacks of December 7/8," 11.

115. Clifford and Okura, *Desperate Diplomat*, 122.

116. State Department Memorandum of Conversation, December 7, 1941, Hull Papers, box 60; Hull, *Memoirs*, 2:1096–1097.

117. As recalled by Kurusu in Clifford and Okura, *Desperate Diplomat*, 122.

118. At least this is what Harry Hopkins wrote in his account at the time, gleaned from Hull's report of the scene to him and Roosevelt that afternoon. In his memoirs, Hull would deny having "cussed out" the envoys. Hopkins memorandum of day's events, December 7, 1941, in *Roosevelt and Hopkins*, 431. Hull's denial in Hull, *Memoirs*, 2:1097.

119. Hotta, *Japan 1941*, 280.

120. Clifford and Okura, *Desperate Diplomat*, 123.

121. Admiral Nomura diary, December 7, 1941, in *The Pacific War Papers: Japanese Documents of World War II*, eds. Donald M. Goldstein and Katherine V. Dillon (Washington, DC, 2005), 213. Nomura and his fellow Japanese diplomats were immediately placed under close FBI surveillance.

122. Clifford and Okura, *Desperate Diplomat*, 123.

123. Stimson diary, December 7, 1941, Stimson MSS.

124. Lilienthal, *Journals*.

125. Jay Taylor, *The Generalissimo: Chiang Kai-shek and the Struggle for Modern China* (Cambridge, MA, and London, 2011), 188. The time there is given as 1 a.m. on December 8, but that is a little too early, as the attacks had not yet taken place. Of course, it is possible that he was brought news of the earlier landings in Malaya then.

126. Thus, Pankaj Mishra, "Land and Blood: The Origins of the Second World War in Asia," *New Yorker*, November 18, 2013, www.newyorker.com/magazine /2013/11/25/land-and-blood.

127. Taylor, *Generalissimo*, 188 (with quote).

128. See Robert Smith Thompson, *Empires on the Pacific: World War II and the Struggle for the Mastery of Asia* (Oxford, 2001), 106.

129. Quoted in Mitter, *Forgotten Ally*, 236.

130. Halifax diary, December 7, 1941, Halifax Papers, Borthwick Institute for Archives, York University.

131. Roberts, *Holy Fox*, 383.

132. Halifax diary, December 7, 1941, Halifax Papers, Borthwick Institute for Archives, York University.

133. From Washington to Foreign Office, Halifax No. 5649, December 6, 1941, National Archives.

134. From Washington to Foreign Office, Viscount Halifax, No. 5664, December 7, 1941, National Archives.

135. See Hugh Phillips, "Mission to America: Maksim M. Litvinov in the United States, 1941–43," *Diplomatic History* 12, no. 3 (July 1988): 261–275.

136. Memorandum by Mr. Joseph E. Davies of Washington, Memorandum of Conference Had with Ambassador Litvinov upon His Arrival, December 7, 1941, FRUS.

137. Joseph E. Davies, Litvinov Arrives in Washington, December 7, 1941, Joseph E. Davies Papers, Library of Congress.

138. Memorandum by Mr. Joseph E. Davies of Washington, Memorandum of Conference Had with Ambassador Litvinov upon His Arrival, December 7, 1941, FRUS.

139. Memorandum by Mr. Joseph E. Davies of Washington, Memorandum of Conference Had with Ambassador Litvinov upon His Arrival, December 7, 1941, FRUS.

140. James S. Hernden and Joseph O. Baylen, "Colonel Philip R. Faymonville and the Red Army, 1934–43," *Slavic Review* 34, no. 3 (September 1975): 500. The attaché in question was Major Ivan Yeaton, and he continued to predict imminent Soviet collapse as late as October. See also Michael Jabara Carley, "Grand Strategy and Summit Diplomacy," in *A Companion to Europe, 1900–1945*, ed. Gordon Martel (Malden, MA, 2006), 431.

141. Hill, *Red Army and the Second World War*, 288–292.

142. Mark Harrison, "The Soviet Union: The Defeated Victor," in *The Economics of World War II: Six Great Powers in International Comparison*, ed. Mark Harrison (Cambridge, 1998), 273–274.

143. December 5, 1941, in Gabriel Gorodetsky, ed., *Stafford Cripps in Moscow 1940–1942: Diaries and Papers*, 217.

144. Van der Vat, *Pearl Harbor*, 125.

145. Van der Vat, *Pearl Harbor*, 85. One of the older Japanese planes, the type 97, was in fact often mistaken for the German BF 109. See Stephen L. Moore, *Pacific Payback: The Carrier Aviators Who Avenged Pearl Harbor at the Battle of Midway* (New York, 2014), 97.

146. Hopkins memorandum of day's events, December 7, 1941, in *Roosevelt and Hopkins*, 431.

147. Stimson diary, December 7, 1941, Stimson MSS.

148. Linda Lotridge Levin, *The Making of FDR: The Story of Stephen T. Early, America's First Modern Press Secretary* (Amherst, NY, 2008), 252.

149. Cooper, *Old Men Forget*, 300–301 (quote 300).

150. Quoted in Dower, *War Without Mercy*, 10.

151. Huybertie Hamlin, "Some Memories of Franklin Roosevelt," April–May 1945, Hamlin Papers, box 358, folder 14.

152. Thus, Halina Rodzinski, *Our Two Lives* (New York, 1976), 211–212.

153. Thus, Jackson, *A Certain Idea of France*, 203. The nature of the repast is in dispute. It must have been supper rather than lunch because the attacks did not take place until later in the day.

154. Pawle, *War and Colonel Warden*, 143.

155. Harriman, "Foreword."

156. Churchill, *Grand Alliance*, 539–540.

157. Robert Sherwood, "The Secret Papers of Harry Hopkins," *Collier's*, July 10, 1948, p. 27.

158. Churchill, *Grand Alliance*, 539–540.

159. John Martin, Letter to Martin Gilbert, September 3, 1982, in *Churchill War Papers*, 3:1577.

160. Halifax diary, December 7, 1941.

161. Churchill, *Grand Alliance*, 539–540. This was "purplest passage of a rather monochrome volume" as noted by David Reynolds, *In Command of History: Churchill Fighting and Writing the Second World War* (London, 2004), 264.

162. Hopkins memorandum of day's events, December 7, 1941, in *Roosevelt and Hopkins*, 431.

163. Grace Tully, *F.D.R., My Boss* (New York, 1949), 254–255.

164. Both quoted in Goodwin, *No Ordinary Time*, 289.

165. Himmler, *Dienstkalender*, 286.

166. Otto Dietrich, *Zwölf Jahre mit Hitler* (Munich, 1955), 85–86.

167. Thus, Harald Sander, *Hitler: Das Itinerar. Aufenthaltsorte und Reisen von 1889 bis 1945. Band IV, 1940–1945* (Berlin, 2018), 1976. See also Mawdsley, *December 1941*, 186–187, 317, on the difficulties of establishing exactly when Hitler heard the news.

168. Keitel, *Mein Leben*, 343.

169. See Otto Lebrecht Meissner, *Staatssekretär unter Ebert, Hindenburg, Hitler: Der Schicksalsweg des deutschen Volkes von 1918–1945 wie ich ihn erlebte* (Hamburg, 1950), 576; Keitel, *Mein Leben*, 343.

170. Franz von Sonnleithner, *Als Diplomat im "Führerhauptquartier"* (Vienna, 1989), 120–121.

171. Quote in Paul Schmidt, *Statist auf diplomatischer Bühne, 1923–45: Erlebnisse des Chefdolmetschers im Auswärtigen Amt mit den Staatsmännern Europas* (Bonn, 1953), 553.

172. As quoted in Sonnleithner, *Als Diplomat*, 121. The author's emphasis on plans to bring Japan into the war against Stalin reflects his own priorities, and perhaps Ribbentrop's, but not those of Hitler.

173. Hayes, *Subhas Chandra Bose*, 73.

174. Cooper, *Old Men Forget*, 300–301 (quote 300); Bailey, "The Attacks of December 7/8," 13.

175. Quoted in Thompson, *Empires on the Pacific*, 119.

176. Barry Gough, "*Prince of Wales* and *Repulse*," 6.

177. Herde, *Italien, Deutschland*, 91; thus, Martin, *Deutschland und Japan*, 43.

178. See the recollection of Sonnleithner, *Als Diplomat*, 21.

179. Quoted in Carl Boyd, *Hitler's Japanese Confidant: General Oshima Hiroshi and Magic Intelligence, 1941–1945* (Lawrence, KS, 1993), 36.

180. Kennan, *Memoirs*, 1:134–136.

181. Hull, *Memoirs*, 2:1098.

182. December 7, 1941, part 2 (folder 2), John Toland Papers, FDR Library.

183. Tully, *F.D.R., My Boss*, 256.

184. Sumner Welles Papers, Speeches and Writings—Speech Draft, December 8, 1941, FDR Library.

185. Sherwood, *Roosevelt and Hopkins*, 432.

186. *December 7: The First Thirty Hours* (New York, 1942) 31–36.

187. Associated Press, "War Fails to Halt Anti-War Rally," *Baltimore Sun*, December 9, 1941, p. 28.

188. FRUS, 1941, 4:732–733.

189. Admiral Layton to the Admiralty, December 8, 1941, John Martin papers, in *Churchill War Papers*, 3:1577.

190. C. in C. Middle East to the War Office, 1642, December 7, 1941, 20/46/38, Churchill Papers.

191. All these telegrams are in Gilbert, *Churchill War Papers*, 3:1579–1580.

192. *War Diaries of Oliver Harvey*, 70.

193. Ivan Mikhailovich Maisky, *Vospominaniya sovetskogo diplomata, 1925–1945 gg.* (T.: Uzbekistan, 1980), 530–531, http://militera.lib.ru/memo/russian/maisky_im1/index.html. We thank Kristina Nazariyan for drawing our attention to this source.

194. Maisky, *Vospominaniya sovetskogo diplomata*, 530–531.

195. December 7, 1941, in *War Diaries of Oliver Harvey*, 70.

196. Thus, Rodzinski, *Our Two Lives*, 212. We thank Steven McGregor for drawing this source to our attention.

197. Quoted in Hotta, *Japan 1941*, 3.

198. Robert Guillain, *I Saw Tokyo Burning: An Eyewitness Narrative from Pearl Harbor to Hiroshima* (London, 1981), 1–3.

199. Thus, at any rate, the recollection of his son-in-law Morisada Hosokawa in Hotta, *Japan 1941*, 11

200. Kase, *Missouri*, 64.

201. Gerhard Krebs, *Japan im Pazifischen Krieg: Herrschaftssystem, politische Willensbildung und Friedenssuche* (Munich, 2010), 268–269.

202. Quoted in Reinhardt, *Moskau*, 205.

203. Bock diary, December 7, 1941, p. 342.

204. SKL diary, December 7, 1941, p. 102.

205. Schmider, *Hitler's Fatal Miscalculation*, 291.

206. Thus, Johannes Hürter, *Hitlers Heerführer: Die deutschen Oberbefehlshaber im Krieg gegen die Sowjetunion, 1941/42* (Munich, 2006), 321.

207. Bock diary, December 7, 1941, p. 342.

208. Quoted in Horst Boog et al., eds, *Das Deutsche Reich und der Zweite Welt-krieg*, vol. 4, *Der Angriff auf die Sowjetunion* (Stuttgart, 1985), 906.

209. SKL diary, December 7, 1941, p. 103.

210. Unfortunately, the records of the Government War Risks Insurance Scheme in National Archives BT 228 have not yet been digitized for the Second World War. We also consulted the digitized "movement cards" of each ship in the Admiralty Records in National Archives BT 389.

211. Kotelnikov, *Lend-Lease and Soviet Aviation*, 45.

212. Richard Woodman, *Arctic Convoys, 1941–1945* (London, 1994), 46, 49.

213. See the list in Bob Ruegg and Arnold Hague, *Convoys to Russia, 1941–1945* (Kendal, 1993), 24.

214. See Admiralty war diary, December 11,1941, National Archives, ADM 237 (referring to earlier events).

215. Woodman, *Arctic Convoys*, 48.

216. Leonard diary, December 7, 1941 (diary of Gunner Leonard Chapman, Royal Fusiliers; cited with the kind permission of his daughter). We thank Bruce Hudson of the Russian Arctic Convoy Museum, Aultbea, Scotland, for his very helpful advice and for making primary material available to us.

217. Chapman diary and subsequent, December 7, 1941 (this diary is cited by kind permission of his daughter Edwina Goodwin). Bruce Hudson points out that, in fact, the *Empire Wave* was sunk five hundred kilometers east of Greenland en route for Halifax.

218. Churchill, *Grand Alliance*, 437.

219. For a list of the ships in the WS-12X convoy, see Samuel Eliot Morison, *History of United States Naval Operations in World War II*, vol. 1, *The Battle of the At-lantic, September 1939–May 1943* (Boston, 1947), 111.

220. Peter Fyans, *Captivity, Slavery and Survival as a Far East POW: The Conjuror on the Kwai* (Barnsley, 2011) 54; and "Anckorn, Fergus Gordon (Oral History)," 22926, Reel 1, Imperial War Museum, April 16, 2002, www.iwm.org.uk/collections/item/object/80021489.

221. Nigel West, *Historical Dictionary of Naval Intelligence* (Lanham, MD, 2010), 20.

222. Fyans, *Captivity, Slavery*, 60.

223. Diarist 5003, December 7, 1941, Mass Observation Archive, Brighton, University of Sussex (hereafter MOA).

224. Diarist 5427, December 7–8, 1941, MOA.

225. Diarist 5333, December 7, 1941, MOA.

226. Kellner diary, December 7, 1941, p. 205.

227. Chrisanf Laskevic, December 7, 1941, in *Sowjetunion mit annektierten Gebieten I*, eds. Bert Hoppe and Hildrun Glass (Munich, 2011), 391.

228. Nathorff diary, December 7, 1941, p. 192.

229. John Modell, ed., *The Kikuchi Diary: Chronicle from an American Concentration Camp* (Champaign-Urbana, IL, 1993), 42–43; Charles Kikuchi, "A Young American with a Japanese Face," in *From Many Lands*, ed. Louis Adamic (New York, 1940), 185–234.

230. Sherwood, *Roosevelt and Hopkins*, 433.

231. Kido diary, December 8, 1941, p. 323.

232. Tully, *F.D.R.: My Boss*, 255.

233. Hamilton, *Mantle of Command*, 64–65.

234. *First Thirty Hours*, 15–16.

235. Merriman A. Smith, *Thank You, Mr. President: A White House Notebook* (New York, 1946), 116.

236. Henry Morgenthau Jr. Diaries: Volume 470, December 7, 1941, FDR Library.

237. SKL diary, December 7, 1941, p. 102.

CHAPTER 4: MONDAY, DECEMBER 8, 1941

1. "Was geht in Deutschland vor?," no date (mid-December 1941), in, *Flugblätter aus der UdSSR, September–Dezember 1941*, ed. Klaus Kirchner (Erlangen, 1988), 441.

2. Bomber Command war diary, 7/8 December 1941, in *The Bomber Command War Diaries, 1939–1945: An Operational Reference Book*, eds. Martin Middlebrook and Chris Everitt (Barnsley, 2014), 224.

3. Ugaki diary, December 8, 1941, p. 44.

4. See Shores and Cull, *Bloody Shambles*, 81.

5. Jonathan Fennell, *Fighting the People's War: The British and Commonwealth Armies and the Second World War* (Cambridge, 2019), 193.

6. Ugaki diary, December 8, 1941, p. 44.

7. Crocker diary, December 8, 1941, Edward S. Crocker II and Lispenard Seabury Crocker Papers, box 11, Library of Congress.

8. Kase, *Missouri*, 62.

9. Grew affidavit, PHA, part 2, 570–571.

10. Robert A. Fearey, "My Year with Ambassador Joseph C. Grew, 1941–1942: A Personal Account," *Journal of American-East Asian Relations* 1, no. 1 (Spring 1992): 112.

11. Crocker diary, December 8, 1941, Crocker Papers, box 11, Library of Congress.

12. First quote ("hands trembling") in Joseph Grew, *Ten Years in Japan* (New York, 1944), 493. Second and third quotes in Crocker diary, December 8, 1941, Crocker Papers, box 11, Library of Congress.

13. Valerie Reitman, "Japan Broke U.S. Code Before Pearl Harbor, Researcher Finds," *Los Angeles Times*, December 7, 2001.

14. Tokyo, Crocker diary, Crocker Papers II, Library of Congress.

15. Eleanor Roosevelt Papers, Speech and Article File, December 1941–January 1942, FDR Library.

16. Mrs. Roosevelt also told Corporal Jimmy Cannon, who was in the studio that night: "The Japanese Ambassador was with my husband today. That little man was so polite to me. I had to get something. That little man arose when I entered the room." Quoted in Goodwin, *No Ordinary Time*, 291.

17. "How to Tell Japs from the Chinese," *Life* 11, no. 25 (December 22, 1941): 81–82.

18. Eleanor Roosevelt Papers, Speech and Article File, December 1941–January 1942, FDR Library.

19. Roll, *Hopkins Touch*, 162.

20. Prange, *December 7, 1941*, 386.

21. Huybertie Hamlin, December 7, 1941, "Visit at the White House," Hamlin Papers, box 358, folder 15, Library of Congress.

22. Lynne Olson, *Citizens of London: The Americans Who Stood with Britain in Its Darkest, Finest Hour* (New York, 2010), 144–146. See also Phillip Seib, *Broadcasts from the Blitz: How Edward R. Murrow Helped Lead America Into War* (Lincoln, NE, 2011), 156–157.

23. Huybertie Hamlin, December 7, 1941, "Visit at the White House," Hamlin Papers, box 358, folder 15, Library of Congress.

24. Weintraub, *Long Day's Journey*, 562.

25. Copp, "Defence of Hong Kong," 6–7, and Macri, "Canadians under Fire," 237–256. See also Philip Cracknell, *The Battle for Hong Kong: December 1941* (Stroud, 2019), 34–44.

26. Thus, Taylor, *Generalissimo*, 188.

27. Susan Butler, *Roosevelt and Stalin: Portrait of a Friendship* (New York, 2015), 223.

28. Quoted in Horne, *Race War!*, 75.

29. We follow here the interpretation of Nicole Elizabeth Barnes, "Worldly Medicine in Wartime China: An Exploration of Pearl Harbor's Unintended Consequences," in *Beyond Pearl Harbor*, 123–124, whose scope is much wider than the title suggests. "Declaration of the Chinese Communist Party Regarding the War in the Pacific," in *Mao's Road to Power*, 7:844; "Directive of the Central Committee of the Chinese Communist Party Regarding the Pacific Anti-Japanese United Front," December 9, 1941, in *Mao's Road to Power*, 7:846.

30. Dull, *Imperial Japanese Navy*, 22.

31. Dull, *Imperial Japanese Navy*, 29.

32. Capozzola, "The Philippines," 165 (with quote). See also the very detailed description in William H. Bartsch, *December 8, 1941: MacArthur's Pearl Harbor* (College Station, TX, 2003), 255–424.

33. Maria Cynthia B. Barriga, "The Asia-Pacific War in the Davao Settler Zone, December 1941," *Philippine Journal of Third World Studies* 30 (2015): 56–90, especially 71–73.

34. Robert Fisk, *In Time of War: Ireland, Ulster and the Price of Neutrality, 1939–45* (London, 1985), 323.

35. Quoted in John Bowman, *De Valera and the Ulster Question, 1917–1973* (Oxford, 1982), 246.

36. The Earl of Longford and Thomas P. O'Neill, *Eamon de Valera* (London, 1970), 393.

37. Fisk, *In Time of War*, 324.

38. Sherwood, *Roosevelt and Hopkins*, 433.

39. Cabinet Meetings, 1941, Francis Biddle Papers, FDR Library.

40. Frances Perkins Interview, part 8, session 1, *Oral History Research Offices: Notable New Yorkers*, Columbia University Library, 67, www.columbia.edu/cu/lweb/digital/collections/nny/perkinsf/transcripts/perkinsf_8_1_67.html.

41. Frances Perkins, *The Roosevelt I Knew* (New York, 1946), 379.

42. PHA, part 19, 3503–3504.

43. Frances Perkins Interview, part 8, session 1, *Oral History*, Columbia University Library, 81.

44. December 7, 1941, Cabinet Meetings, 1941, container 1, Francis Biddle Papers, FDR Library.

45. "Remarks to Cabinet Members and Legislative Leaders" (Speech File 1399a), December 7, 1941, box 63, FDR, Master Speech File, FDR Library.

46. Hull, *Memoirs*, 2:1099.

47. Stimson diary, December 7, 1941, Stimson MSS.

48. US Department of Defense, *The "Magic" Background of Pearl Harbor* (Washington, DC, 1977), 208.

49. PHA, part 20, 4523.

50. December 7, 1941, Cabinet Meetings, 1941, Biddle Papers. In his memoirs, published seven years later, Cordell Hull was more certain that Berlin and Tokyo had a "definite undertaking" to jointly declare war on the United States, and the majority sentiment in cabinet was "that it was inevitable that Germany would declare war on us" (Hull, *Memoirs*, 2:1099). It's likely that Biddle's formulation, written contemporaneously and subtly different to Hull's account, is more accurate, not least as it more faithfully reflects the intelligence gleaned from the MAGIC intercepts.

51. Hull, *Memoirs*, 2:1099

52. Stimson diary, December 7, 1941, Stimson MSS.

53. Stimson diary, December 7, 1941, Stimson MSS.

54. Sherwood, *Roosevelt and Hopkins*, 433.

55. Cabinet Meetings, 1941–1942, Claude Wickard Papers, FDR Library.

56. Quoted in Kaiser, *No End Save Victory*, 333.

57. Quoted in Richard R. Lingeman, *Don't You Know There's a War On?: The American Home Front, 1941–1945* (New York, 1970), 27.

58. John J. Stephan, *Hawaii Under the Rising Sun: Japan's Plans for Conquest After Pearl Harbor* (Honolulu, 1984), 95–96.

59. "Remarks to Cabinet Members and Legislative Leaders," December 7, 1941, FDR—Master Speech File, FDR Library.

60. Stimson diary, December 7, 1941, Stimson MSS.

61. PHA, part 19, 3504–3506.

62. "Remarks to Cabinet Members and Legislative Leaders," December 7, 1941, FDR—Master Speech File, FDR Library.

63. "Remarks to Cabinet Members and Legislative Leaders," December 7, 1941, FDR—Master Speech File, FDR Library.

64. Frances Perkins Interview, part 8, session 1, *Oral History*, Columbia University Library, 81.

65. William Doyle, *Inside the Oval Office: The White House Tapes from FDR to Clinton* (London, 1999), 39.

66. December 7, 1941, Cabinet Meetings, 1941–1942, box 13, Claude Wickard Papers, FDR Library.

67. Samuel Ideo Yamashita, "Popular Japanese Responses to the Pearl Harbor Attack: December 8, 1941, to January 8, 1942," in *Beyond Pearl Harbor*, 90.

68. Guillain, *I Saw Tokyo Burning*, 6.

69. Yamashita, "Popular Japanese Responses," 77.

70. Yamashita, "Popular Japanese Responses," 76.

71. Yamashita, "Popular Japanese Responses," 77.

72. Thus, Togo, *Japan im Zweiten Weltkrieg*, 197.

73. Hotta, *Japan 1941*, 7.

74. Jeremy A. Yellen, "Japan and the 'Spirit of December 8,'" in *Beyond Pearl Harbor*, 69.

75. Eri Hotta, *Pan-Asianism and Japan's War, 1931–1945* (New York, 2007), 179–189.

76. Yellen, "Japan and the 'Spirit of December 8,'" 63.

77. Quoted in, Thorne, *Issue of War*, 1.

78. See Hotta, *Pan-Asianism*, 189–191.

79. Quoted in Dower, *War Without Mercy*, 36.

80. Quoted in Kazuo Tamayama and John Nunnelly, *Tales by Japanese Soldiers* (London, 2000), 26.

81. Yellen, "Japan and the 'Spirit of December 8,'" 59, 65, 67, and 68.

82. Quoted in Donald Keene, *So Lovely a Country Can Never Perish: Wartime Diaries of Japanese Writers* (New York, 2010), 16.

83. Hotta, *Japan 1941*, 8.

84. Quoted in Yamashita, "Popular Japanese Responses," 87.

85. Quoted in Yamashita, "Popular Japanese Responses," 92.

86. Yamashita, "Popular Japanese Responses," 95.

87. Yamashita, "Popular Japanese Responses," 96.

88. Yamashita, "Popular Japanese Responses," 77.

89. Kido diary, December 8, 1941, p. 323.

90. Text in "Botschaft des Tenno an die Japanische Nation," December 8, 1941, in *Der Weg zur Teilung der Welt: Politik und Strategie 1939–1945*, ed. Hans Adolf Jacobsen (Koblenz and Bonn, 1977), 187.

91. Gregory J. W. Urwin, *Facing Fearful Odds: The Siege of Wake Island* (Lincoln, NE, 1997), 225–284.

92. Dull, *Imperial Japanese Navy*, 21–22.

93. Yamashita, "Popular Japanese Responses," 94.

94. December 7, 1941, Cabinet Meetings, 1941–1942, box 13, Claude Wickard Papers, FDR Library.

95. Sol Bloom, *The Autobiography of Sol Bloom* (New York, 1948), 260–261.

96. C. P. Trussell, "Congress Decided," *New York Times*, December 8, 1941, p. 1, 6.

97. "Most Congressmen Seem to Favor a Declaration," *Baltimore Sun*, December 8, 1941, p. 2, quoted in Roland H. Worth, *Congress Declares War: December 8–11 1941* (Jefferson, NC, 2004), 16.

98. Quoted in Wayne S. Cole, *Roosevelt and the Isolationists, 1932–45* (Lincoln, NE, 1983), 503.

99. "Japs Didn't Ask U.S. to 'Pink Tea', Wheeler Warns," *Chicago Tribune*, December 10, 1941, p. 10; see also "Wheeler Backs a War on Japan," *New York Times*, December 8, 1941, p. 6.

100. Charles Lindbergh, December 7, 1941, quoted in James P. Duffy, *Lindbergh vs Roosevelt: The Rivalry that Divided America* (Washington, DC, 2010), 203–204.

101. Lindbergh, too, would maintain that Roosevelt was so "determined" to embroil an unwilling United States in the war that he was prepared "to stoop to almost any means," including precipitating the Pearl Harbor attack to achieve it. Quote in Weintraub, *Long Day's Journey*, 310.

102. Justus Doenecke, ed., *In Danger Undaunted: The Anti-Interventionist Movement of 1940–41 as Revealed in the Papers of the America First Committee* (Stanford, CA, 1990), 461.

103. Quoted in Brereton Greenhous and W. A. B. Douglas, *Out of the Shadows: Canada in the Second World War* (Toronto, 1995), 11.

104. December 7, 1941, Diaries of Mackenzie King, Library and Archives Canada.

105. Report of F. von Weiss, Cologne, December 8, 1941, in *Diplomatische Dokumente der Schweiz, 1848–1945. Volume 14 (1941–1943)*, eds. Antoine Fleury, Mauro Cerutti, and Marc Perrenoud (Vienna, 1997), 395.

106. Report of F. von Weiss, Cologne, December 8, 1941, in *Diplomatische Dokumente der Schweiz*, 397–398.

107. December 7, 1941, Cabinet Meetings, 1941, Francis Biddle Papers, FDR Library.

108. Henry Morgenthau Jr. Diaries, volume 470, December 7, 1941, Morgenthau Papers, FDR Library.

109. Henry Morgenthau Jr. Diaries, volume 470, December 7, 1941, Morgenthau Papers, FDR Library.

110. John J. McCloy diary, Sunday, December 7, 1941, John J. McCloy Papers (box DY1, folders 1–3), Archives and Special Collections, Amherst College Library.

111. Leighton and Coakley, *Global Logistics and Strategy*, 1:209, 247.

112. For an in-depth account of Hopkins's health, see Theodore N. Pappas and Sven Swanson, "The Life, Times, and Health Care of Harry L. Hopkins: Presidential Advisor and Perpetual Patient," *Journal of Medical Biography* 26, no. 1 (2018): 49–59.

113. Prange, *December 7, 1941*, 386.

114. Robert Sherwood, interview with Edward R. Murrow, September 16, 1946, Sherwood Papers, box 411, FDR Library, quoted in Roll, *The Hopkins Touch*, 164. See also Edward R. Murrow, *In Search of Light: The Broadcasts of Edward R. Murrow, 1938–1961* (New York, 1967), 108, and Alexander Kendrick, *Prime Time: The Life of Edward R. Murrow* (Boston, 1969), 240.

115. Thus Weintraub, *Long Day's Journey*, 533. For a slightly different account of the meeting but one that still stresses Donovan's uncertainty about Hitler's intentions, see Anthony Cave Brown, *The Last Hero: Wild Bill Donovan* (London, 1982), 67.

116. Malcolm R. Lowell to Colonel Donovan, December 8, 1941, Coordinator of Information, 1941, Franklin Roosevelt, Papers as President, PSF, box 128, FDR Library.

117. See Krebs, "Deutschland und Pearl Harbor," 359, and Peter Herde, *Planungen und Verwirklichung einer Flugverbindung zwischen den Achsenmächten und Japan 1942–1945* (Stuttgart, 2000), 14.

118. Ugaki diary, December 8, 1941, p. 45.

119. Quoted in Yellen, "Japan and the 'Spirit of December 8,'" 61.

120. Yamashita, "Popular Japanese Responses," 94–95.

121. Reichelt, *Lettland unter deutscher Besatzung*, 169–171.

122. Michelson, *I Survived Rumbuli*, 91–92.

123. Hamburger Fremdenblatt Abend-Ausgabe, December 8, 1941.

124. Goebbels diary, December 9, 1941 (for December 8), p. 455.

125. DNB report, December 8, 1941, p. 38

126. DNB report, December 8, 1941, p. 1.

127. DNB report, December 8, 1941, p. 1.

128. DNB report, December 8, 1941, p. 2.

129. Monday, December 8, 1941, Federal Communications Commission, Foreign Broadcast Intelligence Service (November 27–December 18, 1941), Franklin Roosevelt Papers OF, 1059c, box 11, FDR Library.

130. Hamburger Fremdenblatt Abend-Ausgabe, December 8, 1941.

131. "Betrachtung der allgemeinen strategischen Lage nach Kriegseintritt Japan/USA," no date (probably December 8, 1941), in *Die deutsche Seekriegsleitung 1935–1945. Band III. Denkschriften und Lagebetrachtungen 1938–1944*, ed. Michael Salewski (Frankfurt am Main, 1973), 238.

132. Il Presidente della commissione Italiana con la Francia, Vacca Maggiolini, al ministro degli Esteri, Ciano, December 8, 1941, Turin, in *I documenti diplomaticci Italiani. None a serie. 1939–1943. Volume VII, 24 April–11 December 1941)*, ed. Ministero degli affari esteri (Rome, 1987), 850.

133. Monday, December 8, 1941, Federal Communications Commission, Foreign Broadcast Intelligence Service (November 27–December 18, 1941), Franklin Roosevelt Papers OF, 1059c, box 11, FDR Library.

134. Vernadsky diary, December 9, 1941 (referring to December 8, 1941), Vladimir Ivanovich Vernadsky, "'Korenniye izmeneniya neizbezhni . . . '. Dnevnik 1941 goda," Militera (Voyennaya Literatura), Oleg Rubetsky, http://militera.lib.ru/db/vernadsky_vi/index.html. We thank Kristina Nazariyan for locating this source.

135. Vera Inber, *Leningrad Diary* (London, 1971), 35.

136. Luknitskiy diary, December 8, 1941, P. N. Luknitskiy, "Leningrad deystvuyet . . . Frontovoy dnevnik," Militera (Voyennaya Literatura), Oleg Rubetsky, http://militera.lib.ru/db/luknitsky_pn/01.html. We thank Kristina Nazariyan for drawing our attention to this source.

137. Boris Slavinsky, *The Japanese-Soviet Neutrality Pact: A Diplomatic History, 1941–1945*, trans. Geoffrey Jukes (London, 2004), 80.

138. Christopher Andrew and Oleg Gordievsky, *KGB: The Inside Story of Its Foreign Operations from Lenin to Gorbachev* (London, 1990), 219.

139. Dimitri Akulov, "The Soviet Union and the Formation of the Grand Alliance: Soviet Foreign Policy in Cooperation and Conflict with the Western Powers, 1941–1943" (PhD diss., University of California, Santa Barbara, 2012), 226–227, https://pqdtopen.proquest.com/doc/1012372579.html?FMT=AI. We thank Kristina Nazariyan for drawing this source to our attention.

140. December 7, 1941, in *War Diaries of Oliver Harvey*, 70.

141. Cadogan diary, December 8, 1941, Alexander Cadogan Papers, Churchill Archives, ACAD 1, box 10.

142. Ivan Maisky, *Memoirs of a Soviet Ambassador: The War, 1939–43*, trans. Andrew Rothstein (London, 1967), 222.

143. Anthony Eden, *The Eden Memoirs: The Reckoning* (London, 1965), 286.

144. December 8, 1941, in *War Diaries of Oliver Harvey*, 70–71. See also David Dilks, *The Diaries of Alexander Cadogan, O.M., 1938–1945* (London, 1971), 417.

145. *War Diaries of Oliver Harvey*, 70–71. Eden and Winant would both later suggest that Churchill had handed the phone to the US ambassador—Winant suggesting straight after Churchill spoke to Roosevelt on the evening of the seventh and Eden stating it was on the morning of the eighth. It is likely that Harvey's contemporaneous diary, recording that Eden called Winant on the morning of the eighth after speaking to Churchill, is more accurate.

146. *War Diaries of Oliver Harvey*, 70-71. Maisky, *Vospominaniya sovetskogo diplomata*, 531, http://militera.lib.ru/memo/russian/maisky_im1/index.html. We thank Kristina Nazariyan for drawing this source to our attention.

147. *War Diaries of Oliver Harvey*, 70–71, and Dilks, *Diaries of Alexander Cadogan*, 417.

148. Mitter, *Forgotten Ally*, 240.

149. Ciano diary, December 8, 1941, p. 472.

150. Ciano diary, December 8, 1941, p. 472.

151. See the account of his conversation with Ulrich von Hassell, December 21, 1941 (reporting remarks made on the morning of December 8, 1941), in *Die Hassell-Saguache, 1938–1944. Ulrich von Hassell. Aufzeichnungen vom Andern Deutschland*, ed. Friedrich Freiherr Hiller von Gaertringen (Berlin, 1994), 288.

152. Ritter von Leeb diary, December 8, 1941, p. 410.

153. Bock diary, December 8, 1941, p. 342.

154. Hotta, *Japan 1941*, 10.

155. Herde, *Italien, Deutschland*, 92.

156. Martin, *Deutschland und Japan*, 44.

157. Alfieri to Ciano, December 8, 1941, Berlin, in DDI, 846.

158. Hayes, *Subhas Chandra Bose*, 73–74.

159. Churchill, *Grand Alliance*, 542–543.

160. Meeting of the War Cabinet 125 (41), December 8, 1941, CAB 65/20/18.

161. Alex Danchev and Dan Todman, eds., *Field Marshal Lord Alanbrooke: War Diaries, 1939–1945* (London, 2001), 209. While Alan Brooke recorded this, the cabinet minutes surprisingly contain no mention of Churchill's commitment to leave for Washington as soon as possible.

162. Quoted in Bowman, *De Valera*, 247.

163. For Churchill's anxiety about the tank situation see, for example, "Friday 5 December 1941, General John Kennedy, Director of Military Operations, discusses the Middle East with Churchill," in *Witness to War*, 367–368.

164. Meeting of the War Cabinet 125 (41), December 8, 1941, CAB 65/20/18.

165. See the dramatic description in Bock diary, December 8, 1941, pp. 342–343.

166. Reinhardt, *Moskau*, 209.

167. Stephen G. Fritz, *The First Soldier: Hitler as Military Leader* (New Haven, CT, 2018), 221.

168. Engel diary, December 8, 1941, p. 118. Engel's texts, which were later revised by the author, are not a diary in the conventional sense, but their general accuracy is undoubted.

169. Quoted in Joern Happel, *Der Ost-Experte: Gustav Hilger—Diplomat im Zeitalter der Extreme* (Paderborn, 2018), 276–277.

170. Hewel diary, December 8, 1941, ED 100 Hewel 78, fol. 190. The authors assume that these remarks, which were recorded that day, were made then. They could also have been made on December 7.

171. Directive 39, December 8, 1941, in *Hitlers Weisungen*, 171–174.

172. SKL diary, December 8, 1941, pp. 118–119.

173. SKL diary, December 8, 1941, p. 115.

174. Martin Bormann to Franz Xaver Schwarz (Reichsschatzmeister), FHQ, December 8, 1941, IFZ Berlin, 11700379-80.

175. SKL diary, December 8, 1941, p. 114.

176. SKL diary, December 8, 1941, p. 118.

177. Herde, *Italien, Deutschland*, 92.

178. Goebbels diary, December 9, 1941.

179. Hans-Juergen Doscher, *SS und Auswärtiges Amt im Dritten Reich: Diplomatie im Schatten der Endlösung* (Frankfurt, 1991), 222–223.

180. Walter Manoschek, *Serbien ist judenfrei! Militärische Besatzungspolitik und Judenvernichtung in Serbien 1941/42* (Munich, 1993).

181. Rademacher file note, December 8, 1941, Berlin, ADAP, 805.

182. Heydrich to Luther, Prague, December 8, 1941, in *Am Großen Wannsee*, 115. See also Christian Gerlach, "The Wannsee Conference: The Fate of German Jews, and Hitler's Decision in Principle to Exterminate all European Jews," *Journal of Modern History*, 70 (1998): 759–782.

183. See Joachim Lilla, *Statisten in Uniform: Die Mitglieder des Reichstags 1933–1945. Ein biographisches Handbuch* (Düsseldorf, 2004), 419–420, 702–704. See also Hans-Christian Jasch and Christoph Kreutzmueller, eds., *Die Teilnehmer: Die Männer der Wannsee-Konferenz* (Berlin, 2017).

184. Mawdsley, *December 1941*, 206 and 320. Some accounts date this December 5.

185. "Schreiben der Reichsvereinigung der Juden in Deutschland, Bezirksstelle Rheinland," to the Israelitische Kultusvereinigung Luxemburg, Cologne, December 8, 1941, in *Die Verfolgung und Ermordung der europaischen Juden*, vol. 4, ed. Susanne Heim, 223–224.

186. Report of F. von Weiss, Cologne, December 8, 1941, in *Diplomatische Dokumente der Schweiz*, 396–397.

187. Berthold Rudner diary, December 8, 1941, Minsk, in *Die Verfolgung und Ermordung*, ed. Heim, 184–185. We thank Dr. Suzanne Heim for letting us have advance sight of these documents.

188. David Drake, *Paris at War: 1939–1944* (Cambridge, MA, 2015), 230–231.

189. Gerstberger report, December 8, 1941, Prague, in *Deutschland und das Protektorat Böhmen und Mähren. Aus den Akten des Auswärtigen Amtes, 1939–1945*, ed. Gerald Mund (Goettingen, 2014), 583–584.

190. RSHA report, December 8, 1941, in *Germanisierung und Genozid: Hitlers Endlösung der tschechischen Frage. Deutsche Dokumente, 1933–1945*, ed. Boris Celovsky (Dresden, Brno, 2005), 293.

191. SD daily reports 6 and 7, December 8, 1941, Oslo, in *Meldungen aus Norwegen, 1940–1945: Die geheimen Lageberichte des Befehlshabers der Sicherheitspolizei und des SD in Norwegen*, ed. Stein Ugelvik Larsen, Beatrice Sandberg, and Volker Dahm (Munich, 2008), 1:538–541.

192. Report of the Chef der Sicherheitspolizei und des SD, Berlin, December 8, 1941, in *Die "Ereignismeldungen UdSSR" 1941. Dokumente der Einsatzgruppen in der Sowjetunion*, eds. Klaus-Michael mallmann, Andrei Angrick, Juergen Matthaeus, and Martin Cueppers (Darmstadt, 2011), 858–862.

193. Hopkins note, Hopkins Papers, FDR Library, cited in Samuel I. Rosenman, *Working with Roosevelt* (London, 1952), 307.

194. Keith E. Eiler, *Mobilizing America: Robert P. Patterson and the War Effort, 1940–45* (Ithaca, 2018), 232.

195. J. M. Reeves Memorandum for Colonel Greenbaum, December 8, 1941, Robert Patterson Papers, box 143—Lend-Lease, Library of Congress.

196. "Telephone Conversation with Colonel Aurand," December 8, 1941, folder 5, J. J. McCloy, box 137, Edward Stettinius Papers, Special Collections Library, University of Virginia. We would like to thank Anne Causey for her research assistance in helping to locate this source.

197. Herring, *Aid to Russia*, 46.

198. Edward Stettinius to Oscar Cox, Subject—Accounting for Transfer Authority to the Navy, December 8, 1941, Oscar Cox Papers, box 109, FDR Library.

199. Stettinius to Harry Hopkins, Continuance of Lend-Lease Aid, December 8, 1941, Oscar Cox Papers, box 109, FDR Library.

200. Stimson diary, December 8, 1941, Stimson MSS.

201. Quoted in Henry Probert, *Bomber Harris: His Life and Times* (London, 2001).

202. Quoted in Richard Overy, *The Bombing War: Europe, 1939–1945* (London, 2013), 240.

203. Harris to Wilfried Freeman, September 15, 1941, quoted in Probert, *Bomber Harris*, 120.

204. Arthur Harris, *Bomber Offensive: Marshal of the R.A.F. Sir Arthur Harris* (London, 1947), 66.

205. Quoted in Overy, *Bombing War*, 240.

206. Winston S. Churchill Speech ("Hansard"), December 8, 1941, in *Churchill War Papers*, 3: 1584.

207. "Henry Channon: Diary ('Chips')," December 8, 1941, in *Churchill War Papers*, 3:1581.

208. December 7 and 8, 1941, in Henry Channon, *Chips: The Diaries of Sir Henry Channon*, ed. Robert Rhodes James (Harmondsworth, 1970), 313.

209. Thomsen report, December 8, 1941, AA R29807 Nr 1405, fol. 44746.

210. Dilks, *Diaries of Alexander Cadogan*, 417.

211. Leonard diary, December 8, 1941.

212. Herde, *Italien, Deutschland*, 93.

213. Huybertie Hamlin, December 8, 1941, "Visit at the White House," Hamlin Papers, box 358, folder 15, Library of Congress.

214. It was the largest daytime audience yet recorded for a broadcast in the United States. Alan Barth to R. Keith Kane, "Intelligence Report No. 1," December 15, 1941, Office of Facts and Figures, box 161, Franklin Roosevelt Papers, PSF, FDR Library.

215. "Address to Congress—Declaring War on Japan (speech file 1400) [known as Day of Infamy address], December 8, 1941," in Franklin D. Roosevelt, Master Speech Files, Franklin Roosevelt Presidential Library, box 63.

216. Huybertie Hamlin, December 8, 1941, "Visit at the White House," Hamlin Papers, box 358, folder 15, Library of Congress.

217. "Address to Congress—Declaring War on Japan (speech file 1400) [known as Day of Infamy address], December 8, 1941," in Franklin D. Roosevelt, Master Speech Files, Franklin Roosevelt Presidential Library, box 63.

218. Stimson diary, December 7 and 8, 1941, Stimson MSS.

219. When a White House aide had contacted Edith Wilson to invite her, the former first lady had tearfully remarked that "she knew how hard it was for the President to face such a crisis—she would never forget how hard it was for President Wilson." Huybertie Hamlin, December 8, 1941, "Visit at the White House," Hamlin Papers, box 358, folder 15, Library of Congress.

220. Herbert Hoover to Robert Taft, December 8, 1941, Robert Taft Papers, Library of Congress, box 34.

221. Stimson diary, December 8, 1941, Stimson MSS.

222. Henry L. Stimson and McGeorge Bundy, *On Active Service in Peace and War* (New York, 1948).

223. Hall and Wrigley, *Studies of Overseas Supply*, 173.

224. McMeekin, *Stalin's War*, 385–386.

225. Order of the Commander of the VVS of the Leningrad Front, December 8, 1941, in *Great Patriotic War*, 176.

226. Sir William Palmer (second secretary, supply), Memorandum, December 8, 1941, "Effect on Supplies Under Lend Lease of United States Entry into the War—1941," AVIA 12/123.

227. Mackensen memorandum, December 8, 1941, ADAP, 800.

228. Rosenman, *Working with Roosevelt*, 307–310.

229. Litvinov to the People's Commissariat for Foreign Affairs (Narkomindel), December 8, 1941, quoted in Phillips, "Mission to America," 263.

230. Sumner Welles, Memorandum of Conversation, December 16, 1941, FRUS 1941, 1:665.

231. Sumner Welles, Memorandum of Conversation, December 9, 1941, FRUS 1941, 4:738.

232. Anatoly Koshkin, "Roosevelt Asked Stalin to Help in the War with Japan Immediately after Pearl Harbor," 2017, https://regnum.ru/news/2328766.html. We thank Nora Topor-Kalinskij for drawing this source to our attention.

233. Tomaszewski diary, December 9, 1941, p. 147 (referring to events the day before).

234. Quoted in Stahel, *Retreat from Moscow*, 30.

235. "Press Release," December 8, 1941, Franklin D. Roosevelt Official File 198, Germany Folder—1941–43, Roosevelt Papers, FDR Library.

236. Thus, Schmider, *Hitler's Fatal Miscalculation*, 387.

237. Moreno, "Spain," 208–209.

238. Oleg Beyda, "France," in *Joining Hitler's Crusade*, 315.

239. Stahel, *Retreat from Moscow*, 40.

240. Bücheler, *Hoepner*, 160.

241. Bock diary, December 8, 1941, pp. 343–344.

242. Quoted in Reinhardt, *Moskau*, 214.

243. Quoted in Stahel, *Retreat from Moscow*, 35.

244. Heinrici to his wife and daughter, December 8, 1941, Grasnowo, in *Notizen aus dem Vernichtungskrieg: Die Ostfront 1941/42 in den Aufzeichnungen des Generals Heinrici*, ed. Johannes Hürter (Darmstadt, 2016).

245. Joachim Kuropka, ed., *Meldungen aus Münster, 1924–1944: Geheime und vertrauliche Berichte von Polizei, Gestapo, NSDAP und ihren Gliederungen, staatlicher Verwaltung, Gerichtsbarkeit und Wehrmacht über die politische und gesellschaftliche Situation in Muenster* (Münster, 1992), 557.

246. "Meldung wichtiger staatspolitischer Ereignisse. Politischer Katholizismus," December 8, 1941, Berlin, in *Berichte des SD und der Gestapo über Kirchen und Kirchenvolk in Deutschland 1934–1944*, ed. Heinz Boberach (Mainz, 1971), 602–603.

247. December 8, 1941, in *Meldungen aus dem Reich*, 8:3069–3072.

248. Hillgruber, *Hitlers Strategie*, 698.

249. Quotes in Mawdsley, *December 1941*, 210.

250. Secret Ministry of Information, Home Intelligence Weekly Report No. 63, December 17, 1941.

251. Undated note, Folder: Chron File December 1–19th 1941, Harriman Papers, box 161, Library of Congress.

252. Churchill to King George VI, Churchill Papers 20/20, December 8, 1941, in *Churchill War Papers*, 3:1585.

253. "Japanese Ambassador, Berlin, Reports Ribbentrop's Statement on German War Plans," December 4, 1941, "Government Code and Cypher School: Signals

Intelligence Passed to the Prime Minister, Messages and Correspondence," HW 1/297, National Archives, Kew. For the American intercept, see No. 822, Berlin to Tokyo, November 29, 1941, US Department of Defense, *"Magic" Background*, vol. 4, A-382-4. What is striking is that while the British intelligence intercept refers to "no question of Germany making a separate peace with England," the American version refers to a "separate peace with the United States."

254. See Krebs, "Deutschland und Pearl Harbor," 350–351.

255. No. 831 and No. 833, *Magic Background to Pearl Harbor*, vol. 4, A.387–A.389. Churchill had access to the same sources, as noted in Mawdsley, *December 1941*, 213.

256. Churchill to King George VI, Churchill Papers 20/20, December 8, 1941 in *Churchill War Papers*, 3:1585.

257. Lovell to Donovan, December 8, 1941, Coordinator of Information, 1941, Franklin Roosevelt, Papers as President, PSF, box 128, FDR Library.

258. Ribbentrop to German Embassy Washington, December 8, 1941, AA Pol Arch. R29891.

259. Il Presidente della commissione Italiana con la Francia, Vacca Maggiolini, al ministro degli Esteri, Ciano, December 8, 1941, Turin, in *I documenti diplomaticci Italiani*, 849–853.

260. Tomaszewski diary, December 9, 1941, p. 147.

261. December 9, 1941, Zygmunt Klukowski, *Tagebuch aus den Jahren der Okkupation, 1939–1944*, ed. Christine Glauning and Ewelina Wanke (Berlin, 2017) (hereafter Klukowski diary), 318.

262. See Gottwaldt and Schulle, *Judendeportationen*, 126–127.

263. Sebastian diary, December 8, 1941, p. 450.

264. Kellner diary, December 8, 1941, pp. 205–206.

265. Diarist 5067, December 8, 1941, MOA.

266. Diarist 5004, December 8, 1941, MOA.

267. Diarist 5001, December 8, 1941, MOA.

268. Kikuchi diary, December 9, 1941, p. 44.

269. Quoted in Thorne, *Issue of War*, 25.

CHAPTER 5: TUESDAY, DECEMBER 9, 1941

1. Bomber Command war diary, December 9, 1941, p. 225.

2. Urwin, *Facing Fearful Odds*, 285–292.

3. Ribbentrop to Ott, December 8, 1941, Berlin (sent December 9, 1941), in ADAP, XIII/2, 799.

4. Thus, Herde, *Italien, Deutschland*, 94.

5. Thomsen open telegram, December 8, 1941, Washington, AA R29807, nr. 1405, fol. 50.

6. Thomsen report, December 9, 1941, Washington, Pol Arch AA, R29807, fol. 44760.

7. Thomann report, December 9, 1941, Washington, Pol Arch, R29807, nr. 1405, 44779.

8. Barnet Nover, "The Die Is Cast: War Breaks Out in the Pacific," *Washington Post*, December 8, 1941, p. 13.

9. Both quoted in Hill, *Hitler Attacks Pearl Harbor*, 114.

10. See Paul Schroeder, *The Axis Alliance and Japanese-American Relations, 1941* (Ithaca, NY, 1958), 22–23.

11. Prange, *At Dawn We Slept*, 583.

12. Walter Trohan, "Report Pacific Fleet Reduced Below Japan's," *Chicago Tribune*, December 9, 1941, p. 1. For other examples, see Hill, *Hitler Attacks Pearl Harbor*, 51.

13. "War with Japan," *New York Times*, December 8, 1941, p. 22. For more examples of American doubts about Berlin's intentions, see "Berlin Shy About Aid to Tokyo," *Los Angeles Times*, December 8, 1941.

14. "Man on the Street," Washington DC, December 8, 1941, AFS 6358A, "Location: continued from Palace Theater," Library of Congress.

15. "Man on the Street," Burlington, NC, December 8, 1941, AFS 6365A, Library of Congress.

16. "Man on the Street," Washington, DC, December 8, 1941, AFS 6359A, "Location: possibly outside the billiard hall," Library of Congress.

17. December 8, 1941, in Charles A. Lindbergh, *Wartime Journals of Charles A. Lindbergh* (New York, 1970), 560.

18. Quoted in A. Scott Berg, *Lindbergh* (London, 1998), 432.

19. "Well, We're in It," *New York Daily News*, December 8, 1941, p. 31.

20. *Congressional Record*, 77th Cong., first session, vol. 87, part 9, November 26, 1941, to January 2, 1942 (Washington, DC, 1941), 9523.

21. Folder—Public Reaction, December 8, 1941, President's Personal File PPF 200B, Roosevelt Papers, FDR Library. For Roosevelt's taking account of correspondence after addresses, and his analysis of public opinion in general, see Steven Casey, *Cautious Crusade: Franklin D. Roosevelt, American Public Opinion and the War Against Nazi Germany* (Oxford, 2001), 18–19.

22. From Washington to Foreign Office, Viscount Halifax, No. 5691, December 8, 1941, CHAR 20//46/58-59, Churchill Papers, Churchill Archives.

23. Stimson diary, December 8, 1941, Stimson MSS.

24. December 8, 1941, Joseph Lash Papers, box 31, Folder—Journal, 1939–1942, FDR Library; Roosevelt, *This I Remember*, 236.

25. McCloy diary, December 8, 1941, McCloy Papers, box DY1, folders 1–3, Amherst Library.

26. December 8, 1941, Joseph Lash Papers, box 31, folder—Journal, 1939–1942, FDR Library.

27. Goodwin, *No Ordinary Time*, 296.

28. "Too Many Lights; Crowd Runs Wild in Protest," *Seattle Times*, December 9, 1941, p. 1.

29. Stephan, *Hawaii Under the Rising Sun*, 92.

30. Ugaki diary, December 9, 1941, p. 46.

31. Kido diary, December 9, 1941, p. 322.

32. Quoted in Yellen, "Japan and the 'Spirit of December 8,'" 65.

33. Quoted in Yellen, "Japan and the 'Spirit of December 8,'" 62.

34. Quoted in Hotta, *Pan-Asianism*, 190.

35. Quoted in Keene, *So Lovely a Country*, 16–17.

36. Quoted in Yamashita, "Popular Japanese Responses," 94.

37. Ugaki diary, December 9, 1941, p. 46.

38. Quote in Dower, *War Without Mercy*, 101.

39. Quoted in Thorne, *Issue of War*, 7.

40. Helen Jones, *British Civilians in the Front Line: Air Raids, Productivity and Wartime Culture, 1939–45* (Manchester, 2006), 86.

41. "Opinion," *Daily Express*, December 9, 1941, p. 2.

42. "World War," *The Times*, December 9, 1941, p. 5.

43. "Our London Correspondence: Parliament," *Manchester Guardian*, December 9, 1941, p. 4.

44. "Fighting Spirit in U.S.: Nation United by Unprovoked Attack," *Manchester Guardian*, December 9, 1941, p. 5.

45. "The United States and the Axis: Japan's Expectations," *Manchester Guardian*, December 9, 1941, p. 8.

46. Tuesday, December 9, 1941, Federal Communications Commission, Foreign Broadcast Intelligence Service (November 27–December 18, 1941), Franklin Roosevelt Papers OF, 1059c, box 11, FDR Library.

47. "The United States and the Axis: Japan's Expectations," *Manchester Guardian*, December 9, 1941, p. 8.

48. "Nazi Demands on Spain" and "Opinion," *Daily Express*, December 9, 1941, p. 1.

49. Quoted in Thorne, *Issue of War*, 8.

50. Gottwaldt and Schulle, *Judendeportationen*, 127.

51. Antonia Kimel to Moritz Uhrmann, Litzmannstadt, December 9, 1941, in *Litzmannstadt*, 213.

52. Arthur Lorch to Julius and Jeanette, December 9, 1941, in *Briefe aus den Lagern: Briefe der Brüder Arthur und Rudi Lorch aus Gurs, Noé und anderen Lagern in Südfrankreich*, ed. Renate Dressen (Pfungstadt, 2014), 179–180.

53. Klemperer diary, December 9, 1941, p. 693.

54. Quoted in Kempowski, *Das Echolot*, 366–367.

55. Klukowski diary, December 9, 1941, p. 318.

56. Tuesday, December 9, 1941, Federal Communications Commission, Foreign Broadcast Intelligence Service (November 27–December 18, 1941), Franklin Roosevelt Papers OF, 1059c, box 11, FDR Library.

57. DNB, December 9, 1941, p. 58.

58. DNB, December 9, 1941, p. 51.

59. Goebbels diary, December 10, 1941, p. 467.

60. Tuesday, December 9, 1941, Federal Communications Commission, Foreign Broadcast Intelligence Service (November 27–December 18, 1941), Franklin Roosevelt Papers OF, 1059c, box 11, FDR Library.

61. SKL diary, December 9, 1941, p. 133.

62. "Materials Required from USA," AVIA 12/123, Ministry of Supply, Effect on Supplies Under Lend Lease of United States Entry into the War—1941, UK National Archives.

63. See, J. M. A. Gwyer, *Grand Strategy: June 1941–September 1942* (London, 1964), 389.

64. Sir William Palmer to C. P. Morris, December 12, 1941, Extn. 903, AVIA 12/123, Ministry of Supply, Effect on Supplies Under Lend Lease of United States Entry into the War—1941, UK National Archives.

65. "Materials Required from USA," AVIA 12/123, Ministry of Supply, Effect on Supplies Under Lend Lease of United States Entry into the War—1941, UK National Archives.

66. Bill Clements, *Britain's Island Fortresses: Defence of the Empire, 1756–1956* (Barnsley, 2019), 245.

67. December 9, 1941, Valentine Lawford diary, LWFD 2/4, April–December 1941, Valentine Lawford Papers, Churchill Archives.

68. US 41/209/ FO 954/29A/334, UK National Archives.

69. C.O.S. (41) 414th Meeting, December 9, 1941, CAB 79/16/14 UK National Archives.

70. See Gabriel Gorodetsky, *Soviet Foreign Policy, 1917–1991: A retrospective* (London, 1994), 97–98.

71. See Peter Jahn, *Blockade Leningrads, 1941–1944: Dossiers* (Berlin, 2004), 149.

72. See Hill, *Great Patriotic War*, 157.

73. Report of XXVIII AK to AOK 18, December 9, 1941, quoted in Jahn, *Blockade Leningrads*, 122.

74. Quoted in Kempowski, *Das Echolot*, 373.

75. December 9, 1941, Leonid Ivanovich Timofeev, "Dnevnik voyennikh let," Militera (Voyennaya Literatura), Oleg Rubetsky, http://militera.lib.ru/db/timofeev _li/index.html (there are no page numbers). We thank Kristina Nazariyan for drawing our attention to this source.

76. Thus, SKL diary, December 9, 1941, p. 135.

77. *Soldatenzeitung*, December 9, 1941.

78. Quoted in Soviet General Staff, *The Battle of Moscow 1941–1942: The Red Army's Defensive Operations and Counter-offensive Along the Moscow Strategic Direction*, ed. and trans., Richard W. Harrison (Warwick, 2015), 285.

79. Kellner diary, December 9, 1941, p. 206.

80. DNB report, December 9, 1941, Archiv Institut für Zeitgeschichte, Z2044, fol. 34.

81. Reinhardt, *Moskau*, 211.

82. Stahel, *Retreat from Moscow*, 24.

83. Quoted in Stahel, *Retreat from Moscow*, 39, 41–42.

84. Stahel, *Retreat from Moscow*, 87.

85. Stahel, *Retreat from Moscow*, 51.

86. Bock diary, December 9, 1941, p. 344.

87. Schmider, *Hitler's Fatal Miscalculation*, 389–390.

88. SKL diary, December 9, 1941, p. 136.

89. Karl Doenitz, *Zehn Jahre und zwanzig Tage* (Frankfurt am Main and Bonn, 1963), 190.

90. Thus, Below, *Hitlers Adjutant*, 295.

91. Goebbels diary, December 10, 1941, pp. 464–465.

92. Goebbels diary, December 10, 1941, pp. 468–469.

93. Martin Bormann, Rundschreiben Bettr Behandlung sowjetischer Kriegsgefangener, FHQ, December 9, 1941, in BA Lichterfelde, NS 6 1336.

94. Quoted in Schmider, *Hitler's Fatal Miscalculation*, 392.

95. Quoted in Dower, *War Without Mercy*, 101.

96. B.A.D. Washington to Admiralty, December 9, 1941, Subject File 10, Copy No. 3, CAB 122/29, National Archives, Kew.

97. C.O.S. (41) 415th Meeting, December 10, 1941, CAB 79/16/15, UK National Archives. Portal was not convinced by the War Department's rationale for reallocating the planes and advised Churchill that "Staff Conversations should take place before any large releases of equipment should be made."

98. Churchill, *Grand Alliance*, 609.

99. Halifax diary, December 9, 1941, Halifax Papers, Borthwick Institute, York University.

100. Eden to Churchill, December 9, 1941, CHAR 20/46/66, Churchill Papers, Churchill Archives.

101. King George VI private diary, Tuesday, December 9, 1941, Royal Archives, Windsor Castle.

102. "Most Secret, Only to Be Handled in a Box," December 8, 1941, Premier papers, 3/458/3, Churchill Archives.

103. C. in C. Middle East to War Office, December 9, 1941, 1644 Cipher, December 9, 1941, CHAR 20/46/57, Churchill Papers.

104. John Gordon, "What Went Wrong?," *Sunday Express*, December 7, 1941, p. 2.

105. Moorehead, *Desert War*, 106.

106. Erwin Rommel to Lu Rommel, December 9, 1941, in *The Rommel Papers*, ed. Basil Liddell Hart (London, 1984), 172.

107. Scheffler and Schulle, *Buch der Erinnerung*, 1:17.

108. See Angrick, *Besatzungspolitik und Massenmord*, 338–339.

109. Record of meeting of Zentrale der Jüdischen Kultusgemeinden in Ost-Oberschlesien, December 9, 1941, in *Die Verfolgung und Ermordung*, ed. Loose, 10:209.

110. Wurm memorandum, December 9, 1941, and Wurm to Kerrl, December 1941, in *Landesbischof D. Wurm und der nationalsozialistische Staat, 1940–1945: Eine Dokumentation in Verbindung mit Richard Fischer*, ed. Gerhard Schaefer (Stuttgart, 1971), 275–286. Both documents were actually submitted to the Imperial Chancellery the following day (December 10). See also Diana Jane Beech, "Between Defiance and Compliance: The Lutheran Landesbischoefe of Hanover, Bavaria and Wuerttemberg in the Third Reich" (PhD diss., University of Cambridge, 2010), 157–158.

111. Volker Koop, *In Hitlers Hand: Die Sonder- und Ehrenhäftlinge der SS* (Cologne, Weimar, Vienna, 2010), 102–103.

112. Harold Nicolson diary, December 9, 1941, and Nicolson to Vita, December 11, 1941, in Harold Nicolson, *Diaries and Letters* (London, 1967), 254.

113. Monday, December 9, 1941, Federal Communications Commission, Foreign Broadcast Intelligence Service (November 27–December 18, 1941), Franklin Roosevelt Papers OF, 1059c, box 11, FDR Library.

114. Meissner, *Staatssekretär*, 576. We are assuming from the context that these remarks were made on December 9, 1941.

115. Freytag memorandum, "Unneutrale, beleidigende und herausfordernde Reden des Präsidenten Roosevelt," December 9, 1941, Berlin, Pol Arch AA, R29807 Nr 11405.

116. Below, *Hitlers Adjutant*, 296.

117. E.g., SKL diary, December 9, 1941, p. 137.

118. Goebbels diary, December 10, 1941, p. 468.

119. SKL diary, December 9, 1941, p. 137.

120. Colonna to Ciano, December 9, 1941, Washington, in DDI, 853–854. We are grateful to Francesco Lefebvre for drawing this source to our attention.

121. Gooch, *Mussolini's War*, 211.

122. Memorandum meeting between Ribbentrop and Alfieri, Berlin, December 10, 1941, in ADAP, 809.

123. Stettinius to Hopkins, December 9, 1941, Folder Book 5: FDR and HLH Actions, Post December 7. Hopkins Papers, box 308: Sherwood Collection, FDR Library.

124. The Administrator of Lend-Lease (Stettinius) to the President's Special Assistant (Hopkins), Washington, December 9, 1941, Hopkins Papers, FRUS, Conferences at Washington, 1941–1942, and Casablanca, 1943.

125. John J. McCloy, "Memorandum for the Secretary of War and the Chief of Staff," December 8, 1941, Patterson Papers, box 143, Library of Congress.

126. Stimson diary, December 9, 1941, Stimson MSS.

127. Stettinius to Hopkins, December 9, 1941, Folder Book 5: FDR and HLH Actions, Post December 7, Hopkins Papers, box 308: Sherwood Collection, FDR Library.

128. Tuesday, December 9, 1941, Federal Communications Commission, Foreign Broadcast Intelligence Service, Franklin Roosevelt Papers OF, 1059c, box 11, FDR Library.

129. Domarus, *Hitler: Reden und Proklamationen*, 4:1793.

130. "Aus der Aufzeichnung des Gesandten Schmidt über die Unterredung zwischen Adolf Hitler und dem Großmufti von Jerusalem Hadji Mohammed Amin al Hussein [*sic*]," November 28, 1941, in *Teilung der Welt*, 129–131 (quotes 130–131). See also Klaus Gensicke, *Der Mufti von Jerusalem: Amin al Hesseini und die Nationalsozialisten* (Darmstadt, 2007), 86–92.

131. Ott to Ribbentrop, December 9, 1941 (received 1505), Washington, Pol Archiv R29891, fol. 25091.

132. Thus, Boyd, *Oshima*, 44.

133. Thomsen report, December 8, 1941 (received December 9, 1941, 1510), Washington, AA, R29807 Nr 1404.

134. Thomsen report, December 8, 1941 (received December 9, 1941, 1510), Washington, AA, R29807 Nr 1404.

135. Thomsen report, December 9, 1941, Washington, Pol Arch AA, R29807, Nr 1405, fol. 44762.

136. Drake, *Paris at War*, 230–234.

137. Morgenthau diary, December 9, 1941, book 470, 226–227, Morgenthau Diaries, FDR Library.

138. Morgenthau diary, December 10, 1941, book 471, 55, Morgenthau Diaries, FDR Library.

139. Halifax diary, December 9, 1941, Borthwick Institute, York University.

140. Sherwood, *Roosevelt and Hopkins*, 441.

141. Lord Halifax to Prime Minister, December 9, 1941, Correspondence with Winston Churchill, Halifax, A4, 410, 4/11, Papers of Lord Halifax, Hickleton Papers, Borthwick Institute of Historical Research, University of York. We thank Lydia Dean, archives assistant at the Borthwick, for locating this letter.

142. Quoted in Roberts, *Holy Fox*, 384.

143. Halifax to Prime Minister, December 9, 1941, Correspondence with Winston Churchill, Halifax, A4, 410, 4/11, Papers of Halifax.

144. "Far Eastern War: Question of German and Italian Participation," No: 698722, December 9, 1941, Japanese Ambassador, Berlin, to Foreign Minister, Tokyo (sent December 8, 1941), Government Codes and Cypher School: Signals Intelligence Passed to the Prime Minister Messages and Correspondence, HW 1/310, from Secret Files from World War to Cold War, secretintelligencefiles .com.

Notes to Chapter 5

145. "Japan and the Axis: Proposed Three-Power Pact," No: 6986968, December 1941, Foreign Minister, Tokyo, to the Japanese Ambassador, Berlin (Sent December 7, 1941), Government Codes and Cypher School: Signals Intelligence Passed to the Prime Minister Messages and Correspondence, HW 1/310, from Secret Files from World War to Cold War, secretintelligencefiles.com.

146. "Japanese Request for Axis Declaration of War on America," No: 6987489, December 1941, Japanese Ambassador, Berlin to Foreign Minister, Tokyo (sent on December 8, 1941), Government Codes and Cypher School: Signals Intelligence Passed to the Prime Minister Messages and Correspondence, HW 1/310, from Secret Files from World War to Cold War, secretintelligencefiles.com.

147. SKL diary, December 9, 1941, p. 146.

148. Halder diary, December 9, 1941, p. 327.

149. Le Chef du service de renseignements et de Securite de "Etat major generale de l'armee, R Masson u chef de l'etat major general de l'Armee, J Huber," Swiss Army Headquarters, December 9, 1941, in *Diplomatische Dokumente der Schweiz*, 14:404.

150. Thomsen report, December 9, 1941, in Pol Archiv, R29807, Nr 1405, fol. 44763.

151. Harris, *Bomber Offensive*, 65.

152. Telephone Call with Under Secretary Patterson, December 9, 1941, Morgenthau diary, book 470, 233, Morgenthau Papers, FDR Library.

153. Roger Daniels, *Franklin D. Roosevelt: The War Years, 1939–1945* (Chicago, 2016), 232–233.

154. McCloy diary, December 9, 1941, McCloy Papers, box DY1, folders 1–3, Amherst Library.

155. "Man on the Street," Austin, Texas, December 9, 1941, AFS 6386B, Library of Congress.

156. "Man on the Street," Austin, Texas, December 9, 1941, AFS 6372A, Library of Congress.

157. "Man on the Street," Austin, Texas, December 9, 1941, AFS 6370A, Library of Congress.

158. Arthur Sears Henning, "F.D.R. Asks and Signs War Bill Within 4 hours," *Chicago Tribune*, December 9, 1941, p. 1.

159. "Japan's Perfidy Unites the American People: An Editorial," *Chicago Tribune*, December 9, 1941, p. 1.

160. Walter Lippmann, "Today and Tomorrow: Wake Up, America," *Washington Post*, December 9, 1941, p. 19.

161. "Norman Thomas Urges War to Be Localized in the East," *Baltimore Sun*, December 10, 1941, p. 6.

162. "U.S. Laggard in Hawaii, Wheeler Thinks," *Minneapolis Star Tribune*, December 9, 1941, p. 11.

462

163. "Address by Breckinridge Long, Delivered at the Annual Convention of the American Farm Bureau Federation at Chicago, Illinois," December 9, 1941, Subject File, State Department, 1939–1944, box 188, Breckinridge Long Papers, Library of Congress.

164. Reinhardt, *Moskau*, 214.

165. Ritter von Leeb diary, December 9, 1941, pp. 410–411.

166. Quoted in Stahel, *Retreat from Moscow*, 48.

167. Halder diary, December 9, 1941, p. 337.

168. Quoted in Reinhardt, *Moskau*, 215. See also Hartmann, *Halder*, 299.

169. Hill, *Red Army and the Second World War*, 309.

170. Thus, the account in Ritter von Leeb diary, December 10, 1941, p. 411n618.

171. See Stahel, *Retreat from Moscow*, 45.

172. Stieff to his wife, December 9, 1941, in *Hellmuth Stieff*, 143–44.

173. OKW Bericht, December 9, 1941, in *Die Berichte des Oberkommandos der Wehrmacht, 1939–1945*, vol. 2, *1 Januar 1941 bis 31 Dezember 1941* (Munich, 2004), 311.

174. Mackensen report, December 9, 1941, Pol Arch R29891, fol. 25087.

175. Dispatch Ott, December 9, 1941, Tokyo [received 2210], ADAP, XIII/2, 807–808.

176. Herde, *Italien, Deutschland*, 95.

177. "First War Press Conference," Confidential, Press Conference #790, Executive Office of the President, December 9, 1941, Series 1: Press Conference Transcripts, Press Conference of Franklin D. Roosevelt, 1933–1945, FDR Library.

178. Document 144, Ruth Sarles to Robert E. Wood, December 10, 1941, in *In Danger Undaunted*, 454.

179. "WW2 People's War: An Archive of World War Two Memories—Written by the Public, Gathered by the BBC," contributed on August 19, 2004, www.bbc .co.uk/history/ww2peopleswar/stories/11/a2931211.shtml.

180. Leonard diary, December 10, 1941.

181. Woodman, *Arctic Convoys*, 46.

182. Danchev and Todman, *Field Marshal Lord Alanbrooke*, 209.

183. Ismay to Churchill, August 6, 1948, Churchill Papers, 4/233.

184. Quoted in Kempowski, *Das Echolot*, 364.

185. Sebastian diary, December 9, 1941, p. 450.

186. Klukowski diary, 318.

187. Konrad Adenauer to Wim J. Schmitz, December 9, 1941, in *Adenauer im Dritten Reich*, ed. Hans-Peter Mensing (Berlin, 1991), 372.

188. Stieff to wife, December 9, 1941, in *Hellmuth Stieff*, 142–143.

189. Tomaszewski diary, December 9, 1941, p. 147.

190. Diarist 5427, December 9, 1941, MOA.

191. Diarist 5001, December 9, 1941, MOA.

CHAPTER 6: WEDNESDAY, DECEMBER 10, 1941

1. Thomsen to AA, December 9, 1941, Washington, Pol Arch R106102, f. 192145. For the American press release of these proclamations, see "Information Digest," Office of Government Reports, Washington, DC, December 9, 1941, No. 353, in *Information Digest, Volumes 321–390* (Washington, DC, 1942).

2. Halifax to Churchill, December 9, 1941, CHAR 20/46/68, Churchill Papers, Churchill Archives.

3. See his comment the following day: Ciano diary, December 11, 1941, p. 473.

4. The Chargé in Italy (Wadsworth) to the Secretary of State, Rome, December 9, 1941, 740.0011 European War 1939/17230: Telegram, FRUS 1941, vol. 1.

5. As described in Ciano to Alfieri, December 10, 1941, Rome, DDI, 858.

6. For the story of "Force Z," see Mawdsley, *December 1941*, 230–234. We have also used a very useful timeline drawn up by Samuel Clements on the basis of printed and archival documents.

7. Thomsen report, December 9, 1941, Washington, Pol Arch R29807 Nr 1405, fol. 44776-77.

8. Donovan to the President, December 9, 1941, Coordinator of Information, 1941, Franklin Roosevelt, Papers as President, PSF, box 128, FDR Library.

9. Bomber Command war diary, December 9 and 10, 1941, p. 225.

10. Mackensen to Rintelen, Rome, December 10, 1941, Pol Arch AA, R29891, 25094.

11. Prime Minister to Mr. Duff Cooper, December 9, 1941, CHAR 20/46/47-49, Churchill Papers. See also Paul Hasluck, *The Government and the People* (Canberra, 1952), 45.

12. Cooper, *Old Men Forget*, 301.

13. Memorandum by Heilingbrunner of the Ständiger Politischer Dienst, December 9–10, 1941, Pol Arch AA, R29807, Nr 1405, fol. 44780.

14. Halifax to Churchill, December 9, 1941, CHAR 20/45/65, Churchill Papers, Churchill Archives.

15. Kido diary, December 10, 1941, p. 322.

16. SKL diary, December 10, 1941, p. 80.

17. Quoted in Mark R. Frost and Yu-Mei Blasingamchow, *Singapore: A Biography* (Singapore, 2009), 240.

18. Thus, Haggie, *Britannia at Bay*, 208.

19. Thus, at any rate, the explanation in Shores and Cull, *Bloody Shambles*, 123 (with quote).

20. "Italian Embassy, Washington, Instructed to Prepare for Burning of Cyphers Etc.," No: 698746, December 9, 1941, Foreign Ministry, Rome to Italian Embassy, Washington (sent December 8, 1941), Government Code and Cypher School: Signals Intelligence Passed to the Prime Minister, Messages and Correspondence, HW 1/312, from Secret Files from World War to Cold War, secretintelligencefiles.com.

21. Churchill to Eden, December 10, 1941, CHAR 20/46/62, Churchill Papers, Churchill Archives.

22. Kido diary, December 10, 1941, p. 322.

23. Kathleen Hill, conversation with Martin Gilbert, October 15, 1982, quoted in Gilbert, *Finest Hour*, 6:1273.

24. Churchill to Stalin, November 4, 1941 in *Kremlin Letters*, 65.

25. Churchill, *Grand Alliance*, 551.

26. Danchev and Todman, *Field Marshal Lord Alanbrooke*, 210.

27. *Digest: Decisions and Announcements and Important Speeches by the Prime Minister. No. 11, 8 December to 16 December*, 3–4.

28. Cooper, *Old Men Forget*, 301.

29. Mawdsley, *December 1941*, 275.

30. See Goebbels diary, December 11, 1941, p. 472.

31. DNB, December 10, 1941, p. 14.

32. SKL diary, December 10, 1941, p. 86.

33. Ugaki diary, December 10, 1941, pp. 49–50.

34. Thus, Guillain, *I Saw Tokyo Burning*, 44.

35. Quoted in Yellen, "Japan and the 'Spirit of December 8,'" 65.

36. Quoted in Yamashita, "Popular Japanese Responses," 82–83.

37. Nicolson diary, December 10, 1941, p. 196.

38. Quoted in Kempowski, *Das Echolot*, 380.

39. Leonard diary, December 10, 1941.

40. Fyans, *Captivity, Slavery*.

41. Thomsen report, December 9, 1941 (received 9:10 a.m. on December 10), Washington, Pol Arch AA, R29807, Nr 1405, 44778.

42. Akulov, "The Soviet Union and the Formation of the Grand Alliance," 226–227. We thank Kristina Nazariyan for drawing this source to our attention.

43. Quoted in Koshkin, "Roosevelt Asked Stalin." We thank Nora Topor-Kalinskij for drawing this work to our attention.

44. Wednesday, December 10, 1941, Federal Communications Commission, Foreign Broadcast Intelligence Service (November 27–December 18, 1941), Franklin Roosevelt Papers OF, 1059c, box 11, FDR Library.

45. Koshkin, "Roosevelt Asked Stalin." We thank Nora Topor-Kalinskij for drawing this work to our attention.

46. Koshkin, "Roosevelt Asked Stalin." We thank Nora Topor-Kalinskij for drawing this work to our attention.

47. See Christof Mauch, *The Shadow War Against Hitler: The Covert Operations of America's Wartime Secret Intelligence Service* (New York, 2003), 35–36 (quote 36).

48. Special Correspondent, "Hitler Declares War on U.S. Today," *Daily Express*, December 10, 1941, p. 1.

49. "U.S. and the Axis: Question of Full Belligerence," *The Times*, December 10, 1941, p. 4.

50. "Supply Lines," *Manchester Guardian*, December 10, 1941, p. 4.

51. "The Australian People's Part," *Age*, December 10, 1941.

52. "The Line Up in the World War," *Sydney Morning Herald*, December 10, 1941.

53. *Digest: Decisions and Announcements*, 3–4.

54. Kate Darian-Smith, "Pearl Harbor and Australia's War in the Pacific," in *Beyond Pearl Harbor*, 175.

55. DNB report, December 11, 1941, p. 4.

56. DNB report, December 10, 1941, p. 9.

57. "Japan Says Allies Are Broken at Sea," *New York Times*, December 11, 1941 (referring to broadcasts on December 10, 1941).

58. Wednesday, December 10, 1941, Federal Communications Commission, Foreign Broadcast Intelligence Service (November 27–December 18, 1941), Franklin Roosevelt Papers OF, 1059c, box 11, FDR Library.

59. See now Varley, *Vichy's Double Bind*.

60. See Ciano's account in "Meeting of Ciano with Darlan," December 10, 1941, in DDI, 861–863.

61. See Karine Varley, "Vichy and the Complexities of Collaborating with Fascist Italy: French Policy and Perceptions Between June 1940 and March 1942," *Modern and Contemporary France* 21 (2013): 325 (with quotes).

62. Ciano diary, December 10, 1941, p. 772 (describing meeting in Turin the day before).

63. See Varley, "Vichy and the Complexities," 325 (with quotes).

64. War Cabinet, Chiefs of Staff Committee, Minutes of Meeting Held on December 10, 1941, CAB 79-16-15.

65. "Aufzeichnung Ruhe für Weizsäcker," December 10, 1941, Pol Archiv AA R29891, 25095-6.

66. See the descriptions in Arvid Fredborg, *Behind the Steel Wall: A Swedish Journalist in Berlin, 1941–43* (New York, 1944), 57, and Louis P. Lochner, *What About Germany?* (London, 1943), 262–263. Lochner gives the time of the meeting as 1 p.m., but from the context it was more likely earlier.

67. SKL diary, December 10, 1941, pp. 154 and 158.

68. Quoted in Reinhardt, *Moskau*, 208.

69. See Reinhardt, *Moskau*, 209.

70. Reinhardt, *Moskau*, 210.

71. Quoted in Stahel, *Retreat from Moscow*, 52.

72. Bock diary, December 10, 1941, pp. 344–345.

73. Goebbels diary, December 11, 1941, p. 475.

74. Reinhardt, *Moskau*, 215.

75. Skryabina diary, December 10, 1941.

76. Frank diary, December 10, 1941, p. 449.

77. Goebbels diary, December 11, 1941, p. 76.

78. Herde, *Italien, Deutschland*, 95.

79. Thus, Taschka, *Diplomat ohne Eigenschaften?*, 216.

80. Ribbentrop to Ott, December 10, 1941, Berlin, ADAP, 811–812.

81. Hans-Heinrich Dieckhoff memorandum for Ribbentrop, December 10, 1941, Berlin, Pol Arch AA, R29807, Nr 1405.

82. Weizsäcker diary, December 10, 1941, p. 280.

83. List of journalists in Berlin, December 10, 1941, Pol Arch AA, R29891, fol. 25102.

84. Wörmann to Ribbentrop (via Weizsäcker), December 10, 1941, Berlin, Pol Arch AA, R29891, 2500-5. On Enderis, see Leff, *Buried by the Times*, 66–67.

85. Memorandum for Wörmann by Albrecht, December 10, 1941, Berlin, Pol Arch R29891, 25098.

86. "Henry Channon: Diary ('Chips')," December 10, 1941, in *Churchill War Papers*, 3:1598–1599.

87. The Ambassador in the United Kingdom (Winant) to the Secretary of State, FRUS, Diplomatic Papers, 1941, Far East, vol. 5, 740.0011 P.W./900: Telegram.

88. Danchev and Todman, *Field Marshal Lord Alanbrooke*, 210.

89. Copp, "Defence of Hong Kong," 7.

90. Fisk, *In Time of War*, 325.

91. The Ambassador in the United Kingdom (Winant) to the Secretary of State, FRUS, Diplomatic Papers, 1941, Far East, vol. 5, 740.0011 P.W./900: Telegram.

92. Secret Ministry of Information, Home Intelligence Weekly Report No. 63, December 17, 1941.

93. Home Intelligence Appendix, Public Attitude Towards the U.S.A., December 1941.

94. Secret Ministry of Information, Home Intelligence Weekly Report No. 63, December 17, 1941.

95. December 10, 1941, in *War Diaries of Oliver Harvey*, 71.

96. For information on the SC-57 Convoy, we have drawn on Arnold Hague, *The Allied Convoy System 1939–1945: Its Organization, Defence and Operation* (London, 2000), 133–137; Donald A. Bertke, Gordon Smith, and Don Kindell, *World War II Sea War*, vol. 5, *Air Raid Pearl Harbor: This Is Not a Drill* (Dayton, OH, 2013), 36.

97. S. W. Roskill, *The War at Sea, 1939–1945*, vol. 1, *The Defensive* (London, 1954), 538–539.

98. Diarist 5203, December 10, 1941, MOA.

99. Himmler, *Dienstkalender*, 287.

100. Halder, KTB, December 10, 1941, pp. 337–338.

101. Quoted in Reinhardt, *Moskau*, 216.

102. OKW, KTB, December 10, 1941, p. 809.

103. Quoted in Reinhardt, *Moskau*, 216.

104. *Ereignismeldungen* 144, December 10, 1941, pp. 863–871 (quotes 865).

105. Goebbels diary, December 11, 1941, p. 474.

106. Report from Ribbentrop's Office, December 10, 1941, Berlin, in *Die Einsatzgruppen in der besetzten Sowjetunion 1941/42. Die Tätigkeits- und Lageberichte des Chefs der Sicherheitspolizei und des SD*, ed. Peter Klein (Berlin, 1997), 217.

107. Report from Ribbentrop's Office, December 10, 1941, Berlin, in *Die Einsatzgruppen in der besetzten Sowjetunion*, 220.

108. BDSudSD Oslo, Tagesrapport 9, December 10, 1941, in *Meldungen aus Norwegen*, 543–544 (quote 544).

109. Meldung RSHA, IV, December 10, 1941, in *Germanisierung und Genozid*, 294.

110. Report from Ribbentrop's Office, December 10, 1941, Berlin, *Die Einsatzgruppen in der besetzten Sowjetunion*, 217.

111. OKW, KTB, December 10, 1941, p. 810.

112. Report from Ribbentrop's Office, December 10, 1941, Berlin, in *Die Einsatzgruppen in der besetzten Sowjetunion*, 217–218.

113. Report from Ribbentrop's Office, December 10, 1941, Berlin, in *Die Einsatzgruppen in der besetzten Sowjetunion*, 217–218 (quote 217).

114. Fanny Werner to Fanny Heller, Lodz Ghetto, December 10, 1941, in *Litzmannstadt*, 200–201.

115. See the description and photograph in Scheffler and Schulle, *Buch der Erinnerung*, 1:17, 21.

116. Angrick, *Besatzungspolitik und Massenmord*, 345. There is some doubt as to the exact day this event took place, but historians agree that it was most likely on December 10, 1941.

117. Thus, Angrick, *Besatzungspolitik und Massenmord*, 535–554.

118. Erik Grimmer-Solem, "Selbstständiges verantwortliches Handeln: Generalleutnant Hans Graf von Sponeck (1888–1944) und das Schicksal der Juden in der Ukraine, Juni–Dezember 1941," *Militärgeschichtliche Zeitschrift* 72 (2013): 44.

119. Angrick, *Besatzungspolitik und Massenmord*, 340.

120. Franziszek Piper, "Die Rolle des Lagers Auschwitz bei der Verwirklichung der nationalsozialistischen Ausrottungspolitik. Die doppelte Funktion von Auschwitz als Konzentrationslager und als Zentrum der Judenvernichtung," in *Die nationalsozialistischen Konzentrationslager: Entwicklung und Struktur*, eds. Ulrich Herbert, Karin Orth, and Christoph Dieckmann (Göttingen, 1998), 390–414 (especially 394).

121. Czech, *Kalendarium der Ereignisse*, 152.

122. Quoted in Richard Breitman, "Nazi Espionage: The Abwehr and SD Foreign Intelligence," in *US Intelligence and the Nazis*, 99.

123. A point made by Mawdsley, *December 1941*, 52. On British armored forces in North Africa, see Colin Robins, "Orders of Battle of British Tank Forces and Tank Types at Key Dates in the Western Desert, 1940–42," *Journal of the Society for Army Historical Research* 93, no. 373 (Spring 2015): 52–53.

124. "Moorehead Tells How Libya Panzers Are Being Smashed Westwards," *Daily Express*, December 11, 1941, p. 2.

125. Memorandum Kramarz, December 10, 1941, ADAP, 814.

126. OKW Berichte, December 10, 1941, p. 311.

127. DNB, December 10, 1941, p. 1. See also David Brock Katz, *South Africans Versus Rommel: The Untold Story of the Desert War in World War II* (Guildford, CT, 2018), 154–157.

128. Goebbels diary, December 11, 1941, p. 475.

129. Goebbels diary, December 11, 1941, p. 473.

130. Ritter von Leeb diary, December 10, 1941, p. 412.

131. This included one thousand five-hundred-pound general-purpose bombs, over a million rounds of 30 caliber armor-piercing ammunition, and four 90 mm anti-aircraft guns. "Memorandum from John J. McCloy," December 10, 1941, Sherwood Collection, Folder Book 5: FDR and HLH Actions, Post December 7, Harry Hopkins Papers, box 308, FDR Library.

132. December 9, 1941, Morgenthau diary, book 471, 306, Morgenthau papers, FDR Library.

133. "Telephone Conversation with General Moore, Deputy Chief of Staff," December 12, 1941, Folder 5: J. J. McCloy, box 137, Stettinius Papers.

134. Quoted in Richard C. Lukas, *Eagles East: The Army Air Forces and the Soviet Union, 1941–1945* (Tallahassee, FL, 1970), 58.

135. "Man on the Street," Bloomington, IN, December 10, 1941, AFS 6360A, Library of Congress.

136. December 10, 1941, Morgenthau diary, book 472, 11–12, Morgenthau Papers, FDR Library.

137. Stimson diary, December 10, 1941, Stimson MSS.

138. The Chargé in the Soviet Union (Thurston) to the Secretary of State, FRUS, Diplomatic Papers, 1941, Far East, vol. 4, 740.0011 Pacific War/864: Telegram.

139. Stimson diary, December 10, 1941, Stimson MSS.

140. The Chargé in the Soviet Union (Thurston) to the Secretary of State, FRUS, Diplomatic Papers, 1941, Far East, vol. 4, 740.0011 Pacific War/864: Telegram.

141. Leighton and Coakley, *Global Logistics and Strategy*, 1:270.

142. Woodman, *Arctic Convoys*, 47.

143. Himmler, *Dienstkalender*, December 10, 1941, p. 287.

144. Himmler, *Dienstkalender*, December 10, 1941, p. 287.

145. Dr. Schmidt note for Wörmann, December 10, 1941, Pol Arch AA, R29891, fol. 25115.

146. Mackensen memorandum, December 11, 1941, Rome, ADAP, 817–818 (reporting on events of the day before).

147. See Herde, *Italien, Deutschland*, 98.

148. The cartoon is printed in Dower, *War Without Mercy*, 181.

149. *Minneapolis Morning Tribune*, December 10, 1941, p. 10. The story appeared under different headlines in the *Washington (DC) Evening Star*, December 10, 1941, p. B8; *Cincinnati Enquirer*, December 10, 1941, p. 2; *Nebraska State Journal*, December 10, 1941, p. 1. All cited in Hill, *Hitler Attacks Pearl Harbor*, 60.

150. *Atlanta Journal*, December 11, 1941, p. 29. Cited in Hill, *Hitler Attacks Pearl Harbor*, 51, 116.

151. Paul Mallon, "News Behind the News," *Statesman Journal* (OR), December 10, 1941, p. 4.

152. Poage to Knox, December 10, 1941, in *Blacks in the World War II Naval Establishment*, eds. Morris J. McGregor and Bernard C. Nalty (Wilmington, DE, 1977), 12.

153. *Congressional Record*, 77th Cong., first session, vol. 87, part 9, 9525–9526.

154. For more on Mitchell's evolution and his wartime campaign for civil rights, see Dennis S. Nordin, *The New Deal's Black Congressman: A Life of Arthur Wergs Mitchell* (Columbia, MO, 1997), 240–244. See also Walter C. Daniels, *Black Journals of the United States* (London, 1982), 146.

155. Stimson diary, December 10, 1941, Stimson MSS.

156. Matloff and Snell, *Strategic Planning for Coalition Warfare*, 83.

157. Stimson diary, December 10, 1941, Stimson MSS.

158. December 10, 1941, Morgenthau diary, book 472, 79, Morgenthau Papers, FDR Library.

159. Cable C-139x, in *Churchill and Roosevelt*, 1:284.

160. War Cabinet 126 (41), December 10, 1941, CAB 65/20/19.

161. King George VI to Churchill, December 10, 1941, CHAR 20/20/68, Churchill Papers, Churchill Archives.

162. W.M. (41), 136th Conclusions, Minute 2, Confidential Annex, CAB 65/24/12. See also Reynolds and Pechatnov, *Kremlin Letters*, 72–73.

163. Harriman to Hopkins, December 10, 1941, Cable No. 101839, Folder: Chron File December 1–19th 1941, box 161, W. Averell Harriman Papers, Library of Congress.

164. Harriman to Hopkins, December 10, 1941, Cable No: 101843, Folder: Chron File December 1–19th 1941, box 161, Harriman Papers, Library of Congress.

165. December 10, 1941, AVIA 38, 1049—BSC, Mtg 54, in Jean Monnet Duchêne Cources, JMDS-13, British Supply Council Minutes, 10/07/1940—21/01/1942, Historical Archives of the European Union, European University Institute.

166. An indication of the frequency of calls is contained in McCloy diary, December 8–11 1941, McCloy Papers, box DY1, folders 1–3, Amherst Library.

167. "New Year's Day, 1942," typescript diary, 1941-12, JACB 1/12, Ian Jacob Papers, Churchill College, University of Cambridge.

168. Leighton and Coakley, *Global Logistics and Strategy*, 197.

169. Jean Monnet, *Memoirs* (New York, 1978), 173.

170. Clifford P. Hackett, *The Father of Europe: The Life and Times of Jean Monnet* (Washington, DC, 2018), 76–77.

171. December 10, 1941, AVIA 38, 1049—BSC, Mtg 54, in Jean Monnet Duchêne Cources, JMDS-13, British Supply Council Minutes, 10/07/1940—21/01/1942, Historical Archives of the European Union, European University Institute.

172. December 10, 1941, Morgenthau diary, book 472, 80–81, Morgenthau Papers, FDR Library.

173. Letter to Hiram Johnson Jr., December 13, 1941, in Hiram Johnson, *The Diary Letters of Hiram Johnson*, 7:49.

174. *Congressional Record*, 77th Cong., first session, vol. 87, part 9, 9602.

175. "Document 147, Ruth Sarles to R. Douglas Stuart, Jr., December 10, 1941" and "Document 148, William R. Castle to R. Douglas Stuart, Jr. December 10, 1941," in *In Danger Undaunted*, 462–467.

176. "FDR-Churchill, July-December 1941," vol. 3, Franklin D. Roosevelt Papers as President: Map Room Papers, 1941–1945, FDR Library.

177. Foreign Broadcast Monitoring Service, Federal Communications Commission Daily Report, December 11, FDR Library.

178. Quoted in Kempowski, *Das Echolot*, 383.

179. US Lon 157, December 1941, British Supply Council in North America to Supply Committee, CAB 1222/29.

180. Urwin, *Facing Fearful Odds*, 309–335; Dull, *Imperial Japanese Navy*, 24–25. Because of the time difference, these actions took place on December 11, 1941, local time.

181. Popudrenko diary, December 10, 1941, pp. 30, 34.

182. Ciano diary, December 10, 1941, p. 472.

183. Sebastian diary, December 10, 1941, p. 450.

184. Diarist 5004, December 10, 1941, MOA.

185. Diarist 5001, December 10, 1941, MOA.

186. Diarist 5004, December 10, 1941, MOA.

187. December 10, 1941, Diaries of Mackenzie King, Library and Archives Canada.

188. Kellner diary, December 10, 1941, pp. 206–207.

189. Halder, KTB, December 10, 1941, pp. 338–339.

190. Halder, KTB, December 10, 1941, p. 339.

191. Ribbentrop circular, December 10, 1941, Berlin, Pol Arch AA, R29891.

192. Ribbentrop to Embassy in Washington, December 10, 1941, ADAP, 812–813.

193. AP, *Covering Tyranny: The AP and Nazi Germany: 1933–1945* (New York, 2017), www.ap.org/about/history/ap-in-germany-1933-1945/ap-in-germany-report .pdf.

194. Stephen L. Vaughn, ed., *Encyclopedia of American Journalism*, 38.

195. Kennan, *Memoirs*, 1:134–136.

196. "American Newsmen in Berlin, Reprisal Victims," *Morning Herald* (Union-town, Pennsylvania), December 11, 1941, p. 1.

197. This was what Thuermer was reported as saying, although he claims to have written more colloquially: "Bye-Bye: We Jug-Warding Now." See Angus Mac-Lean Thuermer, "Pearl Harbor in Nazi Berlin," *Nieman Reports* 49, no. 4 (Winter 1995): 70. See also, "Nazis Arrest U.S. Reporters as a Reprisal," *Chicago Tribune*, December 11, 1941, p. 11.

198. Joachim Schröder et al., eds., *Erinnerungsort Alter Schlachthof: Ausstellungskatalog* (Düsseldorf, 2019).

199. DNB report, December 10, 1941, p. 53. See also "Berlin Cuts Off News Wires to U.S.," *Washington Post*, December 11, 1941, p. 1.

CHAPTER 7: THURSDAY, DECEMBER 11, 1941

1. Doenitz, *Zehn Jahre*, 192.

2. SKL diary, December 11, 1941, p. 170 ("Lagebesprechung beim Chef SKL").

3. C. in C. Middle East to the War Office, December 11, 1941, CHAR 20/46/75-76, Churchill Archives.

4. "Berlin Cuts Off News Wires," 1. As the *Post*'s reporter noted, the confirmation that Hitler would address the Reichstag "climaxed a series of reports" throughout the day on December 10 that suggested Hitler seemed poised to issue a declaration of war. If the press was aware of these reports by the evening of December 10, then it is almost certain Roosevelt was too.

5. "FDR-Churchill, July-December 1941," vol. 3, Franklin D. Roosevelt Papers as President: Map Room Papers, 1941–1945, FDR Library.

6. Goodwin, *No Ordinary Time*, 149–154, 263 (both quotes on 153).

7. Quotes in Tor Bomann-Larsen, *Hjemlandest—Haakon and Maud VII* (Oslo, 2016), 198. We thank Hilde Restad for her help with translating this source.

8. Fennell, *Fighting the People's War*, 195.

9. Cooper, *Old Men Forget*, 301–302.

10. Quoted in Masanobu, *Singapore*, 106.

11. "Loss in the Pacific," *The Times*, December 11, 1941, p. 5.

12. "Opinion," *Daily Express*, December 11, 1941, p. 2.

13. "Memorandum to the President: London Press Review," December 13, 1941, PDF: Office of Strategic Services: Donovan Reports, December 12–17, 1941, folder 1, FDR Library.

14. "Lessons from Disaster," *The Times*, December 11, 1941, p. 5.

15. Quoted in Gough, "*Prince of Wales* and *Repulse*," 20.

16. Geoffrey Tebbutt, "The Dark Horizon," *Herald*, December 11, 1941.

17. "Coastal Raids Possible Here," *Daily Telegraph*, December 11, 1941. We thank Josh Abbey for his help in locating these sources.

18. *New York Times*, December 11, 1941. We thank Steve McGregor for drawing this source to our attention.

19. "Berlin Cuts Off News," 1.

20. "Hitler to Address Reichstag Today," *New York Times*, December 11, 1941, p. 1.

21. Lochner, *What About Germany?*, 365.

22. Goebbels diary, December 11, 1941, pp. 481–482.

23. Note by Albrecht, December 11, 1941, Berlin, Pol Arch AA, 29891, fol. 25127.

24. Wörmann note, December 11, 1941, Berlin, Pol Arch AA, R29891, fol. 25110.

25. Goebbels diary, December 11, 1941, pp. 481–482.

26. Gottwaldt and Schalle, *Judendeportationen*, 127.

27. Thus, Yaacov Lozowick, "Documentation 'Judenspediteur': A Deportation Train," *Holocaust and Genocide Studies* 6, no. 3 (1991): 284, and Paul Salitter, "Confidential Report About the Evacuation of Jews to Riga, 11 December to 17 December 1941," December 26, 1941, in "Documentation," 286–287. It should be noted that our picture of this deportation is largely drawn from the account of the perpetrators.

28. Anonymous letter to Emil Hacha, December 11, 1941, Trhove Sviny/Schweinitz, in *Die Verfolgung und Ermordung*, ed. Heim, 705.

29. Salitter, "Confidential Report," 287.

30. Mackensen Memorandum, December 11, 1941, Rome, ADAP, 820.

31. Ciano diary, December 11, 1941, p. 473.

32. SKL diary, December 11, 1941, pp. 176–177 (quote 177).

33. Kido diary, December 11, 1941, p. 322.

34. Salitter, "Confidential Report," 287.

35. December 11, 1941, in *Meldungen aus dem Reich*, 3074.

36. Konferenz, December 11, 1941, in *Wollt ihr den totalen Krieg?*, 197–198.

37. Ciano to Colonna, December 11, 1941, Rome, DDI, 864.

38. See the account (with quotes) in Alfieri to Ciano, December 11, 1941, Berlin, DDI, 867–868.

39. Thus, Bernd Martin, "Die Militaerische Vereinbarung zwischen Deutschland, Italien und Japan vom 18. Januar 1942," in *Probleme des Zweiten Weltkrieges*, ed. Andreas Hillgruber (Cologne and Berlin, 1967), 134 (the phrase here is referring to the agreement of December 11, 1941).

40. "Deutsch-italienische-japanisches Abkommen vom 11.12.1941 über die gemeinsame Kriegfuehrung," Berlin, in *Teilung der Welt*, 132.

41. "War Cabinet, Chiefs of Staff Committee, C.O.S. (41) 417th Meeting," CAB 79-16-17.

42. Danchev and Todman, *Field Marshal Lord Alanbrooke*, 210.

43. "War Cabinet, Chiefs of Staff Committee, C.O.S. (41) 417th Meeting," December 11, 1941, CAB 79-16-17. For more on Turkey's place in British strategy at this time, see Nicholas Tamkin, "Britain, the Middle East and the 'Northern Front,' 1941–42," *War in History* 15, no. 3 (2008): 314–336.

44. Admiralty to B.A.D. 927, Supplies from U.S.A. General, December 12, 1941, CAB 1222/29.

45. "Materials Required from U.S.A.," Ministry of Supply, Effect on Supplies Under Lend-Lease of United States Entry into War—1941, AVIA 12/123.

46. William Palmer to C. P. Morris, December 12, 1941, Ministry of Supply, Effect on Supplies Under Lend-Lease of United States Entry into War—1941, AVIA 12/123.

47. Ciano to Colonna, Rome, December 11, 1941, DDI, 864.

48. Mackensen memorandum, December 11, 1941, ADAP, 820.

49. "Henry Channon: diary ('Chips'), 11 December 1941," in *Churchill War Papers*, 1599.

50. "Diary, December 11, 1941," in *Harold Nicholson Diaries*, 254.

51. Churchill, *Second World War*, 3:552.

52. "Winston S. Churchill (Speech)," in *Churchill War Papers*, 3:1601–1611.

53. "Henry Channon diary ('Chips'), 11 December 1941," and Harold Nicolson, letter to his wife, December 11, 1941 in *Churchill War Papers* 3:1599–1600.

54. Secret Ministry of Information, Home Intelligence Weekly Report No. 63, December 17, 1941.

55. "Winston S. Churchill (Speech)," in *Churchill War Papers*, 3:1609.

56. Harriman to Hopkins, December 11, 1941, Sherwood Collection, Folder Book 5: FDR and HLH Actions, Post December 7, box 308, Hopkins Papers, FDR Library.

57. D. M. Horner, *Inside the War Cabinet: Directing Australia's War Effort 1939–45* (St. Leonards, Australia 1996), 83.

58. Quoted in Horner, *Inside the War Cabinet*, 84; Shedden Manuscript, book 4, box 1, chap. 8., 1, CRS A5954, item 768/13, National Archive of Australia.

59. Horner, *Inside the War Cabinet*, 83; Defence of Australia and Adjacent Areas—Appreciation by Australian Chiefs of Staff—December 1941, CRS A2671, item 14/031/227, National Archive of Australia.

60. Hasluck, *Government and the People*, 41; Cablegram 789, Commonwealth Government to Lord Cranborne, U.K. Secretary of State for Dominion Affairs, December 11, 1941. We thank Mr. Josh Abbey for drawing our attention to these sources.

61. Himmler, *Dienstkalender*, December 11, 1941, p. 288.

62. Thermann report, December 11, 1941, Buenos Aires, ADAP, 815–816.

63. Hitler to Gustav V. Adolf, Führerhauptquartier, December 7, 1941, ADAP, 788–789.

64. Report from Stockholm Embassy, December 11, 1941, Stockholm, 814–815.

65. Fredborg, *Behind the Steel Wall*, 57.

66. Schmidt Protocol, December 11, 1941, Berlin, ADAP, 817. See also, Note handed by Ribbentrop to US charge, December 11, 1941, Plo Arch R29891, fol. 25124-25, and Herde, *Italien, Deutschland*, 99.

67. Schmidt, *Statist auf diplomatischer Bühne*, 554–555.

68. Ciano diary, December 11, 1941, p. 473.

69. "America and the War: Italian Ambassador, Washington, Reports Views of Mr. Phillips," No: 698817, December 11, 1941, Colonna, Washington to Foreign Ministry, Rome (sent on December 9, 1941), Government Codes and Cypher School: Signals Intelligence Passed to the Prime Minister Messages and Correspondence, from Secret Files from World War to Cold War, secretintelligencefiles .com.

70. See the description in DNB, December 11, 1941, pp. 21–22.

71. Czech, *Kalendarium der Ereignisse*, 153.

72. Czech, *Kalendarium der Ereignisse*, 152–153.

73. Angrick, *Besatzungspolitik und Massenmord*, 341–344.

74. Lochner, *What About Germany?*, 366. Just as the speech was about to begin, however, the journalists were transported to a hotel in Grünau.

75. Thus, Fredborg, *Behind the Steel Wall*, 57–58.

76. See the description in DNB, December 11, 1941, pp. 21–22.

77. See the description in DNB, December 11, 1941, pp. 21–22, 30–32.

78. Speech, December 11, 1941, in *Hitler: Reden und Proklamationen*, 4:1794–1811. See also Gerhard Weinberg, "Germany's Declaration of War on the United States: A New Look," in *Germany and America: Essays on Problems of International Relations and Immigration*, ed. Hans L. Trefousse (New York, 1960), 54–70; Eberhard Jaeckel, "Die deutsche Kriegserklärung an die Vereingten Staaten von 1941," in *Im Dienste Deutschlands und des Rechtes: Festschrift für Wilhelm G. Grewe zum 70 Geburtstag am 16 Oktober 1981*, eds. Friedrich J. Kroneck and Thomas Oppermann (Baden-Baden, 1981), 117–137; and Enrico Syring, "Hitlers Kriegserklärung an Amerika vom 11 Dezember 1941," in *Der Zweite Weltkrieg: Analysen-Grundzüge—Forschungsbilanz*, ed. Wolfgang Michalka (Munich and Zurich, 1989), 683–696.

79. Goebbels diary, December 12, 1941, p. 485.

80. Christian Goeschel, *Mussolini and Hitler: The Forging of the Fascist Alliance* (New Haven and London, 2018), 224–225.

81. Ciano diary, December 11, 1941, p. 473. See also Bottai diary, December 11, 1941, in Giordano Bruno Geurri, ed., *Diario, 1935–1944* (Milan, 1982), 292. We thank Bastian Scianna for drawing this and other sources to our attention.

82. Bertram D. Hulen, "Hull Very Frigid to Visiting Envoys," *New York Times*, December 12, 1941, p. 3.

83. Speech, December 11, 1941, in *Hitler: Reden und Proklamationen*, 1809–1810.

84. Goebbels diary, December 12, 1941, p. 485.

85. Quoted in DNB, December 11, 1941, p. 22.

86. Speech, December 11, 1941, in *Hitler: Reden und Proklamationen*, 1810.

87. Thus, Goebbels diary, December 12, 1941, p. 485.

88. Fredborg, *Behind the Steel Wall*, 58.

89. DNB, December 11, 1941, pp. 30–31.

90. Thursday, December 11, 1941, Federal Communications Commission, Foreign Broadcast Intelligence Service (November 27–December 18, 1941), Franklin Roosevelt Papers OF, 1059c, box 11, FDR Library.

91. Ugaki diary, December 11, 1941, p. 52.

92. SKL diary, December 11, 1941, p. 167.

93. SKL diary, December 11, 1941, p. 168.

94. Thus, the summary of SKL diary, December 11, 1941, p. 169.

95. SKL diary, December 11, 1941, p. 169.

96. Quoted in David Brinkley, *Washington Goes to War* (London, 1989). Thomsen ultimately sold his car for a thousand dollars to Olivia Davis, the owner of a nightclub a block from the German embassy.

97. "Re Government Bond Market," Morgenthau diary, December 11, 1941, p. 146.

98. "Re Foreign Funds," Morgenthau diary, December 11, 1941, pp. 157–166.

99. Morgenthau diary, December 11, 1941. The Americans would ultimately have no more success than the British in shifting Dublin's stance.

100. Alfieri to Ciano, December 11, 1941, Berlin, DDI, 867–868.

101. "Message to Congress re Declaration of War on Germany and Italy (Speech File 1402)," December 11, 1941, box 64, Franklin D. Roosevelt, Master Speech File, 1898–1945, FDR Library.

102. Francis Biddle to James F. Byrnes, December 16, 1941, quoted in Sydney M. Milkis and Nicholas F. Jacobs, "Answering the Call: Leaving the Bench to Serve the President—James F. Byrnes and Franklin D. Roosevelt," *Journal of Supreme Court History* 44, no. 1 (March 2019): 71–89.

103. Arthur Schlesinger Jr., *The Imperial Presidency* (London, 1974).

104. FDR, My Boss: Chapter Drafts and Notes, ca. 1947–1949, Sub-Series 3: Writings, box 5, Grace Tully Collection, FDR Library. The remorse was clearly only temporary, as Patterson resumed his attacks on the administration soon after.

105. The Ambassador in France (Leahy) to the Secretary of State, December 11, 1941, FRUS, Diplomatic Papers, 1941, Europe, vol. 2, 851.33/206: Telegram. See also Robert L. Melka, "Darlan Between Britain and Germany, 1940–1941," *Journal of Contemporary History* 8 (1973): 57–80 (with quote on 80).

106. Charles Williams, *Petain* (London, 2005), 401.

107. Quoted in Francois Kersaudy, *De Gaulle et Roosevelt: Le duel au Sommet* (Paris, 2004), 97.

108. Salitter, "Confidential Report," 287.

109. "Message to Congress, December 11, 1941," in Franklin D. Roosevelt, *The War Messages of Franklin D. Roosevelt, December 8, 1941 to April 13, 1945* (Washing-

ton, DC, 1945), 15. The message focused almost exclusively on Germany, mentioning that "Italy also has declared war against the United States" as no more than an afterthought.

110. That is at least the interpretation of one of Roosevelt's most astute analysts. See Kimball, *Forged in War*, 124–125. Evidence that the prewar debates over US foreign policy remained unsettled was provided in the Senate Committee on Foreign Relations that morning. The Roosevelt administration proposed a longer and more elaborate preamble to the war resolution, which went further in "describing the German action as a culmination of its long time plan against us," but this was rejected in favor of what Arthur Vandenberg termed "a more factual statement which avoided the moot question of why we face this challenge." See Vandenberg, *Private Papers of Senator Vandenberg*, 18–19.

111. Sherwood, *Roosevelt and Hopkins*, 442.

112. Quoted in Justus D. Doenecke, *Storm on the Horizon: The Challenge to American Intervention, 1939–1941* (Lanham, 2000), 321–322.

113. Letter to Hiram Johnson Jr., December 13, 1941, in *Diary Letters of Hiram Johnson*, 7:49.

114. Norman Thomas to Maynard Kuefer, December 11, 1941, Norman Thomas Papers, New York Public Library. We thank Jay Mens for locating this source.

115. Vandenberg, *Private Papers of Senator Vandenberg*, 19.

116. Quoted in Frank L. Kluckhorn, "War Opened on US; Congress Acts Quickly as President Meets Hitler Challenge," *New York Times*, December 12, 1941.

117. Quoted in Kempowski, *Das Echolot*, 398.

118. Slavinsky, *Japanese-Soviet Neutrality Pact*, 81–82 (quote 81).

119. "Memorandum of Conversation by the Secretary of State," December 11, 1941, FRUS, Diplomatic Papers, 1941, Far East, vol. 4, 740.0011 Pacific War/1065.

120. Quoted in Phillips, "Mission to America," 261–275, 263.

121. "Memorandum of Conversation by the Secretary of State," December 11, 1941, FRUS, Diplomatic Papers, 1941, Far East, vol. 4, 740.0011 Pacific War/1065.

122. Hopkins to Harriman, December 11, 1941, Chron File December 1–19th 1941, box 161, Harriman Papers.

123. Woodman, *Arctic Convoys*, 48.

124. Ribbentrop circular, December 11, 1941, Berlin, ADAP, 816.

125. Ciano to the Ambassadors in Buenos Aires, Rio de Janeiro, Santiago, and Lima, December 11, 1941, Rome, DDI, 864–865.

126. Ciano diary, December 11, 1941, p. 473.

127. Wörmann file note, December 11, 1941, Berlin, AA Pol Arch, R29891, fol. 25111.

128. Quoted in Himmler, *Dienstkalender*, 287.

129. Goebbels diary, December 12, 1941, p. 484.

130. Salitter, "Confidential Report," 287.

131. Ritter von Leeb diary, December 11, 1941, p. 412.

132. Stahel, *Retreat from Moscow*, 41.

133. Bock diary, December 11, 1941, pp. 346–347.

134. Jackl Hirschbold to Stephan Wellenhofer, December 11, 1941, in *Aus Feld-postbriefen junger Christen, 1939–1945: Ein Beitrag zur Geschichte der Katholischen Ju-gend im Felde*, eds. Karl-Theodor Schleicher and Heinrich Walle (Stuttgart, 2005), 218.

135. Jackl Hirschbold to Stephan Wellenhofer, December 11, 1941, in *Aus Feld-postbriefen junger Christen*, 219.

136. Goebbels diary, December 12, 1941, p. 480.

137. Goebbels diary, December 12, 1941, p. 483.

138. OKW report, December 11, 1941, pp. 311–312.

139. December 11, 1941, in *Meldungen aus dem Reich*, 3073.

140. December 12, 1941, in *Meldungen aus dem Reich*, 3074–3075 (quote 3075).

141. Fredborg, *Behind the Steel Wall*, 59.

142. Erich W. diary, December 11, 1941, in *Mein Tagebuch: Geschichten vom Über-leben, 1939–1947*, ed. Heinrich Breloer (Cologne, 1984), 64.

143. Salitter, "Confidential Report," 287–288.

144. Report of SD Hauptaussenstelle Bielefeld for the period December 10–16, 1941, p. 478.

145. Arthur Kimel to Renee Uhrmann, December 11, 1941, in *Litzmannstadt*, 205.

146. Alexander von Woedtke to Regierungspräsident of Upper Silesia in Kat-towitz, December 11, 1941, Sosnowitz, in *Die Verfolgung und Ermordung*, ed. Loose, 163–167 (quotes 163–164 and 166).

147. John Martin, *Downing Street: The War Years* (London, 1991), 68. For more on Churchill's use of this phrase from the Bible see Darrell Holley, *Churchill's Lit-erary Allusions: An Index to the Education of a Soldier, Statesman and Litterateur* (Jeffer-son, NC, 1987), 9, 18, 27.

148. Winston Churchill, *Winston Churchill: His Complete Speeches, 1897–1963*, ed. Robert Rhodes James (New York, 1974), 6427. This radio speech was broadcast on June 16, 1941, from London to the United States on Churchill receiving the honorary degree of doctor of laws of the University of Rochester, his first honorary degree from an American university.

149. Memorandum of Conversation: Lord Beaverbrook, in London, December 11, 1941, Chron File December 1–19th 1941, box 161, Harriman Papers.

150. Sebastian diary, December 11, 1941, pp. 450–451.

151. Report from Heinrici to his family, December 11, 1941, Grjasnowo, in *Notizen aus dem Vernichtungskrieg*, 115–116.

152. Diary, December 11, 1941, and H. N. to Vita Sackville West, December 11, 1941, in *Harold Nicolson Diaries*, 254–255.

153. Diarist 5004, December 11, 1941, MOA.

154. December 11, 1941, Diaries of Mackenzie King, Library and Archives Canada.

155. Quoted in Gita Sereny, *Albert Speer: His Battle with Truth* (London, 1996), 268 (from an interview with Galbraith).

CHAPTER 8: THE WORLD OF DECEMBER 12, 1941

1. Rexford Tugwell, *The Democratic Roosevelt: A Biography of Franklin D. Roosevelt* (New York, 1957), 15.

2. As his interior secretary Harold Ickes once told him, "You won't talk frankly even with people who are loyal to you and of whose loyalty you are fully convinced. You keep your cards close up against your belly. You never put them on the table." Ickes, *Secret Diary*, 2:659 (recording conversation with FDR on June 21, 1939).

3. An overview of these competing interpretations are sketched out succinctly in Phillips Payson O'Brien, *How the War Was Won: Air-Sea Power and Allied Victory in World War II* (Cambridge, 2015), 171–183; and Harper, *American Visions of Europe*, 73–76. For the argument that Roosevelt continued to hope the United States could avoid formal intervention right up until early December 1941, see Gerhard Weinberg, *A World at Arms: A Global History of World War II* (Cambridge, 1994), 240–241; and Reynolds, *Creation of the Anglo-American Alliance*, 212. For the argument that Roosevelt was moving, at least from mid-1941, toward entrance into the war, see Dallek, *Roosevelt and American Foreign Policy*, 265, 267, 285–289; Patrick Hearden, *Roosevelt Confronts Hitler: America's Entry into World War II* (DeKalb, 1987), 201; and Trachtenberg, *Craft of International History*, 129.

4. Memo of conversation with FDR, March 25–26, 1939, by Sir Arthur Willert, quoted in Harper, *American Visions of Europe*, 73.

5. Quoted in Isaiah Berlin, *Flourishing: Letters 1928–1946*, ed. Henry Hardy (London, 2004), 386.

6. Tugwell, *Democratic Roosevelt*, 97.

7. "Editorial Opinion on Foreign Affairs: The Nation Rallies," December 12, 1941, Alan Barth to Ferdinand Kuhn Jr., Treasury-Morgenthau Henry Jr.—Editorial Opinion Reports, box 80, Franklin Roosevelt Papers, PSF, FDR Library.

8. Dallek, *Roosevelt and American Foreign Policy*, 317.

9. "Radio Address on 150th Anniversary of Bill of Rights (speech file 1404)," December 15, 141, Franklin D. Roosevelt Master Speech Files, 1898–1945, box 64, FDR Library.

10. Alan Barth to R. Keith Kane, "Intelligence Report No. 2," Office of Facts and Figures, December 22, 1941, box 161, Franklin Roosevelt Papers.

11. Alan Barth to R. Keith Kane, "Intelligence Report No. 1," Office of Facts and Figures, December 15, 1941, box 161, Franklin Roosevelt Papers.

12. This proved unsuccessful, despite a prolonged campaign, and the United States eventually reciprocated with declarations of war on all three in June 1942. Weinberg, *World at Arms*, 263.

13. Lochner, *Always the Unexpected*, 275.

14. Clifford and Okura, *Desperate Diplomat*, 124–125, 139.

15. Hull, *Memoirs*, 2:1100.

16. Goebbels diary, December 13, 1941, pp. 494–495.

17. Martin Moll, "Steuerungsinstrument im 'Ämterchaos?': Die Tagungen der Reichs- und Gauleiter der NSDAP," *Vierteljahreshefte für Zeitgeschichte* 49 (2001): 238–243.

18. Goebbels diary, December 13, 1941, p. 498.

19. Alfred Rosenberg, "Vermerk über Unterredung beim Führer am 14.12.1941," in *Alfred Rosenberg: Die Tagebücher von 1934 bis 1944*, eds. Juergen Matthäus and Frank Bajohr (Frankfurt, 2015), 579.

20. See the contrasting views of Christian Gerlach, "The Wannsee Conference, the Fate of German Jews, and Hitler's Decision in Principle to Exterminate all European Jews," *Journal of Modern European History* 70 (1998): 759–812, and Hermann Graml, "Ist Hitlers Anweisung zur Ausrottung der europäischen Judenheit endlich gefunden?," *Jahrbuch für Antisemitismusforschung* 7, 352–362.

21. Report, SD Aussenstelle Minden, December 12, 1941, in *Juden in den geheimen NS-Stimmungsberichten*, 477.

22. Goebbels diary, December 13, 1941, p. 491.

23. Goebbels diary, December 13, 1941, pp. 490–491.

24. Boelcke, *Wollt ihr den totalen Krieg?*, 198–199. See also Willi A. Boelcke, ed., *Die Macht des Radios: Weltpolitik und Auslandsrundfunk, 1924–1976* (Frankfurt am Main and Berlin, 1977), 381–382.

25. Thus, *Landsberger General Anzeiger*, December 12, 1941, p. 1.

26. Klemperer diary, December 12, 1941, p. 694.

27. December 15, 1941, *Meldungen aus dem Reich*, 8:3089–3091.

28. Heinrici to wife, Grjasnowo, December 12, 1941, in *Notizen aus dem Vernichtungskrieg*, 117–118.

29. Quoted in Stahel, *Retreat from Moscow*, 31.

30. Thus, Gooch, *Mussolini's War*, 211.

31. Denis Mack Smith, *Mussolini* (London, 1981), 272–274.

32. See Hans Woller, *Mussolini: Der erste Faschist* (Munich, 2016), 224–226. Our views on this have also been influenced by the unpublished paper of Bastian Scianna, "Mussolini and the US: From Wilsonianism to Pearl Harbor."

33. Quoted in Simms, *Hitler*, 446.

34. DNB, December 12, 1941, p. 44.

35. See Guenter Moltmann, "Nationalklischees und Demagogie: Die deutsche Amerikapropaganda im zweiten Weltkrieg," in *Das Unrechtsregime: Internationale. Internationale Forschung über den Nationalsozialismus. Band I. Ideologie—Herrschaftssystem—Wirkung in Europa*, ed. Ursula Buettner (Hamburg, 1996), 223; and Simms, *Hitler*, 47, 617–618.

36. DNB report, December 12, 1941, p. 44.

37. Quoted in Yellen, "Japan and the 'Spirit of December 8,'" 65.

38. Quoted in Keene, *So Lovely a Country*, 17.

39. "Trial Bares Dream of Harlem Nazi', *New York Times*, December 16, 1942.

40. See Sato Masaharu and Barak Kushner, "'Negro Propaganda Operations': Japan's Short-Wave Radio Broadcasts for World War II Black Americans," *Historical Journal of Film, Radio and Television* 19, no. 1 (1999): 5–26 (especially 7–8).

41. Alan Barth to R. Keith Kane, "Intelligence Report No. 2," December 22, 1941, Office of Facts and Figures, box 161, Franklin Roosevelt Papers, PSF, FDR Library.

42. Alan Barth to R. Keith Kane, "Intelligence Report No. 4," January 5, 1942, Office of Facts and Figures, box 161, Franklin Roosevelt Papers, PSF, FDR Library.

43. "Democracy at Home Abroad," *Pittsburgh Courier*, February 7, 1942, p. 1. For more on this campaign, its origins, and its legacy see Henry Louis Gates Jr., "What Was Black America's Double War?," *Root*, May 24, 2013, www.theroot.com /what-was-black-americas-double-war-1790896568.

44. See Yoji Akashi and Mako Yoshimura, eds., *New Perspectives on the Japanese Occupation in Malaya and Singapore, 1941–1945* (Singapore, 2008). We thank Ce Liang for drawing our attention to this work.

45. Quoted in Thorne, "Racial Aspects," 344 and 370.

46. Thus, Goebbels diary, December 13, 1941, p. 495.

47. Hewel diary, December 16, 1941, Archiv Institut für Zeitgeschichte Munich, ED 100 Hewel 78, fol. 192.

48. Adolf Hitler, December 18, *Monologe im Führerhauptquartier, 1941–1944: Aufgezeichnet von Heinrich Heim, herausgegeben von Werner Jochmann* (Munich, 2000), 69. The "Table Talk/Monologues" should be used with caution; see Mikael Nilsson, *Hitler Redux: The Incredible History of Hitler's So-Called Table Talks* (London, 2021).

49. Thus, Goebbels diary, December 13, 1941, p. 495.

50. Quoted in Simms, *Hitler*, 450.

51. See generally, Motadel, "Global Authoritarian Moment," 843–877.

52. Churchill to Roosevelt, December 12, 1941, CHAR 20-46-85.

53. Churchill to Eden, December 12, 1941, CHAR 20-46-88-89.

54. Quoted in Churchill, *Never Give In!*, 179.

55. Reynolds, "Churchill and the British 'Decision' to Fight On," 147–167.

56. For a critique of Churchill's American diplomacy, see John Charmley, "Churchill and the American Alliance," *Transactions of the Royal Historical Society* 11 (2001): 353–371, especially 355–361 for the prelude to US intervention. For a more positive recent interpretation of Churchill's policies prior to US intervention, see Roberts, *Churchill*, 517–707 (particularly 640, 676). On the background to Anglo-American relations in this period, see also Reynolds, *Creation of the Anglo-American Alliance*, and Kimball, *Forged in War*.

57. Churchill to Clement Attlee and Lord Woolton (Churchill Papers 20/36), December 12, 1941, in *Churchill War Papers*, 1612.

58. Quoted in Danchev and Todman, *Field Marshal Lord Alanbrooke*, 209. Although a number of scholars have assumed this statement was made on December 8, it's not clear exactly when it was made, with Alan Brooke simply saying it occurred "at one of our meetings shortly after the USA had come into the war."

59. King George VI private diary, Friday, December 12, 1941, Royal Archives, Windsor Castle.

60. Schmider, *Hitler's Fatal Miscalculation*; Stahel, *Retreat from Moscow*, 53.

61. Overy, *Russia's War*, 120.

62. Kellner diary, December 12, 1941, pp. 207–208.

63. Luknitskiy diary, December 13, 1941. We thank Kristina Nazariyan for drawing our attention to this source.

64. Klukowski diary, December 13, 1941, p. 319.

65. Luknitskiy diary, December 12, 1941. We thank Kristina Nazariyan for drawing our attention to this source.

66. Quoted from Butler, *Roosevelt and Stalin*, ccxxvi.

67. Oliver Harvey diary, December 16, 1941.

68. C-145x, December 16, 1941/ TOR Dec. 22–25 in *Churchill and Roosevelt*, 1:294.

69. Baron Charles McMoran Wilson Moran, *Churchill: The Struggle for Survival, 1940–1965* (London, 1966), 10.

70. Moran, *Churchill*, 13.

71. "World War" and "The Battle for Supplies," *Economist*, December 13, 1941, pp. 707–709, 713.

72. B.A.D. Washington to Admiralty, December 11, 1941, "Extract from Chiefs of Staff Meeting (41), 418, December 12 1941," W.G. Sterling to F. E. Evans, "12 December 1941," all in CAB 121/340, UK National Archives.

73. British Purchasing Commission Washington, DC, (Archer) to Ministry of Supply (Palmer), December 14, 1941.

74. Stettinius to William Knudsen, "Memorandum: Request for Inventor of Lend-Lease Materials Now at Ports," December 16, 1941, Stettinius Papers, University of Virginia, box 143, Folder 11: Dec. 17, 1941.

75. Alan Barth to R. Keith Kane, "Intelligence Report No. 1," December 15, 1941, Office of Facts and Figures, box 161, Franklin Roosevelt Papers, PSF, FDR Library.

76. Alan Barth to R. Keith Kane, "Intelligence Report No. 2," December 22, 1941, Office of Facts and Figures, box 161, Franklin Roosevelt Papers, PSF, FDR Library.

77. Hall and Wrigley, *Overseas Supplies*, 171–172.

78. Minutes of Meeting Held at Washington, Wednesday, December 17, 1941, AVIA 38/1049 in JMDS-13, British Supply Council Minutes, Jean Monnet Duchêne Sources, Historical Archives of the European Union, European University Institute.

79. Draft memo, Marshall for President, circa December 13, 1941, sub: Aid to Russia, quoted in Leighton and Coakley, *Global Logistics and Strategy*, 552.

80. Memo, Somervell for Chiefs of Staff, December 11, 1941, sub: Shipping Situation, quoted in Leighton and Coakley, *Global Logistics and Strategy*, 209.

81. Draft memo, Marshall for President, circa December 13, 1941, sub: Aid to Russia, quoted in Leighton and Coakley, *Global Logistics and Strategy*, 552.

82. Mikoyan report to Stalin (extract), January 9, 1942, in *Great Patriotic War of the Soviet Union*, 171.

83. Quoted in Goodwin, *No Ordinary Time*, 298.

84. Huybertie Hamlin, December 18, 1941, "Visit at the White House," Hamlin Papers, box 358, folder 15, Library of Congress.

85. W. H. Thompson, *Assignment: Churchill* (New York, 1955), 246. As Britain's war with Germany had begun just over two years before, Thompson was slightly exaggerating.

86. Moran, *Churchill*, 11.

87. Churchill, *Grand Alliance*, 641.

88. Notes, G. C. M. [Marshall], December 23, 1941, sub: Notes on Mtg at White House with President and Br. Prime Minister, Presiding, quoted in Matloff and Snell, *Strategic Planning for Coalition Warfare*, 105.

89. "Churchill Calls for Knockout War," *New York Times*, December 24, 1941, p. 4.

90. "The Speech to Congress," December 26, 1941, in Winston S. Churchill, *The Unrelenting Struggle: War Speeches*, ed. Charles Eade (London, 1942), 339–340.

91. Lilienthal, *Journals*, 1:418.

92. Alan Barth to R. Keith Kane, "Survey of Intelligence Materials No. 3," December 29, 1941, Office of Facts and Figures, box 161, Franklin Roosevelt Papers, PSF, 1933–1945, FDR Library.

93. "Memorandum by the British Chiefs of Staff," December 24, 1941, WW-1 (U.S. Revised), Grand Strategy: Establishment of the Combined Chiefs of Staff, FRUS, Conferences at Washington, 1941–1942, and Casablanca, 1943, 210.

94. Quoted in Dallek, *Roosevelt and American Foreign Policy*, 324.

95. Sherwood, *Roosevelt and Hopkins*, 442.

96. This was proposed by Attlee to Churchill and, by extension, to Roosevelt, who agreed that it was "a distinct advantage to have as long a list of small countries as possible." Initial quote in "The British Lord Privy Seal (Attlee) to Churchill, December 25 1941," and Roosevelt's response in "The President to the Secretary of State, December 27 1941," both in FRUS, Conferences at Washington, 1941–1942, and Casablanca, 1943, 364–370. To list them in the order in which they appeared on the UN Declaration: Australia, Belgium, Canada, Costa Rica, Cuba, Czechoslovakia, Dominican Republic, El Salvador, Greece, Guatemala, Haiti, Honduras, India, Luxembourg, Netherlands, New Zealand, Nicaragua, Norway, Panama, Poland, South Africa, and Yugoslavia.

97. Dan Plesch, *America, Hitler and the UN: How the Allies Won World War II and Forged a Peace* (London and New York, 2011), 33–37 (quotes 34).

98. Dallek, *Roosevelt and American Foreign Policy*, 319.

99. This is a quotation on Churchill's outlook by Sir Ian Jacob, military assistant secretary to Churchill's war cabinet, and referenced in Thorne, *Allies of a Kind*, 103.

100. Herring, *Aid to Russia*, 53.

101. Leighton and Coakley, *Global Logistics and Strategy*, 197.

102. State of the Union Address, January 6, 1942, PPA, vol. 11, 1942, 36–37.

103. Quoted in Goodwin, *No Ordinary Time*, 313.

104. State of the Union Address, January 6, 1942, PPA, vol. 11, 1942, 36–37.

105. First quote in Moran, *Churchill*, 24 and second quote in Winston S. Churchill, *The Second World War*, vol. 4, *The Hinge of Fate* (London, 1951), 78.

106. "Address to Congress," May 19, 1943, in Winston S. Churchill, *Onwards to Victory: War Speeches by the Right Hon. Winston S. Churchill* (London, 1994), 93.

107. Discussion with Oshima, December 13, 1941, in *Staatsmänner und Diplomaten*, 1:682–688.

108. Matthias Rawert, "Die deutsche Kriegserklärung an die USA 1941," *Militärgeschichte: Zeitschrift für historische Bildung* 3 (2011): 19.

109. Discussion with Oshima, January 3, 1942, in *Staatsmänner und Diplomaten*, 2:41. See also Bernd Wegner, "Hitlers Strategie zwischen Pearl Harbour und Stalingrad," in *Das Deutsche Reich und der Zweite Weltkrieg*, 6: 97–107.

110. Schmider, *Hitler's Fatal Miscalculation*, 350–351.

111. "Report of the Commander of Forces of the Western Front to the Supreme High Commander on the Results of the Counteroffensive of the Front from 6 to 10 December, 12 December 1941," in *Russkii Arkhiv: Velikaia Otechestvennaia. T.15 (4-1). Bitva pod Moskvoi. Sbornik Dokumentov*, ed. V.A. Zolotarev (Moscow, 1997), 178–179. We thank Alexander Hill for supplying us with this reference. He notes that while these figures may be exaggerated, they nonetheless give some idea of Soviet perceptions of the success of their operations to date.

112. Bücheler, *Hoepner*, 162.

113. Stieff to wife, December 13, 1941, in *Hellmuth Stieff*, 143.

114. Reinhardt, *Moskau*, 206.

115. Stahel, *Retreat from Moscow*, 110.

116. Thus, Stahel, *Retreat from Moscow*, 131, 142.

117. Thus, Goebbels diary, December 13, 1941.

118. Quoted in Werner Rahn, "Seestrategisches Denken in der Deutschen Marine, 1914–1945," in *Politischer Wandel*, ed. Ernst Willi Hansen, 157.

119. Quoted in Simms, *Hitler*, 456.

120. Guntram Schulze-Wegener, *Die deutsche Kriegsmarine Rüstung, 1942–1945* (Hamburg, Berlin, Bonn, 1996), 19.

121. Thus, Tooze, *Wages of Destruction*, 568–569.

122. "Zurverfügungstellung sowjetischer Kriegsgefangener für die Rüstungswirtschaft," December 24, 1941, in *Führer-Erlasse*, 214–215.

123. Martin, "Die Militärische Vereinbarung," 134–144.

124. Milan Hauner, *India in Axis Strategy: Germany, Japan and Indian Nationalists in the Second World War* (Stuttgart, 1981), 19.

125. Werner Rahn, "Japan and Germany, 1941–1943: No Common Objective, No Common Plans, No Basis of Trust," *Naval War College Review* 46 (1993): 47–68.

126. Thus, Johannes H. Voigt, "Hitler und Indien," *Vierteljahrshefte für Zeitgeschichte* 19 (1971): 55–57.

127. See Glang, "Germany and Chonqing," 885–886.

128. See Alan Donohoe, "Hitler as Military Commander: From Blau to Edelweiss, January–November 1942" (PhD diss., Trinity College Dublin, 2015), 251.

129. Hauner, *India in Axis Strategy*, 20–55, 173–192, 479–509.

130. Thus, Karl-Jesko von Puttkamer, *Die unheimliche See: Hitler und die Kriegsmarine* (Munich, 1952), 51.

131. See Herde, *Planungen und Verwirklichung*, 14–101.

132. Thus, Rotem Kowner, "When Economics, Strategy, and Racial Ideology Meet: Inter-Axis Connections in the Wartime Indian Ocean," *Journal of Global History* 12 (2017): 228–250.

133. "Anckorn, Fergus Gordon (Oral History)," 22926, Reels 1–5, Imperial War Museum, Production Date—April 16, 2002, www.iwm.org.uk/collections/item/object/80021489.

134. Quoted in Thorne, "Racial Aspects," 377.

135. Mark Roseman, *The Villa, the Lake, the Meeting: Wannsee and the Final Solution* (London, 2003).

136. Gerlach, *Extermination*, 99–100.

137. Gottwaldt and Schulle, *Judendeportationen*, 126–128.

138. Jeffrey Herf, "Hitlers Dschihad: Nationalsozialistische Rundfunkpropaganda für Nordafrika und den Nahen Osten," *Vierteljahrshefte für Zeitgeschichte* 2 (2010): 259–286, especially 266–274.

139. Churchill, *Second World War*, 4:54.

140. December 18, 1941, in Henry Channon, *Chips: The Diaries of Sir Henry Channon*, ed. Robert Rhodes James (London, 1967), 315.

141. "War Situation," Commons Sitting, HC Deb, January 27, 1942, Hansard, vol 377, cc619.

142. Churchill, *Second World War*, 4:81.

143. December poll in Gallup Organization, Gallup Poll #1941-0255: World War II/Employment, Gallup Organization, dataset (Cornell University, Ithaca, NY: Roper Center for Public Opinion Research, 1941). February poll in Dallek, *Roosevelt and American Foreign Policy*, 331.

144. Quoted in Mark Stoler, *Allies and Adversaries: The Joint Chiefs of Staff, the Grand Alliance and US Strategy in World War II* (Chapel Hill, NC, 2000), 110.

145. Quotes in Dallek, *Roosevelt and American Foreign Policy*, 334–336. For more extensive accounts, see Stetson Conn, "The Decision to Evacuate the Japanese from the Pacific Coast (1942)," in *Command Decisions*, ed. Kent Roberts (New York, 1959), 88–109, and Roger Daniels, *Concentration Camps USA: Japanese Americans*

and World War II (New York, 1971). An overview of the documentary record in their collections is provided by the Franklin D. Roosevelt Presidential Library and Museum's online exhibit, *Confront the Issue: FDR and Japanese American Internment*, www.fdrlibraryvirtualtour.org/page07-15.asp.

146. Francis Biddle, *In Brief Authority* (New York, 1961), 212–216, 235–238.

147. Quoted in James MacGregor Burns, *Roosevelt: The Soldier of Freedom, 1940–1945* (London, 1971), 216.

148. O'Brien, *How the War Was Won*, 109–201.

149. April 23, 1942, in *Chips*, 327.

150. Danchev and Todman, *Field Marshal Lord Alanbrooke*, 248.

151. See John Glancy, *The Most Dangerous Moment of the War: Japan's Attack on the Indian Ocean* (Philadelphia, 2015).

152. Boyd, *Royal Navy in Eastern Waters*, 355–399.

153. McMeekin, *Stalin's War*, 403–432.

154. Churchill's central analysis is confirmed by Kennedy, *Rise and Fall of the Great Powers*, 347–357.

155. See O'Brien, *How the War Was Won*.

156. Simms, *Hitler*, 456–457, 497–498, 502, 525.

157. See Hill, *Red Army and the Second World War*, 180, 220, 313, 360, 442, 467, 486, 493, 505, 508–509.

158. Quoted in Ian Campbell and Donald MacIntyre, *The Kola Run: A Record of the Arctic Convoys, 1941–1945* (London, 1958), 230.

159. E.g., *Geschichte des Großen vaterländischen Krieges der Sowjetunion. Volume 2. Die Abwehr des wortbrüchigen Überfalls des faschistischen Deutschlands auf die Sowjetunion. Die Schaffung der Voraussetzungen für den Grundlegenden Umschwung im Kriege* (Berlin, 1963), 226–227.

160. V. M. Molotov and Feliz Chuev, *Molotov Remembers: Inside Kremlin Politics* (Chicago, 1993), 61.

161. Vladimir Putin, "The Real Lessons of the 75th Anniversary of World War II," *National Interest*, June 18, 2020.

162. All these figures can be found in Thompson, *A Sense of Power*, 196–197. See also Kennedy, *Rise and Fall of the Great Powers*, 355, and Richard Overy, *Why the Allies Won* (London, 1995), 228–234.

163. Quoted in Daniel Yergin, *The Prize: The Epic Quest for Oil, Money and Power* (New York, 1991), 364.

164. Nobuo, "Die japanische Botschaft in Berlin," 69.

165. Hotta, *Japan 1941*, 13.

166. Ugaki diary, December 10, 1941, pp. 49–50.

167. The counterfactual is posed in Robert Farley, "What if Hitler Never Declared War on the US During World War II?," *National Interest*, September 2, 2016.

INDEX

BRENDAN SIMMS is a professor in the history of international relations and a fellow at Cambridge. He is the author of many books, including *Europe* and *Hitler*. He lives in Cambridge, UK.

CHARLIE LADERMAN is a lecturer in international history in the war studies department at King's College, London. He is the author of books on US–UK foreign policy, including *Sharing the Burden*. He lives in London.